D1476597

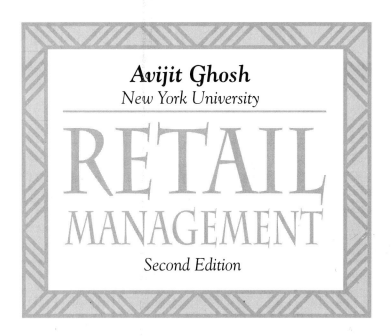

Avijit Ghosh
New York University

RETAIL
MANAGEMENT

Second Edition

THE DRYDEN PRESS
HARCOURT BRACE COLLEGE PUBLISHERS

Fort Worth   Philadelphia   San Diego   New York   Orlando   Austin   San Antonio
Toronta   Montreal   London   Sydney   Tokyo

To Sally, Smita, and Priya

Publisher	Liz Widdicombe
Senior Acquisitions Editor	Lynn Hastert
Senior Developmental Editor	Paul Stewart
Total Concept Services	Bookmark Book Production Services
Text Type	Palatino 10/12

Copyright © 1994, 1990 by The Dryden Press

Address for Editorial Correspondence

The Dryden Press, 301 Commerce Street, Suite 3700, Fort Worth, TX 76102

Address for Orders
The Dryden Press, 6277 Sea Harbor Drive, Orlando, FL 32887
1-800-782-4479, or 1-800-433-0001 (in Florida)

ISBN: 0-03-076749-0

Library of Congress Catalogue Number: 93-72475

Printed in the United States of America

3 4 5 6 7 8 9 0 1 2   048   9 8 7 6 5 4 3 2 1

The Dryden Press
Harcourt Brace College Publishers

Photo Credits:

© Lisa Quinones/Black Star 215; Courtesy of The Body Shop 105; Courtesy of Bullock's/Macy's 556; Everett Collection 25; Courtesy of H & R Block 94; Courtesy of Hertz Systems, Inc. 611; © Nathan Holtz 11; © Susan Holtz 35, 147, 162, 268, 272, 274, 285, 287, 308, 320, 441; Image Works/ © Marc Bernsau 193, 455, © Bob Daemmrich 483, © Charles Fleming 517; Courtesy of IMTECH International, Inc. 549; Courtesy of Jazzercise, Inc. 95; Courtesy of KinderCare 111; Courtesy of Lands' End 20, 479; Courtesy of Marriott 591; Courtesy of T.J. Maxx 167; Courtesy of Miami Subs Corporation 71; Courtesy of Nike Retail 529; Courtesy of Northwest Airlines 414; Courtesy of Oscar Mayer 233; Courtesy of Perfumania, Inc. 399; PhotoEdit/ © Bill Aron 540, © Robert Brenner 323, 329, 373, 381, © Amy Etra 462, © Tony Freeman 129, © Dennis MacDonald 424, © Felicia Martinez 393, © Michael Newman 576, © Mark Richards 291, 349, ©David Young-Wolff 358, 528; Photo Researchers/ © Lawrence Migdale 78, © Arthur Glauberman 430, © Spencer Grant 537, © Tom Hollyman 251; Courtesy of Pizza Hut 283; Courtesy of Piggly Wiggly 139; Courtesy of Radio Shack 44; © Mark Richards 38; Ann States/SABA 123; The San Diego Union/JIM BAIRD 12; Courtesy of The Sherwin-Williams Company 87; Stock, Boston/ © Dean Abramson 446, © John Cole 332, © John Coletti 364, 504, © Bob Daemmrich 4, 125, 156, © Laima Druskis 219, © J. Dunn 613, © Charles Gupton 500, © Jerry Howard 152, © Tom Lei, © Gregg Mancuso 361, © Mike Mazzaschi 51, © Jeffrey Myers 488, © Alan Oransky 220, © Frank Siteman 598, © Cary Wolinsky 232; Courtesy of Underground Atlanta Joint Venture 247; Courtesy of The United States Shoe Corporation 200, 201; Courtesy of Virginia Specialty Stores 457; Courtesy of Vons Companies, Inc. 155; Courtesy of Wal-Mart 594; Courtesy of Waldenbook Company, Inc. 62; Courtesy of Welcome Home 570; Courtesy of F.W. Woolworth 41; Courtesy of F.W. Woodworth, Frankfurt 183.

The Dryden Press Series in Marketing

About the Author

Avijit Ghosh is the Harold Price Professor of Marketing and Entrepreneurship at New York University's Leonard Stern School of Business, where he has taught courses on marketing and retailing since 1980 and where he received the Excellence in Teaching Award. He has taught marketing for executive programs in the United States, France, and Singapore.

Professor Ghosh was born in Calcutta, India. He earned a B.S. degree from Calcutta University, a post-graduate degree in management from Xavier Institute in India and M.A. and Ph.D degrees from the University of Iowa.

Professor Ghosh's research interests are in the area of retail and marketing management, locational analysis, sales forecasting, and the application of location allocation methods for planning service distribution systems. He has served as a consultant to a number of companies, and his research publications have appeared in such journals as *Journal of Marketing, Journal of Retailing, Geographical Analysis, Journal of Marketing Research, Urban Studies*, and *Journal of Business Research*, among others. For two articles published in the *Journal of Retailing*, Professor Ghosh received special awards by the journal's editorial board.

Professor Ghosh was the Editor of the *Journal of Retailing* from 1985 to 1991. He is the co-author of *Location Strategies for Retail and Service Firms* and *Market Centers and Retail Location*. He is the co-editor of *Spatial Analysis and Location Allocation Models* and of *Spatial Analysis in Marketing: Theory, Methods and Applications*. He is a member of the American Marketing Association, The Institute of Management Science, and the American Collegiate Retailing Association. Currently, he is the Director of the Center for Entrepreneurial Studies at New York University.

Preface

Since the publication of the first edition of this book in 1990, the retail industry has faced severe economic pressures forcing many firms to reevaluate their practices and to formulate new strategies for success in an increasingly competitive environment. For retailers, the 1980s brought fundamental transformations. Changes in the marketing environment and in consumer behavior together with innovations in communications and in other technologies gave rise to new retail institutions while established ones reoriented their strategies to sharpen their competitive focuses. Mergers and acquisitions of retail firms in the 1980s led to increased concentration in the hands of fewer retail chains resulting in a new balance of power between retailers and manufacturers and among retailers themselves. Moreover, the economic downturn at the start of the 1990s threatened the financial well-being of many retail firms, large and small. These transformations in the retail environment increased emphasis on the need to better understand the forces of retail competition and to create successful retail strategies.

Retail Management, Second Edition, provides a broad view of the challenges as well as the excitement of retailing. It introduces the reader to the basic principles of retailing, the diversity of the retail industry, emerging trends, and tools for improving retail profitability. It emphasizes the importance of strategic market planning to focus the firm's effort on its customers and external environment and to link marketing and financial decision. The book also exposes the reader to fundamental concepts and techniques for managing retail enterprises. *Retail Management* presents a complete picture of the discipline of retailing as it prepares to enter a new century.

Retail Management contains a number of special features.

- It presents an integrative view of retailing that blends strategic market planning issues with market programming issues.
- It demonstrates the translation of strategic concerns into tactical operational concerns.
- It emphasizes the impact of the consumer, competitive, and technological environments of retail institutions.
- It provides a balanced coverage of different types of retail institutions, drawing on examples from a variety of retail institutions, both domestic and international, small and large.
- It provides up-to-date coverage of emerging forms of retailing such as home shopping, direct retailing, services retailing, and specialty retailing.
- It discusses in detail such trends as the globalization of retail firms and the renewed growth of franchising.
- It integrates new techniques and concepts of retail management such as geodemographic targeting, direct product profit (DPP), and electronic data interchange (EDI), to name a few.
- It stresses the need for coordinating financial and marketing planning and demonstrates the use of important financial control tools.
- It integrates consumer behavior and marketing research issues in each chapter to emphasize their key role in formulating retail strategy.

v

- It looks at retailing from the perspective of large firms as well as the small entrepreneurial start-up.

CHANGES IN THE SECOND EDITION

While the major concern and the key focus of the book remains the same, many changes have been made in this edition to further augment its value. We were fortunate to receive comments from many adopters of the first edition. These have helped us to make the book even better and more useful. The changes include:

- Complete new sets of vignettes and boxed materials to reflect changing trends and industry practices.
- Greater emphasis on how globalization affects the retail industry.
- Expanded discussion of such trends as franchising, merchandise control, retail services, direct retailing, and the impacts of new technology.
- Greater emphasis on the link between retail strategy and the implementation of retail programs.
- Expanded discussion of such new and evolving retail techniques as EDI, DPP, and geodemographics.
- In addition, all examples and statistics in the text have been updated and new examples added throughout the text.

ORGANIZATION OF THE SECOND EDITION

Retail Management is intended for students who plan to pursue careers in the retailing industry, perhaps by opening and operating one or more retail stores of their own, or by joining a large retail chain. It is also intended for students interested in retailing because of its economic and social significance. The goal is to develop an appreciation for the central concerns and challenges of strategic retail management and the tasks facing retail managers. The book is organized into four parts, each of which focuses on an important aspect of the retail management process.

Part One

The first chapter introduces the reader to the retail industry. It demonstrates the diversity of retail operations, while pointing out the common challenges that all retailers face. The next three chapters in the first section deal with the retail environment. Chapter 2 discusses the nature of retail competition. Chapter 3 looks at the relationships between retailers and their suppliers and at different forms of vertical marketing systems such as franchising. Chapter 4 examines the various changes taking place in the demographic, economic, technological, and legal environments and their implications for the retail industry. Changes in these environments often present new opportunities or threaten existing strategies.

Part Two

The five chapters in Part Two focus on strategic planning. The section starts by discussing how retail marketing strategies are formulated through the analysis of customer needs and potential customer segments. But no firm can serve all the needs of all potential customers. The firm selects its target market by analyzing the consumer and competitive environments and then matching its strength to the opportunities presented to it. This is the subject of Chapter 5. Many large retail firms are multiunit conglomerates that operate portfolios of different retail stores. As one of their most important tasks, managers of multiunit firms must integrate the strategies of the individual units to achieve synergy for the firm as a whole. Chapter 6 discusses concepts and analytical tools necessary to achieve this kind of synergy. Any discussion of strategy must examine financial implications. The aim of retailing, after all, is to satisfy consumer needs in a profitable way. The interface between marketing and financial strategies is the subject of Chapter 7. It develops a comprehensive financial control framework for retail firms.

Chapters 8 and 9 focus on location. The location decision is crucial since it determines the number and types of customers the store can attract. Chapter 8 presents a framework for making location decisions and discusses the various factors that influence location strategy. Chapter 9 presents an array of techniques, ranging from simple rules of thumb to sophisticated computerized approaches, for forecasting sales of individual outlets.

Part Three

The five chapters of Part Three deal with merchandise management. Chapter 10 on merchandise strategy illustrates how merchandise decisions affect the overall image of a store and discusses the retail manager's key merchandising decisions. Chapter 11 presents the various planning tools that retail managers use to make and monitor merchandise budgets. No merchandising strategy is complete without a decision on how to price the products. Retail managers are faced with the daunting task of pricing thousands of individual items. Chapter 12 provides an overall framework that can be used to approach this task and discusses such fundamental concepts as *markups* and *markdowns*. Retail stores typically have a large portion of their assets invested in inventory. One of the lessons of the last decade is that retail profitability depends critically on the firm's ability to manage and monitor its investments in merchandise inventory. Chapters 13 and 14 explain the principles underlying an effective merchandise evaluation and control system.

Part Four

The merchandise is the heart of the retailing machine. But the merchandise has to be supported by augmenting the value of the merchandise by providing customers with information and services and by creating a pleasant shopping atmosphere, as discussed in Part Four. Chapter 14 looks at how retailers enhance value for their customers through effective shopping atmosphere and efficient transactional services. Chapter 16 focuses on communication through media and direct mail advertising as well as through in-store announcements. Two other ways in which retailers increase the value of their merchandise, personal selling and ancillary services, are discussed in Chapter 17. This concluding chapter also discusses some of the special characteristics of service retailing and how customers evaluate service quality.

PEDAGOGY

Each chapter of Retail Management is designed to reinforce the major concepts presented in the chapter. A number of innovative features were introduced in the previous edition to achieve this goal. These elements have all been retained in the Second Edition, but each has been revised and updated to provide students with current information. These features include:

Opening Vignettes Each chapter begins with a description of a retail situation that introduces students to the concepts discussed in that chapter. The vignettes provide a context for the concepts discussed in the chapter, and introduce current industry practices as well as some of the nation's leading retailers.

Learning Objectives and Summary Learning objectives at the beginning of each chapter guide reader's studies. The end-of-chapter summaries parallel these objectives for further reinforcement.

Entrepreneurial Edge Small firms play an important role in retailing. Each year thousands of new retail stores are opened, but only a few of them become successful. With this in mind, each chapter contains one or more boxed features that highlight a successful new venture and the reasons for its success. These features are designed to further reinforce the concepts discussed in the chapter.

Strategy in Action Each chapter features real-world examples of how retailers apply the concepts in the chapter. These examples appear both within the text and in boxes entitled "Strategy in Action."

Research Report Throughout, the text introduces readers to current research findings. In addition, a number of "Research Report" boxes highlight important research findings and industry trends.

End-of-Chapter Review Questions Thought-provoking questions encourage the reader to review and apply concepts discussed in the chapter. Various types of questions are listed at the end of each chapter. Some questions test readers' comprehension of text material, others require them to solve specific problems using the concepts in the book, or apply the concepts to understand retailing in their home towns.

Cases   Two types of cases appear in the book. Nineteen problem-oriented short cases give readers the opportunity to apply concepts directly to real-world situations. In addition, a video case and six longer, more comprehensive cases are also provided.

Supplementary Materials   An extensive set of materials for both the professor and the student supplement the text, including:

- An *Instructor's Manual* which provides background and suggestions for each chapter and case.
- A large *Test Bank* of true/false, multiple-choice and short-answer questions.
- A computerized version of the *Test Bank*, for use with IBM PC microcomputers.
- *Transparency Masters* of new items and key figures and tables from the book.
- A computer disk containing a financial model that can be used in solving problems.
- A video of Wal-Mart Stores, Inc., with an accompanying video case in the text.

All of these materials are available to adopters. For further details of the many unique features of the supplements, please contact your Dryden Press sales representative.

ACKNOWLEDGMENTS

Although a single name appears on the cover of this book, numerous people have helped to produce it. The text has benefited immensely from hundreds of suggestions from colleagues and friends who reviewed earlier drafts. I would like to thank the following people who reviewed drafts of the current or the earlier edition:

Larry Audler, University of New Orleans; William Black, Louisiana State University; Bixby Cooper, Michigan State University; Ronald Dornoff, University of Cincinnati; Chloe Elmgren, Mankato State University; Gwen Fontenot, University of North Texas; John Gifford, Miami University of Ohio; Thomas Greer, University of Maryland; Larry Gresham, Texas A&M University; Douglas Harms, Iowa State University; Mark Johnson, University of Colorado; Robert M. Jones, California State University, Fullerton; Robert F. Krampf, Kent State University; Michael Little, Virginia Commonwealth University; Dolly Loyd, University of Southern Mississippi; Douglas MacLachlan, University of Washington; Ray Marquardt, University of Nebraska; Martin Meloche, East Carolina University; Joseph Miller, Indiana University; William Panschar, Indiana University; Michael Pearson, Bowling Green University; Michael O'Neill, California State University, Chico; James Robertson, Indian River Community College; Thaddeus Spratlen, University of Washington; Ruth A. Taylor, Southwest Texas State University; Lillia Verner, University of Minnesota.

Special thanks are also due to Dale Achabal of Santa Clara University, Charles Ingene of the University of Washington, Michael Levy of Miami University, Vijay Mahajan of Southern Methodist University, Gina O'Connor of RPI, and the faculty of New York University, especially Sam Craig, for their encouragement and inspiration throughout the project.

Karen Goldstein made numerous trips to the library and photocopied innumerable reference materials. More importantly, her sense of order and organization kept the project from getting out of hand. I also thank Sophie Henderson who helped with the revisions and contributed many of the boxed materials and chapter opening vignettes.

The staff at The Dryden Press played a special part in this project. I thank Lynn Hastert for planning this edition; Paul Stewart for his encouragement and advice; and the staff of Bookmark Book Production Services, especially Lynn Edwards for shepherding the book through production.

I thank, too, the hundreds of students who took my retailing classes at New York University. Their perceptive comments, questions, and observations have improved my own understanding of retailing. Some of them read photocopied drafts of the text and provided helpful comments to improve it. A special thanks to them.

Finally, I thank my family—Sally, Smita, and Priya—and my parents for their patience and support. To them the book is dedicated.

Avijit Ghosh

Contents

PART I
Understanding the Retail Environment

This book, which is divided into four parts is about strategic market planning for retail firms. The four chapters in the first part of the book introduce readers to the environment of retailing. Chapter 1 presents a broad overview of the central concerns and challenges of strategic retail management and the tasks facing retail managers. It discusses the important role that retail institutions play in the economy and introduces the reader to the different classifications of retail stores.

The remaining three chapters of Part One discuss the environment in which retail stores operate. Chapter 2 deals with the retail competitive environment, and presents a framework for understanding retail market structure. Reasons for the increasing pace of globalization in retailing are also discussed in this chapter. Chapter 3 looks at the relationship between retailers and their suppliers. It describes the organization of marketing channels—and explores the role of the retailers in the channel. Franchising and its growth in recent years is also discussed in this chapter. Chapter 4 examines the changes taking place in the consumer, economic, technological, and legal environments and their implications for the retail industry.

CHAPTER 1
Retailing: The Business of Creating Value

Retailing is an integral part of the world we live in. Wherever people need products and services, there are retailers. Furthermore, retail is the primary point at which most people have contact with the world of business. Retailing is such a common part of people's daily lives that its institutions are taken for granted. Similarly, the challenges and demands of retail management tend to be underestimated. Every year thousands of new retail ventures are initiated; however, many of them fail because of poor management and lack of appreciation of the special demands of retailing. Successful retailing requires hard work, dedication, and keen managerial skills. This book presents the concepts, methods and techniques, and, most importantly, the understanding necessary for managing retail firms skillfully and profitably.

The world of retailing is dynamic, exciting, and extremely diverse. At one end of the spectrum are firms such as Sears, K mart, and Radio Shack that operate large chains of outlets. At the other end are small, neighborhood retail outlets owned and operated by individual entrepreneurs—the mom-and-pop businesses. Altogether, there are nearly two million retail outlets in the United States; about 300,000 of these belong to retail chains

with more than four outlets. Although the small, independent retailer is still a vital part of the retail industry, the dominance of large retail chains is growing steadily.

The diversity of retailing derives from more than differences in firm size. There are many types of retail stores which sell such a wide variety of merchandise that it is impossible to catalog all of them. They range from convenience-oriented neighborhood stores to prestigious fashion-outlets such as Neiman-Marcus, Bonwit Teller, Bergdorf Goodman, and Nordstrom. Large discount chains such as K mart, Target, Caldor, and Wal-Mart exist alongside department stores such as Macy's, Bloomingdale's, Marshall Fields, Jordan Marsh, Dayton's, Dillard's, and The Broadway, and specialty stores that sell limited lines of merchandise, such as The Limited, The Gap, Toys R Us, Waldenbooks, RiteAid, Safeway, A&P, and ComputerLand.

There is also tremendous diversity in the geographic scope of retail firms. Many firms operate only in local markets, while others serve regional, national, or international markets. Prior to World War II, even the largest retail firms operated primarily in regional markets. But in the post-World War II period, the geographic scope of retail firms has increased dramatically. Chain stores such as

After studying this chapter, the reader will be able to:

- *Define retailing and recognize its importance to the economy.*
- *Understand how retailers create value for consumers.*
- *Describe how macroenvironmental factors affect retailing.*
- *Understand the importance of creating differential advantage over competitors.*
- *Recognize the elements of the retail mix.*
- *Know the various elements of the retail strategic planning process and the tasks and functions of retail management.*
- *Understand the criteria by which retail stores are classified.*

J.C. Penney, Sears, Montgomery Ward, K mart, The Limited, and The Gap have established national networks of outlets. During the past two decades retailing has become increasingly internationalized, too. Many U.S. firms have aggressively entered foreign markets by opening their own outlets, through joint ventures, or by granting franchises. McDonald's, Burger King, and Kentucky Fried Chicken, for example, earn a significant portion of their sales and profits from foreign outlets. Similarly, foreign firms such as Ikea, Conran's, and Benetton are significant players in the U.S. market. Other foreign firms have entered the U.S. market through direct acquisition. Some of the well-known U.S. retailers that are wholly or partially owned by foreign firms include Dillard's, Spiegel, Brooks Brothers, and A&P.

This first chapter provides an overview of the retail management process, explains the functions of **retailing**, and discusses its importance in the economy. We then provide an overall framework for developing retail strategy and outline the tasks and functions of retail management. The second section of the chapter presents some common schemes by which to classify retail stores.

THE MEANING OF RETAILING

Retail firms are business organizations that sell goods and services to customers for their personal or household use. The retailers' customers are the ultimate or final consumers who buy products or services for their own use and not for resale to others. This differentiates retailers from manufacturers and wholesalers. Manufacturers and wholesalers sell goods to other businesses who resell them, in the same or in different forms. Manufacturers sell products to wholesalers, who, in turn, sell them to retailers. It is the retailers who sell the products to the ultimate consumers. Retailers, therefore, are the final link in the channel through which goods flow from manufacturers to consumers.

Not all retailing, however, takes place in store settings. During the latter half of the nineteenth and the early part of the twentieth century, mail-order catalogs from Sears, Roebuck and Montgomery Ward were the major sources of merchandise for many farming communities. The importance of catalogs and other types of **nonstore retailing** such as computer shopping, TV shopping programs, door-to-door selling, telemarketing, and vending machines increased in the 1980s and 1990s.

Another major trend is the growth of **service retailing**. Although most people tend to associate retailing with the sale of products, the sale of services is an important part of many retail businesses. Until recently both Sears and K mart offered real estate, insurance, and brokerage services to their customers. Moreover, such diverse businesses as hair salons, dry cleaners, banks, hospitals, dental clinics, car rental agencies, and hotels are also retail organizations, since they all provide service to the ultimate consumer.

Retailing is a vital part of the national economy. Exhibit 1.1 shows the growth of retail sales in the United States since 1975. These statistics, published by the Department of Commerce, include sales at retail stores and through mail-order catalogs, and exclude other forms of nonstore retailing and sale of services. In 1975, total retail sales were $588 billion, which translates to per capita sales of about $2,700. By 1980, retail sales in the United States reached $1 trillion per year. In the next seven years, sales increased by another $500 billion to total approximately $1.5 trillion in 1987. In 1990, total retail sales reached $1.807 trillion.[1] This is more than $5,000 for every man, woman, and child in the country, and this total does not include the money spent on services.

Exhibit 1.2 shows the breakdown of retail sales according to the type of products sold. Food-related sales (sales at food stores, restaurants, bars, and liquor stores) account for about 33 percent of total retail sales. This is closely followed by automobile-related sales (car dealers, gasoline stations, auto parts, and so on), which accounts for approximately another 30 percent of total sales. Thus, food- and auto-related sales together account for over 60 percent of the total. The remaining sales are distributed among six other categories of stores. In order of importance these stores include general merchandise, building material and hardware, apparel and accessories, furniture and home furnishings, liquor, and nonstore retailers.

Exhibit 1.1   *Total Retail Trade Sales*

Source: *Statistical Abstract of the United States*, 1991 (Washington, D.C.: Department of Commerce).

Employment potential also makes retailing important to the economy. The Department of Labor estimates that retail firms employ about 19 million people, or approximately 16 percent of the total labor force in the country.[2] Most observers believe, however, that this estimate is too low. During busy periods, many retailers rely on seasonal and part-time workers who may not be included in this count. Moreover, the official figures tend to underestimate the number of people employed by small, family-run stores.

The economic importance of retailing can also be gauged by looking at some of the top retailers in the country. The 1990 sales of Sears, Roebuck and Company, the nation's largest retailer, was nearly $56 billion, more than the gross national product of Greece. Sears is the sixth largest corporation in the United States with sales more than double that of Philip Morris, the largest consumer packaged-goods company. In 1990, sales of the top 25 retail firms together exceeded $335 billion, as shown in Exhibit 1.3.

It is important to note the diversity among the top 25 firms. The list includes general merchandisers (Sears), department stores (Macy's), discount stores (Wal-Mart and K mart), supermarkets (Safeway and Kroger), convenience stores

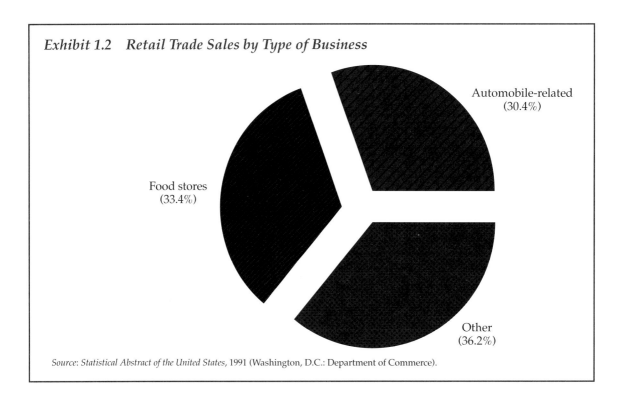

Exhibit 1.2   Retail Trade Sales by Type of Business

Automobile-related
(30.4%)

Food stores
(33.4%)

Other
(36.2%)

Source: *Statistical Abstract of the United States,* 1991 (Washington, D.C.: Department of Commerce).

(Southland, operator of 7-Eleven stores), restaurants (McDonald's), and specialty stores (Toys R Us, The Limited). Diversity also shows up in the way these retail businesses operate. Some, such as Sears, K mart, J.C. Penney, the supermarkets, and McDonald's, concentrate predominantly on a single type of store. Other more diversified companies operate portfolios of different kinds of retail stores with distinctive identities of their own. Dayton Hudson, for example, owns department stores (Dayton's and Hudson's), discount stores (Target), soft-good stores (Mervyn's), and hard-good stores (Lechmere). Until a few years ago, the company also owned the B. Dalton bookstore chain and an off-price apparel chain called Plums. Note, too, the diversity in the pattern ownership. Except for McDonald's, all the top firms are publicly held companies that own and operate their own chain of outlets. McDonald's is a franchisor, most of its outlets are owned and operated by individual franchisees and not by the company.

THE RETAIL EXCHANGE PROCESS

At the heart of every business transaction is an **exchange**. Simply stated, an *exchange is the act of obtaining a desired object from somebody by offering something in*

Exhibit 1.3   Top 25 Retail Firms, 1990

Rank by Sales	Company	Sales (millions of dollars) (1990)	Profits (millions of dollars) (1990)
1	Sears, Roebuck, Chicago, IL	55,971.7	902.2
2	Wal-Mart Stores, Bentonville, AR	32,601.6	1,291.0
3	K mart, Troy, MI	32,080.0	756.0
4	American Stores, Salt Lake City, UT	22,155.0	182.4
5	Kroger, Cincinnati, OH	20,261.0	82.4
6	J.C. Penney, Dallas, TX	17,410.0	577.0
7	Safeway, Oakland, CA	14,873.6	87.1
8	Dayton Hudson, Minneapolis, MN	14,739.0	412.0
9	Great Atlantic & Pacific Tea, NJ	11,164.2	146.7
10	May Department Stores, St. Louis, MO	11,027.0	500.0
11	Woolworth, New York, NY	9,789.0	317.0
12	Winn-Dixie Stores, Jacksonville, FL	9,744.5	152.5
13	Melville, Rye, NY	8,686.8	385.3
14	Albertson's, Boise, ID	8,218.6	233.8
15	Southland, Dallas, TX	8,037.1	(276.6)
16	R.H. Macy, New York, NY	7,266.8	(215.3)
17	McDonald's, Oak Brook, IL	6,639.6	802.3
18	Supermarkets General Holdings, Woodbridge, NJ	6,126.0	(41.5)
19	Walgreen, Deerfield, IL	6,063.0	174.6
20	Publix SuperMarkets, Lakeland, FL	5,820.7	149.0
21	Food Lion, Salisbury, NC	5,584.4	172.6
22	Toys R Us, Paramus, NJ	5,521.2	326.0
23	Price, San Diego, CA	5,428.8	125.4
24	Vons, Arcadia, CA	5,333.9	82.2
25	The Limited, Columbus, OH	5,253.5	398.4

Source: The 1991 Directory of U.S. Corporations, The FORTUNE SERVICE 500, Sept. 30, 1991, p. 62.

return.[3] An exchange, therefore, requires two parties, each of whom has something to offer that the other values (See Exhibit 1.4). Retailing is no exception. Retailers must offer to sell products and services that customers value and the customers must be willing to pay for what they buy (the retailer values the customers' payments). Since the creation of value through the exchange process is a critical part of retailing, it is important to understand the ways in which retailers create value for their customers.

The **value** that a retailer creates for its customers depends on two factors: the utility of the retailer's products and services, as perceived by the customer, and the price the customer has to pay for those goods and services. Although the notion of price is quite clear, the concept of utility requires discussion. **Utility** is the

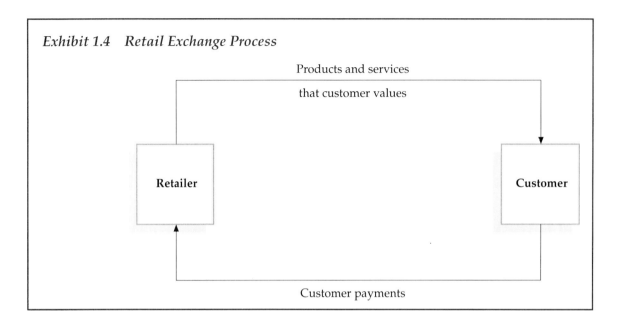

Exhibit 1.4   Retail Exchange Process

benefit or worth of the retailer's offering as perceived by the customer. The greater the perceived benefit, the higher the utility. Since utility depends on customer perceptions, different customers may have different levels of utility for the same set of goods and services. Individual needs, tastes, and preferences determine the level of utility each consumer perceives.

A customer who gets more satisfaction from a retailer's offering perceives a greater level of utility. Thus, one way to increase utility is to offer goods and services that closely match the customer's needs. For example, a person shopping for a pair of jeans is unlikely to find utility in a formal suit, however high its quality. The suit simply does not match the person's need at the time, so it does not create any value for the customer. By stocking products and services desired by customers, the retailer creates utility and with it the potential for exchange.

A consumer's perception of utility also depends on the manner in which the retailer offers its products and services. For example, knowledgeable, helpful sales personnel and shopping services such as delivery and gift wrapping can enhance the value of the retailer's offering. A convenient location that saves the customer from traveling far to patronize the store also enhances utility. If two stores sell the same brand of jeans at the same price, the customer will likely choose the more conveniently located one.

The utility of the retailer's offering and **price** jointly determine the value the retailer creates for its customers. Since the perceived utility of an offering determines how much a customer will be willing to pay for it, the greater the utility relative to price, the higher the value of that offering to the customer (see Exhibit 1.5). Higher value, in turn, makes the consumer more willing to purchase from the retailer, completing the exchange process.

When the asked price exceeds utility, the perceived value for the retailer's offering becomes negative and there is no potential for exchange. The customer may forego the purchase or patronize a different retailer who offers a better value. The customer will have no demand for the retailer's offering if perceived utility is less than the asked price.

Consumers have access to many competing retail stores but they will shop only at those that create value for them. One major goal of retail strategy is to find new, innovative ways to enhance value to potential customers. Retail managers must continuously strive to increase utility and at the same time monitor their costs in an effort to reduce the prices they have to charge. Implemented in tandem, these actions will enhance value and attract more customers to the store.

How Retailers Create Value

Good retailers continuously search for ways to create value for their customers. The many ways in which retailers enhance value can be grouped into the five categories shown in Exhibit 1.6: (1) create utility by offering the right merchandise, (2) create utility by having a good shopping atmosphere, (3) create utility by decreasing the risk of shopping, (4) create utility by making shopping convenient, and (5) reduce price by controlling costs.

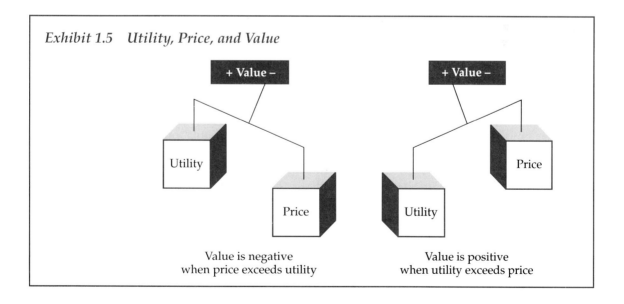

Exhibit 1.5   Utility, Price, and Value

Value is negative when price exceeds utility

Value is positive when utility exceeds price

Exhibit 1.6   How Retailers Create Value

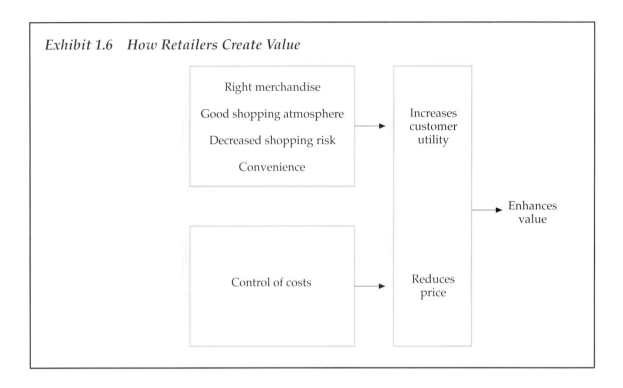

The Right Merchandise

A retailer's **merchandise**—the products and services it offers for sale—fundamentally determines the utility of the retailer's offer. Consumers expect retailers to provide products and services:

- That satisfy their needs and wants.
- In quantities and packages that are convenient for them.

Although a retailer does not manufacture products, it creates utility for consumers by bringing together at a single location a combination of products and services that are varied but related. A department store, for example, sells a wide variety of merchandise that typically includes apparel, housewares, furniture, toys, electronic goods, and cosmetics. Within each of these different merchandise lines, it also carries various brands, styles, colors, sizes, and so on. This range of choice within a merchandise line is referred to as the level of assortment. Because of the variety of merchandise and the level of assortment, the total number of items carried by a large department store can exceed hundreds of thousands. Similarly, an average supermarket carries about 25,000 items, and a combination supermarket and drugstore may offer as many as 40,000 to 50,000 items.

Discount stores such as Target are one of the mainstays of retailing in the United States. The Target chain is operated by Dayton Hudson Company, which also operates department and soft- and hard-goods stores.

The merchandise offered for sale is one of the major factors influencing the consumer's decision to shop at a particular store. Although other factors also influence the ultimate purchase decision, the potential for exchange will never be created if the retailer does not carry the products and services consumers need. The retailer must anticipate what products and services its customers will want and procure them from manufacturers or wholesalers. The retailer thus acts as the consumer's purchasing agent.

The retailer's role as a purchasing agent significantly benefits consumers, since it increases the efficiency of shopping. Consider consumers' difficulty if they had to deal with many different food producers separately instead of buying all groceries they required at a supermarket. This would be so inconvenient and time consuming that it would be practically impossible. The same holds true for buying a dress or a suit. The consumer can visit a retail store and inspect and compare all available dresses and suits instead of having to deal with hundreds of manufacturers located around the world.

To fulfill its role as a purchasing agent properly, the retailer must carry merchandise that meets the needs and expectations of its customers. Different groups of consumers have different needs and expectations; their tastes and preferences also vary. Each retailer must, therefore, match the items it carries to the needs and

Retailing is extremely diverse, and comprises both large chain stores with hundreds of outlets and small, independent stores such as this jewelry store. Jewelry stores typically have low sales but high margins.

expectations of the customers it wants to attract. Few people would shop at K mart or Wal-Mart for a $300 dress. Similarly, no one expects fashionable stores like Bloomingdale's and Jordan Marsh to sell hardware and lumber.

To satisfy diverse consumer needs, a variety of retail institutions, including department stores, discount stores, supermarkets, drugstores, specialty apparel stores, etc., has emerged. Each satisfies a different set of consumer needs. Consumers have expectations about the kinds of goods and services sold by each type of store and the variety and assortment of its merchandise offering. For example, consumers expect variety stores (Woolworth or Ben Franklin) and discount stores (Wal-Mart or K mart) to sell a wide variety of merchandise, but offer limited assortments within each product line. Specialty stores, on the other hand, concentrate on a few types of merchandise, but offer wide selections within those lines. Consider, for example, The Gap, a well-known apparel chain. Gap stores sell only a limited variety of clothing, but have many sizes, colors, and styles of the jeans, sweaters, shorts, and tee shirts that suit the tastes of their teenage and young adult customers. Department stores (Macy's, Jordan Marsh, or Dillard's) and general merchandisers (Sears) follow a more balanced strategy that offers variety as well as assortment.

Even when two types of stores carry similar products, their merchandise strategies can differ. Books, for example, are sold at specialty book chains (such as Waldenbooks, B. Dalton, and Barnes and Noble), book sections of department stores, convenience stores (gift stores at airports), supermarkets, and drug stores. The merchandising strategies of these stores, however, are quite different.

Specialty book stores stock the greatest assortment of book titles in both hardcover and paperback. At the other extreme, convenience stores, supermarkets, and drug stores typically carry only best-selling paperbacks, since they are in greatest demand. Department stores fall in between these two extremes. In addition to paperback novels, department stores also sell hardcover books of general interest. Campus book stores, on the other hand, follow a strategy that is quite distinct from all of these types of stores. They cater to the needs of students and, therefore, carry mostly textbooks for classes at the local college or university.

The merchandise offering is the most important vehicle through which retailers create utility for their customers. To be successful, retailers must match their merchandise offerings with customer expectations. A well-defined merchandise offering creates a clear image about the store in the consumer's mind. When each store carries a well-defined and consistent merchandise assortment, the consumer can limit the search for goods to a small number of stores likely to carry what he or she wants to buy. If retail stores continuously change their merchandise policy, consumers must spend much more time searching for products and services at different stores, and the entire shopping process would become very inefficient. Consumers will, therefore, pay premium prices at stores that serve their needs consistently.

The Shopping Atmosphere

Although the merchandise is a key element in determining utility, as discussed earlier, it is not the only one. Utility can be further enhanced by supporting the merchandise with a good **shopping atmosphere**. In making a purchase decision, consumers "respond to more than the tangible product or service that is being offered."[4]

The physical environment in which the product or service is sold is also an integral part of the exchange process. The aesthetic atmosphere of the store influences the customer's perceived utility and therefore the value of the exchange. This is often described as psychic utility, since it derives from the psychological feeling generated by the physical environment. By creating a shopping atmosphere that evokes pleasant feelings, retailers can enhance the perceived value of what they sell. The store's decor, color, layout, merchandise displays, and even its piped-in music are important in creating a proper shopping atmosphere.

In designing the shopping atmosphere, the retailer must consider the type of customers it wants to attract. Just as the merchandise must match the needs of the customers, the shopping atmosphere, too, must be consistent with customer expectations. The atmosphere must fortify the attitudes and emotional feelings customers expect from the store.

Reducing Shopping Risk

Buying products and services can be risky and stressful to consumers. Retailers can enhance their perceived value by reducing this **shopping risk**. Retailers provide consumers with merchandise information, as one way to decrease the risk of shopping for consumers. Too many products and brands are available for a consumer to know much about all of them. Consumers learn a great deal about products and services from retail salespeople. By providing this merchandise information, sales personnel can greatly enhance the value of the retailer's offering to consumers.

Liberal policies for accepting returned merchandise and warranties also reduce risk. This is especially important for mail-order firms and other direct retailers who must overcome consumer resistance to buying products sight unseen. Most mail-order firms, therefore, have very liberal return policies to reduce the risk of shopping by mail. For example, the Company Store, which sells down coats and comforters by mail, will not only fully refund the price of any item that a customer wants to return, but will also arrange for free pick-up by United Parcel Service. This policy has attracted many consumers who might otherwise have found mail-order shopping too risky.

Shopping Convenience

Making shopping more convenient for potential customers is another important way to increase utility and value. Dual-career households in today's time-pressed society make **shopping convenience** very important.

Retailers can increase shopping convenience in many ways. Proper location increases shopping convenience by reducing the time customers have to spend traveling to the store. Keeping stores open longer hours, especially late at night, also increases convenience. Shopping convenience is one reason for the growth of mail-order retailing. Many consumers find it more convenient to shop from their own homes than to travel to retail stores.

Adequate customer service can also enhance shopping convenience. Acceptance of credit cards and personal checks, for example, makes shopping easier for consumers by eliminating the need to carry large amounts of cash. Gift wrapping and alterations are two other examples. Many department stores even offer personalized shopping assistance to help customers complete their shopping quickly and conveniently.

Shopping convenience can also be enhanced by making it easier for consumers to find what they need. Signs along aisles in supermarkets and store directories in department stores are just two of the many ways in which retailers make the task of shopping easier for their customers.

Controlling Costs

As mentioned earlier, utility and price jointly determine value. Therefore, in addition to increasing utility, retailers must continuously control their costs so that they can price their merchandise competitively. Four major types of costs in retail operations are: (1) cost of land and buildings, (2) labor costs, (3) cost of goods, and (4) inventory carrying costs. Efficiently controlling these costs gives the firm the ability to keep prices lower than competitors and yet earn adequate profits. These and other costs affecting retail operations are discussed in more detail in later chapters.

The hallmark of successful retailing is the ability to create value for customers through proper merchandise selection, supporting the merchandise with good shopping atmosphere, reducing shopping risk, increasing shopping convenience, and controlling costs. Astute retailers continuously search for new and innovative ways to increase customer utility. In this way they give consumers reason to shop at their stores as opposed to those of their competitors.

STRATEGIC RETAIL MARKETING

Retailing is an intensely competitive industry. The nearly two million retail outlets in the country continuously and vigorously compete to attract customers. Although total retail sales has been growing in nominal terms, in recent years it has held more or less constant in terms of real (that is, inflation-adjusted) dollars. This means that much of the increase in retail sales is due to inflation and not because people are buying more. The early 1990s were particularly hard for many retailers. Because of adverse economic conditions, Christmas and holiday sales were negatively affected in both 1990 and 1991, putting many retailers—large and small—in financial trouble.

Without a growing level of total demand, individual retailers can expand only by taking customers away from their competitors. As a result, the level of competition in the retail industry has reached historic proportions. As one observer of the industry put it, "It's constant war out there—24 hours a day."[5]

The Search for Differential Advantage

To survive in a highly competitive environment, a business must create a competitive advantage and differentiate itself from competitors. The retailer must offer superior value to give customers more reason to visit its store than those of its competitors. In a nutshell, this is the challenge of retail management—*to find profitable avenues for creating competitive **differential advantage***. No business can survive without a sustainable differential advantage over its competitors.

Retailers create differential advantage in many ways. Stores such as Bloomingdale's and Neiman-Marcus, for example, are well-known for their innovative merchandising. Their unique, fashionable merchandise follows the latest styles and trends, giving customers a reason to visit these stores. Nordstrom and Parisian's, two apparel chains, are well-known for the high level of personal service they provide. The high service level differentiates these chains from other apparel stores.

For another example consider Domino's Pizza. Domino's was successful in differentiating itself in the highly competitive fast-food market by offering free delivery service. Domino's promises free delivery within 30 minutes of placing an order. If the pizza is not delivered within 30 minutes, it is given to the customer at a discount. Although other chains, too, now offer delivery service, Domino's has been able to retain the advantage it gained initially. Warehouse stores, such as Costco, on the other hand, gain their differential advantage through low prices. Convenience stores such as 7-Eleven have the advantage of convenient locations. These are just a few examples of how retailers create differential advantage. These and many other examples will be discussed in more detail throughout the book.

Principles of Strategic Retail Marketing

To meet the challenge of creating and sustaining competitive advantage, retail firms need to adopt the **strategic retail marketing** approach. Strategic marketing focuses the firm's efforts on the consumer and the external environment of the business. The strategic marketing approach is a way of thinking based on the philosophy that *the goal of all business is to create value by satisfying consumer needs at a profit*. When applied to retail firms, this yields four important principles:

1. As their primary goal, retail firms seek to earn profits by creating value for their customers.
2. To create value, retailers must satisfy the needs and expectations of their customers better than their competitors.
3. The goal of customer satisfaction must permeate the entire organization and integrate all the activities of the firm.
4. Retailers must have a long-term view and respond to threats and opportunities created by shifts in the business environment.

These principles demonstrate that the primary focus of the marketing concept is **customer orientation**. To do this well, retailers must look at their business from the customers' perspective and channel all efforts towards satisfying their needs and expectations. Success hinges on the ability to gauge changing customer needs and respond to them quickly and efficiently. A manager of Safeway, one of the nation's largest supermarket chains, stated it this way:

Marketing in now our prime focus. In the past, we ran our business by giving [consumers] what we thought they wanted. Now we have got to find out what they want and then develop the products.[6]

Another observer puts it this way:

Merchants will live or die on how well their strategic planning creates value for their customers. . . . New merchandise, new presentations, new market, better values lead to solid, dramatic long-term growth.[7]

The Retail Environment

Although an organization's strategy must focus on the customer, other groups and forces also influence its activities. As shown in Exhibit 1.7, the retailer's environment can be viewed as comprising two layers. The first is the actions of competitors and suppliers. The second layer comprises demographic, economic, technological, and legal forces.

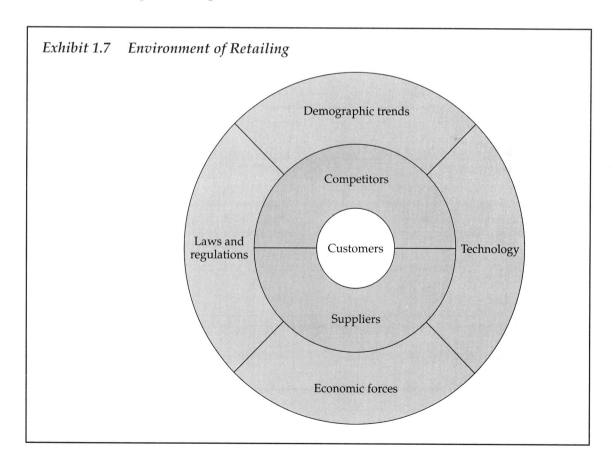

Exhibit 1.7   Environment of Retailing

Starting Your Own Retail Business Requires a Good Idea and Lots of Hard Work

Starting a business and making it successful involves the combination of many elements: hard work, a willingness to live with uncertainty, staying power while the business gets going, and good business skills. But perhaps the most important element to starting a business is having a good idea— an idea that will sell. And for many people that is the real challenge.

Which ideas will work? Ideas that work are the ones for products or services that consumers want and need, and of course, are willing to pay for. This doesn't mean that the product or service has to be glamorous or unusual, often it is the most practical idea that succeeds.

The idea for Garrett Boone and Kip Tindell's chain, *The Container Store*, came in a flash of light, says Boone. The two were seeking *the* idea, the one that would launch their careers, and they simply happened upon the idea to sell containers. The partners, urban dwellers themselves, realized that urban dwellers need to store things in an organized and efficient manner. Based on this perceived need, the partners decided to open a retail store specializing in containers, of every shape and sort, for storing almost anything. Thus was born a successful entrepreneurial venture.

Boone and Tindell knew their target audience well; after all, they were part of it:

consumers seeking a way to make efficient use of limited closet space or a way to ensure that their small kitchens could hold all the necessities. In 1978, Boone and Tindell set up the first Container Store in a 1,600-square-foot location. A small but neatly organized store was the best way, they thought, to demonstrate the usefulness of the products they sold. Consumers clearly agreed with the idea. The Container Store now boasts ten locations, of more than 23,000 square feet each, with annual sales topping $36 million.

Both founders agree that a good part of the chain's success is due to the fact that they have remained focused on their original merchandising concept of selling multifunctional, well-designed storage products for the home or office. Neither has waved from this core idea in their 13 years of business. The company has resisted many possible ideas for diversification. This focus has ensured that there is no confusion by management or consumers about what The Container Store sells. While the stores may not have diversified, they have certainly expanded, and Boone and Tindell look forward to continuing growth.

Source: "Retailing's Entrepreneurs of the Year," *Chain Store Age Executive*, December 1991, pp. 28–50.

The actions of competitors directly affect the firm's performance. Firms must monitor their competitors' strategy closely and, when competitors' actions threaten their well-being, respond quickly with their own plans to protect their competitive positions. Constant maneuvering by firms, each trying to establish superior competitive position, creates rivalry among them. The nature of rivalry and competition in retailing is the subject of the next chapter.

Suppliers also influence retailers' strategies. Retailers do not typically produce the merchandise they sell, but rather obtain it from manufacturers and wholesalers. Each retailer is thus part of a **marketing channel**, which is the *set of institutions that distribute goods and services from the manufacturer to the final consumer.* Manufacturers rely on retailers to sell their products and retailers depend on manufacturers for their suppliers. This interdependency imparts some special characteristics to retail institutions which will be explored fully in Chapter 3.

The retailer and its customers, competitors, and suppliers are all influenced by macroenvironmental factors. Firms must monitor and respond to changes in those environments when they create opportunities for growth or threaten the firm's very existence. Exhibit 1.7 shows four major forces—demographic, technological, economic, and legal—that make up the macroenvironment. While the impact of each of these forces on retail strategy will be examined in detail in Chapter 4, the following examples illustrate their importance:

- Over the last two decades more and more women have joined the ranks of professional managers. Many department stores have increased their selection of women's career suits and dresses to cater to the clothing needs of the working women. Many specialty apparel stores, too, have taken advantage of this trend by specializing in clothes for working women. For example, the specialty clothing retailer, Barney's—until recently the bastion of businessmen—now gives equal attention to the businesswoman.
- Working women have less time to spend in stores. Mail-order retailers such as L.L. Bean, Land's End, Williams-Sonoma, and Spiegel have responded to this trend very successfully. The number of mail-order retailers and the amount of merchandise bought from them has been increasing each year. Supermarkets and convenience stores have also responded to this trend by extending store hours—some even staying open for 24 hours a day—to allow customers to shop at their own convenience.
- One of the most important changes taking place in the United States is the change in the demographic composition of the population. The American population is aging. Nearly 30 million people, comprising over 11 percent of the population, are over 65 years old. The elderly demand many services, particularly travel, leisure activities, health care, and home maintenance. They also frequently buy financial services, furs, jewelry, and expensive clothing.[8]
- Changing demographics have also propelled the kids' apparel and toy markets to a place among the fastest growing retail segments. Children's clothing chains such as Kids R Us, Espirit Kids, and GapKids have expanded rapidly in the last few years. To exploit this growth opportunity, Sears entered into a licensing agreement with McDonald's to sell specially designed children's clothing, and Woolworth opened a chain of off-price clothing outlets for children.[9]
- Today's consumers pay close attention to their health and diet. A retail store called Sweet Victory saw an untapped opportunity in this trend. It sells low-

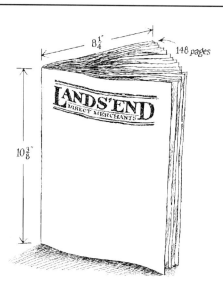

THE STORE WE MIND

Our store is 10⅜ inches tall, 8¼ inches wide, and 148 pages deep.**
It has no crowded parking lots, clogged elevators or hidden rest rooms.

It displays over 775 pieces of merchandise. And by the time you count colors and sizes and shapes and variations, you are up to 18,000 items you can shop from—assembled under one "roof" from the four corners of the earth, wherever quality calls.

Most of these items are shown on or with models so much like you they could live in your neighborhood. Every item is unconditionally guaranteed by the world's shortest guarantee. In two words: **GUARANTEED. PERIOD**.

We mind our store 24 hours a day, 7 days a week. You can buy from us in the comfort of your own home. But first, remember, we're only a phone call away—wherever you live. The toll-free telephone number: 1-800-356-4444. Or send in the coupon at right for a free look at our "store."

Oh, yes—we accept Discover, Am Ex, MC, or VISA. And we deliver by UPS, U.S. Mail, or Federal Express.

of fine wool and cotton sweaters, Oxford buttondown shirts, traditional dress clothing, snow wear, deck wear, original Lands' End soft luggage and a multitude of other quality goods from around the world.

**This describes our "store" for April '93. The dimensions may vary by season, but you can always count on the quality, price, and service.

©1993, Lands' End, Inc.

Please send free catalog,
Lands' End Direct Merchants
Dept. 2-??
1 Lands' End Lane
Dodgeville, WI 53595

Name _____
Address _____
_____ Apt. _____
City _____
State _____ Zip _____
Phone ( ) _____

Or call toll-free:
1-800-356-4444

Direct retailers such as Land's End represent one of the fastest growing segments of retailing. Customers can shop from the convenience of their homes without making a trip to the store. The growth of direct retailing has been helped tremendously by the proliferation of credit cards and by the swift means of delivering merchandise to customers.

calorie, hand-dipped ice cream and chocolates to satisfy the needs of the diet-conscious ice-cream and chocolate lovers.

- Changes in technology also create opportunity for retailers. The combination of cable television and new satellite communication technology has fueled the recent growth of electronic home shopping, one of the newest forms of retailing. Improvements in satellite communication technology have also spurred the use of electronic data interchange between retailers and their suppliers, changing the way in which retailers manage their inventories.
- The concern for the earth's physical environment is rising worldwide. This is reflected in the demand for products made of natural ingredients. Consumers are also demanding packaging made of recyclable materials. McDonald's has responded to this by replacing environmentally harmful packages with those made of recyclable materials. Another retailer which has responded to this trend is the Body Shop. This international retailer sells cosmetics and body-care products made of natural ingredients.
- The overall economic climate has a profound impact on retailing, since the amount of money people spend in retail stores is affected by it. The poor economy of the last few years has adversely affected even some of the largest of the nation's retailers. Many have sought bankruptcy proceedings under Chapter 11, while others have closed their doors permanently.

The Target Market

One of the primary tasks in formulating marketing strategy for a retail store is to choose the customer group the store will serve. Consumers' needs differ and so do their perceptions of value. These differences arise from variations in socioeconomic status, age, education, lifestyle, psychographic, and other factors. A single retailer cannot satisfy all needs of all people. The retailer must choose the specific group of customers that it wishes to serve by fulfilling certain of their needs. This group of customers is called the retailer's **target market**, the one or more specific segments of potential consumers toward whom it will direct its marketing program.[10] The retailer must gear its marketing strategy to the needs and expectations of that target market.

Concentration on the needs of its target market has contributed to the success of Wal-Mart. The company has established itself as the nation's premier provider of basic value to predominantly middle-class families residing in small and medium-sized towns. The company's mission is to be the store of first choice for these families. Its entire retail operation, from the merchandise it sells and the locations of its outlets to the way its advertises, seeks to serve this target market.

In contrast to Wal-Mart, such stores as Neiman-Marcus, Saks Fifth Avenue, and Bergdorf Goodman gear their strategies to meet the needs of more fashion-conscious consumers with high incomes. They carry fashion-forward merchandise with up-to-date styles, colors, and designs. The store interiors and customer services also seek to please high-income customers. The stores are located primarily in large cities or high-income suburban areas where the target customers typically reside.

The Retail Mix

With the target market selected, the retail manager must determine the appropriate retail mix to satisfy it. **Retail mix** refers to the combination of marketing activities such as choosing a location, selecting merchandise, advertising, providing customer service, pricing, and so on by which the retail managers must determine the optimum mix of activities and coordinate the elements of the mix. While many elements may make up a firm's retail mix, the basic ones are:

- Location
- Merchandise
- Store atmosphere
- Customer service
- Price
- Advertising
- Personal selling
- Sales incentive programs

Each retail store has a distinct **retail image** in consumers' minds, which emerges from its combination of the various elements of the retail mix. The retail mix must be very carefully planned so that it creates the desired image. Each element of the mix must be consistent with the others or the image will be confused. To attract upper-income customers for high-priced, fashionable clothes, a store must create an inviting shopping atmosphere and an ambiance that suits the merchandise. It would be inconsistent for such a store to be located along a shopping strip next to car dealers and lumber yards. The store must have properly trained salespeople to help its customers, and it must accept checks and credit cards. The store must properly orchestrate the elements of the retail mix to create the desired image.

Because of the importance of the retail mix, each of its elements will be discussed in detail in later chapters of the book. It is, however, important to note at this point a crucial difference between the elements of the retail mix and the environmental factors discussed earlier. The environmental factors sometimes create new opportunities for the firm and at other times pose threats to its very existence. Retailers can adapt and respond to these forces, but they cannot control them. Retailers can control the retail mix elements, though. Retail managers can decide where to locate a store, what type of merchandise to sell, what price to charge, the kind of atmosphere the store should have, what services to provide, and how to advertise and promote the merchandise. Through these decisions the manager creates the store's image and responds to the environment. The retail mix elements are the weapons for fighting the competitive war, while the environmental factors define the terrain on which the battles will be fought.

ENTREPRENEURIAL EDGE

Transforming a Hobby into a Business

Retail ventures get started in many different ways. Sometimes the efforts are well-planned, carefully thought out ventures of large corporations or individual entrepreneurs. Some businesses are started by individuals confronted with what seems like a great idea. And a few spring from the personal hobbies of their owners.

Take, for example, Gloria Jean and Ed Kvetko, owners of *Gloria Jean's Coffee Bean*. They went to buy coffee one day, and ended up buying a business. The Kvetkos, self-taught coffee connoisseurs, were always on the lookout for a good cup of coffee, but they were rarely able to find gourmet coffee that suited their tastes. As a hobby, they began importing coffee from around the world for their personal consumption. They enjoyed trying out a myriad of coffees, from dark Turkish roasts, to light, sweet, liqueur-flavored coffees. The Kvetkos travelled a great deal, finding some of their coffees while touring the world. Whenever they heard or read about a new type of coffee, they ordered directly from the producer.

Slowly, the Kvetkos built up a list of sources and suppliers for some of the finest coffees available in the world. Without realizing it, they had acquired one of the most important ingredients of a successful new business: knowledge of product sources. Not only did they know *where* to get the coffees, but they had tested each of the varieties available and had learned their prices. In essence, they gave their business a trial-run before actually setting up shop.

Then in 1979, they found a gourmet coffee shop that was for sale, and they knew they had found their dream. The store was unprofitable, but the Kvetkos believed that the causes were poor products and high prices. Armed with their knowledge of coffee types and sources, the couple decided to buy the coffee store and restock it with the great coffees they had already been importing for their personal consumption. The Kvetkos knew where to get the best coffee, knew how much they should be paying, and what real coffee connoisseurs (like themselves) would be willing to pay for a cup of "gourmet joe."

After the store became successful, the owners then turned to franchising their concept. Franchising transformed Gloria Jean's Coffee Bean from a neighborhood success story to a national phenomenon. It is now a 132-store national chain earning over $80 million in revenues annually, and plans are being made for international expansion. The Kvetkos clearly understood the basic principles of the coffee business, and through their own love of coffee, they were able to turn their hobby into a thriving business. In fact, Gloria Jean and Ed Kvetko were named one of 1991's retailing entrepreneurs of the year by *Chain Store Age Executive*, providing that the combination of good ideas and tasteful research really pays off!

Sources: "Retailing's Entrepreneurs of the Year," *Chain Store Age Executive*, December 1991, pp. 28–50; and Janean Huber, "Franchise Forecast," *Entrepreneur*, January 1993, pp. 72–75.

The Challenge of Retail Management

Retail managers face a challenging task (see Exhibit 1.8). As discussed, the role of retail management can be described as generating profits for the firm by creating value for target consumers. This goal can be achieved only if the retailer is able to create a differential advantage for the store. Without a sustainable differential advantage, customers will have little reason to patronize that store over others, and success will be elusive. To maintain their competitive position, retail managers must keep abreast of changes in competition and the other elements of the macroenvironment, select and keep their focus on the target market, and coordinate the retail mix elements. Throughout this book the reader will find illustrations of how firms have achieved success by following customer-oriented marketing strategies and providing superior value to their customers. One such example is McDonald's.

On Friday, April 15, 1955, Ray Kroc opened his first restaurant in Des Plaines, Illinois. That day he sowed the seeds for one of the most remarkable stories of modern-day corporate America. Today McDonald's is not just a symbol of corporate success, but a part of Americana itself. In 1992, McDonald's had nearly 10,000 outlets in the United States and over 3,000 outlets located in 53 foreign countries. Its golden arches are one of the most widely recognized corporate icons in the world.

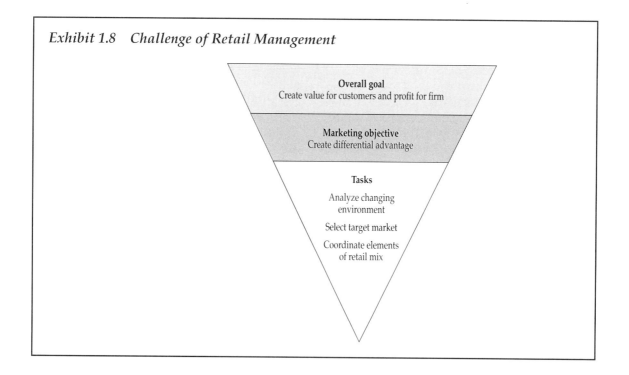

Exhibit 1.8   Challenge of Retail Management

Overall goal
Create value for customers and profit for firm

Marketing objective
Create differential advantage

Tasks

Analyze changing environment

Select target market

Coordinate elements of retail mix

Few will argue that McDonald's is one of the most successful business organizations of recent times. Underlying McDonald's success are two criteria of good strategic management—its focus on its customers and its ability to differentiate itself from competitors in those customer's minds.

The reasons for this phenomenal success can be explained in one simple word: Value. McDonald's has consistently provided value for its customers, and it has reaped the benefits. Ray Kroc did not invent the hamburger or the french fry, but he did realize how quality, service, cleanliness, and convenience can increase the value of the food.

Another reason for McDonald's success is its steadfast focus on the target market: people wanting fast, convenient, light meals. Although McDonald's customers come from virtually every demographic segment of the population—families with young children, adults, teens, and seniors—they all perceive value in McDonald's offering. McDonald's also meticulously plans and implements its retail mix. The locations are convenient, the restaurants are simple, yet clean and attractive, service is efficient, and prices are reasonable. The final reason for McDonald's success, and the one that differentiates it from its competitors, is its image of consistency and trustworthiness. Later chapters of this book will return more than once to draw insights from this retailer without par.

In today's highly competitive environment, no firm, not even McDonald's, can afford to relax its customer orientation. McDonald's value position was somewhat eroded in the late 1980s by other fast-food retailers such as Taco Bell and Pizza

Hut. McDonald's was, however, able to respond by introducing new menu items and by lowering prices on some items.

How do retailers respond to rapidly changing environments, keep their focus on the consumer, and sustain their competitive advantage? They must have a strategic plan driven by a marketing orientation. In recent years, retail firms have had to increase their emphasis on formal strategic planning to determine what they need to do to become and remain successful.

Strategic planning is not really a new concept. All business success results from implementation of a good, long-term strategy. Unfortunately, too many retailers tend to focus attention primarily on short-term decisions rather than chart long-term growth of the company. They have also tended to be internally oriented, rather than focusing on the external environment. Good planning must, however, "continually look outward and keep the business in line with the outside environment."[11] Today's rapid environmental change requires long-term strategic thinking that capitalizes on new opportunities and builds value for customers. Without a well-planned strategy, a firm wanders like a rudderless ship continuously buffeted by changing environmental forces.[12] The strategic plan charts the firm's future course and directs the activities of all the parts of the organization toward achieving long-term goals. The various elements of a well-formulated strategy are discussed in detail in Chapters 5 and 6.

TYPES OF RETAIL INSTITUTIONS

Retailing is extremely diverse. Many different types of retail stores compete for shares of the market. Although they all share the common focus of selling to ultimate consumers, retail stores have different formats, sizes, policies, and marketing strategies. Diverse types of organizations operate these different retail outlets. Some large retailers operate hundreds of outlets, while other retailers are small, independent businesses with one or two outlets. Also, franchised stores and voluntary chains, although independently owned, belong to large networks of stores. Several classification schemes have been proposed to categorize retail stores into groups based on similarities in strategies and operational procedures. A list of some of the many ways in which retail forms can be classified appears in Exhibit 1.9. This section discusses some of these schemes.

Store versus Nonstore Retailing

At the broadest level, retail institutions can be distinguished based on whether the selling takes place at a store or not. Vending machines, door-to-door sales, and direct retailing are the major forms of nonstore retailing. Direct retailers are currently growing by reaching consumers through mail, telephone, television, radio, magazines, or computer networks. After learning about the retailer's offerings, consumers can order by mail, telephone, or through electronic networks. L.L. Bean,

---

Exhibit 1.9 Retail Store Classification Schemes

1. Store versus nonstore retailing
2. Service versus product retailing
3. By type of merchandise: food, apparel, automotive, drug
4. Departmentalized versus specialty retailing
5. By margin and turnover
6. By location: downtown, mall, free-standing
7. By type of ownership: independent, chain, franchise
8. By strategic group

Spiegel, Company Store, CompuStore, and Home Shopping Network are some prominent retailers who rely exclusively on direct retailing techniques. In addition, some of the large chain stores, such as J.C. Penney and Bloomingdale's, also sell merchandise through catalogs mailed to consumers' homes. In fact, until it decided to close its catalog operations in 1993, Sears was the largest mail-order retailer in the United States.

Avon, Tupperware, and Mary Kay, three other prominent nonstore retailers, rely on agents who sell directly at the consumer's home or workplace. Many insurance agents and encyclopedia salespeople also go directly to the customer's home. Retailers whose salespeople call on customers at their homes or workplaces are called direct-selling retailers.

Goods versus Service Retailing

A distinction can also be made between retailers that sell goods and those that sell services. Service retailers do not sell tangible products to their customers, but provide them with personal services. Like nonstore retailing, service retailing is growing in importance.

The strategies of service retailers vary considerably depending on the type of service they provide and their degree of contact with the customer. Hotels, motels, airlines, hospitals, banks, and hair salons have high degrees of customer contact. In high-contact services, customers' satisfaction with the service depends critically on their perception of the quality of the service personnel. On the other hand, the level of customer contact can be much lower in such services as car rental, automated laundromats, and parking garages. The customer may never need to see a service person at all.

Type of Merchandise

Most government publications classify retail outlets based on the type of merchandise predominantly sold by the store. Exhibit 1.10 shows the classification scheme used by the Census of Retailing published by the U.S. Department of Commerce. Because most government statistics on retailing are organized in this fashion, this classification scheme is useful for comparing historical trends and sales for different types of stores. This type of classification has some serious drawbacks though.

First, because retail stores often sell a variety of products, it is not always possible to assign them precisely to one of the groups shown in Exhibit 1.10. Consider, for example, a combination store that sells food and grocery products as well as health and beauty aids. The Census Bureau will assign this store to either the food category or the drugstore category depending on which kind of merchandise predominates. This reduces the accuracy of the classification. For a second problem, such a broad classification masks changing sales patterns and categories. For example, while total sales at food stores have grown only modestly, combination store sales have grown markedly. Such changes in sales pattern within merchandise and retail categories goes unnoticed in the broad classifications in the Census of Retailing. Finally, this classification scheme does not provide insight into the stores' strategies or operations.

Merchandise Strategy

Retail stores can also be classified according to their levels of merchandise specialization. A key distinction separates stores that concentrate on limited merchandise lines and those that sell a wide variety of products. **Specialty stores** sell a limited variety of products, but offer a wide choice within their product lines. Consider the following examples:

- The Gap, The Limited, Benetton, Brooks Brothers (apparel)
- Lucky Stores, Safeway, A&P, Kroger, Grand Union (food)
- Rx Place, Rite-Aid, Genovese, Revco (drugs)
- The Wiz, Circuit City, Radio Shack (electronic goods)

Specialization gives each of these retailers the opportunity to offer a large selection of brands, models, styles, and sizes within their product lines.

Very different merchandise strategies characterize department stores (Macy's, Dayton's, Dillard's), discount outlets (K Mart, Wal-Mart, Target, Zayre), variety stores (Woolworth, Ben Franklin), and mass merchandisers (Sears). Instead of concentrating on narrow product lines, these stores sell a wide variety of merchandise covering different types of products and services. The stores are typically organized around a number of separate merchandise operations such as apparel, appliances, cosmetics, furniture, and so on. The physical organization of these stores, their merchandise displays, and even their management hierarchies reflect this departmental structure. For this reason they are referred to as **departmentalized operations**.

Departmentalized operations derive a major competitive strength from facilitating one-stop shopping. Consumers who need to purchase a variety of items can

---

Exhibit 1.10 *Classification Scheme: Census of Retailing*

Automotive dealers
  Motor vehicle dealers
  Miscellaneous automotive supply dealers
  Auto and home supply stores

Furniture, home furnishings, and equipment dealers
  Furniture and home furnishings stores
  Household appliances, radios, and TV stores
  Other stores

Building materials, hardware, garden supplies, and mobile home dealers
  Building materials stores
  Hardware stores
  Other stores

Apparel and accessories stores
  Men's and boys' clothing and furnishings
  Women's clothing
  Specialty stores
  Furriers
  Shoe stores
  Other apparel and accessories stores

Drug stores

Eating and drinking places

Food stores
  Grocery stores
  Other food stores

Gasoline service stations

General merchandise stores
  Department stores
  Variety stores
  Other general-merchandise stores

Liquor stores

Mail-order houses (department store merchandise)

---

simply visit one of these stores rather than make separate trips to different specialty stores. However, because they carry a large variety of merchandise, departmentalized stores offer only limited choice within each product line compared to a specialty store that concentrates on that line of merchandise. For instance, the selection of toys in department stores is very limited compared with the selection at a specialty toy store like Toys R Us. The electronics department at a department store will not carry nearly as wide a selection of televisions, VCRs, and calculators as a specialty electronics retailer.

The Margin-Turnover Classification

A useful way to differentiate the strategies of different types of retail stores is to categorize them based on the two fundamental dimensions of any retail strategy—gross margin and inventory turnover.[13] Because of their fundamental importance in retailing, the concepts of margin and turnover will be discussed in more detail in later chapters. Only a brief explanation is provided here. To measure **margin**, subtract the retailer's cost of goods sold (the amount the retailer paid the supplier) from its sales revenue. A retailer with higher margins makes more money from each dollar of sales. **Turnover** measures the number of times the retailer sells its average inventory during the year. It reflects how quickly the merchandise sells once it is offered for sale.

These two concepts underlie the retail categorization scheme shown in Exhibit 1.11. Based on their margins and turnovers, all retail stores fall in one of the four quadrants shown in the exhibit. Jewelry stores, especially those selling high-priced diamonds and gems, are typical of stores with high margins and low turnovers. The jeweler's inventory doesn't turn over very quickly, but the margin on a piece of jewelry sold is high. A supermarket, on the other hand, trades off margin for turnover. Supermarket inventories turn over very quickly, but they provide very low margins. Cost of goods typically accounts for 80 cents of each dollar of supermarket sales. The cost of land, building, labor, advertising, and so on, can account for another 18 to 19 cents for each dollar of sales, leaving a supermarket with only 1 or 2 cents of profit per dollar of sales. The average net profit margin for supermarkets is about 1.4 cents per dollar of sales.

Marketing strategies of most retail stores stress either margin or turnover. Some stores, however, get both high margins and high turnovers by creating local monopolies. Two examples are neighborhood convenience stores and concessions at ball parks. Because of their access to customers, they can charge comparatively high prices (thereby maintaining high margin) and still turn their merchandise over quickly.

The final quadrant is the disaster scenario. In the long run, no store can survive with low margins together with low turnover.

Classification by Strategic Group

Another way of classifying stores is to group them based on similarities along key competitive dimensions. Such groups, called **strategic groups**, represent stores having the same or very similar customer focus and marketing strategy. Stores in the same strategic group, therefore, face similar consumer and competitive environ-

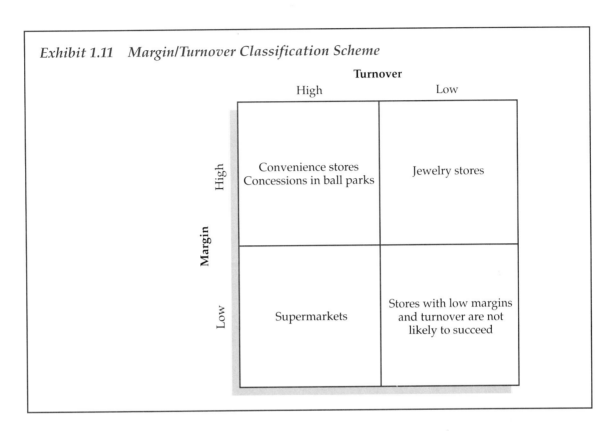

Exhibit 1.11   *Margin/Turnover Classification Scheme*

Turnover

	High	Low
High	Convenience stores Concessions in ball parks	Jewelry stores
Low	Supermarkets	Stores with low margins and turnover are not likely to succeed

Margin

ments. The concept of strategic groups and their implication for retail strategy are discussed in more detail in the next chapter.

Summary

1. Retail firms are those businesses that sell goods and services to customers for their personal or household use. Retailing is the primary institution through which most people come in contact with the world of business. Retailers exist wherever people need products or services. Retail companies comprise large chains with hundreds of outlets as well as small, neighborhood outlets operated by individual entrepreneurs. Nonstore and service retailing are important parts of the retail economy.
2. For retail exchange to take place, the retailer must offer to sell products and services that customers value, and customers must be willing to pay for them. Retailers create value for customers by (1) offering the right merchandise, (2) creating a pleasant shopping atmosphere, (3) decreasing shopping risk, (4) increasing shopping convenience, and (5) reducing price by controlling costs.

   To survive in today's competitive environment, retail firms must adopt the marketing philosophy that the goal of all business is to satisfy consumer needs at a profit. The marketing philosophy must permeate the organization and integrate all activities of the firm.

3. Although the customer must be central to an organization's strategy, the retailer must also pay close attention to competitors, suppliers, and the macroenvironment. Macroenvironmental forces are largely beyond the firm's control. These include demographic, economic, technological, and regulatory forces. Changes in the environment may create new opportunities or pose threats to the firm.

4. The foundation of a successful retail marketing strategy is the choice of the target market—the group of consumers the firm seeks to serve—and the way in which the firm differentiates itself from competitors. A well-established differential advantage gives consumers a reason to choose one firm's outlet over another.

5. The retail mix elements are tools for creating value and differential advantage. While many elements make up the retail mix, the most important are location, merchandise, store atmosphere, customer service, price, advertising, personal selling, and promotions. Retail managers must plan and coordinate each element of the retail mix carefully. The elements must all be consistent with the store's overall strategy and with each other.

6. In recent years, firms have begun to place a great deal of emphasis on a formal marketing strategy to determine what they need to do to become and remain successful. The overall goal of marketing strategy is to create value for customers and profits for the firm. The marketing strategy must identify how the firm will respond to changing environments, the target market it will serve, and how it will coordinate the elements of the retail mix to create differential advantage.

7. Retail stores can be classified in a number of ways including: by type of merchandise, level of merchandise specialization, margin and turnover, and strategic groups.

Key Concepts

Retailing	Differential advantage
Retail firms	Strategic retail marketing
Nonstore retailing	Customer orientation
Service retailing	Target market
Exchange	Retail mix
Value	Retail image
Utility	Specialty stores
Price	Departmentalized operations
Merchandise	Margin
Shopping atmosphere	Turnover
Shopping risk	Strategic groups
Shopping convenience	

Discussion Questions

1. Explain the following terms: (1) target market, (2) differential advantage, (3) retail mix, (4), retail image, (5) merchandise specialization.

2. Describe with examples the different ways in which retailers can create value for their customers?

3. Choose two local retailers and briefly describe their target markets. What are the differential advantages of these stores? Explain how these retailers have utilized the elements of the retail mix to enhance value for their customers?
4. How would you explain retailing and its importance to the economy to someone not familiar with the subject?
5. Explain the principles of strategic retail marketing.
6. What are the components of the retail environment. Give an example of a retail store that has either prospered or suffered due to changes in the macroenvironment. What new opportunities for retailers are currently arising due to changes in the environment?
7. Describe three approaches to classifying retail stores, other than by merchandise category.
8. Explain the margin-turnover scheme for classifying retail stores. How does an understanding of this classification help in formulating retail strategy?
9. Suppose that you are planning to open a new women's apparel store in your community. Describe the type of consumers you would target. How would you create differential advantage for your store compared to existing stores in your community?

Notes

1. The retail sales figures reported in this section are from various annual issues of the *Statistical Abstract of the United States* (Washington, D.C.: Department of Commerce, Bureau of Statistics).
2. U.S. Department of Labor, Bureau of Labor Statistics.
3. Philip Kotler, *Marketing: Analysis, Planning and Control* (Englewood Cliffs: Prentice-Hall, 1991), p. 7.
4. Philip Kotler, "Atmospherics as a Marketing Tool," *Journal of Retailing* 49 (Winter 1973), p. 48.
5. Samuel J. Cohen quoted in R. Johnson, "Retailers Refashioning Their Operations," *Kansas City Times*, March 7, 1983, p. D1.
6. See "Marketing: A New Priority," *Business Week*, Nov. 21, 1983, p. 99.
7. D. Kirk Davidson, "Merchants: Stick to Your Merchandising," *Marketing News* 26 (8), 1992, p. 4, 8.
8. Ganesan Viswabharaty and David Rink, "The Elderly: Neglected Business Opportunities," *Journal of Consumer Marketing* 1, no. 4 (1984), p. 39.
9. "Toddlers in $90 Suits? You Gotta Be Kidding," *Business Week*, September 21, 1987, p. 52.
10. Eric N. Berkowitz, Roger A. Kerin, and William Rudelius, *Marketing* (St. Louis: Times Mirror/Mosby 1986), p. 13.
11. George S. Day, *Strategic Market Planning* (St. Paul: West 1984), p. 3.
12. Ibid., p. 6.
13. Ronald Gist, *Retailing: Concepts and Decisions* (New York: John Wiley and Sons 1968), pp. 37–40.

CHAPTER 2
The Nature of
Retail Competition

Stores Reposition to Attract New Customers

As the consumer of the nineties grows ever more price-sensitive and value-oriented, apparel stores are struggling to find a profitable position for themselves within the industry. Gone are the days when consumers had extra time and money to devote to shopping. Now consumers seek high-quality, low-priced, long-wearing clothes; they want value and good service quickly. Retailers must now balance their merchandise offering with prices that create profit for them and value for their customers.

To create value for their customers, retailers must balance the quality of their merchandise, service, and shopping atmosphere with the price they charge. In other words, they have to take positions along the shopping opportunity line. As discussed later in this chapter, the shopping opportunity line has four basic positions for apparel retailers: discounter, mass merchandiser, department store, or high-fashion boutique. Store movement along the line can result in an overall repositioning that will attract a new customer base and offer new retailing opportunities.

From its founding in 1913 until the 1980s, J.C. Penney was a traditional mass merchan-

diser, offering everything from auto parts to clothing for the whole family. Its biggest competitor was Sears, and the two firms competed successfully for many years all over the United States. By the 1980s, however, these mass-merchandise stores were being squeezed out by the discounters on one side and the department stores on the other. Consumers were seeking a new form of quality and value—either through the low-priced discounter or the more fashion-oriented department store. A store such as J.C. Penney, whose offering was priced higher than the discounters but whose quality was below that of the department store, began to lack appeal for the consumer. Given this trend away from their traditional store category, J.C. Penney made the decision to revamp its image in an effort to become more competitive with department stores and upscale apparel retailers such as Nordstrom.

For J.C. Penney, such a move required significant changes in its retailing strategy. Penney's began by reducing its durable goods (auto parts, home furnishings, and so on) and by expanding the areas of men's, women's, and children's apparel. Management sought to improve not only the selection but also the quality in these areas, and began selling both private label and national

After studying this chapter, the reader will be able to:
- *Understand the characteristics of retail competition.*
- *Use strategic group analysis to analyze the nature of retail competition in a geographic market area.*
- *Explain how the level of competition among strategic groups is related to their positions on the shopping opportunity line.*
- *Describe how retailers can differentiate themselves from competitors within the same strategic group.*
- *Explain the forces affecting competitive rivalry among retail firms.*
- *Understand the reasons why the retail industry is becoming increasingly globalized.*

The change that the J.C. Penney chain has undergone throughout the 1980s is a prime example of how stores reposition to attract new target markets.

brands. Penney's included such department store favorite labels as Liz Claiborne and Halston, filling its selection with more fashion-oriented, high-quality, stylish clothing. Other areas expanded included accessories, such as cosmetics and belts, handbags and men's and women's shoes.

This new emphasis on fashion made it necessary for J.C. Penney to improve the stores' physical appearance. To sell higher fashion items, the stores needed to look the part. Penney's tried to emulate the decoration and arrangement of the traditional department store, adding better lighting and ornamentation, cleaner, more attractive display areas, wider aisles, and more dressing rooms. Service and salesperson training was also increased. Overall, the look of J.C. Penney was transformed into that of a department store, and despite an initially difficult financial period due to their expansion coinciding with an economic downturn, the repositioning succeeded in capturing a new customer base and created the fashionable department store image that J.C. Penney sought.

Other apparel industry repositioning efforts include The Avenue, which replaced Lerner Woman. The name change helped support a whole new fashion image and upscale design shift, similar to Penney's. The store's new owners decided to shift the previously dowdy store for women's plus sizes to a moderately priced fashion store with an upscale environment. While vogue fashions will always sell, The Avenue management felt that women over size fourteen—over 40 percent of the U.S. population—desired a more fashionable store that catered to them. The Avenue has thus far succeeded by emphasizing more fashionable styles and extras such as increased customer service and an elegant shopping atmosphere. The redesign also included the introduction of a store credit card and such finishing touches as wrapping purchases in tissue paper rather than putting them directly into shopping bags. The overall increase in sales has allowed The Avenue to keep prices moderate and increase the service and the frills at the same time. The response has been overwhelmingly positive, and expansion is expected to continue.

However, movement in the opposite direction, down the shopping opportunity line, is also very common. For example, when Sears was experiencing the same squeeze from discounters and department stores as was J.C. Penney, the chain opted to shift its image and reposition in order to compete with discount-

ers, such as Wal-Mart and K mart. Even big name designers and department stores are eager to downscale areas of their offerings in order to attract and retain the more price sensitive consumer. Examples include Nordstrom, the store synonymous with service and high-quality merchandise, which plans to open off-price stores in 1993, and designers such as Donna Karan and Giorgio Armani. Armani has three lines, each sold in its own outlet, ranging from suits from $2,500 to casual wear for $100 and below, and Donna Karan launched the DKNY line, featuring less expensive leisure wear for women. These secondary lines help to maintain profitability for the designers, often covering the costs of the haute-couture lines, and in and of themselves, have become phenomenally successful.

Sources: Susan Caminite, "The Pretty Payoff in Cheap Chic"; *Fortune*, February 24, 1992, p. 71; Marianne Wilson, "The Avenue Replaces Lerner Women"; *Chain Store Age Executive*, October 1991, pp. 25–26; and Jill Lettich, "J.C. Penney Struggles to Maintain Upscale Image"; *Discount Store News*, October 7, 1991, p. 34.

The nature of competition in any industry results from the interplay of supply and demand. In retailing, supply depends on the number and type of retail stores, and demand derives from the need and expectations of consumers and their ability to pay. The nature of demand cannot be appreciated by looking at supply and demand conditions separately; one must look at consumer demand in relation to supply. Moreover, changes in the environment affect both supply and demand (see Exhibit 2.1). The competitive conditions in an industry are never static. During the last decade, for example, wholesale clubs and television shopping networks have become prominent in the United States. The development of such new types of retail institutions causes major changes in the competitive environment. The economic condition also affects competition: consumer expenditures drop during unfavorable economic conditions, intensifying the level of competition.

This chapter's five sections focus on the nature of retail competition. The first section discusses some of the characteristics that make competition among retail stores different from competition in other industries. The subject of the second section, strategic group analysis, is essential for understanding how stores selling similar merchandise compete with each other. The third section presents a framework for understanding how the intensity of competition among stores relates to similarities in their marketing strategies and how firms can differentiate themselves in order to reduce competition. The fourth section reviews some reasons the inten-

Exhibit 2.1 The Nature of Competition Is Affected by Supply, Demand, and Environmental Factors

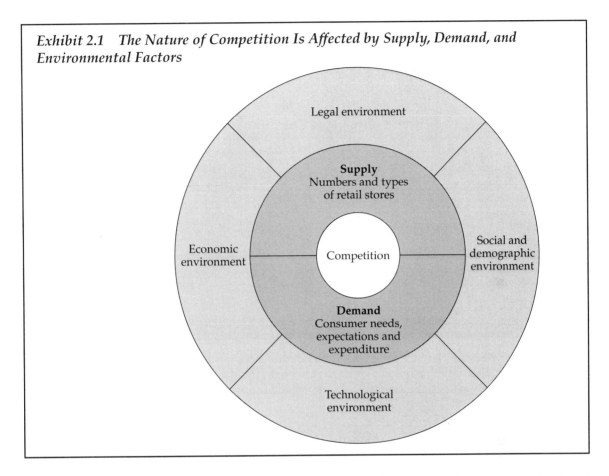

sity of competition in retailing is increasing. The final section discusses the global dimensions of retail competition.

CHARACTERISTICS OF RETAIL COMPETITION

Today's retail environment is extremely competitive. Whatever they sell, however large they are, or whoever owns them, all retail stores must aggressively compete to attract their share of the money consumers spend in retail stores. Competition creates rivalry among firms because each firm has to continuously improve its position in the marketplace. Although the nature of competition is governed by the general economic principles of supply and demand, there are some unique characteristics in each industry. Three characteristics of the retail industry need special mention.

First, a distinction must be made between intratype and intertype retail competition. The second special characteristic of retailing is the coexistence of large retail chains that operate hundreds of outlets with small, independent businesses that

Stores such as the Price Club outlet shown in this picture create their differential advantage through low prices. But to do so, the store must tightly control its expenses and have lower costs than competitors.

operate just one or two stores. Although the concentration of retail stores in chain outlets is increasing, the small, independent retailer remains a vital part of the retail industry. The third characteristic that makes retail competition different is its local market orientation. Retail competition takes place at the local level where neighboring outlets seek customers from the same market area. The level of competition can vary considerably from one market to another, depending on the number and types of stores.

Two Types of Retail Competition

It is quite easy to identify IBM's competitors in the market for personal computers (PCs) as other PC manufacturers such as Apple, Compaq, Epson, Leading Edge, Zeos, and so on. Identifying the competitors of a supermarket or a hypermarket, however, is not that easy. A supermarket competes directly with other food retailers in the area. In addition, it may also compete with drugstores and discount stores, depending on the range of merchandise it carries. Similarly, because hypermarkets sell food, groceries, appliances, hardware, health and beauty aids, electronic equipment, and even clothing, they compete with many different types of retail stores, at least to some extent. Because retailers can face competition from a variety of sources, it is useful to differentiate between intratype and intertype competition.

Intratype Competition   Direct competition between two similar types of retail stores, such as two supermarkets or two discount stores, is called **intratype competition**. The closer two or more stores' locations and the more similar their products and services, the greater the intensity of competition between them. To reduce the impact of competition, stores must differentiate themselves from their intratype competitors on the basis of customer service, store atmosphere or merchandise offering.

Intertype Competition   Retail competition is not limited to rivalry between similar stores. One feature of retailing today is the emergence of many different types of retail institutions selling similar goods and services. In any market area one can find supermarkets, drugstores, discount stores, convenience stores, department stores, and a whole array of specialty stores. In addition, consumers have the opportunity to shop by mail, telephone, or electronically, by using computer terminals. The existence of so many different types of retailers blurs distinctions among them since the merchandise offering of different types of stores overlap considerably. This leads to competition among them. Competition among different types of retail institutions selling similar merchandise is called **intertype competition**. For example, department stores and specialty stores both sell clothes and, therefore, compete to attract customers. Similarly, since department stores, discount stores, supermarkets, drugstores, and direct retailers (Avon, for example) all sell health and beauty aids, they all compete to some extent. A supermarket and a drugstore both try to sell toothpaste and shaving items to the same group of customers and thus compete with each other. All of these are examples of intertype competition.

The level of intertype competition is increasing as new forms of retail institutions emerge and as retailers add new merchandise lines to increase their sales. The emergence of warehouse clubs, for example, has increased intertype competition, since the merchandise lines carried by these stores overlaps with those of many other types of retail institutions. Similarly, many supermarkets have, in recent years, added paperback books to their merchandise line. This has created intertype competition for book sales (although supermarkets' share of book sales is still very small).

Chain Stores and Concentration

At one time, independently owned firms that operated only one or two stores dominated retailing. However, things began to change around the 1920s with the growth of retail chains. *A **retail chain** consists of multiple centrally owned and, to some degree, centrally managed outlets with the same name that sell similar merchandise, have similar appearance, and follow similar business procedures.*[1] The Great Atlantic and Pacific Tea Company (A&P) and F.W. Woolworth are generally considered to be the earliest examples of successful retail chains. A&P started its chain of stores in 1859 and Woolworth followed in 1879.[2] The rapid expansion of supermarkets and variety stores fueled the growth of chain stores in the 1920s and 1930s. Another period of growth in chain stores was in the 1960s when discount store chains and specialty chains moved into the many new shopping malls which were constructed during that period.

Advantages of Chain Stores

Chain stores offer a major advantage in the opportunity to standardize retail operations and gain economies of scale. Since all outlets belonging to the same chain have the same or very similar merchandise, a common advertising and promotional campaign can be developed for the entire chain. Pooling these resources reduces the amount of money that each outlet spends on advertising. Compared to independent stores, chains also have access to more varied advertising media. Large national chains can advertise in network television programs and national magazines, in addition to local newspapers and radio.

Chains can also gain scale economies in distribution and information systems. A large chain, for example, can gain cost efficiencies by performing its own shipping, storing, and order processing, thereby reducing its reliance on wholesalers. Because of their large size, chain stores can invest in large computers and other data processing equipment that are beyond the means of smaller competitors. Wal-Mart, for example, has established an electronic communication link among its stores, warehouses, and many of its suppliers. The link helps the chain to better manage its inventory by reducing delivery times and stock-outs. A Wal-Mart store employee can use this electronic link to directly transmit an order to the warehouse, from where, in turn, the order is forwarded to the supplier, if necessary. This electronic link gives Wal-Mart a competitive edge. Independent retailers, or even small chains, can rarely afford the cost of establishing such systems.

Retail chains gain another important advantage in their bargaining power with suppliers. By virtue of their size, chains can get special concessions from manufacturers that small retailers cannot. As chains get larger, its power to bargain with suppliers increases. For example, it has been reported that large computer chains, such as ComputerLand, paid manufacturers only 60 to 65 percent of list price, while independent computer retailers paid nearly 75 percent of the list price.[3] The chain outlets, therefore, enjoyed a cost advantage over smaller outlets. Manufacturers are also likely to cooperate much more willingly with large chains in training salespeople and ensuring adequate supplies.

These advantages have made large chains a dominant force in U.S. retailing. An examination of the names of some popular stores illustrates the importance of retail chains in our economy. Sears, K mart, Target, Venture, Mervyn's, Wal-Mart, The Gap, The Limited, Safeway, A&P, Krogers, Lucky Stores, J.C. Penney, Radio Shack, Target, Toys R Us, and Caldor, to name just a few, are all chain stores. Ac-

A&P and F.W. Woolworth are generally considered to be the earliest examples of successful retail chains in the United States. Pictured here is one of the early "Five and Dime" stores operated by F.W. Woolworth.

The First 5 & 10c. Store in the United States. Opened by F. W. Woolworth, June 21st, 1879, at Lancaster, Pa.

cording to the U.S. Department of Commerce, the 50 largest firms accounted for just over 20 percent of total retail sales.[4] More broadly, firms that own 11 or more outlets accounted for 38 percent of total retail sales in 1990, although as shown in Exhibit 2.2 this figure varies considerably by line of trade.[5] This is not to say that independent businesses do not have an important role in this sector. Single-unit firms still account for nearly 80 percent of all outlets and just under 50 percent of sales. But the proportion of total retail sales accounted for by single-unit businesses has been declining steadily over time.[6]

Concentration Ratio   Despite the rapid growth of chain stores, the level of **retail concentration** is still quite low compared to other industries. Concentration refers to the dominance of an industry by large firms. To measure the level of concentration in an industry, economists calculate an index called the **concentration ratio** as the share of the total sales of an industry accounted by the four largest firms. Exhibit 2.3 shows the 1990 sales of the four largest supermarket chains in the United States. These four firms had a combined sales in 1990 of just under $69 billion, less than 25 percent of all food store sales in the country for that year. In

Exhibit 2.2   Sales of Multiunit Organizations (11 or More Stores) by Kind of Business, 1990

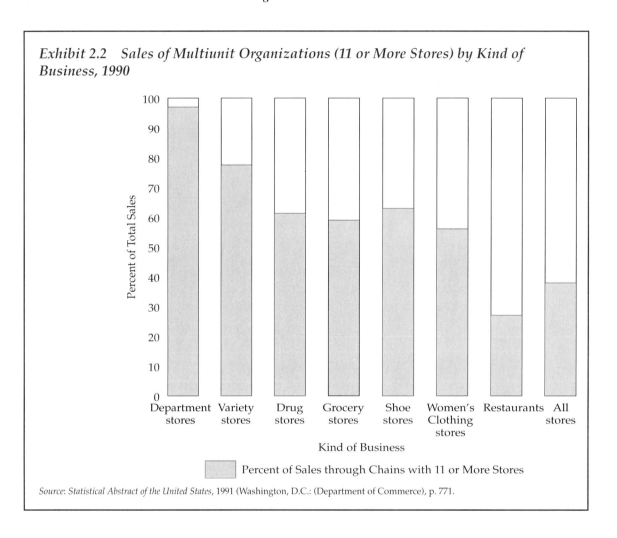

Percent of Sales through Chains with 11 or More Stores

Source: *Statistical Abstract of the United States*, 1991 (Washington, D.C.: (Department of Commerce), p. 771.

contrast, the top three manufacturers of breakfast cereals, General Mills, Kelloggs, and General Foods, account for more than 75 percent of all cereal sales. The top three manufacturers of detergents sell nearly 90 percent of all detergents.

Barriers to Entry   One reason for the low concentration level in retailing is the industry's low barriers to entry. *Barriers to entry are industry conditions or competitive strategies that deter new firms from entering the industry.* High capital requirements, heavy advertising expenditures, restricted access to suppliers, and switching costs are some common entry barriers.

High capital requirements bar entry into industries such as oil refining, aircraft manufacturing, and automobiles, which require large production facilities. Because retailing does not depend on large production facilities, small firms and entrepre-

Exhibit 2.3 *Sales of Four Largest Supermarket Chains, 1990*

Company	Sales (millions of dollars)
American Stores	22,155
Kroger	20,261
Safeway	14,873
Great Atlantic & Pacific Tea (A&P)	11,164
Four-firm total	68,453

Source: *1991 Directory of U.S. Corporations*, The Fortune Service 500, September 30, 1991, p. 62.

neurs can enter the business easily. Starting a new retail store requires only modest levels of resources, and every year thousands of new stores open throughout the country.

Level of advertising is another potential barrier to entry. Consumer goods manufacturers (such as Coca-Cola, Procter and Gamble, and Anheiser-Busch) spend millions of dollars in advertising, often as much as 10 to 15 percent of their sales revenue, making it difficult for a new firm to establish its own brand name. Compared to consumer goods manufacturers, the level of advertising in retailing is relatively low except for some of the fast-food restaurants. McDonald's, for example, spends about 4 percent of its total sales in advertising. Sears and K mart spend approximately 2 percent of sales. Supermarkets typically spend between one-tenth and two-tenths of one percent of sales on advertising. For large chains, however, even this low a percentage translates into a substantial amount in absolute terms, creating a barrier for new firms.

Lack of access to suppliers also creates a barrier to entry. Because of the large number of potential suppliers for almost all types of merchandise, most retailers can get easy access to them. Lack of access to suppliers does, however, limit the entry of small, independent retailers into the department store business. Large apparel manufacturers and well-known designers often prefer to deal exclusively with large chains to protect their brand image; thus small, independent retailers often find it difficult to procure name-brand apparel. This is the reason why department store sales are so heavily concentrated in firms with 10 or more units.

Barriers to entry can also arise due to switching costs. These are the costs consumers have to incur in changing from one supplier to another. Switching costs can create a considerable barrier to entry for high technology products. A company that already owns IBM computers may not be willing to buy from other manufacturers if the equipment is not compatible with IBM's. In retailing there are, however, no significant switching costs. Consumers can easily shift their patronage from one store to another without incurring any costs, although there are situations in

Radio Shack outlets, which sell electronic goods manufactured by the parent company Tandy Corporation, are examples of vertical marketing systems.

which store loyalty and habit deters a consumer from switching stores.

Low barriers to entry gives retailing a dual character with many small firms coexisting with large retail chains. It is for this reason that the concentration ratio in retailing is much lower than that in other industries. The low level of entry barriers allows many small retailers to exist along with large chains.

Local-Market Orientation

One of the distinguishing features of retail competition is its **local-market orientation**. To generate sales, retail outlets, whether they belong to large chains or small firms, must attract customers from the local market areas. And in doing so they must compete with other outlets located in the same market. Retail managers, therefore, need to be more concerned about the nature of local competition in individual markets rather than competition at the national level.

At the local level, retail sales are usually much more concentrated than at the national level. The data in Exhibit 2.4 show the level of supermarket concentration in four metropolitan areas. In all the cities, the top two or three largest firms

Exhibit 2.4 **Concentration of Supermarket Sales in Four Metropolitan Areas**

Chain	Number of Stores	Percentage of Area Grocery-Store Sales
Chicago		
Jewel	148	46.0
Dominick's	88	23.0
Certified Grocer's	123	12.0
Central Grocers	45	5.0
Total—top four	404	86.0
San Diego		
Vons	65	36.9
Lucky	30	19.1
Ralph's	17	15.5
Alpha Beta	17	6.5
Total—top four	129	78.0
Atlanta		
Kroger	70	33.0
Winn Dixie	61	19.2
Super Value	60	16.0
Big Star	46	16.4
Total—top four	237	84.6
Washington, D.C.		
Giant Food	107	45.8
Safeway	105	30.0
Shoppers Food Warehouse	22	10.3
Basics/Food-A-Rama	13	3.7
Total—top four	247	89.8

Source: SN Distribution Study of Grocery Store Sales (New York: Fairchild Publications, 1992).

command a large portion of total food sales in the area. These firms are typically large supermarket chains with many outlets in the same market area. Because of their size, the large firms have considerable advantage over their smaller competitors in the same area. The level of competition among the top chains in the market is, however, very intense. Each will continually strive to maintain or increase its market share. Any competitive move initiated by one chain, such as price cuts or double couponing, is likely to be quickly imitated by the other chains.

Local-market orientation reduces the value of national data summarizing information from all over the country for understanding the nature of retail competition. Each market area must be analyzed separately since their levels of competition can vary considerably, as can competition among types of retail stores. In formulating their strategies, managers of individual stores must analyze competition at a local level by looking at the number and type of competitors that are located nearby.

STRATEGIC GROUPS

In designing their own marketing strategies, retailers must consider the competitive environment in which they operate. The competitive environment is shaped by the interactive process that results as firms seek ways to satisfy customers more effectively than their competitors. The marketing decisions made by an individual firm influence consumer responses in the market place; and they also affect the marketing strategies of their competitors. It is this interaction among the marketing strategies that creates competitive rivalry and shapes the competitive environment. It is important, therefore, to clearly understand how retail stores compete with each other and how their marketing strategies interact.

Understanding competitive rivalry in retailing requires insight into the nature of competition among different types of retail stores operating in the same market area. What, for example, is the nature of competition between traditional department stores such as Macy's, Dillard's, and Rich's, on the one hand and Sears, on the other? Or what is the nature of competition between Sears and K mart? Although these outlets have different target markets and marketing strategies, they compete with each other, to some extent, because they sell similar types of merchandise. The nature of this rivalry can be understood through strategic group analysis, which originated in a branch of economics called industrial organization.[7]

Most market areas contain many stores that sell the same type of merchandise. Clothing, for example, is sold by department stores, discount stores, apparel specialty stores, mass merchandisers, and off-price outlets. Although all of them sell clothes, each of them has a different customer focus, and a different marketing strategy. The quality and fashion orientation of the merchandise, store atmosphere, and the level of customer service also differs from store to store. Another difference is the price. Depending on the characteristics of the merchandise, the typical price charged by different kinds of stores also varies.

Although each store is somewhat unique, there is some degree of commonality in their marketing strategies. To understand the nature of retail competition in an area, these commonalties must first be identified and then the different stores in the area categorized into strategic groups based on those common elements. A **strategic group** is a group of stores that has the same or similar target market and marketing strategy. The identification of strategic groups is an important step in analyzing retail competition, because it provides the framework for understanding how outlets selling similar merchandise compete with each other.

Key Competitive Dimensions

The first step in strategic group analysis is to identify the key competitive dimensions in an industry. **Key competitive dimensions** are the aspects of firm strategy with key importance in the industry. In retailing, two key competitive dimensions are price and merchandise offering. They determine the type of customers the store will attract and how the stores will fulfill the expectations of those customers.

The merchandise offering of a store can be characterized in a number of ways depending on the type of products and services that it sells. The merchandise offerings of apparel stores, for example, can be characterized by their quality, fashion orientation, and selection. Supermarkets' merchandise offerings, on the other hand, must be judged by the freshness and quality of meats and produce and by the selection of branded grocery items. The merchandise offering of restaurants differs in the quality of cooking, uniqueness of the menu, and the restaurant's ambiance.

With the key competitive dimensions identified, the next step is to classify competing stores into groups based on their similarities along those dimensions. Stores that have similar price and merchandise offerings fall into the same strategic groups. In this way each strategic group represents stores having the same or very similar customer focus and marketing strategy. For example, while both K mart and Neiman-Marcus sell women's clothing, their merchandise offerings and prices differ significantly. K mart and Neiman-Marcus, therefore, belong to different strategic groups. On the other hand, Saks Fifth Avenue and Neiman-Marcus belong in the same strategic group because they have similar price and merchandise offerings. For the same reason, traditional department stores such as Macy's, Robinson's, and Rich's all belong to one strategic group.

Any retail market contains stores belonging to a number of strategic groups, each with characteristic prices and merchandise offerings. The organization of these strategic groups is an important determinant of the nature of retail competition. To understand the competitive relationship among the different groups, it is helpful to map the positions of the strategic groups on the key strategic dimensions—merchandise and price. Exhibit 2.5 shows an example of such a map for general merchandise retailers. The merchandise offering of general merchandise stores can be characterized by its quality, fashion orientation, and selection. Quality and fashion, however, are usually correlated with price. Higher quality, more fashionable merchandise commands higher prices.[8] The diagonal line in the exhibit, the **shopping opportunity line**, indicates possible combinations of price and merchandise offering. The association of high quality and fashion with high prices causes the shopping opportunity line to slope upward.

The shopping opportunity line in Exhibit 2.5 is drawn as a straight line making a 45-degree angle with both axes. This may not always be the case. The slope of the shopping opportunity line depends on the particular way in which consumers trade off merchandise quality and price. Greater sensitivity to price makes the line

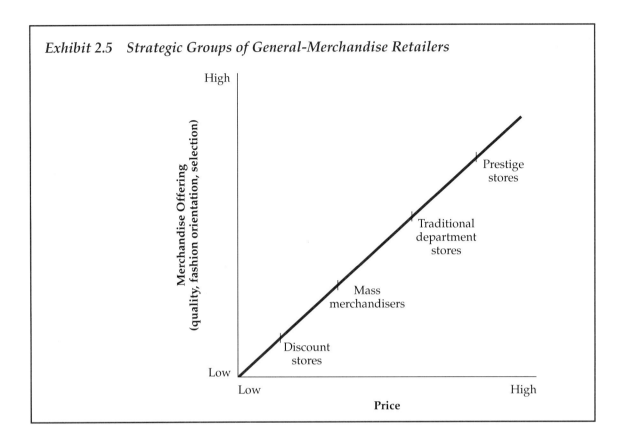

Exhibit 2.5   *Strategic Groups of General-Merchandise Retailers*

steeper. A lower price sensitivity, on the other hand, makes the line flatter.   Note, however, that since rational consumers will never prefer less quality to more at the same price, the shopping opportunity line always slopes upward from left to right.

A map of strategic groups places retail stores along the price and merchandise continuum represented by the shopping opportunity line. A discount store, for example, combines low-price and low-fashion merchandise, so it falls at one end of the shopping opportunity line. At the other extreme of the shopping opportunity line fall prestige stores and boutiques that offer high-priced, fashionable merchandise. Department stores and mass merchandisers lie between these two extremes on the shopping opportunity line. Each of the four types of retail stores shown in Exhibit 2.5 is a strategic group, since the merchandise and price differ among the types.

It is important to realize that, while a store's position on the shopping opportunity line dictates its marketing strategy, this does not determine its profit. Profits depend on how well the firm implements its marketing strategy. For example, department stores as a group do not necessarily earn greater profits than discount stores, just because they charge higher prices.

Strategic Map of Supermarkets

Strategic group analysis is not limited to general merchandise retailers. It can be applied to all forms of retail outlets. To map the strategic groups for any form of retailing, the first step is to determine how consumers evaluate the merchandise offerings for that particular kind of store. Fashion is an important criteria for judging apparel and accessories, but has little to do with the merchandise offering of supermarkets. Freshness, quality, and selection are important factors for judging the merchandise offering of different supermarkets. This yields three strategic groups in the supermarket industry:[9]

Limited Assortment (Box) Stores   These are typically small grocery stores with very limited product selection (between 500 to 1000 items). They usually have no perishable departments and a limited assortment of packaged dry goods. Limited assortment stores have low service, and merchandise is usually sold directly from cartons in which it was received.

Warehouse Stores   Like limited assortment stores, warehouse stores offer little customer service and sell products directly from cartons. They do, however, have larger product assortments. The product assortments stress dry goods with only a limited choice of meats and other perishables. These stores carry only a limited number of brands in each product category in order to reduce costs. They reduce costs further by opportunistic buying of national brands from manufacturers on special deals. As a consequence, brand assortments often lack continuity; a brand featured one week may not be stocked the next week, if the manufacturer withdraws the deal.

Conventional Supermarkets   Conventional supermarkets offer a full line of groceries, meat, and produce, and often carry as many as 25,000 to 30,000 items (some superstores carry as many as 50,000 items). Items are stocked individually in racks rather than in cartons. Conventional supermarkets carry a balanced assortment of national and private label brands. Most conventional supermarkets offer free bagging, accept personal checks, and are conveniently located.

A **strategic map** of the supermarket industry is shown in Exhibit 2.6. The vertical axis differentiates the three different kinds of supermarkets on the basis of merchandise quality, freshness, and assortment, and the horizontal axis measures pricing strategies. As one might expect, larger selections of better-quality packaged goods and fresher produce means higher prices. Limited assortment stores typically have the lowest price, while prices are highest at conventional supermarkets. Prices at warehouse stores fall in between these extremes.

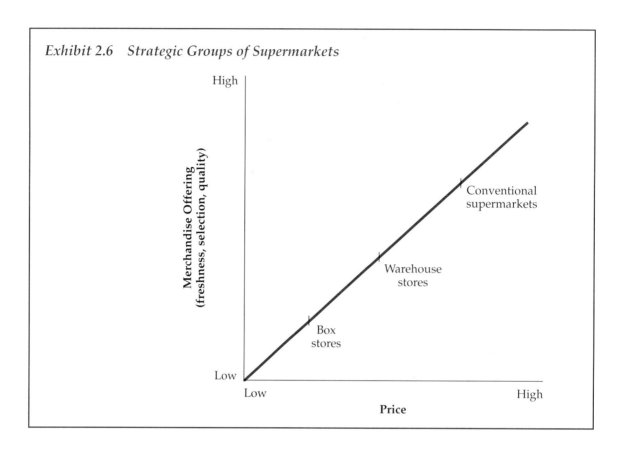

Exhibit 2.6   Strategic Groups of Supermarkets

Strategic Groups and Retail Strategy

Because of their different merchandise offerings and price levels, stores belonging to different strategic groups have different target markets and marketing strategies. Store atmosphere, service, location, and promotion strategies differ from one strategic group to another. Prestige stores, for example, are usually located in downtown sites in large cities or in fashionable shopping malls in affluent suburban areas. Discount stores, on the other hand, are usually free-standing or located in smaller shopping complexes. The ambiance and store atmospheres also differ. Compare, for example, the spartan interiors of a K mart with the glittering displays at a Neiman-Marcus or a Bloomingdale's store. Contrast the wide aisles and well-stocked shelves of a conventional supermarket with the cramped interior of a limited assortment store filled with open and unopened packing cases.

Certain characteristics differentiate each strategic group from other types of stores in the consumers' mind. Consumers have well-formed expectations regarding the quality and fashion orientation of the group's merchandise, the quality of

Retailing is the business of providing goods and services to customers for their personal or household use. The diverse world of retailing is made up of innumerable stores, differing in size and format, and selling a vast array of items. Traditional department stores, such as the venerable Bloomingdale's on New York's Fifth Avenue, are giants of retailing. The woman in this cosmetics department at the Broadway in Phoenix is enjoying the customer service and one-stop shopping a department store can offer.

Specialty stores are another important segment of retailing. In contrast to department stores' wide variety of items, specialty stores limit their variety, but offer wider selections within their merchandising categories. Just Us Books, Inc. in Detroit offers childrens' books on African-American themes and E.A.T., a food store in Manhattan, specializes in gourmet creations. In recent years, specialty stores have grown in prominence and continue to be very popular with consumers.

© Robert Brenner/PhotoEdit
© Andy Levin/Photo Researchers

Convenience and value are important to today's consumer. Supermarkets can offer one-stop shopping and a vast array of fresh and packaged products that are competitively priced. At this Food Lion in New Jersey, free bagging and carryout and the acceptance of credit cards are also offered. Franchise stores, like this Supercuts in Los Angeles, offer walk-in service and standard pricing. The owner of this store benefits from his franchisor's national advertising and development of new service offerings.

© Will McIntyre/Photo Researchers
© Tony Freeman/PhotoEdit

Fast-food retailing continues to be one of the great success stories of modern American business. McDonald's, which set the stage in the mid-'50's, and its numerous competitors have focused on quality, service, cleanliness, convenience, and value. Taco Bell, by specializing in Mexican food, became extremely popular in the late '80's and eroded the market of the hamburger/french fry restaurants.

© Richard Hutchings/Photo Researchers
© David Young-Wolff/PhotoEdit

One advantage large superstores have over other kinds of retailers is the opportunity for one-stop-shopping. The large array of merchandise carried by these stores attracts many customers.

the shopping environment, and the level of service appropriate for different kinds of stores. To compete effectively, a store must adopt a strategy that is consistent with customer expectations of that kind of store. A prestige department store, for example, should be fashion forward and should introduce the latest fashions and styles first. Mass merchandisers and discount stores, on the other hand, usually adapt to fashions that have been accepted by a large segment of the population. In this way, each strategic group is differentiated from the others: each has a market focus of its own.

Evolution of Strategic Groups

The retail industry undergoes continuous change. New retail institutions constantly emerge to challenge established stores. The competitive environment also reflects existing stores' changing strategies to improve their competitive positions. Strategic groups, therefore, are not static, they change as the competitive environment changes.

Considering the emergence of upscale discount stores shows how new strategic groups evolve. Exhibit 2.5 classified all discount stores as a single strategic group, but the increasing fashion orientation of stores such as Target and Caldor seems to have created a new upscale department store group positioned between discount stores and mass merchandisers on the shopping opportunity line (see Exhibit 2.7). They offer more fashionable merchandise than typical discount stores (e.g., Wal-Mart, K mart) but do not reach the level of Sears or Penney's.

The changes implemented by J.C. Penney in recent years described at the beginning of the chapter give another example of how strategic groups shift.[10] Penney's strategy may be viewed as an attempt to move the firm higher and to the right on the shopping opportunity line as shown in Exhibit 2.8. The objective was to make Penney's more competitive with regional department store chains such as Davidson's and Rich's and with specialty clothing stores that are typically located in the same shopping centers as Penney's. This change in Penney's position on the shopping opportunity line also differentiates it from Sears, its traditional rival. Sears, too, had attempted, although in a more modest way, to reposition itself as a more fashion-oriented store. Recently, however, Sears has been changing its strategy to compete more directly with discount stores.

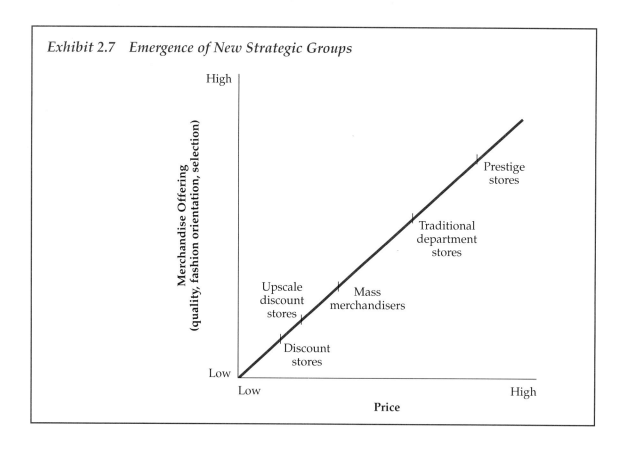

Exhibit 2.7   *Emergence of New Strategic Groups*

To shift its position along the shopping opportunity line, J.C. Penney implemented numerous changes in its retail strategy. First, the customer focus shifted more towards working women. To appeal to this new target group, the firm emphasized apparel over home electronics, sporting goods, and automotive repair. In 1981, men's, women's, and children's apparel together accounted for 63 percent of total sales. By 1989 this had increased to 84 percent.[11] In 1982, to appeal to more fashion-oriented shoppers, Penney's signed a design and licensing agreement with Halston Enterprises, a well-known designer of women's clothing and marketer of fragrances and cosmetics. As many as 600 Penney's stores started selling women's apparel specially designed for the company by Halston. More recently the company has started Mixit, a store within Penney stores. Mixit sells contemporary clothes and accessories.[12]

Repositioning to emphasize fashion and style also necessitated upgrading store atmosphere. New stores had contemporary looks creating an ambiance that customers associated with fashion-oriented stores. A number of existing stores were closed or extensively remodeled. New stores were located in shopping malls rather than at the downtown sites of Penney's old stores.

Strategic group analysis is an important step in understanding the nature of retail competition and the strategies of different retail institutions competing in the same geographic area. The next section employs the concept of strategic groups to develop a framework which explains in detail how stores located in the same market area compete.

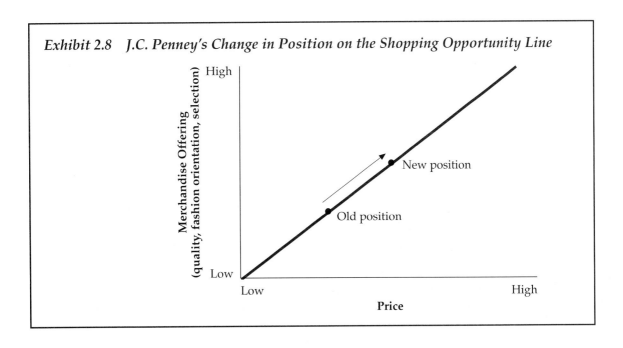

Exhibit 2.8   *J.C. Penney's Change in Position on the Shopping Opportunity Line*

THE STRUCTURE OF RETAIL COMPETITION

Knowledge about competitors is essential for effective management of retail stores. Retail managers must monitor the actions and strategies of competitors. To provide a systematic framework for understanding how different stores in the same market area compete, this section classifies competition into three levels: (1) generic competition, (2) competition among strategic groups, and (3) competition within strategic groups.

Generic Competition

In a broad sense, all stores located in the same market area compete to some extent, even those that sell different types of products and services. For example, a bowling alley, a game arcade, an amusement park, and a movie theater compete for consumers' expenditures on leisure activities. Similarly, fast-food outlets and supermarkets compete since the more people eat in fast-food restaurants the less they purchase from supermarkets. This most general type of competition is called **generic competition**. Generic competition is the most difficult to predict since it occurs among firms offering products and services that are substitutes in the broadest sense of the word.

Competition among Strategic Groups

The second level of competition is that among stores that sell similar merchandise but belong to different strategic groups. Consider, for example, competition among a mass merchandiser (Sears), a department store (Macy's, Dillard's), and a discount store (K mart). Although each of these three types of store forms a different strategic group (since they have different price and merchandise offerings), to a certain degree they all compete to attract customers.

The intensity of competition between two stores belonging to different strategic groups depends on the relative positions of their strategic groups on the shopping opportunity line. Competition is greatest among groups that are located near each other on the shopping opportunity line because their target market will have some degree of overlap. On the other hand, strategic groups that fall far apart on the shopping opportunity line will tend to have very different target markets. Consequently, competition between these stores will be less vigorous. In general, the intensity of competition between stores belonging to different strategic groups depends on the proximity of the strategic groups on the shopping opportunity line. Groups that fall closer on the line compete more intensely.

Exhibit 2.9 illustrates the relationship of competition among different stores to the positions of their strategic groups on the shopping opportunity line. As an example, consider the nature of competition among Neiman-Marcus, Macy's, and K mart. A Neiman-Marcus store faces significant competition from a Macy's lo-

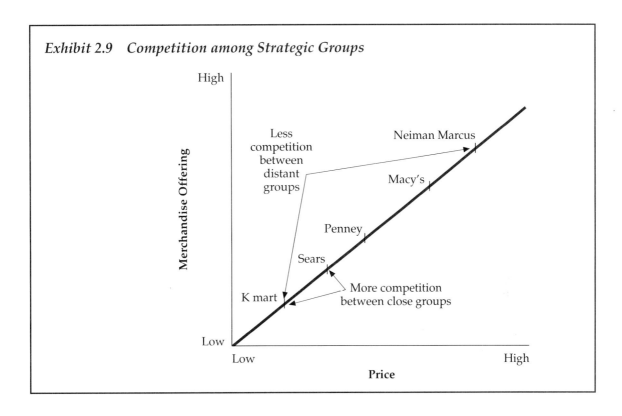

Exhibit 2.9   Competition among Strategic Groups

cated in the same market area. However, it faces relatively little competition from a K mart, since the two stores have very different target markets. The relative positions of Macy's, Sears, and K mart on the shopping opportunity line also imply that the level of competition between Macy's and Sears is greater than that between Macy's and K mart. K mart faces more competition from Sears than Macy's, since Sears' position on the shopping opportunity line is closer than Macy's to K mart's.

When a strategic group is positioned between two other groups, it faces competitive pressures from both of them. Department stores, for example, have to compete with prestige stores as well as stores like J.C. Penney. As noted previously, Penney has been changing its strategy in order to move closer to department stores on the shopping opportunity line. As it moves closer, it will exert greater competitive pressure on department stores.

Competition within Strategic Groups

Thus far, the discussion has focussed on competition between stores that belong to different strategic groups. But what is the nature of competition between stores

ENTREPRENEURIAL EDGE

Creating Trends in Video Retailing

Michael Landes, chairman and CEO of RKO Warner Video, loves movies. He describes himself as an enthusiastic fan. Enthusiastic, to say the least, as he found a way to turn his hobby into a wildly successful career. A lawyer by training, Landes left the profession in 1980 to found a company that grew into the RKO Century Warner Theaters. Landes liked showing movies, but felt that he had little control over what was to be shown. In 1986, he sold his part of that business to a larger theater chain, Cineplex Odeon, in a deal that allowed him to keep the RKO Warner name as well as some of its video units. He used these assets to develop the RKO Warner Video stores. Based in Manhattan, Landes now has 40 stores, with over $40 million in sales annually, and RKO has leaped to the top of the video retail industry because of his innovative strategies. Barely five years old, the chain now ranks in the top three video retailers in Manhattan, a notoriously difficult and competitive market, and has sales of over $800,000 per unit annually. That's a lot of videos!

Landes' success stems from his ability to read the emerging trends in this relatively new retailing field. He pioneered the hands-on approach to video rental, and most consumers can't even remember the time when they had to know the name of the film desired in advance, and then ask for a salesperson to retrieve it. In the RKO stores, all the videos are displayed on shelves, allowing the customer to browse and choose the film. He also developed the video "superstore," which has a wide range of videos—from action adventure to sci-fi or documentaries—as well as video accessories such as blank tapes, popcorn, and VCR repair kits. This retailing strategy has now become the standard for the industry.

Another reason for RKO's success is Landes' aggressive merchandising and advertising strategies, offering discounts for volume rentals, and special deals for RKO members. RKO advertisements look like movie posters, and draw the customers into the store, so that RKO benefits from impulse as well as planned video rentals. Once in the store, there are so many deals to choose from that customers, even those who just wanted to browse and check out the new releases, will find rental specials that suits their video

that belong to the same strategic group? For example, how does a supermarket compete with another one located nearby? What is the nature of competition between two department stores or two drug stores located in the same market area? Stores within the same strategic group offer merchandise at comparable prices and focus on similar customers. These similarities make the stores rather homogenous to consumers.

This perceived homogeneity intensifies the competitive rivalry between stores belonging to the same strategic group and increases the role of price as a competitive weapon. Consider, for example, gasoline retailing. In general, consumers do

needs of the moment, as well as ones that keep them coming back for more rentals.

Lew Kennedy, president of Minnesota-based Title Wave music and video stores, takes Landes' concept one step further by combining video rentals with music sales. Kennedy's background had included many stints in the electronics business, as everything from merchandising manager for Target's electronics and music departments to marketing executive at The Wherehouse Entertainment, a California-based music and video chain. While at The Wherehouse, he realized the potential of combining the two entertainment markets. Kennedy saw an opportunity in his area for one-stop video rental and music shopping, and he seized the chance. He expanded The Wherehouse concept and in 1986 launched his own company, Title Wave in Minneapolis.

Kennedy's concept of one-stop shopping for videos and movies garnered an enthusiastic reception from the outset. Title Wave stores have bright, high-tech interiors. Supported with aggressive promotion and advertising, the stores attract urban customers by offering retail environment filled with light, sound, and entertainment at every turn. Title Wave relies on internal growth, rather than on borrowing, to expand, and has grown to ten superstores—each over 10,000 square feet—in just five years. Kennedy plans to open three to five stores annually, and hopes to take the concept to other geographic markets by the end of the 1990s.

A key part of Title Wave's success involves hiring the right kind of people and recognizing their achievements. Kennedy believes that a company is successful only if it has a well-trained and motivated staff, and he fosters a feeling of kinship among employees. Clearly, the customers like the stores too, as Title Wave has annual sales exceeding $13 million—with only ten stores—and sales show no signs of slowing down.

Sources: "Retailing's Entrepreneurs of the Year," *Chain Store Age Executive*, December 1991, pp. 28–38; and "Retailing's Entrepreneurs of the Year," *Chain Store Age Executive*, December 1990, pp. 28–38.

not perceive much difference in the quality of gasoline or in the services offered by different gasoline stations. Of two gasoline stations located next to each other, most motorists will choose the one with the lower price. The same is true for two neighboring conventional supermarkets or dealers of GM cars. Prospective customers will most likely compare the price at the two stores and then buy from the one with the lowest price, unless one of them has a nonprice differential advantage that the other cannot match.

As consumers perceive two stores to be more homogenous, the degree of competition between them increases. To gain an advantage over its competitors, a store must separate itself from other stores in the same strategic group. An examination of the shopping opportunity line indicates two general ways this can be achieved. First, a store can gain competitive advantage by lowering price while offering the same merchandise quality. Another strategy is to improve merchandise quality without a commensurate increase in price. Both these strategies give competitive advantage because they lead to superior positions relative to other stores in the same strategic group.   Note that these strategies result in a leftward or upward shift in the store's position in the shopping opportunity line (see Exhibit 2.10). A shift to the right or below the shopping opportunity line, on the other hand, would make the firm weaker and must be avoided.

To be effective, **differentiation** strategies must be implemented carefully. While a lower price can attract more customers, sole reliance on lower price as a competitive strategy can be risky. Competitors can change their prices in order to maintain their own competitive position. A price cut by one store often initiates a cascading effect as competitors cut their prices too. Then the store is forced to cut its price once again, to be followed by a new series of price cuts by competitors, and so on. The result is a price war like those that are frequently observed among gasoline stations, car rental companies, and airlines.

Unless properly implemented, a competitive strategy based on price can have a disastrous effect on a store's profit. Although sales may increase, profits can fall

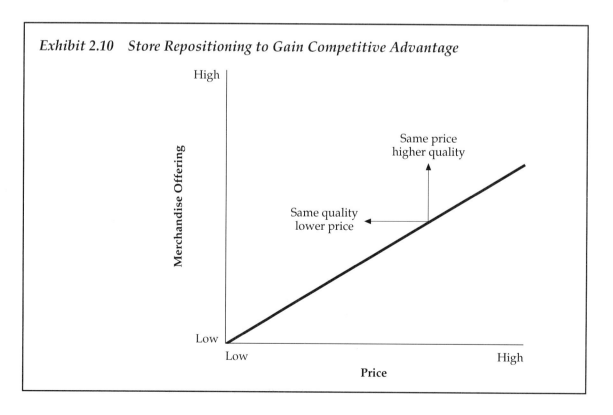

Exhibit 2.10   Store Repositioning to Gain Competitive Advantage

because of lower margins. The impact of A&P's WEO ("where economy originates") program on supermarket profits is a good example. In the early 1970s A&P initiated an aggressive strategy to gain back some of the market share it had lost in the 1960s. The strategy relied heavily on cutting prices to attract customers. A&P's sales increased as a result of the WEO program, but the price cuts reduced the firm's profit margin (the amount of profit per dollar of sales) from 0.9 percent to 0.2 percent between 1970 and 1973. A&P's competitors also suffered heavily as they were forced to reduce their prices too. Their profit margin fell from 0.9 percent to 0.4 percent during the same period. In contrast, supermarkets that did not compete with A&P were able to maintain their profit margin of 1.4 percent. Thus, both A&P and its competitors suffered as a result of the WEO program.[13] Car rental agencies met with the same fate when Avis and Hertz, the two largest chains, cut their prices to attract customers. Both chains lost substantial amounts of profit in the process, without any significant change in their respective market shares. The fare wars among airlines in the summer of 1992 also resulted in lower profits for the industry as a whole, with no company benefiting from it.

A low price strategy can be successful only if the store has significant cost advantages over its competitors. Competitors will then find it hard to match the lower price without affecting their profits significantly. One source of cost advantage is economies of scale. As mentioned earlier, this is one advantage chain stores have over independent stores. For this reason chain stores can charge a lower price and yet have higher profitability than a similar store that is independently owned. Witness, for example, the inability of small, independent merchants to be price-competitive with chain stores such as Wal-Mart.

The Differentiation Triangle

In addition to price and quality, stores can also differentiate themselves based on the other retail mix elements. The **differentiation triangle** shown in Exhibit 2.11 focuses on three retail mix elements—location, service, and store atmosphere—that are typically used to differentiate stores from competitors in the same strategic group.

Although such differentiation does not move a store away from its position on the shopping opportunity line, these elements are important since they give customers more reason to visit the outlet. Location, for example, is a very important competitive tool in retailing. When choosing among similar stores, a consumer is likely to select the one that is most conveniently located as long as the other retail mix elements do not differ significantly. A store that is located at a site that is accessible to large numbers of its target customers can, therefore, attract more customers. The closer the store is to where consumers are, the greater its competitive advantage compared to a distant store. The impact of location on a store's ability to draw customers is discussed in more detail in Chapters 8 and 9.

Stores can differentiate, too, by improving store atmosphere and customer service. Service differentiation is a powerful competitive tool. Unfortunately, many

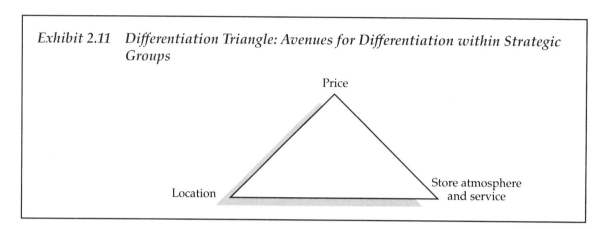

Exhibit 2.11   Differentiation Triangle: Avenues for Differentiation within Strategic Groups

retailers have ignored its potential and allowed service quality to deteriorate in pursuit of cost savings. Just as American manufacturers are rediscovering the importance of product quality, retailers must concentrate on improving service quality to build long-term relationships with customers. A pleasant store atmosphere, too, can give a differential advantage by attracting customers away from other stores. All retail marketing plans must aim to effectively create and sustain differential advantages for the firm. Given its importance, strategies for differentiation will be discussed in detail throughout the later chapters of the book.

DETERMINANTS OF COMPETITIVE RIVALRY

Retail stores compete with each other to attract customers and generate sales. As mentioned earlier, competition creates rivalry because each firm tries to differentiate itself in order to improve its position compared to competitors. In **competitive rivalry**, competing stores "jockey for favorable positions"[14] using the elements of the retail mix as competitive tools. When a store changes its marketing policy it affects all of its competitors, possibly forcing them to retaliate with their own counter strategies to protect their competitive positions. These competitive moves and counter moves determine the level of rivalry among firms. Some reasons for the high and rising level of competitive rivalry in retailing are discussed below.

Slow Market Growth

In expanding markets, firms can grow by merely keeping pace with the level of industry growth. When demand ceases to grow or the rate of growth slows down, individual stores must take customers away from their competitors in order to increase sales. Each store, therefore, has to compete aggressively to protect its own share of the market. Thus competitive rivalry is more intense in markets that are not growing or growing very slowly.

Many sectors of retailing have reached maturity—demand is growing very slowly, if at all. For example, in the early 1980s, demand for electronics goods increased 20 percent or more a year "when one electronics product after another caught the public's fancy."[15] In contrast, growth in recent years has been minimal, or not at all. The number of retail stores, however, continues to increase, which means that "more retailers are scrambling for a piece of the same pie."[16] To lure customers into their stores, retailers are resorting to steep price cuts, resulting in lower profits for all. This has forced a number of chains into serious financial distress.

Growth of Branded Goods

Most manufacturers have come to rely heavily on advertising and branding to market their products. A large and growing amount of advertising features cameras, TVs, personal computers, and other electronic goods. Even branded apparel such as designer jeans are now heavily advertised on TV, in magazines, and on billboards. Consumers of heavily advertised branded goods become less reliant on retail stores for information on products, thus reducing the influence of the retail store personnel on purchase decisions. Moreover, when the same brand is available at different stores, price becomes the most important competitive tool. This again intensifies competitive rivalry among retail stores, since stores find it difficult to differentiate themselves based on merchandise selection.

Overstoring

In 1946, Jack Pearltone, a home builder who moved into shopping center development, built what is considered to be the first shopping mall in the United States, a 250,000-square-foot complex anchored by Hochschild Department Stores in Seattle.[17] Since then the number of shopping centers has grown explosively. Between 1960 and 1990, the total gross leasable area in shopping centers increased from 600 million to over 4.5 billion square feet.[18] This amounts to more than 15 square feet of shopping center space for every person in the country! The number of free-standing stores and shopping strips has also grown dramatically. The phenomenal growth in shopping space has resulted in what some observers call the era of overstoring. Overstoring increases competitive rivalry since each store must fight even harder to protect its own market share.

With most major cities now overcrowded with stores, secondary markets in smaller cities have grown in importance. Secondary markets are not yet well served by large chains and the level of competition is significantly less than that in the major metropolitan markets. Of many chains targeting their growth in cities with

---

STRATEGY IN ACTION

The Changing Face of Book Retailing

Book retailing has undergone significant changes recent years. The era of cramped mall stores with limited selection may be on the way out. Several book retailers are now opening large superstores which offer customers a wide selection of titles, space to browse, and sometimes, a place to eat. Much of this change in selling patterns is due to the near-saturation of the mall market, and many of the national bookstore chains are scrambling to open freestanding superstores that cater to a different consumer. The target book consumer is the more literate, educated reader who wants as wide a selection in bookstores as in supermarkets.

These new superstores come equipped with coffee bars, comfortable furniture, piped-in classical music, and an improved "browser-friendly" attitude. The chains are hoping that the stores will attract custom-

ers away from the smaller mom and pop bookstores which have traditionally been freestanding stores in downtown shopping areas. Barnes & Noble has opened 17 superstores in the past few years, Crown Books 16, and Borders Book Shop has operated its 18 outlets as superstores since the

---

populations of less than 50,000, the most successful has been Wal-Mart. Wal-Mart has outperformed most other retailers in terms of sales and profit growth. Ames department stores had also profited from concentrating in secondary markets. The chain, however, ran into financial problems after merging with Zayre's.

Emergence of New Retail Institutions

Competitive rivalry is generally intense when competing firms utilize very different strategies and operating procedures to achieve different goals and objectives. Retailing has always been a diverse industry with a wide variety of institutions, and the level of diversity keeps increasing as new retail institutions emerge to challenge established ones.

Consider, for example, the emergence of off-price apparel retailers in the early part of the 1980s. Off-price retailers, sell name-brand clothes at 30 to 50 percent

day they opened. Waldenbooks launched its first superstore in June 1992 and plans to open several more over the next year. While these chains have begun their superstore launch in such densely populated urban areas as New York City, Chicago, and Los Angeles, the chains are also seeking locations in smaller cities such as Portland, Maine, Providence, Rhode Island, and Iowa City, Iowa. The attraction of these smaller cities is in the customer potential of students and professors from nearby colleges and also in the lack of competition in these areas than in the large urban sites.

A typical freestanding superstore is over four times the size of the average mall shop: 15,000 square feet, compared with 2,500 square feet. They also carry about four times the number of books, with an average of 100,000–150,000 titles in stock. Title collections include bestsellers as well as books on a broad range of subjects, such as expanded sections on history, psychology, philosophy, and literature.

The trend toward superstores, or megastores, as they are sometimes called, is not limited to book retailing. Take, for example, the store that Nike recently opened on Chicago's Michigan Avenue. The three-story Nike Town store has a half-court basketball court, life-sized statues of Michael Jordan and Bo Jackson, and display cases of sports memorabilia. Michigan Avenue is also the home to Sony's giant electronic store and a three-story F.A.O. Schwarz retail outlet.

Sources: Carrie Goerne: "Now Book Browsers Can Munch Brownies as They Shop for Browning," *Marketing News*, July 6, 1992, pp. 1, 9; and "Megastores that Entertain and Educate May Signal the Future of Merchandising," *The Wall Street Journal*, March 11, 1993, pp. B1, B9.

less than regular department store prices and have dramatically affected department store strategies. By 1983, off-price retailers accounted for between 4 and 6 percent of all apparel sales. Off-price stores such as Hit n' Miss, T.J. Maxx, Loehman's, Marshall's, National Brand Outlet (NBO), and Syms are now an important part of the American retailing scene.

The entry of new types of institutions always changes the nature of competition since they bring with them new strategies and policies, and often just new ways of doing old things. The emergence of off-price retailers, for example, forced department stores to reconsider their relationships with vendors who supplied off-price retailers. As a result many have reduced their reliance on designer apparels and are promoting their own house brands instead. Others have refused to buy from suppliers who distribute their goods through off-price outlets.

Toys R Us provides another example of how new competitors can change established ways of doing things, and thereby change the nature of rivalry in the industry. For a long time, toys were mainly sold at toy departments in department stores and by specialty toy stores. Department stores tended to neglect the toy department except during the Christmas season. Toy specialty stores, on the other hand, are generally small operations (except a few like F.A.O. Schwarz).

Toys R Us changed the situation completely. It sells a large selection of popular toys in stores that are typically around 40,000 square feet. It organizes its stores like supermarkets with wide aisles and tall shelves. It also borrowed from supermarkets its policy of self-service and self-selection by customers. Another important element of Toys R Us strategy is pricing. The Toys R Us price, on average, is about 30 percent less than what department stores charge for similar merchandise. Specialty chains like Toys R Us have hurt department stores, in many cases forcing them to abandon or severely curtail their own toy operations.

Changes in technology, especially electronics, and telecommunication, also spawn new types of retail institutions. In the 1930s, advancements in refrigeration and packaging technologies brought the first supermarkets. In the 1980s, new communication technologies ushered in the era of computer and television shopping. Companies like Compushop and Home Shopping Network are the latest institutions to enter the retail arena.

GLOBALIZATION OF RETAILING

Because retail stores cater to local markets with their own norms and expectations it is often said that retailing travels slowly. Compared to manufacturers, retail firms have been slow to expand internationally. This situation, however, has changed dramatically in the last two decades. Many retailers have expanded into international markets by starting their own branches or subsidiaries. Others have entered through direct investments in foreign companies or through franchising and licensing. In the **globalization of retailing**, the expansion has been in both directions, with U.S. retailers entering foreign markets and foreign retailers entering U.S. markets, as well.

Foreign Retailers in United States

The history of foreign retailers' entry into the U.S. market date at least as far back as 1939 when Loblaw, a Canadian firm, opened food stores in New York, Pennsylvania, and Ohio. Later, in 1955, Loblaw also acquired National, a chain of supermarkets operating primarily in the Midwest.[19] The flow of foreign direct investments in U.S. retailing increased substantially in the 1970s and the early 1980s. For example, the acquisitions of Allied Stores and Federated Department Stores made Canada-based Campeau Corporation one of the largest operators of department stores in the United States. Although the company encountered financial difficulties soon after the acquisition, Federated reemerged from bankruptcy early in 1992. Other large U.S. retailers owned, wholly or partially, by foreign firms include A&P,

Giant Food Stores, Hardee's, Dillard, Spiegel, and Brooks Brothers. Some foreign firms entered the U.S. market by opening and operating their own stores or through licensing. Conran's, Ikea, Benetton, Laura Ashley, and the Body Shop are some examples of these.

There are various reasons for the influx of foreign retailers into the U.S. market. These can be divided into "push" factors emanating from the European countries and "pull" factors in the United States, as shown in Exhibit 2.12.[20] The push factors include high levels of competition in European retail markets due to market saturation and overstoring. The competitive intensity in many European retail sectors was especially high during the late 1970s and early 1980s. In addition, local zoning and planning regulations in most European countries—especially in Great Britain, Belgium, and Italy—severely restricted the ability of large European retailers to expand in their home markets. These factors led European retailers to search for growth opportunities in foreign markets.

A number of pull factors attracted European retailers to the United States. First, during the 1970s the U.S. dollar declined significantly in value compared with major European currencies. This decline led to sharp drops in the value of U.S. stocks and made it easier for foreign companies to acquire U.S. firms. Second, to European retailers the U.S. offered a large market that was socio-culturally similar, to some degree, with their home markets. Third, the business practices followed by U.S. firms were, in general, fairly similar to those of European firms, although they varied in detail. Finally, U.S. laws and business practices did not discriminate against foreign companies operating in the country.

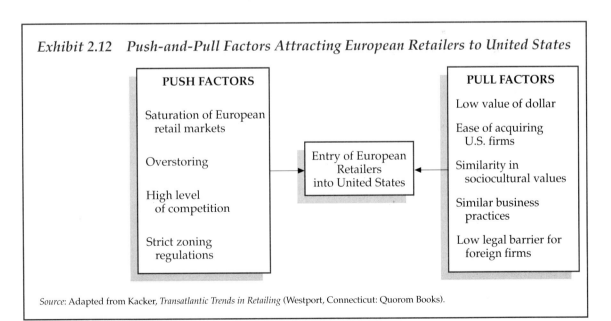

Exhibit 2.12   *Push-and-Pull Factors Attracting European Retailers to United States*

PUSH FACTORS

Saturation of European retail markets

Overstoring

High level of competition

Strict zoning regulations

Entry of European Retailers into United States

PULL FACTORS

Low value of dollar

Ease of acquiring U.S. firms

Similarity in sociocultural values

Similar business practices

Low legal barrier for foreign firms

Source: Adapted from Kacker, *Transatlantic Trends in Retailing* (Westport, Connecticut: Quorom Books).

International Expansion of U.S. Retailers

A number of U.S. firms, such as J.C. Penney, K mart, Safeway, Sears, and Woolworth have had significant presence in foreign markets for a long time. Woolworth expanded into Canada and Great Britain at the turn of the century, and established itself as the leading variety store chain in those countries. Sears entered Cuba in 1942, and Safeway entered the Canadian market in 1929 and the European and Australian markets in the 1950s.[21] More recently, Safeway has initiated joint projects in Saudi Arabia and Japan. J.C. Penney and K mart also have significant presence in foreign markets. To these companies, foreign markets represented new market opportunities that enabled the firm to expand their operations quickly.

There was considerable variation in the speed with which these firms ventured into foreign markets. Woolworth, for example, sought opportunities in foreign markets early in its history, long before consolidating its domestic network. Sears, too, started its Latin American operations before expanding in the Northeastern United States. Like most supermarket chains, Safeway has chosen to retain a regional, rather than a national focus, in the United States, while expanding into foreign markets. Others, however, entered foreign markets only after consolidating their operations in the United States.

A new wave of foreign expansion has taken place during the last two decades. Unlike the earlier one, this expansionary wave has been, and continues to be, led by franchisors. With their domestic markets highly saturated, franchisors such as McDonald's, Burger King, Kentucky Fried Chicken, Wendy's, and Pizza Hut, have expanded into foreign markets in search for growth. For example, in 1991 McDonald's had 3,355 franchised outlets abroad in 53 countries. It is estimated that by 1995 profits from McDonald's overseas operations will exceed domestic profits.[22] While smaller in comparison to McDonald's, Burger King's international presence is also substantial: in 1991 Burger King had 199 company owned and 653 franchised outlets overseas.[23] In the same year the 4,579 foreign outlets of Pizza Hut, Kentucky Fried Chicken, and Taco Bell, three fast-food chains owned by Pepsico, generated $3.7 billion in sales.[24]

Market opportunity is the major reason U.S. franchise operators have expanded into international markets aggressively. After years of rapid growth, the U.S. fast-food (or quick service, as it is often called) market seems to have reached saturation. Industry sales have grown very modestly and severe competition has put pressure on profit margins. Another problem facing the industry is the lack of attractive sites for expansion. With the prime sites already taken, franchisors are finding it difficult to expand their network in domestic markets. The trend toward foreign markets is likely to continue for some time. Most expansion, so far, has been limited to Great Britain, Canada, Australia, continental Europe, and, to a smaller extent, Japan. The newly emerging economies of Eastern Europe, Russia, and Asia are still significantly underpenetrated. Leading franchise organizations are competing aggressively to capture the prime locations in such cities as Beijing, Moscow, Prague, and Budapest.

The list of U.S. retailers selling internationally has now been joined by a number of mail order catalogs. With the value of the U.S. dollar at its historic low in comparison with major European currencies, some mail order companies are aggressively courting customers overseas. According to one estimate, a British customer could save nearly $1,600, even after paying all import duties, by purchasing an Apple computer from a U.S. mail order catalog than by buying one in Britain.[25] Such differences in price have created a booming export business for U.S. mail order houses. One such firm is Express Technology, Inc., of Scottsdale, Arizona. This computer software company sells only to overseas shoppers. In one week during July, 1992, the firm sold $100,000 worth of products to foreign customers ordering by phone.[26] The mail-order giant, L.L. Bean, started an international department to sell to foreign customers and generated $38 million in sales in 1991 compared with only $2 million in foreign sales in 1986.[27]

Summary

1. Retailing is an extremely competitive industry. All retail stores have to compete aggressively to attract their share of the money that consumers spend in retail stores. Although, like all industries, retail competition is governed by the general principles of supply and demand, three special characteristics make retail competition somewhat unique:
   a. Retailers face both *intratype* competition which comes from similar stores (e.g., competition between two supermarkets) as well as *intertype* competition from other types of stores that sell the same merchandise (e.g., competition between a supermarket and a drug store).
   b. Large chain stores and small, independent stores coexist, giving retailing a dual character. Although large chains are increasing their share of total retail sales nationally, retailing is not very concentrated compared with other consumer industries. Extremely low barriers to entry into retailing, account, in part, for the low concentration.
   c. Another distinguishing feature of retailing is its local market orientation. Since stores attract customers from their local market areas, retail managers must focus on competition at the local level.
2. Strategic group analysis classifies stores into different groups based on similarities in their market focus. Strategic group analysis is important because it provides the framework for understanding how retail stores compete with each other. It also helps in classifying retail stores based on their marketing strategies.
3. Competition among stores belonging to different strategic groups varies with the relative positions of the groups on the shopping opportunity line. The closer together two groups are on the shopping opportunity line, the more intense the competition. Conversely, groups that lie farther apart on the shopping opportunity line compete less intensely.
4. Competition among stores belonging to the same strategic group can be quite intense, and the intensity increases as stores become more homogenous in consumers' minds. Retailers must differentiate their stores from other stores in the same strategic group. Price, location, store atmosphere, and service are some avenues for achieving such differentiation. Price differentiation may be risky since profits can suffer. Service and locational differentiation can insulate the store from price competition.

5. Four forces are increasing the intensity of competitive rivalry among retailers: slow market growth, growth of branded goods, overstoring, and emergence of new retail institutions.
6. The retail industry is becoming increasingly globalized. Many retailers have expanded into international markets through direct investments in foreign companies, joint ventures, or starting their own branches or subsidiaries. The flow has been in both directions, with U.S. retailers entering foreign markets and foreign retailers entering U.S. markets as well. A number of push-and-pull factors have contributed to this movement.

Key Concepts

Intratype Competition
Intertype Competition
Retail chain stores
Retail concentration
Concentration ratio
Barriers to entry
Local-market orientation
Strategic Group
Key competitive dimensions

Shopping opportunity line
Strategic map
Generic competition
Evolution of strategic groups
Differentiation
Differentiation Triangle
Competitive rivalry
Globalization of retailing

Discussion Questions

1. Using some local retailers as examples, explain the difference between intratype and intertype competition.
2. Jackie Smith owns a small department store in Topeka, Kansas. Over the years, Jackie has watched her family-owned store lose sales to regional and national chains. Prepare a report for Jackie explaining the advantages the chain department stores can have over small firms. Suggest some ways in which independent stores can improve their competitive position.
3. In any market area, a large number of stores usually sell women's clothing. Explain how the concepts of strategic groups helps in understanding the nature of competition among these stores.
4. Draw a strategic group map of some local clothing stores. Explain how the level of competition among these stores depends on their positions on the shopping

opportunity line. Has any store in the area attempted to shift its position on the shopping opportunity line? How did the store achieve this? Has the repositioning strategy succeeded, in your view?
5. Using the strategic map, explain how marketing strategies of stores in various strategic groups differ.
6. Stores that belong to the same strategic group have a degree of homogeneity in consumers' minds. Discuss how these stores can differentiate themselves from competitors. Draw examples from practices of local retailers.
7. Why has competitive rivalry increased among retail firms?
8. What forces led to the influx of foreign retailers into the U.S. market during the 1970s? Why have U.S. retailers expanded into foreign markets lately?

Notes

1. Roger Dickinson, *Retail Management* (Austin: Austin Press, 1984), p. 50.
2. Ibid.
3. Joel Dryfuss, "More Power to PC Chains," *Fortune*, May 1, 1984, pp. 83–88.
4. *1987 Census of Retail Trade, Retail Trade—Subject Series* (Washington D.C.: Department of Commerce), p. 1–119.
5. *Statistical Abstract of the United States, 1991* (Washington D.C.: Department of Commerce), p. 768.
6. See various issues of *Census of Retail Trade* (Washington, D.C.: Department of Commerce.
7. See, for example, Michael Porter, *Competitive Strategy* (New York: Free Press, 1980). The meaning of the term *strategic group* differs somewhat here from its meaning in the industrial organization literature. There, strategic groups are determined based on similarities among financial, technological, and marketing strategies, Here, strategic groups are determined solely by market focus.
8. On competition among general merchandise and department stores, see Elizabeth Hirshman, "A Descriptive Theory of Retail Market Structures," *Journal of Retailing*, 54 (Winter 1978), p. 29–48.
9. The following description is based on John Quelch, *Shopfair Supermarkets* (Harvard Business School case 9-581-158).
10. Avijit Ghosh and Sara McLafferty, *Location Strategies for Retail and Service Firms* (Lexington, MA: Lexington Books, 1987).
11. "The Newly Minted Penney: Where Fashion Rules," *Business Week*, April 17, 1989, pp. 88–90.
12. Ibid.
13. Robert Lusch, *Retail Management* (Boston: Kent Publishing, 1983).
14. Porter, *Competitive Strategies*, p. 17.
15. Isadore Barmash, "Breaking Out of the Low Price Pack," *New York Times*, June 28, 1987, p. F12.
16. Ibid.
17. E. Winkelman and J. C. Bieri, "The Impact of the Development Process," in *Store Location and Store Assessment Research* ed. by R. L. Davies and D. S. Rogers (New York: John Wiley and Sons, 1984), pp. 91–98.
18. The 1960 figure is from Winkelmam and Bieri, op. cit.; the 1990 figure is from Avijit Ghosh and Sara McLafferty, "The Transformation of Metropolitan Retailing in the United States," Working Paper 91-2, Stern School of Business, New York University.
19. Madhav P. Kacker, *Transatlantic Trends in Retailing* (Westport CT: Quorom Books), p. 24.
20. This section is based on Chapters 4 and 5 of Kacker, *Transatlantic Trends in Retailing.*
21. Madhav P. Kacker, *Transatlantic Trends in Retailing* (Westport CT: Quorom Books), p. 23.
22. Lois Therrien, "McRisky," *Business Week*, October 21, p. 116.
23. Burger King Corporation Fact Sheet.
24. Pepsico, Inc. *1990 Annual Report.*
25. "Shopping Sans Frontières," *The Economist*, August 22–28, 1992, p. 52.
26. Andree Brooks, "The Latest Buzzwords: Mailed From America," *New York Times*, August 16, 1992, p. F4.
27. Ibid.

CHAPTER 3
The Retailer in the Marketing Channel

The Growth of Regional Franchises

Franchises now come in all varieties, from the conventional fast-food stores, to newer types of firms such as cleaning services or income tax preparation. Traditionally, the success of franchising was due to its ability to respond to changes across markets and customers more rapidly than other types of stores. Now, however, some franchises are so large, like McDonald's or Burger King, that they are unable to respond to local market demands as quickly as they once were, and there is a whole new breed of franchises—regional chains—that are rapidly filling in this gap. Furthermore, the consumer of the nineties is changing. This consumer seeks good quality, value, and low prices. The regional chains' ability to respond to these kinds of demands faster than the national chains with improved customer service, a tighter focus, and a wider variety of low-priced, better quality products or services, is helping these regional chains to grow and *flourish.*

Because of their regional status, these franchises have more flexibility in their marketing techniques, and are better able to focus on local customer needs and preferences. The regional stores can offer more services within their niches such as longer operating hours, widely varied menus, and promotions and store designs suited to local flavor. While large, national franchises are attempting to respond to increased local demands, they cannot match the speed at which a regional chain can change its menu, pricing scheme or portion size to suit local preferences. Furthermore, the national chains cannot alter the overall theme of the chain too drastically in any one area without the risk of hurting their national image.

One example of this newly successful breed of franchises is Florida-based Miami Subs, owned and licensed by QSR, Inc. Miami Subs began in the Southeastern United States and now has grown to 75 locations nationwide. QSR, Inc., licenses the franchise by region—for example, the boroughs of Manhattan, Staten Island, and the Bronx make up one "region"—and regions are owned and operated separately, and each has their own distinct characteristics. While all the stores have the same colorful tropical theme and similar menus, the regional affiliates are free to alter any part of the business to suit their locale. For example, the Southeastern locations serve champagne to add the flair and flashiness often associated with Miami and other resort areas, and the New York stores are open until midnight and offer delivery for the busy and long-working hours of that target market. Miami Subs is positioned between McDonald's (fast-food and quick service) and Friday's (casual, family dining with

LEARNING OBJECTIVES

After studying this chapter, the reader will be able to:
- *Understand the retailer's role in making merchandise available to consumers in an efficient manner.*
- *Describe the functions that marketing channels perform.*
- *Understand the sources of power and conflict in marketing channels.*
- *Explain the advantages and disadvantages of different forms of vertical marketing systems.*
- *Describe the organization of franchise systems, their advantages and disadvantages, and the guidelines for evaluating franchise opportunities.*

Since the 1960s, fast-food franchises have been one of the fastest growing segments of retailing. Chains such as McDonald's, Burger King, and Kentucky Fried Chicken are now well-established in the retail landscape. However, these established chains are now facing increased competition from newcomers such as Miami Subs.

fresh food served quickly and without frills). The menu has a wide selection, ranging from hot and cold subs, gyros, and pizza, to salads, yogurts, and desserts, with entree prices from $2 to $5. This formula of fast, fresh food at low prices has created such value for cus-

tomers that they keep coming back, and in droves.

A crucial element to Miami Subs' success is in its low overhead. Rather than building new stores for each location, which would cost over $1 million, Miami Subs' regional affiliates remodel failed *restaurant* locations where commercial development is permitted, bypassing the expensive and time-consuming zoning process. Because the property is distressed, QSR, Inc., can lease the property at low rates, keeping the rent low for their affiliates. The conversion costs then run from $200,000 to $250,000—only 25 percent of what it would cost to buy the property and build—and the conversion time usually is only three to four months, cutting start-up time in half. This method has proved both time and cost efficient for Miami Subs.

Miami Subs' principal competitors are Subway and TCBY. To compete with these giants, Miami Subs uses two strategies to woo customers: its off-the-street attraction and its unique and varied menu. While Miami Subs uses no advertising, it draws customers into the stores with its bright store designs and colorful signage. Once in the restaurants, the customers often find the menu ad welcome change from the typical fast food, and they have responded positively to the variety of foods offered. The chain then keeps its customers coming back because of its cheerful atmosphere, its seating areas suited to family dining, and, most importantly, its good value.

Miami Subs believes that there are only two ways to win repeat customers: offer low-priced food with quick service, and create value through a unique and varied menu. Clearly, Miami Subs has found the formula to do both. The chain recognized that the fast-food customer was changing: fast service wasn't enough; customers began seeking variety and freshness, service with a smile, and with health and nutritional considerations included. There is a whole generation of consumers who grew up on fast food, but as they reach their thirties and forties, they want fresher, more healthful food at low prices for themselves and their families. Miami Subs was quick to respond to this new kind of customer preference, serving salads and sandwiches with fresh ingredients while the giants were still serving pre-cooked food and caloric fries. Sales for Miami Subs continue to increase, to over $950,000 per location annually at the beginning of 1992. It seems that despite the size and strength of chains like Subway or McDonald's, Miami Subs is here to stay, and will continue its vigorous expansion.

Sources: Milford Prewit, "Miami Subs Explodes into Growth Mode," *Nation's Restaurant News*, February 10, 1992, p. 45; and Jack Hayes, "Regionals Battle the Big Boys with Localized Marketing," *Nation's Restaurant News*, January 7, 1991, pp. 1, 7.

Retailers do not manufacture the products they sell. They procure them from manufacturers and wholesalers and sell them to consumers. A retailer depends critically on suppliers (or vendors, as they are often called) to satisfy the merchandise needs of its customers. A stronger link with vendors increases the retailer's ability to compete for customers. Retailers, manufacturers, and wholesalers have to join together to form the channel or pipeline through which goods can flow from their point-of-production to the point-of-sale. This is the **marketing channel**, the *set of institutions responsible for making goods and services available to consumers.*

When consumers buy shirts at department stores or soft drinks at supermarkets, or when they rent videos at neighborhood convenience stores, they experience the benefits of the marketing channel. Each of these goods reaches the consumer through a marketing channel; although the consumer may not realize how the channels are organized. Exhibit 3.1 shows how marketing channels for consumer goods are commonly organized. As shown in the diagram, some channels involve manufacturers and retailers only.   For example, department stores typically get their supplies directly from the manufacturer, without a wholesaler acting as an **intermediary**. Because of their large size, retail chains like Sears, K mart, J. C. Penney, and Toys R Us, obtain their products directly from manufacturers. Similarly, catalog retailers such as L. L. Bean, Spiegel, and Land's End sell consumers merchandise they obtain directly from manufacturers. In addition, retailers of high-priced consumer goods such as car dealers and computer retailers obtain merchandise directly from manufacturers. In each case, the retailer acts as an intermediary between the manufacturer and the consumer.

Exhibit 3.1   Marketing Channels for Consumer Goods

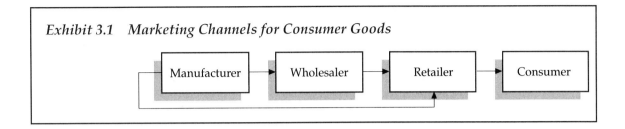

In other cases, two levels of intermediaries lie between manufacturers and consumers: retailers and wholesalers. This two-tier system is commonly used, for example, to distribute beer and soft drinks. Beer manufacturers typically sell to beer wholesalers (or distributors), and soft drink manufacturers sell concentrated syrup to bottlers. Beer wholesalers and soft drink bottlers supply individual stores, bars, and restaurants. Frequently purchased, low-priced consumer goods such as candies, cigarettes, and chewing gum are distributed through marketing channels that have one or more intermediaries between manufacturers and retailers. In each case, however, it is the retailer who makes the product available to consumers.

Exhibit 3.1 shows that retailers are part of the larger system of institutions that bridge the separation between producers and consumers. Simple, subsistence-oriented economies rely on direct transactions between producers and consumers. But as economies become more specialized, producers and consumers tend to get separated and deal with each other through intermediaries rather than directly. Because of economies of scale in manufacturing processes, the most efficient scales of production tend to be far greater than the most efficient scales of consumption. Consider, for example, chewing gum. Most consumers buy chewing gum in small packets of five or ten sticks. Production, on the other hand, takes place in highly automated plants that must produce large quantities to be efficient. Producers rely on intermediaries to bridge the gap between the scale of production and the scale of consumption. The intermediaries achieve this by **breaking bulk**; that is, each intermediary sells lot sizes that are smaller than the lot size they purchase. Large scale production also creates a geographic separation between producers and consumers. Production takes place in a few large factories while consumers are geographically dispersed. Intermediaries are also essential in overcoming this geographical separation between producers and consumers. In this way, by acting as intermediaries, retailers make the marketing channel more efficient and benefit producers as well as consumers.

While intermediaries are typically needed to distribute products efficiently, they are bypassed in situations in which there is no separation between producers and consumers. A custom tailor, for example, is a marketing channel without an intermediary. To have their clothes made to order, customers go directly to the tailor, the manufacturer in this case. The tailor can maintain direct relationships with customers because there is no discrepancy between the scales of production and consumption. The tailor makes each piece of clothing only when the customer places an order.

Most consumer services are distributed without intermediaries. Dentists, lawyers, banks, and restaurants all provide services directly to their customers. In each of these cases, like the tailor shop, the service is provided only when it is required. Another feature of service retailing is that services are produced and consumed at the same place, eliminating the need for intermediaries to distribute services. Because service providers interact directly with their customers, confusion often arises as to whether they are manufacturers or retailers. Although in some sense they are both, the term service retailer is more common than service manufacturer and will be used here.

This chapter focuses on understanding the functions of marketing channels for consumer goods and the retailer's role in that channel. The chapter begins by discussing the various functions performed by members of a marketing channel. The second section looks at coordination of activities of channel members to reduce conflict and increase effectiveness. The final section deals with vertical marketing systems. Throughout, the chapter places special emphasis on understanding the relationship between retailers and their suppliers.

FUNCTIONS OF MARKETING CHANNEL MEMBERS

Marketing channels are conduits through which merchandise flows from producers to consumers. Marketing channel members need to perform a variety of **channel functions** to ensure that goods and services reach consumers in an efficient manner. The channel functions performed by retailers can be broadly classified into three main categories: (1) maintaining inventory; (2) advertising, promotion, and service; and (3) maintaining information flow (see Exhibit 3.2). These three types of functions are discussed below.

Maintaining Inventory

One of the major tasks of channel members is to maintain an adequate inventory of merchandise. The flow of goods through the channel stops if channel members do not have the right amount of merchandise at the right time and the right place. A retailer must order and stock the merchandise that customers want in adequate quantities. As one basic function, retailers ensure the flow of goods from manufacturers to consumers by breaking bulk and maintaining merchandise inventory. To maintain adequate merchandise inventory, retailers must order, buy, transport, and store merchandise regularly.

Maintaining inventory entails significant costs, and when retailers take title to merchandise and assume its ownership, they bear these costs. The most important is the opportunity cost of capital invested in inventory. Most retailers have a

Exhibit 3.2 Functions of Marketing Channels

MAINTAINING INVENTORY	ADVERTISING PROMOTION AND SERVICE	INFORMATION FLOW
Order and stock merchandise that customers want in adequate quantities	Display merchandise	Collect market information
Monitor and manage inventory	Provide in-store and after-sales service	Provide information to customers
Assume risk of maintaining inventory	Advertise in mass media and at point-of-sale	Provide information to suppliers

significant portion of their capital tied up in inventories. By tying up this capital, the retailer looses the opportunity to invest it elsewhere. Larger inventories require larger investments and hence increase this opportunity cost.

Maintaining inventory creates considerable risk, because holding inventory is always a speculative venture. Sometimes the demand for a piece of merchandise is lower than expected and it has to be sold at a price that is lower than the anticipated price. The holder of the inventory has to then absorb the loss due to the lower price. Merchandise obsolescence due to spoilage or change in consumer preferences also adds to the risk of holding inventory. The channel member who holds title to the merchandise has to bear the risks associated with maintaining merchandise inventory. Inventory risks also increase with the level of inventory.

In addition to risks and opportunity costs, there are also direct expenses associated with maintaining inventory. These include the cost of warehousing, handling, insurance, and taxes. These costs, too, typically increase with the volume of inventory.

The total cost of maintaining inventory, including risk, opportunity cost, and direct expenses, is typically referred to as the **inventory holding cost**. For most retailers, inventory holding cost is a significant portion of their operating costs because retail businesses rely on readily available inventory of merchandise. An important goal for retailers, therefore, is to control inventory costs without sacrificing customer demand. One important key to better inventory management is faster inventory turn-around. That is, merchandise should sell as soon as possible after it is put on the shelf. Fast turn-around reduces the level of inventory that the retailer has to maintain to meet consumer demand. Better inventory management also requires constant monitoring of sales and inventory levels of individual items. Because they carry many thousands of items, many retailers have tended to monitor merchandise inventory at broad, aggregate levels. For example, they monitor the inventory of men's shirts rather than the inventories of individual brands and colors of shirts. One of the most significant changes taking place in retail management is the shift in this focus. Retailers are now paying much more attention to item management; that is, monitoring and managing the inventory, sales, and profits of individual merchandise items.

To monitor and manage inventory better, many retailers are relying on computerized inventory management and record-keeping systems that track each of the merchandise items carried by the store. Large retailers such as Dillard's, May Company, Wal-Mart, and Federated Department Stores have developed their own system to automate inventory and sales records. The system developed by Federated, called Sabre, for example, tracks inventory from the time the order is placed with a vendor through the delivery and distribution process until a sale is made. The inventory management system is linked to the point-of-sale cash registers, allowing a user to find out exactly how much inventory is available at any time. This allows the company to meet customer demand with less inventory on hand and mark down less merchandise.[1]

Inventory management is equally important for small retailers. A number of software programs for inventory management suitable for small retailers are commercially available. Because of their importance, issues related to merchandise inventory control will be discussed in more detail in Chapter 12. It is important here, however, to stress the importance of having a proper inventory merchandise system that focuses on item management. It is no exaggeration to state that the potential for retail profit depends strongly on the quality of inventory management.

Advertising Promotion and Service

Merchandise sales depends not only on its physical qualities, but also on advertising, promotion, and service. All channel members participate in this function to some extent. Retailers advertise merchandise, display it attractively, promote it at the point-of-sale, and provide after-sales service to customers. Without the cooperation of retailers, manufacturers would find it difficult to market their products effectively. Small manufacturers, especially, rely heavily on wholesalers and retailers to promote their merchandise. Providing promotion and service is another important function of marketing channels.

Information Flow

As another important function, marketing channels maintain the flow of information between producers and consumers. Customers need information about products and services, and manufacturers need information about consumption patterns and customer characteristics. Information must, therefore, flow in both directions. The marketing channel provides a conduit for the flow of information between manufacturers and consumers. Retailers participate very actively in collecting market information. In the marketing channel they are the first to know of changes in customer tastes, preferences, and buying habits. The point-of-sale scanning equipment used by retailers tracks the sales levels of different brands, styles, and sizes in a continuous manner. The scanners can also be used to monitor sales of new products and how price changes affect sales. Retailers also participate in the reverse flow of information. They pass along product information provided by the manufacturer to the consumer.

Allocation of Channel Functions

For marketing channels to function effectively, all the channel functions are essential. But all channel members do not necessarily participate in all functions. Rather, each channel member tends to specialize in one or more of the functions. Such specialization creates efficiency since each channel member can "offer other channel members more than they can usually achieve on their own."[2] The activities of the different channel members must, however, be coordinated to ensure that all the necessary functions are performed and that the channel operates in an efficient manner.

The degree to which channel members participate in different channel functions depends on their expertise and the resources available to them. Large retailers typically participate in all channel functions ranging from carrying inventory to providing after-sales service. A car dealer, for example, typically:

- Maintains inventory of cars.
- Displays the cars.
- Advertises in local media.
- Provides information to prospective customers.
- Provides after-sales service.
- Helps arrange for car loans for customers.

All of these functions facilitate the exchange process and are important. If a car dealer fails to perform one or more of these functions, the channel will become ineffective and consumers will be dissatisfied. In contrast to large retailers, small retailers tend to participate in only a few functions. The functions of newspaper vendors, for example, is typically limited to making the newspaper physically available to customers. They rarely do any advertising or promotion except for some point-of-sale displays. Because they often have limited financial resources, newspaper vendors typically do not assume the risk of maintaining inventory. Maintaining newspaper inventory is quite risky because they are highly perishable (yesterday's unsold newspapers do not have any value today). Newspaper publishers or distributors (wholesalers), therefore, assume the inventory risk and provide credit to newspaper vendors. The vendors receive a supply of newspapers every day and pay at the end of the day only for the copies that were sold. This way the vendor does not bear any risk of maintaining inventory.

Stores can differentiate themselves from competitors by providing customers with increased shopping convenience. Convenience stores, such as this one, compete on that basis.

Because of their limited resources, small neighborhood grocery and convenience stores, too, do not assume the risk of inventory for many products. They receive goods from manufacturers or from **rack jobbers** (a type of wholesaler) on consignment. The manufacturer or the rack jobber retains title to the merchandise and charges the store only for the merchandise that is sold. The rack jobber determines the variety and assortment of the merchandise that the retailer should carry and periodically visits the store to replenish stocks. Like newspaper vendors, the major function that these stores perform is to make the merchandise widely available to consumers.

This is not to imply, however, that newspaper vendors and neighborhood convenience stores are unimportant to their respective marketing channels. On the contrary, their roles in the channels are critical. They enhance consumer convenience by bridging the geographic separation between producers and consumers. Consider how inconvenient it would be if people had to travel long distances to buy the daily newspaper or a can of soda. The sale of these products is highly dependent on the products being available conveniently. To ensure locational convenience, the newspaper vendor and the neighborhood convenience stores (in many cases they are one and the same) are integral to the proper functioning of their respective marketing channels.

Irrespective of how channel functions are allocated among the channel members, they must all be performed well. Each channel function is essential for meeting consumer needs effectively and efficiently. There is considerable truth in the saying that "one can eliminate an intermediary, but not the functions of the intermediary." To eliminate an intermediary, another channel member must assume the functions of that intermediary. If newspaper publishers decide to eliminate the vendors from the channel, they, or their distributors, will have to perform the vendor's task by operating newsstands themselves. It is unlikely that they can reach their customers without the newspaper stands. Similarly, retailers have to rely on their suppliers for merchandise. Without them, they would have to produce the merchandise themselves.

CHANNEL COORDINATION AND CONFLICT

Marketing channel members are independent organizations or individuals linked together by the common goal of distributing merchandise to consumers. The relationship between retailers and their suppliers has often been a struggle for **channel power**. The manufacturer's desire to distribute their products widely at low cost often conflicts with the retailer's need to manage its operations efficiently and make the most effective use of shelf space.[3]

Manufacturer Power

At one time manufacturers always held the most power in the marketing channel. They typically assumed the role of channel captains and took the lead in directing and coordinating the activities of all channel members. Large manufacturers such as Procter and Gamble, Coca-Cola, and Anheiser-Busch still have considerable influence over the behavior of other channel members. Strong consumer demand for their products gives large manufacturers the power to set standards and conditions for all channel members.

Manufacturers derive their power in the channel from a number of sources. First is the strength of their brand name. Retailers prefer to carry brands with well-recognized names since they are easier to sell than those without any name recognition. Thus, the more recognizable the brand name, the greater the power of the manufacturer. Consumer advertising and promotion undertaken by manufacturers enhance their brand names and lead to greater power for the manufacturer. Another source of manufacturer power is sales and trade promotions. The greater the level of such promotions by a manufacturer, the more incentive retailers have to carry the manufacturer's products. Finally, the more dependent a retailer is on a manufacturer for supplies, the greater the manufacturer's power over the retailer. Consider, for example, the relationship between Ford Motor Company and the individual dealers who sell Ford cars. The individual dealers are highly dependent on Ford—they simply have no other sources of supply. They are also dependent on Ford for national advertising and promotion of the brand and for a steady source of inventory. Individual car dealers also depend on the manufacturers to provide consumer and trade promotions to boost sales. An individual car dealer is highly dependent on the manufacturer and has little bargaining power over it. To counter balance the manufacturer's power, auto dealers group together in trade associations which actively promote the interests of individual dealers.

Retailer's Power

In the last decade, the balance of power between manufacturers and retailers has gradually shifted toward retailers. Today, the typical retail firm wields considerably more power over the channel than it did 10 years ago. Indeed, some argue that retailers now have an upper hand over their suppliers. There are many reasons for this shift in power from manufacturers to retailers, the text below discusses some prominent ones.

Increased Size of Retail Chains   During the 1960s and 1970s, many retail chains expanded into suburban locations, attracted by the growing suburban population and available retail space in shopping malls. As a result, many large chains now exceed the size of their suppliers, so they wield considerable power over them. In many cases, the suppliers rely heavily on these chains, since the chains buy almost all the merchandise the suppliers produce. Consider, for example, a manufacturer of casual socks. J.C. Penney, Sears, and K mart may collectively buy all the socks this manufacturer produces. When a manufacturer's reliance on a few retailers increases, so does those retailers' bargaining power with the manufacturer.

Increased Concentration   Hand-in-hand with increased size of the retail chains has come increased concentration in the retail industry. Toys R Us, for example, now controls approximately 25 percent of the toy retailing industry in the United States. Unless this chain carries its products, a manufacturer will be locked out of a significant portion of its potential market.[4] A similar situation now prevails in the appliance industry. It used to be that most household appliances (refrigerators, dishwashers, ovens, and so on) were sold through small appliance dealers who carried one or two brands. These retailers relied heavily on the manufacturers; and the manufacturers, in turn, held considerable power over them. Currently, however, power has shifted to large discount-oriented appliance chains that carry multiple brands and promote them aggressively. These large appliance chains prefer to deal with manufacturers who carry a full line of appliances. As a result, manufacturers such as Maytag, who specialize in one type of appliance only, have been forced to broaden their product line to gain retailer cooperation.

The recent spate of mergers among department stores, supermarkets, and drugstores, has increased the power of these consolidated retailers over their suppliers. Indeed greater bargaining power over suppliers is often cited as a major reason for retail mergers. By merging together, retailers can consolidate their buying. In addition to decreasing administrative costs (which occur typically, but not always), this gives them greater power over their suppliers.

Increased Competition among Manufacturers   The markets for many consumer goods have reached the maturity stage of their life cycles. That is, demand for these goods and services is growing at a very slow rate, if at all. To improve their competitive positions in these mature markets, manufacturers have introduced many new products that are quite similar to each other. From this wide array of products retailers can pick and choose the ones they wish to carry, once again increasing their bargaining power.

Increased Attention to Item Profitability   As mentioned earlier, retailers are now looking more closely at the performance of individual brands in order to control inventory costs. With increased availability of detailed sales and cost information, they are now using direct product profit (DPP) criteria to decide which products they will keep on their shelves. As discussed in more detail in Chapter 13, DPP essentially allocates all the retailer's cost to every item on the shelf to determine the net profit each generates. Detailed calculations of product profitability allow retailers to assess how much each product contributes to their bottom lines. As the number of new products increases, retailers will use DPP to decide which to keep and which to discontinue. Even when they carry a product, retailers use DPP calculations to negotiate better terms and conditions with manufacturers.[5]

Implications of Increased Retailer Power

There are a number of indications of the retailer's increased influence in the marketing channel. The most controversial one is the **slotting fee** many supermarkets now charge for carrying new products. *This is a one-time fee that a retailer charges the manufacturer of a new product as consideration for providing shelf space for the new product.* A new product manufacturer who refuses to pay the slotting fee may find it difficult to obtain shelf space for the new product. Slotting fees have raised considerable controversy in the industry and many consider them to be illegal, since they discriminate against smaller retailers who do not have the power to extract such fees from manufacturers. Large chains, who have many outlets and buy in large quantities, are the ones who typically charge slotting fees. According to one estimate, it may cost a manufacturer $70,000 or more in slotting fees to introduce a new six-item line into a 50-store chain.[6] Despite the controversy, the fee seems to be taking hold and becoming the normal practice in the supermarket industry.

The increased level of trade promotions in the supermarket industry is another sign of increased retailer power. Manufacturers have been forced to sacrifice some of their margin in the form of sales incentives and temporary price promotions in order to get business from retailers. Retailers have demanded and obtained from manufacturers various forms of trade promotions such as off-invoice allowance, special packs, late payment terms, advertising allowances, and so on. Some supermarket and drug store chains will only carry those brands that manufacturers promote to the trade with special deals. Manufacturer trade promotions and deals have been extremely attractive to retailers. Most supermarkets, for example, do not pass on the cost saving to customers in the form of lower prices. The money from trade promotions and slotting fees add directly to the supermarkets' bottom line. Given the supermarket industry's low margins, money from promotions can make a significant difference in profits.

Another reflection of the shift in channel power is the reorganization of sales and marketing departments of many consumer product companies. The salesforce of most consumer product manufacturers is typically organized to reflect the company's own divisional structures. Some, however, are reorganizing their salesforce around key retail accounts in recognition of the retailer's importance.

Some large manufacturers have begun to resist pressure from supermarkets on trade promotions and deals and to flex their own muscle more. In the first half of 1992, Procter and Gamble instituted a new pricing policy that drastically reduced trade promotions in favor of everyday low prices. The company is also rationalizing its product lines to reduce the total number of items it sells. Some retailers, however, are resisting this move and refusing to carry the company's products. It has, however, won the support of retailers like Wal-Mart, which stress "everyday low prices" themselves. Manufacturers and retailers seem to be drawing the battle lines over the issue of pricing policy.

Channel Conflict

Despite attempts to coordinate the functions of the channel, conflicts do occur and relationships among channel members do break down. In fact, since channel members are independent businesses, each with its own goals and objectives, some degree of **channel conflict** is often the rule rather than the exception. Consider the following situations:

- Many department stores refuse to carry apparel lines that are also sold by off-price retailers.
- Manufacturers threaten to discontinue supply to retailers who discount prices heavily.
- Wholesalers refuse to cooperate with manufacturers who also sell directly to retailers and retailers complain when manufacturers sell directly to consumers.
- Franchisors complain about high prices for required purchases from franchisors.

Each of these represents a potential conflict between channel members. Such conflict can ultimately lead to a breakdown of the channel. Given the negative impact that conflict typically has on channel performance, it is important for retailers to understand the potential sources of conflict and take steps to reduce its harmful effects.

Sources of Conflict

Conflict commonly arises from four sources: (1) failure by a channel member to perform an assigned role; (2) goal incompatibility; (3) domain dissension; and (4) vertical competition.

Failure to Perform Assigned Role   Conflict most commonly arises due to failure of a channel member to perform its assigned role in the channel. Retailers, for example, expect large manufacturers to market their products aggressively and advertise them to consumers. Manufacturers, on the other hand, expect retailers to run local advertising and promote the products in the store. Failure by manufacturers or retailers to perform these functions can lead to conflict. Many franchisees, for example, complain that their franchisors fail to introduce new products or coordinate national advertising and promotional campaigns effectively. This can lead to dissatisfaction with the franchisor and can result in conflict as was the case recently with Burger King.

Goal Incompatibility   Another source of conflict is incompatibility of the goals of the different channel members. Consider, for example, the relationship between a manufacturer of exclusive gift items and its retailers. The manufacturer wants to project a high-status, high-quality image for its products. Some of the retailers, on the other hand, are more interested in high turnovers and are willing to sacrifice margins to increase sales. The incompatibility of the goals of the manufacturer and the retailers creates the potential for conflict. Similarly, many small manufacturers rely on retailers to expand their markets by opening new outlets or aggressively promoting the merchandise carried in the store. The goals of such a manufacturer will be incompatible with a retailer uninterested in expansion, leading to the possibility of conflict between them.

Domain Dissension   Conflicts also arise due to disagreements over who has the authority to make decisions that affect the channel. Which channel member, for example, should determine the appropriate amount of inventory for each member to hold, how should sales information be provided to customers, and, perhaps most importantly, at what price is the product to be sold? In few channels do members explicitly agree on who will make these decisions or how they will be made. Each channel member's role in the decision-making process evolves over time, depending on the amount of power they assert. Disagreements over the domain of each channel member's authority stimulates a great deal of conflict among channel members.

Disagreements over price and inventory decisions, for example, commonly cause conflict between manufacturers and retailers. Retailers argue that they must have complete freedom to determine the final price. Some manufacturers, on the other hand, would like to control or have considerable input into the decision. Although manufacturers have no legal control over the price of their merchandise after they sell it to retailers, they do attempt to control prices indirectly.[7] Some manufacturers attempt to coerce retailers in following its "recommended" prices. Such coercion can lead to conflict between the manufacturer and retailers.

Vertical Competition   Another source of conflict between manufacturers and retailers is **vertical competition**. *Vertical competition occurs when manufacturers and retailers (or wholesalers) compete for the same consumers.* For example, Gucci products are available at department stores as well as from outlets operated by the manufacturer. Gucci outlets and department stores, therefore, compete for customers wanting to purchase Gucci products. This is vertical competition between the manufacturer and retailers.

Retailers can also initiate vertical competition. Many supermarket chains actively promote their house brands of grocery products. The house brands compete with manufacturer brands the retailers sell, resulting in vertical competition. Vertical competition frequently generates conflict as retailers view manufacturer's actions as encroachments on their business and vice versa.

Managing Conflict

The failure to perform assigned tasks, goal incompatibility, domain dissension, and vertical competition can all potentially lead to conflict between retailers and the manufacturers they represent. Some degree of conflict is almost inevitable in marketing channels. In fact, some conflict may be beneficial since it reminds channel members of their interdependency. However, channel members must work together in controlling the level of conflict.

Conflict between channel members can be categorized into three levels: latent, perceived, and manifest. Most commonly, conflict remains latent and does not surface. In this type of **latent conflict**, relationships between channel members are often in a state of tension as they attempt to fulfill their own respective goals. But, such tension is typically not dysfunctional and is seen as a normal aspect of the relationship. Conflict reaches the **perceived conflict** stage when channel members start voicing disagreements about specific issues, either formally or informally. Some common sources of disagreement between manufacturers and retailers are pricing, cooperative advertising funds, promotional support, merchandise display, and the trade allowance pass through. This last issue is a major source of friction between manufacturers and retailers. When manufacturers give special price incentives to retailers, they expect retailers to pass on the savings to consumers in the form of lower prices, although this is typically not a legal requirement. Many retailers, however, do not pass on the deal to the consumers; they simply use it to increase their margins. Finally, **manifest conflict** results in overt behavioral actions such as a manufacturer refusing to supply retailers or threatening to discontinue advertising or promotional support or a retailer refusing to carry a manufacturer's products. Ideally, conflict should be anticipated and controlled before it reaches the manifest stage and breaks down channel relationships. Typically, however, conflict is detected only "after it is well-developed and obvious."[8] At this late stage, the conflict may have done its damage and become difficult to control.

One way to anticipate potential conflict is to periodically review the relationships between channel members. The most effective way to perform such reviews is to form a channelwide committee composed of representatives from all channel members.[9] In the soft drink industry, for example, channelwide committees consisting of representatives of the manufacturers and bottlers periodically review channel relationships. Because it includes representatives from both the manufacturer and bottlers, the committee can take all perspectives into account in making channelwide decisions.[10]

To avoid manifest conflict, the channel committee must arrive at a set of goals that benefits both manufacturers and bottlers, along with systemwide performance standards such as inventory levels, advertising, promotion, and new account generation. The resources of the channel members must be considered in setting these performance standards.

VERTICAL MARKETING SYSTEMS

So far, our discussion has concentrated on traditional or conventional marketing channels, the members of which—manufacturers, wholesalers, and retailers—are independent organizations, each with its own goals and objectives. In conventional channels, these independent institutions form a loose alliance to distribute goods and services to consumers. Members of conventional channels bargain aggressively with each other to define their roles in the channel. As a result, channel conflict is common in conventional channels. To overcome this problem, new types of channel organizations called **vertical marketing systems** have become popular in recent years.

Vertical marketing systems are marketing channels that are centrally coordinated to perform channel functions efficiently and increase market impact.[11] Vertical marketing systems clearly specify the role and tasks of each channel member, and typically a designated channel member leads and coordinates the entire channel. In contrast to conventional channels, vertical marketing systems (VMS) are managed as a system, reducing the potential for conflict and increasing channel efficiency. Vertical marketing systems take three common forms: (1) corporate systems; (2) administered systems; and (3) contractual systems (see Exhibit 3.3).

Corporate System

In sharp contrast to conventional channels, in the ***corporate system*** *all channel operations are completely integrated by a single corporate entity.* The same firm that pro-

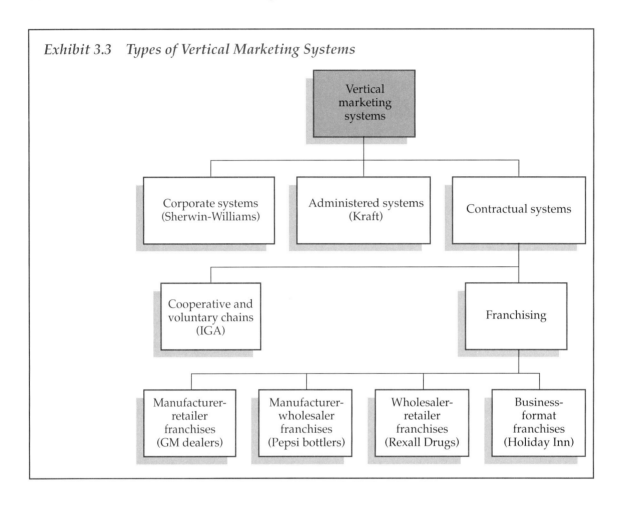

Exhibit 3.3   Types of Vertical Marketing Systems

duces the merchandise also performs all other channel functions. For example, Hart Shaffner and Marx, a manufacturer of men's clothing, also owns and operates retail stores that sell the clothing that it manufactures. Another example is Sherwin-Williams. The company manufactures the paints and accessories sold in Sherwin-Williams retail paint stores. Recently, Sony has opened retail stores to sell products manufactured by the company. This, too, is an example of the corporate system.

Advantages of Corporate Systems   As their major advantage, corporate systems maintain control. Since a single organization performs all the functions of the channel, it can achieve a high degree of coordination and control. Corporate systems can integrate planning since all channel members have common goals and the locus of control is well defined. As a result, merchandise can be distributed more effectively and conflict can be eliminated. The manufacturer, for example,

In a corporate system, such as Sherwin-Williams, the same firm that produces the merchandise also performs all other channel functions, thereby integrating all channel operations.

can set the retail price for the product and change it when desired without opposition from other channel members. In recent years many manufacturers have been concerned that heavy price discounts offered by some retailers could hamper their efforts in creating a prestige-oriented image for their products. Through corporate systems, aggrieved manufacturers can gain complete control over the distribution of their products.

Disadvantages of Corporate Systems   Corporate systems, however, have significant risks, too. The most important one is their cost. Since the wholesaling and retailing functions in the corporate system are limited to the products of a single manufacturer, they may be costly compared to having independent wholesalers and retailers. Independent retailers, for example, can achieve significant economies of scope by spreading their costs over a large number of products. Further, when a manufacturer integrates the wholesaling and retailing functions, or a retailer integrates to perform manufacturing, they enter into areas where they might have limited expertise.

Finally, lack of product variety and assortment limit the development of corporate systems. As discussed in Chapter 1, retail outlets benefit consumers by

ENTREPRENEURIAL EDGE

Food Shopping Made Luxurious

Everyone shops in supermarkets, and consumers have many supermarkets from which to choose. Given this, how does a supermarket go about attracting customers? If you are Robert Onstead, chairman and CEO of the 42-store Randall's Food Markets chain, based in Houston, you create stores that emulate feelings of warmth and empathy. Warmth and empathy for a 55,000-square-foot supermarket? Onstead's markets definitely have a friendly ambiance, and he is adamant that this ambiance is the key to his company's success precisely because it is so different from the usual supermarket atmosphere.

Randall's was founded in 1966 when Onstead and a partner bought two struggling Houston food stores. Onstead saw a challenge in making the markets succeed, and in the first three months they doubled the weekly revenues at both stores. The changes they made were drastic: improved customer service, better layout and design of the stores, better-quality products, more fresh offerings (deli, produce, butcher, and so on). With these changes, the Randall's concept was launched. Onstead has always believed that—no matter what the situation—the customers come first in terms of products and service, and customers should *always* get what they want in a Randall's store. Onstead and his partner have kept their company private, so that they can be free to do whatever is needed to keep the customer "Number 1" without having to worry about the reactions of stockholders.

Randall's stores are all clean and well-lighted and well designed to promote ease of shopping. The aisles are wide and the carts large. The stores offer a wide variety of merchandise and services, including food and staples, pharmacy, deli, florist, butcher, and bakery. Furthermore, the design of the stores allows customers to see most of the food preparation, so they feel that they know exactly what they are purchasing in every department, and can ask for changes or additions. And finally, the staff is top-notch: floor staff is always nearby to answer questions about products, or to reach boxes on the top shelves. In fact, the employees are required to take part in a customer-service training program to ensure that friendliness and helpfulness is displayed by all the Randall's employees.

Clearly, Onstead knows what his customers want. Sales for Randall's have topped $1 billion, and show no sign of slowing. The sales volume and customer base increases each year, as does its share of the Houston market, which is currently at a whopping 24 percent. Onstead says that his vision succeeds because he fosters a true family feeling among his staff, from the top down, and he insists on a team-oriented, friendly atmosphere among his employees, because he wants that feeling to filter back to the customers. For Onstead, this ambiance is vital to his stores, and it seems that his customers agree.

Source: "Retailing's Entrepreneurs of the Year," *Chain Store Age Executive*, December 1990, pp. 28–38.

offering a wide variety and assortment of products at one place. The retail outlets of the corporate system cannot create much variety or assortment since they sell merchandise produced by a single manufacturer only. This makes it difficult for most manufacturers to open their own retail stores. Many manufacturers of consumer durables, for example, would like to perform their own retailing to gain more control over the channel. However, the lack of product assortment makes it difficult for them to open their own corporate system.

Administered Systems

In comparison to corporate systems, administered systems lie on the other end of the spectrum of vertical marketing systems. Unlike corporate systems but similar to conventional channels, **administered systems** are made up of independent organizations. The activities of channel members in an administered system, however, are coordinated to reduce conflict and maximize market impact. Despite their formal independence, members of administered systems have a more systemwide perspective than members of conventional channels.

The channel member with the greatest size and power, be it the retailer, wholesaler, or manufacturer, usually coordinates the activities of an administered system. A common coordinating mechanism is **programmed merchandising**. In programmed merchandising, channel members agree to mutually acceptable standards of performance and formally assign responsibility to one member to maintain those standards. In the food industry, for example, cheese producers like Kraft and Dorman Cheese use program merchandising. The merchandising agreements between Kraft and supermarkets specify standards of inventory replenishment and display, smoothing those areas of potential conflict between manufacturers and supermarkets. By agreeing to specific standards, supermarkets and manufacturers reduce the possibility of conflict. A list of some other manufacturers who use programmed merchandising is shown in Exhibit 3.4. Because of their size, large retailers like Sears and K mart also exert power over their suppliers to develop merchandising and promotional programs.

Contractual Systems

The third type of vertical marketing system is contractual systems. *A* **contractual system** *defines relationships between independent channel members bound together in a contractual agreement.* The contractual agreement specifies the responsibilities of each channel member and the manner in which the activities of the channel are to be coordinated. Of the three types of vertical marketing systems, contractual systems are the most common. There are two types of contractual systems: (1) cooperatives and voluntary chains, and (2) franchise systems.

Exhibit 3.4   *Manufacturers Operating Administered Channels*

Company	Product
Armstrong Cork	Floor coverings
Baumritter (Ethan Allan)	Furniture
Corning Glass	Cookware and china
General Electric	Household appliances
Kellogg	Cereal
Kraft	Food products
Magnavox	Consumer electronic products
Scotts	Lawn products
Sealy	Mattresses
Villager	Women's apparel

Source: Bert Rosenbloom, *Marketing Channels* (Hinsdale, IL.: The Dryden Press, 1987), p. 366.

Cooperatives and Voluntary Chains   To increase efficiency and gain some bargaining power with suppliers, small, independent retailers often join together to form retail cooperatives or voluntary chains. In a retail cooperative, individual retailers pool their resources and collectively conduct their own wholesaling operation. By pooling their buying power, the members of the cooperative can obtain better terms from the manufacturer than they could if they act individually.

Voluntary chains are similar to retail cooperatives except that a wholesaler leads the channel rather than a group of retailers. In a wholesaler-sponsored voluntary chain, a wholesaler develops a "contractual relationship with small, independent retailers to standardize and coordinate the buying practices, merchandise programs, and inventory management efforts."[12] The motivation for retailers to join wholesaler-sponsored chains, like that for joining retail cooperatives, is to obtain merchandise at lower prices, which helps them compete against large retail chains. As part of a larger buying group, small retailers can obtain discounts and promotional support from manufacturers that would most likely be denied to them if they purchased independently.

As their most important function, retail cooperatives and voluntary chains create economies of scale for small retailers by pooling their individual buying power. In addition, the cooperative or the wholesaler sponsoring the voluntary chain often provides such services as quality control, product development, packaging, promotion, and advertising. Some, such as the IGA (Independent Grocers' Alliance), even develop their own private label program. Overall, these services make small retailers more competitive and increase their ability to meet customer needs and expectations.

Cooperatives and voluntary chains are most prominent in the food, drug, and hardware industries. Some well-known examples include IGA, Associated Grocers, Super Duper, and Topco in the food industry, Associated Druggists and Good Neighbor Pharmacies in drug retailing, and Sentry and Pro in hardware.

The second type of contractual system is franchising, which is the most common type of vertical marketing system. Every year thousands of people enter into franchise agreements to fulfill their dreams of running an independent business. Given the importance of franchising to the economy and its role in fostering entrepreneurship and new business growth, the remainder of this chapter is devoted to a detailed discussion of franchising as a retail format.

FRANCHISING

Franchising is the most common type of vertical marketing system. *In a franchise system, an individual franchisee and a franchisor (the parent company) enter into a contractual agreement that permits the franchisee to operate a business using the franchisor's name or trademark and approved trade practices and receive assistance in establishing and operating the business.* For this the franchisor pays an initial fee to join the franchise, a continuing royalty fee based on the level of sales, and, in many cases, an advertising fee to the franchisor and agrees to operate the business by prescribed norms.

Franchising is an important part of retailing in the United States, generating more than $700 billion of retail sales every year (see Exhibit 3.5). Over 600,000 franchised outlets compete in such varied fields as fast food, hotels and motels, car rental, laundry and dry cleaning, soft drink bottling, auto dealerships, campgrounds, and convenience stores, to name just a few. Some of the largest retail businesses in the country are franchise operations, including McDonald's, Burger King, Holiday Inn, Kentucky Fried Chicken, Pizza Hut, Ford auto dealers, Century 21 real estate, Dunkin Donuts, and H&R Block tax services.

The concept of franchising is not new, it dates back to the 1800s. Singer Sewing Company, for example, opened a number of franchised retail stores soon after the Civil War.[13] The advent of the automobile industry in the late nineteenth century brought the first franchised auto dealerships in 1898. These were followed by Rexall Drugs in 1902, Western Auto in 1909, A&W Root Beer in 1919, and Howard Johnson in 1926.[14] A number of other well-known franchises, such as SuperValue and Ace Hardware emerged during the Great Depression years of the 1930s.[15] Although automobile and gasoline outlets still dominate franchising, service franchises—such as fast-food restaurants, hotels and motels, car rentals, and convenience stores—have been the growth areas since 1960. Exhibit 3.6 lists the 20 largest franchisers in the United States.

Types of Franchises

Franchise systems can be categorized into four groups based on the channel members that participate in the franchise agreement (see Exhibit 3.3). The earliest form

Exhibit 3.5   *Major Types of Franchising in the Economy, 1990*

Kinds of Franchise	No. of Outlets (in thousands)	Sales (in billions)
TOTAL	533.0	716.4
Auto and truck dealers	27.6	362.3
Gasoline stations	111.7	115.1
Restaurants	102.1	76.5
Non-food retailing	54.1	28.6
Soft drink bottlers	0.8	25.8
Hotels and motels	11.1	23.9
Business aids and services	67.3	19.5
Automotive products and services	38.6	13.6
Convenience stores	17.5	14.4
Food retailing	25.4	11.9

Source: Statistical Abstract of the United States, 1991 (Washington, D.C.: Department of Commerce). Table 1369.

of franchising was the **manufacturer-retailer franchise**, in which a manufacturer sells its products through a chain of franchised retailers. This type of franchising is still common in the auto industry. Auto manufacturers and oil companies typically sell their products through franchised auto dealers and gas stations. The franchise agreement between a car manufacturer and auto dealers specifies the minimum size and configuration of the facility that the dealer must maintain and sets standards of inventory and after-sales service. In exchange, the auto manufacturer agrees to protect the dealer's monopoly by not opening competing outlets within a specified distance.

A second type of franchise is the **manufacturer-wholesaler franchise**. This type of franchise agreement binds the wholesaler to the manufacturer, but there is no contractual agreement between the manufacturer and retailers. To reach consumers, wholesalers distribute the product through independent retailers. This type of franchise is common in the soft drink industry. Soft drink manufacturers like Coca-Cola and PepsiCo sell concentrated syrup to franchised bottlers, who put the drink in bottles and cans which they distribute through retail stores, vending machines, restaurants, and bars. The franchise agreement is quite similar to that in a manufacturer-retailer franchise, except, of course, in this case it is between a manufacturer and a wholesaler. The agreement requires the bottler to make specified investments in bottling and distribution facilities while granting it an exclusive territorial right. Without such territorial rights, neither the auto dealer nor the bottler would be motivated to make the financial investments required.

The third type of franchise, the **wholesaler-retailer franchise**, binds a wholesaler to a number of retailers. Rexall Drugs and True Value hardware stores are two examples of this type of franchise agreement. This type of franchising is quite similar to the wholesaler-sponsored voluntary chains discussed earlier.

Exhibit 3.6 *Fifteen Largest Franchise Systems*

Franchisors	Number of Outlets
1 McDonald's	13,900
2 7-Eleven Stores	12,000
3 H&R Block	9,000
4 Kentucky Fried Chicken	8,800
5 Century 21	7,000
6 Pizza Hut	5,600
7 Dairy Queen	5,140
8 Domino's Pizza	4,650
9 Servicemaster	4,600
10 Jazzercise	4,000
11 Wendy's	3,770
12 Budget Rent-A-Car	3,650
13 Baskin-Robbins	3,406
14 Hardee's	3,450
15 Electronic Realty Associates	2,840

Source: Dennis Foster, *The Encyclopedia of Franchises and Franchising* (New York: Facts on File) 1989.

The final type of franchise agreement is the **business format franchising**. These types of franchises are used by firms that have developed a unique business format incorporating a novel service or merchandising concept. The franchise agreement grants individual franchisees the right to use the franchisor's trade name, business format, and merchandising programs and gives them access to the parent firm's expertise in return for a fee. Business format franchises are common in a wide variety of fields including fast-food restaurants, convenience stores, hotels, motels, tax preparation services, and auto repair, to name just a few. Business format franchises have grown in recent years in terms of sales generated and the number of outlets as well as the variety of businesses. Some well-known examples are the fast-food chains such as McDonald's, Kentucky Fried Chicken, and Domino's Pizza, hotels and motels such as Holiday Inn and Day's Inn, auto repair outlets such as Aamco Transmission and Midas Muffler, and service outlets such as Century 21 and H&R Block.

Advantages of Franchising

Franchise systems are popular because they have advantages for both franchisors and franchisees. The franchisor's most important advantage is the ability to grow rapidly. The franchisor can fund the growth of the company through the resources invested by individual franchisees, without requiring large amounts of debt or equity capital. It is doubtful that firms such as Kentucky Fried Chicken, McDonald's,

Service franchisees such as those in real estate, car rental, auto repair, and the H&R Block tax preparation service pictured here, are a rapidly growing area of retailing.

Burger King, Wendy's, or Holiday Inn could have grown as fast as they did if they had tried to open their own retail outlets rather than franchising.

By franchising instead of building their own outlets, franchisors can also reduce overhead expenses. Since the franchise stores are independently owned and operated, the franchisor must do less direct supervision, saving it the expense of a large management team. Another advantage of franchise systems, it is argued, is that individual franchisees are likely to be more motivated than salaried employees.

Each new outlet provides the franchisor with a fixed start-up fee and a source of royalty paid by the franchisee. The royalty is usually a fixed percentage of the annual revenue earned by the franchisee. This provides the franchisor with a steady source of income and cash flow. There is incentive, therefore, for the franchisor to open new outlets. Unfortunately, sometimes franchisors expand too rapidly in order to increase short-term cash flow. This can sacrifice the long-term viability of the entire chain.

Franchise operations also have many advantages for franchisees. First, a franchise agreement gives the franchisee the right to use a trade name that is familiar to consumers and a mode of operation that has proved successful. A prospective businessperson feels mush more confident investing in a proven concept rather than in a completely new business. Experience has demonstrated that franchisees have a much greater chance of succeeding than similar independent businesses.

The franchisee can also rely on the parent company's experience and expertise in operating the business. This can give the franchise store owner considerable advantage over a similar independent business. The owner of a McDonald's or Domino's Pizza outlet is likely to have a competitive advantage over an independent fast-food outlet because of the strong consumer acceptance of the McDonald's and Domino's name. The high levels of advertising undertaken by these chains and their ubiquitous presence heightens this competitive advantage.

Services Provided by Franchisors

Franchise outlets provide a major advantage over independent stores in the service provided by franchisors. Most franchisors provide a variety of services to support individual franchise members (see Exhibit 3.7). Some one-time services are provided when the store opens, while others are continuing services. One of the important services provided by most major franchisors is help with market analysis and site selection. The selection of a good location is one of the most important prerequisites for success of a retail outlet. As will be discussed in more detail in Chapters 8 and 9, proper site selection requires detailed analysis of demographic characteristics of

Entrepreneurs such as Judi Sheppard Missett, the founder of Jazzercise, often rely on franchising to expand their business. Ms. Missett is shown here conducting a class in Wisconsin.

Exhibit 3.7   *Services Provided by Franchisors*

Initial Services	Continued Services
Site selection	Centralized advertising and promotion programs
Operating manuals	Field supervision
Operations training	Access to new product ideas
Financing	Customer research
Store design	Centralized purchasing
Lease negotiations	Access to group insurance

---

consumers and the location of competitors. Such analysis is an important one-time service provided by many franchisors. Another is store design. In many cases franchisors also help franchisees obtain financing and negotiate leases. Another very important service is the training provided by franchisors. For example, prior to opening their stores all new McDonald's franchisees undergo extensive training in restaurant operations, food preparation, accounting and personnel management. Such training can make the difference between success and failure.

As their most important continuing service, franchisors coordinate advertising and promotional campaigns for the chain. The name recognition and consumer awareness created by the advertising campaign is important for individual franchisees. Although individual franchisees usually have to pay for the advertising, a coordinated campaign is more efficient since the resources from all franchisees are pooled together. Pooling resources also allows access to regional and national media that are more cost efficient than the local media typically used by independent retailers. By projecting an unified image for the entire system in regional and national media, the advertising campaign achieves a synergy that cannot be obtained from local advertising by individual franchisees.

New product introduction is another important service provided by franchisors. Fast-food franchisors continuously research and develop new menu items to keep pace with changing consumer eating habits. Individual franchisees benefit from these new product introductions. For example, in recent years McDonald's has introduced an array of new products including Chicken McNuggets, McLean Deluxe, Chicken Burritos, and green salads. Sales of individual franchise stores have benefited greatly from these new products (many of these new product ideas originally came from individual franchisees).

In many cases an important service provided by franchisors is centralized customer access. Franchised motel operators and car rental outlets, for example, rely on the franchisor to maintain the central reservation system that allows customers to use a single phone number to make a reservation at any outlet belonging to the system. This benefits the entire system by making it competitive with other chains. Good franchisors also help their franchisees with information on business trends, changes in industry practices, laws, and regulations, consumer behavior, and related matters.

Conflict in Franchise Systems

Even in a franchise system conflicts do occur. An inherent source of conflict in many franchise agreements is the required royalty payment. Under most franchise agreements, the amount of royalty payable by the franchisee is determined as a percentage of sales rather than profits. This often results in the franchisor pushing for programs that increase sales, but are not profitable for the franchisee. Moreover, with royalty pegged to sales, franchisees may have to pay a large amount of money to the franchisor even when the business is losing money. In addition, franchise agreements typically give franchisors considerable control over the activities of individual franchisees to maintain service standards and product quality. These often become a source of conflict between franchisors and franchisees. A franchisee, for example, may be unable or unwilling to incur the cost of renovations demanded by the franchisor or refuse to participate in special promotional programs or new product introductions.

Some franchisees complain that franchise contracts are often unfair and that franchisors coerce them to follow policies that are to the detriment of the franchisees. **Tying Agreements**, stipulated in many franchise agreements, are the source of many such complains. For example, Chicken Delight, a retailer of fried chicken products, had a tying agreement in its franchise contract that forced all franchisees to purchase all their supplies including chicken, spices, and paper products from the franchisor. The company argued that such stipulations were necessary to protect the quality of the product and hence the reputation of the brand. However, franchisees complained that they were forced to pay significantly more than what other suppliers of comparable products charged. When the franchisees brought suit against the company, the court ruled that the tying agreement was illegal. It allowed Chicken Delight to set quality control standards, but gave franchisees the right to choose their suppliers.[16] Tying agreements are justified only when the franchisor can establish that they are essential to maintain the quality of the product or a trade secret. In the Chicken Delight case, for example, the franchisor could insist that the franchisees had to obtain the spice mixture from it. Similarly, Coca-Cola bottlers are required to buy the syrup from the Coca-Cola Company.

Another potential source of conflict between franchisors and franchisees centers on location. A group of Kentucky Fried Chicken franchisees, for example, recently charged the company with violating the territorial restriction clause in the franchise agreement.[17] A **territorial restriction** agreement in franchising is a promise by a franchisor not to grant a new franchise within a specified distance of an existing outlet. The Kentucky Fried Chicken franchisees charged that the company was violating this clause and locating new franchising close to existing ones in order to increase systemwide revenues. The revenues of existing franchisees, according

STRATEGY IN ACTION

Franchising Offers a Second Career Opportunity

Franchises come in all shapes and sizes, from the ever-present fast-food restaurant and motels to national chains of real-estate agents, tax preparers, or investment advisors. They are a way for people from all walks of life—first-time entrepreneurs, corporate drop-outs, or billionaires with a vision—to be their own bosses and make a decent profit in the process. Some franchises are sold one outlet at a time, like a McDonald's. Others grant area franchises which allows the franchisee to open a network of outlets within a geographical area. Some franchisees obtain licenses from multiple franchisors who sell related products and open outlets at the same site.

Whatever their form and legal arrangement, it is clear that franchises are an important part of the national economy and provide employment to millions of people. According to one estimate, franchises added approximately 380,000 new jobs to the economy in 1991. This at a time when large corporations were laying off employees by the thousands. A number of corporate executives have started a second career in franchising, and they have been highly successful at it.

One such success story is Harry Edgar, who left his job as senior vice-president in charge of 102 Lerner and The Limited stores in 1985 to buy the rights to one franchise area for The Maids. The Maids is an Omaha-based residential cleaning service. Suffering from corporate burnout, Edgar wanted a change. He now owns the rights to 11 franchise areas, and earned $1 million in revenues in 1991.

Another example is Jeffrey Clements, who shed his suit and tie for sweatshirts and shorts when he bought a franchise of Discovery Zone, a children's fitness center. He was sick of meetings and schedules and wanted to be his own boss, and while he

to them, were being curtailed in the process. Conflict over territorial restriction clauses are quite common in the auto industry, where manufacturers typically grant dealers an exclusive territory through the franchise agreement. In some states, such protection to franchise auto dealers is even granted by state legislation. When granting new franchises, car dealers are required to demonstrate that the location of the new outlet will not violate the protected territory of an existing one. Dealers, however, often charge manufacturers with violating territorial agreements in pursuit of their own profits. To avoid such conflict the franchisor's goal of maximizing systemwide revenue and the individual franchisee's goal of maximizing the profit of a specific outlet must be considered simultaneously in developing the locational plan for franchised distribution systems.[18]

Advertising and promotion is another common source of conflict in franchise systems. Franchisors often complain that while they have to pay a fee to the franchisor, they do not always receive commensurate benefit. In some instances franchisees do not approve the advertising theme or promotional program initi-

probably works longer hours than he did as a corporate executive, he loves the work. For an hourly fee, kids are allowed free reign on an indoor playroom filled with fitness equipment disguised as toys: mazes of tunnels and slides, pyramids designed to develop coordination and upper-body strength, as well as areas for tumbling and running. Parents can play for free, and often do. The idea is catching on; Clements' first location quickly netted $18,000 a week, and he expects to be earning his old corporate salary in no time.

The new breed of franchise owners is changing the face of franchising. Today's average franchisee is 40 years old and is likely to be college educated. About 20 percent of them are women and 11 percent minorities. And more than one-third of them are "corporate refugees."

The advantage of franchises such as The Maids or Discovery Zone is that the plan-

ning and marketing is mapped out by the franchisor, and good managers like Edgar and Clements can quickly succeed with careful management and dedication to the new business. It is clear that franchises are a new multibillion-dollar industry, covering everything from vitamin stores to pet centers and tax services. In fact, the International Franchise Association, the Washington, D.C., trade group that represents franchisors, reports that goods and services provided by franchises grew to over $759 billion in 1991, and the figures are expected to increase each year.

Sources: Andrew E. Serwer, "Stand by Your Franchise," *Fortune*, January 25, 1993, p. 104; Susan Caminiti, "Look Who Likes Franchising Now," *Fortune*, September 23, 1991; pp. 125–30; and Janean Huber, "Franchise Forecast," *Entrepreneur*, January 1993, pp. 72–75.

ated by the franchisor. Forcing unwilling franchisees to participate in special price promotions can also lead to conflict. These types of conflict can often be resolved with the help of channel committees consisting of selected franchisees and representatives of the franchisor.

Guidelines for Evaluating Franchise Offerings[19]

For over a century now franchising has provided individuals with the opportunity to own and manage a small business. Every year thousands of people join hundreds of established or new franchises. Not all franchises are successful, however. It is important that a prospective investor carefully evaluate the franchise before joining it. Some of the key items to evaluate are:

- The franchise should be an on-going business. The longer the history of the firm, the less the risk in the venture. Critical questions to ask a prospective franchisor are: How many stores does the system have and for how long? And have they been consistently profitable?

- The franchisor should have a well-established mode of operation with a trademark that has strong consumer acceptance. A new franchisor must be able to demonstrate the viability of the business concept and have access to financial and professional resources to implement a good roll-out plan.

- The franchisor should have a strong, experienced management team that has realistic and effective plans for supporting and helping individual franchisees. It is critically important to ensure that the franchisor has the resources to provide these services to franchisees. Many franchisors promise services that they cannot deliver. Perhaps the worst case of this was the Minnie Pearl's Fried Chicken chain. Minnie Pearl sold 1,800 franchises. But only 161 outlets were actually opened, all of which eventually failed.[20]

- Most franchises require the franchisee to pay an initial start-up fee, and a royalty on sales. In addition, franchisees are typically required to contribute toward a common advertising fund. But fees and royalties, as well as the initial investments required to start the business vary depending on the franchise. Prior to signing the franchise agreement, potential franchisees should compare these fees with the fees charged by similar businesses (Exhibit 3.8). Prospective franchisees should prepare a detailed business plan to ensure that the franchisor's estimates of costs and expected sales and profits are realistic for the proposed market area.

- One major benefit of joining a franchise system is the national and regional advertising and promotional program. Prospective franchisees should carefully evaluate the quality of the franchisor's communication effort. Similarly, the quality of other services provided by the franchisor must be evaluated carefully.

- Conflict, as mentioned before, can arise from a variety of reasons. In extreme form, conflict in franchise systems manifests in litigation brought against the franchisor by disgruntled franchisees. A franchisor with a long history of litigations should be avoided. One must, however, distinguish between lawsuits initiated by genuinely aggrieved franchisees from legal actions taken by the franchisor to protect its own trademark.

- Under what conditions can the franchisor terminate the franchise agreement? There should be provisions for adequate notice and due process prior to termination.

The law requires franchisors to make full disclosure regarding their business in a prospectus. The prospectus must be provided to a buyer at least 10 days prior to the signing of the agreement. The Federal Trade Commission's trade regulation Rule 436 specifies the information that must be disclosed by the franchisor.[21] This includes information on past history of the firm, background of the principals and the management team, litigation history, fee structure, and anticipated start-up costs. A number of states (for example, New York, California, Illinois) impose additional disclosure requirements. The prospectus, or the UFOC (uniform franchise

Exhibit 3.8 **Examples of Franchise Royalty and Fee Structures**

Franchise	Royalty (% of sales)	Advertising Fee (% of sales)	Initial Payment to Franchisor ($'000s)	Initial Investment Required to Start ($'000s)
Aamco	7%	Varies	30	95
Baskin-Robbins	0.5–1.0%	1.5–4%	None	95–185
Budget Rent-A-Car	7.5%	None	15& up	Varies
Realty World	3–6%	2%	14–16	12–41
Super 8 Motels	4%	3%	20	150
McDonald's	3.5%	4%	22.5	Varies
Wendy's	4%	4%	25	250
Blockbuster Video	4–8%	2–3%	20–55	365–695

Source: "Annual Franchise 500" *Entrepreneur*, January 1993, pp. 129–221.

offering circular), as it is often called, provides valuable information, and a thorough study of its contents prior to entering a franchise agreement is a must.

Despite the rules requiring full disclosure, there have been many complaints regarding the quality of information franchisors provide to prospective franchisees. The rule requiring substantiation of claims of franchise earnings that the franchisor provides to potential franchisees has drawn the most fire. It is believed that many franchisees inflate earnings figures or base them on their most successful franchisees instead of the system norm. Regulators are urging for more openness by franchisors and are insisting that franchisors make no claim about franchise earnings unless it is well documented. They are also preparing new guidelines to make the UFOC easier to understand.[22]

Summary

1. Marketing channels are the pipelines through which goods and services flow to consumers. Retailers play a crucial role in the marketing channel, since they make goods and services available to the final consumer. Intermediaries in a marketing channel help overcome the separation between producers and consumers by breaking bulk and making products available over a wide geographic area.

2. The functions of a marketing channel can be categorized into three broad groups: (a) inventory, (b) advertising, promotion, and service, and (c) information flow. The activities of channel members must be coordinated to ensure proper performance of all these channel functions. If any channel member fails to perform its task properly, the entire channel will become ineffective and customers will be dissatisfied.

3. In the last decade, the balance of power between manufacturers and retailers has shifted in favor of retailers, although some manufacturers are taking steps to regain their power. Some reasons for this shift are: (a) increased size of retail chains, (b) greater concentration among

retailers, (c) increased competition among manufacturers, and (d) increased attention by retailers to item profitability.

Since channel members are independent organizations with their own goals and objectives, conflicts often arise in marketing channels. Failure of one channel member to perform its assigned role, goal incompatibility, domain dissension, and vertical competition are common sources of conflict. Channelwide committees are often formed to coordinate activities within the channel and reduce the potential for conflict.

4. Vertical marketing systems attempt to reduce conflict by centrally coordinating the activities of all channel members. There are three types of vertical marketing systems: (a) corporate systems, (b) administered systems, and (c) contractual systems. In corporate systems, all channel functions are completely integrated by a single corporate entity. The activities of administered systems are coordinated by the channel member with greatest size and power, typically through programmed merchandising. In a contractual system, a contractual agreement specifies the manner in which the activities of the channel are to be coordinated.

5. The most common type of vertical marketing system is franchising, which has a long history in the United States. The importance of franchising in the economy has grown in recent years, due to the growth in the number of service franchises. Franchising provides both the franchisor and the franchisee with a number of advantages. Although the franchise agreement eliminates some common sources of conflict found in conventional channels, it often raises complaints from franchisors because of tying agreements and territorial restrictions.

Key Concepts

Marketing channel	Vertical marketing system
Intermediary	Corporate system
Breaking bulk	Administered system
Channel function	Programmed merchandising
Inventory holding cost	Contractual system
Rack jobbers	Franchising
Channel power	Manufacturer-retailer franchise
Slotting fee	Manufacturer-wholesaler franchise
Channel conflict	Wholesaler-retailer franchise
Vertical competition	Business format franchising
Latent conflict	Tying agreement
Perceived conflict	Territorial restriction
Manifest conflict	

Discussion Questions

1. It is often said that "One can eliminate the intermediary but not the functions of the intermediary." Do you agree with this statement? Explain the functions that intermediaries perform.

2. Why does conflict arise among channel members? How can the potential for conflict be reduced? How should conflict be managed?

3. Visit the campus bookstore and a local supermarket. Determine the functions these intermediaries perform in the distribution of books and groceries, respectively. What are the potential sources of conflict in these

channels? If possible, speak to the store managers about how potential conflict is managed in these channels.

4. How has channel power shifted from manufacturers to retailers in recent years?

5. Identify the types of vertical marketing systems. Explain how each type of vertical marketing system reduces the potential for conflict.

6. How do wholesaler-sponsored voluntary chains and retailer cooperatives help individual store owners compete with chain stores?

7. What advantages does a manufacturer have in operating a corporate vertical marketing system? What are the disadvantages?

8. What are some reasons for entering into a franchise agreement from both the franchisor's and franchisee's point of view? How can conflict arise in a franchise system?

9. Interview two local franchisees and determine the types of services their franchisors provide for them.

Notes

1. Stephanie Strom, "Helping Stores to Track What's Hot, and What's Not," *The New York Times*, May 20, 1992, p. D6.

2. Philip Kotler, *Marketing Management: Analysis, Planning and Control* (Englewood Cliffs: Prentice-Hall, 1989), p. 418.

3. Brent H. Felgner, "Retailers Grab Power, Control Marketplace," *Marketing News*, Jan. 16, 1989, p. 1.

4. Ibid.

5. Ibid.

6. "Want Shelf Space at the Supermarket: Ante Up," *Business Week*, August 7, 1989, p. 60.

7. Bert Rosenbloom, *Marketing Channels: A Management View* (Hinsdale, IL: The Dryden Press, 1991), p. 109.

8. Ibid.

9. Larry J. Rosenburg, "A New Approach to Distribution Conflict Management," *Management Horizon*, October 1974, p. 67–74.

10. Ibid.

11. Bert C. McCammon, Jr., "Perspectives for Distribution Programming," in *Vertical Marketing Systems*, ed. by Louis P. Bucklin (Glenview, IL: Scott, Foresman, 1970), p. 43.

12. Ibid.

13. Rosenbloom, *Marketing Channels*, p. 304.

14. Raymond A. Marquardt, James C. Makens, and Robert G. Roe, *Retail Management: Satisfaction of Consumer Needs* (Hinsdale, IL: The Dryden Press, 1974), p. 91.

15. Raymond J. Munna, *Franchise Selection* (Kenner, LA: Granite Publishers, 1987), p. 29.

16. "Cramping the Business Style of Franchisers," *Business Week*, June 16, 1975, p. 82; and Rosenbloom, *Marketing Channels*, p. 457.

17. S. Hume, "Franchisees to Sue KFC on Territorial Rule," *Advertising Age*, May 21, 1990, p. 23.

18. For a discussion of an analytical approach to this locational problem, see Avijit Ghosh and C. Samuel Craig, "FRANSYS: A Franchise Distribution System Location Model," *Journal of Retailing*, 1991, 61 (4), p. 466–95.

19. This section is based on "Guidelines for Evaluating Franchise Offerings," *Inc.*, Jan. 1992, p. 89; and Steve A. Fox, *Keys to Buying a Franchise*, (Hauppauge, NY: Barron's Education Services, Inc. 1992).

20. Munna, *Franchise Selection*, p. 30.

21. Munna, *Franchise Selection*, p. 32.

22. Jeffrey A. Tannenbaum, "Regulators Press for Wider Disclosure by Franchisers," *The Wall Street Journal*, August 13, 1992, p. B2.

CHAPTER 4
The Changing Retail Environment

Green Marketing Is Good Business

During the 1980s, there was a change in the view of many Americans about the environment and society's role in protecting it. People realized that treating the earth better—by recycling, helping distressed areas and peoples, protecting plants and animals— was really a way of treating themselves better. This new conservationist view of the earth was in sharp contrast to the habits of the typical American consumer who was used to a whole range of products to satisfy everyday needs, from clothing to food, from cosmetics to medicines, presented with elaborate packaging, synthetic ingredients, and nonrecyclable materials.

As the environmental movement grew, and everyone from toddlers to grandmothers joined groups to save the earth and their local communities, many consumers began to shun the products that they once bought. Consumers clamored for fresh and natural products that had recyclable packaging and no artificial ingredients. This new trend in consumer preferences gave rise to a new type of consumer product, and a walk down any store aisle will show the range of new products available, from biodegradable detergent to fat-free, low cholesterol food. With the ad-

vent of "green products," companies needed a new form of marketing, one that promoted the environmental and socially conscientious aspects of their products, and thus "green marketing" was hatched.

A whole new breed of companies joined the market: companies that cared about the earth and its people as much as profits, and who offered products that were natural and straightforward. These companies were both environmentally concerned and socially conscious, each for their own reasons: some because they truly believed in it, some because it helped business, but all because it became better business practice. Companies responded differently to the new consumer challenge: some use their social activism as a marketing tool, some use their natural products and fresh ingredients as a sales device, while some simply incorporated these concerns into their missions, unbeknownst to their consumers. The number of companies that use this type of green marketing is growing quickly, and many are having astounding success.

Examples of these new forms of marketing are numerous, ranging from The Gap, which makes generous charitable contributions to the communities in which it operates, and whose employees are encouraged to

After studying this chapter, the reader will be able to:

- *Understand how the macroenvironment affects retailers.*
- *Discuss the impact of the changing age structure of the population on the demand for retail goods and services.*
- *Describe the geographical shifts in the U.S. population.*
- *Understand how consumer lifestyles are changing and the effect of these changes on retail operations.*
- *Discuss how changes in technology affect retailers.*
- *Explain how laws and regulations affect business operations.*
- *Describe the frameworks used to explain changes in retail institutions.*

Anita Roddick, the founder of Body Shop, is a strong believer in responsibility toward the environment. The Body Shop philosophy is to make a difference to customers and the environment.

contribute to these communities through volunteer work, often on company time. Even the giant cosmetics company Estée Lauder joined the green craze, launching a line of natural body and skin products, Origins, whose use of natural ingredients has been such a successful sales tool that sales have been unusually high for a new product in the saturated cosmetics and body care market. While The Gap does not publicize its environmental and social activities, Origins uses its environmentally safe ingredients as its strongest marketing tool. The scope of green marketing is broad, encompassing all varieties of consumer products and companies of all sizes.

For example, Patagonia, an outdoor-wear company with annual sales of $100 million, has a plan for social action built into its corporate mission. Founder Yvon Chouinard's original intent was to become as large as possible in order to generously support different environmental groups. Recently, however, he decided to slow the growth of his company because he wanted to show other consumer product companies that business can be profitable without excessive growth and consumption. Patagonia still gives 10 percent of its *pre-tax* profit to environmental groups, and Chouinard believes that this strategy will show other companies how, like Patagonia, their companies can be a tool for social change. However, he believes that bigger is not necessarily better for the environment, and he instills these values in everyone who works at Patagonia. All employees must donate time to environmental groups in the communities where they work, on company time of course. Chouinard knows that corporate America watches his company very carefully: it is a small business with great success and everyone wants in on their secret. Patagonia's philosophy—take care of the environment and it will take care of you—is practiced by a growing number of firms, and they are examples to all businesses—that green marketing can be very profitable.

Another company that relies on its social concerns as its largest marketing tool is the Body Shop. The Body Shop does not advertise—initially because it could not afford to and presently because there is sufficient word of mouth about the store to generate a whopping $238 million annually in sales of hair and skin products. The Body Shop has stores in 40 countries, and profits are expected to grow 35 percent annually through the 1990s. The Body Shop's philosophy is simple and straightforward: natural products, simple packaging, and no hype. Customers find this view refreshing, and are loyal to this company that concerns itself not just with its products, but also with the community, the environment, and "the big wide world beyond cosmetics."

The Body Shop philosophy is multipronged: to make a difference to their customers, the business community, the planet, and to everyday life. How does a cosmetics company achieve this ambitious goal? The customers gain because they can buy pure and natural products without hype or idealized notions. The different product forms, believes the Body Shop, meet the needs of real people, simply and honestly. The business community gains because the Body Shop has created fair trade deals with its suppliers and has established innovative trading programs with people all over the world. The Body Shop makes a difference in everyday life by supporting many human rights and environmental organizations through generous charitable contributions, and all staff (corporate to salesclerks) must devote time to local volunteer work on company time. And finally, the planet gains because all of the company's products are natural, all the packaging recyclable, and no animals are used in the product testing. When you make a purchase at the Body Shop, you are encouraged not to take a shopping bag unless necessary, and the only ones available are simple brown paper (recycled) stamped with the reminder "Buy only what you need." "Reuse—Refill—Recycle." This formula of green marketing has proved undeniably successful for the Body Shop.

Sources: Angus M. Thuermer, Jr., "Patagonia Philosophy," *Jackson Hole News*, June 19, 1991, pp. 1, 22A; Rahal Jacob, "What Selling Will Be Like in the Nineties," *Fortune*, January 27, 1992.

The environment in which firms operate is never static. The pattern of consumer demand changes constantly, as does technology. In order to develop sound strategies, retailers must track changes in the environment to identify trends that might affect their ability to compete effectively. They must then respond to change in a manner that protects the firm's performance.

This chapter examines trends in the consumer, economic, technological, and legal environments that affect retail firms. As discussed in Chapter 1 (see Exhibit 1.8) these forces interact to define the macroenvironment in which all firms operate. This chapter demonstrates how changes in these factors create opportunities and pose threats to retail firms. The final section of the chapter analyzes how the environment has shaped the historical pattern of evolution of different retail institutions.

THE CONSUMER ENVIRONMENT

The demographic characteristics of the population, such as age, sex, occupation, family size, and residential location, along with dominant social and cultural values, determine the pattern of demand for goods and services. The 1980s saw major changes in the demographic characteristics of the American population, and retailers have responded to those changes. Consider the following examples:

- The decline in the number of teenagers and young adults affected retailers such as The Gap. To decrease its reliance on this age group, the company expanded its GapKids chain.
- To cater to the growing number of young children, WaldenBooks opened a chain of outlets selling children's books. Attracted by the same group, Sears introduced a new line of children's clothing under license from McDonald's.
- With more women now working, American families are very time-pressed. To respond to this trend, supermarkets now stay open later—often 24 hours a day. They also offer more fresh-baked goods, salad bars, and prepared meals to appeal to shoppers with little or no time to cook.
- The mature market—those over 65 years old—commands increasing attention as its size and spending power has increased. Hotel chains such as Quality Inn have increased their share of this market by instituting special discounts and promotions for older customers.[1]

As the above examples illustrate, changing demographics concerns retailers deeply. Some important demographic trends in the United States are discussed below.

The Graying of America

Perhaps the single most important change taking place in the United States today is the changing age structure, sometimes called **the graying of America**. On the average, the American population is aging. The total population of the United States in 1990 was 248 million, and the median age was 32.9 years. (A median age of 32.9 years means that half the nation's population is older than 32.9 years and half younger than that age.) The 1990 median age of 32.9 years is 5.2 years higher than the median age in 1970 and 2.9 years higher than that in 1980. By the year 2000, the population is expected to reach 270 million, and the median age will be much higher.[2]

The graying of America can be best illustrated by comparing **age pyramids** from different years. An age pyramid shows the percentage of the total population within different age segments.[3] Exhibit 4.1 shows the age pyramids for 1960, 1980, and 2000. The figures for 1960 and 1980 are based on actual statistics, while the figures for the year 2000 are estimates. In 1960 the population was concentrated in younger age groups. Nearly 35 percent of the population was younger than 17, and only 9 percent was over 65 years of age. By 1980 about 30 percent of the population was in the middle age brackets (18 to 34) and the above-65 population increased to 11 percent. The pyramid for the year 2000 is "top heavy" with a large concentration of people in the older age groups. By that year the number of people more than 65 years old is projected to be more than one and a half times the number in 1960, and the bulk of the population will be in the 25–54 age bracket.

Why is the population aging? The graying of America is a result of two forces: (1) the changing pattern of births and (2) increasing life expectancies.

Births   As shown in Exhibit 4.2, the pattern of the annual number of births in the United States over the last 50 years can be divided into four distinct periods. The first phase, the period between 1935 and 1945, was marked by relatively few births due to the economic depression and the Second World War. The annual number of births increased after 1945, and the period from 1945 to 1964 is known as the **baby boom period** because of the large number of babies born during that period. At least 4 million babies were born each year between 1954 and 1964. The baby boom peaked in 1957 when 4.3 million new babies were born in the United States.

The third period, from 1965 to 1980, was marked by a low number of births. From its height in 1957, the annual number of births dropped to only 3.2 million by the mid-1970s. In contrast to the baby boom, this period is often referred to as the **baby bust**. The final phase started in 1980 and is still continuing. The low births of the previous 15 years was reversed as the children of the baby boom years reached childbearing age and started families of their own. This has created a boom of its own. The number of births per year has been increasing every year since 1976, with over 4 million births in 1990. This often is referred to as the **ripple effect**, and the post-1980 period as the **echo boom period**. The number of births are expected to decline again later in the 1990s as the baby boomers leave their childbearing years.

Life Expectancy   The second reason underlying the changes in the age structure is increased life expectancy. Improvements in living conditions and in medical science have increased longevity. The current average life expectancy of 76 years is 27 years longer than the expected life span in 1900. The average life expectancy varies by sex: current expectancies are 78 years for females, and 70 for males. This means that more females than males survive into the older age groups. In the under-18 category, males outnumber females and the two sexes are closely balanced

Exhibit 4.1   Age Pyramids for 1960, 1980, and 2000

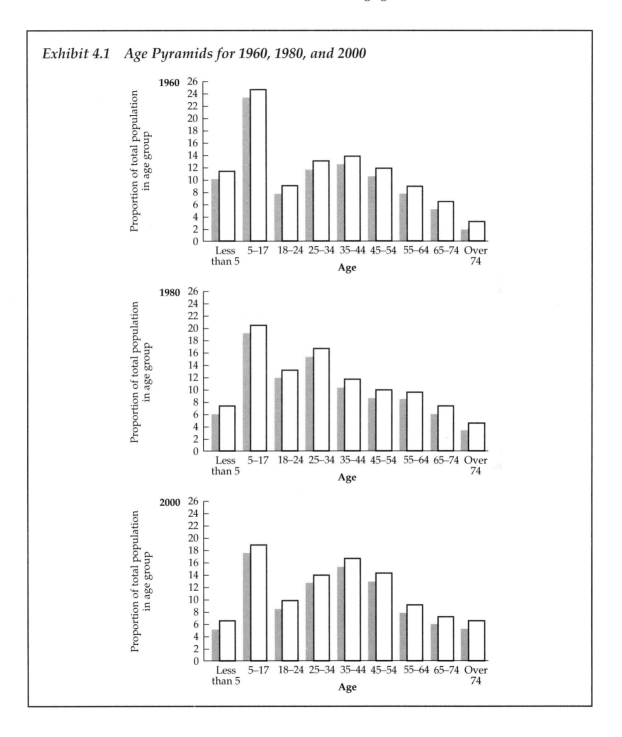

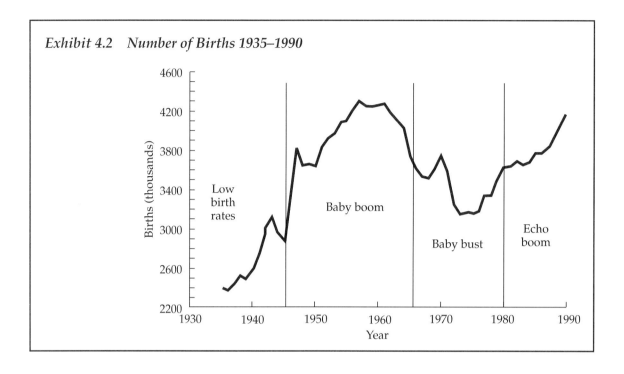

Exhibit 4.2   Number of Births 1935–1990

in the 18–24 age group. However, women account for 60 percent of the population above the age of 65.[4]

There are also considerable differences in life expectancies by race and ethnic groups. Longevity for African-Americans is significantly less than that of whites. The shorter life spans reflect poor health conditions and lack of access to health care for many members of these groups.

Age Structure and Demand Patterns

Changes in the age structure affect **demand for goods and services** in significant ways, and retailers have to respond to these changes. The impact of each of the age-groups on retail demand is considered below:

The Echo Boom Period   The low birthrates of the 1970s had sent the baby food market spiralling downwards, but the ripple effect has turned it around. The 1990 birthrate of 4.1 million was the highest in 15 years, creating renewed demand for infant and baby items. Compared with their counterparts of the 1950s and 1960s, today's parents are older, better educated, and seemingly willing to spend more on children. Stores selling baby foods, infant clothes, toys, and furniture are enjoying an unprecedented boom. Also, many of today's parents both work, nearly half of the mothers returning to work within a year of giving birth. This affects the demand for child care. Kinder-Care Learning Centers, which operates a chain of day-care centers, has nearly tripled its revenues since 1980.

The birth rate will not, however, stay high for long. It is expected to decline later in the 1990s as women of the baby boom generation move beyond childbearing age. The market for infant care products and services will, therefore, decrease during the last few years of the century.

The Baby Bust Period   The low number of births during the baby bust period means fewer teenagers and young adults in the 1990s. This has affected retailers of records, clothing, electronic equipment, and soft drinks. Because of the fewer number of teenagers, Levis has diversified from jeans to more formal clothing for the adult market. Enrollments at high schools and colleges are lower and so is attendance at movies and amusement parks.

The lower number of teenagers has also affected the labor market for retailers. Fast food restaurants and supermarkets are finding it especially difficult to fill vacancies. The shortage of teenage workers prompted McDonald's to broadcast a series of television advertisements encouraging senior citizens to work in its restaurants.

Despite their smaller numbers, studies have found that the amount spent by the members of this age group is increasing. There are two reasons for this. First,

The growth in birth rates and dual-career households increased the need for organized day-care facilities. These children are in the KinderCare facility in Montgomery, Alabama.

they have more money, since many of them work part- or full-time. Second, teenagers have assumed the role of purchasing agents in many dual-career households. According to one estimate, the shopping for as much as 40 percent of family food expenditures is done by teenagers.[5]

The Baby Boom Period   During the 1960s and 1970s, when they were teenagers, the baby boomers filled the nation's schools and colleges as well as its fast-food restaurants, jean's shops, record stores, and drive-in movies. Today they are shopping for houses, cars, stereos, frozen foods, premium ice creams, and other packaged foods. Their immense purchasing power and their matching desire to spend makes the baby boomers very important.

Although not all baby boomers are affluent, many have well-paying professional jobs and working spouses. During the 1980s, two-income families—often without children and the accompanying expenses—wielded their purchasing power to buy premium, upscale products and services. Marketers and retailers of sports cars, home appliances, better clothing, and gourmet food benefited from the spending habits of these baby boomers. As the baby boomers move into their fifties, they will represent the major portion of the country's buying power. It is estimated that people from the baby boom generation account for 50 percent of all consumer expenditures.[6] The baby boom generation has influenced and will continue to influence consumer demand in an important way. One observer stated:

> As the baby boomers grew older, it became evident that this generation, in its lifetime, would always be dominant, compelling attention through the magnetic pull of its numbers and its vast buying powers.[7]

The Mature Market   The over 60 million people born prior to 1945 comprise the **mature market**. The mature market is only one-fourth of the country's population, but they represent nearly half of its buying power and control over three-quarters of its assets.[8] The size of this market is growing and will continue to do so through the 1990s and the start of the next century. According to a Census Bureau estimate, the number of Americans over 50 will increase to more than 100 million by 2025, more than a third of the population.[9]

Mature consumers have high demand for home care, recreational services, and health care. Higher disposable income also allows them to travel frequently and buy luxury cars. By one estimate, they account for 80 percent of all leisure-travel related expenditures and 50 percent of all purchases of domestic cars.[10] They are also frequent buyers of stocks, bonds, furs, jewelry, and expensive clothing.[11] As the size of the mature market grows, retailers must cater to the needs of these shoppers and adapt to their shopping habits. Most retailers, however, have traditionally neglected mature consumers and given priority to younger customers.

As a first step, it is important to recognize that not all mature customers are alike. The mature market can be divided into four subgroups, each with distinct spending patterns. The four groups are: 50–64-year-olds (representing nearly half the market), 65–74, 75–84, and 85 and older. The bulk of the purchasing power is concentrated in the 50–64-year group. Many of them are at the peak of their earning power, but the cost of buying a home and raising children are behind them. Those in the two middle groups spend money on traveling and buying gifts for children. Those in the last group may spend large amounts on health care.

Geographical Pattern of Population

When people migrate from one state to another, from the city to the suburb, or from the farm to the city, they affect the spatial pattern of retail demand. The map in Exhibit 4.3 shows the percent change in population of each state from 1980 to 1990. As is evident from the map, during the last decade the western and middle-Atlantic states, and Florida have grown the most. The rest of the states have grown minimally. Wyoming, North Dakota, Iowa, and West Virginia actually lost population during the 1980s. The map in Exhibit 4.4 shows the absolute growth in popu-

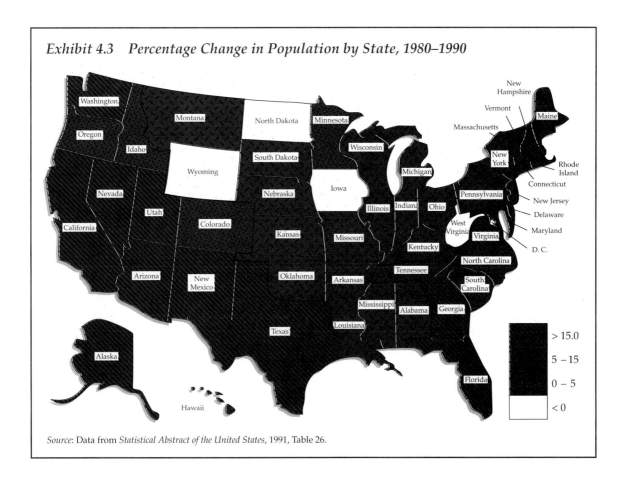

Exhibit 4.3 Percentage Change in Population by State, 1980–1990

▓	> 15.0
▒	5 – 15
░	0 – 5
□	< 0

Source: Data from *Statistical Abstract of the United States*, 1991, Table 26.

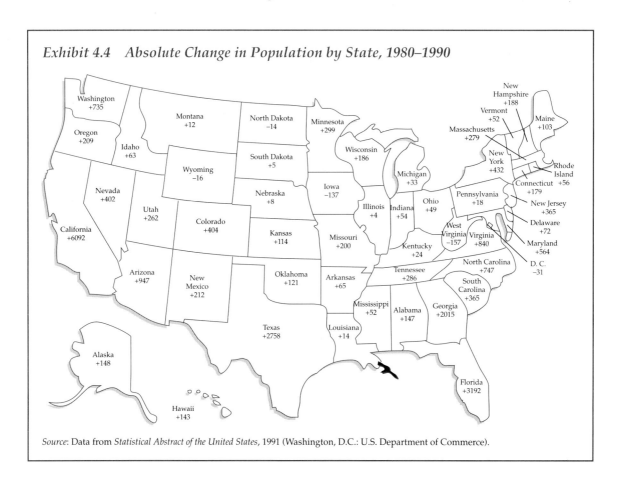

Exhibit 4.4   Absolute Change in Population by State, 1980–1990

Source: Data from *Statistical Abstract of the United States*, 1991 (Washington, D.C.: U.S. Department of Commerce).

lation for each state during the same period. The states with the highest population growth between 1980 and 1990 were California, Florida, and Texas. Many retailers opened new stores in these states during the 1980s, although the growth in Texas and California has slowed considerably.

The historical pattern of population movement from the northeastern and midwestern states to the South and the West has caused the nation's center of population to shift dramatically. The center of population is the point at which equal proportion of populations lie in all four directions. Exhibit 4.5 shows how the center of the population has progressively moved west and a little to the south over the years. As the population shifts geographically, the spatial pattern of demand for goods and services changes, opening up opportunities for new retail outlets and closing down others.

Suburbanization   Another important geographic shift has been the growth of suburban areas since the end of the Second World War. Although suburbs existed

Exhibit 4.5 **Shifting Center of U.S. Population**

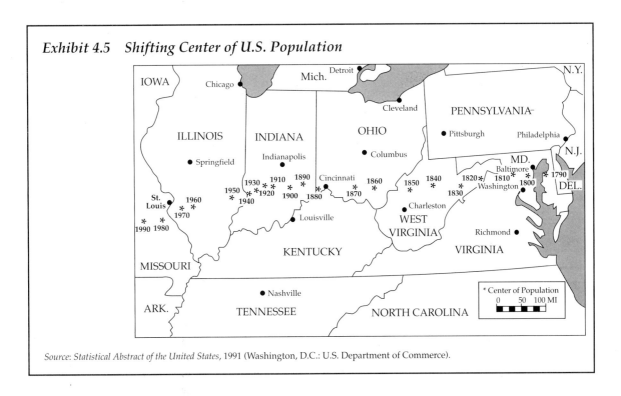

Source: *Statistical Abstract of the United States*, 1991 (Washington, D.C.: U.S. Department of Commerce).

prior to the 1940s, the rate of **suburbanization** increased dramatically since 1950. In 1950, 40 percent of the U.S. population lived in central cities; by 1970 that figure had dropped to about 30 percent. Almost half of all Americans now live in suburban areas.[12] Access to private transportation and the building of the interstate highway system were the key to the massive expansion of suburban areas. Low mortgage rates in the 1960s also contributed.

Suburban growth had a profound impact on retailing. Retailers had to shift from downtown retail centers to suburban locations to bring shopping closer to where people lived. Although department stores initially resisted the move to the suburbs, the large market represented by the middle and upper income suburban shoppers was too attractive to forego. Department stores moved into the suburban shopping malls as "anchor" tenants, joining mass merchandisers (Sears, Penney) and discount stores (K mart, Venture, Target) who also moved into suburban sites in large numbers. Suburbanization and the consequent growth of suburban shopping malls also stimulated the growth of specialty store chains like The Limited.

Exurbia During the 1970s, suburban growth took a different form, with people moving into smaller towns (the "exurbia") rather than moving into suburban areas that are contiguous to metropolitan areas.[13] The economic importance of small towns in the vicinity of the metropolis grew rapidly as a result of people's search for cleaner environments, simplicity, and a lower cost of living.[14] Although the rate of growth of exurbs seems to have slowed,[15] as the population becomes dispersed retailers will have to continually expand their network of stores to be where the consumers are. One retailer who has been able to take good advantage of this trend to **exurbanization** is Wal-Mart. As mentioned in Chapter 2, Wal-Mart concentrated its stores in smaller, secondary markets, where the level of competition from other discounters was low.

The geographical distribution of population clearly impacts retail location decisions, since outlets must be located at sites that are accessible to people. In Chapter 8 a detailed scheme is developed for examining local populations and measuring retail demand in specified areas.

The Changing American Family

The changing population structure is altering society's values and attitudes and the norms by which it lives, resulting in a **changing family structure**. Retailers must monitor these trends since they alter the marketplace.

American households have become increasingly diverse. Description of the typical American family as a household with one or more children, a working father and a home-making mother no longer rings true. This profile fit 70 percent of all households in 1950, but only about 15 percent of the population now match this description.[16] It may be difficult to come up with a description for the typical American family of the 1990s. Both husband and wife may work full time and have only one or no children, or a single parent may be raising a child, or two previously divorced adults may live with their children from earlier marriages. Here are some ways in which the American family is changing.

Smaller Families   One trend that has been apparent for some time is the shrinking size of the American family as well as American households. During the 1980s, average family size fell from 3.29 to 3.17 persons, and average household size fell from 2.76 members to 2.63 members. Some reasons for these changes are increases in the number of single-parent families, childless married couples, and people living alone.[17]

Late marriages are another reason for this trend. Although most American adults get married, they are marrying at a later age. In 1970, 45 percent of men and 64 percent of women in their early twenties had married; by 1985 the comparable figures had dropped to 34 percent and 41 percent, respectively.[18] Not only are people marrying later, they are also postponing the decision to have children, and having fewer children when they do.

The Blended Family   The divorce rate is another factor affecting the family structure. About 50 percent of all first marriages now end in divorce—the highest divorce rate in the world. Most divorcees ultimately remarry, often to a formerly divorced person. This has lead to the growth of blended families consisting of two divorced or separated individuals and their children from previous marriages.

Single Adult Households   The rise of the single adult household is another phenomenon impacting the traditional family structure. In 1980, 35.6 percent of households had only one adult—either living alone or with a child. By 1990, that number had risen to 39.4, an increase of approximately 9 percent.[19]

Working Women   One of the most important social changes of recent years is the growth in the number of working women. The proportion of women in the labor force increased from 33 percent in 1950 to 43 percent in 1970 and 57 percent in 1989. Projections indicate that this proportion will continue to grow for the rest of this century.[20] As more women join the workforce, the disposable income of dual-career households increases. The median incomes of dual-income households are significantly more than that of households with only one wage earner. Because of their higher disposable income, two-wage families are inclined to spend more and are less likely to delay purchases.

LIFE STYLE TRENDS

Changes in demographic characteristics and values have affected the lifestyles of American consumers. **Lifestyles** refers to the consumers' mode of living that is identified by their activities, what they consider important and their opinions about themselves and the world in general. A number of broad changes in lifestyle have occurred in the 1980s, and retailers have had to change the way they operate in order to respond to those changes. This section discusses four of the most important changes.

Poverty of Time

Increasing numbers of women working outside the home have given rise to **time-pressed consumers**. "Many people appear genuinely pressed for time; they seemed hurried and overbusy."[21] The time pressure is even more severe for these dual-worker families when they have children. The poverty of time has had severe and far-reaching implications for retailers.[22] On the one hand, it has stimulated the growth of such time-saving devices as microwave ovens, food processors, and prepared foods; on the other hand, it has stimulated the growth of convenience stores, fast-food outlets, and direct marketing.

Retailers are responding to this need for convenience in a number of ways. Many stores now stay open for 24 hours or close late so that consumers can shop after work. The retailers are also scheduling deliveries and repairs during weekends and late evening hours. The growth of sales through mail order and electronic

RETAIL RESEARCH REPORT

Will Hypermarkets Ever Succeed in the U.S?

What is a hypermarket? Based on an idea imported from Europe, these are huge stores carrying thousands of products that combine a drugstore, supermarket, and discount store under one roof. Hypermarkets usually have four basic departments: food, apparel, drugs, health and beauty aids, and hard goods (including home and automotive supplies, gardening, and sports equipment). Similar to a Wal-Mart with food, a family can take care of *all* their shopping needs in one stop. However, while the concept has worked successfully for decades in Europe, the American consumer has had a very lukewarm reaction to these superstores.

The brain-child of French retailer Marcel Fournier, the first hypermarket, Carrefour (French for "crossroads"), was opened in the early 1960s near Paris. Totalling more than five times the space of a typical American supermarket, these enormous stores offered a fast, efficient alternative to neighborhood markets. In addition, prices were much lower because Fournier negotiated with manufacturers the same credit they gave to smaller stores. Since Carrefour's turnover was much higher than that of smaller stores, the manufacturers effectively financed Carrefour's inventory. French customers responded positively to the hypermarket idea, and by 1988 Carrefour had 55 hypermarkets in France, generating $7 billion in annual sales.

The high sales figures generated by the European hypermarkets—up to $140 million annually per store—has attracted many American retailers to the concept. The average discount store in the United States generates $20 to $25 million annually and the average supermarket about $15 million. However, U.S. hypermarkets have proven unsuccessful for a number of reasons. For one, some American shoppers feel that one-stop shopping is more of a bother than a con-

catalogs is another example. Supermarkets and convenience stores are offering more varieties of ready-to-eat and frozen prepared foods. To help consumers do their grocery shopping in less time, a number of supermarket chains now accept orders by phone or fax and then deliver the order to the customer's home free of cost or for a nominal charge. Retailers that can help consumers reduce time pressure by offering time-saving goods and services and shopping convenience will have a differential advantage over their competitors.

Blending of Traditional Male-Female Roles

The increased number of working women and changes in traditional family structure have resulted in a shift away from earlier lifestyles. As working women have less time for cooking and housekeeping, husbands increasingly assume more re-

venience—think of the size of the final purchase, if one buys all the family's grocery needs as well as clothing and housewares! Furthermore, there are considerably higher overhead costs associated with running a store of this scale, and some of them are passed onto the consumer in certain categories. And finally, as local supermarkets have grown in size and expanded their selection, they have begun to pose a formidable threat to the fledgling hypermarket.

One chain, however, is proving that the hypermarket concept can work in America. Leedmark, which calls itself a *hybrid*market rather than a *hyper*market, is striving to combine the good aspects of the European stores with a more recognizable American format. Leedmark uses American technology and merchandising expertise to customize the traditional European hypermarket for American shoppers. Differences from other hypermarkets include a smaller selling space

(on average, a mere 130,000 square feet), a more decentralized management and buying structure that will allow each Leedmark to respond better to local tastes and preferences, a more targeted merchandising mix, cooperative ownership, and a consumer-friendly atmosphere. Owned by the French company Leclerc, which is one of the most successful hypermarket chains in Europe, Leedmark feels that it has a better chance at success than other hypermarkets because of its more carefully customized strategy. Leedmark still has to convince the American public that one-stop shopping is truly better, a challenge that has proved difficult for many of its competitors.

Sources: James L. Heskett: *Managing in the Service Economy*,(Cambridge, MA: Harvard Business School Press, 1986), pp. 5–6; Marianne Wilson: "Leedmark: A Hypermarket by Any Other Name," *Chain Store Age Executive*, August 1991, pp. 28–29; and Iris S. Rosenberg, "Hypermarket Now," *Stores*, March 1986.

sponsibility for shopping. Recent surveys have found that a significant number of men are now involved in grocery shopping. On the other hand, "as women's purchasing power has increased, they have become more influential in traditional male dominated purchasing decisions."[23] The trend is toward a more androgynous behavior, a blending of male and female purchase roles. In the past, husbands and wives had separate and clearly defined purchase domains, now they make more purchase decisions jointly.[24]

Shopping for Value

The economic downturn of the 1970s caused many consumers to fundamentally change their shopping habits. The lack of growth in real incomes made consumers more sensitive to price, as they struggled to maintain their standard of living.

Although the economy improved during the 1980s this attitude has not changed. They still shop actively for sale items to reduce expenditures. The economic hardships of the 1970s and early 1980s have caused a permanent change in life style that continues to emphasize value for the dollar.

Concern for the Environment

There has been a change in Americans' view of the environment. Many of today's consumers prefer products with natural ingredients and recyclable packaging. For example, a survey of New York State residents conducted in 1990 found that one-fourth had stopped buying products of at least one company they believed to be an environmental polluter.[25] As described in the vignette at the beginning of the chapter, many retailers have responded to this "green movement" with success.

In response to the concerns of their consumers, both K mart and Wal-Mart use in-store signs to announce environmental actions by their suppliers. When Dow Chemical, for example, started packaging Zip-lock bags in recycled packaging, Wal-Mart's announcement read, "Wal-Mart salutes Dow for sharing its environmental concern."[26] Some retailers are introducing lines of environmentally friendly products to appeal to consumers. Sales of the "green" line exceeded projections at Loblaw, the Canadian supermarket chain.[27] McDonald's, long criticized for its use of environmentally harmful packaging, has begun using bags made of recycled paper. The trend towards environmental concern and environmentally safe products is sure to continue in the future.

THE ECONOMIC ENVIRONMENT

Consumer Income

Consumers' buying habits are strongly related to **consumer income**, both current and anticipated. Retailers must monitor trends in consumer incomes, savings, debt, and expenditure patterns.

Exhibit 4.6 shows the change in median family income from 1970 to 1990. Half the nation's families have incomes above the median and the other half earn less than that level. The exhibit illustrates the historic pattern of family incomes both in terms of current and constant dollars. Constant dollar figures adjust for yearly changes in purchasing power due to inflation. While family incomes have grown steadily over the years in terms of current dollars, real income in terms of constant dollars has not changed much. The decline in real incomes during the 1970s had a major consequence for retailers. Faced with lower real incomes, consumers became more price-conscious and searched for better values. Discount stores benefited significantly from this trend. Lead by chains like K mart, Target, Caldor, and Venture, the growth of discount stores far outstripped that of department stores. Compa-

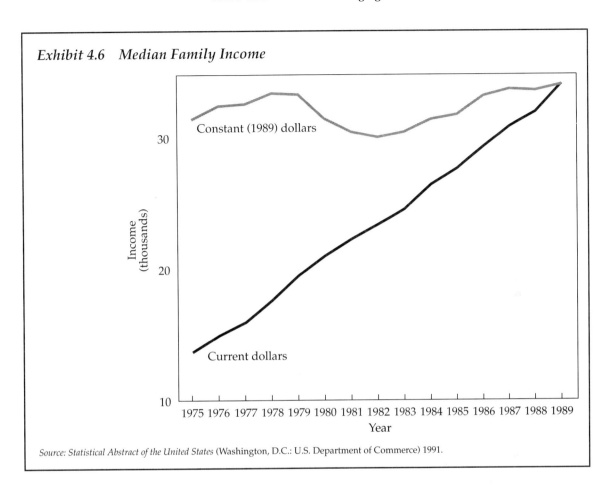

Exhibit 4.6   Median Family Income

Constant (1989) dollars

Income (thousands)

Current dollars

30

20

10

1975 1976 1977 1978 1979 1980 1981 1982 1983 1984 1985 1986 1987 1988 1989

Year

Source: Statistical Abstract of the United States (Washington, D.C.: U.S. Department of Commerce) 1991.

nies like Dayton Hudson funneled money away from department stores to finance the growth of discount chains (Target and Mervyn's). Because of their focus on lower prices, warehouse supermarkets and limited assortment grocery (sometimes called "box" stores) outlets also came into prominence during this period.

Savings and Debt   Retail sales are also affected by the level of consumers' **savings and debt**. Consumers who save more have less discretionary income, while the availability of credit enhances consumer expenditures. Compared to other countries, the rate of savings in the United States is low and the use of credit is high. Many economists claim that the low level of consumer savings is having a negative impact on the U.S. economy. Others, however, argue to the contrary that consumer expenditures fuel economic growth. Whatever may be the case, the rate of savings and expenditures depends ultimately on the consumers' confidence in their future earning power and economic well being.

STRATEGY IN ACTION

Origins: "Green Marketing" in Department Stores

Many observers agree that there has been a clear shift in consumer preferences, across many product groups, away from the luxury and excess of 1980s' materialism. Consumers have begun to look for simpler, more environmentally friendly products. This trend has been evident especially in the cosmetics industry, as the mantra "beauty without cruelty" took hold and won over many consumers. Consumers wanted products that were environmentally safe, ones that were not tested on animals, and had natural ingredients and recyclable packaging. Many firms sought to capitalize on this trend by introducing "natural" lines. One example in the United States was Estée Lauder's Origins line of natural cosmetics, which was launched in 1990 for department store consumers.

Estée Lauder has long pioneered trends in department store cosmetics, and it was logical for the company to try to tap into that consumer segment, even though many of Lauder's "green" competitors have had success in other venues: opening specialty boutiques (The Body Shop), or adding products to their existing lines (Revlon). Bringing a green line to a department store was a radical move for a cosmetics company, but Estée Lauder felt that the growing concern for the environment and natural ingredients created the opportunity to capture two markets in the department stores: one, the current department store customer now seeking a natural line; and two, the younger customer, who is not a department store shopper. In fact, department stores were losing many younger consumers to mass merchandise and specialty stores. Estée Lauder hoped to lure them to the department store with the new line. All products in the Origins line are based on the principle of respect for customers, animals, and the environment. All products are dedicated to preserving the earth, and all printing and packaging use recycled paper. In addition, the Origins line is priced well below most department store lines, with items retailing between $8 and $30, which is attractive to the younger consumer.

While Estée Lauder will have some free-standing Origins stores, the main focus of their sales will be in department stores. Origins is currently sold at all outlets where other Lauder products are sold; and the company has plans for 500 free-standing stores by 1996. This is a most ambitious plan for the company, but Lauder hopes that with such an aggressive plan they will be able to ride the crest of the wave of mixing social consciousness with the cosmetics industry. Already the line has proved successful.

The introduction of the product line was not accompanied by conventional advertising and promotional campaigns. A great deal of the visibility of the new product line has been obtained through good press and word-of-mouth advertising. Estée Lauder's public relations campaign has targeted the media, consumers, and leading department stores. Press conferences have been held to introduce the product line to the editors of major nationwide magazines, and special events, such as the Run for the Earth marathon, help to publicize the product line.

Sources: Pat Sloan, "Cosmetics: Color It Green," *Advertising Age*, July 23, 1990, p. 1; Cyndee Miller, "Cosmetics Industry's Marketing Approach," *Marketing News*, June 10, 1991, p. 2.

Many of today's consumers are concerned about the environment. Wal-Mart uses in-store signs to announce environmental actions by suppliers.

TECHNOLOGICAL ENVIRONMENT

Advancing technologies, especially computer applications, communication, and electronics are having a dramatic impact on retailing. In the last decade, changing technology has made numerous retail innovations possible, including:

- Computerized checkout counters equipped with optical scanners and voice synthesizers that recite merchandise price.
- Automatic teller machines (ATMs) at banks.
- Electronic shopping systems such as Videotex.
- Computer assisted design (CAD) to plan store layouts.
- Store catalogs on videodiscs.
- Home shopping through cable television.
- Electronic data interchange (EDI) between retailers and their suppliers.

As these examples illustrate, the accelerated pace of technological change is affecting all facets of retailing. The impact has been so pervasive that no retailer, small or large, can survive any longer without concern for the **technological environment**. Like good merchandise and good location, technology is now a fundamental competitive tool in retailing.

The effects of new technologies can be grouped into three categories. New technologies have: (1) given rise to new forms of retailing, (2) made retail transactions more efficient, thereby increasing retail productivity, and (iii) improved control of retail operations.

New Forms of Retailing

Videotex systems and home shopping through cable television are two examples of new forms of retailing made possible by advances in communications technology. **Videotex** is a generic name for interactive electronic systems in which data and graphics are transmitted through telephone lines or coaxial cables and displayed on a subscriber's television or computer monitor.[28] A subscriber to a videotex system can gain access to information on the merchandise offerings of different retailers. The shopper first selects the product category of interest and then views on the screen the different brands, styles, colors, and sizes that are available and the price of each item. To make a purchase, the shopper can directly order through a home computer and charge the amount to a credit card. In addition to shopping information, videotex systems usually provide other services such as home banking, news, weather information, stock market quotes, and so on.

One system that has been operating since 1983 is Comp-U-Card, a buying service for subscribers who pay an annual fee. Subscribers can call a toll-free number to access the company's data base which contains information on more than 30,000 products. The data base also contains the names of the lowest priced suppliers of branded items. Subscribers can compare the price of different brands and place an order, if desired. Home computer owners can directly access the information and place orders through their terminals. The company also operates "The Shopping Channel," a shopping program for cable TV viewers.

Home shopping television programs broadcast through cable television channels can potentially reach many more people than videotex systems. Cable TV subscribers have free access to the programs, while videotex users typically have to pay a monthly fee. However, the potential shopper has no control over the cable program's schedule. A videotex system allows a shopper who wants to buy a new dishwasher to skip over information on other products and go directly to the section on dishwashers. In cable programs, the viewer has to patiently wait and watch in the hope that the show will feature a dishwasher. This inconvenience has kept many shoppers away from TV shopping programs. An ideal electronic home shopping system would combine cable television's potential for reaching wide audiences with the interactive capability of videotex systems.

Such an interactive shopping channel was recently tried in Chicago. To use Teleaction, which debuted in 1987, shoppers tune to a special interactive cable channel and dial a local phone number. The TV displays merchandise from a selected group of retailers. The shopper can use the buttons on the phone to select and guide the video display through different merchandise categories and then use

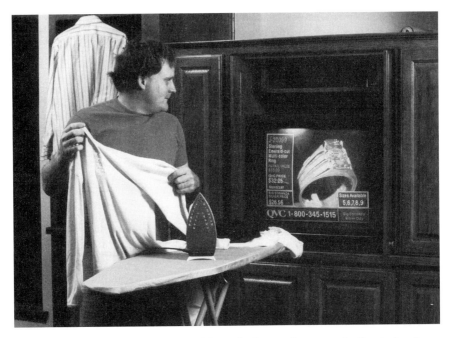

A product of changing consumer habits and advanced communication technology, electronic shopping has emerged as an important retail institution.

the phone to order goods.[29] When Teleaction was introduced it was heralded as the wave of the future. Many experts still believe that interactive home shopping is an innovation whose time has come. But, J.C. Penney, which had invested $106 million dollars into the project, "pulled the plug" on Teleaction in 1989.[30]

Future of Electronic Retailing

Despite many experiments and the millions of dollars that have been invested in it, electronic retailing is still in the early stages of its development. Many consumers consider shopping through mail, telephone or interactive devices to be risky. Many resist buying products from nonstore retailers. One reason for this reluctance is the consumer's inability to physically examine the quality of the products offered by nonstore retailers. In contrast, at retail stores consumers can physically touch and feel the product and get immediate delivery, as well. The limited merchandise selection offered by many nonstore retailers is also a drawback, since it limits the potential for comparison shopping. Moreover, many Americans value the retail stores as an important part of the social and cultural landscape and consider shopping an important form of entertainment. Video catalogs cannot match the excitement of well-displayed merchandise, changing window displays, and the

STRATEGY IN ACTION

Is There Home Shopping in Your Future?

Since 1982, when Florida ad-man Roy Speer launched the Home Shopping Network (HSN) on a local television station, consumers with cable TV have been able to buy everything from vacuum cleaners to gold chains 24 hours a day right from their living rooms. Overall, the TV home shopping industry now has sales of over $2.2 billion, and the numbers keep growing as the technology becomes more flexible. While there are only two major players in the industry, HSN and Pennsylvania-based QVC (Quality, Value, Convenience), there are many local home shopping channels across the country.

Sales for HSN have been in the millions from the beginning, thanks to its aggressive sales tactics and its cutting-edge technology capabilities. Products on HSN are hawked by perky hosts who deliver constant sales pitches and offer many sales incentives and extras, assertively putting pressure on the viewer to buy, buy, buy. HSN has 23,000 incoming phone lines, answered by an automated service that can field up to 20,000 calls a minute, as well as 2,000 human operators.

Most of HSN's consumers communicate directly with the network's computer through their touch-tone phones. The computer takes orders, confirms credit, and sends the order to the nearest warehouse, registering sales faster than an army of human operators ever could.

The real symbol of HSN and its aggressive selling methods is the company's "sales screens." During the broadcast, sales information is simultaneously rechanneled to the on-air hosts and network management via the sales screens, which show the item offered, the number of buyers calling, and the sales being generated. This information is further broken down into sales per item, per minute, and per show. Updated every 15 seconds, the sales screen is the driving force of HSN, keeping the executives on the edges of their seats, and sending on-air hosts into selling frenzies as the numbers climb.

QVC, on the other hand, is decidedly different in temperament. There is less focus on impulse buying, with programming including longer shows about the products and their uses. Unlike HSN, items on QVC

glitter of shining showcases. The future of electronic retailing is still unfolding and while it will grow in importance with time, "the details of the end result are almost impossible to anticipate."[31]

More Efficient Retail Transactions

In addition to giving rise to new forms of retailing, technological advances are also making retail transactions more efficient. Consider, for example, the video order-

are offered all day, and customers are given time to think about how and if they could use the products available. The hosts, while using hard-sell pitches to make sales, will not over-sell the products with promises that they will change one's life. Furthermore, items are somewhat higher-end than those on HSN, attracting a more upscale audience. Most different, however, is that at QVC there is definitely less fascination with technology. QVC has only 3,100 phone lines, which all staff—executives as well as secretaries—answer when necessary, and there is no such equivalent to the sales screens.

QVC, entering the home shopping industry later than HSN, has grown through acquisition of smaller home shopping channels, most importantly Cable Value Network and J.C. Penney TV. After a period of false-starts, QVC now boasts booming sales and a loyal audience.

In November 1992, the merger of HSN and QVC was announced, and in December, former Fox chairman Barry Diller, whose vast experience in television programming turned Fox into a fourth major network, announced plans to take over the helm of the new company. With HSN's technology and QVC's upscale audience, which offers more commercial potential, the company's possibilities seem unlimited. Diller has visions of an interactive network where consumers can choose which items they wish to see, and he plans to offer a wide array of services, from videos to banking advice and bill payment services. QVC is poised on the brink of the twenty-first century, and as the technology begins to catch up with Diller's ideas, home shopping appears to be the mode of retailing in the future.

Sources: Joe Schwartz, "The Evolution of Retailing," *American Demographics*, December 1986, pp. 30–37; Sydney P. Freedberg, "Home Shopping Shakeout Forces Survivors to Find Fresh Approach," *The Wall Street Journal*, November 4, 1987; Joe Agnew, "Home Shopping TV's Hit of the Season," *Marketing News*, March 13, 1987, p. 1; Calvin Sims, "Diller Acquires QVC Stake," *The New York Times*, December 11, 1993, pp. D1, D5; and Peter Carlin, "Is this Television's Future?", *The New York Times Magazine*, February 28, 1993, pp. 36–41.

ing system recently introduced by Florsheim. Shoe stores cannot carry thousands of different styles and sizes in which shoes are available. Customers are disappointed when the store does not have their preferred style in the correct size. Now a customer entering the store can view all of the different styles Florsheim offers on a video monitor. If the store does not have the customer's preferred style or size in stock, he or she can order it directly at the video counter using a credit card and get delivery at home through United Parcel Service.

J. P. Stevens Company has developed a similar system called "Bed and Bath Fashion Center." A video monitor can display all the items in Stevens' product line. After shoppers make their selections, the entire order is printed out at the video station. The shopper presents the printout at a sales desk for payment and pickup.[32] Balfour, Inc., operates another interactive system which allows students to order class rings through video kiosks.[33]

Devices such as optical scanners and voice synthesizers improve efficiency at retail checkout counters. Optical scanners can quickly read and interpret the Universal Product Code (UPC) on packages, retrieve the price of the product from a central computer, and calculate the total amount of sale. Voice synthesizers announce each item's price and the total amount to the customer.

These technological innovations are helping both consumers and retailers. For example, high-tech checkout counters speed up check out and help eliminate the long lines at many supermarkets. Optical scanners also save labor by eliminating the need to mark prices on each item. Instead, prices are displayed on large cards attached to shelves. Some states, however, require that the price of each item be individually marked. Since price information is retrieved from a computer, checkout personnel need not punch in the price of each item at the counter. This eliminates a common source of error and delay. It is also easy for the retailer to change prices by simply reprogramming the computer with the new price information. When prices are individually marked on items, a price change entails much labor since each item must be physically restamped with the new price.

Improved Control of Retail Operations

Computerized checkout counters (often called POS or point-of-sale systems) not only help reduce lines and labor costs, but give retailers ready access to up-to-date information on sales and inventories.

A large selection of computer software especially designed for retailers is now available. Coupled with an electronic POS system, these software packages track sales and inventory levels and automate merchandise ordering, receiving, and pricing. They can also perform routine calculations of markups, margins, and other data necessary for merchandise valuation. Computers also help prepare payrolls and maintain accounting records.

Computers are affecting large and small retailers alike. The owner of a small drug store described their impact this way: "The computer is now a competitive tool. I wouldn't be in retailing if there were no computers." The store uses a personal computer and an electronic point-of-sale unit to track inventory and sales. At the end of each day, a summary report displays the sales of each item and the amount of inventory on hand. The price at which each item was bought and sold, and the current wholesale price also appears on the summary. The summary sheet shows the direct product profit (DPP) of each item and its sales trend. Based on these data, the owner then decides which items to order and which to mark down. Finally, the owner places the order directly through a computer link with the wholesaler. Electronic data interchange (EDI) systems linking retailers to their suppliers enable retailers to manage their inventory more efficiently and thereby reduce in-

Computerized check-out counters, like this one used by J.C. Penney, make retail transactions more efficient and give retailers more control over their operations.

ventory investments. EDI will be one of the most important technological trends in retail operations in the 1990s.

Computers are revolutionizing retail information systems and merchandise control procedures for both large and small retailers. They are changing the way merchandise performance is evaluated and how it is controlled. Chapter 13 discusses in more detail the use of computerized retail information systems to control merchandise performance.

LEGAL ENVIRONMENT

Retail businesses are strongly affected by federal, state, and local laws and regulations. Legislation affecting business has increased steadily over the years and it is impossible in this space to discuss all of the legislation. This section considers some major legislation; additional examples of how the **legal environment** affects the actions of retailers appear throughout the book.

Legislation affecting businesses in the United States fall generally into four categories: (1) antitrust laws to protect business competition, (2) laws to protect firms from unfair business practices, (3) laws to protect consumers, and (4) laws to regulate store operations.

Antitrust Laws

During the late nineteenth and early twentieth centuries a number of federal laws were passed to protect competition. These laws, the Sherman Antitrust Act, the Clayton Act, and the Federal Trade Commission Act, sought to deter the formation of monopolies. They prohibited the concentration of business in the hands of only a few firms, because, supporters argued, in a free enterprise system the threat of competition motivates businesses to act in a manner that increases consumer and social well-being.

The Sherman Antitrust Act of 1890 was one of the first laws enacted to protect business competition. At that time, large railroad companies were accused of colluding to fix their shipping rates. After intensive lobbying by midwestern farmers, Congress passed the Sherman Act which expressly forbade contracts or combinations which restrained free trade and formation of or attempts to form monopolies in any part of trade or commerce. In 1914, the Clayton Act and the Federal Trade Commission (FTC) Act were passed to supplement the Sherman Act. The Clayton Act (1) expressly prohibited manufacturers and wholesalers from discriminating among retailers based on price, (2) prohibited manufacturers from requiring wholesalers and retailers to refrain from dealing with their competitors, and (3) prohibited interlocking directorates that lessened competition. The FTC Act created the Federal Trade Commission and gave it investigatory powers to enforce antitrust legislation.

In recent years, the Federal Trade Commission (FTC) has invoked the provisions of the Sherman Act on a number of occasions to deter mergers among retail firms. Using its powers under the Federal Trade Commission Act, the FTC scrutinizes the potential anticompetitive impact of horizontal retail mergers, that is, a merger among stores serving similar consumer markets. A horizontal merger can reduce competition if the merged firm commands a large share of the market. This can create monopolistic tendencies and create a barrier to entry for new firms.

During the 1980s, the upsurge in retail mergers and acquisitions kept the FTC active in scrutinizing their potential harmful effects. The FTC objected to many contemplated mergers, sometimes forcing the parties to reduce the scope of their operations. For example, when the May Department Stores and Associated Dry Goods agreed to merge in 1986, the FTC objected because the merged company would own all the department stores in the Pittsburgh area. This potential monopoly was deemed to be anticompetitive. The FTC removed its objection only after the May Department Store agreed to sell one Pittsburgh-area department store chain to local businesspeople. Similarly, the government allowed Revco to merge with the Skillern Drug Department of Zale Corporation after Revco agreed to sell off some outlets in Texas.[34]

The Sherman Act also had an effect on the merger between Campeau Corporation (which previously had acquired Allied Stores) and Federated Department Stores. Since the merger of the two companies would create potential monopolies over department stores in New York and California, many people expected FTC to object. To allay this likely objection, Campeau sold some of the Federated divisions to other department store operators such as Macy's, thereby reducing the potential anticompetitive effect of the merger.

It is interesting to note that the FTC judges the potential anticompetitive effects of retail mergers by the resulting concentration in local rather than national markets. This implies that even mergers among firms that have very small shares of the national market may be deemed undesirable if they create local monopolies. This reflects the local orientation of retail competition, as discussed in Chapter 2.

The Sherman Act also prohibits collusion among groups of retailers or between retailers and their suppliers. For example, retailers who engage in horizontal price fixing, that is, those who agree with their competitors to charge the same price on similar merchandise, are liable for prosecution under the Sherman Act. Similarly, manufacturers who attempt to set minimum retail prices at which their products must be sold, called vertical price fixing, may violate antitrust laws. In one incident, Panasonic Company agreed to return as much as $16 million to consumers after New York State charged it with vertical price fixing. According to the State Attorney General's office, Panasonic threatened to cut off supplies from retailers unless Panasonic products were sold at prices dictated by the firm. The Consumer Goods Pricing Act expressly prohibits such activities.

Laws to Protect Firms from Unfair Business Competition

The Robinson-Patman Act is the most important piece of legislation enacted to protect firms from unfair business competition. This 1936 act prohibits the practice of "predatory" pricing, or pricing artificially low to injure one or more competitors. It also requires manufacturers to give quantity discounts and promotional allowances to retailers in strict proportion to the volume purchased by the retailer. Without such legislation, manufacturers may favor large retailers over smaller ones, reducing the ability of small retailers to compete.

Laws to Protect Consumers

During the past 30 years many laws have been enacted to protect consumers. A prime example is the Equal Credit Opportunity Act of 1975, which prohibits discrimination in any aspect of a credit transaction. It also requires stores to notify customers of actions taken regarding their credit applications and to provide detailed reasons on all adverse decisions.

Laws Affecting Store Operations

Many state and local laws affect how retailers operate their stores. For example, some localities enact "blue laws" to prohibit retailers from opening their store on

Sundays. Local ordinances may also restrict the size and type of signs and billboards. The location of the store itself is subject to zoning regulations that restrict businesses from locating in certain residential areas.

Hiring and firing practices and working conditions are also subject to government regulations. The Fair Labor Standards Act of 1938, for example, requires that all employees must be paid at least the current minimum wage. It also requires that all employees working more than 40 hours a week must receive overtime benefits. Retailers must also pay worker's compensation and unemployment insurance for their employees and conform to the guidelines of the Occupational Safety and Health Administration (OSHA).

As is evident from this brief discussion, the legal environment affects all aspects of the retail business. More detailed discussions of laws that affect pricing and advertising practices appear in Chapters 14 and 16, respectively.

INSTITUTIONAL CHANGE IN RETAILING

Changes in the retail environment affect not only the fortunes of individual firms, but ultimately the competitive structure of the industry as a whole. As individual firms respond strategically to changes in consumer demand and technology, new forms of retail institutions often emerge. This changes the competitive positions of different types of retail stores over time.

Consider the department store as an example. The downtown department store originated in the middle of the nineteenth century with the opening of such stores as Marshall Field's in Chicago, John Wanamaker's in Philadelphia, and A. T. Stewart and Macy's in New York City. Until the 1940s, department stores grew in importance and their share of total retail sales increased steadily. At their height in the 1940s, downtown department stores accounted for 8.5 percent of all retail sales in the country. By 1975, however, the downtown department store's share of total retail sales had fallen to a mere 1.1 percent.[35] What forces affected the fortunes of department stores so drastically?

There is no simple explanation of institutional change, nor can any theory accurately predict the futures of all different types of retail institutions. Environmental forces affect each type of institution in a unique way that cannot be generalizable to other forms of retailing. Certain frameworks and concepts have, however, proven useful in describing the way retail institutions change over time.

The Wheel of Retailing

One of the best known theories of how retail institutions change is the **wheel of retailing** hypothesis proposed by Malcolm P. McNair. According to McNair, changes in retail institutions move in a cycle consisting of three phases—entry, trading up, and vulnerability. Exhibit 4.7 illustrates the three phases of McNair's

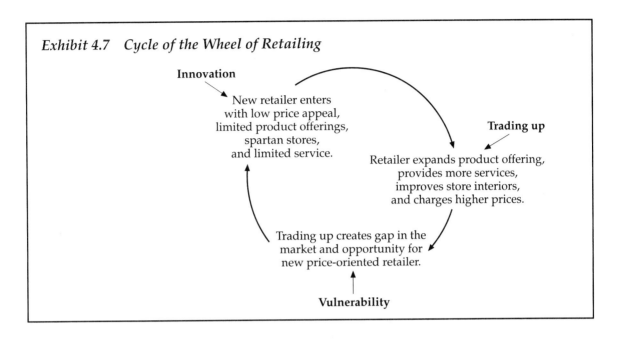

Exhibit 4.7 Cycle of the Wheel of Retailing

Innovation

New retailer enters
with low price appeal,
limited product offerings,
spartan stores,
and limited service.

Trading up

Retailer expands product offering,
provides more services,
improves store interiors,
and charges higher prices.

Trading up creates gap in the
market and opportunity for
new price-oriented retailer.

Vulnerability

retail cycle and how the repetition of those phases creates a pattern of continous movement.

The movement of the wheel through its cycles can best be explained by applying the concept of the shopping opportunity line discussed in Chapter 2. Recall that the shopping opportunity line represents the continuum of the possible combinations of merchandise quality and service, on the one hand, and price on the other. Exhibit 4.8 shows the relationship between McNair's cycle and the shopping opportunity line.

In the entry phase of the cycle, a new retail institution enters the market at the lower end of the shopping opportunity line. Its differential advantage over existing competitors is its low price. To offer low prices, the institution controls its cost strictly by limiting store services, by locating at low rent sites, and by often lowering store standards and merchandise quality. To maintain its low prices, the innovator sometimes sacrifices profit margins compared to the more established competitors.

If the innovation succeeds, emulators copy it over time and increase the level of competition. In response to competitive pressure, the stores then add services and improve quality to create differential advantage. Higher merchandise prices usually accompany such store upgrade, or "trading up." In other words, competition from within the strategic group forces the stores to move to the right along the shopping opportunity line. This creates the opportunity for new institutions to enter at the lower end of the shopping opportunity line. In this way the cycle continues.

Exhibit 4.8   *Wheel of Retailing and Shopping Opportunity Line*

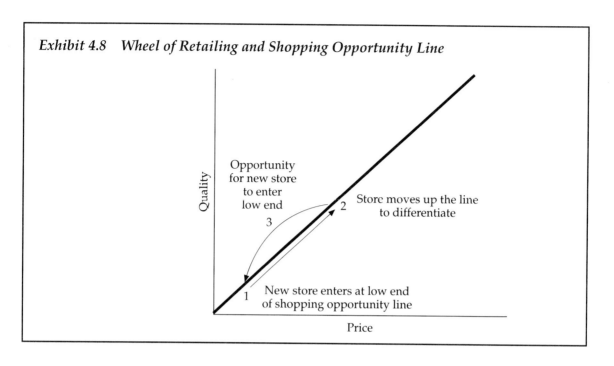

The wheel of retailing concept has the been subject of numerous studies.[36] It is generally agreed now that, although it cannot explain all retail changes, it does provide considerable insight into how low-end retail stores emerge and develop. The evolution of discount stores, catalog showrooms, and warehouse stores all seem to follow the pattern of the wheel. Prestige boutiques and specialty stores, however, are examples of some institutions that did not follow this model. They did not begin at the low end of the shopping opportunity line.

Does the wheel still continue to revolve? Many observers of the retail industry have asked themselves this question. The answer is both yes and no. The wheel still continues to revolve but perhaps at a slower pace.

The wheel still revolves because stores continue to shift their position along the shopping opportunity line. J.C. Penney's strategic change is one example of such a move. As discussed in Chapter 2, that company has implemented a number of changes to move its stores further to the right along the shopping opportunity line (see Exhibit 2.14). This resembles the trading up phase of McNair's cycle.

However, the movement of the wheel may be slowing because retail firms are now tailoring their outlets to match specific positions along the shopping opportunity line. This shows up clearly in diversified companies that operate stores at different positions along the shopping opportunity continuum. A firm that operates both discount stores and department stores will control the trading up process of the discount store so that its market focus remains distinct from that of the department store's in order to prevent the stores from cannibalizing each other's sales.

In general, the realization is growing among retail managers that each store must have a well defined market focus geared to serve a specific customer group.

The Dialectic Process

The **dialectic process** is another model that describes the emergence and growth of retail institutions. It views retailing as an evolutionary system in which different retail institutions adapt to each other, in the process generating new retail formats. The central premise of the dialectical model is that "when challenged by a competitor with a differential advantage, an established institution will adopt strategies and tactics in the direction of that advantage, thereby negating some of the innovators' attraction."[37] The new institution then modifies its strategy to maintain its competitive advantage. These mutual adaptations gradually move the two retailers together in terms of merchandise offerings, service, and price.[38]

The emergence of the discount department store is perhaps the best example of how the dialectical process works. As shown in Exhibit 4.9, department stores were traditionally located in downtown areas and offered high levels of customer service. They also had relatively high prices and high margins. In the 1950s, discount

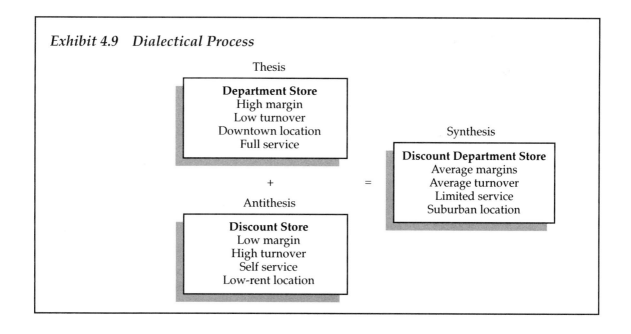

Exhibit 4.9   Dialectical Process

Thesis

Department Store
High margin
Low turnover
Downtown location
Full service

+

Antithesis

Discount Store
Low margin
High turnover
Self service
Low-rent location

=

Synthesis

Discount Department Store
Average margins
Average turnover
Limited service
Suburban location

stores (such as Korvette's) emerged as a competitive force challenging department stores. The early discount store was generally located at suburban sites, had lower prices, and offered no customer services. In contrast to the department store, its managerial philosophy stressed lower margins to create greater merchandise turnover. As department stores and discount stores adapted to each other over time, discount department stores such as K mart evolved, blending the two opposing forces. Discount department stores combined the strengths of both department stores and discount stores and created a competitive position of their own.

Retail Life Cycles

The **retail life cycle** is another concept that describes the process of institutional change in retailing. This model states that retail institutions pass through a life cycle that can be divided into four stages: (1) introduction, (2) growth, (3) maturity, and (4) decline (see Exhibit 4.10).

New types of retail institutions first appear at the introduction or innovation stage, as downtown department stores did in the 1860s. Similarly, franchised fast-food outlets were at this stage of their life cycle in the 1950s and early 1960s. Dur-

---

Exhibit 4.10   Retail Life Cycle

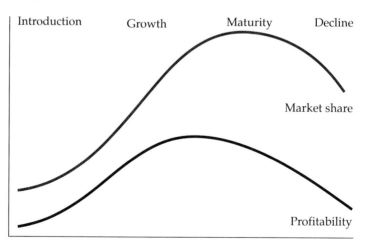

Note: The duration of the stages (the horizontal scale) varies depending on many circumstances. The four stages are portrayed equally on the time scale for schematic purposes only.

Source: Adapted by permission of *Harvard Business Review.* An exhibit from "The Retail Life Cycle," by William R. Davidson, Albert D. Bates and Stephen J. Boss, vol. 54 (November–December 1976), pp. 89–96. Copyright © 1976 by the President and Fellows of Harvard College; all rights reserved.

ing this stage the new retail concept has a marked competitive advantage over conventional outlets.[39] This advantage may be based on price, merchandise assortment, convenience, or a new approach to sales and promotion.

The competitive advantage propels the institution into the second stage of the life cycle, which is characterized by growth in both sales and profits. This stage is also marked by the emergence of new competitors who imitate the original concept. As competition increases, firms expand their chains geographically to reach new markets and increase sales. Between 1983 and 1985, for example, large electronic retail chains, such as Circuit City, Video Affiliates, and The Wiz, expanded their network of outlets into a number of new markets to establish a dominant position in those markets.[40] By expanding their own network, these chains restricted new competitors from entering into this sector of retailing.

The stage of rapid growth is inevitably followed by one of maturity when the speed of market growth slows and sales start to stagnate. Currently drug stores, athletic shoe stores, and electronic stores seem to be in this stage of their life cycle. After growing rapidly during the first part of the 1980s, total sales at these stores have slowed down considerably. In the early 1980s, the consumer electronics market grew by more than 20 percent a year.[41] In contrast, there has been little or no growth in the 1990s. As growth slows, competitive rivalry intensifies, since firms fight aggressively to maintain their share of the market. Consequently, profits start to decline during this stage of the life cycle.

The final stage is one of decline. Both sales and profits are low during this period. The lack of competitive advantage often leads to the total demise of the institution. However, failure can often be avoided by repositioning or by a reversal of environmental trends. Downtown department stores, for example, got a new lease on life when, in the middle 1970s, many cities initiated urban renewal projects to attract more shoppers to downtown areas.

Although one can never forecast the duration of an institutional life cycle with certainty, considerable evidence suggests that life cycles are accelerating. As shown in Exhibit 4.11, the time taken for institutions to reach the maturity stage is becoming shorter with each new kind of retail innovation. Whereas traditional department stores took approximately 80 years to reach maturity, later innovations such as home improvement centers and fast-food outlets matured in only 15 years. More recent innovations, such as off-price retailers, may reach maturity even faster. The **acceleration of the retail life cycle** reflects increased competitive pressures in the retail industry and the rapid pace of environmental change. Neither of these processes is expected to slow down in the future.

The Life Cycle and Environmental Change

What forces affect the shape of the life cycle? The life cycle pattern reflects fundamental shifts in the competitive position of different types of retail institutions

Exhibit 4.11 *Acceleration of Retail Life Cycles*

Institution	Approximate Date of Innovation	Approximate Date of Maturity	Years to Reach Maturity
Downtown department store	1860	1940	80
Variety store	1890	1955	65
Supermarket	1930	1965	35
Discount store	1950	1975	25
Home improvement center	1965	1980	15
Electronic superstore	1980	1987	7

Source: William R. Davidson, Albert D. Bates, and Stephen J. Bass, "The Retail Life Cycle," *Harvard Business Review* 54 (November–December, 1976), pp. 88–96.

caused by changes in the consumer environment. Analysis of the life cycle of department stores and supermarkets illustrates the relationship of the life cycle to the environment.

Department stores   Department stores emerged as a retail institution in the middle of the nineteenth century. Prior to that time, the dominant force in retailing was the full-line general store. However, the growth of industrialization and urbanization changed this situation beginning in the mid-1800s. The sewing machine was also invented during this period, leading to the development of the ready-to-wear apparel industry. These two trends together sowed the seeds for the growth of the department store industry. As cities grew in population and public transportation made travel to "downtown" areas easier, downtown department stores blossomed into a major force in retailing. Broader newspaper circulation, which made mass advertising feasible, also contributed to this movement.[42]

A. T. Stewart, one of the first department stores, opened its doors in New York City in 1863. R. H. Macy, Marshall Field, and Jordan Marsh followed soon after. By the end of the century, downtown department stores were open in all the major U.S. cities and sales at department stores continued to grow until the middle of the twentieth century. In 1899, department stores were estimated to account for 1.6 percent of total retail sales. By 1929 this figure had risen to 8.9 percent and reached 10.7 percent in 1967.[43] From this point, the downtown department stores' share of retail sales has generally decreased, although the decline has reversed slightly in recent years.

Piggly Wiggly, America's first self-service grocery store, was founded in 1916. This is Piggly Wiggly's first store in Memphis, Tennessee.

What led to the decline of downtown department stores? Just as urbanization stimulated their growth, suburbanization led to their decline. As mentioned earlier in the chapter, during the late 1950s and early 1960s increasing numbers of Americans chose to live in suburban areas rather than in central cities. As people moved out of the city, they shopped more in suburban shopping malls and less in downtown areas. Mass merchandisers like Sears and J.C. Penney and discount stores like K mart, Target, and Venture grew more important and eroded the dominance of downtown department stores.

Supermarkets The opening of the first Piggly Wiggly food store in 1916 heralded the start of the supermarket industry. It introduced the idea of self-selection and self-service by customers and the use of centralized check-out counters. Another early innovator was The Big Bear Market, which opened in an abandoned automobile plant in Elizabeth, New Jersey in 1932. Attracted by its low prices, customers reportedly traveled as much as 100 miles to shop at The Big Bear Market. Even though its margin was about one-third of the prevailing rate of 30 percent, Big Bear achieved annual sales of $3 million—a figure unheard of until then.[44]

Five environmental trends drove the evolution of supermarket retailing:[45]

1. Consumers in the 1930s were very price conscious because of the Great Depression, so lower prices at supermarkets attracted them.
2. The wider availability of automobiles made possible longer shopping trips and more purchases per trip.
3. Advances in refrigeration technology allowed both stores and consumers to store perishable commodities.
4. Evolving packaging technology allowed consumer-sized packages to replace barrels and crates, making consumer self-service possible.
5. Brand advertising by food product manufacturers allowed self-selection by customers without help from store personnel.

The conventional supermarket grew unabated for more than 40 years until the middle of the 1970s, when limited assortment (box) stores and warehouse stores emerged to challenge it. Stung by inflation during the 1970s, consumers patronized these new types of stores because of their lower prices.

In recent years another new format has emerged in the supermarket industry—the combination supermarket and drug store. This too is a result of changes in the environment. As society becomes more time-pressed, the convenience of one-stop shopping offered by the combination stores creates a competitive advantage for them over conventional supermarkets.

As the history of department stores and supermarkets illustrates, various environmental forces shape the development of retail stores. As the environment changes, so does the relative competitive positions of different types of retail stores. For this reason retail managers must pay special attention to the environment in which they operate and continuously monitor new changes. The changes may open up new opportunities for growth or they may foreshadow future decline and demise.

Summary

1. In order to create sound strategies, retailers must keep abreast of changes in the consumer, economic, technological, and legal environments. Environmental changes sometimes create new opportunities and at other times pose threats to the firm's very existence.
2. One of the most important changes in the consumer environment is the changing age structure of the U.S. population. As the number of people in different age groups change, so does the pattern of demand for different kinds of retail goods and services. People

born during the baby boom period are asserting a major influence on consumer expenditure patterns. Retailers also have to adapt to the growing number of elderly in the population.

3. The U.S. population is still shifting to the Sunbelt areas, although the rate has slowed compared to the last decade. A new phenomenon is the growth of the exurbia. Population shifts create opportunities for locating new retail outlets.

4. Three broad changes in consumer life styles occurred in the 1980s and are expected to continue into the 1990s. First, with more and more women joining the work force, American society is becoming time-pressed. Second, there is a trend toward the blending of traditional male and female purchase roles. Third, consumers continue to put emphasis on value for their money despite current increases in income. Retailers have had to change the way they operate in order to respond to these changes.

5. Advancing technologies in the areas of computer applications, communications, and electronics are: (a) giving rise to new forms of retailing such as cable shopping networks and videotex systems; (b) making retail transactions more efficient; and (c) improving control of retail operations.

6. The legal environment is made up of federal, state, and local laws and regulations. These fall into four categories: (a) laws to protect business competition; (b) laws against unfair business practices; (c) laws to protect consumers; and (d) laws to regulate store operations.

7. Changes in the retail environment ultimately change the competitive structure of the industry. Three frameworks suggested for describing how retail institutions change are: (a) wheel of retailing; (b) dialectic process; and (c) retail life cycle.

Key Concepts

The graying of America
Age pyramid
Baby boom
Baby bust
Ripple effect
Echo boom
Demand for goods and services
Mature market
Suburbanization
Exurbanization
Changing family structure

Time-pressed consumers
Consumer income
Savings and debt
Videotex
Technological environment
Legal environment
Wheel of retailing
Dialectic process
Retail life cycle
Acceleration of retail life cycles

Discussion Questions

1. What forces in the environment have made possible the evolution and growth of TV retailing in the last decade? What factors do you think will shape the future of this form of retailing?

2. What is meant by these terms: (a) graying of America, (b) the echo boom, (c) life styles.

3. Has the changing population age structure affected any retailers in your town?

How have these retailers responded to the change? What suggestions would you have for these retailers?

4. Changes in the traditional family structure have resulted in a blending of male and female roles in purchasing decisions. Discuss how such blending may affect retailers and how retailers can respond to this trend.

5. This chapter presents a number of examples of retailers' use of new technologies to improve their competitive positions. Discuss some examples of how retailers in your area have responded to changing technology.

6. In recent years, the Federal Trade Commission has invoked the antitrust laws to deter mergers among retail firms. Supporters of such actions argue that increased retail concentration would be harmful to consumers. Others, however, feel that larger companies will be more efficient and therefore able to charge lower prices. Which argument do you support? Why?

7. Describe the stages in the retail life cycle. Describe the factors that influenced the life cycle of department stores. Are retail life cycles accelerating, why, or why not?

8. Discuss the propositions of the *wheel of retailing* hypothesis. Give some examples of retail institutions that have followed this evolutionary path.

Notes

1. "The Rich Autumn of a Consumer's Life," *The Economist*, September 5, 1992, p. 67.

2. See Judith Waldrop, "Secrets of the Age Pyramid," *American Demographics*, August 1992, p. 51; "Median Age of America Climbs to 31.7 years, Study Finds," *The New York Times*, October 2, 1987, p. A13; and U.S. Department of Commerce, Bureau of the Census, *Statistical Abstract of the United States, 1991* (Washington, D.C.: U.S. Government Printing Office, 1991).

3. Ibid. (Waldrop)

4. Ibid. (*The New York Times*)

5. "Teenagers: Rising in Income and Firm in Brand Loyalty," *Business Week*, April 23, 1984, p. 51; and "Targeting Teens," *American Demographics*, February 1985, p. 51.

6. "Invest in the Baby Boom," *American Demographics*, July 1984, p. 14.

7. "Baby Boomers, A Beautiful Bulge," *Sales and Marketing Management*, October 26, 1981, p. 39.

8. "Older Consumers Adopt Baby Boomer Buying Behavior," *Marketing News*, February 15, 1988, p. 8.

9. "The Rich Autumn of a Consumer's Life," *The Economist*, September 5, 1992, p. 67.

10. "U.S. Companies Go for the Gray," *Business Week*, April 3, 1989, p. 67.

11. Ganesan Viswabharaty and David Rink, "The Elderly: Neglected Business Opportunities," *Journal of Consumer Marketing* 1, no. 4 (1984), p. 39.

12. *American Demographics*, March 1991.

13. Alan Bates, *Retailing and Its Environment* (New York: D. Van Nostrand, 1979), p. 10.

14. Leonard L. Berry, "The New Consumer," in *Competitive Structures in Retail Markets: The Department Store Perspective*, ed. by Ronald W. Stampfl and Elizabeth C. Hirschman (Chicago: American Marketing Association, 1981), p. 1.

15. *American Demographics*, March 1991.

16. Paul Glick, "How American Families Are Changing," *American Demographics*, January 1984, pp. 21–25.

17. *American Demographics*, March 1991.

18. "Families in America," *Data Track*, American Council of Life Insurance, no. 17, December 1987, p. 1.

19. *American Demographics*, March 1991.

20. Henry Assael, *Consumer Behavior and Marketing Action*, p. 271, "Women at

Work," *Business Week*, January 28, 1984, pp. 80–87; "How Women Have Changed," *American Demographics*, May 1983, pp. 21–24.

21. Leonard L. Berry, "The Time Buying Consumer," *Journal of Retailing* 55 (Winter 1979), p. 58.

22. Ibid.

23. Henry Assael, *Consumer Behavior and Marketing Action* (Boston: PWS-KENT Publishing, 1992), p. 298.

24. Ibid. p. 297.

25. "Green Consumers Influence Buying," *Advertising Age*, September 25, 1989, p. 19.

26. "Wal-Mart's 'Green' Campaign to Emphasize Recycling Next," *Adweek's Marketing Week*, February 12, 1990, pp. 60–61.

27. "A New Sales Pitch: The Environment," *Business Week*, July 24, 1989, p. 50.

28. Videotex: What It Is All About," *Marketing News*, November 25, 1983, p. 16.

29. "Teleaction: Is It Ready for Prime Time?," *Chain Store Age Executive*, July 1988, pp. 16–19.

30. "The Newly Minted Penney: Where Fashion Rules," *Business Week*, April 17, 1989, p. 88.

31. Malcolm McNair and Eleanor May, "The Next Revolution of the Retailing Wheel," *Harvard Business Review*, 56 (September–October 1978), pp. 81–91.

32. Joan Paganetti, "High Tech Adds Gleam to Service with a Smile," *Advertising Age*, July 1983, p. M24.

33. Robert F. Lusch, Patrick Dunne, and Myron Gable, *Retail Management* (Cincinnati: South-Western Publishing, 1990), p. 198.

34. "Revco Sets Accord with Justice Department on Buying Zale Unit," *The Wall Street Journal*, February 9, 1981, p. 2.

35. William H. Davidson, Alan Bates, and Stephen J. Bass, "The Retail Life Cycle," *Harvard Business Review*, 54 (1976), pp. 89–96.

36. See, for example, Arieh Goldman, "The Role of Trading Up in the Development of the Retail System," *Journal of Marketing*, 39 (January 1975), pp. 54–62; Arieh Goldman, "Institutional Change in Retailing: An Updated Wheel of Retailing Theory," in *Foundations of Marketing Channels*, ed., by A. G. Woodside, J. Y. Sims, D. M. Lewison, and I. F. Wilkinson (Austin: Lone Star Publishing, 1978); Stanley C. Hollander, "Oddities, Nostalgia, Wheels and Other Patterns in Retail Evolution," in *Competitive Structure in Retail Markets*, ed. by R. Stampfl and E. Hirschman (Chicago: American Marketing Association, 1980), pp. 78–87.

37. Thomas J. Maronick and Bruce J. Walker, "The Dialectic Evolution of Retailing," in *Proceedings*, Southern Marketing Association, ed. by Burnett Greenburg (Atlanta: Georgia State University, 1974), p. 147.

38. Louis W. Stern and Adel I. El-Ansary, *Marketing Channels* (Englewood Cliffs: Prentice-Hall, 1981), p. 64.

39. Bates, *Retailing and Its Environment*, p. 21.

40. "Electronic Superstores Are Devouring Their Rivals," *Business Week*, June 24, 1985, pp. 84–85.

41. Isadore Barmash, "Breaking Out of the Pack," *The New York Times*, June 28, 1987, p. F12.

42. Stern and El-Ansary, *Marketing Channels*, p. 33.

43. Louis P. Bucklin, *Competition and Evolution in the Distributive Trade* (Englewood Cliffs: Prentice-Hall, 1972), pp. 55–60.

44. Ibid.

45. Ibid.

PART II
Designing Retail Strategy

Having examined in Part One the environment in which retail firms operate, we now shift our focus to strategic planning for retail firms.

Whether a firm operates one or many retail units, it must have a well-defined marketing strategy that gears the store's efforts toward a specific target market and differentiates it from competitors. The steps in developing such a marketing strategy are described in Chapter 5. Today, many retail firms are multiunit conglomerates that operate a portfolio of retail stores, each with its distinctive name, customer focus, and marketing strategy. An important concern for such firms is to integrate the strategies of the individual units to achieve synergy. Chapter 6 discusses the special planning concerns of such multiunit firms.

Marketing and financial strategies are the two pillars on which successful retail programs stand. Even the most detailed marketing plan will not succeed without proper financial planning and control. Chapter 7 provides a comprehensive discussion of financial planning for retail firms. Chapters 8 and 9 focus on location decisions—another important aspect of retail strategy. The store's location determines the number and type of customers it will attract.

CHAPTER 5
Retail Marketing Strategy

The Tale of Three Toy Retailers

During the 1980s, the toy industry—like the retail industry—split into distinct selling positions to cater to the changing toy consumer. These shifts reflected the changing preferences of toy consumers who were seeking new forms of value: some wanted deep discounts on items and accepted no-frills shopping atmospheres; others wanted the selection and convenience offered by mall shopping; and still others wanted novel toys, continued customer service, and engaging shopping atmospheres. Each position requires its own strategy and specific merchandise offering. This gave rise to three distinct kinds of toy stores: the discount toy supermarket, such as Toys R Us and Child World; mall stores like Kay-Bee; and boutique stores like F.A.O. Schwarz.

In 1990, Toys R Us sales reached $5.5 billion. It is the largest U.S. toy retailer, operating 457 domestic stores, 98 international stores, and 164 Kids R Us children's clothing stores. The company's merchandising strategy is to offer brand name goods (both clothing and toys) in its stores, and keep selection wide, inventory deep, and price competitive. Toys R Us does not hold sales, but rather relies on everyday low prices to compete. To support the huge number of stores, Toys R Us maintains 20 distribution centers, its own transportation fleet, and a very sophisticated computerized inventory system.

With this many stores, Toys R Us dominates toy retailing in the United States. It is called the toy supermarket because of its policy of selling wide and deep assortments of toys in outlets that typically enclose about 40,000 square feet. Like supermarkets, but in distinct contrast with most other toy specialty stores, Toys R Us relies on customer self-service and self-selection. The stores also resemble supermarkets, with toys stacked on shelves arranged in regimented aisles. Like supermarket shoppers, customers use shopping carts and pay at centralized checkout counters near the exit.

Toys R Us locates its outlets along major traffic arteries near suburban shopping malls. To control costs, the stores are freestanding or located in small shopping centers, rather than inside shopping malls. The chain's unique pricing policy makes cost control very important. Toys R Us sets its prices, on average, about one-third below those charged by department stores for comparable merchandise. The firm follows this low-price policy year round and offers no special price promotions. This unique approach to pricing has been one of the key forces behind the store's success in attracting customers. To maintain customer loyalty, the company has a very liberal return policy and communicates this to

customers through advertising and in-store signs.

However, while the business world's attention has been focused on the success of Toys R Us, Kay-Bee has moved steadily to become a different kind of powerhouse in toy retailing. Without attracting much attention, the chain grew to over 770 stores across the country in the late 1980s, with 1989 sales totaling $724 million (up from $410 million in 1985). By most industry accounts, Kay-Bee now dominates the other pole of toy retailing: mall stores. While Toys R Us builds huge freestanding stores offering over 40,000 items, Kay-Bee operates mall stores averaging 3,500 square feet offering about 3,000

items. Despite the similar inventory, given this size and location difference, the marketing strategies of the two giants differ greatly.

Toys R Us positions itself as a "destination store," a store customers must make a special trip to visit because they are looking for a special item. The chain thus relies on a pull strategy to draw the customers to the store, as demonstrated by its pricing and wide selection. Kay-Bee, however, relies much more on a push strategy, because a visit to the store is much more likely to be unplanned. Here, the mall is the destination, and customers stop at Kay-Bee on impulse, especially if they have children with them. For this to work, the stores must be bright, attractive, and attention-getting, and the sales staff must be friendly and available. The customers come into the stores on a whim, and the strategy is to gently push them into purchases, and thus far, the strategy has been effective.

The third kind of toy retailer, the boutique or specialty store, is exemplified by F.A.O. Schwarz. The first F.A.O. Schwarz outlet opened in 1862 in Baltimore. The firm, which describes itself as the most unique toy store, offers new, trendy, and fancy children's toys of high quality at full price. The firm targets customers who are status- and prestige-conscious, and who are willing to pay high prices for what they consider to be special merchandise. The merchandise ranges from such basic items as stuffed animals to customized model cars and doll houses priced at several thousand dollars. Consistent with its merchandise policy, the store maintains a high level of customer service and an exciting shopping atmosphere. Customers can always find sales people ready to answer questions or help with shopping. Instead of high stacks and wide aisles, the store organizes nearly 100 boutiques around such themes as trains and clowns.

To cater to its high-income target market, F.A.O. Schwarz locates its outlets at prime re-

tail sites in urban areas. The flagship store is located on Manhattan's Fifth Avenue, one of the world's premier retail districts. The location attracts not only residents, but also shoppers from the suburbs who are willing to travel great distances to visit the store. In addition, the location is a popular shopping area for tourists from all over the world.

Sources: Courtesy Toys R Us, Courtesy Retail Planning Associates; M. McGlade, *Toys R Us Company Report*, Paine Webber, Inc., October 28, 1991; David Megehan, "A Berkshire Toy Empire," *The Boston Globe*, Tuesday, October 9, 1990.

The contrasting strategies of Toys R Us, Kay-Bee, and F.A.O. Schwarz demonstrate how stores selling the same type of merchandise may have different marketing strategies. Note, for example, the difference in the types of customers that Toys R Us and F.A.O. Schwarz attract: Toys R Us serves mostly suburban families with children who shop for popular, nationally advertised toys. Schwarz's more cosmopolitan customers want unique, novel or European toys. These differences in customer characteristics dictate vastly different locations, merchandise selection, and in-store atmosphere. Similarly, the level of in-store service at the two stores reflects the expectations of their customers. Since Toys R Us customers generally buy popular toys that are heavily advertised, they need very little in-store service. The novel toys sold by F.A.O. Schwarz, on the other hand, need to be demonstrated and explained to customers.

Despite their different strategies, these stores are all successful because they have clearly defined the way in which they will deliver value to their target markets. Simply put, *they know their customers well*, and in developing their marketing strategies they have kept their customers continuously in mind. In every element, from locating stores, advertising, and pricing to displays of individual merchandise items, the strategies aim to satisfy the target customer. This is the foundation of all successful marketing strategies and a valuable lesson for all retailers.

DEVELOPING MARKETING STRATEGY

In business, success comes to those who have a clear strategy for winning marketplace competition. To win marketplace competition firms must have a **marketing strategy** that clearly describes the firm's overall program for differentiating itself from competitors and delivering value to its customers. According to Webster's dictionary, the word *strategy* originates from the Greek word *strategia* meaning generalship. In the context of business planning, strategy refers to the use of the organization's resources efficiently to compete most effectively. Strategic planning, therefore, sets long-term goals for the firm and determines the actions necessary to fulfill those goals. Just as military strategy has winning the war as its objective, marketing strategy has the objective of winning marketplace competition by providing value to customers and creating a sustainable differential advantage over competitors.[1]

Steps in Developing Marketing Strategy

This chapter deals with the process of developing and monitoring marketing strategy. The marketing strategy must specify the firm's target market and how it will position the various retail mix elements to satisfy the needs of the target market.

To develop its marketing strategy, the retailer must take several key steps as shown in Exhibit 5.1. The process starts with the analysis of potential customers. Customer analysis involves understanding differences in customer behavior and identifying potential market segments. Based on customer analysis, the firm has to select the target market it will serve, which is the second step. This requires measuring the potential of each segment and the level of competition within each segment. To be viable, the chosen segment must represent adequate market potential to ensure the volume of sales and profits needed to make the venture economically feasible.

The third step is to identify how the firm will position itself to create a sustainable differential advantage in the marketplace. The chosen competitive position must reflect the firm's strengths compared with its competitors. With the target market chosen and the desired competitive position determined, the firm must then plan its retail mix elements to implement its marketing strategy. Finally, the firm must monitor performance to make sure it is achieving the desired results. In addition to monitoring sales and profits, retailers must also track the store's image in the minds of the consumers. Since the store's image is influenced by the elements of the retail mix, studying the image provides important feedback for fine tuning the marketing strategy.

This chapter discusses each of these steps in the development of marketing strategy. In addition, an appendix to the chapter describes a number of marketing research techniques used to measure store image.

The Need for Marketing Strategy

At one time most retailers survived, and some even prospered, without strategic planning. Today, however, few retailers can succeed without well-formulated strategies. Competition has simply become too intense, and, as discussed in the previous chapter, key environmental forces, as well as consumer behavior patterns, are

Exhibit 5.1   Steps in Developing Marketing Strategy

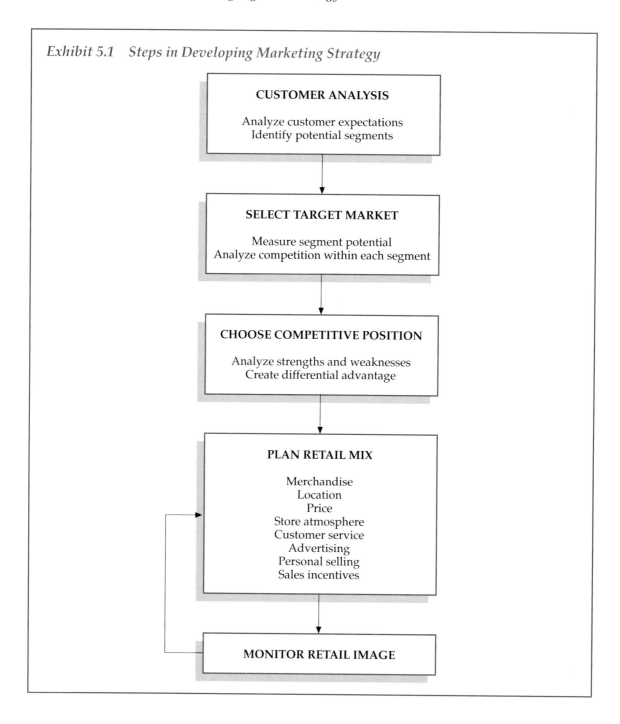

changing too fast. In this rapidly changing business environment, the lack of a clear marketing strategy too often leads to a lack of focus and inability to deal with changing market conditions.

The marketing strategy integrates the different functions of a retail business. For example, the target market defined in the marketing strategy guides the real estate department when choosing locations for outlets. Similarly, the buyers for the store make their purchases with the same target consumer in mind. In this way the marketing strategy keeps the different activities of the firm focussed on the same objectives. Without a clear strategy, the real estate department may locate outlets in high-income neighborhoods while buyers select merchandise with families of moderate income in mind. Such a lack of coordination would make the firm an ineffective competitor.

A clear strategy helps the firm respond to changes in the external environment. As mentioned in Chapter 4, changes in the environment can open new business opportunities or pose a threat to the firm's very existence. An important part of the developing strategy is to assess the changes taking place in the environment and determine how best the firm can respond to them. In this way the strategic planning process ensures that the firm is not caught off-guard by changes in the environment.

Strategy and Tactics

Strategies, of course, have to be implemented to provide returns. **Tactics** are the specific actions taken to implement a strategy. In a war, the strategy might be to take control of a hill. Landing airborne forces on top of a hill might be a tactic to implement this strategy. Tactics are associated with executions of plans, while strategies identify their objectives.

A firm must adopt tactics that are consistent with its strategies. For example, in order to provide families with young children with "food and fun," McDonald's provides play areas in the outlets and "Happy Meals" for children. The tactic of serving beer or selling cigarettes would be inconsistent with McDonald's strategy.

ANALYZING CUSTOMER EXPECTATIONS

No single store can serve all consumers. In fact, it is often said that a store that tries to serve all consumers ends up serving none. Consumers have different tastes, preferences, and perceptions of value. These differences create the potential for dividing the total market into several relatively homogenous market segments. Each retail store must focus its efforts on the segment or segments that it can serve best; this is the store's target market. An important step in the strategic planning process is to analyze customer expectations to identify potential segments in the market.

Play areas and Happy Meals are two among many ways in which McDonald's attracts families with children.

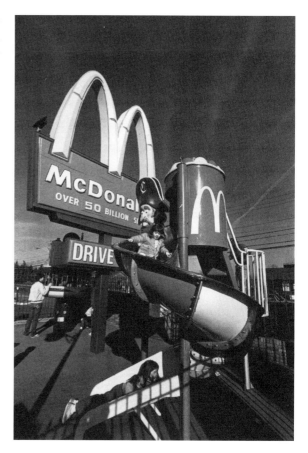

Segmenting Consumer Markets

The essence of **segmentation** is to group together people who evaluate the benefits of a retail offering, and, therefore, retail stores, similarly. The total market can be viewed as containing a number of these segments. All consumers belonging to the same segment will respond similarly to the retailer's marketing strategy, since they have similar expectations about their shopping experience. On the other hand, consumers from different segments have different expectations and, therefore, respond differently. A retailer must choose the segment it wants to serve and design a marketing program that most effectively meets the expectations of customers in that segment. Market segmentation, therefore, is *the means of relating retail strategy to differences in consumer needs and expectations.*

Because it recognizes differences among groups of customers instead of treating the entire market as homogenous, segmentation makes the marketing program more efficient. By understanding the differences among segments, a retailer can match its resources to consumer needs most effectively. The retailer can combine the retail mix elements to gain the maximum response from the chosen target market. Segmentation also allows a better focus on competition, since not all firms compete for the same customer segments. By determining the firms that focus on the same customer segment, a retailer can determine the stores with which it will have the greatest competitive rivalry.

Consider, for example, the market for women's clothing. The total market—all potential purchasers of women's clothing—is vast. But not all of these customers have the same expectations when they shop for clothing. They differ in terms of the relative importance they give to fashion and price in the purchase decision. The apparel market can thus be divided into segments based on these criteria. Exhibit 5.2, for example, shows a scheme for segmenting the women's apparel market based on a study done for *Glamour* magazine. As shown in the exhibit, the women's apparel market can be divided into four groups—(1) fashion-enthusiasts, (2) style-seekers, (3) classics, and (4) timids and uninvolveds. Each group has different levels of fashion involvement. At one extreme are the fashion-enthusiasts. They are highly motivated by style, social status, and high-quality clothing. At the other extreme is the timid and uninvolved segment. They do not enjoy

Exhibit 5.2   *Segments in Women's Apparel Market*

Segment	Percent of Consumers	Shopping Behavior
Fashion Enthusiasts	8 percent of consumers. With style seekers account for 58 percent of all expenditures on clothing	Confident. Highly motivated by style, social status, and high-quality clothing
Style Seekers	12 percent of consumers. With fasion enthusiasts account for 58 percent of all expenditures on clothing	Keep close eye on latest styles. More oriented towards quantity than quality
Classics	20 percent of consumers and expenditures on clothing	Look for traditional, good quality styles that have stood the test of time.
Timids and Uninvolveds	60 percent of consumers account for only 22 percent of expenditures.	Little or no interest in fashion. Shop only when they have to and spend as little as possible.

Source: Based on study conducted by *Glamour Magazine* reported in Susan Kraft, "Discount Drives Women to Clothes," *American Demographics*, February 1991.

shopping, give little or no importance to fashion, and are very price conscious. According to the study, the fashion-enthusiasts and style-seekers together comprise 20 percent of all shoppers, but account for 58 percent of all expenditures on women's clothing. On the contrary, the timid and uninvolved segment make up 60 percent of all shoppers but account for only 22 percent of expenditures.

It is unlikely that a single store can meet the expectations of all of these segments. To meet the expectations of fashion-enthusiasts, a store must stock up-to-date, fashionable clothes; otherwise these customers will not patronize the store even if its prices are low. The buying decisions of the uninvolved or timid segment, on the other hand, are more influenced by price than fashion. They may be willing to accept a not-so-fashionable dress, if the price is low.

Their different attitudes towards fashion and price give the segments different preferences for shopping atmospheres. Customers of high-priced, fashionable merchandise expect stores to employ salespeople who know the latest trends in fashion and designer names. On the other hand, members of the timid segment may prefer self-selection and self-service. Similarly, the ambience and decor that may suit one group may not please the other. Because of the differences among the groups, it is difficult, if not impossible, for a single store to meet the needs of all the segments.

As another example, consider the differences between customers who patronize full-service camera stores and those who buy cameras from discount stores. Patrons of full-service camera stores are willing to pay higher prices because they derive considerable benefit from the services offered by these stores. These customers are typically uncertain about camera features and how to choose among alternative models and brands of cameras. Therefore, they value the help they get from the sales personnel of full-service stores. Discount store shoppers, on the other hand, are willing to forego such help but seek lower prices. Because of the differences in their shopping behavior—in terms of the type of service they require—the customers of full-service and discount camera stores constitute different segments.

The furniture market provides yet another example. Although a wide spectrum of consumers buy furniture, there are distinct differences among them. Some are first-time homemakers. They seek affordable yet attractive furniture that they can easily replace when they move or their families grow larger. The furniture they buy often comes in modular form, which customers assemble on their own. Ikea and Conran's are two stores that cater to this segment of customers. Other stores, in contrast, cater to customers who view furniture as investments. They are willing to pay more for furniture they plan to keep for a long time. The two types of furniture buyers, too, make up different segments, since the types of merchandise they seek are different because of the customers' different motivations for buying furniture.

As the preceding examples illustrate, markets can be grouped into different segments based on differences among consumers in terms of their motivation for shopping, the benefits they seek, the types of merchandise and service they desire, and

STRATEGY IN ACTION

Tianguis Brings Fiesta Atmosphere to Hispanic Community

Von's Grocery Company has found success in Southern California by targeting the large population of Hispanic shoppers there. The company has opened stores, named Tianguis, targeted especially to this market. The stores provide an atmosphere and selection of merchandise designed to make Hispanic customers feel at home.

With Hispanics comprising about 30 percent of the population of Los Angeles County, the area seems a prime target market for Tianguis. Furthermore, the Hispanic population of the United States has risen by more than 30 percent since 1980. Before opening its first Tianguis store, Von's conducted a two-and-a-half-year market study. The company learned that at least two million Hispanics resided in Los Angeles County, and that these families tended to shop frequently and spend significantly more per week on groceries than families from other ethnic groups.

Research proved to Von's that Hispanic consumers typically view shopping as a fun, social event. They want to enjoy food and music while they shop at leisure. In response, Tianguis set up stands to sell a wide variety of Mexican food in outdoor patios. Brightly colored interiors with piñatas hanging from the ceiling and live Mariachi bands add to the festive atmosphere.

Tianguis also gears its merchandise to the Hispanic community. The shelves hold such items as *empanadas*, *chorizos*, and handmade *tortillas*. The produce section carries *frijoles* and at least a dozen types of *chilies*. The store also has services that are unusual in U.S. stores. Customers can use gold and silver exchanges and Western Union booths to wire money home to Mexico.

Staffing plays a key role at Tianguis. So that the customers feel more comfortable shopping, Tianguis hires Spanish-speaking employees. In fact, most of the employees are immigrants themselves, so they can empathize with the customers.

Meeting the special needs of the Hispanic customers has paid off handsomely for Von's.

Sources: Alfredo Corchado, "Hispanic Supermarkets Are Blossoming," *The Wall Street Journal*, January 23, 1989, p. B1; and John Nielsen, "California Store Woos Hispanic Community," *The New York Times*, February 11, 1987, pp. C1, C6.

their sensitivity to price. These are the fundamental bases for market segmentation. Once these differences among segments are understood, each segment must then be described in terms of the demographic, socioeconomic, psychographic or other observable consumer characteristics. This makes the segments *identifiable* and *measurable*. By describing segments in terms of identifiable demographic, socioeconomic, and psychographic characteristics, retailers can easily differentiate the members of the segment from the rest of the population. It also makes it possible for the retailer to measure (at least roughly) the number of people or households that belong to the segment.

Demographic Segmentation

Most retailers describe market segments in terms of consumer demographic and socioeconomic characteristics. They consider these characteristics—age, sex, income, occupation, stage in life cycle, and so on—because:

Market segments are typically described in terms of demographics and socioeconomic characteristics. The Home Depot caters mainly to its suburban homeowner segment.

1. Information on demographic and socioeconomic variables can be easily obtained from secondary sources and they are easy to measure and interpret.
2. These characteristics are highly related to product preference and usage. For example, teenagers and young adults patronize jeans stores and record stores more than any other population group. Similarly, young couples are quite likely to buy furniture and home appliances.

A vast amount of demographic and socioeconomic information is available from secondary sources to help retailers describe market segments. Exhibit 5.3 shows some of the frequently used variables. Consumer markets can be segmented with reference to one or more of these variables. For example, age and income may help describe the market for apparel retailers. A store such as Neiman-Marcus, for example, appeals to high-income, female adults. Compared with them, the typical customer of a Gap store is younger and less affluent. Similarly, household appliance and furniture retailers can best segment their market by stage of life cycle. For example, Conran's targets its furniture and kitchenware outlets toward young people making their first major investment in furniture and home decoration. As another example, consider customers of do-it-yourself (DIY) home supply stores such as Home Depot, Rickels, and Pergament. Their customers are more likely to be home owners than renters and more likely to live in suburban areas.

Exhibit 5.3 *Common Demographic Variables for Segmenting Retail Markets*

Variable	Typical Breakdown
Age	Infants, Toddlers, Teens, Adults under 35 Adults 36–55, Adults over 65
Sex	Male, Female
Family size	1, 2, 3–4, 5, More than 5
Income	Under $15,000, $15,000–$25,000, $25,000–$35,000, $35,000–$50,000, More than $50,000
Occupation	Professional, Managerial, Clerical, Agricultural
Stage in life cycle	Young single, Young married with no children Married with preschool-age children, Married with high school-age children, Married with children living away from home, Retired
Education	Grade school or less, High school, College, Graduate degree
Housing	Own, Rent

ENTREPRENEURIAL EDGE

Selling the Outdoors

Stores that specialize in outdoor active-wear and accessories have often faced a difficult obstacle: how to help customers choose the right products for their next camping or fishing trip. For the seasoned outdoorsperson, there is no problem, but for the novice, it can be a daunting task. Stores are often staffed with untrained sales clerks who are not themselves outdoor enthusiasts, and who can't help the customers make the connection between what is on the shelf and what they need for a specific outdoor activity. However, one store, Turner's Outdoorsman, a small, California chain specializing in hunting and fishing gear, has solved the problem with specialized merchandising and rigorous employee training.

Founder and president Shirley Links is an avid hunting and fishing enthusiast who saved every penny from the time she was in high school in order to open up her own business. When she finally had enough savings to go solo, combining her interests with a retail venture in hunting and fishing accessories was a natural fit. The first store opened in 1971, and Turner's Outdoorsman now has seven stores with annual sales of more than $34 million. More stores are planned in the next five years, and Links sees no sign of her company's slowing down.

Links believes that the key to the success of her stores is the high level of customer service and the wide range of items offered in the very specialized market of hunting and fishing accessories. Links wanted to create stores that were both pleasant and friendly, so that everyone, from the most avid hunter to the novice, would feel welcome. Her employees have a rigorous training program that they must complete before they can work with customers. The program is designed to educate them in how to best serve the customer. The employees also participate in frequent seminars and training sessions, so that they are familiar with the

Lifestyle Segmentation[2]

Although demographic segmentation has traditionally been the most popular basis for describing segments, consumer lifestyle or psychographic characteristics can also be used to develop more detailed pictures of different consumer segments. A **lifestyle** is broadly defined as a mode of living that is identified by how people spend their time (activities), what they consider important in their environment (interests), and what they think of themselves and the world around them (opinions).[3] Retailers typically develop lifestyle or psychographic profiles of consumers through the AIO method. In surveys, they ask consumers to agree or disagree with a list of statements dealing with activities, interests, and opinion (AIOs). Some

products as well as the latest trends. This way they are able to answer all possible customer queries.

Most of Turner's Outdoorsman's employees are outdoors enthusiasts themselves. Links believes that together they create a solid team that sells the equipment not just because it is their job, but because it is what they too like to do in their spare time. In this way, customers are made to feel like part of a big family of hunters and fishermen, and they trust the advice and equipment found at Turner's Outdoorsman. Clearly, Links has tapped into the right vein of customer needs and wants in this industry. Both the store's customer base and sales have increased each year.

Links' mission is to help her customers get out into the outdoors, and everyone on the staff works very hard to meet this end. She does not cater to the one-time outdoor enthusiast, but rather tries to ensure that this type of customer will become a true outdoor

activity fan. When customers come into the store, her staff takes pains not to rush sales, and even discourages sales when the staff thinks the person is over-doing it. There is nothing more frustrating than finding yourself in the woods (or at home or in the office) with all the latest equipment, and no idea of how to make it work. Links will walk her customers through each step, suggesting that they buy one item at a time and see how they like it before coming back for more. Rather than buying all the fishing equipment available, she asks her customers to start with a simple rod and reel and work their way up to tackle boxes, fancy flies, gaiters, and clothing. Clearly, this strategy has worked, as her customers have grown to trust her advice, and they keep coming back for more.

Source: "Retailing's Entrepreneurs of the Year,"*Chain Store Age Executive*, December 1990, pp. 28–38.

common dimensions in AIO surveys appear in Exhibit 5.4. This information, combined with basic demographic variables such as age, sex, income, occupation, and stage of life cycle, provides richer descriptions of consumer segments.

Perhaps the most well-known system of lifestyle segmentation is the **Values and Lifestyles Programs (VALS2)** developed by the Stanford Research Institute. The VALS2 approach introduced by this company is a comprehensive classification of Americans based on their lifestyles. VALS2 groups consumers into eight segments as shown in Exhibit 5.5. These segments are differentiated on two dimensions. The vertical dimension represents the amount of resources (money, education, self-confidence) available to members of the segment. As shown in the Exhibit, *Actualizers* have the most resources, and *Strugglers* have the least. The horizontal dimension

Exhibit 5.4   *Common Dimensions in AIO Surveys*

Activities	Interests	Opinions about
Work	Family	Themselves
Hobbies	Home	Social issues
Social events	Job	Politics
Vacations	Community	Business
Entertainment	Recreation	Economic issues
Club membership	Fashion	Education
Community	Food	Products
Shopping	Media	Future
Sports	Achievement	Culture

Source: Henry Assael, *Consumer Behavior and Marketing Action* (Boston: Kent Publishing, 1987), p. 261.

separates the segments into three groups depending on their self-orientation. Principle-oriented consumers are guided by their own views of the world; status-oriented consumers are guided by the opinions of others; action-oriented consumers are guided by the desire for activity, variety, and risk-taking.

Many retailers focus their marketing strategy on serving consumers with particular lifestyles. The Limited, for example, has implemented this type of strategy with great success. The Limited specializes in selling medium-priced apparel to women between the ages of 16 and 35 with a distinctive lifestyle. The company describes its target consumer as follows:

> The Limited's target market is the 16–35 year old female. She is well educated, affluent, gregarious, fashion oriented and more often than not she is a working woman who lives in or near a major metropolitan area. The Limited is her favorite place to shop because of our fashion and quality.[4]

Geodemographic Segmentation

One method of segmentation that has gained popularity in recent years, especially with direct retailers, is **geodemographic segmentation**. As a fundamental principle, geodemographics assumes that individuals residing within the same neighborhood tend to have similar consumption patterns and that neighborhoods repeat themselves across the country. It seeks to group neighborhoods into similar market segments. A number of firms have developed standardized geo-demographic segments that individual firms can use to define their own target markets. One example of such a segmentation system is the *MicroVision* system developed by Equifax National Decision Systems.[5]

Exhibit 5.5   The VALS 2 Consumer Segments

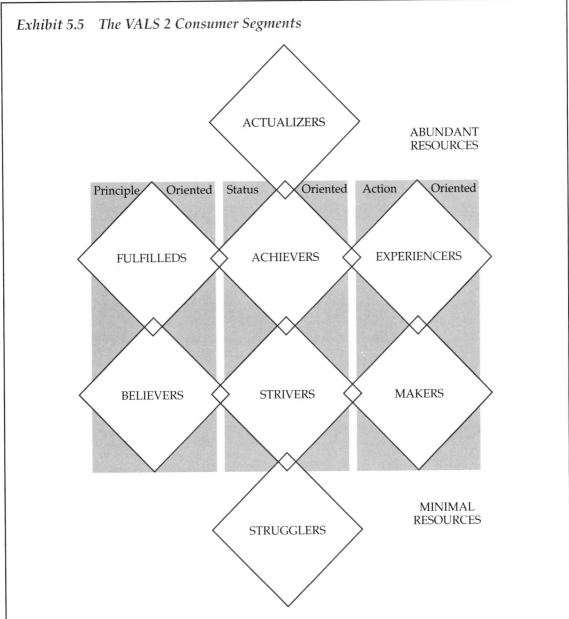

Source: SRI International, Menlo Park, CA as shown in Martha Farnsworth Riche, "Psychographics for the 1990s," *American Demographics*, July 1989, p. 26. Reprinted with permission. © American Demographics, July 1989.

Many retailers direct their marketing toward people with certain lifestyles. The Limited successfully attracts young, urban, working women who are fashion-forward.

MicroVision classifies every neighborhood in the United States into one of 48 segments, based on the demographic and socioeconomic characteristics of the neighborhood and the purchasing patterns of the residents. It defines each market segment so that consumption, purchasing, and financial behavior is homogenous within segments. The MicroVision system assigns each 9-digit zip code in the country to one of the segments. Exhibit 5.6 describes two of these segments.

The first segment, *The Upper Crust*, includes predominantly white, professional households with the highest levels of income and wealth in the country. They reside in single family dwellings in major metropolitan areas. The Upper Crust are big spenders as well as big savers. They tend to own expensive cars, and spend heavily on travel and leisure activities, theaters, restaurants, magazines, and books. They probably eat out often but not at fast-food restaurants.

Another segment is *Successful Singles*. Demographically, they are predominantly between 25 and 34 years of age. They are well educated and primarily employed as managers and professionals. They live in condominiums and multi-family apart-

Exhibit 5.6   Description of Two MicroVision *Segments*

Upper Crust (MicroVision Group 1)

Metropolitan Families, Very High Income and Education, Managers/Professionals; Very High Installment Activity

UPPER CRUST is a middle-aged segment (ages 45 to 54), predominantly white, and almost half have college and/or graduate degrees. They primarily work in the managerial and professional fields, with the highest income in the nation. The majority of these families, with teenagers, own homes built in the 60s and early 70s. Their financial activity is high, with installment account balances much higher than the national average. City dwellers, they watch morning news programs, read *The Wall Street Journal,* attend live theater, and travel to foreign lands. Aerobics and jogging keep them fit and trim.

Successful Singles (MicroVision Group 9)

Young, Single Renters, Older Housing, Ethnic Mix, High Education, Medium Income, Managers/Professionals; Very High Bankcard Accounts, Very High Installment Activity, Very Low Retail Activity

This is yet another young segment (ages 25 to 34). Well-educated, these households have an ethnic mix. It represents the largest percentage of East Europeans and a significant Asian population. This segment has the most college and/or graduate degrees, and is primarily employed in managerial and professional specialty occupations, with a medium-income level. Most of this young single segment rents an apartment in urban multi-unit complexes (10-plus units) which were built before 1939. SUCCESSFUL SINGLES have more bankcards than any other MicroVision segment, but their balances are par with the nation. These folks watch prime time soap operas and listen to rock music. They stay active with aerobic classes and tennis. They enjoy live theater and foreign excursions. They consult a financial planner and keep in touch reading *The Wall Street Journal.*

Source: Reprinted with permission from Equifax National Decision Systems, a leading provider of customer segmentation systems, San Diego, CA.

ment complexes. Compared to other segments, they make more foreign trips and enjoy live theater and sports. They buy heavily through direct mail.

The use of geodemographics has increased significantly in recent years due to the availability of geographical databases that combine demographic and socioeconomic information from the Census of Population with purchase pattern and lifestyle information from syndicated panels. The combination of information from different sources into a single database creates considerable synergy and rich descriptions of potential consumer segments. The use of geodemographics for selecting locations for retail stores and for targeting direct mail campaigns are discussed in more detail in Chapters 8 and 16, respectively.

SELECTING THE TARGET MARKET

Once the retailer has analyzed potential customers and identified a number of viable segments, it can choose the target market it wishes to serve. To accomplish this, the retailer must evaluate each segment in terms of two criteria:

1. The market potential of the segment.
2. The competitive environment of the segment.

Based on these criteria, the retailer can judge the desirability of targeting a particular segment.

Market Potential

A viable target market must generate a volume of sales and profits adequate to make the venture economically feasible. The segment's **market potential** is affected by the size of the segment and the expected growth rate.

Size   The number and purchasing power of customers in a segment determine the level of sales the retailer can generate from that segment. This factor, called market size, is important in determining whether the segment is worth pursuing. The retailer usually estimates the size of the segment from secondary data sources.

As an example, consider the decision facing Emily Swain, a young entrepreneur planning to open a pizzeria in a town of about 15,000 people. No restaurant in town currently serves pizza, although it does have a number of coffee shops and diners and a Dairy Queen. Based on her experience and talks with pizza restaurant owners in other towns, Ms. Swain believes that single people in the 15 to 35-year-old age group and families with young children would be ideal targets for her restaurants. To measure the size of these targets Ms. Swain needs to find the number of single people in town between the ages of 15 and 35 and the number of families with young children. This information is readily available from the *Census of Population* published by the Department of Commerce, copies of which can be found in many libraries. The *census* provides detailed information about the number of people residing in a town and the age and sex breakdown of the population.

The census is an example of a **secondary data** source, since the information in it is not collected especially for Ms. Swain, but for general use. The biggest advantage of the census is that the information is easily available for free in many libraries. The town or county planning department will also probably have access to the census for the local area. Exhibit 5.7 lists a number of other publications that can also be useful in measuring market size.

Sometimes needed information cannot be obtained from secondary sources. For example, Ms. Swain might not find information on pizza-eating habits of people in her town from secondary sources; she will have to collect that information her-

Exhibit 5.7   Secondary Sources of Consumer Information

Sales and Marketing Management Survey of Buying Power gives data for cities, counties, metropolitan areas, states, and total United States on population, number of households, per capita income, retail sales in total and nine categories, plus indices of buying power and sales activities.

Editor and Publisher Marketing Guide profiles 1,500 newspaper markets in terms of variety of standard measures (population, housing, transportation, employment) as well as information on principal industries, housing, retail outlets, and shopping days.

A Guide to Consumer Markets contains information on population, prices, employment, on statewide and larger regional unit bases. Information on ownership of durables and spending by product categories are also given.

Rand McNally Commercial Atlas and Marketing Guide contains population figures plus numerous other statistics on each county in the United States.

County Business Reports summarize information on business activities in different areas including monthly reports on retail sales by product category.

Source: Based on Donald R. Lehman, *Market Research and Analysis* (Homewood, Illinois: Richard D. Irwin, 1989), pp. 83–85.

self. Such **primary data** can be obtained either through direct observations of people's behavior or by conducting a survey administered through personal interviews, by mail or over the telephone.

Expected Growth   A small segment may still be attractive if its size is expected to increase in the future. Growing segments are typically better than stagnant ones. For example, a number of retailers entered the eye-care business in the 1980s to take advantage of the growing number of people reaching 40: such people typically need some form of eye care. As the population ages, the size of the eye-care market will continue to grow. For another example, consider The Body Shop. This chain of skin care and personal grooming products stores has grown rapidly by targeting its stores toward the increasing number of consumers who want personal care products made only of natural ingredients.

The Competitive Environment

To systematically evaluate the attractiveness of each segment, the retailer must gather information on the levels of competition within them. Information on competition can be summarized in a **competitive environment matrix** like the one in Exhibit 5.8. The matrix shows the active competitors for each segment of the women's clothing market in a small town. The town has long been the home to a Sears and a K mart. Two years ago, a regional off-price clothing chain called Dress

Exhibit 5.8   *Competitive Inventory Matrix*

	Sears	K mart	Sophie's	Dress Barn	Marie's Fashion	The Clothing Store
Fashion Enthusiasts			X			
Style-Seekers			X		X	
Classics	X		X			
Timids	X	X		X		X
Uninvolveds	X	X		X		X

Barn also opened an outlet in town. In addition, there are a number of local stores that sell women's clothes. Three of the largest local stores are shown in the matrix. As is evident from the matrix, there is a high level of competition for the more price-sensitive segments of the market. But only two stores currently target fashion-enthusiasts and style-seekers. Note, however, that the lack of competition in the fashion-oriented segments does not necessarily make it attractive to a new entrant. The potential of this segment may not be very high in this town. On the other hand, the presence of many competitors, including two national chain stores, reduces the attraction of price-sensitive segments to a new entrant. In this town, the middle market may represent the best opportunity for a new entrant.

CREATING SUSTAINABLE DIFFERENTIAL ADVANTAGE

Having selected a target market, the retailer must now choose how it will compete in the marketplace. The goal must be to create a sustainable competitive advantage over other stores catering to the same target market. The retailer must give the members of its target market a reason to choose its store over those of its competitors. In other words, the store must be able to differentiate itself from competing stores. Recall from the discussion in Chapter 2 that the various ways stores differentiate themselves can be grouped into five main categories: price, merchandise, location, customer service, and store atmosphere. Some examples of how stores have used these elements to differentiate are discussed below.

Sources of Differential Advantage

Some stores create differential advantage by pricing their merchandise lower than their competitors. Electronic discount stores such as The Wiz, 47th Street Photo, and J & R Music World are some examples of stores that follow this strategy. These stores sell nationally advertised brands of electronic appliances such as televisions, VCRs, personal computers, camcorders, and cameras. Because these branded appliances are widely available, customers seek the store with the lowest price. To create a differential advantage the stores try to keep their prices as low as possible and promote their low price image through television and newspaper advertisements. The Wiz's advertising slogan, "Nobody beats the Wiz," typifies this approach.

Off-price apparel retailers also follow price differentiation strategies. Off-price stores such as Hit or Miss, T.J. Maxx, Marshall's, NBO, and Syms offer branded (often designer) merchandise at prices 30 or 40 percent below what department stores charge. The price attracts customers who want to buy fashionable clothing but do not wish to pay the high price charged by department stores. To keep their prices low, the stores lower operating costs by locating at freestanding sites along major suburban traffic arteries. The rents at these sites are considerably lower than at the mall and downtown locations of department stores. They also advertise less than department stores and, like the electronic stores, have spartan store interiors. Another way these stores reduce their costs is opportunistic buying of end-of-season or excess merchandise.

T.J. Maxx draws customers interested in fashionable clothing by offering prices 30 to 40 percent below department store prices.

The uniqueness of a store's merchandise is another potential source of differentiation. Much of the aura surrounding stores such as Neiman-Marcus, Bloomingdale's and Saks Fifth Avenue comes from their unique, hard-to-find-elsewhere, merchandise. Their buyers travel the world to locate sources of new and innovative merchandise that appeals to their target markets. Neiman-Marcus's annual *his-and-her gift* items and Bloomingdale's periodic country fairs support their overall philosophies of creating an atmosphere of excitement through innovative merchandising that differentiates them from other stores.

High levels of customer service can also provide differentiate advantage. For example, Nordstrom, the well-known apparel retailer, is reputed for its high level of service. Despite its relatively high prices and its few sales or markdowns, Nordstrom maintains a competitive advantage because its competitors have failed to match this level of service. This strategy has paid-off well, since Nordstrom has one of the highest levels of sales per square foot in the apparel business.

Even supermarkets can successfully implement service-oriented strategies, although most tend to compete on low price. Consider, for example, Stew Leonard's in Norwalk, Connecticut, Draeger's in California, Byerly's in Minnesota, and Lofino's in Dayton, Ohio. These stores have differentiated themselves from other supermarkets by resisting the industry trend towards reduced service. Not only do they offer such traditional services as free bagging and check cashing, but they also accept credit cards, maintain in-store home economists, and offer free cooking classes. Such services differentiate them from the rest of the industry, as do their high margins compared with typical supermarkets.

Sustaining Differential Advantage

For long-term success firms must be able to sustain their differential advantage. A competitive advantage is sustainable only if the source of the advantage is strongly secured by the firm's operations. Consider, for example, a store competing on the basis of low price. It will be impossible for the store to maintain its low prices unless its cost of operation is also low. To sustain its low price advantage, the store must also be able to develop low-cost sources of merchandise, have an efficient distribution and logistics system and have low overheads. Without them a low-price strategy will become unprofitable and cannot be sustained. A few years ago, Sears adopted an "Everyday Low Price" strategy to become more price competitive with K mart and Wal-Mart. Many observers feel, however, that Sears has been hard pressed to sustain this strategy because its operating cost (as a percentage of sales) is higher than that of its competitors. Unless Sears is able to reduce its operating costs significantly, the low price strategy is unlikely to be profitable.

A strong corporate culture and management philosophy is also necessary to sustain competitive advantage. As noted earlier, Nordstrom has built a reputation for customer service that many of its competitors have tried but failed to duplicate. Nordstrom is able to sustain its high-quality service because customer service is a strong and integral part of its corporate philosophy and the firm's top management is fully committed to it. They hire well-qualified salespeople and provide them with incentives for improving service. Another example is McDonald's. McDonald's continued leadership in the fast-food business is not a matter of accident. It has sustained this leadership by its commitment to training and by its support for its franchise operators.

RETAIL MIX PLANNING

No single marketing strategy suits all retailers. Each store has to formulate its own strategy and implement it by selecting the correct **retail mix** elements to achieve the desired differential advantage. This is an important task since the store's combination of retail mix elements will determine its overall image. The store's location, the merchandise it carries, the prices it charges, its shopping atmosphere, the services it provides, the knowledge and helpfulness of the salespeople, and the way in which it advertises and promotes the merchandise all influence how the target market perceives the store. The retail mix is the vehicle through which a store's marketing strategy is implemented. We will discuss various issues in planning these retail mix elements in detail in later chapters. However, it is important now to draw attention to three principles that must guide all retail mix planning:

1. The retail mix must be consistent with the expectations of the target customers.
2. The elements of the retail mix must be consistent with each other to create synergy.
3. A store's retail mix must be responsive to competitive strategy.

Consistency with Customer Expectations

The first principle states that all retail mix elements must be consistent with the expectations of the store's target market. This consistency of retail mix with target market expectations is one of the main reasons for the success of Wal-Mart. The marketing policies of this discount chain meet the needs of and expectations of middle-income customers in small towns and rural areas. In its location selection, for example, Wal-Mart has concentrated on sites in rural areas and small-town markets and has mostly avoided the metropolitan areas typically targeted by its main competitors like Target and K mart. Wal-Mart stresses basic merchandise in a simple setting. The location, size, decor, and merchandising policies of Wal-Mart stores are all consistent with the expectations of its target market. This successful strategy has produced one of the highest levels of profitability per square foot among discount store operators.

At the other end of the spectrum from Wal-Mart is Bijan's, a fancy men's clothing store, located in such exclusive shopping areas as Rodeo Drive in Beverly Hills and Manhattan's Upper East Side. Customers enter the stores by appointment only after being screened by white-uniformed doormen. Decorated with authentic Persian rugs, Austrian chandeliers, and antique armor, the stores sell $100 silk ties, $400 shoes, and leather jackets costing more than $3,000. The owner claims that the quality of the merchandise justifies these prices. Silk for the shirt is purchased in China, dyed in Milan, and stitched in Florence. On a typical day the store serves only six or seven customers, but each is likely to spend several thousand dollars.[6]

Target markets, of course, vary from store to store. High income Beverly Hills residents may go to Bijan's and the other fancy stores on Rodeo Drive, while small-town residents shop at Wal-Mart and Ben Franklin. Young adults and teenagers shop at The Gap and The Limited for their clothes, but older customers go to department stores. Bargain hunting shoppers patronize Filene's Basement and off-price stores, and typical middle-American consumers shop at Sears or K mart. Whatever the characteristics of its target market, no store can compete effectively without keeping all policies consistent with the expectations of its target customers.

Synergy among All Retail Mix Elements

The second principle seeks to create synergy by making each component of the retail mix consistent with the others. The store's merchandise, atmosphere, customer service, advertising, and price must evoke the same feeling in the customer. It would be inconsistent for Bijan's, for example, to promote a storewide reduction sale. The comparison of the policies of Toys R Us and F.A.O. Schwarz described at the beginning of the chapter illustrates the importance of internal consistency. Each store keeps its location, merchandise, store design, service, and pricing policies consistent with each other and in line with the expectations of the target market.

Responding to Competitors' Actions

The actions of competitors can never be ignored in planning the retail mix. Retailers must identify their competitors and monitor their marketing strategies to anticipate the effects of competitive actions on their own policies. A table like the one shown in Exhibit 5.9 helps track competitors' offerings. The amount of detail provided in the table will vary from one market to another depending on the competitive environment. Exhibit 5.10, for example, shows detailed price information that one department store gathered for its men's shirt department. The store's managers use this information to decide their own pricing policy and how to divide the inventory among the different price points.

Exhibit 5.9 Tracking Competing Supermarkets' Marketing Programs

	Store A	Store B	Store C
Target market	Families	Ethnic groups	Young professionals
Merchandise	Emphasis on house brands; on-premise deli	Salad bar	Best meat and produce; no generics
Price	Below average; limited specials	Weekly specials on 500 items	Higher than average
Location	Busy street; inadequate parking	Shopping cluster; easy parking	Next to shopping cluster
Convenience	Open 7 a.m.–10 p.m., 7 days	Open 7 a.m.–11 p.m., 7 days	Open 24 hours
Advertising	Fliers every Wednesday	Every Wednesday and Sunday	Every Wednesday; some television
Other remarks		Needs to expand	

STORE IMAGE

Human behavior, it is said, is not directed by raw knowledge and information, but is a product of the images that people perceive.[7] Retail behavior is no exception. Each store evokes an image in the minds of consumers. These **store images**— how consumers perceive stores—significantly influence shopping behavior since

---

Exhibit 5.10 Competitive Price Monitoring by a Department Store

	Distribution of Stock by Price Range (percentages)					
	Under $10	$10–$15	$15–$20	$20–$25	$25–$30	Over $30
Store A	0	15	30	30	15	10
Store B	10	25	40	25	0	0
Store C	0	10	50	40	0	0
Store D	20	30	35	10	5	0
Store E	0	10	10	40	25	15

they determine to a large extent a consumer's predisposition toward various stores.

A store's image results from its marketing strategy. The type of customer a store attracts, the way it differentiates itself, as well as the store's location, merchandise, atmosphere, price, advertising, and service, all influence its image. Every retailer must periodically monitor its image, for only in this way can it know how it is positioned relative to competitors in the consumers' minds. For example, a store that wants to differentiate itself on the basis of high-quality service must ascertain how the consumers rate its service relative to the competition to be sure that its image is consistent with its strategy. Since the image is a representation of the store in the consumers' minds, systematic research is necessary to measure store image. Exhibit 5.11 is an example of a **perceptual map**, which is one of the common ways in which store images are represented.

The perceptual map represents consumer perceptions of similarities among stores. The dimensions of the map represent the characteristics that the consumers use to evaluate the store. In the map shown in Exhibit 5.11, which is based on

Exhibit 5.11   *Perceptual Map of Women's Clothing Stores*

surveys of young-adult women residing in the New York metropolitan area, the horizontal dimension represents the consumer evaluation of the merchandise, while the vertical dimension represents perceptions of value. The position of a store on these two dimensions represents the store's image to this group of consumers. Saks Fifth Avenue, for example, has an image of carrying highly fashion-forward clothing but is not perceived to offer good value for money. The image of Urban Outfitters is distinctly different: it's considered to be very trendy and casual and to offer moderate value for the money. Century 21, a popular off-price clothing store, on the other hand, is viewed as offering good value for moderately fashionable clothing.

The closer together the positions of two stores on the map, the greater their similarity in the consumers' minds. Thus, to this group of consumers, the images of Bergdorf Goodman and Saks Fifth Avenue are very similar. The images of both of these stores, however, are distinctly different from The Limited both in terms of fashion and value. On the other hand, Sears and Century 21 are considered to be similar in fashion but very different in value. Since stores located close together on the perceptual map have greater perceived similarity, they are also likely to have greater competitive rivalry. Thus the two prestige stores (Bergdorf Goodman and Saks Fifth Avenue) compete much more with each other than they do with Sears or The Gap. Because it indicates likely level of competition among stores, the perceptual map provides a useful pictorial summary of the competitive structure of the market.

The appendix to this chapter provides more detail about perceptual mapping, also called multidimensional scaling (MDS) and other market research techniques used to measure store images.

Summary

1. Each store must specify in a well-formulated marketing strategy how it will compete in the marketplace and attract customers to its outlets.
   Development of the marketing strategy takes place in five major steps: (a) customer analysis to identify potential market segments, (b) selecting the target market, (c) identifying how the firm will create a sustainable differential advantage in the marketplace, (d) planning retail mix elements, and (e) assessing store image.
2. Consumers differ in terms of their tastes, preferences, and the way they perceive value from the shopping experience. These differences create the potential for dividing the market into several relatively homogenous customer groups. The total market can thus be viewed as comprising a number of smaller market segments.
3. Retailers commonly describe segments based on consumer demographic, socioeconomic, and lifestyle characteristics. Consumption patterns and shopping behavior have been found to be strongly related to these factors.
4. Once it has identified segments, the retailers must choose one or more of them as its target market. To select the target market, each segment's market potential and

competition level must be analyzed. Market grids are often used to summarize this information and identify potential market opportunities.

5. With the target market selected, the retailer must choose how it will compete in the marketplace. It must create a sustainable differential advantage over stores catering to the same target market.

6. To differentiate, the retailer must set up a retail mix of location, merchandise, shopping atmosphere, price, advertising, customer service, personal selling, and sales promotion. The elements of the retail mix must be consistent with (a) customer expectations, (b) competitors' actions, and (c) each other.

7. A store's image is a perception of it in the shoppers' minds. The image is based partly on the functional qualities of the store and partly on psychological attributes. Free response, semantic differential scales, and multidimensional scaling are three common methods for measuring image.

Key Concepts

Marketing strategy	Market potential
Tactics	Secondary data
Segmentation	Primary data
Lifestyle	Competitive inventory matrix
Values and Lifestyles Programs (VALS)	Retail mix
Geodemographic segmentation	Store image
Target market	Perceptual maps

Discussion Questions

1. What is meant by the terms *market segment* and *target market*?

2. What are some of the bases for segmenting retail markets? How are retail market segments typically described?

3. How would you describe the target markets for Toys R Us and F.A.O. Schwarz?

4. What is the market opportunity grid? How does the grid help in selecting target markets?

5. Based on your observations, create a market opportunity grid for women's apparel market in your town (if necessary, select a sample of the stores in your town).

6. Why is it important for stores to have a sustainable differential advantage? Select three local stores and describe how they have created differential advantage over their competitors.

7. What are the elements of the retail mix? Explain the principles of consistency that must guide all retail mix planning.

8. Explain the term *store image* and discuss, with examples, the factors that influence store image.

9. Select two stores in your town that sell similar merchandise (for example, two supermarkets, two clothing stores, two bookstores, and so on). Based on your observations, discuss the elements of their marketing strategy. This should contain descriptions of their target markets, their respective differential advantages, the store images, and the elements of the retail mix.

Notes

1. Robert E. Stevens and Philip K. Sherwood, *Market Opportunity Analysis* (Lexington, MA: Lexington Books, 1987), p. 5.
2. This section is based on Martha Farnsworth Riche, "Psychographics for the 1990s," *American Demographics* (July 1989), pp. 25–31 and Chapter 7 of Henry Assael, *Consumer Behavior and Marketing Action* (Boston: PWS-KENT Publishing 1992).
3. Henry Assael, *Consumer Behavior and Marketing Action* (Boston: PWS-KENT Publishing 1992), p. 294.
4. Quoted in Roger D. Blackwell and W. Wayne Talarzyk, "Lifestyle Retailing: Competitive Strategies of the 1980s," *Journal of Retailing* 59 (Winter 1983), pp. 7–28.
5. MicroVision is the registered trademark of National Decision Systems. ACORN and PRIZM are two other popular geodemographic systems.
6. Hal Lancaster, "Trendy Men's Store Finds Locking Door Is a Key to Success," *The Wall Street Journal*, January 22, 1988, p. 1.
7. Kenneth E. Boulding, *The Image* (Ann Arbor: University of Michigan Press, 1956), p. 6.
8. Pierre Martineau, "The Personality of a Retail Store," *Harvard Business Review* 36 (January–February 1958), p. 47.

Appendix 5A

Market Research for Measuring Store Image

A store's image is a perception held in the shopper's mind, determined partly by the functional qualities of the store and partly by the aura of psychological attributes.[8] Functional qualities are such observable characteristics as merchandise selection, price, location, and credit policies. In addition to these functional qualities, the store's image is also affected by the emotional feelings evoked in shoppers by such intangible, psychological factors as the warmth and friendliness of salespeople or feelings of excitement and interest evoked by the store's ambience. Moreover, an image is more than the sum of its parts. It represents interactions among the functional characteristics and the shoppers' emotions. As one author aptly put it: "It is less like a photograph than like a highly interpretive portrait."[1]

COMPONENTS OF IMAGE

It is somewhat difficult to make a comprehensive list of all factors that influence image, since every aspect of a store will influence it to some extent. The factors also vary from one store to another, depending on the type of operation. Previous research on store image does, however, suggest a general classification of relevant store characteristics. Such a list would include the following categories:

1. Merchandise
2. Price
3. Types of services offered
4. Physical characteristics of stores
5. Convenience
6. Types of advertising and promotion
7. Store ambience
8. Characteristics of shoppers
9. Characteristics of store personnel

Items 1 through 5 represent tangible factors. Items 6 and 7 can be grouped together since they evoke emotional responses from the consumers. The style and content of a store's advertising create images in the minds of potential shoppers. Similarly, the layout, display, decor, and other aspects of a store's ambience also create images. Items 8 and 9 fall into a third group. The store's clientele, for example, may create an image that "The best people shop there."[2] The store's sales personnel can also create a negative or a positive image.

Three methods are commonly used to measure a store's image: (1) free response, (2) semantic differential scales, and (3) multidimensional scaling. Although the three methods are quite different, they all share two common features. First, all involve eliciting information from actual or potential shoppers. Second, each measures a store's image relative to those of its competitors.[3]

FREE RESPONSE METHOD

A very simple approach to evaluating a store's image is to ask a group of shoppers directly their opinions about different stores. This can be done in a focus group interview, in which a small group of consumers (typically between 10 and 15) are invited to discuss their shopping experiences. A moderator leads the discussion to foster interaction among the participants and gauge the strengths of their feelings.

In an alternative free-response method, one surveys a number of consumers about what they liked or disliked about shopping at different stores. The results from one such survey appear in Exhibit 5A.1 The survey asked respondents to list what they liked most and least about two stores. Store A is a department store and

Exhibit 5A.1   Customer Comments from a Free Response Interview

Liked Most	Store A	Store B
Sales personnel		
courteous/helpful/friendly	51	53
Merchandise suitability		
good selection	33	40
good quality products	11	13
Post-transaction satisfaction		
money-back guarantee/reputable store	37	1
good service after purchase	4	1
Store atmosphere		
good layout	6	10
good displays	5	11
pleasant surroundings	11	7
Value for price		
good bargain	1	13
Store services		
air conditioned/packing/delivery/etc.	9	5
Location		
good location	7	0
Nothing	33	38
No answer/unclassifiable	1	2
	209	194
Liked Least		
Sales personnel		
hard to get a clerk	31	2
unhelpful/unfriendly/discourteous	12	2
pushy salespeople	1	29
Merchandise suitability		
not enough stock/variety	9	4
low-quality products	3	4
Post-transaction satisfaction		
poor service after payment	3	5
bad experience	7	5
Store atmosphere		
crowded/too big/etc.	13	3
poor layout	5	1
Value for price		
prices too high	19	15
Store services		
poor parking/slow elevators/etc.	14	4
Location		
poor location	—	6
Advertising		
can't believe their ads/dishonest	3	9
Nothing	84	104
Unclassifiable	5	1
	209	194

Source: G. H. G. McDougal and J. N. Fry, "Combining Two Methods of Image Measurement," *Journal of Retailing* 50 (Winter 1974), pp. 56–57.

Store B a promotion-oriented specialty store. The responses indicate that the sales-people and the merchandise elicited the most reactions, along with the department store's money-back guarantee.

The free-response method brings a major advantage in that it can uncover the critical factors covering a store's image. For example, the department store's money-back guarantee is an important component of its image. This is indicated by the large number of responses it elicited. Free-response questions capture customers' feelings very closely and make it easy for the retailer to take action. In this case both stores need to correct the negative assessments of their sales-people.

One disadvantage of the free-response method is that many consumers tend to say that they neither liked nor disliked anything about the store. Note that more than 100 respondents said that they disliked nothing about Store B and 84 said the same of Store A. Although some people may have genuinely felt that the stores had nothing wrong, it is more than likely that they simply did not want to answer the question.

SEMANTIC DIFFERENTIAL SCALE

The semantic differential scale asks consumers to choose between bipolar adjectives (opposites) describing a store. In contrast to the free-response method, in this method the researcher provides the respondent with a set of characteristics or dimensions on which to evaluate the store. Exhibit 5A.2 gives an example of a semantic differential scale for rating store image on six characteristics. For example, a store would receive a rating of one of seven positions from unpleasant to pleasant depending on the consumer's belief about its atmosphere. The results of the semantic differential scale are typically illustrated on graphs like the one shown in Exhibit 5A.2.

Semantic differential scales have several advantages. They are easy to administer, the respondents have to spend very little time in answering the questions, and the results can be easily summarized with graphs. There are, however, two major disadvantages. First, the number of dimensions on which information is to be collected must be limited to keep the data collection manageable. The extremely limited set of scales shown in Exhibit 5A.2 has only six categories. This weakness can be partly overcome by breaking down each of the categories into subcomponents. Exhibit 5A.3, for example, shows how different semantic scales can reach more deeply into the factors influencing consumer perceptions of price and service personnel. However, the need for detail must be judiciously balanced against the ease of data collection and analysis.

The second, and perhaps the most important, disadvantage of using semantic differential scales is that they force people to respond to certain predefined char-

Exhibit 5A.2 Semantic Differential Scale

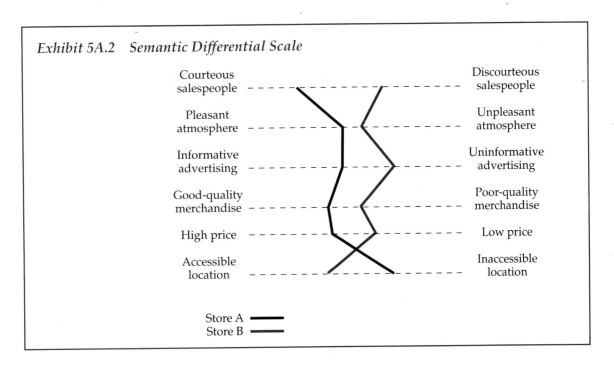

Courteous salespeople	Discourteous salespeople
Pleasant atmosphere	Unpleasant atmosphere
Informative advertising	Uninformative advertising
Good-quality merchandise	Poor-quality merchandise
High price	Low price
Accessible location	Inaccessible location

Store A ▬▬▬
Store B ▬▬▬

Exhibit 5A.3 Detailed Feedback on Consumer Perceptions of Price and Store Personnel

Prices

Low compared to other stores	High compared to other stores
Low values for money spent	High values for money spent
Large number of items specially priced	Small number of items specially priced

Personnel

Courteous	Discourteous
Cold	Friendly
Unhelpful	Helpful
Adequate number	Inadequate number

acteristics about the store. Shoppers cannot give their opinion on characteristics not included in the survey. Thus, responses to semantic differential scales may not give a complete picture of the shoppers' perceptions of retail offerings.

MULTIDIMENSIONAL SCALING (MDS)

The third approach to studying store images is multidimensional scaling. This is the method used to create the perceptual map shown earlier in Exhibit 5.11. Recall that the perceptual map presents a pictorial representation of the images of stores based on the *perceived* similarity among stores.

To measure the perceived similarity among stores, each store shown in Exhibit 5.11 was paired with each of the remaining seven stores to form 28 pairs. Consumers then rated on a seven point scale how similar the stores were to each other. Based on these responses each pair was ranked according to the perceived similarity of the two stores. This rank order information was then analyzed by a multidimensional-scaling computer program, which determined the relative position of each store on the perceptual map. This created a map on which the distance between each pair of stores is as close as possible to the rank order of similarities given by consumers.

MDS has a major advantage in that the information needed from consumers is straightforward. They simply have to judge the similarity between pairs of stores. Unlike the semantic differential scale, one need not list characteristics on which to rate the stores. Instead, consumers base their responses on their overall images of the stores. For a second advantage, the perceptual map provides a nice pictorial summary of the results.

MDS has disadvantages, too, though. For one, the dimensions of perceptual maps may be difficult to interpret. The dimensions will change from one study to another, and the researcher must interpret what they mean. Also, perceptual maps can have more than two dimensions. The number of dimensions is related to the number of major factors consumers use to judge similarities between stores. Exhibit 5A.4 illustrates a perceptual map with three dimensions. In some cases, however, more than three dimensions are required to represent consumer judgments adequately, making it impossible to represent the results on a single map.

Notes

1. Alfred R. Oxenfeldt, "Developing a Favorable Price Quality Image," *Journal of Retailing* 50 (Winter 1974), p. 8.
2. Ibid.
3. For some other related methods see: Arun Jain and Michael Etgar, "Measuring Store Image Through Multidimensional Scaling of Free Response Data," *Journal of Retailing*, 52 (Winter 1976), pp. 61–70. Linda Golden, Gerald Albaum, and Mary Zimmer, "The Numerical Comparative Scale: An Economical Format for Retail Image Measurement," *Journal of Retailing* 50 (Winter 1987), pp. 393–410. Mary Zimmer and Linda Golden, "Impressions of Retail Stores: A Content Analysis of Retail Images," *Journal of Retailing* 64 (Fall 1988), pp. 265–93. Jordan J. Louviere and Richard D. Johnson, "Using Conjoint Analysis to Measure Retail Image," in A. Ghosh and C. A. Ingene (Ed.), *Spatial Analysis in Marketing: Theory, Methods and Applications* (Greenwich, CT: Jai Press 1991).

Exhibit 5A.4 *Three-Dimensional Perceptual Map*

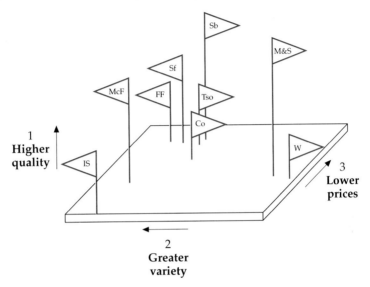

Source: Peter Doyle and Ian Fenwick, "How Store Image Affects Shopping Habit in Grocery Chains," *Journal of Retailing*, Vol. 50 (Winter 1974), pp. 39–52. Reprinted with permission.

CHAPTER 6
Managing Growth and Diversification

From Five-and-Dime to Specialty Chains: The Story of Woolworth's Diversification

In 1982, Woolworth began a major restructuring of its business. Long known to generations of shoppers as a leading five-and-dime store chain, Woolworth began to make a name for itself as a diversified, international specialty retailer. The company closed its floundering Woolco chain of discount stores in the United States, started a long process of revitalizing existing stores, and began the search for specialty stores and formats into which the company could diversify. Why the big changes? Woolco had become a huge drain on profits, and management wanted to focus attention on new areas of growth. Malls were becoming America's way of shopping, and Woolworth's freestanding variety, clothing, and shoe stores, situated in downtown shopping areas were begin threatened as shopping patterns changed.

The chairman and CEO of the company, Harold Sells, took a long, hard look at the different stores Woolworth then owned, including Kinney Shoes and Richman (a chain of men's clothing stores), as well as the product lines of the core variety stores, to decide into which areas Woolworth would expand. Sells believed that Woolworth had the expertise in specialty retailing because of their successes with Kinney and Richman through the 1960s and 1970s. Furthermore, the company was organized into divisions according to store product lines, which meant that each management team was focused on their one area of specialty within the retailing industry. The divisions included Kinney U.S.—which oversaw all of Woolworth's specialty stores—and general merchandising—which oversaw the Woolworth and Woolco variety stores. Sells believed that getting his stores into malls would be critical for their success, and so the majority of the Woolworth specialty stores are now mall retailers. Some have freestanding stores in busy urban areas, but all have a presence in shopping malls across the United States. Building from each area of expertise and specialty, Sells shaped Woolworth into a specialty retailing giant, poised to face the economic challenges of the 1990s and beyond.

One of the most successful chains that Woolworth used for its specialty expansion was Foot Locker, the athletic footwear and apparel chain. Foot Locker is currently in 85 percent of U.S. malls, and has opened store extensions such as Lady Foot Locker and Kids Foot Locker. Woolworth built on its knowledge of the footwear industry to open this chain, and now, building on their success and knowledge of running athletic footwear chains, Woolworth has revitalized overseas operations with versions of Foot Locker, most notably in Germany. Woolworth is also

LEARNING OBJECTIVES

After studying this chapter, the reader will be able to:
- *Know the key steps in developing a corporate strategy for growth.*
- *Understand how a corporation's missions, goals, and objectives affect its strategy.*
- *Know how retailers can increase the sales of their existing stores.*
- *Recognize the role of diversification and geographical expansion in achieving growth.*
- *Know the criteria used to screen potential growth opportunities.*
- *Understand the importance of monitoring the business portfolio.*

Woolworth's Moderna/Schuh store in Walsvode, Germany.

poised for expansion throughout Europe with plans for about 1,000 Foot Lockers by the year 2000 in Western Europe. Woolworth already operates 1,500 Foot Lockers in the United States and Canada, and plans for expansion continue.

Other expansions came from formats within the variety stores. Woolworth currently operates more than 400 Afterthoughts stores, which sell women's costume jewelry. The category had been sold in their Woolworth variety stores for over a century,

and management understood what consumers wanted. It was simply a matter of taking the division out of the variety stores and opening it in its own 1,000 square-foot outlet. Another example is the company's The Best of Times chain of stores selling watches, clocks, and timepieces. Again, this had been a successful department in the variety stores for decades, and Woolworth had the expertise to turn the format into stores of their own. Other examples include The Party Shop, which sells party goods, stationery, and greeting cards, and Northern Reflections, a chain of women's outdoor sportswear. All of these stores are overseen by a newly created division, Woolworth U.S., as each sprang from a department of the traditional variety stores.

Two areas where the company is retrenching rather than expanding are in the Woolworth stores and in Kinney Shoes stores. Many of the original stores are being closed, as their downtown locations become less and less profitable. Woolworth stores are being replaced by Woolworth Express, which are general merchandise convenience stores and a streamlined version of their large variety stores. The Express stores sell such high volume merchandise as health and beauty aids, and have been able to earn roughly double the sales per square foot of the old stores. The number of Kinney Shoes stores has also been reduced, from over 1,600 in

183

1982 to under 1,300 in 1990, as stores like their Kids Foot Locker and Footquarters, a family shoe store chain, replace them, and draw in new customers in their new mall locations.

For its expansion, Woolworth relied mostly on internal funds rather than acquiring large amounts of additional debt. Sells advocates that companies that are highly leveraged cannot afford to expand, especially in the 1990s, or even to remodel and revitalize existing stores. Another factor contributing to Woolworth's success is its strong presence in Europe. More than 40 percent of the company's revenues now come from outside the United States, giving the company a buffer against recession in any of the countries where it operates. Times were especially tough in 1990, when earnings fell a whopping 55 percent, but Woolworth was sheltered by its diversity: Foot Locker's sales quadrupled to $1.5 billion in that year, and the company's stars in Germany (Foot Locker, the variety store, and the Moderna/ Der Schuh family shoe stores) continued to reap profits. Woolworth can take the bumps, and it is more than ready for the challenges of the 1990s.

Sources: Penny Gill: "Sells: Key Players in Woolworth Renaissance," *Stores,* May 1991, pp. 25–34; Laura Zinn: "Why 'Business Stinks' at Woolworth," *Business Week,* November 25, 1991, pp. 72–73.

No organization likes to be stagnant. In business, standing still is often considered to be a sign of weakness. Like other businesses, retail firms continuously seek new avenues for growth. The previous chapter focussed on the importance of a clearly defined marketing strategy. The focus on the customer, the competitors, and other aspects of the retailing environment has a far-reaching effect on a firm's performance. This focus is also important in charting a firm's strategy for growth. This chapter continues the discussion of retail marketing strategy by exploring the key decisions involved in developing a corporate strategy for growth. It describes the components of corporate strategy, with a focus on identifying avenues for growth. It concludes with a number of analytical techniques commonly employed to screen growth opportunities and manage diversified firms.

CORPORATE STRATEGY

As mentioned in the previous chapter, a strategy matches a firm's resources to the opportunities presented by the environment. A well-formulated strategy uses the organization's resources efficiently to compete most effectively. A corporate strategy has two major goals. First, it provides a view of the future. It projects the consequences of continuing current practices into the future and defines changes to present activities needed in light of expected future conditions. It is important to note, however, that the objective of **strategic planning** is not to determine what actions should be taken in the future, but what actions need to be taken today in anticipation of the future.[1]

An important goal of corporate strategy is to chart a plan for growth. The need to increase sales and profits requires retail firms to continually seek new avenues for growth, screen available opportunities, and select those that are consistent with the firm's mission. The strategic plan must match the firm's resources and strengths with the available opportunities and select the most attractive among them. A firm's corporate strategy provides the framework within which such decisions must be made. A firm must take four key steps to develop its corporate strategy:

1. Define the business mission.
2. Formulate corporate objectives.
3. Identify opportunities for growth.
4. Screen opportunities for growth.

In addition, it must have in place analytical planning procedures for managing diversified units in its portfolio of stores. Each of these steps is discussed below.

BUSINESS MISSION

Every organization must be guided by a **business mission** that defines the purpose for its existence. To define its mission, each firm must seek answers to three fundamental questions: What is our business? Who is our customer? How are we positioned in the market? The answers to these questions provide the foundation for developing strategy. Although they sound simple, these questions are most difficult for a firm to answer. One major company took two years to write a satisfactory statement of its corporate mission.[2]

All retailers must meet certain needs in the marketplace to survive and grow. Each retailer, however, fulfills these needs in a unique way that reflects the philosophy of that organization. The mission statement describes this philosophy and the way in which the organization will conduct its business. A clear understanding of the business mission delineates the types of merchandise and services the firm will sell, the geographic scope of the business and the ways in which it will compete. Without a stated mission the firm is likely to loose its focus.

Mission Statements Examples

Consider the following mission statement of a small firm selling personal care products:

> Our mission is to sell high-quality, environmentally safe, skin-care and personal-care products for women through a chain of retail stores located in northeastern United States.

Notice how the statement answers the questions raised earlier. It clearly defines the type of business the firm will be engaged in (skin and personal care), the type of customers it will serve (women), the geographic scope of the business (the Northeast), and how it will compete (high-quality, environmentally safe products). Business opportunities that violate this mission will not be acceptable to this firm. For example, a store in California would be inconsistent with the firm's mission. Similarly, the firm would consider unacceptable any proposal to sell products that are not environmentally safe or that are not, in its opinion, of high quality. This mission statement clearly demonstrates how a firm's activities are influenced by its mission.

Now consider the mission statement of the Dayton Hudson Corporation. Although very different from the earlier one, this statement, too, illustrates how the mission statement and the corporate philosophy it embodies influence the organization's strategy. Dayton Hudson defines its mission this way:

> Dayton Hudson is a diversified national retailer whose business it is to serve the American consumer through the retailing of dominant assortments of merchandise that represent quality, fashion and value. The company's stated policy is to be premier in every facet of its business.[3]

Clearly, the scope of this mission statement is much broader than the earlier one. Dayton Hudson aims at a national market and intends to be a leader in diverse retail segments. To achieve its stated mission, the company has developed a portfolio of retail formats that caters to the needs of diverse consumer segments. The retail units operated by Dayton Hudson include:

• Department Stores (Dayton's, Hudson's, and Marshall Fields).
• Discount Stores (Target).
• Soft-good stores (Mervyn's).
• Hard good specialty stores (Lechmere).

In the past, the company had also owned and operated B. Dalton Booksellers and Plums, an off-price apparel chain. It sold those units because it could not achieve a premier position in those markets.

Corporate Culture

The corporate mission also reflects the organization's philosophy regarding the way in which it will conduct its business and its **corporate culture**—*the set of values that are shared by everyone in the firm.* For example, McDonald's corporate mission is to provide quality food, quick service, and convenience to budget-conscious families. In keeping with this mission, the corporate culture stresses the themes of quality, service, convenience, and value (QSCV) which are repeatedly emphasized throughout the organization. The QSCV slogan is an integral part of McDonald's corporate culture and guides all of its activities.

The attitudes of the top level managers towards other employees of the firm are also reflected in the corporate culture. Wal-Mart's culture stresses the involvement of all employees in managerial decision-making and is reflected in its slogan: "We care about people." The senior managers of the company encourage all employees to get involved in managing the company, a policy started by Sam Walton, the founder. Wal-Mart's policy of encouraging all employees to provide input into managerial decisions and its broad-based profit-sharing plan that also includes lower level employees are reflections of the corporate culture.

CORPORATE OBJECTIVES

Objectives and goals *state the results that the firm wishes to achieve.* They translate the corporate mission into specific performance standards for the firm's managers. Retail firms usually set their objectives in terms of financial performance (profits), market position (sales, market share) or productivity (inventory turnover, sales per square foot). Firms commonly have multiple goals ranked in order of importance.

The mission statement of the May Department Stores illustrates the relationship between a company's mission and its objectives. To fulfill its corporate mission, the May Company has set for itself the overall objective of "achieving top-quartile performance among relevant competition . . . as measured by return on common stockholder's investment." This is the firm's primary objective. Its statement of objectives also recognizes the need for a high-level of sales growth and return on net assets. These secondary objectives are consistent with its overall mission.

Criteria for Objectives

Corporate objectives provide the basis for monitoring the firm's actions and evaluating its performance. The firm's actual results must be compared against its stated objectives. These objectives are the yardsticks for measuring how well the firm is actually performing. For this reason, the firm must translate the general objectives into specific goals that are (1) measurable, (2) realistic, and (3) consistent with each other.

Measurable   Often goals are stated too generally, that is, they're not specific enough. For instance, goals to "earn adequate profits" or "increase productivity" are not very useful. Goal statements must specify the levels of profit and productivity improvement that the firm will consider adequate and the time frame for achieving these levels. These goals would be better stated as "earn a 15 percent return on equity in 1995," or "increase labor productivity by 10 percent next year."

Realistic   Goals are useless if they merely state the firm's good intentions.[4] They must be realistic within the organization's strengths and resources. Only then can they provide a meaningful benchmark for judging the firm's actual performance. It would be unrealistic, for example, for a firm with limited resources to set a goal of increasing sales by 100 percent in a highly competitive market.

Internally Consistent   Finally, goals must be internally consistent. One store manager, for example, was asked to increase sales by 20 percent and to cut advertising and promotion expenditures by 20 percent at the same time. To increase sales, however, the store needed to spend more on advertising and promotion to attract more customers. Cutting these expenditures at the same time as trying to increase sales is inconsistent. Inconsistent objectives create confusion and blur the company's overall strategy.

As mentioned earlier, retail firms set their corporate objectives in terms of financial performance, market position, or productivity. Exhibit 6.1 presents a list of measures commonly used to translate these objectives into specific goals. Each measure is briefly described below. More detailed discussions are provided in later chapters.

Financial Performance

As their ultimate objective all retail firms seek to earn profits. Profits—the difference between total revenues and total expenses—are the company's reward for taking the risks of doing business. Without profits a firm cannot survive. It is not surprising, therefore, that firms most commonly measure performance in terms of financial criteria. A number of financial measures are typically used to measure performance:

Profit   The actual amount of money earned by the firm during a time period is the most fundamental measure of financial performance. This is the basis for measuring most other financial results.

Return on Assets   Profits in relation to the level of resources (assets) used. Typically abbreviated as ROA.

Exhibit 6.1   *Measures of Retail Performance*

Financial Performance	Profit
	Return on net worth (RONW)
	Earnings per share
Market Position	Sales revenue
	Market share
	Margin
Productivity	Inventory turnover
	Sales per square foot
	Sales per employee

Return on Net Worth   RONW, also called return on equity (ROE), measures profit in relation to the amount of money provided by the owners of private companies and stockholders of publicly held companies.

Earnings per Share   Also called EPS, this measure divides profits by the number of shares of common stock issued by the firm and is important for firms with publicly traded stocks. Outside investors use this criterion to determine the likely future value of the stock.

Market Position

Profits derive from a firm's ability to market its products well and manage its operation properly. Consequently, market position is a good indicator of a firm's performance. Some common measures of market position include:

Sales Revenue   Sales revenue is a common measure of performance used by most firms. This is simply the total sales dollars earned by the firm. For comparison purposes, retail firms use *same store sales* to monitor performance. This is the annual increase in sales of stores operating for more than one year.

Market Share   This is the measure of the firm's sales as a portion of the sales of all competing retailers that sell similar merchandise.

Margin   Margin is the percentage by which revenue earned from sales of merchandise exceeds the cost of the goods sold. It measures the firm's ability to control expenses.

Productivity

Productivity measures how efficiently a firm utilizes its resources. The three major types of resources used by retail firms correspond with the following three measures of productivity in retailing:

Inventory Turnover   This measures the productivity of the firm's investment in merchandise inventory and is calculated as the number of times the average stock is sold during a year. In essence, turnover reflects the speed with which the firm was able to sell its merchandise.

Space Productivity   Space is one of the most important resources of a retail firm. Sales per square foot is the most common way of measuring space productivity. Other indicators include sales per linear foot of shelf space and sales per square foot of display area.

Employee Productivity   Like most businesses, retailers need to maintain the productivity of their employees. A common procedure is to calculate sales per

RESEARCH REPORT

Sears Ends an Era

In January 1993, after years of decreasing profits and losses in market share, Sears, Roebuck, America's third largest retailer, announced a dramatic restructuring plan to turn the ailing giant around. In an attempt to overhaul its crumbling retailing business, Sears revealed that it would cut 50,000 full- and part-time jobs (nearly 15 percent of its 350,000 merchandising employees), close more than 100 unprofitable stores, and close its 97-year-old catalogue operation.

Change was long in coming to Sears, which saw a dizzying decline in its retailing share during the 1980s, culminating in the company losing its long-held title of "America's Number 1 Retailer" to Wal-Mart. According to industry analysts, Sears failed to keep pace with changes in the retail industry, loyally sticking to traditional items and not updating their technology as fast as their competitors. With losses for the catalogue alone totalling in excess of $175 million, company losses topped $3.9 billion. With many of its stores showing continued losses, the dramatic changes were clearly

necessary. Having closed or sold off many of its financial and insurance subsidiaries, Sears insisted that the only way to turn the company around would be to downsize and become more focused in its retailing efforts.

By far the most dramatic part of the plan was the closing of the catalogue, known as the "big book." Started in 1896, the catalogue has been part of American households for generations, and Americans have used it to buy everything from sewing machines and farm equipment to clothes and groceries and even houses. Sears began losing market share in the 1980s, as specialty catalogues gained ground. Customers did not want to wade through the 1,500-page catalogue that had no index to find items, and most believed that the services offered were old-fashioned. For example, until the late 1980s, the only credit card a catalogue customer could use was the Sears card, and there was no toll-free order number until 1990. Furthermore, Sears took weeks to fill orders, much longer than its competitors. If that didn't dissuade customers, the traditional,

employee. Although it is easy to calculate, this measure ignores the variability of skills and wages of employees. An alternative is to express total wages and salaries as a percent of sales.

IDENTIFYING GROWTH OPPORTUNITIES

Retail firms continuously look for growth opportunities. A particularly useful way to conceive of the avenues for retail growth is in terms of outlets and merchandise. Some of the most crucial strategy decisions faced by retail firms revolve around

less stylish items offered in the catalogue did, and sales began to decline. In recent years, as losses for the catalogue mounted ($135 million annually between 1989 and 1991, and $175 million in 1992 alone) Sears took steps to cut the losses of the catalogue division, trimming the inventory by one-third (more than 33,000 items). At its peak, the big book had a 15-million-household mailing list and over $4 billion in sales, and given this, the decline of the catalogue is truly the end of an American era, and a sad moment in America's retailing history.

In its time the catalogue had revolutionized retailing. While Sears' competitors of the era, R.H. Macy and John Wannamaker, focused on the big cities, Richard Warren Sears, a former railroad agent, realized that anything that could be put in a box could be shipped, and he believed that the new technology of the era, the railroad, could change merchandising. With careful insights into advertising, demographics, and consumer psychology, Sears and his catalogue single-handedly changed the face of Ameri-

can retailing. Offering sewing machines for $10.45 that were retailing in stores for more than $50, Sears was selling a machine a minute by 1902. To the isolated families of the Midwest, who had only heard of the luxurious merchandise available in the cities, the big book was a dream come true. In 1900, only four years after it was started, the catalogue was already reaping over $10 million in sales, and by the 1930s it was said that Sears knew more about the socioeconomic breakdown of America than the federal government. In this context, it is tragic that while the advent of new technology in the 1890s made the catalogue a winner, the new technology of the 1990s—credit card orders, toll-free numbers, and high-tech distribution systems—and Sears' inability to keep pace with these innovations were the reasons for its ultimate failure.

Sources: Richard S. Tedlow, *New and Improved,* (New York: Basic Books), pp. 259–343; Gregory A. Patterson and Christina Duff, "Sears Trims Operations, Ending an Era," *The Wall Street Journal,* January 26, 1993, pp. B1, B8; Timothy D. Schellhardt, "Closing the Book on an American Tradition," *The Wall Street Journal,* January 26, 1993, p. B1; and Paul Farhi, "Goodbye, Book of Dreams," *The Washington Post,* January 26, 1993, pp. C1, C3.

making investments in existing outlets or in new ones, and in existing or new merchandise categories. These choices are reflected in the **retail expansion grid** shown in Exhibit 6.2. The expansion grid shows six avenues for firms to grow, each involving a choice of outlet and merchandise strategy.

Consider the case of the Island Food Company, a firm which currently operates one supermarket in a medium-sized town called Orange. The firm's managers have to first look for opportunities to increase the sales of this outlet. As shown in the expansion grid, there are two ways to increase sales of existing outlets. First, the firm can increase **category penetration** of the different categories of merchandise currently carried by the supermarket. In other words, the firm has to increase the

Exhibit 6.2   The Retail Expansion Grid

		EXISTING MERCHANDISE	NEW MERCHANDISE
EXISTING OUTLETS		Category penetration	Scrambled merchandising
NEW OUTLETS	EXISTING MARKET AREA	Market penetration	Diversification
	NEW MARKET AREA	Geographic expansion	Diversification and geographic expansion

sales of the merchandise it currently carries in the store. Another avenue for increasing sales of the outlet is **scrambled merchandising**. That is, the store adds new merchandise categories to its current merchandise selection. Many supermarkets, for example, now sell items such as wrist watches and paperback books as well as grocery and perishables.

The number of potential customers residing in the local area can, however, put a limit on sales. The firm must therefore grow by opening new outlets. The expansion grid identifies four different scenarios for this type of growth based on where the new outlet is located and whether the merchandise is similar to or different from that carried by the existing store. The firm can increase its sales by opening new outlets in the same town (market area). This is the **market penetration** strategy. Another possibility is **geographical expansion**; that is, opening outlets in new market areas. Another avenue for growth is **diversification** into new retail formats as exemplified by Woolworth's strategy described at the beginning of the chapter. The new, diversified stores can be located in the market area in which the firm currently operates or in different geographical areas.

Increasing Sales of Existing Stores

Two avenues for increasing sales of existing stores are category penetration and scrambled merchandising. In both cases, the firm aims to increase the sales of existing outlets by attracting a larger share of the total retail sales generated within their respective trade areas. An outlet's **trade area** is the geographical area from

This store carries a great deal of merchandise in a rather small space. Is this a productive use of retail space?

which the store draws most of its customers. The size of the trade area is determined partly by the distance people are willing to travel to shop at the store and partly by competition. Since the number of people an outlet can attract depends on the size of the trade area, retail sales potential is determined by the spending pattern of the population within the trade area. The trade area, therefore, sets a spatial limit to the store's market potential. For further discussion of trade areas and their impact on market potential see Chapter 9.

The level of sales generated by an outlet is affected by three factors as shown in the following sales equation:

Annual sales = Number of customers
× Number of visits a year
× Average expenditure per trip

Therefore, to increase sales one or more components of the sales equation has to be changed. The store can change the number of customers who patronize it, the number of times the customers come to the store, and the amount they spend per trip. An increase in any one of these factors will increase sales.

Category Penetration   **Category penetration** increases sales of existing outlets by impacting the components of the sales equation. The supermarket, for example, can increase sales of its fresh produce department by carrying a better and more varied selection. This may induce some customers to buy more fruits and vegetables, thus increasing the amount they spend at the store. Moreover, customers who make filler trips to fruit and vegetable stands to purchase produce, may stop that practice and frequent the supermarket more often. It may also induce customers from other supermarkets to switch patronage. In this way all three components of the sales equation can increase sales.

To increase category penetration, a store must offer value to customers so that they have more reasons to patronize it rather than competitor's outlets. Better merchandise, better service, lower prices, and increased advertising and promotion are some tactics for implementing penetration strategies. Increasing sales through category penetration is especially important when retailers compete with many similar stores located nearby. For example, apparel stores located in a shopping center typically face intense competition from other apparel retailers and department stores located in the same center. They have to pursue aggressive strategies to attract customers and increase sales.

Category penetration strategies should be implemented with considerable care. An aggressive pursuit of sales often invites competitive retaliation and may prove costly to implement. Witness, for example, the costly marketing battles fought by different fast-food restaurants located in the same market area. Often these outlets are located in close proximity to each other and compete for the same customers. Each outlet has to advertise and promote vigorously to maintain its market share. Similarly, in the airline industry, fare reduction by one company is swiftly matched by others resulting in lower profitability for all the firms. The price war of the summer of 1992, for example, brought a record number of passengers but also financial losses for all the leading airlines.[5]

A market penetration strategy is most successful when it is based on strengths that competitors cannot easily match. For instance, when Nordstrom, the Seattle-based apparel chain, first opened its outlets in California, its strategy of providing superior service that its competitors could not easily match won customers for Nordstrom.

Scrambled Merchandising   **Scrambled merchandising** is another strategy for increasing sales of existing stores in which retailers sell new products and services that may be unrelated to the store's existing merchandise. Many supermarkets are now providing video rentals and selling paperback novels, watches, and lottery tickets. These are all examples of scrambled merchandising, since they are unrelated to the supermarkets' core food-related merchandise. Scrambled merchandising leads to more frequent visits and more expenditure per trip by current customers. It can also attract new customers because it facilitates one-stop shopping. Thus, scrambled merchandising, too, has an impact on all three components of the sales equation.

One example of a successful scrambled merchandising strategy is the introduction of breakfast sales by McDonald's and Burger King. The breakfast menu at fast-food restaurants tends to attract a different group of customers than the regu-

ENTREPRENEURIAL EDGE

Food Shopping without the Frills

Food Lion, the Salisbury, North Carolina-based supermarket chain with 663 stores, is a thriving company today. Food Lion was started in 1957 by Ralph Ketner. The first decade of operation was sluggish: more than half the new stores opened were closed shortly after, and Ketner entered his second decade of ownership losing money. Desperate for new ideas to make the company succeed, Ketner travelled to Ohio to learn about the wildly successful Food Town chain, which had become popular and profitable by employing a new practice in the supermarket industry: reducing prices. What Ketner learned was that he could slash prices on some of his inventory, and the effect on profit would be positive because of greater sales.

Ketner's idea was more than a smash hit in North Carolina: sales jumped a whopping 80 percent in the first year the new plan was implemented, and over 650 percent in the next three years. However, cutting prices wasn't the only piece to the puzzle, and Ketner struggled to cut costs and still make ends meet. Thus, the first in a long line of "no-frills," warehouse-style supermarkets was born. Stores were stripped of their fancy decorations, and products were unglamorously stacked up on shelves. In the early 1970s when Ketner introduced this concept, it was completely new. Today, no one thinks twice about shopping at "no frills" stores—for everything from food, clothes, and health and beauty aids to household appliances. But when Ketner first introduced the concept, it was his alone. For many customers, giving up atmosphere for the substantially lower prices was more than a fair trade-off.

Ketner's ideas have had an impact across the industry for the warehouse devotee and nondiscount shopper alike. Many chains have followed his lead, and those who don't follow have felt the impact. Each time a Food Lion opens its doors, other supermarkets in the area are forced to lower their prices as much as 6 percent to be competitive. Ketner feels that he helps his customers greatly all over the South, where Food Lion operates, and no doubt his customers are happy to oblige him by shopping in his no-frills, good value stores to the tune of $5 billion annually.

Source: "Retailing's Entrepreneurs of the Year," *Chain Store Age Executive*, December 1990, pp. 28–38.

lar menu. The addition of breakfast thus increases sales by attracting new customers rather than by cannibalizing the regular-menu sales.

Opening New Outlets

Trade-area size limits the scope for increasing sales of existing stores. To achieve further growth, retail firms must increase market penetration, expand geographically, or diversify, all of which involve opening new outlets to increase market coverage.

Market Penetration   One way in which the Island Food Company can increase sales is to increase **market penetration** by opening new supermarkets in the town of Orange. In this way the company can reach new customers in Orange since each outlet will have a different trade area and hence attract different customers. Supermarkets, banks, fast food outlets, and specialty and convenience stores have commonly followed this kind of expansion strategy.

For example, Exhibit 6.3 shows the network of outlets operated by The Gap in Manhattan, New York. Each Gap outlet can only attract customers from its immediate neighborhood. Each store, therefore, caters to customers from a small geographic area. By opening multiple outlets, the firm can reach more customers and increase its overall sales potential.

In addition to increasing sales, a coordinated strategy of increasing market penetration also creates potential for scale economies in advertising, promotion, and distribution. All the outlets, for example, can share the cost of advertising in local newspapers and TV. Since the total cost of advertising remains virtually constant irrespective of the number of stores in the area, increasing the number of outlets reduces the advertising expense per outlet. Outlets located near each other can also share warehouse space and other support services, again resulting in lower expenditures per store.

Developing a network of local outlets requires skills in location analysis. The location of each outlet must be chosen carefully to avoid cannibalizing each other's sales. Chapters 8 and 9 discuss methods for selecting optimal locations for local area networks.

Geographic Expansion   Market potential can also be increased by **geographic expansion**. Instead of expanding within the same city or market area, the retailer can open outlets in new market areas, and make its outlets accessible to even larger numbers of people. Many fast-food restaurants and national chain stores such as The Limited, K mart, Sears, and J.C. Penny have expanded this way. There are more than 2,200 K mart outlets and more than 1,500 J.C. Penney stores in the United States. Tandy Corporation also follows this strategy, operating a nation-wide network of 7,000 Radio Shack outlets.

Not all firms, however, have the resources to expand nationally. Moreover, a widely spread network of outlets can be difficult to operate. Managerial supervision and distribution logistics are especially difficult in large, widely spread networks. As a result, many firms adopt regional expansion strategies. In the supermarket industry, for example, each major chain has concentrated its store locations in one part of the country. Most department store chains have similarly located their outlets in regional clusters and limited the geographic area served by their outlet networks. Such regional concentration keeps the sizes of their networks manageable.

Exhibit 6.3   The Gap Map

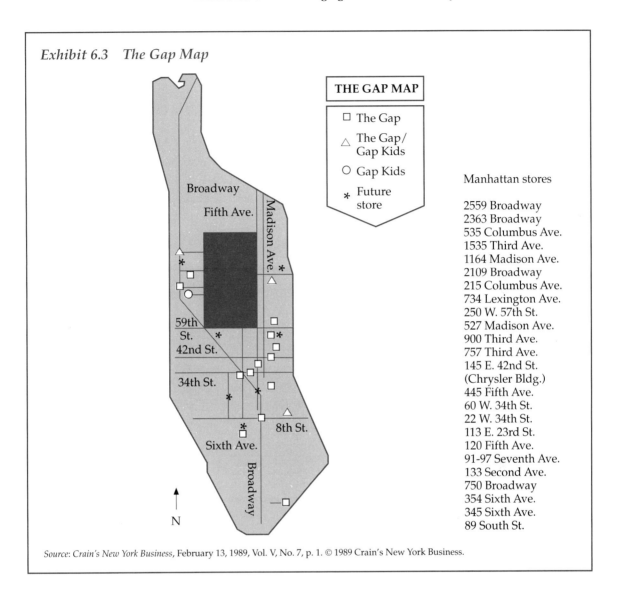

THE GAP MAP

□ The Gap
△ The Gap/ Gap Kids
○ Gap Kids
* Future store

Manhattan stores

2559 Broadway
2363 Broadway
535 Columbus Ave.
1535 Third Ave.
1164 Madison Ave.
2109 Broadway
215 Columbus Ave.
734 Lexington Ave.
250 W. 57th St.
527 Madison Ave.
900 Third Ave.
757 Third Ave.
145 E. 42nd St.
(Chrysler Bldg.)
445 Fifth Ave.
60 W. 34th St.
22 W. 34th St.
113 E. 23rd St.
120 Fifth Ave.
91-97 Seventh Ave.
133 Second Ave.
750 Broadway
354 Sixth Ave.
345 Sixth Ave.
89 South St.

Source: Crain's New York Business, February 13, 1989, Vol. V, No. 7, p. 1. © 1989 Crain's New York Business.

Regional expansion also allows firms to respond to changing economic environments of different areas in the country. For example, during the 1970s many retailers, especially department stores, targeted their expansion in cities such as Phoenix, Dallas, and Houston to follow the population growth in the Sunbelt areas. Later, department stores opened new outlets in Florida to take advantage of the growing population in that state.

Many firms that expand geographically do so by franchising their operations to expand quickly without incurring tremendous financial liabilities. Franchising

The Price Club is a good example of rapid geographic expansion. It originated in San Diego, California, and in just a few short years has expanded throughout the United States and into Canada and Mexico.

also reduces the need for day-to-day supervision of each outlet. Companies such as McDonald's, Burger King, Kentucky Fried Chicken, and Day's Inn have successfully expanded their network of outlets through franchising.

Geographic expansion strategies need not be limited to the borders of this country. As discussed in Chapter 2, many U.S. firms have expanded into international markets to increase sales volumes. Exhibit 6.4 shows the countries with Burger King outlets. Other chains such as Wendy's, Sears, J.C. Penney, and Toys R Us have also expanded internationally.

Diversification   **Diversification** involves developing new store formats and operating them as separate units. For instance, a department store operator may start

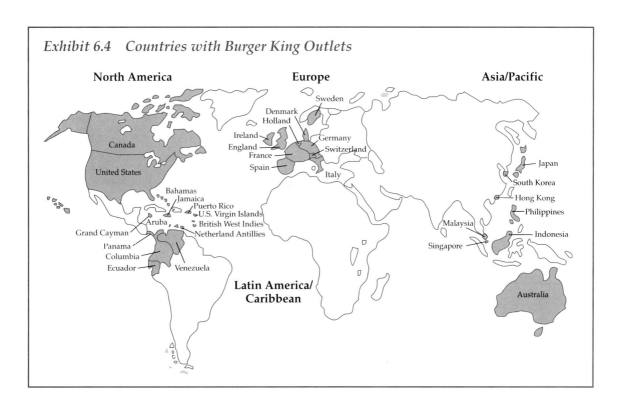

Exhibit 6.4   Countries with Burger King Outlets

a chain of discount stores or open another store with a different target market. Island Food, for example, can diversify from the supermarket business into selling hardware or appliances. Diversification allows firms to expand by entering attractive, growing businesses. By diversifying, the organization can develop a "portfolio" of retail operations, each of which appeals to different customer groups and serves different customer needs. By spreading its resources among different types of retail operations, the firm can take advantage of emerging opportunities and reduce the risk of concentrating on a single business. In essence, the idea is similar to individuals creating a portfolio of stocks rather than investing all their money into the stocks of just one company.

Diversification strategies can take various forms. Some firms diversify by opening retail formats that are related to their existing operations. One example is Woolworth Corporation, which operates a number of different retail formats—Foot Locker, Lady Foot Locker, Kinney's Shoes—to sell shoes. Similarly, The Limited operates a portfolio of women's apparel and accessory stores. This type of **related diversification** allows the firm to leverage off its core competence. **Unrelated diversification**, such as Woolworth's opening of the discount drug store chain called RX, on the other hand, requires firms to develop new business skills. Below are some examples of diversification strategies implemented by retail firms.[6]

One way companies can continue to grow is through diversification. U.S. Shoe Corporation diversified into such specialty shops as Casual Corner for women's apparel and Lenscrafters for eyeglasses. Easy Spirit is one of their many specialty shoe stores.

Dayton Hudson Corporation   The portfolio of stores operated by Dayton Hudson includes department stores, discount stores, soft goods stores and hard goods stores. By operating a variety of different types of stores, the firm has created a portfolio that is well positioned to respond to major consumer trends that are changing the nature of the retail marketplace. For example, in the late 1970s, when the competitive position of department stores was weak, Dayton Hudson put most of its resources into expanding the network of Target and Mervyn's outlets. In 1977, department stores accounted for 50 percent of the total sales of the company. By 1981 it had dropped to less than 30 percent.

The U.S. Shoe Corporation   To reduce its reliance on shoes, U.S. Shoe has diversified into a number of different specialty stores selling shoes as well as apparel. Its store portfolio includes August Max, J. Riggins, Outrigger, Ups 'N Downs, Proving Ground, and T.H. Mandy all of which sell apparel. In addition, the company owns Papagallo and Hahn shoe stores, and the Lenscrafter chain of eyeglass stores.

By entering into emerging specialty retail sectors, a company can keep its total sales growing. There are certain advantages to concentrating on only one or two kinds of specialty stores, rather than diversifying into different types of retail institutions like Dayton Hudson has done. Since the store operations are quite similar, U.S. Shoe can easily transfer its experience from one operation to another. In addition, since most of the stores occupy similar space in shopping malls, the company can interchange locations of different stores if necessary.

The Limited, Inc.   The Limited follows a strategy that is quite similar to U.S. Shoe's. It has developed a diversified portfolio of specialty stores, all of which focus on women's apparel and accessories (see Exhibit 6.5). In this way the firm creates synergy among all its units and, like U.S. Shoe, can transfer its experiences from one store to another. Most of The Limited's outlets, too, are located in shopping malls, allowing it the possibility of interchanging locations of the outlets. Having mul-

tiple sites within the same mall gives the firm tremendous bargaining power with mall developers and leasing agents.

Albertson's, Inc.   Albertson's strategy illustrates yet another form of related diversification. The company has developed several supermarket formats which include conventional supermarkets, combination food and drug stores, superstores, and warehouse stores (See Exhibit 6.6). In response to changing consumer attitudes towards food shopping and changing industry trends, the company moved away from the smaller conventional stores to the larger formats. In 1982, for example, the company had 266 conventional supermarkets, 84 combination stores, 52 superstores, and 14 warehouse stores. In the next four years, 66 conventional stores were either closed or converted to other formats. By then Albertson's was operating 102 combination stores, 124 superstores, and 26 warehouses.

The Gap   This company initiated its diversification strategy when it acquired the Banana Republic chain. At present, the company operates three chains—The Gap, GapKids, and Banana Republic. Although both The Gap and Banana Republic sell casual clothing, they target different customers. Thus, outlets of both stores can be located in the same geographic market area without fear of extensive cannibalization of sales. In fact, all three stores are located right next to each other in some places.

Screening Growth Opportunities

The previous examples illustrate many opportunities for firms to grow, but not all of them may be relevant for any specific company. Each firm must screen the growth opportunities, and decide which it should actively pursue. A number of different criteria must be used to screen each growth opportunity as suggested in Exhibit 6.7.

Exhibit 6.5   *The Limited's Store Portfolio*

Store Name	Number of Outlets	Description
The Limited	778	This women's specialty clothing store started by Leslie Wexner is how the portfolio started.
Lerner	858	Value-oriented fashion clothing.
Lane Bryant	752	Fashionable clothes for large sizes.
The Express	549	Women's clothing.
Victoria's Secret	442	Fast expanding women's lingerie chain.
Structure	152	Men's clothing and accessories.
Limited Too	108	High fashion, high quality, moderate-priced clothes for girls.
Bath and Body Works	27	Sells personal care products made of natural ingredients sold in natural market atmosphere.
Abercombie & Fitch	27	This 100-year-old chain sells high quality men's clothing and accessories.
Lingerie Cacique	51	High quality European-style lingerie.
Victoria's Secret Bath Shops	109	Quality English bath products.

Consistency with Environment   The best opportunities are consistent with the emerging trends in the environment and allow the firm to respond to changing consumer needs and competitive conditions. For instance, in the beginning of the 1980s, off-price apparel stores selling well-known brand-name merchandise at deep discount prices, represented the most prominent growth area in retailing. As a result a number of firms opened off-price chains, including Zayre (T.J. Maxx, Hit or Miss), U.S. Shoe (T.H. Mandy), Associated Dry Goods (Loehmann's), and Melville Corporation (Marshall's).

The downturn of the U.S. economy during the early 1990s shifted consumers toward no-frill stores offering quality products at reasonable prices. This has prompted a number of firms to venture into this arena by operating warehouse

---

Exhibit 6.6   *Albertson's Supermarket Formats*

Combination food–drug units
The fastest growing sector of the supermarket industry is the combination food–drug unit. Such a store carries all the merchandise lines typically found in large drugstores as well as those sold at supermarkets. The combination unit carries over 40,000 items. Sized from 48,000 to 60,000 square feet, it sells all merchandise through a common set of checkout counters. A single unit manager directs the entire operation.

Superstores
The superstore is a smaller version of the combination store. It carries a full selection of supermarket items and selected high-volume items sold in drug stores. An Albertson's superstore typically carries about 30,000 items and may range from 35,000 to 46,000 square feet in size.

Conventional supermarkets
A conventional supermarket carries approximately 20,000 items including groceries, fresh meat, produce, dairy products, and a limited line of nonfood merchandise. Some stores have in-store bakeries and delicatessens.

Warehouse stores
Albertson's operates warehouse stores that range from 24,000 to 73,000 square feet, although 50,000 square feet is typical. These full-line merchandise stores offer significant savings, with special emphasis on discounted meat and produce.

---

stores and wholesale clubs. Leaders among them are Costco, Sam's Wholesale Club, and Price Club. Even Nordstrom, long well-known for full-service and full-price, is trying to fit into this trend. The firm will soon expand its chain of discount-oriented apparel stores.

Consistency with the Firm's Resources   Does the firm have (or will it be able to acquire) the resources necessary to succeed? A small firm that currently operates only one store cannot hope to be able to develop a national network or diversify into new businesses immediately. Market penetration or scrambled

---

Exhibit 6.7   *Criteria for Screening Growth Opportunities*

■ Is the opportunity consistent with emerging environmental trends?

■ Does the firm have adequate resources?

■ Does the firm have (or can it acquire) competencies required to succeed in this business?

■ Does the profit potential justify the risks?

STRATEGY IN ACTION

The Gap: Good Value for the Customer and the Community

The philosophy of The Gap, Inc., is good value and good quality, and this vision permeates all Gap stores, in terms of how business is done, and in terms of the clothing offered in each. While one would imagine that this notion of value and quality would refer only to the clothing manufactured and sold by the company, The Gap, Inc., believes that the company itself should offer value and quality in a larger context by giving back to the communities in which the stores operate. According to many observers, this kind of corporate culture makes The Gap one of the most socially progressive companies in the United States.

The examples of The Gap's social responsibility are many. On a very basic level, the company gives a sizable portion of its pre-tax income to a variety of charities, both locally and nationally. The company also has an aggressive recycling program, which has been in place at all company stores and offices since long before the "green" wave took over corporate America in the late 1980s. Furthermore, all Gap employees, at all levels, from top management to salesclerks, are required to do volunteer work in their communities, on company time.

Many companies use their social and environmental works to promote their products in the eyes of their customers. But most Gap customers have no idea of the level of charitable works performed by the company, nor of the company's commitment to these good works. Although all of this information is listed in the company's annual report and other shareholder statements, very little of it actually filters down to the consumer. There are no signs or plaques in the stores, and their advertising has not taken the route of Esprit or Benetton by focusing on these points. Gap advertisements, for all of their stores, focus mainly on the kind of person who wears Gap clothes, rather than on the clothes per se. The highly acclaimed "Individual of Styles" campaign in the late 1980s focused on the personality of the "individual" wearing the clothes, and later campaigns, such as "A Gap for Every Generation," focused on the image of Gap customers: people doing ordinary things like shopping, reading, or walking with their kids. The closest the company has come to promoting its social activism has been in the Banana Republic (a division of The Gap, Inc.) campaign launched in the summer of 1992 that proclaimed, while showing close-up shots of multiethnic groups of young people, "We better stop worrying that we don't share the same past and start worrying that we'll have the same future." The Gap says it will continue its good works, and will not use them to promote the image or sales of the company, even though consumer awareness of these good works would probably make the company even more popular.

Sources: Russell Mitchell, "How The Gap's Ads Got So-o-o Cool," *Business Week*, March 9, 1992, p. 64; and Maria Shao, "Everybody's Falling into The Gap," *Business Week*, September 23, 1991, p. 36.

merchandising may be more appropriate strategies for it to follow. If it does decide to open new outlets, it is most likely to be in the vicinity of the current one.

Consistency with the Firm's Competence   Each successful firm develops a unique set of distinctive competencies that gives it a differential advantage over competitors. Similarly, each line of business has a set of factors that are critical to success. In the fast-food industry, for example, a critical success factor is the ability to manage franchisor-franchisee relationships. A company that has no experience in managing franchise systems may not have the competence to succeed in the fast-food business. Hence, an important question in screening new opportunities is: Do the firm's competencies match the required success factors of the new business?

Rewards and Risks   The ultimate test of new opportunities is the sales and profit it can potentially generate. Faced with a choice between two potential opportunities, firms will tend to choose the one that is likely to give more rewards compared to the risk the firms must take. This requires an in-depth analysis of the attractiveness of different markets and the firm's own strengths in that industry.

Many companies use an analytical technique called the business planning grid to screen growth opportunities systematically. This and some other analytical planning techniques are discussed in the next section.

MANAGING DIVERSIFIED FIRMS

Diversified firms with different business units face a major management challenge. In such firms, a major function of strategic planning is to formulate a long-run strategy for each constituent unit and to determine how resources should be allocated among the units. This step is often called **business portfolio planning**. Not all the different units operated by a corporation are equally attractive at the same time. Some may be growing fast, others may be holding their own and growing steadily, while yet others may be declining. The resources needed by each type of business will differ depending on its situation. Portfolio planning allow managers to evaluate the different units on a common basis, much like an investment manager evaluates an investment portfolio.[7] The goals and objectives of each unit and their overall strategy will also vary. The essence of portfolio planning is to ensure that the various units of the firms are managed as a balanced portfolio. Capital and resources are allocated to each to serve the interest of the firm as a whole in order to achieve balanced growth with acceptable risk. In essence, the organization must foster the growth of the strong units and either improve or pare down the weak ones.

To allocate resources across the different units, managers must assess the strengths and weaknesses of all the units. A planning tool known as the **business planning grid** is useful for this purpose.

Business Planning Grid

Three concepts underlie the use of business planning grids: First, the long-run profit potential of a business unit depends on the attractiveness of the industry relative to other industries. Second, a firm's expected profit depends on its strengths relative to competition. Third, investments should be made in accordance with the overall strength of a unit as measured jointly by industry attractiveness and business strength. These ideas are combined into a grid, as depicted in Exhibit 6.8, in which industry attractiveness is crossed with business strength. These grids are typically divided into a 3 × 3 matrix in which each dimension is rated high, medium, or low.

Exhibit 6.9 shows the six steps required to use planning grids.[8] As shown, the six steps are divided into two phases: situation assessment and strategy development.

Situation Assessment   The first step in the situation phase is to establish the unit of analysis. The analysis can be performed at various levels with units differentiated in various ways. The resulting units, typically called **strategic business units (SBU)** are divisions or parts of an organization that are treated as separate business units because each has its own (1) customer focus, (2) set of competitors, (3) marketing strategy, and (4) manager.[9] Retail organizations can define SBUs in a number of ways.

1. *By store groups* One way of defining SBUs is in terms of the different groups of stores (department stores, supermarkets, specialty stores, and so on) operated by a diversified firm. For example, for organizational purposes Woolworth Corporation divides the U.S. operations of the firm into two main divisions: the

---

Exhibit 6.8   Business Planning Grid

		Business Position		
		High	Medium	Low
Market Attractiveness	High	GROW	BUILD	SUPPORT
	Medium	REINFORCE	SUPPORT	HARVEST
	Low	MAINTAIN	HARVEST	DIVEST

Exhibit 6.9 *Six Steps in Using Planning Grid*

Situation Assessment
1. Establish unit of analysis
2. Identify factors that make markets attractive and firms competitive
3. Assign weights to factors to reflect their relative importance
4. Assess the *current* position of each unit on each factor and combine to determine overall position on market attractiveness and business strength

Strategy Development
5. Project the future position of each unit, based on forecasts of environmental trends and continuation of current strategy
6. Explore possible changes in the position of each of these units

Woolworth division, which operates the "five-and-dime" stores, and the Kinney division, which contains all the specialty stores. At the broadest level these two divisions constitute the firm's SBUs.

2. *By different formats within a group* Examples are the different chains operated by The Limited Corporation. Since each chain has different customer orientations, faces different competitive environments, and has different marketing strategies, they each can form an independent SBU.

3. *By merchandise category* Because of the large variety of products sold in department and discount stores, each major merchandise category (health and beauty aids, kitchen accessories, toys, and so forth) is typically used to define SBUs. Each merchandise category is an SBU, since it faces different competitive environments.

4. *By geographical location* Large retailers who operate national or international networks of outlets of the same store, typically define SBUs based on geography, since competitive conditions can vary significantly across different regions. Woolworth, for example, treats its Canadian and U.S. stores as constituting different SBUs. Similarly, Macy's distinguishes its California and New York operations into separate units for planning purposes.

Once the firm has delineated the units, the second step in applying the grid is to identify the relevant factors that make markets attractive and measure the competitive position of a business. This requires an understanding of why some markets are more attractive than others and how firms create competitive advantage. While the factors considered can vary from one application to another, some of the factors typically used to measure industry attractiveness include:

- Market factors: market size, cyclicity, seasonality
- Expected growth rate

- Number and size of competitors, degree of concentration in market
- Bargaining power of suppliers
- Margins

Common measures of business strength include:

- Sales and market share
- Market share relative to leading competitors
- Quality of managers relative to competition
- Relative efficiency
- Financial resources
- Relationship with suppliers

Once the relevant factors are identified, weights are assigned to the factors based on their relative importance. These "make explicit different managers' implicit weightings" of the different factors.[10] As one observer notes: "Forcing managers to try to assign weights and then to defend those assignments reveals the hidden assumptions different managers are using and aids the process of reaching consensus."

The final step in the assessment stage is to rate each business on the various factors and to combine the ratings into indices of industry attractiveness and business strength. Each SBU is then placed on the grid based on its rating on industry attractiveness and business strength.

Strategy Development   The two steps in the strategy development phase involve projecting the units' position in the future. While the objectives of the steps are quite simple, it requires full participation of and considerable discussion among the managers. Critical assumptions about the industry, the environment, and the firm's competitive strengths surface during these discussions.

The projections in the first step is based on the assumption that current strategies and environmental trends will continue into the future. Typically, the projections are made for five years into the future, but this period may vary. In the final step, the future position of different units under new strategies are projected.

The position of an SBU in the grid reflects its overall attractiveness and suggests the course of action that the firm should take in reference to the unit. The strongest units are those that lie in the upper left-hand corner of the grid: SBUs with high business strength in highly attractive industries. The firm should allocate resources to these units to maintain its leading position. Units in the other corner of the grid, on the other hand, are potential candidates for disinvestment or divestiture. The industry has little attractiveness and the firm has little competitive advantage within the industry. The cells in between these two corners represent various levels of attractiveness and call for different types of strategies as shown in Exhibit 6.8.

Monitoring the Portfolio

To maintain balance in its portfolio, the firm should monitor the performance of each SBU. The **growth-gain matrix** is an useful tool for monitoring SBU performance over time. The growth-gain matrix indicates the degree to which the growth of each SBU is keeping pace with growth in market size.[11] Like the business-planning grid, the growth-gain matrix also has two dimensions (see Exhibit 6.10). The vertical axis measures the change in total sales of the SBU and the horizontal axis measures how the size of the industry to which the SBU belongs has changed. The position of each SBU along these two dimensions is then plotted. As shown in the exhibit, a 45-degree diagonal line is drawn through the figure to help interpret it. The sales of SBUs that lie above the diagonal line on the matrix have grown faster than the total sales of their industries. This means that these units must have increased their market shares. SBUs following a build strategy should, therefore, be in this section above the diagonal. Business units that lie along the diagonal are maintaining their market share, since their sales have kept up with the industry. Businesses below the diagonal have not grown as fast as the industry—they have lost market share. Businesses that are being harvested are most likely to be in this section. The market position of a business that is being harvested is allowed to deteriorate in order to gain cash flow.

By plotting the position of each SBU in the growth-gain matrix, a manager can determine whether the businesses are all performing according to plan. For example, SBUs that are receiving additional resources to build their strength should never lie in the middle or the bottom sections of the growth-gain matrix; they should be above the diagonal line in the matrix. Similarly, businesses following a hold

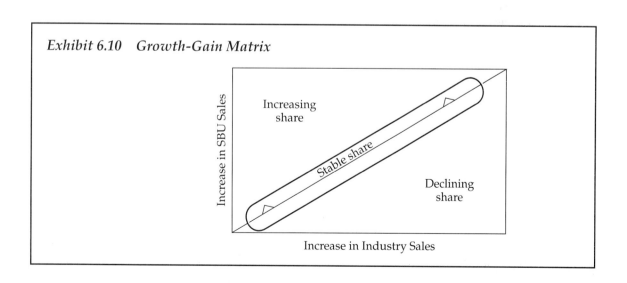

Exhibit 6.10 **Growth-Gain Matrix**

strategy should not be in the lower section, since that would indicate a loss of market share.

Problems with Portfolio Planning Approaches

Although portfolio planning models revolutionized the application of strategic planning in the 1970s,[12] they have their limitations. They can be time-consuming to implement because of the amount of data required to measure industry attractiveness and business strength. Moreover, the selection of factors for measuring these dimensions may itself be controversial and difficult.

Another difficult issue for retailers is the correct definition of market boundaries for each SBU. A proper market boundary definition is crucial for measuring market share correctly. Although it appears to be a simple task, it is usually difficult in practice. Consider a business unit that operates a chain of ten department stores in Pennsylvania. How should it define its relevant market to calculate market share? Should it include all other department stores? Should mass merchandise outlets and specialty stores also be included? There is also the question of whether sales by stores outside Pennsylvania should be included in the calculation of the total market size. Theoretically, all stores that compete to meet a similar need for the same customer group belong to the same market. Practically, this may be difficult to determine and considerable judgment and experience will be required. Despite their limitations, however, the business planning grid and the growth-gain matrix are useful aids to the strategic planning process. They are good diagnostic tools and provide a comprehensive graphical representation of the overall market position of all of the organization's SBUs. They force managers to view all the different components of the firm in a holistic fashion rather than to look at them only individually. Without looking at all the SBUs together, it is unlikely that the firm will be able to coordinate the strategies of its different businesses.

STRATEGIC MARKET PLANNING: A POSTSCRIPT

Although most companies now engage in strategic planning, many have been disappointed with the effectiveness of their strategic planning efforts because they have neglected some of the fundamental tenets of strategy development as listed below.

- Effective strategies must be market and customer oriented. They must exploit the firm's strengths, derived from a proper understanding of environmental trends and competitive behavior, and create and sustain a competitive advantage.[13]
- The strategic planning process must never lose contact with the customer. One of the characteristics of excellent companies is their closeness to the customer. The customer orientation must permeate throughout the organization.[14]
- Effective strategies are implementable. Plans have no value unless they "degen-

erate into work."[15] The firm must translate plan objectives into specific tasks for specific managers to accomplish. The firm's senior managers must commit themselves to the plan, and they must reward individual managers who achieve plan targets.

Summary

1. An important goal of corporate strategy is to chart a plan for growth. A firm's corporate strategy provides the framework for identifying growth opportunities, screening them, and selecting those that are consistent with the firm's resources and competencies. A firm must take four key steps to develop its corporate strategy: (a) define the business mission, (b) formulate corporate objectives, (c) identify opportunities for growth, and (d) screen opportunities for growth. In addition, it must have in place analytical planning procedures for managing diversified units in its portfolio of stores.

2. The corporate mission is a written statement that describes the way in which that organization will conduct its business. A clear statement of the company mission is necessary to delineate the company's activities and define the company's business domain. Retail businesses must formulate clear objectives and set specific performance goals. Goals are stated in terms of financial profitability, market position, or productivity. They must be measurable, realistic, and internally consistent.

3. One way to grow is to increase sales of existing stores. Category penetration and scrambled merchandising are two avenues for achieving this. Both these strategies affect the components of the sales equation. The size of the trade puts a limit to the sales of specific outlets.

4. Geographical expansion and diversification are two other avenues for growth. By expanding into new geographical areas firms can reach new groups of customers, either within the same market area or in new markets.
Diversification is another avenue for growth. The company can start a new retail operation of its own, merge with another firm, or acquire another company. The new businesses could be related or unrelated to the firm's current line of business.

5. Growth strategies will succeed only if the firm can take advantage of emerging environmental trends and its own distinctive competence. They must also be consistent with the firm's resources. The ultimate test is the potential rewards of pursuing the strategy and the level of risk it entails.

6. To allocate resources across the different units, managers must assess the strengths and weaknesses of all the units. A planning tool known as the business planning grid is useful for this purpose. The grid evaluates business units based on the attractiveness of the industry relative to other industries and the company strengths relative to competition. The growth-gain matrix is useful for monitoring the performance of business units. It provides a pictorial summary of the units that are gaining market share, those that are losing their share, and those that are holding on to their share.

Key Concepts

Strategic planning
Business mission

Corporate culture
Objectives and goals

Retail expansion grid
Trade area
Category penetration
Scrambled merchandising
Market penetration
Geographic expansion
Diversification

Related diversification
Unrelated diversification
Business portfolio planning
Business planning grid
Strategic business units (SBU)
Growth-gain matrix

Discussion Questions

1. Explain briefly the key steps in developing a firm's corporate strategy.
2. Why is it important for a firm to have a well-articulated mission statement? How does the mission statement differ from a statement of corporate objectives?
3. What criteria do retailers use to measure their performance and set their objectives? What are the three desirable characteristics of corporate objectives?
4. By what avenues can retail firms grow? Give examples of retail firms that have used each of these avenues.
5. What is the distinction between a strategy of category penetration and market penetration? When would a company be likely to use one or the other as the primary vehicle for growth? Give examples.
6. By what criteria should a firm screen alternative growth opportunities?
7. Compare and contrast the differences between related and unrelated diversification strategies. What are the advantages and disadvantages of each of these strategies?
8. What is a strategic business unit (SBU)? On what bases do retail firms define SBUs?
9. Describe the construction of a business planning grid and discuss how the grid can help retail planning.

Notes

1. George S. Day, *Strategic Market Planning* (St. Paul: West Publishing, 1984), p. 2.
2. Philip Kotler, *Marketing Management: Analysis, Planning and Control* (Englewood Cliffs: Prentice-Hall, 1985), p. 66.
3. Dayton Hudson Corporation, *1981 Annual Report*.
4. Peter Drucker, *Management: Tasks, Responsibilities, Practices* (New York: Harper and Row, 1974), p. 101.
5. Edwin McDowell, "Airlines Tally the Damage from Summer's Fare War," *New York Times*, September 12, 1992, p. 1, 34.
6. The information on different companies are from the annual reports of the respective companies.
7. John A. Czepiel, *Competitive Marketing Strategy* (Englewood Cliffs: Prentice-Hall, 1992), p. 375.
8. This section is based on George S. Day, *Analysis for Strategic Market Decisions* (St. Paul: West Publishing Company, 1986), chapter 7; and John A. Czepiel, *Competitive Marketing Strategy* Englewood Cliffs: Prentice-Hall, 1992), chapter 11.
9. Derek Abell and John S. Hammond, *Strategic Marketing Planning* (Englewood Cliffs: Prentice-Hall, 1979), p. 10.
10. Czepiel, *Competitive Marketing Strategy,* p. 394.
11. Abell and Hammond, *Strategic Market Planning*, p. 180.

12. For more detailed discussion of portfolio planning, see, among others, George S. Day, "Diagnosing the Product Portfolio," *Journal of Marketing*, 41 (2) (April 1977), pp. 29–38. Peter Patel and Michael Younger, "A Frame of Reference for Strategy Development," *Long Range Planning* 11 (April 1978), pp. 6–12, and Arnoldo C. Hax and Nicolas S. Majluf, *Strategic Management* (Englewood Cliffs: Prentice-Hall, 1984), chapter 9.

13. Day, *Strategic Market Planning*, p. 206.

14. Thomas J. Peters and Robert H. Waterman, Jr., *In Search of Excellence* (New York: Harper and Row, 1982), p. 156.

15. Drucker, *Management*, p. 128.

CHAPTER 7
Financial Strategy and Planning

Will Macy's Debt Burden Prove to Be too Much?

In February 1992, Macy's, one of the nation's leading department store chains and a veritable New York institution, filed for Chapter 11 bankruptcy. This filing came after a long succession of poor management decisions and failed attempts to save the chain, and the news rocked the retail industry. Founded in the mid-nineteenth century, Macy's was one of the original department stores and the model upon which many chains were founded. The chain grew into a shopper's mecca, *the store where everybody shopped.* Shopping at Macy's was an event: the service and the shopping atmosphere were unparalleled for many customers, and the stores attracted visitors from all over the world. When Macy's filed for bankruptcy, it seemed to many to mark the end of an era and the end of the great department store tradition in the United States.

In 1986 Edward Finkelstein, chairman of R.H. Macy Co., organized a management-led leveraged buyout (LBO) of the retail chain. At the time, it was the largest management-led LBO ($3.7 billion, nearly all of it borrowed). By taking the company private, Finkelstein hoped to free-up cash flow and centralize decision-making in order to ex-

pand the company's holdings. One year after the buyout, the strategy seemed to have worked: Macy's had a adequate operating cushion and enough cash flow to pay all interest expenses plus capital spending, and still had $54 million left over.

However, in 1988, Finkelstein entered a bidding war with Canadian-based Campeau Corp. over the Federated Department Stores, and while he finally succeeded in purchasing the Los Angeles-based Bullocks and San Francisco-based I. Magnin divisions of Federated, chains that he had long coveted, he put Macy's at great risk. Industry analysts felt that both Campeau Corp. and Macy had paid very inflated prices for the Federated divisions. While this meant that Finkelstein added another $1 billion to the initial debt load, he felt justified in the move because it offered increased presence in the very lucrative California market, which, Finkelstein says, would have taken ten years or more to build from scratch. The overall debt level for the company was staggering, requiring an estimated half-billion dollars annually in interest payments, roughly 10 cents on every sales dollar. But for two years, until the disastrous 1989 Christmas season, Macy stayed afloat, covering all of its interest payments, and still showing a positive cash flow.

214

The greatest effect of the Federated purchases was that the deal increased the amount of cash that Macy had to generate in order to cover its interest payments. The deal also came at a time when the economy was softening, and consumers were tightening their belts. As the retail industry headed into a slump in 1989, analysts felt that Macy, saddled with huge debt and high interest payments, was headed for financial trouble. The first real signal for Macy came after the disappointing Christmas season of 1989. Both Finkelstein and his staff misjudged the con-

sumer mood and optimistically ordered more goods than were eventually purchased. This left the stores with a surplus of costly inventory, and the cost of maintaining that inventory reduced Macy's cash flow—the lifeblood of leveraged companies. All during 1990 this pattern was repeated—Finkelstein's declaring an imminent recovery, goods being ordered, and sales not meeting expectations—as Macy struggled to meet its interest payments, supplier payments, operating expenses, and even payroll costs.

At the end of fiscal year 1990, Macy brought in a new chief financial officer, Diane Baker, former head of the retail banking group at Solomon Brothers. Baker was an expert at restructuring and was known on Wall Street as a top advisor to companies facing serious financial difficulties. By the end of 1991, Macy was close to bankruptcy, but managed to avoid it, with an infusion of cash from the board and some investors, most notably G.E. Capital Corp. and Laurence A. Tisch, head of CBS.

Macy tried to stave off insolvency in a number of ways during 1991, including raising cash by selling assets, asking investors to increase their stakes, and renegotiating the terms of their bank debt 23 *times*. But, by the end of 1991, Macy was again barely afloat, and while all of the company's stores remained open, bankruptcy seemed imminent. Finally, in January 1992, Tisch made an eleventh-hour bid to buy the struggling company and rescue it from the huge debt load. Tisch's proposal fell through within weeks, however, and Macy was finally forced to file for Chapter 11 bankruptcy protection.

This decision effectively put Macy, one in a long line of American retailers, in a very vulnerable position, and it left suppliers and investors little hope of getting money back or their outstanding bills paid. While business was conducted as usual in all the Macy, Bullocks, and I. Magnin stores, management was given time to put together a plan to get the chain back on its feet by reducing its debt load and restoring its balance sheet without having to continue to borrow in order to keep up with interest and supplier payments. The protection effectively put the creditors on hold until the company could draw up a plan to balance the company's cash flow with its costs. In the interim, Macy acquired a $600 million short-term loan to pay its outstanding merchandise and utility bills as well as its payroll. In the spring of 1992, Macy's lawyers were confident that it would be no longer than a two-year process, similar to Bloomingdale's 1989–1990 slump into Chapter 11, and that Macy would emerge a much healthier and stronger company. In February 1993, Macy announced its decision to close stores in 11 locations in New York and California as part of its reorganization plan.

Sources: Subatra N. Chakravarty, "The Benefits of Leverage," *Forbes*, May 1, 1989, p. 42; Steve Lohr, "Reality Spoiled a Merchant's Dream," *The New York Times*, January 28, 1992, p. D6.

Marketing and financial strategies are the two pillars that support successful retail programs. The preceding chapter discussed facets of retail marketing strategy, and this chapter focuses on developing financial strategy. Like all businesses, retail firms must be concerned about their financial well-being. Even the most elaborate marketing strategy will fail without an adequate, well-conceived financial plan. This chapter demonstrates how a firm's marketing strategy affects its financial performance. It develops a framework for evaluating that performance and presents a systematic approach to financial planning for retail firms.

Financial planning is important for both large and small firms. Firms with poor financial performance cannot survive in today's performance-oriented business environment; in fact, it is estimated that more than 50 percent of all small retailers fail within three years of establishing the business.[1] Although, on average, large firms tend to do much better than small stores, the failure of such large retail firms as W. T. Grant, Korvettes, Allied Supermarkets, and R. H. Stearns and the recent bankruptcy filings by Revco, Best Stores, and Macy's bear testimony to the importance of financial planning and the need to integrate marketing and financial strategies to develop a successful retail program.

ANALYZING FINANCIAL PERFORMANCE

Although all retailers will agree that financial planning is important, many do not give it adequate attention. For both a large firm with many outlets or a small one that operates only a single store, proper financial planning is an essential ingredient of success. A key task in developing the firm's financial strategy is to analyze current performance and set future targets. Because financial analysis requires information from the firm's balance sheet and income statement, it is useful to first review these two accounting statements.

The Income Statement

Whether or not they engage in any formal financial planning, nearly all retailers prepare **income statements**. The income statement summarizes the financial results of the firm for a specific time period such as a quarter, six months, or a year. It reports the revenues earned by the firm and the sources and amounts of all expenses incurred during that time period. Based on these revenues and expenses, the profit (or loss) for that period can be calculated. The income statement is a concise summary of the financial impact of the firm's operations during the specified time period.

Exhibit 7.1 presents the income statement of the Alpine Ski Shop for the year 1991. Two friends opened the Alpine Ski Shop in a New England town in 1983 after graduating from a local university with degrees in marketing and retailing. The store sells ski equipment, camping and hiking gear, athletic shoes, and outdoor clothing. It serves the local population as well as the many tourists who visit the area. Although the store struggled for the first few years, it has recorded increasing sales and profit each year since 1987.

In 1990, convinced that the teething period was finally over, the owners hired a full-time manager to run the store on a daily basis. The two friends now devote most of their time to operating a motel located a few miles from the store. They continue, however, to closely oversee the operations of the ski shop.

Five elements of the income statement summarize key dimensions of the firm's operations for the year. These are: (1) sales; (2) cost of goods sold; (3) gross margin; (4) selling, general, and administrative (SGA) expenses (also called operating expenses); and (5) profit. It is important to first clearly define what each of these elements measure.

Sales   For the year 1990 the gross sales for Alpine Ski Shop were $272,200. Gross sales reports the total amount of money obtained from customers through the sale of merchandise and services. Some of the money, however, had to be returned to customers who brought back defective items. The amount after accounting for such returns and other adjustments is **net sales**. In 1990 the net sales for the ski shop were $270,000. When a reference is made to a store's "sales," it usually means net sales.

Exhibit 7.1   *Income Statement for Alpine Ski Shop, 1991*

Gross sales	$272,200		
Less: returns	2,200		
Net sales			$270,000
Beginning inventory (at cost)	85,000		
Purchases during year	170,000		
Freight	1,000		
Inventory available for sale		$256,000	
Less: ending inventory		80,000	
Cost of goods sold			176,000
Gross margin			94,000
Wages and salaries	38,200		
Rents and occupancy	24,400		
Selling expenses	8,000		
General expenses	6,000		
Total SGA expenses			76,600
Net profit			17,400

Cost of Goods Sold (COGS)   To generate $270,000 worth of sales, the store had to purchase merchandise from various suppliers. This merchandise cost the Alpine Ski Shop $176,000. This is the **cost of goods sold**. Cost of goods sold is usually the largest expense item for retailers. It tends to be highest for supermarkets where it typically represents 80 to 85 percent of net sales. In department and apparel stores, the cost of goods is about 60 to 65 percent of revenues.

The cost of goods sold is the total expense the retailer incurred to put together the merchandise it sold to customers. For example, an apparel store will include its cost of all clothes it sold during the year. It will also include any cost it incurred in transporting the merchandise and the cost of alterations. In supermarkets, COGS includes the cost of all packaged goods as well as the costs of items such as meat and produce. For restaurants, the costs of all food supplies and cooking ingredients is included in the cost of goods sold. In addition, if the restaurant uses disposable napkins, plates, and tableware, it includes the costs of those items too.

Gross Margin   The difference between sales revenue and cost of goods sold is called **gross margin**. This is an important measure because it indicates the amount of money that is available to cover expenses. In 1990 the ski shop's gross margin was $94,000 ($270,000 – $176,000). The firm needed this amount to cover its oper-

For this fast food restaurant the cost of its disposable cups, napkins, and packaging is part of the cost of goods sold.

ating expenses such as rents, wages and salaries, advertising, promotion, and so forth. Gross margin is often expressed as a percentage of net sales:

$$\text{Gross margin percentage} = \frac{\text{Net sales} - \text{COGS}}{\text{Net sales}} \times 100$$

The Alpine Ski Shop's gross margin percentage can be calculated as follows:

$$\text{Gross margin percentage} = \frac{\$270{,}000 - \$176{,}000}{\$270{,}000} \times 100 = 34.8 \text{ percent}$$

This means that for every dollar of sales it generated, the ski shop got 34.8 cents to cover costs. The remaining 65.2 cents went directly to cover the cost of the merchandise.

Selling, General and Administrative (SGA) Expenses   **SGA expenses** include all expenses the retailer incurs except its cost of goods sold. SGA expenses are also called operating expenses. The total SGA expenses for Alpine Ski Shop for 1990 amounted to $76,600. Total SGA expenses can be divided into four major groups as shown in Exhibit 7.1.

The largest expense for this ski shop is the cost of the merchandise it buys from its various suppliers.

- *Wages and Salaries* represent the cost of paying all personnel working for the firm. Salaries as well as the cost of providing health, retirement, and other benefits to sales personnel, clerical staff, and managers are included in this category.
- *Rent and occupancy* covers costs of renting the store site or the cost of the mortgage. Utility expenses and real estate taxes also fall in this category.
- *Selling expenses* are the direct costs of selling the merchandise. Advertising and promotion account for a major part of selling expenses. Some firms pay salespeople commissions based on the amount of sales they are able to generate. The amount of such commission is also included under selling expenses.
- *General expenses* include such items as depreciation and interest.

Profit   The final element of the income statement is **net profit**. This reports the amount the firm earned (or lost, if net profit is negative) during the period covered by the income statement. It is found by subtracting the cost of goods sold and total SGA expenses from net sales. As shown in Exhibit 7-1, Alpine Ski Shop's 1991 net profit before taxes was $17,400. Subtracting the amount of tax payable by the store from this figure yields the net profit after taxes.

The Balance Sheet

Firms prepare a second financial report called the **balance sheet**. Exhibit 7.2 shows the balance sheet for Alpine Ski Shop as of December 31, 1991. The top portion of the balance sheet lists the monetary value of the firm's assets. The lower portion labeled liabilities and net worth shows the sources of the firm's funds.

The balance sheet usually divides the firm's **assets** into two categories: current assets and fixed assets. Current assets include items that can easily be converted into cash—such as cash on hand, accounts receivables, any short-term investments made by the firm, and the value of the merchandise inventory. Fixed assets, on the other hand, are items that are used for the operation of the business and are not intended for resale or immediate conversion to cash. Fixed assets include such items as land and buildings, fixtures, display racks, and delivery

---

Exhibit 7.2   Alpine Ski Shop, Balance Sheet: December 31, 1991

Assets

Cash	$7,400	
Accounts receivables	600	
Inventory	80,000	
Total current assets		$88,000
Equipment and fixtures	28,000	
Vehicles	12,000	
Total fixed assets		40,000
Total assets		128,000

Liabilities and Net Worth

Accounts payable	$3,500	
Short-term loan	5,000	
Taxes payable	2,500	
Total current liabilities	$11,000	
Long-term debt	33,000	
Total liabilities		44,000
Net worth (stockholders' equity)		84,000
Total liabilities and net worth		128,000

vehicles. The essential difference between the two types of assets is that the current assets are resources needed for day-to-day operations, while fixed assets represent long-term investments.

The second part of the balance sheet shows the firm's **liabilities** and net worth, the sources from which the firm received money to fund its assets. Liabilities include monies owed to banks and other creditors, divided into short term or long term. The firm expects to pay off short-term liabilities within a year, while long-term liabilities are debts taken for longer periods. Net worth represents the total funds the firm's owners provide to it, or the owner's equity in the firm. Note that on the balance sheet the total of liabilities and net worth equals total assets. This must always be true since the firm cannot have more assets than the total amount of funds available to it.

It is important to note that the balance sheet shows the assets and liabilities of the firm at a particular point of time, in this case December 31, 1991. The income statement, on the other hand, summarizes the ski shop's operation for the entire year 1991. The balance sheet gives valid information to evaluate the firm's performance for the year only if the year-end data represents the typical conditions during the year. For example, if a significant amount of assets is added just prior to the end of the year, the balance sheet would not represent the typical conditions over the year.

MARGIN MANAGEMENT

The income statement and balance sheet provide the information necessary to analyze a firm's financial performance. One important indicator of a firm's performance, its **net profit margin** or return on sales (ROS), measures profit as a percent of sales. In 1991 Alpine Ski Shop earned $17,400 on sales of $270,000. Its net profit margin, therefore, was:

$$\text{Net profit margin} = \frac{\text{Net profit}}{\text{Net sales}} \times 100$$

$$= \frac{\$17,400}{\$270,000} \times 100$$

On average, every dollar of sales generated 6.44 cents of profit. Retailers evaluate profit margin rather than absolute profit because they can compare profit margin among firms. Profit margins also allow historical comparison of a firm's performance in different years.

The Margin Model

By comparing profits to sales, the net profit margin indicates how well the firm has managed its cost in relation to its sales revenue. **Margin management** is an important task for retail managers since it determines much of a firm's profitability. To see more clearly how net profit margin reflects the store's operations, Exhibit 7.3 presents the information from the Alpine Ski Shop's income statement in a slightly different format. This format provides a better visual picture of the relationship among the different elements of the income statement.

Net profit margin depends primarily on the relationship among three factors: sales, cost of goods sold, and SGA expenses. A change in any one of these factors will affect the firm's profit margin. To manage the margin, the retailer controls the relationship among these three factors to achieve the desired rate of profitability.

Since the profit margin depends on the relationship between revenues and costs, it is sensitive to the firm's marketing and operating policies. Any policy that changes

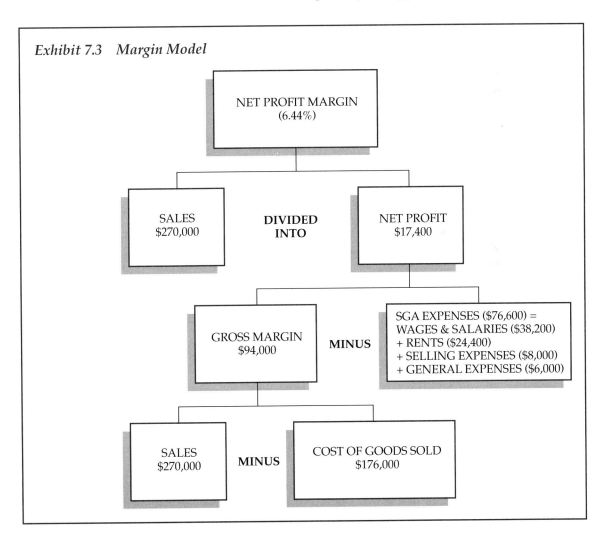

Exhibit 7.3   Margin Model

NET PROFIT MARGIN
(6.44%)

SALES
$270,000

**DIVIDED
INTO**

NET PROFIT
$17,400

GROSS MARGIN
$94,000

MINUS

SGA EXPENSES ($76,600) =
WAGES & SALARIES ($38,200)
+ RENTS ($24,400)
+ SELLING EXPENSES ($8,000)
+ GENERAL EXPENSES ($6,000)

SALES
$270,000

MINUS

COST OF GOODS SOLD
$176,000

RESEARCH REPORT

Financing Your New Retail Venture

If you plan to open a new retail business, one of the major challenges you will face is to secure financing. You will require money to furnish the store, procure merchandise, advertise, and arrange for working capital to cover salaries, insurance, utilities, and so on. Most entrepreneurs are faced with the question of how to raise money. Here is a list of some common sources of entrepreneurial capital:

Personal Sources Entrepreneurs initially use some of their personal resources for start-up capital. Many entrepreneurs, for example, tap into their personal savings, obtain second mortgages on their house, or cash-in life insurance policies to obtain start-up capital. Loans from family members and close friends are another popular source. Outside investors will typically insist on some equity participation from the entrepreneur before agreeing to invest in the new venture.

Private Investors Beyond friends and family, many wealthy individuals may want to invest in your business in hopes of sharing future profits. This is often called *informal risk capital*. Your ability to tap into this source depends on your personal contacts and your ability to network. Typically, you will need a written business plan in order to obtain informal risk capital. If you form a corporation, you can obtain capital through *private placement* of stock equity. A private placement is a limited sale of stock to pri-

the levels of net sales, cost of goods, or other expenses will impact on profit margin. Maintaining a proper relationship among these factors is an important aspect of financial management of retail firms. A change in marketing strategy can have disastrous consequences for the firm's financial health, if the balance among sales, expenses, and profit is not maintained. Retailers often implement special promotional programs and change their pricing strategy to increase sales. While sales do increase, often net profit margin drops significantly and leads to poor financial results. Proper margin management requires a thorough understanding of the impact the firm's policies have on sales revenues and the costs of generating those sales.

Impact of Sales and Costs on Margin

Impact of Sales Increase   What impact would a change in pricing strategy have on the Alpine Ski Shop's profit margin? Suppose the ski shop selectively raises price on some of its merchandise. Assume that the price increase boosts

vate parties under the 1982 SEC Regulation D guidelines.

Venture Capital   Venture capital refers to a professionally managed pool of funds that are invested in new ventures. Venture capital firms seek high rates of return to balance the riskiness of their ventures. Venture capitalists, however, are quite reluctant to invest in the early stages of a new business, although there are some who do provide seed capital. Venture capital may be more appropriate for financing an expansion once the store has become well established.

Debt Capital   Debt is another source of capital for new businesses. Commercial banks, of course, are the most popular source of debt. Banks lend against a com-

pany's assets such as inventory and store fixtures. A new retailer can get help from the Small Business Administration (SBA) to secure bank loans. The Small Business Investment Company (SBIC) and the Minority Enterprise Small Business Investment Company (MESBIC) provide equity and debt financing to small corporations. Sometimes debts can be obtained from suppliers and vendors, too.

Sources: David H. Holt, *Entrepreneurship*, (Englewood Cliffs, NJ: Prentice-Hall), 1992; and Howard H. Stevenson, Michael J. Roberts, and H. Irving Grousbeck, *New Business Ventures and the Entrepreneur*, (Homewood, IL: Irwin), 1989.

sales by 3 percent without any increase in the cost of goods sold or SGA expenses. The impact of this price change is shown in Exhibit 7.4. A 3 percent increase raises net sales to $278,100. In the absence of any cost increase, net profit increases to $25,500 ($278,100 – $176,000 – $76,600). These new levels of sales and profits yield a net profit margin of 9.17 percent. This is a 42.4 percent increase from the current level of 6.44 percent. A 3 percent increase in sales revenue results in a 42 percent increase in profit margin!

This surprising increase occurred because none of the costs increased even though sales increased. Since both cost of goods and SGA expenses remain unchanged, net profit increased by the same amount as the revenue gained by the price increase (3 percent of $270,000). Every dollar of increased sales reaches the bottom line intact.

Impact of Expense Control   Retailers can also increase net profit margin by controlling expenses. If they can maintain the same level of sales with lower costs, net profit margin will increase. Suppose, for example, that Alpine Ski Shop reduces its cost of goods sold by 5 percent by taking advantage of trade discounts pro-

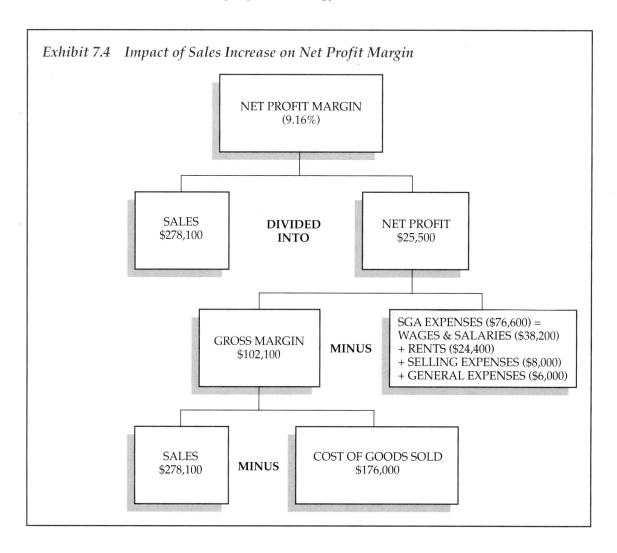

Exhibit 7.4   Impact of Sales Increase on Net Profit Margin

vided by some suppliers and controlling freight and delivery charges. What impact do these savings have on profit margin?

A 5 percent decrease reduces cost of goods sold to $167,200 and this increases margin to $102,800 ($270,000 – $167,200). Net profit in this scenario comes to $26,200 ($102,800 – $76,600), yielding a net profit margin of 9.70 percent. Thus, the store increases profit margin by more than 50 percent by reducing cost of goods sold by 5 percent. Again, a small change in costs results in a substantial improvement in net profit margin.

Joint Impact of Increasing Sales and Reducing Cost   How will the ski shop's profit margin change if it increases net sales by 3 percent and decreases cost of goods by 5 percent at the same time? Surely profit margin will increase. If a 3 percent increase in net sales raises profit margin to 9.14 percent and a 5 percent reduction in cost of goods sold increases it to 9.70 percent, what will the profit margin be if sales increase and cost reduction occur simultaneously?

Exhibit 7.5 demonstrates the joint impact of sales increase and cost reduction on the ski shop's profit margin. Changes in sales and cost affects all components of the income statement, ultimately including the profit margin. In the new scenario, net sales of $278,100 and cost of goods sold of $167,200 give a gross margin of $110,900 ($278,100 − $167,200). Subtracting the SGA expenses from the gross margin gives a net profit of $34,300. The net profit margin is 12.33 percent, which is nearly double the actual 1991 level of 6.44 percent.

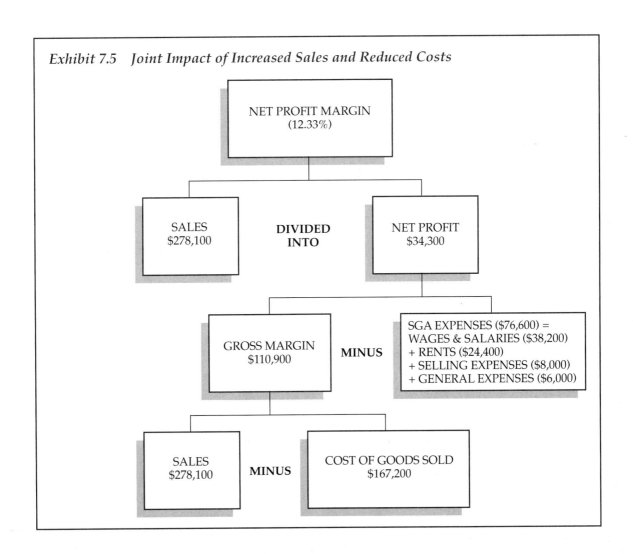

Exhibit 7.5   *Joint Impact of Increased Sales and Reduced Costs*

These examples illustrate the sensitivity of profit margins to the firm's marketing and operating policies. It is important to realize that even a small change in sales or expenses can greatly affect profit performance. To set effective profit goals or targets, the retail manager must understand these relationships well.

ASSET MANAGEMENT

Managing profit margin is a crucial component of the overall financial planning for the firm, since the margin determines the level of profit the firm will be able to earn. Margins do not, however, provide a complete picture of the firm's financial performance because the calculations do not consider the amount of resources used by the firm. If two firms earn exactly the same amount of profits, but consume different amounts of resources, then their performance is not equal despite identical profits. To measure financial performance in light of resource utilization, sales and profit levels must be judged in relation to the amount of resources the firm consumed to generate them. Only then can one measure show how productively the firm's assets have been used.

Asset Turnover

One measure of asset productivity, **asset turnover**, examines the relationship between sales and total assets of the firm. Asset turnover is calculated as follows:

$$\text{Asset turnover} = \frac{\text{Net sales}}{\text{Total assets}}$$

Asset turnover measures the sales generated per dollar of assets owned by the firm. Since the assets represent the resources used to run a business, asset turnover measures how productively a firm employed its resources. Higher turnover indicates a higher level of sales per dollar of assets.

The Alpine Ski Shop's 1987 asset turnover can be calculated by dividing the net sales figure from the income statement by the total asset figure from the balance sheet, giving:

$$\text{Asset turnover} = \frac{\$270,000}{\$128,000} = 2.11$$

This means that for every dollar of assets the store generated revenues of $2.11.

Factors Affecting Asset Turnover

How can a firm improve the productivity of assets? Since the asset turnover rate depends on the balance between sales and assets, it can be increased by increasing sales, decreasing assets, or both. In the earlier example, if the ski shop increased its sales by 3 percent, it would increase asset turnover to 2.17 ($278,000/$128,000), as long as it consumed no new assets in increasing sales. Similarly, if it reduced the size of total assets without sacrificing sales, it would increase asset turnover. A reduction in any of the asset categories—inventory, account receivables, or fixed assets—increases asset turnover. Consider, for example, that the store was able to reduce inventory costs from $80,000 to $72,000 and used the released funds to pay off some debts. If sales do not change, the asset turnover would increase to 2.24 ($270,000/$120,000).

Return on Assets

The analysis of Alpine Ski Shop's financial performance in 1991 reveals two important insights:

- The firm had a net profit margin of 6.44 percent for the year. On average, each dollar of sales generated 6.44 percent of profit.
- The firm had an asset turnover of 2.11 for the year. On average, every dollar of assets generated sales of $2.11.

Since net profit margin measures profits per dollar of sales, and asset turnover measures sales per dollar of assets, combining the two ratios yield profit per dollar of assets:

$$\frac{\text{Net profit}}{\text{Net sales}} \times \frac{\text{Net sales}}{\text{Total assets}} = \frac{\text{Net profit}}{\text{Total assets}}$$

The right side of this expression measures the **return on assets (ROA)**, while the two ratios on the left-hand side measure net profit margin and asset turnover, respectively. In other words:

$$\text{Net profit margin} \times \text{Asset turnover} = \text{Return on assets (ROA)}$$

This expression gives a return on assets for Alpine Ski Shop for 1991 of:

$$\frac{\$17,400}{\$270,000} \times \frac{\$270,000}{\$128,000} = \frac{\$17,400}{\$128,000}$$

$$6.44 \quad \times \quad 2.11 \quad = 13.59 \text{ percent}$$

For every dollar of assets, the Alpine Ski Shop generated 13.59 cents of profit.

Return on assets (ROA) is an important indicator of financial performance. It combines profit margin and asset turnover figures into a single ratio that measures the productivity of the firm's assets in terms of profits. A single ROA figure has an advantage over individual return on sales and asset turnover in that ROAs of different types of firms can be directly compared. Return on sales and asset turnover, on the other hand, depend on the characteristics of the firm and cannot be compared across different types of retail operations.

For example, jewelry stores and high-end specialty and department stores generally have lower asset turnover rates and higher profit margins than discount stores, convenience stores, or supermarkets. The marketing strategies of high-end stores stress margin over turnover, while supermarkets and discount stores stress turnover over margin. Comparing the profit margins and asset turnovers of firms that follow different marketing strategies yields little meaningful information, but because all firms must earn an adequate return on their assets, the return on assets of different types of firms can be directly compared.

Balancing Profit Margin and Asset Turnover

To survive, all firms must achieve an adequate return on their assets. A firm that does not stress fast asset turnover must earn high margins. Similarly, firms with low profit margins must have high asset turnover. Compare, for example, the 1991 financial results of May Department Stores, a diversified firm that operates department, discount, and specialty chains, and Costco Wholesale, a warehouse club chain:

Company	Net Profit Margin	Asset Turnover	ROA
May	4.85	1.23	5.96
Costco	1.64	4.22	6.92

Note how each firm balanced asset turnover and margin. As is typical of warehouse stores, Costco stressed turnover more than margins. The marketing strategies of warehouse stores stress low prices which keep their margins low. But they achieve profitability through high asset turnover. Department stores cannot achieve the same asset turnover as warehouse clubs. May generated sales of just 1.23 times its assets, but its net profit margin was 4.85 percent compared to Costco's margin of 1.64 percent. Retail firms must strike a balance between turnover and margin to ensure adequate returns on their assets.

Improving Return on Assets

Retailers must continuously monitor the impact of marketing and operating policies on return on assets since in sales, profits, costs, or assets can all change ROA. To monitor the effect of firm policies on ROA, it is best to combine information from the income statement and the balance sheet into a single ROA model like that shown in Exhibit 7.6, that shows all the factors that affect a firm's return on assets. In the exhibit, ten boxes representing primary operating variables are highlighted. The primary operating variables are the keys to profitability. A change in any of these variables will affect ROA. The retail manager must continuously monitor and control these factors and seek ways to improve ROA by changing the relationship among them.

Firms may use different avenues to improve return on assets. Some examples are discussed briefly below.

Exhibit 7.6   Return on Assets (ROA) Model

Sales $270,000	−	Cost of goods sold $176,000	=	Gross margin $94,000

Wages and salaries $38,200	+	Rent and occupancy $24,400	+	Selling expense $8,000	+	General expense $6,000	=	Total expenses $76,600

Gross margin $94,000	−	Total expenses $76,600	=	Net profit $17,400

Net profit $17,400	÷	Sales $270,000	=	Net profit margin 6.44%

Inventory $80,000	+	Accounts receivable $600	+	Other current assets $7,400	=	Total current assets $88,000

Total current assets $88,000	+	Fixed assets $40,000	=	Total assets $128,000

Sales $270,000	÷	Total assets $128,000	=	Asset turnover 2.11

Asset turnover 2.11	×	Net profit margin 6.44%	=	Return on assets 13.59%

Increasing Sales   One way to improve ROA is to increase sales while controlling costs and assets. Since sales revenue depends in part on price, it may be possible to increase revenue by changing the price of the merchandise. However, retailers should exercise caution when changing prices to keep them consistent with

Filene's in Boston increases sales by using special markdown policies.

the firm's overall strategy. Supermarkets, discount stores, and many appliance stores and electronics retailers build their competitive advantage through low prices. The intense price competition in these industries leaves these firms little room to increase price. On the other hand, a price decrease could increase revenues if it increased demand adequately. This depends on the price elasticity of the goods sold by the store. The relation between price elasticity and retail prices is discussed in more detail in Chapter 14.

At the other end of the spectrum, customers of exclusive stores, such as Gucci, Neiman-Marcus, and Tiffany's, pay more attention to nonprice factors. The status appeal of their exclusive merchandise strongly influences the customer's purchase decision. These stores thus have more latitude to increase price.

Retailers can also increase total revenue by controlling the amount of markdowns taken during special "sale" periods. Since markdowns indirectly reduce the price of the product, by offering fewer markdowns the retailer may increase revenues without any increase in the original price of the merchandise. Retailers should control their inventories closely to reduce the need to sell merchandise at marked-down prices. Markdown policies are discussed in more detail in Chapter 12.

Unusual promotions can increase sales. Oscar Mayer's "wiener car" travels the country promoting its hot dogs.

A store's sales revenue reflects the success of its overall retail strategy. The store's merchandise, advertising, promotion, display, service, and price together determine sales. Thus, improved merchandise selection, more effective advertising and promotion, and better service can all lead to increased sales. Many retailers lose substantial sales because they run out of stock. Proper inventory control procedures can increase sales by maintaining adequate stock of merchandise. Similarly, in-store promotions of merchandise—such as special displays and signs—can also increase sales.

Controlling Cost of Goods Sold   Cost of goods sold is a major component of the retailer's costs, and the retailer must continuously monitor suppliers' prices and payment terms to control it. Retailers must continuously search for lower prices and better payment terms without sacrificing the quality of the merchandise. Many opportunistic buying practices, such as purchasing more items during periods in which manufacturers give special price discounts and trade deals, can reduce the cost of goods. A typical supermarket, for instance, may purchase 50 to 60 percent of its grocery merchandise on deal. Warehouse supermarkets, however, reduce their costs by purchasing almost all of their merchandise on special deals. This way they can charge a lower price to the consumers and yet maintain their margin and return on assets.

Off-price clothing retailers such as T.J. Maxx and Marshall's take advantage of opportunistic buying to be able to offer their customers a significant discount from department store prices for similar merchandise. Manufacturers of national brand and designer clothing are willing to sell to off-price chains at a lower price because: (1) off-price retailers do not ask for cooperative advertising and markdown allowances from the manufacturer; (2) off-price retailers rarely return goods once they are bought; (3) off-price retailers pay promptly; and (4) off-price retailers buy end-of-season merchandise and mixed size lots. These opportunistic buying practices induce manufacturers and vendors to offer off-price retailers 30 to 40 percent discounts from their regular prices. As a result, off-price retailers can offer merchandise to customers at a significant discount and yet maintain healthy profit margins.[2]

Controlling SGA Expenses   SGA or operating expenses determine how much of its gross margin the store will convert to net profit. By reducing these costs relative to gross margin a store can raise its net profit margin. In order to control total operating costs, each cost item—wages, salaries, advertising, displays, rent, and occupancy, and so on—must be closely monitored.

Cost cutting programs must, however, be implemented carefully. During the late 1970s, many department stores reduced services and the number of sales personnel in order to control costs. This damaged the image and competitive position of department stores. Department store shoppers commonly complain about inadequate service and unqualified sales help and this has contributed to the success of specialty apparel chains. Many department stores are now trying to enhance their service quality to reacquire their lost reputations.

Controlling Assets   The fourth avenue for improving return on assets is to control the size of the firm's assets. By controlling assets, retailers can increase productivity, if they maintain sales.

For most retailers, merchandise inventory represents the largest portion of current assets. Although retailers must maintain adequate merchandise inventories, they may have opportunities for controlling inventories and reducing costs without decreasing customer convenience or without reducing merchandise selection. All items should be examined to check whether the level of stock reflects the pattern of demand. Retailers must institute proper inventory control measures to keep each item of inventory in balance with demand, keeping less stock of slow-moving items and more of items that sell well. Inventory investments can also be reduced by pruning the number of brands and sizes of each product. Since retailers typically carry many merchandise items, they may find it feasible to eliminate some slow-moving or out-of-fashion items without any negative impact on sales volume.

Good logistics and distribution systems are essential ingredients in controlling inventory investments. Inventory investments can be reduced significantly by reducing the *lead time*—the time from placing an order to receiving the merchandise in the store. Many retailers have been able to shorten their lead times by streamlining their distribution systems. Recent advances in communication technology that allow direct electronic data interchange between retailers and manufacturers and the adoption of just-in-time (JIT) inventory systems have become important tools for inventory management. Many observers believe that a key reason for Wal-Mart's success is their state-of-the-art distribution and logistics system.

LEVERAGE AND PROFITABILITY

How good an investment is Alpine Ski Shop for its owners? Unfortunately, ROA does not answer this question. Although return on assets is an important measure, it does not consider how much the firm pays its owners. As noted, ROA measures the productivity of the total assets used by the firm. Since the firm finances some assets through loans from banks and other creditors rather than by investments of its owners, a different measure is required to gauge performance from the owner's perspective. Examine, for instance, the Alpine Ski Shop's 1991 balance sheet (Exhibit 7.2). At the end of 1991, the store had total assets of $128,000. The owners had provided $84,000 to fund these assets. This is the net worth of the firm, or the owners' equity in it.

For their $84,000 investment, the owners' of the ski shop received an income of $17,400 in 1991. This is an annual return of 20.66 percent:

$$\frac{\$17,400}{\$84,000} \times 100 = 20.66 \text{ percent}$$

This is the firm's **return on net worth (RONW)** or **return on equity (ROE)**. In general RONW is calculated as follows:

$$\text{Return on net worth (RONW)} = \frac{\text{Net profit}}{\text{Net worth}} \times 100$$

Since it compares profit to amount of funds invested by the owners, RONW measures the firm's financial performance from the owners' perspective: it indicates how much profit the firm has earned for its owners. In publicly held corporations, the net worth is the sum of the monies the firm has received through stock sales and its retained earnings.

Relation of RONW to ROA

How does a firm's RONW relate to its ROA? The ski store's ROA for 1991 was 13.59 percent, but its RONW for the same year was 20.7 percent. Why is the RONW greater than ROA? The answer is that Alpine Ski Shop finances some of its assets with debt. When a firm finances assets by debt, return on net worth exceeds return on assets. Firms typically use some debt, so RONW usually exceeds ROA, as can easily be seen by comparing the expressions for RONW and ROA:

$$RONW = \frac{\text{Net profit}}{\text{Net worth}} \qquad ROA = \frac{\text{Net profit}}{\text{Total assets}}$$

The numerators in both expressions are the same. Therefore, as net worth declines compared to total assets, RONW increases compared to ROA. The two ratios will be equal if net worth equals total assets; that is, if the firm has no debt. ROA can never exceed RONW since net worth cannot exceed the firm's total assets.

Leverage Ratio

The **leverage ratio** provides one way to measure the relation between net worth to total assets:

$$\text{Leverage ratio} = \frac{\text{Net worth} + \text{Total liabilities}}{\text{Net worth}}$$

Note that since the sum of net worth and total liabilities must equal the total assets of the firm, the leverage ratio can also be defined as:

$$\text{Leverage ratio} = \frac{\text{Total assets}}{\text{Net worth}}$$

The leverage ratio for the Alpine Ski Shop can be calculated as follows:

$$\text{Leverage ratio for Alpine Ski Shop} = \frac{\$128,000}{\$84,000} = 1.52$$

The smaller the portion of the total assets funded by the owners, the higher the leverage ratio. A firm described as highly leveraged has a small owner's equity in relation to its total assets. Highly leveraged firms depend heavily on debt to operate. There is a direct relationship between a firm's leverage ratio and its debt-to-equity ratio, since the latter is determined by the relative proportion of debt and equity used to finance the firm. Consider, for example, a firm with a debt-to-equity ratio of 1:1. Such a firm has the same amount of net worth and liabilities, thus giving it a leverage ratio of 2.0. Similarly, a firm with a debt-to-equity ratio of 2.0 would have a leverage ratio of 3.0.

Impact of Leverage on RONW

The same level of ROA can result in different levels of RONW depending on the leverage ratio. The following expression states the relationship among RONW, ROA, and leverage ratio:

$$\frac{\text{Net profit}}{\text{Net worth}} = \frac{\text{Net profit}}{\text{Total assets}} \times \frac{\text{Total assets}}{\text{Net worth}}$$

$$\text{i.e., RONW} = \text{ROA} \times \text{Leverage ratio}$$

To illustrate the impact of leverage on RONW, Exhibit 7.7 shows Alpine Ski Shop's RONW for five levels of net worth. Each case has the same ROA, but a different net worth. As net worth changes, the leverage ratio changes and so does RONW.

As evident from Exhibit 7.7, for a given level of ROA, the return on the owner's investment can be increased by increasing leverage. In other words, more debt relative to equity gives a greater RONW for a given level of ROA. Consider, for example, the financial results of Home Depot and K mart corporations. The two firms' ROAs, leverages, and RONWs for 1991 were as follows:

Company	ROA	Leverage Ratio	RONW
Home Depot	9.94	1.57	15.61
K mart	5.39	2.89	15.58

The two firms had very different levels of ROA but almost equal RONW. K mart's greater use of debt boosted its return to the stockholders despite a lower ROA compared with Home Depot.

Although high leverage increases RONW, it brings with it significant risks. High levels of interest payments can severely strain the firm's resources and force it to cut expenses in marketing and merchandising. Moreover, because of high interest payments, any downturn in cash flow can become disastrous. Ultimately, the greatest risk is that of bankruptcy, when firms fail to pay creditors on time, as has happened in recent years with a number of major retailers including Federated Department Stores, Macy's, Best Corporation, Southland Corporation (7-Eleven), Carter Hawley Hale, and Revco, to name just a few.

STRATEGIC PROFIT MODEL

Return on net worth is a key financial measure by which firms set future performance targets. Meeting the target RONW is an important strategic objective and

---

Exhibit 7.7 *Impact of Leverage on RONW*

1	2	3	4	5
			Leverage	RONW
ROA	Total Assets	Net Worth	(2 ÷ 3)	(1 × 4)
13.59	$128,000	$128,000	1.00	13.59
13.59	128,000	100,000	1.28	17.39
13.59	128,000	84,000	1.52	20.66
13.59	128,000	64,000	2.00	27.18
13.59	128,000	44,000	2.91	39.55

STRATEGY IN ACTION

Excessive Debt Topples a Giant

In January 1990, less than two years after Toronto-based Campeau Corporation took over Federated Department Stores, Inc., and Allied Stores Corporation, it filed for bankruptcy protection under Chapter 11. The company, which had $7.5 billion in debt, sought protection from its creditors. The bankruptcy filing enabled the company to keep its 260 stores—belonging to Bloomingdale's, Abraham & Strauss, Stern's, Jordan Marsh, Burdine's, Rich's, Lazarus and Bon Marché chains—open and operating. Retailers and industry analysts alike were shocked, because despite the recent downturn in retailing, all of the stores owned by Allied and Federated were clear moneymakers. The problem was simply that Campeau Corporation had taken on too much debt to purchase the chains. Forced to make huge interest payments to stay afloat, the otherwise profitable retailer had no choice but to declare bankruptcy.

The 1980s were a kind of gold-rush on Wall Street, and raising money to purchase companies was easy, investors and lenders both believed that the value of good companies would continue to rise. This gold-rush spirit allowed Canadian real-estate entrepreneur Robert Campeau to borrow $3.6 billion in 1986 to buy Allied and another $6.6 billion two years later to buy Federated. By 1989, Campeau Corporation was issuing high-risk junk-bonds to investors, in order to meet their interest payments. What Campeau needed was billions annually to service his debt, and he was not able to squeeze the chains or improve operations enough to meet those payments. By the end of 1989, it was clear to many investors that the retailing giant was in trouble, and suddenly money for Campeau dried up. Unable to meet his payments, squeeze his stores for another dollar, or borrow to meet loan obligations, Campeau was forced to file for protection.

Just prior to filing for bankruptcy Campeau obtained fresh loans in excess of $700 million to meet obligations for payroll and supplies. This sent suppliers and em-

firms must develop financial plans to attain this goal. This section of the chapter presents a comprehensive framework for this financial planning called **strategic profit model**, which combines the various aspects of financial planning into a single framework that focuses on return on net worth. Many retailing and nonretailing firms alike employ the strategic profit model—sometimes called the Du Pont model after the well-known chemical manufacturers that first proposed it as a formal financial planning tool.

Three Avenues to Profitability

It has already been observed that a firm's return on net worth (RONW) is related to its return on assets (ROA) in the following manner:

ployees dashing to the bank in order to deposit the checks and get them cleared before the bankruptcy papers were filed. Some suppliers even went as far as to open accounts in the states where the checks were issued in order to clear the checks faster, but many suppliers and employees lost their money in any case. Some suppliers were resigned about it, saying they hoped that Allied and Federated, as great retailing clients, would get themselves back on their feet. But others were furious at the company for plunging all those great stores into failure unnecessarily. Across the board, however, everyone believed in the potential of all the stores involved, and believed that with careful management all the Federated and Allied stores could again be profitable. According to industry analysts, the problem was the debt burden, and not a downturn in retailing.

Criticism of the crumbling empire took a very personal approach, putting most of the blame on Robert Campeau himself. At odds with the Canadian banking and retailing industries for many years, Campeau was seen by many as a retail upstart. Blocked by the Toronto business establishment in 1980 from purchasing one of Canada's largest financial houses, Campeau complained that the Canadian business community was against him and turned his attention to U.S. retailers. In the heady days of 1986 when his billion-dollar deals to purchase Allied and Federated were approved, the Campeaus threw lavish parties at their homes in Toronto and Palm Beach, inviting world-famous fashion and entertainment figures, and Campeau himself graced the covers of many major business publications. However, after the Chapter 11 filing, the nicest thing that anyone seemed to be able to say was that he had overextended himself, his company, and American retailing as a whole in his quest for social legitimacy.

Sources: Floyd Norris, "Campeau Invokes Bankruptcy for Its Biggest Stores: Loan Spree Seems Over," *The New York Times*, January 16, 1990, pp. A1, D6; and Isadore Barmash, "Campeau Invokes Bankruptcy for Its Biggest Stores: $7.5 Billion in Debt," *The New York Times*, January 16, 1990, pp. A1, D5.

$$\text{RONW} = \text{ROA} \times \text{Leverage ratio}$$

Further, recall that ROA also has two components:

$$\text{ROA} = \text{Net profit margin} \times \text{Asset turnover}$$

Combining these two relationships leads to the following expression:

$$\text{RONW} = \text{Net profit margin} \times \text{Asset turnover} \times \text{Leverage ratio}$$

Or,

$$\frac{\text{Net profit}}{\text{Net worth}} = \frac{\text{Net profit}}{\text{Net sales}} \times \frac{\text{Net sales}}{\text{Total assets}} \times \frac{\text{Total assets}}{\text{Net worth}}$$

This expression, which summarizes the strategic profit model, shows the three components of the retail financial program and how they combine to determine a firm's return on net worth.

The relationship among the three components of the strategic profit model can be examined by filling in the model for the Alpine Ski Shop. The store's strategic profit model for 1991:

$$
\begin{aligned}
\text{RONW} &= \text{Net profit margin} \times \text{Asset turnover} \times \text{Leverage ratio} \\
&= \frac{\$17{,}400}{\$270{,}000} \times \frac{\$270{,}000}{\$128{,}000} \times \frac{\$128{,}000}{\$84{,}000} \\
&= 6.44\% \times 2.11 \times 1.52 \\
&= 20.66 \text{ percent}
\end{aligned}
$$

Note that this is the same figure obtained earlier.

A reason for the importance of the strategic profit model is that it clearly identifies three avenues for improving a firm's financial performance. Return on net worth can be improved through proper management of (1) margins (the relationship between sales and expenses), (2) asset turnover (the relationship between sales and assets, and (3) leverage ratio (the relationship between debt and equity). Each of these three components must be coordinated to get the best financial results and a change in any one of them will affect RONW. For example, compare the scenario that the Alpine Ski Shop is able to raise prices and increase its net sales by 3 percent without any increase in its COGS or SGA expenses and without opening any additional outlets. How would this affect the firm's RONW? As seen earlier in Exhibit 7.4, a 3 percent sales increase boosts sales to $278,100 and the net profit margin to 9.17 percent. The higher sales also increase asset turnover to 2.17 ($278,100 / $128,000), since no additional assets are used. The leverage ratio remains at 1.52 since no new debt or equity is involved. The new return on net worth then is:

$$
\text{RONW} = 9.17\% \times 2.17 \times 1.52 = 30.25\%
$$

This is a 46 percent increase over the current RONW level.

Now suppose that the firm had taken a long-term debt of $10,000 for new fixtures requiring an annual interest payment of $1,200. The additional interest payment reduces the net profit from $25,500 to $24,300, resulting in a net profit margin of 8.74 percent. Asset turnover also decreases since $10,000 of new assets are now being used to generate the extra sales. The asset turnover in this scenario is 2.02 ($278,100 / $138,000). The leverage ratio, on the other hand, increases since the firm is now using relatively more debt than before. The new leverage ratio is 1.64 ($138,000 / $84,000). The return on net worth in this case is:

$$
\text{RONW} = 8.74\% \times 2.02 \times 1.64 = 28.95
$$

The three components of RONW—margin, asset turnover, and leverage—depend directly on the firm's marketing and operating policies. Exhibit 7.8 presents the strategic profit model figures for a number of well-known retail firms. It is interesting to observe from these examples how different combinations of margins, asset turnover, and leverage result in similar return on net worth.

Exhibit 7.8 *Strategic Profit Model for Selected Retail Firms*

Firm	Net Profit Margin	Asset Turnover	Leverage	Return on Net Worth
Wal-Mart	3.66%	2.84	2.41	25.0
Sears, Roebuck	2.00	0.54	8.09	8.7
Home Depot	4.85	2.05	1.57	15.6
K mart	2.46	2.19	2.89	15.5
Toys R Us	5.55	1.24	2.29	15.7
The Limited	6.55	1.74	2.08	23.7
J.C. Penney	3.05	1.38	3.15	13.3
May Department Stores	4.85	1.23	3.82	22.8
Food Lion	3.18	3.23	2.41	24.8
The Gap	9.13	2.20	1.69	33.9
Albertson's	2.97	3.97	1.87	22.1
Dayton Hudson	1.97	1.70	3.91	13.9
Dillard Department Stores	5.10	1.15	2.36	18.0
Walgreen	2.87	3.14	2.00	12.4
Costco Wholesale	1.64	4.22	1.87	12.9

Source: Computed from data in *The 1992 Business Week 1000*.

Using the Strategic Profit Model

The strategic profit model aids retail managers in three important ways. First, the model helps them monitor and evaluate current performance and identify potential problem areas. Second, the strategic profit model helps in setting future targets. Third, it can predict the financial implications of proposed changes in store policy.

Evaluating Current Performance   A simple way to judge a firm's current performance is to compare it with past results. Historical comparisons indicate whether the firm's performance has improved over time, held ground, or deteriorated. Simply meeting past standards is not reassuring, however, if the firm has consistently performed poorly in the past. It is important, therefore, to compare a firm's financial results with those of other, similar firms. A comparison with industry-wide figures indicates whether a firm has kept pace with its peers' performance. The firm's overall RONW as well as the figures for the components of the model should be compared to identify its weaknesses and strengths.

Industry-wide financial results are available from a variety of secondary sources. Dun and Bradstreet compiles the most widely used source, Industry Norms and Key Business Ratios, covering 24 categories of retail firms. For each category the average return on sales, return on assets, and return on net worth of good performers (upper quartile), average performers (median), and poor performers (lower quartile) are reported. An example appears in Exhibit 7.9. Another source is the annual S*tatement Studies* published by Robert Morris Associates, an association of bank loan officers. Many trade associations also publish industry-wide financial ratios.

Setting Financial Targets   The strategic profit model helps in setting future goals for the company. Consider, for example, a jewelry store that achieves a 2 percent return on sales. As evident from Exhibit 7.8, this is well below the average performance for the industry. The average ROS for median performers was 5.5 percent. Noting that the store's profit margin falls short of industry norms, the managers of the store can concentrate on this factor in future years. First, they must ask why the profit margin is lower than industry average. Next, they must set targets for the future. Finally, they must devise strategies that will help them reach the target without negatively affecting other aspects of the firm's business.

Financial Impact of New Strategy   The strategic profit model can also help evaluate the financial implication of changes in the firm's marketing or operating strategies. Before implementing a new strategy, managers can attempt to predict its impact on financial results by anticipating how the strategy will affect sales, cost of goods sold, interest expenses, inventory costs, and other factors that determine the three components of the strategic profit model. Such *what-if analysis* is a useful tool for managerial decision-making, since it allows reasoned judgment about future courses of action. Firms can also modify and improve plans based on the analysis. The increasing use of spreadsheet software programs on personal computers has made what-if analysis (also called simulation) a popular managerial tool.

Advantages of Strategic Profit Model

The strategic profit model is a versatile tool for financial analysis and planning. Specific strengths include:

1. The model brings together information from the income statement and the balance sheet into a single, comprehensive framework.
2. It sets return on net worth as the principal yardstick for measuring a firm's financial performance.
3. It clearly identifies three avenues—margin management, asset management, and leverage management—for improving return on net worth.
4. It provides easy comparison of the firm's performance against industry-wide figures to determine areas for future improvement.
5. It can be used as a spreadsheet for performing what-if analysis.

One of the retailer's most important decisions is choosing the location of the store. Stores can be located in suburban shopping centers, such as this one in Southern California, or in isolated sites like this hardware store in San Diego. Shopping malls draw great numbers of people which can be very beneficial to small specialty stores. An isolated site can help a store develop a small but loyal clientele, providing a steady sales volume.

Specialty malls like this one in Trump Towers in Manhattan cater to the buildings' tenants and tourists from all over the world. The main-street of this small Ohio town continues to meet the needs of both consumers and retailers, just as it has for over one hundred years.

The central business district, has historically been the center of big city retailing and the birthplace of most major department stores. The Macy's outlet in New York is one of the largest stores in the world. The movement to the suburbs accelerated in the years following World War II, stimulating the growth of small planned shopping centers. The neighborhood center in the San Fernando Valley suburbs of Los Angeles is typical.

Stores catering to a particular market or ethnic group can enhance business by locating near one another. Koreatown Plaza in Los Angeles contains many Korean-owned businesses and restaurants. A street in Queens, New York, is home to retailers selling goods from India.

© Bill Aron/PhotoEdit
© Robert Brenner/PhotoEdit

Exhibit 7.9 *Profitability Ratios by Store Type*

	Upper Quartile	Median	Lower Quartile
Department stores 5311			
Return on sales	3.8	1.4	(0.1)
Return on assets	7.0	2.8	(0.2)
Return on net worth	12.1	5.3	(0.1)
Family clothing stores 5651			
Return on sales	11.1	4.3	0.9
Return on assets	16.4	6.7	1.5
Return on net worth	25.4	10.7	2.4
Furniture stores 5712			
Return on sales	8.3	3.3	0.6
Return on assets	12.7	5.4	0.9
Return on net worth	25.9	10.2	2.5
General merchandise 5399			
Return on sales	7.5	3.3	0.7
Return on assets	14.9	6.3	1.0
Return on net worth	27.0	9.8	1.8
Grocery stores 5411			
Return on sales	3.5	1.4	0.5
Return on assets	12.8	6.6	2.1
Return on net worth	35.5	15.1	5.9
Liquor stores 5921			
Return on sales	7.6	3.4	0.7
Return on assets	17.8	7.8	1.7
Return on net worth	46.2	16.5	4.5
Men's/boys' clothing 5611			
Return on sales	11.7	4.0	1.0
Return on assets	17.7	6.9	1.5
Return on net worth	28.9	12.1	3.2
Electronic stores 5731			
Return on sales	11.8	5.1	1.2
Return on assets	19.7	8.2	2.1
Return on net worth	33.6	15.3	4.6
Shoe stores 5661			
Return on sales	13.0	6.4	1.7
Return on assets	26.2	10.9	3.3
Return on net worth	50.3	21.2	6.8
Women's accessories 5632			
Return on sales	13.6	5.5	0.7
Return on assets	28.1	9.9	1.4
Return on net worth	146.1	19.3	3.0
Women's clothing 5621			
Return on sales	11.0	4.8	0.8
Return on assets	20.1	7.5	1.3
Return on net worth	35.5	14.1	2.1
Drug stores 5912			
Return on sales	7.4	3.1	0.9
Return on assets	20.0	8.4	2.3
Return on net worth	41.9	16.6	5.1

Summary

1. Financial planning is important for both small and large retail firms. Lack of proper financial planning can disrupt even the most elaborate marketing strategies. Since a firm's marketing strategy directly affects its financial performance, it must coordinate marketing and financial strategies properly to yield profitable results.
2. The income statement and the balance sheet are two basic accounting statements used by almost all retail firms. The income statement summarizes the revenues earned and the sources and amounts of all expenses incurred during a specific time period. Five key elements of the income statement are: (a) sales; (b) cost of goods sold; (c) gross margin; (d) selling, general, and administrative expenses; and (e) profit.
3. The balance sheet shows the firm's assets, liabilities, and net worth. Current assets fund day-to-day operations and fixed assets are longer-term resources. Liabilities are debts owed to banks and other creditors. Net worth is the owner's equity in the firm.
4. From information on the income statement and balance sheet, retailers calculate three important financial ratios: (a) net profit margin, (b) asset turnover, and (c) leverage ratio. Net profit margin shows the amount of profit earned for each dollar of sales. Asset turnover measures the amount of sales generated per dollar of assets. These two ratios combine to measure return on assets (ROA)—profits earned per each dollar of assets. The leverage ratio measures the relationship between a firm's liabilities and net worth.
5. Net profit margin, asset turnover, and leverage determine the firm's return on net worth (RONW), which is also called return on equity (ROE). RONW measures how well the firm is performing financially for its owners.
6. The strategic profit model is an integrated financial planning tool. It sets RONW as the principal yardstick for measuring the firm's financial performance and identifies the avenues for improving RONW. It helps the firm compare its performance historically and identify areas for improvement. The strategic profit model also helps the company set financial goals and evaluate financial implications for alternative marketing strategies through what-if analysis.

Key Concepts

Income statement	Net profit margin
Net sales	Margin management
Cost of goods sold	Asset turnover
Gross margin	Return on assets
SGA expenses	Return on net worth
Net profit	Return on equity
Balance sheet	Leverage ratio
Assets	Strategic profit model
Liabilities	What-if analysis

Discussion Questions

1. What aspect of a firm's performance does return on assets (ROA) measure? What are the two components of ROA? What does each component measure?

2. In what ways can a firm improve its profit margin and asset turnover?
3. What is meant by the term *leverage*? How does leverage affect the financial returns the owners receive from their investment in the firm?
4. What are the three components of the strategic profit model? How are these components calculated? What aspects of a firm's performance does each measure?
5. How can the strategic profit model benefit retail managers?
6. A department store achieved a net profit margin of 3.2 percent and return on assets of 6.0 percent. What was the store's asset turnover? If the store earned a return on net worth of 15 percent, what portion of the firm's assets is funded through long-term debt?
7. A jewelry store achieved a profit margin of 10.0 percent and had an asset turnover of 1.5. If the store's debt-to-equity ratio is 7:5, what is its RONW?

8. Some financial highlights of the Woolworth Corporation for the years 1981 and 1990 appear below. Construct the firm's strategic profit model, and comment on the changes in its performance during that period.

(in millions of dollars)	1981	1990
Net sales	5,130	9,789
Net profit	272	639
Total assets	2,698	4,305
Shareholders' equity	1,372	2,340

9. Using the data in Exhibit 7.8, comment on the performance of Sears, The Gap, and Food Lion. If possible, obtain information on each company for the previous year from annual reports or industry surveys published in *Fortune* or *Business Week*. Compare how the performance of these companies changed.

Notes

1. Alvin D. Starr and Michael Z. Massel, "Survival Rates for Retailers," *Journal of Retailing*, 57, Summer 1981, p. 87.

2. See *Off Price Retailing: Current Issues and Trends in Marketing of Branded Merchandise* (New York: NYU Institute of Retail Management 1983).

CHAPTER 8
Developing Retail Locations Strategy

The Evolution of Shopping Malls

Shopping malls have changed American shopping habits. Once featureless agglomerations of apparel and home furnishings stores, malls have expanded to include everything from stores to movies and restaurants in elaborately designed and decorated buildings. After World War II, malls sprouted up all over the United States, and they have become a way of life in America. In cities across the country, shopping patterns have shifted from downtown areas to malls. Malls attract customers not only to shop, but to stroll, meet friends, eat, take in a movie, and spend the day. They are clean, well-lit places where people can pass their time in a safe and comfortable environment and where they can come to socialize or get away from the dirty and sometimes dangerous aspects of urban shopping. While the mall formula is consistent across the country, many malls are trying to create an atmosphere and flavor that captures their region and that responds directly to the needs and preferences of local customers. As malls become the substitutes for the town centers in some areas, becoming more attuned to local preferences in terms of offering and atmosphere is increasingly important to the success of the mall.

One example is the Danbury Fair Mall, located in Danbury, Connecticut. The mall sits on the site of the old fairgrounds, where for 112 years there was an annual fair. Festooned with a myriad of lights, a grandstand, and zany facades, everyone who grew up nearby remembers the fair. For that reason, the mall architects wanted to evoke the flavor of the fair, which was dismantled in the late 1960s, to bring some of it back to the community in the form of a mall. There are Tivoli lights on the food court and an old carousel—all of which hark back to the old fair. Mall employees describe it as Main Street, U.S.A., but a main street free of litter, panhandlers, or cold winters. Visitors to the mall, on the other hand, see it as a 1.3 million square foot, seven-day-a-week show where one can relax, shop, and see all types of people.

Another successful mall concept is Underground Atlanta, a shopping and entertainment center in the heart of that city. Underground Atlanta features a mix of retail stores, restaurants, and nightclubs, that developers think offers something for everyone. Daniel O'Connel, director of leasing for Time-Out Family Amusement Centers, believes that having an entertainment anchor as the keystone of a mall is a logical offshoot for mall development. As mall developers have added food courts, theaters, and other attractions to extend a mall's leisure time activities, including more entertainment has become the next step for attracting visitors and customers.

Entertainment-oriented anchors can also give a mall the extra competitive advantage

After studying this chapter, the reader will be able to:
- *Know the steps in developing locational policy.*
- *Understand the importance of the locational decision to the retailer's marketing strategy.*
- *Calculate the attractiveness of different geographical market areas.*
- *Analyze the spatial characteristics of subareas within different market areas.*
- *Understand the advantages and disadvantages of different types of location.*
- *Evaluate the characteristics of individual sites.*

Shopping centers that combine retailing with entertainment and dining have helped revitalize many urban areas.

it will need to successfully compete with other malls in the area. Says O'Connel, "Most enclosed malls offer the same fare these days—The Gap, The Limited, food courts, etc., as a standard, but a destination entertainment anchor can make the mall stand out from its competition." Experts claim that given the choice of a number of area malls, families will tend to frequent the one with an entertainment anchor, which increases the

traffic for all the retailers and promotes the overall success of the mall. While some of the entertainment anchors are simply upscale restaurants or clubs, Underground Atlanta hopes to capture a customer base with attractions like the New Georgia Railroad, an old-fashioned train that makes an 18-mile loop from Underground Atlanta around the city, with excursions to Stone Mountain Park.

Yet a different kind of mall, scheduled to open in summer 1993, is a value mall planned for the Seattle, Washington, suburb of Auburn. Called The SuperMall of the Great Northwest, the mall will be a value-oriented center. It is designed in a hexagonal plan that will allow visitors to pass all the stores and arrive back to their point of entry without backtracking, and this race-track type design will reduce the fatigue that comes with walking around the typical mall, and then having to backtrack to return to the car. There are roughly 200 value-oriented and outlet retailers scheduled for the mall, and eight major anchors (from Nordstrom Rack and Sears Outlet to a huge entertainment center). SuperMall will have four entries and courts, each with its own theme (aviation, forestry, rail, and shipping), designed to celebrate the heritage and geography of the Pacific Northwest. There will be a video system to keep shoppers entertained and informed, with large monitors located throughout the mall. And most importantly, the 150-acre site was carefully chosen, located midway between Seattle and Tacoma and with key freeway interchanges for the rest of the state. While the SuperMall will have an elaborate decor and a full entertainment center, the stores will remain value oriented, catering to the economically depressed region. Developers feel that while this set of consumers requires discount and outlet stores, there is no need to set the stores in a bland or "discount/no-frills" atmosphere, and that the appeal of an elegant and exciting shopping atmosphere will be an important factor in drawing customers.

Sources: William Glaberson, "The Heart of the City Now Beats in the Mall," *The New York Times*, March 27, 1992, pp. A1, B4; "Amusement Anchors: New Mall Headliners," *Chain Store Age Executive*, August 1989, pp. 54–55; "Value Mall Planned for Seattle Suburb," *Chain Store Age Executive*, November 1991, pp. 60–61.

It is often said that the three secrets to success in retailing are location, location, and location. Although this oft repeated adage may seem to exaggerate somewhat, the importance of location in the retailer's overall marketing strategy can hardly be overstated. Whether selling goods or services, the retailer may make its most important decision in choosing an outlet location.

A number of considerations make this decision so critical. To a large extent, the location determines the type and number of people the store will attract. Good locations provide ready access to large numbers of target consumers and increase potential sales. In today's highly competitive retail environment, even a slight difference in location can have a significant impact on market share and profitability. A poor location is a liability that is not easy to overcome. In the development of competitive strategies, retailers can match prices, extend and improve services, duplicate merchandise, and imitate promotion, but an effective location strategy is difficult to assail or neutralize.[1]

Opening a new store is inherently risky, entailing significant monetary costs, including the rising costs of real estate and construction. Since location decisions cannot be changed easily, the greatest risk in opening a new outlet is the possibility that it will never achieve its sales potential. The failure of a store at a new location can have significant negative impact on the store's image. A retail chain that operates many outlets in the same area may feel the effect of the failure of any one store throughout the entire chain. Even for a firm that operates only a single store in an area, store closure or relocation can be quite damaging. A relocated store may lose many of its loyal customers to whom the new site is inconvenient, requiring the firm to rebuild its customer base at the new site. The long-term nature of the store location decision and the substantial financial investments it puts at risk compel the retailer to make the decision carefully.

Any firm that operates retail outlets must implement a well-thought-out location policy that is consistent with its overall marketing strategy. In addition to traditional retail firms such as department stores, discount outlets, specialty stores, and supermarkets, locational planning is important for such diverse organizations as banks, hospitals and medical clinics, restaurants and fast-food outlets, drug stores, convenience outlets, and movie theaters, to name only a few.

This chapter discusses the various aspects of a retailer's location decision and the types of analyses it must perform in order to develop a coherent locational policy. The chapter provides a systematic framework to follow in selecting market areas and specific sites in which to locate new outlets. Each step in the locational decision-making process is discussed in detail with special emphasis on the types of data needed and their sources.

STEPS IN DEVELOPING LOCATION POLICY

The location policy is the blueprint for achieving the firm's marketing objectives and expansion plans. It translates the firm's marketing strategy into a concrete policy that is sensitive to the spatial pattern of demand and the availability of desirable sites, and targets the firm's investments toward specific locations and market areas. A series of steps is required to formulate a coherent location policy as shown in Exhibit 8.1.

The process starts with analysis of the firm's marketing strategy and an understanding of its target market. As was stressed earlier, the location decision, like other retail mix decisions, must be consistent with the firm's overall strategy. Next, the firm must analyze the spatial aspects of different geographic market areas. The spatial analysis process starts with **regional analysis**, which is the identification of regional markets such as cities, towns, and metropolitan areas in which to locate new stores. The retailer is concerned here with regional variations in demand for retail goods and services and variations in the level of retail competition. The retailer compares regional demand and supply and then ranks regional areas according to their potential for supporting new outlets.

Even within a city or town, however, population characteristics and the level of retail activity can vary spatially. Thus, the next step, which is called **areal analysis**, focuses on the immediate area surrounding potential sites. The demographic

---

Exhibit 8.1   Steps in Developing Location Policy

Step	Factors to Consider
Marketing strategy	Target market and position on shopping opportunity line
Regional analysis	Regional variations in economic potential and level of competition
Areal analysis	Demographics of population surrounding potential site
Site evaluation	Type of location, traffic flow, accessibility, cost of occupancy, and so on

and socioeconomic characteristics of the population surrounding each site must be carefully evaluated, since they will ultimately determine the sales potential of the site. The final step in the process is **site evaluation**, which focuses on the characteristics of the sites at which a new store may be located. The characteristics of each site are analyzed in detail with respect to traffic flow, access patterns, compatibility, and terms of occupancy.

Each of the steps in developing the location policy is discussed in detail below.

MARKETING STRATEGY AND LOCATION POLICY

Since each type of store has a unique target market, each has its own locational requirements. Home improvement centers, for example, rely on home owners for a major portion of their sales. Therefore, in selecting a location for this type of store, the managers must pay special attention to the number of home owners who will be attracted to the site. A supermarket, on the other hand, is more concerned with the general level of population in the area than just with home owners specifically. Similarly, in selecting a site for a children's clothing store, the number of families with children requires careful attention, whereas an audio specialty store must look at the number of teenagers and young families in the area, since these population groups patronize audio stores most frequently.

Even stores selling similar types of merchandise may have different locational requirements, because their positions on the shopping opportunity line may differ. As already discussed in the previous chapters, stores with different positions on the shopping opportunity line attract different clienteles. Thus, although both discount stores and specialty boutiques sell clothing, they attract quite different consumer groups. This difference in target markets gives them different locational requirements. Fashion-oriented clothing stores tend to locate in central business districts or regional shopping centers, whereas discount stores are often located in smaller shopping centers, in suburban shopping strips, or as freestanding units.

The location policies of service retailers also differ because of differences in their marketing strategy. The impact of marketing strategy on location policy can be seen especially clearly in the case of restaurants. High priced, fancy restaurants usually locate in high-income neighborhoods. Family-oriented restaurants, on the other hand, tend to locate in middle-income suburbs with large numbers of children.

Even the ideal locations for fast-food restaurants differ. Some that cater to lunch-time crowds seek locations near busy commercial areas. Other fast-food outlets serve travelers and locate near highways, airports, and tourist spots. Finally, yet another group of fast-food restaurants locates in neighborhoods where many families with children live. The specific population segment served by each type of fast-food restaurant dictates to a large extent its location policies.

Because a firm's location policy must be consistent with its policies on price, promotion, and merchandise, a change in the marketing strategy often necessitates a change in location policy, too. An analysis of the changes made by the J.C. Penney

Locational analysis is important for restaurants. The location of this upscale restaurant in San Francisco attracts many business-people.

Company in the early 1980s demonstrates this very well. As mentioned in earlier chapters, J.C. Penney changed its marketing strategy in order to create a new, more fashion-oriented image. The new strategy focused on working women who are major purchasers of women's clothing. Repositioning to emphasize fashion and style made it necessary to upgrade store atmosphere and change locations. Originally, many Penney outlets were located in downtown sites in urban areas. To reach its new target market more effectively, locations in shopping malls—where most working women shop for apparel—were favored. The mall locations also made Penney outlets more competitive with regional department store chains and specialty clothing stores. The contemporary decor of the new stores created an ambience that customers associate with fashion-oriented stores. A number of the existing outlets were either closed or extensively remodeled to reflect the new image.

As another example, consider the locational changes made by the Woolworth Corporation. As mentioned in Chapter 5, Woolworth undertook a major change

STRATEGY IN ACTION

Outlet Stores: Do Manufacturers Compete with Their Own Retailers?

As the allure of price shopping increases and the self-indulgent 1980s give way to the self-disciplined 1990s, outlet stores have become all the rage. There was a time when a stigma surrounded outlet stores because they sold only "seconds" or slightly defective goods. Not any longer, it seems. From 1988 to 1990 alone, the number of outlet stores nearly doubled, and the annual sales increased to $6.3 billion, making outlets one of the fastest growing segments of the retail industry. Now, most of the items found in these outlets are unblemished, and the stores offer both a deep selection and just-off-the-line items. Why? With retailers purchasing roughly 80 percent of their manufacturers' capacity, the manufacturers produce the last 20 percent for the outlet stores they operate themselves.

Items available at the outlet stores are discounted, anywhere from 25 to 70 percent off retail prices. And manufacturers are finding that selling directly to the customer offers them significant savings. Cutting out the retail buyers keeps the costs down, and opens up the goods to a whole selection of customers who otherwise would not be purchasing the items, thereby increasing the number of sales. Customers who can't afford the department store price rush to the outlet stores, and this increases profits for the manufacturers.

What's more, as sales continue to rise and profits become consistent for the manufacturers, they are able to pass back the earnings to their customers in terms of better prices and increased service. In fact, service levels at outlet stores are at times better than at department stores, and this keeps the customers coming back. In the early 1980s, finding a salesperson or a private fitting room was unheard of at these stores, but now most customers would not recognize the difference between the outlet stores and their favorite department store.

Many retailers view these outlet stores as a growing threat. What irks them most is that this competition is not from a rival store, but from the suppliers themselves. Many of the outlet stores opt to locate in outlet malls that are strategically located near regular malls. With names like Coach, Donna Karan, Esprit, and Liz Claiborne joining the fray, customers often find it much more appealing to go to the outlet mall rather than the shopping center down the street.

Source: Kevin Helliker, "Thriving Factory Outlets Anger Retailers as Store Suppliers Turn into Competitors," *The Wall Street Journal*, October 8, 1981, pp. B1 and B8.

in strategy when it closed the Woolco discount chain and many Woolworth stores in the United States to concentrate more on specialty stores such as Foot Locker, Lady Foot Locker, Champs, and Afterthoughts. Although the company was opening new specialty stores at the same time as it was closing down other outlets, the specialty stores could not be located in the sites being vacated by Woolworth and Woolco stores. The locational requirements of the specialty stores were very different from what the vacated Woolworth and Woolco sites offered. The new specialty formats are mostly located in regional shopping centers, while many of the vacated sites were in downtown areas or in smaller shopping centers. Since many of the specialty formats were not destination stores (that is, people do not make a trip specifically to visit the store), their success is highly dependent on locating in a mall that attracts many shoppers.

As these examples illustrate, the location policy of a firm is an integral part of its overall marketing strategy, and it must be consistent with the other elements of the retailer's marketing mix. The marketing strategy dictates the criteria by which the firm evaluates different market areas and selects the sites at which to locate new outlets.

REGIONAL ANALYSIS

Once the firm sets overall locational goals in light of its marketing strategy, it can proceed to evaluate geographic markets and select potential sites. The first step in this spatial evaluation process is regional analysis (see Exhibit 8.2). The objective of regional analysis is to select the geographic market in which to open new outlets. This is a vital step since the potential of the market ultimately determines the profitability of outlets located in the area.

The retail potential or attractiveness of a region depends on the interplay between the demand for and supply of retail goods and services. To support a new outlet, an area must have adequate population and income to create sufficient demand. Moreover, the demographic and socioeconomic characteristics of the population must be consistent with the firm's target market. However, higher levels of supply (that is, more existing stores) make regions less attractive for new stores.

Retailers usually rely on secondary data sources to calculate the potentials of geographic markets. Common sources include the *Census of Population* and *Census of Retailing* published by the U.S. Department of Commerce, *Survey of Buying Power* published annually by the *Sales and Marketing Management* magazine, and the *Editor and Publisher Marketing Guide*. In addition, many federal, state, and local government agencies and trade organizations collect population information and make it available to the public.

Many commercial firms also compile demographic and socioeconomic information for different geographic markets from a variety of sources and make it available to retailers. Many of these data bases can be accessed through on-line computers or are available on microcomputer disk. These machine-readable data bases have greatly enhanced a retailer's ability to obtain geographic information.

Measuring Demand

Retail demand in an area can be measured in a number of ways. For example, the number of people living in the region provides a quick but approximate estimate

Exhibit 8.2   Three Levels of Spatial Analysis

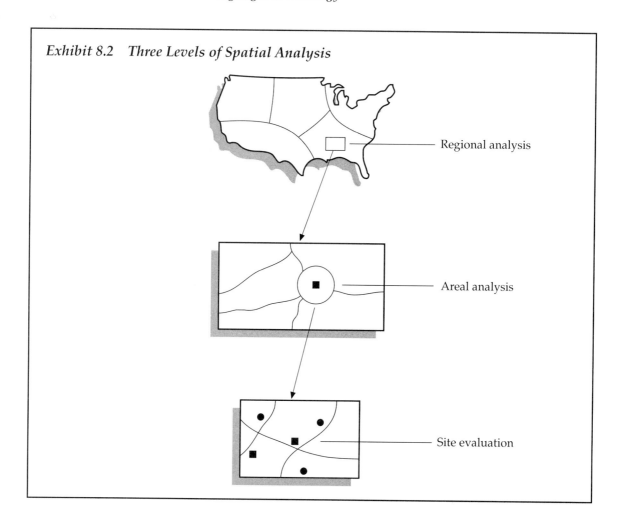

of demand. More specifically, however, one should look at the total retail purchasing power in the region. This depends on both the size of the population and how much they spend. This information is available from secondary sources. The *Census of Population* contains data on population size and composition for all geographic regions in the United States. Information on per capita expenditure is available from the Bureau of Labor Statistics.

Of course, a retailer will not always rely on total population size and income to measure demand. Depending on the target market of the store, it may be more appropriate to focus on specific population groups. For example, in measuring demand for a children's clothing outlet, the number of families with young children is more relevant than total population. Likewise, some stores may look only at the number of higher-income families because of the nature of their target market. For the purpose of measuring demand, it is common to define the target market in terms of:

- demographic characteristics (age, sex).
- household characteristics (family size, number of children).
- socioeconomic characteristics (annual family income, type of housing).

The Buying Power Index

Many retailers rely on the **Buying Power Index** published annually by the *Sales and Marketing Management* magazine. The magazine publishes the Buying Power Index (BPI) for states, counties, metropolitan areas, cities, and television viewing areas. The BPI measures the overall retail demand in an area expressed as a percentage of total demand in the United States. In essence, the Buying Power Index measures "the market's ability to buy."[2]

The index is a weighted average of the area's population size, income, and total retail sales in the preceding year, computed as follows:

$$BPI = 0.5 \times \text{(percentage of U.S. effective buying income)}$$
$$+ 0.3 \times \text{(percentage of U.S. retail sales)}$$
$$+ 0.2 \times \text{(percentage of U.S. population)}$$

Of the three factors, most importance is given to effective buying income (that is, an individual's income after taxes). The index gives the least weight to population size, and the preceding year's retail sales gets an intermediate weight. The weights are based on the perceived importance of each factor in predicting the total retail demand in an area.

Exhibit 8.3 shows the BPI for all 50 states along with some other useful demographic information. As shown in the second-to-last column, California has the highest BPI, accounting for 12.66 percent of the total retail buying power in the country. It is followed by New York and Texas with BPIs of 7.46 percent and 6.67 percent, respectively. In contrast, Vermont, North Dakota, South Dakota, Wyoming, Delaware, and Alaska have very low buying power, each with less than 0.3 percent of the total retail purchasing power in the country. This is not surprising given these states' small populations.

The table also shows for each state the total retail sales, the percent of U.S. population residing in the state, and retail sales by store groups. Finally, the table provides two indices that indicate the strength of the buying power in that state. The **Sales Activity Index** is obtained by dividing an area's percent of U.S. population into its percent of U.S. retail sales. A high Sales Activity Index indicates a strong influx of nonresident purchasers. Note, for example, the high index for Hawaii. This indicates that the retail sales in that state is much higher than what one would expect given its population size. The quality index is calculated by dividing a market's BPI by its percent of U.S. population figure. A high index number

Exhibit 8.3   Retail Sales and Buying Power Index by State

S&MM Estimates: 12/31/91   Retail Sales by Store Group   Sales/Advertising Indexes

Region State	1991 Total Retail Sales ($000)	% of U.S.	Per Household Retail Sales	Food ($000)	Eating & Drinking Places ($000)	General Merchandise ($000)	Furniture/Home Furnish. Appliance ($000)	Automotive ($000)	Drug ($000)	Sales Activity	Buying Power	Quality
New England	**110,944,410**	**6.0913**	**22,236**	**22,366,971**	**12,954,414**	**10,917,917**	**4,925,164**	**22,691,055**	**4,029,082**	**116**	**5.9473**	**113**
Connecticut	26,543,565	1.4574	21,415	5,207,937	2,773,378	2,542,966	1,312,357	5,479,628	884,459	112	1.5854	121
Maine	10,091,828	.5541	21,309	2,299,183	1,003,858	874,504	326,376	2,062,787	328,340	113	.4896	100
Massachusetts	52,089,985	2.8599	23,084	10,178,102	6,773,641	5,231,570	2,339,084	10,475,713	2,048,847	120	2.7376	115
New Hampshire	11,008,774	.6044	25,946	2,313,889	1,051,528	1,212,648	533,157	2,493,847	303,827	134	.5270	117
Rhode Island	6,760,389	.3712	17,753	1,361,202	859,268	752,495	244,909	1,254,545	331,996	93	.3848	96
Vermont	4,449,869	.2443	20,716	1,006,658	492,741	303,734	169,281	924,535	131,613	108	.2229	99
Middle Atlantic	**266,597,624**	**14.6370**	**19,004**	**59,025,410**	**25,322,384**	**27,896,591**	**14,503,502**	**51,255,070**	**10,864,333**	**98**	**15.8607**	**106**
New Jersey	63,209,987	3.4704	22,428	13,969,509	5,504,942	6,161,258	3,792,936	13,353,800	2,148,313	113	3.7379	121
New York	122,445,952	6.7227	18,337	27,261,298	12,517,081	12,504,449	6,996,850	21,203,382	5,333,929	94	7.4575	104
Pennsylvania	80,941,685	4.4439	17,856	17,794,603	7,300,361	9,230,884	3,713,716	16,697,888	3,382,091	94	4.6653	99
East North Central	**303,829,171**	**16.6812**	**19,322**	**53,901,240**	**30,930,088**	**40,346,662**	**14,779,379**	**62,482,843**	**13,665,510**	**100**	**16.6412**	**100**
Illinois	84,709,929	4.6509	20,058	14,534,017	8,736,103	10,332,174	4,335,131	16,500,985	4,450,752	102	4.8229	106
Indiana	39,881,962	2.1896	19,132	6,847,712	3,899,381	5,084,060	1,723,908	8,593,231	1,959,398	99	2.1074	96
Michigan	67,760,980	3.7203	19,626	11,360,029	6,614,209	9,988,017	3,453,911	14,692,619	2,832,641	101	3.6620	99
Ohio	76,294,964	4.1888	18,534	14,819,701	7,910,163	10,489,958	3,506,954	15,862,737	3,252,915	97	4.1514	96
Wisconsin	35,181,336	1.9316	19,041	6,339,781	3,770,232	4,452,453	1,759,475	6,833,271	1,169,804	99	1.8975	97
West North Central	**128,510,344**	**7.0557**	**18,900**	**24,659,571**	**12,213,664**	**17,716,256**	**4,278,349**	**29,615,329**	**4,077,297**	**100**	**6.8616**	**98**
Iowa	19,511,756	1.0713	18,288	4,145,952	1,762,415	2,572,930	587,218	4,581,874	704,883	98	1.0456	95
Kansas	17,159,623	.9421	17,931	3,506,359	1,621,325	2,362,154	589,213	4,060,782	498,179	95	.9621	97
Minnesota	35,159,987	1.9304	20,921	6,233,195	3,296,937	5,027,848	1,293,943	7,518,861	1,103,209	110	1.7865	102
Missouri	36,427,985	2.0000	18,334	6,873,603	3,586,959	5,178,776	1,125,059	8,773,988	1,093,314	98	1.9700	96
Nebraska	10,693,370	.5871	17,649	2,105,295	1,078,200	1,404,096	417,776	2,373,020	348,138	94	.6012	96
North Dakota	4,669,914	.2564	19,434	837,427	423,305	640,806	123,243	1,138,900	149,525	103	.2343	94
South Dakota	4,887,709	.2684	18,663	957,740	444,523	529,646	141,897	1,167,904	180,049	97	.2619	95
South Atlantic	**328,761,764**	**18.0499**	**19,327**	**65,620,961**	**33,303,284**	**37,893,988**	**17,073,930**	**71,254,943**	**14,076,957**	**102**	**17.4816**	**99**
Delaware	6,060,409	.3327	23,907	1,101,065	546,870	860,249	317,169	1,240,106	237,228	123	.2938	109
District of Columbia	3,606,373	.1980	14,732	603,563	864,527	326,968	193,629	158,821	225,597	84	.2508	106
Florida	109,570,910	6.0158	20,446	21,180,699	11,553,056	12,530,333	5,706,809	25,134,086	4,905,995	113	5.4837	103
Georgia	46,910,489	2.5755	19,136	9,115,269	4,743,524	5,819,539	2,319,119	9,951,630	1,948,537	97	2.4916	94
Maryland	36,385,417	1.9977	20,248	7,004,319	3,515,550	4,323,855	1,956,132	7,920,047	1,413,999	103	2.0884	108
North Carolina	46,077,984	2.5298	17,862	9,345,315	4,584,845	4,788,865	2,545,790	9,943,912	2,009,410	95	2.4717	93
South Carolina	24,219,853	1.3297	18,795	5,260,477	2,378,824	2,583,664	1,202,547	4,908,057	1,007,465	95	1.2514	89
Virginia	45,782,963	2.5136	19,485	9,571,321	4,274,672	5,170,456	2,452,584	9,971,367	1,800,101	100	2.5765	103
West Virginia	10,147,366	.5571	14,777	2,438,933	841,416	1,490,059	380,154	2,026,917	528,625	79	.5737	82
East South Central	**97,306,693**	**5.3424**	**17,010**	**19,319,392**	**8,555,642**	**13,760,162**	**4,305,738**	**22,350,600**	**4,236,131**	**88**	**5.2871**	**87**
Alabama	26,132,246	1.4347	17,130	5,108,264	2,198,114	3,478,780	1,125,321	6,408,158	1,072,720	89	1.4153	88
Kentucky	24,097,976	1.3231	17,358	5,027,576	2,270,832	3,448,368	1,036,416	4,901,506	1,156,788	91	1.2868	88
Louisiana	28,996,995	1.5920	19,271	7,422,896	2,567,235	4,032,646	1,160,649	5,815,331	1,369,526	95	1.4910	89
Mississippi	13,692,446	.7517	14,916	3,090,897	1,056,031	2,088,592	518,723	2,994,535	630,934	74	.7861	77
Tennessee	33,384,025	1.8329	17,677	6,092,655	3,030,665	4,744,422	1,625,278	8,046,401	1,375,689	94	1.7989	92
West South Central	**190,942,239**	**10.4833**	**19,404**	**43,080,583**	**17,437,745**	**24,936,799**	**7,929,968**	**45,097,518**	**6,149,471**	**98**	**10.0518**	**94**
Arkansas	15,583,945	.8556	17,281	3,380,575	1,124,173	2,252,135	557,396	3,838,975	474,685	91	.8105	87
Oklahoma	20,200,258	1.1091	16,678	4,583,266	1,876,097	2,570,442	805,314	5,016,942	605,816	89	1.0786	87
Texas	126,161,041	6.9266	20,275	27,693,846	11,870,240	16,081,576	5,406,609	30,426,270	3,699,444	101	6.6717	97
Mountain	**96,491,074**	**5.2977**	**18,546**	**21,897,517**	**10,301,863**	**11,440,509**	**4,765,900**	**18,359,835**	**3,226,442**	**95**	**5.2111**	**94**
Arizona	26,893,039	1.4765	18,797	6,370,820	2,787,201	3,153,320	1,398,892	5,238,692	1,151,244	98	1.3978	93
Colorado	25,216,404	1.3844	19,207	5,400,945	2,930,401	3,168,889	1,317,249	4,663,772	614,976	104	1.3684	103
Idaho	6,191,970	.3399	16,853	1,487,719	587,925	627,788	282,285	1,259,747	218,274	84	.3548	88
Montana	5,472,882	.3005	17,810	1,331,343	612,675	547,509	231,162	1,000,427	188,963	95	.2911	92
Nevada	9,825,951	.5395	19,496	2,141,904	1,049,525	1,158,810	437,164	1,827,683	400,428	105	.5242	102
New Mexico	9,645,014	.5296	17,217	2,095,622	1,062,822	1,170,116	410,931	1,882,706	346,969	86	.5260	85
Utah	10,451,699	.5739	18,958	2,451,729	964,586	1,313,376	593,942	1,977,942	235,580	82	.5842	84
Wyoming	2,794,115	.1534	16,543	617,435	306,728	300,701	94,275	508,866	70,008	86	.1646	92
Pacific	**298,002,617**	**16.3615**	**20,750**	**60,382,962**	**38,173,074**	**32,584,632**	**17,277,022**	**52,536,839**	**14,669,048**	**102**	**16.6576**	**104**
Alaska	4,740,158	.2603	24,197	1,245,707	685,740	600,732	150,999	550,015	124,896	116	.2594	115
California	220,871,295	12.1266	20,563	43,854,436	28,043,773	23,276,783	13,607,131	39,890,413	11,222,119	99	12.6608	104
Hawaii	11,411,804	.6266	31,095	2,224,365	2,095,424	1,527,201	409,262	1,390,280	729,847	140	.5312	118
Oregon	23,262,179	1.2772	20,575	4,582,412	2,721,017	3,102,492	1,145,947	4,477,243	820,429	111	1.1470	100
Washington	37,717,181	2.0708	19,575	8,476,042	4,627,120	4,077,424	1,963,683	6,228,888	1,771,757	105	2.0592	104
Total United States	**1,821,385,936**	**100.0000**	**19,443**	**370,254,607**	**189,192,158**	**217,493,516**	**89,838,952**	**375,644,032**	**74,994,271**	**100**	**100.0000**	**100**

Source: *Sales & Marketing Management*, August 24, 1992.

reflects either above average buying power of residents, influx of nonresident shoppers, or both.[3]

Buying Power Indices offer a useful summary of the retail potential in an area. They can be used to compare and rank different markets according to their potential. For many applications, however, the state is too large a geographic area to analyze retail potential, given the wide differences that might exist among parts of the state. BPIs for counties, cities, and metropolitan areas provide a more detailed look at the distribution of retail potential within a state. Compare, for example, the two Arizona towns of Scottsdale and Tempe. Although the towns have very similar population sizes, their retail potentials are quite different. Scottsdale's BPI is .0808 and Tempe's is .0635 (see Exhibit 8.4). While this indicates the greater attractiveness of Scottsdale for locating a retail store, many retailers will need to look at potentials within specific target groups to decide on the relative attractiveness of these two towns for their stores. Exhibit 8.4 illustrates how such a customized index of demand can be constructed.

Consider, for example, a video-rental store interested in locating in either Scottsdale or Tempe. The general BPI is not likely to be very helpful to this firm, since the target customers of video-rental stores are different from the general population. To calculate a customized BPI, the analyst must first define the target customer group in terms of income and age. The population within the age group of 18 to 34, rather than total population, is a better indicator of the potential for this video store. In addition, the company targets families with effective buying incomes (EBIs) above $20,000. The final step in the selection process is to determine whether sales within a particular store group—such as food stores, drug stores, general merchandise, furniture, and so on—is a better indicator of potential than total retail sales. As shown in Exhibit 8.3, *Sales and Marketing Management* magazine provides information on retail sales for six different categories. According to the managers of the video store, the total of all nonauto related retail sales is likely to be a good indicator of the potential for their store.

Exhibit 8.4 provides the basic information needed to compute the potential for video stores in Scottsdale and Tempe. To compute customized indices for the two towns, it is necessary to compare local activity to that for the United States as a

---

Exhibit 8.4   **Calculating Customized BPIs**

	BPI	Population 18–34 (thousands)	Households w/EBI $20,000 + (thousands)	Nonauto Retail Sales (millions)	X (%)	Y (%)	Z (%)	Customized BPI
Scottsdale	.0808	34.3	47.1	1.35	.0498	.0716	.0934	.0651
Tempe	.0635	60.4	40.8	1.06	.0877	.0620	.0733	.0771
U.S.	100.00	68,834	65,775	1,445.7				

whole, producing a ratio for the three factors—age, income, and retail sales. As shown in Exhibit 8.4, only 34,300 of Scottsdale's population are between 18 and 34 years old, the store's target group. Tempe, on the other hand, has more than 60,000 people in this age group. There is a difference, too, in the income distribution: there are more households with Effective Buying Incomes greater than $20,000 in Scottsdale than there are in Tempe. Finally, the retail sales patterns are also different. On the whole, family incomes and the current retail sales pattern seem to favor Scottsdale, but Tempe's population better matches the target market in terms of age.

To examine the age, income and retail sales in a systematic manner, it is necessary to compute indices for each component as follows:[4]

$$\frac{\text{Market's Population 18–34}}{\text{U.S. Population 18–34}} = X$$

$$\frac{\text{Market's Hshlds. w/EBIs \$20,000 +}}{\text{U.S. Hshlds. w/EBIs \$20,000 +}} = Y$$

$$\frac{\text{Market's Nonauto Retail Sales}}{\text{U.S. Nonauto Retail Sales}} = Z$$

These calculations are shown in Exhibit 8.4 for both Scottsdale and Tempe. The final step in computing the customized BPI is to multiply each ratio by its appropriate weight and adding the resulting totals. In this case, the retailer assigned weights of .5 to age, .3 to income, and .2 to retail sales, based on the perceived importance of the three factors in predicting video store sales. The resulting *customized BPIs* are shown in the last column of Exhibit 8.4. Clearly, Tempe has a greater potential for this video store chain than Scottsdale.

Index of Retail Saturation

Purchasing power indices, such as the BPI or those constructed from census data, measure the retail demand in an area. The attractiveness of an area, however, depends on more than demand. The interplay of demand and supply creates market opportunities. An area with high demand may not be suitable for locating new stores if its level of competition is already high. An area of low demand, on the other hand, may be attractive if the level of competition is low.

To ascertain an area's potential for supporting a new store, retailers need a measure that compares both demand and supply. One such measure, the **Index of Retail Saturation (IRS)**, measures the potential demand per square foot of selling space for a given type of retail store in a particular market area.[5] By comparing demand and supply, the IRS measures the level of store saturation in the area as follows:

$$\text{Index of retail saturation} = \frac{\text{Demand}}{\text{Square feet of retail selling space}}$$

Since the IRS measures demand relative to supply, a low value indicates overstoring in the area since this means the level of supply is high relative to demand. Thus a high index of retail saturation indicates an attractive area for new store openings.

Any of the measures of demand discussed earlier can be used to determine the level of saturation. Exhibit 8.5 shows two example calculations of retail saturation for discount stores. The first case takes BPI as a measure of retail demand in the area. The second case calculates demand from census information. Multiplying the census figure for the total population in the area by the per-capita discount store sales yields the sales potential for the area. Both cases measure supply by total square footage of discount store space in the area.

Like indices of this type, the IRS is meaningful only in comparison to some kind of norm, possibly a standard set by management based on previous experience. Alternatively, the relative attractiveness of different market areas can be assessed by calculating the index for each area and ranking them. In Exhibit 8.5, Market Area A is the most attractive, since it has the highest IRS value, with potential sales of $160 per square foot. The figure is slightly higher than that of Area B ($152) and substantially above that of Area C. However, the retailer's previous experience may dictate a minimum potential of $175 per square foot for a new discount store to be profitable. In such a case, none of the three markets would be suitable for opening new outlets.

Market Expansion Potential

The index of retail saturation reflects the existing level of demand and supply in an area, as determined by existing buying patterns and expenditures. The attractiveness of different market areas also depends on the scope for expanding the market.[6]

Exhibit 8.5 *Indices of Retail Saturation for Three Areas*

	Area A	Area B	Area C
Population	120,000	240,000	400,000
Annual per-capita discount-store sales	$280	$260	$225
Discount-store sales potential	$33,600,000	$62,400,000	$90,000,000
Square feet of discount-store space	210,000	410,526	614,438
BPI	.1221	.1620	.2210
IRS[1]	.0058	.0039	.0036
IRS[2]	160	152	146

$$1 \quad \frac{\text{BPI}}{\text{Square feet of discount store space}} \times 100$$

$$2 \quad \frac{\text{Discount store sales potential}}{\text{Square feet of discount-store space}}$$

The existing potential is partly reflective of the marketing skills of retailers already located in the area. A low per-capita retail expenditure in an area may reflect the inability of existing retailers to satisfy consumer needs completely. This leads to outshopping and sales leakage from the area. Outshopping occurs when consumers patronize stores in other areas because of better merchandise, selection, price, service, or convenience. Often, consumers are willing to travel extra distances to visit stores or shopping centers in other nearby towns to take advantage of better prices and wider selections.

Significant levels of outshopping prevent the IRS from truly reflecting the attractiveness of the area. A good retailer can enter a low-IRS market and still be successful by reducing the level of outshopping and generating new demand in the area by presenting consumers with an attractive local store to shop in. For this reason, the retailer must consider an area's potential for creating new demand, its **market expansion potential (MEP)**, along with its IRS to assess its attractiveness for locating new outlets.[7]

One way of calculating the potential for market expansion is to measure the level of outshopping by estimating the amount of money the residents of the area spend at retail stores outside the area. As outshopping increases, so does the potential for market expansion.

The sales activity and quality index published by *Sales and Marketing Management* also measures the potential for expanding a market. These indices show the extent to which the market's quality is above or below par.[8] A market area with an activity or quality index below 100, the par value, has less than average buying power, signifying the possibility of high levels of outshopping. These markets' high expansion potential afford opportunities to astute retailers to increase total sales in the area.

Market Classification Scheme

Evaluation of the desirability of opening new stores requires consideration of both the IRS and the MEP for an area. IRS indicates existing conditions while MEP is more future oriented. Exhibit 8.6 presents a **market classification scheme** based on both IRS and MEP.

The most attractive markets, those with high ratings on both IRS and MEP, appear in the upper left-hand quadrant. The high IRS values indicate low saturation in the markets, so competition is not too intense. In addition, these markets have high expansion potentials; that is, their total demand can be increased. The markets in the lower right-hand quadrant, on the other hand, are low on both IRS and MEP, indicating highly competitive markets with little scope for expansion, which would discourage new stores.

The attractiveness of markets in the other two quadrants depends on the entering firm's competitive strength. Markets in Quadrant 2 have low levels of existing competition (high IRS), but lack growth potential (low MEP). The lack of growth potential reduces the attractiveness of these markets, despite the relatively mild

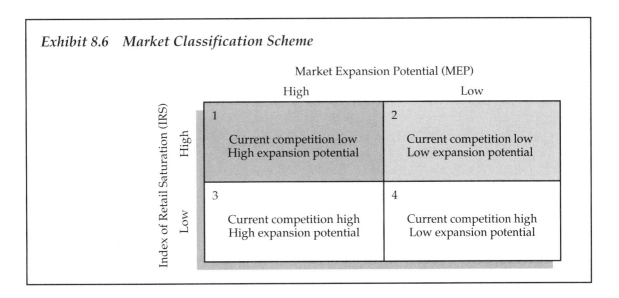

Exhibit 8.6   Market Classification Scheme

competition. Markets in Quadrant 3 have high growth potentials, but they also have high levels of existing competition (low IRS). This implies that the new entrant can gain sales only by aggressively taking sales away from existing stores.

Other Considerations

The classification scheme presented in the previous section provides a useful tool for comparing the attractiveness of geographic areas. However, factors other than market potential also influence selection of regions for expansion. For instance, it is very important to assess the overall economic base of the area. The future economic viability of an area depends critically on its economic base. A retailer might find an area with its economy based on a single industry unattractive. Examples of such areas are a mining town or a town dominated by a single large factory. A prolonged strike or temporary closure of the mine or factory can affect the entire town and reduce retail sales significantly. For this reason, areas with a single economic base are quite risky.

Some firms must consider accessibility to a system of warehouses as another important factor in selecting areas for expansion. Outlets of chain stores often receive merchandise from a few strategically located warehouses. Proximity to these warehouses is a major consideration in selecting markets for these firms. Such proximity is especially important for regional chains that gear their distribution systems to serve a particular region of the country.

In addition, some other points that must be considered are:

1. Availability and cost of media for advertising.

2. Availability and cost of labor.
3. Responsiveness of the local government to new business.
4. The regulatory and legal environment.

These factors, of course, should be secondary to concerns for market attractiveness and retail potential.

A Caution on Overstoring

Prior to concluding this section, a word of caution is necessary regarding market selection decisions. An area that attracts one firm based on demand potential is also likely to attract the firm's competitors. A market area with high potential might lose its attractiveness if a number of firms were to open new stores there at about the same time. Markets quickly become overstored as many new stores open within a short period of time.

This happened in a number of cities in the "Sun Belt" during the last decade. Attracted by the population migrating to the Sun Belt, many retailers, especially department stores, targeted their expansion to cities in Florida, Arizona, and Texas. Many new stores opened within a short time span, fundamentally affecting the level of competition in the area. Some of the retailers may have stayed away from these cities if they had anticipated these new store openings.

AREAL ANALYSIS

Based on regional analysis, a retailer can identify attractive geographic markets in which to locate new outlets. The geographic scope of this type of analysis is necessarily broad, comparing entire states, counties, cities, or metropolitan areas. It is not enough, however, just to examine the attractiveness of the region as a whole. The retailer must consider spatial variations in market potential and attractiveness within a region. Land-use and housing patterns vary considerably within cities and give rise to significant intracity variations in market attractiveness. In large metropolitan areas, especially, retail potentials vary considerably among different parts of the region. To select sites for new stores, the location analyst must, therefore, focus on the characteristics of local areas within the region. This step in the site selection process is called *areal analysis*.

The central objective of areal analysis is to measure the retail potential in the area from which the store is likely to attract its customers. Thus, the first step in areal analysis is to identify the feasible sites for new stores. Then the demographic and socioeconomic characteristics of the population around the sites are studied to measure the potential. Like regional analysis, the key question in areal analysis, too, is the extent to which the demographic characteristics of a subarea match the target market of the store. A department store's target market may, for example, consist predominantly of middle- and upper-income groups. Thus, these stores will count the number of families with annual incomes above $25,000 or so. A supermarket, on the other hand, will be more concerned with overall population size, since it targets a broader market. Similarly, stores selling children's clothing and toys will be more interested in the number of families with children living in each subarea and the expected growth of this demographic group.

To systematically consider all the relevant demographic and socioeconomic factors, it is necessary to get detailed information about the population surrounding the potential site. A number of market research firms specialize in providing demographic data for small, user-defined areas. These companies maintain demographic and socioeconomic data bases on computer systems that can easily supply data on any geographic area. To utilize this kind of service the analyst has to first identify the address of the potential site. Next the analyst has to determine the approximate area from which the new store is likely to attract its customers. The extent of this area depends on the type of store being located and the characteristics of the site.

Examining the total population is not enough when stores have more specific target markets. For example, a home improvement center may consider the following three factors as important in selecting locations for its stores: (1) median annual household income of $30,000; (2) at least 30 percent of the households owning their homes; and (3) median property value of $125,000. It is evident from Exhibit 8.7 that Site A is better suited for a home improvement center than Site B. Even though Site A has less population surrounding it, the characteristics of this population better match the target for home improvement centers.

Competitive Inventory

Just as regional analysis requires consideration of both demand and supply factors, both population and competitive factors must be examined in areal analysis. There are many ways in which to measure the level of competition within a subarea. Indices such as the number of stores, stores per capita, and selling space per capita often serve this purpose. To obtain a visual picture of the competition in an area,

---

Exhibit 8.7 **Example of Areal Analysis**

	Site A	Site B
Population	147,569	165,820
Median annual HH income	$32,476	$29,213
Percent owning home	36.21%	24.71%
Median property value	$143,200	$117,280

ENTREPRENEURIAL EDGE

Putting Stores Where the Customer Travels

Don Paradies, president of the Paradies Shops, the Atlanta-based airport and hotel stores, sets up his stores with an unusual retail goal: to attract customers whose real purpose is not to shop, but to kill time. Purchases in his stores are typically made on impulse, rather than as carefully planned acquisitions. Travelers in a rush do not arrive at the airport (or their hotel) with a shopping list in hand; they may have left behind shampoo or a toothbrush that they need to replace, but rarely do they plan on buying clothing or other nonconvenience items. Paradies, however, stocks a wide variety of items in his stores, displayed to attract harried travelers and entice them to come in and browse. Once in the stores, the customers are tempted by a whole selection of items, from shirts and souvenirs to shampoo and shoes. More often than not, the customers leave the store with both the needed shampoo and a shirt bought on a whim.

Don Paradies and his brother opened their first store in the Atlanta airport. The brothers were then in the distribution business, and were looking for a career change. Their second airport store opened almost three years later, and the first hotel store five years after that. Notwithstanding the slow start, Paradies shops can now be found in hotels and airports nationwide,

and the 200 stores, each averaging roughly 1,200 square feet, rack up annual sales of over $100 million.

Paradies cites the main reason for the success of his stores to his unique merchandising formula that ideally fits the characteristics of the location. The stores all carry an unusual merchandise mix, offering more than the typical travel convenience items, and showcased in eye-catching and unusual ways. Paradies carries brand-name apparel, from Izod shirts to Reebok sneakers, along with newspapers and toothpaste in store environments that soothe the weary traveler. While most airport stores and their hotel counterparts are merely utilitarian-looking, stores (or lounges or restaurants) that offer a brief respite from the hustle-bustle of the waiting area are very much welcomed by travelers. There is nothing like the dreaded prospect of having to kill time, and when travelers come upon a Paradies store, which offers both an exciting and an enticing place to wait, the customers almost can't help but buy something.

Paradies Shops' success will continue as long as the company follows its retail location strategy.

Source: "Retailing's Entrepreneurs of the Year," *Chain Store Age Executive*, December 1990, p. 28–38.

---

the analyst can map locations of competitive stores to create a **competitive inventory** as shown in Exhibit 8.8. Before constructing such maps it is important, however, to properly identify relevant competitors.

Exhibit 8.8 shows locations of two types of competitors. First, direct competitors appear who operate outlets similar to the new outlet. In the example, these

Exhibit 8.8   Competitive Inventory for Census Tracts

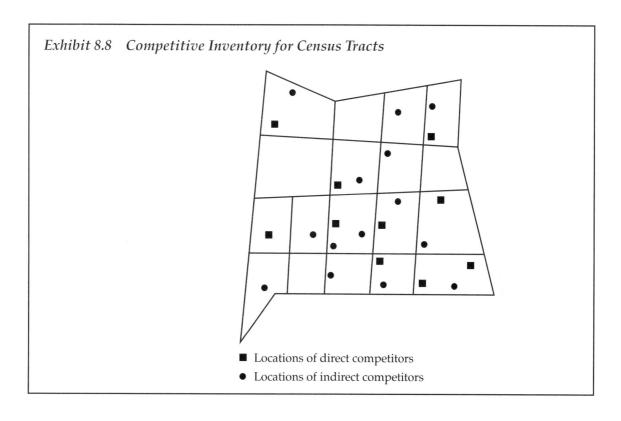

■ Locations of direct competitors
● Locations of indirect competitors

are other home improvement centers. Location of a second category of major intertype competitors (hardware stores, paint stores, electrical suppliers, and so forth) also appears on the map. Only by comparing demand with the level of competition can the attractiveness of an area be determined. Often, areas of high demand also have many established stores, reducing the potential for a new store to locate there.

It is evident that the retail analyst relies heavily on first-hand market knowledge as well as on secondary data sources for conducting regional and areal analysis. Exhibit 8.9 lists some common sources of information for market analysis. Exhibit 8.10 illustrates a page from yet another source: the *Editor and Publisher Market Guide.*

SITE EVALUATION

Having completed regional and areal analyses, the location analyst can now proceed to the final step of the location selection process, **site evaluation**. Site evaluation systematically evaluates the characteristics of each site to determine their feasibility as locations for new outlets.

Exhibit 8.9   Retail Industry Directories

Shopping Center Directory, published by the National Bureau of Research, provides information on the number, size, age, and tenant mix of shopping centers by market.

Department Store Directory, published by Chain Store Age Publishing Company, gives location of department stores by market area.

Discount Department Store Directory, published by Chain Store Age Publishing Company, gives location of discount stores by market area.

Market Guidebook, published by the Progressive Grocer, gives locations of supermarkets by market area.

It is often said that the essence of site evaluation is to find a 100 percent location, one that has all the desirable characteristics of a good site.[9] Unfortunately, finding a 100 percent location may not be an easy task. One must first determine what characteristics to look for, since desirable characteristics vary from one type of store to another. The 100 percent location for a specialty apparel store may not be appropriate for a fast-food restaurant.

What characteristics make a site good for locating new outlets? Although the specific factors firms look for in individual sites vary from one situation to another, five broad types of factors must always be considered:

1. Type of location.
2. Accessibility and traffic flow patterns.
3. Store compatibility.
4. Physical characteristics of site.
5. Terms of occupancy.

Type of Location

Broadly speaking, it is possible to distinguish among four types of sites. First, are sites located in the **central business districts** of urban areas. Second, are sites within planned **shopping centers or malls**. Business districts are usually unplanned store clusters found mainly in urban areas. Shopping centers and malls, on the other hand, are a carefully planned, well-balanced mix of stores within a single complex typically located in suburban areas. Two other types of locations complete the regional mosaic of shopping opportunities. One type is **ribbon (strip) developments**, which result from freestanding stores located near one another along major traffic arteries. The fourth type is **freestanding sites** located in relatively isolated places that are not a part of any store cluster.

Exhibit 8.10   Information for Market Analysis from Editor and Publisher Market Guide

ITHACA

1 - LOCATION: Tompkins County, E&P Map D-4, County Seat. S central part of western state. On State Hwys. 13, 34, 79, 89, 96. Eastern & Southern gateway to the Finger Lakes Region. 240 mi. NW of N.Y.C.; 150 mi. E of Buffalo; 55 mi. SW of Syracuse; 35 mi. NE of Elmira; 30 mi. N of Pennsylvania border. Education; dairy; some fruit and mfg. Home of various agric. enterprises.

2 - TRANSPORTATION: Railroads-Lehigh Valley (freight).
Intercity Bus Lines-Interstate; Greyhound.
Airlines-USAir; Piedmont.

3 - POPULATION:
Corp. City 80 Cen. 28,732; E&P 87 Est. 28,035
CZ-ABC: (80) 44,754
RTZ-ABC: (80) 42,331
County 80 Cen. 87,085; E&P 87 Est. 91,574
City & RTZ-ABC: (80) 87,085
Demographic Information available from Newspaper. See paragraph 14.

4 - HOUSEHOLDS:
City 80 Cen. 14,105; E&P 87 Est. 9,080
CZ-ABC: (80) 14,105
RTZ-ABC: (80) 15,443
County 80 Cen. 29,548; E&P 87 Est. 31,933
City & RTZ-ABC: (80) 29,548

5 - BANKS	NUMBER	DEPOSITS
Commercial	3	$138,000,000
Savings	1	$102,000,000
Savings & Loan	1	$31,000,000

6 - PASSENGER AUTOS: County 41,615

7 - ELECTRIC METERS: Residence 32,336

8 - GAS METERS: Residence 11,063

9 - PRINCIPAL INDUSTRIES: Industry, No. of Wage Earners-Mach. Shop Mfg. 2,850; Textiles 150; Tooling 175; Cornell Univ. 10,000; Ithaca College 500.

10 - CLIMATE: Min. & Max. Temp.-Spring 26-94; Summer 32-98; Fall 4-82; Winter 2-66. First killing frost, Oct. 9; last killing frost, May 5.

11 - TAP WATER: Alkaline, soft; not fluoridated.

12 - RETAILING: Principal Shopping Center-4 blocks on State St., 1 on Green St., 1/2 on Seneca St. (these 3 parallel); 3 on Aurora St., 3 on Tioga St., 3 on Cayuga St. (these 3 crossing).
Neighborhood Shopping Centers-Triphammer, NE; The Plz. to SE College Town (2 blocks on College Ave., 1 on Dryden Rd., 1 on Eddy Cayuga Mall, NE on College Ave., 1 on Dryden Rd., 1 on Eddy St., near Cornell. Univ.); Community Corners, about 3 mi. NE, beyond vlg. of Cayuga Heights; Pyramid Mall NE.

Nearby Shopping Centers

Name (No. of stores)	Miles from Downtown	Principal Stores
Corners Community(20)	NA	IGA
East Hill(12)	NA	Rite Aid, P&C
Ithaca Plz.(13)	NA	Grand Union
Triphammer(15)	NA	A&P, Sears, Jamesway
Cayuga Mall(8)	NA	Grand Union, Zayre
Pyramid Mall(80)	NA	JCPenney, Howlands, J.W. Rhodes, Hill's, Mont. Ward

Principal Shopping Days-Thur., Fri., Sat.
Stores Open Evenings-Downtown-Thur.; Malls-every night except Sun.

13 - RETAIL OUTLETS: Department Stores-JCPenney; Woolworth; Hills; J.W. Rhodes; Steinbach; Montgomery Ward; Iszard's.
Discount Stores-Jamesway; Clinton; Rite Aid; Down Town; Fay's; K mart.
Chain Drug Stores-The Hills; Rite Aid.
Chain Supermarkets-A&P; Grand Union; P&C 2; Great American; Tops; Payless.
Other Chain Stores-Fanny Farmer; Outdoor; Triangle; Singer Co.; Firestone; Goodyear; Thom McAn; Sears (catalog); Sherwin-Williams; Mary Carter Paints.

14 - NEWSPAPERS: JOURNAL (e) 19,815; Mar. 29, 1987 ABC.
Local Contact for Advertising and Merchandising Data: Gary Bucciero, Adv. Dir., JOURNAL, 123 W. State St., Ithaca, NY 14850; Tel. (607) 272-2321.
National Representative: Gannett National Newspaper Sales.

The Central Business District

The CBD, the familiar downtown district, has historically been the center of urban retailing where most major department stores started operations. In the latter part of the nineteenth century, urbanization made downtown shopping clusters promi-

San Diego's central business district had lost most of its retailers. When Horton Plaza was built there in the mid-1980s, the city center was revitalized.

nent parts of the city. As people moved into cities from rural areas, commercial establishments followed them and clustered in the city center. The process accelerated further in the early part of this century with the growth of mass transportation systems, which provided easier access to the CBD and expanded the geographic area from which downtown stores could draw their customers.

Advantages of Locating in the CBD   The *Central Business District or CBD*, with its high concentration of commercial buildings and retail stores, remains one of the most important parts of the urban structure. Retail stores gain an advantage from the CBD's high drawing power, since the district draws people from all over the metropolitan region. In many cities, the CBD also attracts tourists and visiting business people. It is estimated, for example, that over 60 million people annually pass by the stores located on parts of Fifth Avenue in Manhattan, New York City's central business district.[10]

The concentration of commercial activities and tourist attractions and the availability of mass transit bring many people into the CBD. While each store may not be able to draw customers across large distances, as part of the CBD, each benefits from its drawing power. This is the greatest strength of a CBD location. The CBD usually offers a varied assortment of stores with different prices and store images.

In most cases, this includes one or more large department stores, mass merchandise outlets, specialty outlets, and many small stores. The flagship stores of many leading department store chains are located in CBDs. San Francisco's CBD is a good example. In this city's thriving central business district around Union Square are located outlets of such well-known retail chains as Macy's, I. Magnin, Emporium, Nordstrom, The Gap, F.A.O. Schwarz, and Gucci, along with many smaller stores.

Disadvantages of CBD Locations   Unfortunately, a CBD location's strengths often become liabilities. For example, traffic drawn to the CBD by its commercial activities can create congestion and shortage of parking space that keep shoppers away from the area. Further, it is often difficult to attract shoppers to the CBD on weekends and after office hours. Another weakness of the CBD is its poorly planned development. Since the organization of stores in most CBDs developed without much planning, the physical layouts of many CBDs are not very conducive to shopping. For another drawback, the lack of control over the types of retailers that locate in the CBD often keeps its shopping image out of focus. Consumers do not have a clear perception of the type of stores that they can expect to find there.

Planned Shopping Centers

As the population movement to suburban areas accelerated in the years following World War II, suburban shopping centers grew in response. During the 1960s and 1970s, this type of shopping location multiplied at a phenomenal rate, increasing between 1965 and 1979 from an estimated 9,200 to 20,400.[11] During the same period, shopping center sales increased nearly five-fold from about $8 billion to $38 billion. Sales in stores located in shopping centers now account for over 50 percent of total retail sales in the country.[12]

Shopping centers are planned shopping clusters constructed and managed by developers. The developer keeps the mix of stores located in a center well-balanced to cater to the needs of the surrounding population. A unified image is created for each center by carefully planning the types of stores allowed to locate in it. This contrasts sharply with the CBD and other urban shopping clusters, whose images tend to be confused by the wide diversity of stores located there.

Types of Shopping Centers   The *regional center* is the largest type of planned shopping center. Usually enclosed malls, regional centers average from 75 to 150 stores anchored by two or three department stores or mass merchandisers. Some larger centers house as many as 250 to 300 stores with five or six anchor stores and cover two million or more square feet of space (these large centers are sometimes called super regional centers). With so many stores in one place, the regional mall can attract shoppers from a wide geographic area, often 20 to 30 miles, sometimes even more.

The two smaller types of shopping centers, *community shopping centers* and *neighborhood centers*, resemble regional shopping centers, on a much smaller scale. The

RESEARCH REPORT

The Suburbanization of Retailing

The shift of retailing activities from central cities to suburbs has been the most significant spatial change in retailing in the post-World War II period. Before the war, the central business district (CBD) ranked as the preeminent metropolitan shopping district, offering a vast array of goods and services and attracting shoppers from throughout the metropolitan region. That premier position has fallen dramatically since the 1950s, however.

Four factors were key to the phenomenal growth of suburban shopping centers in the post-war period: (1) suburban residents' need for easy access to shopping opportunities; (2) retail industry's need for access to the suburban population; (3) local governments' need to diversify their tax base; and (4) availability of financing and tax advantages of investing in commercial real estate.

After the 1950s, retail activities declined in the metropolitan core and grew rapidly in the suburban periphery. This pattern of retail dispersal clearly reflected the spatial redistribution of population and income in the metropolitan areas. During the 1950s, the suburban areas grew five times faster than the central cities. The central city not only lost population but income as well. The exodus from the central city contained a relatively higher proportion of middle- and upper-income groups who preferred a home in the suburbs to living in the city. The redistribution of population and income contained in it the seed of suburban retailing growth.

The establishment of shopping centers was greatly encouraged by suburban municipal governments. Lacking any substantial industrial base, local governments viewed shopping centers as a major source of real estate and sales taxes. They actively welcomed and helped shopping center developers, leading in many cases to competition among municipalities to attract new developments.

Capital-intensive projects such as shopping centers require access to large amounts of financing. The relatively low interest rates in the years following World War II greatly facilitated the growth of shopping centers. Real Estate Investment Trusts, or REITs, which allowed individuals and institutions to invest in securities that were backed by mortgage or rental income, also aided the proliferation of shopping centers. Through REITs, financial institutions such as pension funds and insurance companies became dominant players in financing shopping center developers.

Source: Avijit Ghosh and Sara McLafferty, "The Transformation of Metropolitan Retailing in the United States," Working Paper, Stern School of Business, 1991.

community shopping center usually groups 20 to 30 stores anchored by a variety store, a small department store, or a mass merchandiser. They draw their clientele from the people living within 10 to 15 minutes driving time by car. The smaller neighborhood center usually features about 10 stores, often anchored by a supermarket or a convenience store. These centers serve the needs of the local population residing in the immediate vicinity of the center. Exhibit 8.11 summarizes the characteristics of the major types of shopping centers.

In addition to these three types of centers, there has been a recent trend toward the establishment of *specialty centers*. Instead of housing a wide variety of stores, these specialty centers serve a more defined market segment with assortments of similar stores. At one type of specialty center, the factory outlet or off-price center, specialty stores offer merchandise at a discount from regular prices. Because they focus on low prices, these centers tend to be located in low-rent areas that are often quite distant from major cities. In contrast to off-price factory outlet centers, some specialty centers specialize in high-fashion specialty apparel stores that cater to high-income consumers. Located mainly in high-income suburban neighborhoods, these centers typically combine specialty stores, designer outlets, and high-end department stores. Auto care malls are another example of specialty centers.

Benefits of Locating in Shopping Centers   Locating in a shopping center, especially a large one, brings a major benefit in increased drawing power. By locating in a mall, a store can draw far more people than it could by itself. This is especially true for small specialty stores, which benefit greatly from large stores located in the same malls. The large store attracts customers who tend also to visit the specialty stores located in the same center. For this reason these stores are said to "anchor" malls. Typically, department stores and mass merchandisers such as Sears and Penneys serve as **anchor stores** in large regional malls; variety stores and smaller department stores, and mass merchandisers are anchors at community centers. Small neighborhood centers are typically anchored by supermarkets. In addition to attracting customers, the anchor stores impart some of their own store

---

Exhibit 8.11   *Characteristics of Major Types of Shopping Centers*

	Size (square feet)	Type of Anchors	Population Served	Drive Time (minutes)	Number of Stores
Neighborhood	50,000–200,000	Supermarket	10,000	5	5–15
Community	75,000–300,000	Discount store	40,000+	15	20–30
Regional	400,000–600,000	Two major department stores	150,000+	15–20	75–150
Super regional	750,000–1 million	Three to six major department stores	150,000+	30–45	150+

The neighborhood shopping centers, like this one in El Cajon, California, draw their clientele from people living within a 10- to 15-minute drive.

images to the malls they anchor. This critical role commonly earns anchor stores lower rents per square foot than smaller stores.

Gathering different stores in a shopping center makes shopping convenient for consumers, since they can visit a variety of outlets on a single trip. Grouping stores together also facilitates comparison shopping, since consumers can easily check product availability and prices in different stores in the center. Moreover, enclosed malls provide a more pleasant shopping environment and protect shoppers from inclement weather. Consumers often bypass freestanding stores located near their homes and travel farther for the convenience of shopping at a shopping center.

Another advantage of a shopping center location is that individual stores benefit from the promotional activities of the center. Shopping center developers sponsor advertisements on local television and also in newspapers and promote activities such as special shows, entertainment, and activities for children. Individual stores also benefit from sharing the cost of maintaining parking facilities and pedestrian areas. Of course, store owners compensate the developer for these costs through the rent they pay.

Disadvantages of Shopping Centers   Stores suffer certain disadvantages, however, when they locate within a shopping center. As part of the collection that makes up the mall, each individual store must follow certain norms and guidelines regarding store operations. All stores, for example, are expected to open and close at the same hours. The mall may also enforce restrictions on the design of store exterior. Further, the store operator is often restricted from changing the type of merchandise it sells or in reducing the size of the store. Also, the level of competition in a shopping center can be quite high. Specialty stores, for example, may face intense competition from the anchor department stores, as well as from other specialty stores located in the center.

Freestanding Sites

In contrast to stores located in shopping districts or centers, a freestanding store forms no direct part of any retail group. Two types of freestanding sites can be distinguished. The first type is a site in a *ribbon* or *strip development*. The second type of freestanding stores is an *isolated site* that is not connected to any shopping cluster.

Ribbon and Strip Developments   These types of developments typically lie along major roads connecting urban and suburban neighborhoods. In some cases, strips or ribbons of commercial development follow along major roads connecting two shopping centers. Stores locate next to each other along the traffic arteries, but usually have separate entrances, exits, and parking facilities. Since many stores locate close together and along both sides of the roadway, individual sites enjoy the benefits of a shopping cluster without being a direct part of a shopping complex.

Strip locations have an advantage in the large volume of traffic on the streets along which they are located. The stores depend on this traffic flow to attract customers. For another advantage, rent is lower than for locations inside shopping centers. Thus, furniture retailers and auto dealers, who require large display areas, often locate in ribbon developments. Toys R Us, the discount toy chain, also favors freestanding sites over shopping centers, since the large size of its outlets would make the cost of comparable mall locations prohibitive. Strip locations also attract convenience outlets, as evidenced by the many fast-food restaurants and 7-Eleven stores that can be found there.

The Isolated Site   The isolated site lies in relative isolation from other shopping opportunities. Two types of stores tend to locate in this type of site. A small neighborhood outlet catering to a small client base living near the store is one type. This could be a neighborhood grocery store, dry cleaner, drugstore, or pizza parlor. Large retailers that can attract customers even in a relatively isolated location might also locate at an isolated site. A store that can do this can benefit from the lower rent of the isolated store compared with sites of similar sizes in shopping centers. Historically, many discount stores located in freestanding sites because shopping centers barred discount stores from their premises fearing damage to

Pier 1 is a large retailer that can enjoy the advantages of an isolated site and still attract many customers.

the images of the centers. Thus, stores like K mart and Jamesway, a discount-store chain in the Northeast, used to locate in freestanding sites, although now they occupy space in many shopping centers, too.

The isolated site has a number of advantages. First, it enjoys some monopoly power because of its isolation. Although it doesn't benefit from the drawing power of a planned center, it does not have to share its clientele with other stores, either. It may develop a small, loyal clientele who provide a steady sales volume. The second advantage is the lower rent of isolated sites compared to mall locations. Low rent is especially attractive to lumber yards, home repair centers, and large hardware stores, which require large amounts of space for showrooms and storage facilities.

As the preceding discussion indicates, each type of location has its own advantages and disadvantages. To find a good site, the retailer must carefully weigh the benefits and costs and determine the type of location that is most appropriate for its outlet. The type of merchandise the store sells and its target market both have major influences on this decision. Department stores, for example, tend to locate in regional malls and CBDs because they have to attract shoppers from large geographic areas. Supermarkets, on the other hand, favor neighborhood centers. Final evaluation of the desirability of a potential site must also consider other factors besides the type of location. As mentioned earlier these include accessibility and traffic flow patterns, neighborhood compatibility, physical characteristics of the site, and terms of occupancy.

Accessibility and Traffic Flow

Since retail outlets serve customers who travel from various distances, ease of access to the outlets is a critical determinant of their success. **Accessibility** ultimately determines the number of customers the site can attract, depending on several factors such as the quality of the roads surrounding the site, the ease of entry and exit from the site, and physical and psychological barriers to travel in the area. To assess accessibility one must ask questions such as: Can potential customers reach the site easily? Do major streets link the site to the surrounding area? Are the roads too congested? Do barriers such as railway crossings or limited-access highways impair access to the site?

An important component of site evaluation is a quantitative enumeration of the level and composition of **traffic flow** around the site. In general, higher levels of traffic flow increase sales potential. However, it is important to investigate the composition of the traffic flow. A large volume of truck traffic not only does not generate sales, it may actually deter shoppers from patronizing the site because of congestion. One must evaluate even pedestrian traffic to make sure that the characteristics of the pedestrians correspond to those of the target market of the outlet to be located. In evaluating a site for a women's clothing store, for example, a traffic flow consisting mainly of male office workers would add little value. As has been stressed throughout the book, very few retail decisions can be made without studying and defining the characteristics of the store's target market.

Assessing traffic flow requires a quantitative enumeration of pedestrian and vehicular traffic around the site. Data pertaining to vehicular traffic patterns are often available from local planning agencies and highway departments. Pedestrian traffic data is scarce among secondary sources, and the analyst usually must collect it at the site. A good pedestrian count should include data on the total number of pedestrians who pass by the site, broken out by sex and age. The age breakdown for this purpose can be quite broad (for example, children, teenagers, and adults). Since traffic patterns vary significantly during the day and between weekdays and weekends, the traffic count must compare data for different days of the week and different parts of the day to accurately depict total traffic flow. The traffic count figures can be augmented by interviews with a randomly selected subset of the people passing by the store. The interviews should aim at finding: (1) the proportion of pedestrians who are potential shoppers, (2) the stores they typically visit, and (3) the average frequency with which people visit the area.

Store Compatibility

Most retail sites are part of some shopping cluster. Whether a site is in an urban shopping district or a suburban shopping center, other stores will be located nearby.

In evaluating a potential site, one must study the number and composition of stores in the immediate area to assure **store compatibility**.

The compatibility of adjacent stores depends on the level of affinity between two types of outlets. Specialty apparel outlets, for example, have strong affinity for department stores. Small specialty stores benefit greatly from locating close to large department stores, since the smaller stores can share in the superior drawing power of the larger department store. An apparel store, on the other hand, has very little affinity for hardware outlets. A paint store, a lumber yard, and a hardware store, on the other hand, have strong affinity for each other, since consumers may have to visit all three on the same trip. By locating next to each other, they facilitate multipurpose shopping, allowing consumers to visit all three stores on a single trip. This affinity benefits all three types of stores, since the increased traffic increases sales for all of them.

Some stores may have a strong affinity for competing outlets. Before they purchase many types of goods, shoppers like to compare the offerings of competing outlets before making a purchase. Examples of such goods are automobiles, furniture, and antiques. These outlets tend to cluster in the same area in order to facilitate comparison shopping and maintain close links with competitors. Such clustering of competitive stores benefits individual outlets as it creates synergy and increases the volume of traffic in the area. To gain competitive advantage, each store in the cluster tries to differentiate its merchandise, price, or service level.

Physical Site Characteristics

The physical characteristics of a site determine the type of structure that can be built there, the visibility for potential customers, and the ease with which they can enter and exit. A vacant piece of flat land with good visibility and access is ideal. However, a vacant piece of land can be costly to develop. Alternatively, if an available site has an existing structure, a retailer must decide whether the existing structure can be remodeled or the entire structure or any part of it needs to be demolished.

Whether a potential site is a vacant piece of land or a vacant store, its **visibility** is important. A store that has a small frontage at the end of a shopping center or in a small side street is not as easily visible as one located on a major street or near the main entrance of a mall. Similarly, a site in a strip development that is set back far from the major roadway may not be easily visible to potential customers driving along the road. Although this can sometimes be remedied by constructing large, clearly visible signs, there is always the potential for losing a significant amount of business.

Along with visibility, the position of the site is another important consideration. This is especially true for sites in strip developments. Generally a corner site at the intersection of two roads is better than one in the middle of a block. Many stores will pay higher rents to gain the easier access of corner sites. Corner sites also provide greater opportunity for window displays and separation of exits and entrances to the parking lot.

Another important physical characteristic of a site is the availability of parking space. Most shopping centers provide adequate free parking facilities. In central business districts, however, parking can be a major problem. Although in many CBDs, parking is provided by municipal governments or through cooperative arrangements among downtown stores, it often falls short of need. Even when parking is available, it tends to be costly. In order to make it easier to shop in the CBD, some downtown stores have arranged for free parking with proof of purchase. Despite these efforts, the lack of parking can be a major deterrent to shopping in a CBD.

Terms of Occupancy

The final step in assessing the desirability of a site is to compare the attractiveness of the site with its cost. A retailer must be willing to pay adequately for a high-quality site. However, the critical issue is how the cost compares with similar sites. Since no two sites are exactly similar, this is not an easy comparison to make. Moreover, the cost and **terms of occupancy** can be structured in a variety of ways. The retailer must rely on expert knowledge and past experience to analyze the benefits of different terms of occupancy and compare them to the cost.

Retailers can occupy sites in two ways: they may own the site or lease it. The lease arrangement itself can take various forms. The lease payment could, for example, be a fixed annual or monthly rent per square foot, or a fixed percentage of the store's revenue. A typical arrangement is a two-part price, in which the retailer pays a flat, fixed fee per square foot and then a percentage of sales, if sales exceeds a prespecified level. Many large retailers engage in sale-and-lease-back arrangements in which they first develop the site according to their needs and then sell it to a real estate firm which leases it back to the retailer. By selling the property, the retailer recoups the financial capital invested in the site, but by agreeing to a long-term lease, it keeps the use of the site.

Developing a Checklist

To keep track of the large number and wide variety of factors that affect site evaluation, analysts commonly develop a checklist covering all the relevant factors to aid the evaluation process. An example of a site evaluation checklist is shown in Exhibit 8.12. The checklist helps the location analyst compare the desirability of alternative sites by rating them with respect to each factor on the list. A judgment about the relative desirability of each site can then be made by comparing the overall evaluations.

The checklist makes the site evaluation procedure systematic. Although the data may be quite subjective, it standardizes data collection and ensures comparability

Exhibit 8.12   Checklist for Site Evaluation

Traffic Flow and Accessibility
   Number and types of vehicles
   Number and types of pedestrians
   Access to highway system
   Availability of mass transit
   Quality of streets

Retail Structure
   Number of competitors in area
   Complementarity of neighboring stores
   Proximity to commercial areas
   Joint promotions by retail merchants

Site Characteristics
   Number of parking spots available
   Distance of store to parking area
   Visibility of site
   Ease of entrance and exit
   Condition of lot and/or existing building

Legal and Cost Factors
   Type of zoning
   Length of lease

of information collected for different sites. The relative ease with which the checklist method can be implemented and its reliance on expert opinions and judgments give it two more advantages.[13]

Creating Market Coverage

Preceding sections outlined the various steps in selecting regions, market areas, and sites for locating retail outlets. The emphasis has been on selecting single sites that are attractive for opening new stores. In today's competitive environment, however, many retail firms create competitive advantage for their outlets by establishing a strong presence in a market area through **market coverage** by multiple outlets. Many retail chains attempt to saturate an existing market prior to expanding into new ones.

K mart has consistently followed this strategy. For example, when the firm entered the Columbus, Ohio, area in 1975, it opened five stores at the same time located along major highways so that "78 percent of the area residents lived within five miles of one of the new stores, making it possible for a resident to drive to one of the K mart stores in 15 minutes or less."[14] Many supermarkets, fast-food, and appliance chains, as well as retail banks follow this type of market saturation strategy.

Locating multiple units in one market has a number of advantages. It creates market presence so that all consumers in the market area have relatively easy access to the store. Multiple outlets also create managerial efficiencies as well as scale economies in distribution, warehousing, and transportation costs. In addition, it increases the efficiency of advertising and promotion expenditures in the local market. Concentrating outlets in an area can create synergy, improving the performance of individual outlets that are a part of a larger local network.

Creating a network of outlets in an area requires special attention to their locations. Selecting the best individual sites is not enough since the location of each outlet relative to the firm's other outlets is critical. Sites that may be desirable when considered individually, may lose attractiveness when the entire network of stores is considered. Two stores located too close to each other may cannibalize one another's sales since they will both compete for the same customers. At the same time, the outlets must be well-located with respect to the distribution of customers and competitive locations. Special procedures and analytical techniques are required for designing the spatial pattern of multiple outlet networks, some of which are discussed in the next chapter.[15]

Summary

1. The location policy is the blueprint for achieving the firm's marketing objectives and expansion plans. It has to be sensitive to the spatial pattern of demand and the availability of desirable sites, and target the firm's investment toward specific locations and market areas. Developing a location policy involves four major steps: analysis of marketing strategy, regional analysis, areal analysis, and site evaluation.

2. Like all retail policies, the location decision must be consistent with the firm's overall corporate goals and marketing strategy. The firm's marketing strategy and the target market it intends to serve strongly influence its location policy. Since each store has a unique target market, each has its own locational requirements. Even stores selling similar types of merchandise may have different locational requirements, because their positions in the shopping opportunity line may differ. A firm's locational policy must also be consistent with its policies on price, promotion, and merchandise. A change in the overall marketing strategy, therefore, often requires a change in location policy.

3. Regional analysis involves the selection of a geographic market at the level of counties, cities, or metropolitan areas in which to locate the outlet. The key to regional analysis is to assess the retail potential in the region by comparing supply and demand. A number of sources provide data to measure demand and supply. Based on these data, the analyst can calculate the index of retail saturation and the market expansion potential of an area. Together these indices indicate the attractiveness of locating a new outlet in a particular region.

4. Once the region is chosen, areal analysis focuses on measuring the retail potential in the area from which the store is likely to attract its customers. It is necessary to get detailed

information about the characteristics of the population surrounding a potential site. This information is used to estimate the relative potential of a site and its suitability for locating a new store. The ideal trade area population characteristics, of course, differ from one application to another. A number of market research firms provide demographic and socio-economic data for small areas.

5. Four types of sites are generally available for locating new stores: (a) sites located in the central business districts of urban areas, (b) sites within planned shopping centers or mall, (c) ribbon (strip) developments, which result from freestanding stores located near one another along major traffic arteries; (d) freestanding sites located in relatively isolated places that are not a part of any store cluster.

6. The final step in selecting a new location is site evaluation. Each site must be evaluated in terms of accessibility and traffic flow patterns, compatibility of neighboring stores, visibility, adequacy of parking, and terms of occupancy. A checklist typically helps make this evaluation systematic.

Key Concepts

Regional analysis	Shopping centers (malls)
Areal analysis	Ribbon (strip) developments
Site evaluation	Freestanding sites
Buying power index	Anchor stores
Sales Activity Index	Accessibility
Index of retail saturation	Traffic flow
Market expansion potential	Store compatibility
Market classification scheme	Visibility
Competitive inventory	Terms of occupancy
Central business districts	Market coverage

Discussion Questions

1. Why is the location decision so critical for a retail firm? What are the steps in developing a location policy?

2. Using examples of some local retailers, explain how a firm's overall marketing strategy affects its location decision.

3. How can one measure retail demand in a county? What other factors besides demand must be considered in measuring the desirability of an area for opening a new store?

4. Explain how the market expansion potential and the index of retail saturation help develop a market classification scheme for evaluating areas for expansion.

5. A department store chain is considering opening a new store in either Cochise or Coconimo county in Arizona. The managers of this firm believe that the demand for their store is determined by: (a) the size of the population over age 25, (b) general merchandise, home furnishings, and appliance sales, and (c) number of households with annual buying income exceeding $35,000. According to the managers, each of these factors is equally important. The relevant information for the two counties are shown on the next page:

   (a) Calculate the customized BPI for the two counties for this department store

   (b) What type of location would be appropriate for the department store? Why?

	BPI	Total Population (thousands)	Percent Population 25+	General Merchandise Sales ($000)	Furniture Home Furnishings Appliances Sales ($000)	Households with EBI $35,000 + ($000)
Cochise	.0297	99.8	61.9	52.1	16.0	10.8
Coconimo	.0337	100.9	53.3	91.7	27.5	10.6
U.S.	100.0	253,629	63.8	217,493	89,839	42,556

6. What factors would you consider in evaluating potential sites for a new department store? How would these factors differ from those you would consider for a fast-food outlet?

7. What are the advantages and disadvantages of a specialty clothing store such as The Gap or The Limited locating in a regional mall? Would a site in a regional mall be appropriate for a supermarket? Why or why not?

8. Why do large furniture stores typically locate in freestanding sites?

9. Explain, with examples, the term "store compatibility."

Notes

1. Arun K. Jain and Vijay Mahajan, "Evaluating the Competitive Environment in Retailing Using the Multiplicative Competitive Interactive Model," in *Research in Marketing*, ed. by Jagdish Sheth, (Greenwich, CT: JAI Press, 1979).

2. "Survey of Buying Power," *Sales and Marketing Management* (August 24, 1992), p. A-7.

3. "Survey of Buying Power," *Sales and Marketing Management* (August 24, 1992), p. A-25.

4. Ibid.

5. Bernard Lalonde, "The Logistics of Retail Location," *AMA Educators' Conference Proceedings* (Chicago: American Marketing Association, 1961).

6. Charles A. Ingene and Robert F. Lusch, "Marketing Selection Decisions for Department Stores," *Journal of Retailing*, 56 (Fall 1980), pp. 21–40.

7. Ibid.

8. "Survey of Buying Power," *Sales and Marketing Management* (August 24, 1992), p. A-7.

9. Rom J. Markin, *Retailing Management* (New York: Macmillan, 1977), p. 177.

10. Mark Meemot, "Snooty Store Sites Aren't Cheap," *USA Today*, April 29, 1987, p. A1.

11. E. Winkelman and J. C. Bieri, "The Impact of the Development Process," in *Store Location and Assessment Research*, ed. by R. L. Davies and D. S. Rogers (New York: John Wiley and Sons, 1986), pp. 91–98.

12. *Monitor*, "A History of the Shopping Center Industry," (August 1990), pp. 11–59.

13. Jac. L. Goldstucker, Danny L. Bellenger, Thomas J. Stanley and Ruth L. Otte, *New Developments in Retail Trade Area Analysis and Site Selection*, Research Monograph No. 78 (Atlanta: Georgia State University, 1978), p. 85.

14. Albert D. Bates, *Retailing and Its Environment* (New York: D. Van Nostrand, 1979), p. 91.

15. For a more detailed discussion of methods for developing multiple outlet networks, see Avijit Ghosh and Sara L. McLafferty, *Location Strategies for Retail and Service Firms* (Lexington, MA: D.C. Heath, 1987).

CHAPTER 9
Trade Area Estimation and Sales Forecasting

American Fast-Food's International Expansion

As the market for fast-food in the United States becomes increasingly saturated, fast-food chains are looking for new markets. These firms must compete fiercely for clients in their home territories, and they want new and profitable markets to provide a cushion for them in the face of declining U.S. fast-food sales. In 1990 alone, burger consumption dropped 2 percent in the United States, totalling close to $1.48 billion of the $74 billion fast-food industry. Consumers are growing more health conscious, and the typically fried fast-food is losing its appeal. Once a uniform market of burgers and fries, new entrants are providing new choices at a dizzying pace, selling everything from subs (Miami Subs) to frozen Yogurt (TCBY) and tacos (Taco Bell), and the industry as a whole must now look towards new and growing markets to satisfy declining profits and changing consumer demands.

Fast-food chains have a double challenge in America: to reach new customers in the face of declining fast-food appeal and to re-attract old customers in the face of stiff industry competition. One way that industry players are reaching out to new consumers is by opening outlets in innovative places, like hospitals, army bases, and airports. These new locations have helped some in-dustry giants find new American customers. Some chains are beginning to change their menus and to offer new services in order to get back their customers, and to compete with new industry players that offer fare other than burgers and fries. These chains are offering more nutritious, tastier foods to ensure that their customers will keep coming back in this age of health consciousness. To step up to this new challenge, chains like McDonald's now serve salads and Kentucky Fried Chicken introduced a lower-fat, skinless broiled chicken dish. Moreover, even in the fast-food environment, customers are demanding higher levels of service. McDonald's and others have met this demand by providing play areas for small children, and all the large fast-food chains now have "Value Meals" to compete with some of their lower priced competitors.

The most attractive area for expansion is in foreign markets, and industry players are flocking abroad in droves. For example, McDonald's has 3,654 international units in 60 countries; total earnings for the international units is expected to surpass those of the 8,764 domestic restaurants by 1995. American-owned restaurants in foreign countries are highly profitable. The highest selling McDonald's is in Moscow's Red Square, and the chain's top ten restaurants in *sales and profits* are all located abroad. In fact, McDonald's income from the interna-

LEARNING OBJECTIVES

After studying this chapter, the reader will be able to:

- *Realize how retail stores' trade areas determine their potential sales.*
- *Understand the factors that determine the sizes, shapes, and other characteristics of retail trade areas.*
- *Know how to identify trade areas of existing stores.*
- *Realize how customer origin maps can be used to make retail decisions.*
- *Explain the different methods to forecast sales of new retail stores.*

tional operations doubled to $700 million between 1987 and 1991. Their profits from abroad are growing nearly three times as those from domestic restaurants. In 1991, for the first time, the company built more overseas locations than domestic ones. Foreign locations do not face the same amount of competition, and can, on average, earn 25 percent more than an American location.

However, there are certain downsides to doing business overseas, especially in the area of quality control, an area in which McDonald's has excelled. For McDonald's, quality is "110 percent of the business," and ensuring the same levels of quality in foreign restaurants as in domestic ones is not always easy. In Beijing, McDonald's sent a team of professionals to train the new employees, and worked for over seven years to develop potatoes suitable for McDonald's french-fries. The same was done in Russia, where scores of farmers vied to grow the perfect potatoes, cucumbers (for pickles), and tomatoes. It took ten years in Russia, but the result is high-quality, fresh produce and vegetables for all the sandwiches. Other negatives include fluctuations in foreign exchange rates, and prices that are often too high. In Moscow, for example, a typical McDonald's meal costs close to 50 rubles, or roughly 50 U.S. cents, but with an average monthly income of 800 to 1,000 rubles, this is often too expensive for the Russian consumer.

Pizza is another example of successful American fast-food sold overseas, and Domino's and Pizza Hut lead the way abroad. The two companies are expanding aggressively into key international markets. Mindful of the U.S. market saturation, they seek markets with high growth potentials. Both chains have been very successful in Mexico, where Pizza Hut has 29 outlets and Domino's has 38. However, the future expansion plans of the two chains are quite different. Domino's is heading into Western Europe and Japan, while Pizza Hut is aiming for Eastern Europe and the former Soviet Union. Hungary's first Pizza Hut, opened in the spring of 1992, had waiting lines to get in for months after the opening. The restaurant is decorated with scenes from Hollywood, complete with portraits of Humphrey Bogart and Superman, and a lifesize mannequin of Marilyn Monroe. While it is the only pizza available in Budapest, the $2.60 price is too high for some, while for others it is the treat of a lifetime. Sales averaged over $6,000

a day in the first months, promising a healthy return for the chain in its first Hungarian venture. Many of these restaurants are not simply selling food, they are selling the glitz of the U.S. culture, and a different kind of life style, and it is this facet of doing business abroad that has made so many of these restaurants so popular *and profitable.*

Sources: Eben Shapiro, "Overseas Sizzles for McDonald's," *The New York Times,* April 17, 1992, pp. D1, D4; "Domino's and Pizza Hut Make a Run for the Border, and Continue Their War," *Marketing News,* November 11, 1991, p. 5.

The previous chapter discussed the important steps in developing retail location policy. By systematically following the four-step procedure outlined, retail managers can identify potential sites for locating new outlets. Typically, a retailer identifies a number of alternative feasible sites by following those steps, and then chooses the site or set of sites for ultimate development by examining the expected sales at each of those sites. These **sales forecasts** are necessary to determine the long-run profitability of retail outlets, and this chapter describes a number of common techniques for doing that job.

Most retail stores generate sales by attracting people who reside in areas surrounding the stores. A store's sales depend, therefore, on two factors: (1) the size of its trade area and (2) its market penetration within the trade area. The *trade area is the geographic area from which the store draws its customers.* In general, as the trade area grows larger, the potential for sales increases. However, the level of sales the store actually achieves also depends on market penetration, that is, the store's share of expenditures made by consumers within the trade area. Thus the first step in sales forecasting for any outlet is **trade area estimation.** The size and population composition of the trade area will determine the number and types of people the store will attract. The chapter begins, therefore, by looking at the concept of trade areas.

Some stores, instead of drawing their customers from the trade area surrounding the store, rely on transient customers to generate sales. Outlets located at airports and along interstate highways are examples of this type of store. Sales at an airport bookstore depend to a large degree on the number of passengers passing through the airport, and not on the number of people residing near the airport. Similarly, gasoline stations along an interstate highway generate sales from cars and trucks using the highway. Trade area analysis is less important for these stores, since they do not serve a local clientele. To manage other types of stores, however,

Retail stores generally attract customers living in the vicinity of the store. Is this true of an airport bookstore?

it is critical to know the size of the trade area and the characteristics of the people within it since they indicate how many customers the store can attract and how much revenue it can generate.

The following section is organized in two parts. The first part looks at factors that affect the sizes and shapes of trade areas, and the second part examines research techniques commonly used to delineate trade areas of individual outlets.

SIZES AND SHAPES OF TRADE AREAS

Trade area size can range from a few blocks to many miles. The trade areas of supermarkets in densely populated urban areas, for example, tend to be quite small, because many shoppers in these areas walk to stores and the level of competition is usually high. In contrast, regional shopping centers have large trade areas because customers are willing to drive long distances to shop there and fewer large shopping centers compete for this business.

The total trading area of a store is often divided into three parts: (1) primary trading area, (2) secondary trading area, and (3) tertiary or fringe trading area (see Exhibit 9.1).

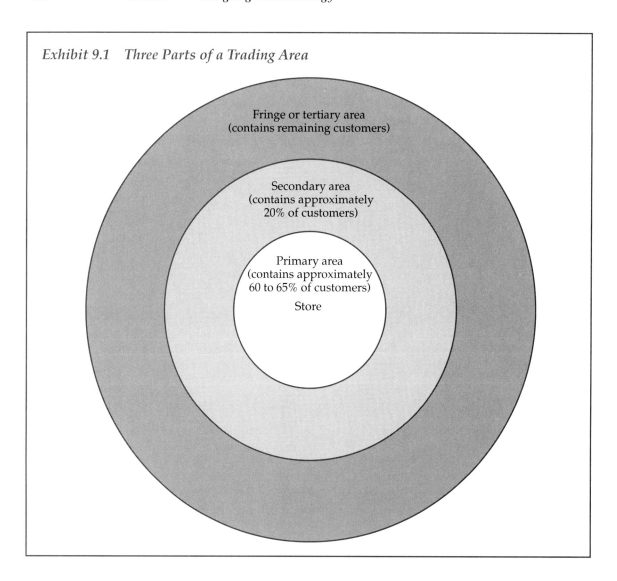

Exhibit 9.1   Three Parts of a Trading Area

Fringe or tertiary area
(contains remaining customers)

Secondary area
(contains approximately
20% of customers)

Primary area
(contains approximately
60 to 65% of customers)

Store

The primary trading area is the area closest to the store that accounts for about 60 to 65 percent of its customers. Within this area the store has a competitive advantage in terms of accessibility and has the highest level of market share. The secondary trading area, the next zone out, accounts for another 15 to 20 percent of the customers. The store has considerable drawing power in this area, but usually competes with other stores to attract these customers. The final zone, the fringe or tertiary trading area, is the area beyond the primary and secondary areas from which the remainder of the store's customers originate. The store's competitive

Shopping centers have large trade areas where customers are willing to drive long distances in order to shop.

position in the tertiary area is weak, since other stores are likely to be more accessible to customers in this area.

The sizes of the different trade areas will vary from one to another and among different types of stores. A suburban discount chain, for example, may have a primary trade area radius of four miles, a secondary area of four miles, and a tertiary area of eight miles.[1] A supermarket's primary trading area, on the other hand, may be less than two miles, and its total trade area less than three miles, because supermarkets attract most of their customers from their local areas.

In addition to attracting customers from the primary, secondary, and tertiary areas, a retail store also generates some sales from customers not residing in the neighborhood of the outlet. These may be tourists and other transient customers passing through the area. This type of customer is generally ignored in determining the trade area of the store.

Factors that Affect Trade Area Size

Since the trade area determines the store's ability to generate sales, it is important to understand the factors that determine its size. Trade area size depends on consumers' willingness to travel to shop at a particular store. As consumers are willing to travel longer distances, the trade area increases. The factors that affect consumer willingness to travel can be grouped into two general categories: (1) store characteristics and (2) characteristics of the site at which the store is located.

Impact of Store Characteristics   Three types of store characteristics affect the size of the trade area: (1) the type of goods the store sells, (2) the size of the store, and (3) its marketing strategies.

1. *Type of Goods Sold*   The t*ype of goods sold* by the store is a major determinant of trade area size. The trade area of a department store, for example, typically far exceeds that of a supermarket because consumers are not usually willing to travel far to patronize convenience-oriented stores that they visit frequently. They are much more willing to travel to department stores because they visit these stores less often and to make special purchases. This difference in willingness to travel causes the trade areas of different types of stores to vary.
2. *Store Size*   The size of the trade area also depends on the *size of the store*. In general, larger stores also have larger trade areas. A small convenience store that sells just cigarettes and candies can attract customers only from the immediate neighborhood. Larger stores offer greater varieties and assortments of merchandise, so they attract more customers. Similarly, people are more willing to travel to large supermarkets than to small grocery stores.
3. *Marketing Strategy*   The *store's marketing strategy* also influences the size of the trade area. Retail managers can enlarge their trade areas by adopting marketing strategies that increase the store's competitive advantage. Consumers will travel farther to a store that offers unique merchandise than to one that sells widely available merchandise. A lower price, too, enlarges the trade area as many consumers will bypass closer stores and patronize a more distant one to take advantage of the lower price. Similarly, superior service and promotional strategies also create competitive advantage and enlarge the size of the trade area.

The implication is that the trade areas of two similar stores in a given market need not be equal in size. By adopting good marketing strategies a store can expand its trade area and attract more customers. Of course, the cost of implementing such marketing strategies must be weighed against the benefits of additional revenues gained by enlarging the trade areas.

Impact of Site Characteristics   In addition to store characteristics, the size of the trade area also depends on the characteristics of the site at which the store is located. Three major site characteristics that influence trade area size are: (1) type of location, (2) quality of transportation, and (3) level of competition.

1. *Type of Location*   The t*ype of location* itself has a major influence on trade area size. A store located in a shopping center will generally draw customers from a larger

trade area than a similar store in an isolated site. As discussed in the previous chapter, this is one of the major advantages of locating in a shopping cluster.

A store that is part of a shopping cluster benefits from the cluster's own ability to attract customers. Larger shopping clusters generally attract more potential customers, increasing the trade areas of the stores in the cluster. Stores located in central business districts (CBDs) and regional shopping centers generally have the largest trade areas.

2. *Quality of Transportation*   Another site characteristic that influences trade area size is the *quality of the transportation network* around the site of the store. Stores located along major roadways have larger trade areas than those located along secondary arteries and side streets because it is easier to travel along major roads. The availability of public transit can also increase the size of the trading area. Barriers to travel, such as congested intersections and railroad crossings, on the other hand, make travel to the store more difficult and decrease the size of the trade area.

3. *Level of Competition*   The final site characteristic that affects trade area size is the *level of competition in the area*. When consumers can choose among many alternatives, they have no incentive to travel long distances to shop. The size of the retail trade area, therefore, is inversely related to the level of competition in an area.

The level of retail competition in an area, on the other hand, depends on the density of the population. Higher population densities allow greater numbers of stores to operate profitably in the area because higher population density results in greater disposable income and retail purchasing power. Therefore, the size of the trade area decreases as the density of population increases. In highly urbanized areas, a supermarket's trade area may be just a few blocks, while the trade area of a similar supermarket in a rural area will tend to be much larger.

Factors that Affect Trade Area Shape

A store's ability to attract customers can vary in different directions. **Trade area shapes** can differ depending on (1) the transportation network in the area, (2) barriers to travel, and (3) the locations of competitors.

Transportation Network   The shape of a trade area depends on the pattern of the transportation network in the vicinity of the site. Trade areas tend to spread along major highways, since people can travel faster along major highways than along minor routes (see Exhibit 9.2A).

Barriers to Travel   Because retail outlets serve a spatially dispersed population, the shape of the trade area depends on physical and social barriers to travel. Physical barriers such as lakes, rivers, and railroad crossings reduce accessibility and

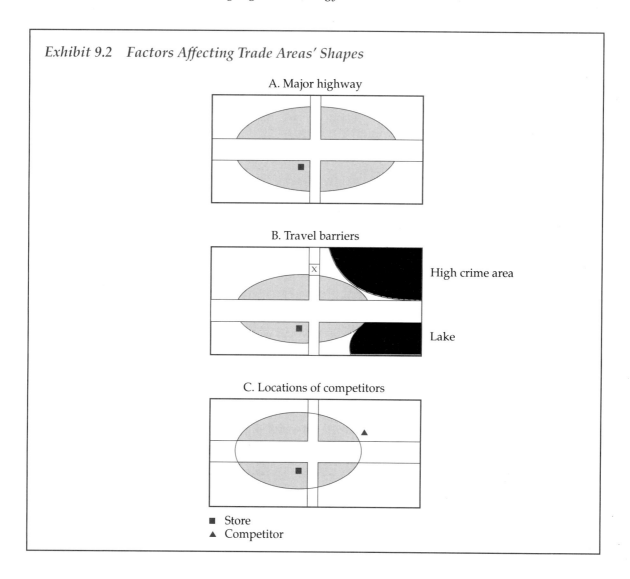

Exhibit 9.2   Factors Affecting Trade Areas' Shapes

A. Major highway

B. Travel barriers

High crime area

Lake

C. Locations of competitors

■ Store
▲ Competitor

affect the shape of the trade area. Social barriers can also reduce accessibility. Potential customers may be unwilling to travel through high-crime areas or blighted neighborhoods (see Exhibit 9.2B).

Locations of Competitors   Another factor affecting trade area shape is the locations of competitors. The trade area of the store shown in Exhibit 9.2C is much longer in the west than in the east because the competitors to the east of the outlet intercept some of the traffic coming from that direction. Since no competing stores lie to the west, the store has greater drawing power in that direction.

DELINEATING THE TRADE AREA

Because the size and the nature of a trade area determine a store's potential to generate revenues, delineating them is an important part of location analysis. To define the geographic area from which the customers of the outlet come, researchers employ a technique known as customer spotting.

Customer Spotting

Popularized by William Applebaum, **customer spotting** helps to determine the spatial extent of a store's trade area.[2] Practitioners of this technique interview a sample of the store's customers to determine their (1) geographic origin (street address), (2) demographic characteristics, and (3) shopping habits.

While customer spotting is simple to do, it must still be done with considerable care to provide accurate results. One important consideration is to ensure that a representative sample of shoppers is interviewed; that is, to ensure that all types of customers and not a particular group of shoppers are contacted. A number of

Delineating a retailer's trade area can be accomplished through a technique known as customer spotting. This surveyor in the Fox Hills Mall in Pennsylvania is asking a shopper where she lives and about her normal shopping habits.

important steps are necessary to ensure a representative sample. First, it is very important that the survey is spread over different days of the week and different times of the day. A survey that interviewed shoppers on weekdays only, for example, may miss important customer groups who shop on weekends. Similarly, interviews should be conducted throughout the day.

Ideally, an independent group, and not the store's regular employees, should conduct the interviews. Experience has shown that when asked to conduct such surveys in addition to their normal work, store employees might ignore the survey when the store is busy. This, however, may be the prime time for conducting interviews. Shopper interviews by store employees are typically conducted at the point-of-sale when the customer is paying. An important drawback of this practice is to slow down the checkout process and potentially alienate customers. The only way to overcome these problems is to hire trained, independent interviewers, although this raises the cost of conducting the survey.

Plotting the address of each interviewed customer on a detailed street map delineates the store's trade area, as shown in Exhibit 9.3. Computers can speed up this rather tedious process by running address-matching software packages which automatically locate and mark addresses on the map.

Exhibit 9.3   Customer Spotting Map

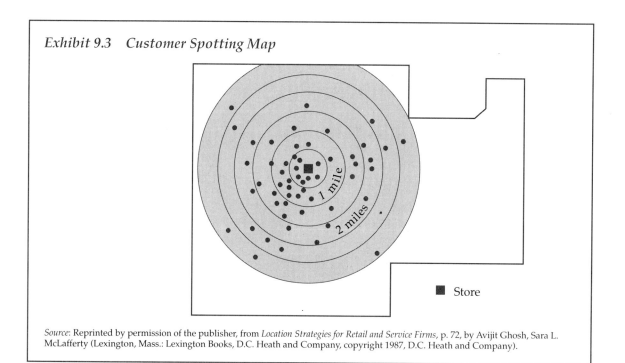

■ Store

Source: Reprinted by permission of the publisher, from *Location Strategies for Retail and Service Firms*, p. 72, by Avijit Ghosh, Sara L. McLafferty (Lexington, Mass.: Lexington Books, D.C. Heath and Company, copyright 1987, D.C. Heath and Company).

Whether drawn manually or with the help of a computer, the **customer origin map** reveals the relationship between distance and the store's ability to attract customers. The customer origin map in Exhibit 9.3 shows a geographic pattern to this relationship. A store's ability to attract customers is greatest in the immediate vicinity of the store, but market penetration decreases as one moves away from the outlet. This inverse relationship between market penetration and distance is a universal pattern called the **distance decay effect**. The distance decay effect reflects the impact of geographic accessibility on store patronage.

Survey of Customer Records   Although the most accurate customer spotting techniques are based on customer interviews, the customer origin map can also be drawn based on addresses from customer checks or store credit cards. Check and credit card information reduces the cost and time requirements of data collection, but they should be used with some caution because the customer origin map may not accurately reflect the store's trade area if it ignores cash customers completely. This is especially true when an analyst draws customer origin maps based only on addresses of credit card customers. Credit card customers may not be completely representative of the store's total customer base. It is advisable, therefore, to sample credit card, check, and cash customers to assure adequate representation of all customer groups.

License Plate Surveys   Customer spotting information can sometimes be generated by listing the license plate numbers of cars in the store's parking lot. Official car registration records can provide the addresses of the car owners. A number of market research firms specialize in performing license plate surveys.

License plate surveys are relatively inexpensive, their major advantage, but they do have a number of serious limitations. The mere fact that a car is in the parking lot does not guarantee that the owner is actually shopping at the store. This is a special problem when a number of stores share the parking lot. For a second drawback, license plate surveys do not provide any information on how much, if any, money the customer spent at the store. Despite these drawbacks, many shopping centers perform license plate surveys to determine their trade areas.

Uses of Customer Origin Maps

Customer origin maps provide important information for retailers. They contribute in a number of ways to the development of various retail policies.

Delineating Trade Areas   The store can determine its primary, secondary, and fringe trade areas by inspecting the customer origin map. Concentric circles of different sizes drawn on the map define these areas with the location of the store as the center, then the cumulative proportion of customers in each circle is calculated starting from the innermost one. For example, in Exhibit 9.3 the innermost circle (with a one-half mile radius) accounts for 14 percent of all customers. Another 22

STRATEGY IN ACTION

Ben & Jerry's Harlem Scoop Shop

In June 1992, Ben & Jerry's, the ice-cream maker, opened a "partnershop" at 125th Street and Fifth Avenue in Manhattan. Located in one of the poorest neighborhoods in the city, the shop's mission is to help homeless people in the area. This "scoop shop" is the result of a carefully worked-out partnership between Harlem businessman Joseph Holland and the Vermont-based ice cream and frozen yogurt maker. Holland visited Vermont in 1989, learned of the socially minded company, and began discussions with founders Ben Cohen and Jerry Greenfield to see if a plan could be worked out to help the poor and needy of Holland's urban neighborhood.

Ben & Jerry's believed that a shop where training and economic development could directly impact the community would be a wonderful idea. The company waived the usual $25,000 franchise fee, Holland found some local financing, and the Harlem scoop shop was born. Holland also runs HARKhomes, a nonprofit program for homeless men in New York City. The scoop shop is staffed by men in the HARKhomes program, and 75 percent of the profits are turned over to the organization. Both Cohen and Greenfield feel that the project demonstrates how business can be a powerful force for progressive social change. For Holland, the mission is more personal— seeking to build bridges between business and the inner city. Says he: "We need to have these alliances, now more than ever, to create healthy communities and empowered people."

Another reason the Harlem location was so attractive to Ben & Jerry's was because there are no similar stores in the area, and the scoop shop can thus count on considerable business due to its novelty. While the shop is in a low-income area, and "designer" ice cream might be considered a luxury purchase, the distinctiveness of the store within the neighborhood assures a continuous flow of customers to the store. In addition, people in the neighborhood both welcome and

percent of the customers come from the second zone. The cumulative proportion of customers from the first two zones is, therefore, 36 percent. In total, 80 percent of the customers come from within a two-mile radius of the store, and 90 percent of them come from within a two and one-half-mile radius.

The trade area boundary can be delineated based on the cumulative proportion of customers from each zone. In Exhibit 9.3, the first three zones define the primary trade area since they account for about 60 percent of the customers. The next zone, from which 20 percent of the customers come, is the secondary trade area. The fringe or tertiary area, the zone between two and two and one-half miles from the store, accounts for 11 percent of the store's customers. The remaining 9 percent of the customers were transient customers.

value the contribution that the company makes to the neighborhood and in turn want to give the scoop shop their business. The combination of a socially and economically conscious mission with a carefully designed and produced product have meant great success for Ben & Jerry's; the customers love the products as much as the company mission, and Ben & Jerry's can count on customers' continued support.

Ben & Jerry's was founded in 1978 in a renovated gas station in Burlington, Vermont, by childhood friends, Ben Cohen and Jerry Greenfield. The company has always been dedicated to the creation and demonstration of a new corporate concept of linked prosperity. The mission consists of three parts: product, social, and economic missions. The underlying goal of the company is to continually seek creative ways to address all three parts. The Harlem scoop shop combines the three mission parts, and Ben & Jerry's is seeking other areas in which similar shops could be set up.

Both Cohen and Greenfield truly believe in the possibility of companies working not just for profit, but also for positive social change and improvement of the quality of life for their communities, local, national, and global. In fact, in addition to their good works through their stores and products, the company gives a full 7.5 percent of their pretax profit to a wide variety of social causes, all the monies for which are funnelled through the Ben & Jerry's Foundation. The only criteria for donation: that the recipients must offer models for imaginative social change. In this way, Ben & Jerry's ensures that all their efforts, both in-house and through their donations, keep sight of the company mission.

Source: Ben & Jerry's Company documents: "About Ben & Jerry's" and "The Ben & Jerry's Herd Hits Harlem: Newest Scoop Shop to Help the Homeless."

Matching Merchandise to Customer Characteristics   With the trade area delineated, the retailer can analyze the demographic and socioeconomic characteristics of its potential customers. Such analysis provides valuable guidelines for streamlining the store's merchandising and pricing policies and for responding more directly to customer needs. For example, a supermarket chain with a number of outlets in an urban area uses trade area analysis to determine the ethnic composition of each store's customer base. It then carefully selects the merchandise at individual outlets to meet the needs of their local customers, since ethnic groups vary in their preferences for grocery items and produce.

Consider another example: After analyzing the pattern of sales at each of its outlets in a northeastern town, a supermarket found that the sales of fresh produce and meat were significantly below average at one of the stores. The chain then assessed the trade area of the store and carefully analyzed its population characteristics. The analysis made evident that there were many single-person households in the trade area of this particular outlet. Single-person households are typically not heavy buyers of fresh produce and meat. The chain decreased the sizes of these departments in this store and increased the size of the prepared food department instead.

Targeting Advertising and Promotion   Trade area analysis is also important in formulating advertising and promotion strategies. Advertising or promotion through a medium that does not reach a store's trade area will be ineffective. At the same time, advertising in a medium that reaches far beyond the trade area will be inefficient. A small convenience store that serves mostly customers from its own neighborhood would waste resources if it advertised in a newspaper with a large regional circulation. The key is to advertise in media that have circulation areas similar to the store's trade area.

A detailed knowledge of the geographic pattern of the trade area also helps a retailer pinpoint promotional campaigns. Having specified its trade area boundaries, the retailer can target promotion and direct mail campaigns toward residents within them. Alternatively, the retailer can target the promotional campaign to neighborhood areas from which it presently may not be attracting customers in an effort to increase the store's market share in those areas.

Gauging Competition   For another important reason, retailers undertake trade area studies to clarify their pictures of their competitive environments. Consider, for example, the trade areas of the three stores shown in Exhibit 9.4. The trade areas of Store A and Store B overlap considerably, as do the trade areas of Stores B and D. Larger overlaps between two stores' trade areas increase the intensity of competition between them. In this case, Store B has the disadvantage of fighting for customers with both Store A and Store D. Store C, on the other hand, has a monopoly in its trade area. In this way, studies of how the trade areas of stores in a market overlap gauge the intensity of competition among them.

Planning Expansion   Trade area analysis also helps retailers formulate plans for expanding their retail networks by opening new outlets. When a retail chain opens a new outlet near an existing one, it must consider carefully the extent to which the new store might cannibalize the sales of the existing one. Trade area analysis contributes essential information toward answering this type of question.

Consider the case of a retailer that operates a restaurant and is considering opening a second outlet in the same town. Having determined that the existing restaurant has a trade area of about three miles, the owner has identified two possible sites for the second store. The first site is four miles east of the existing outlet along the same road. The second potential site is much farther away in a different part of town. Exhibit 9.5 shows the trade area of the existing outlet and those estimated

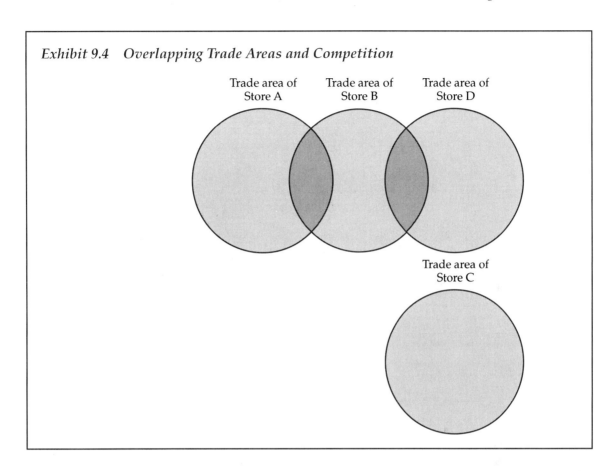

Exhibit 9.4   *Overlapping Trade Areas and Competition*

Trade area of
Store A

Trade area of
Store B

Trade area of
Store D

Trade area of
Store C

for the new sites. Since the new outlet will resemble the existing one, the owner estimates that it, too, will have a trade area of three miles.

Exhibit 9.5 shows that the trade area of a new store located at Site A would overlap considerably with that of the existing store. The two stores would compete with each other, the new outlet cannibalizing the sales of the existing one. Site B, on the other hand, does not compete directly with the existing outlet, since the trade area at that site does not overlap with that of the existing store.

This does not necessarily mean, however, that Site A is less desirable than Site B. To determine the better location, the retailer must calculate the incremental sales that would result from locating at the two potential sites and choose the one that would yield the greatest profit. The density of population around Site B could be too low to support an outlet. A number of techniques for systematically dealing with such network expansion decisions have now been developed. These are especially useful for retail firms that operate multiple outlets in the same market area.[3]

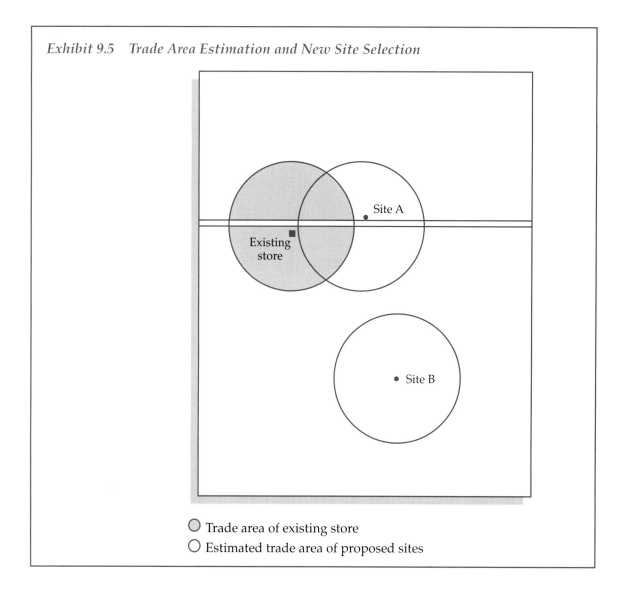

Exhibit 9.5   Trade Area Estimation and New Site Selection

Site A

Existing
store

Site B

◯ Trade area of existing store
◯ Estimated trade area of proposed sites

FORECASTING SALES OF NEW OUTLETS

The final decision whether or not to open a new outlet depends, to a large extent, on the level of sales that the firm can expect to generate at a site. Similarly, when faced with a choice among a number of alternative sites for opening a new store, a retailer will choose the site with the highest sales potential. This criterion makes accurate sales forecasts essential for selecting new sites.

Three common methods for forecasting sales of retail outlets are (1) the analog method, (2) the regression method, and (3) the spatial interaction method. Each method estimates a trade area and the sales it will generate by a different technique. The discussion of these methods stresses their advantages and disadvantages and their appropriateness in different types of applications.

Analog Method

Popularized in 1966 by William Applebaum, the **analog method** was one of the first systematic procedures suggested for forecasting retail sales.[4] To forecast sales for a new store, the analog method studies a similar store that is already in operation as an "analog." The analyst determines the analog store's trade area and market penetration by customer spotting. The sales pattern of the analog store then serves as the basis for forecasting the sales of a new outlet.

The most important step in implementing the analog procedure is to identify an analog store that resembles the proposed new store. The analog store should be similar in terms of size, store services, pricing, and merchandising policies, the level of competition, and site characteristics. The ideal analog is an existing outlet operated by the same chain.

After identifying the analog store, customer spotting reveals the geographic pattern of its customer base. Next, concentric circles of different radii drawn on the customer origin map determine the analog store's trade area. Based on the information from the customer spotting analysis, the firm calculates the drawing power of the analog store and its per capita sales from each distance zone as shown in Exhibit 9.6. That illustration shows that 38 percent of all the analog store's customers live within a half-mile radius. These customers accounted for $19,200 in weekly sales. Secondary sources reported the number of people living within this zone as 4,800. The store's per-capita weekly sales within this half-mile area is, therefore, $4.00 ($19,200/4,800). In a similar manner, the per-capita weekly sales for the other distance zones are calculated, too. Note that only 92 percent of the customers of the analog store came from within a four-mile radius. The remaining 8 percent are transient customers who reside outside the neighborhood of the store.

The pattern of per-capita sales achieved by the analog store is the key to forecasting the sales for the new store. This forecast assumes that the new store will have a sales pattern similar to that of the analog store. This crucial assumption requires that the analog store closely resembles the store that is to be opened. Unless the stores were very similar it would not be reasonable to assume that the patterns of their trade areas would be similar, too.

The basic steps in calculating expected sales at the new site are shown in the bottom part of Exhibit 9.6. First, on a map of the area surrounding the new site, the analyst draws concentric circles with the new site as the center, as was done before for the analog store. Next, the total population residing within each circular zone is found from secondary sources. These figures allow calculation of expected sales for each zone by multiplying the total population in the zone by the analog store's per-capita sales for that zone.

Exhibit 9.6   Analog Forecasting

A. Market Penetration of Analog Store

(1)	(2)	(3)	(4)	(5)	(6)
		Cumulative			Per-capita
Radius	Percentage	Drawing	Weekly		Sales
(miles)	of Customers	Power	Sales	Population	[(4)/(5)]
0–0.5	38%	38%	$19,200	4,800	$4.00
0.5–1.0	24%	62%	12,126	7,100	1.70
1.0–1.5	14%	76%	7,073	11,000	0.64
1.5–2.0	6%	82%	3,031	14,200	0.21
2.0–2.5	4%	86%	2,021	16,800	0.12
2.5–3.0	3%	89%	1,516	14,400	0.11
3.0–3.5	2%	91%	1,010	12,200	0.08
3.5–4.0	1%	92%	505	9,400	0.05

B. Sales Projection for New Site

Radius (miles)	Population	Per-capita Sales	Sales from Zone
0–0.5	4,200	$4.00	$16,800
0.5–1.0	7,600	1.70	12,920
1.0–1.5	14,200	0.64	9,088
1.5–2.0	20,800	0.21	4,368
2.0–2.5	22,600	0.12	2,712
2.5–3.0	21,100	0.11	2,321
3.0–3.5	16,000	0.08	1,280
3.5–4.0	12,600	0.05	630
Total weekly sales			50,119
Adjusted weekly sales			55,119

As shown in the exhibit, 4,200 people reside within a half-mile radius of the new site. For this distance zone, the analog store achieved per capita weekly sales of $4. Thus, the new store can expect weekly sales of $16,800 (4,200 × $4) from this zone. In the same manner, the expected weekly sales from the next distance zone (0.5 to 1.0-mile radius) can be calculated. The zone population of 7,600 times per-capita sales of $1.70 yields total sales from the zone of $12,920.

To find the total expected sales at the new site, the analyst sums the sales expected from each distance zone. This gives a weekly sales forecast of $50,119 for the new store. However, this figure does not consider the sales generated by transient customers and those who live beyond the four-mile radius. To reflect potential sales from these customers, $5,000 has been added to the total forecast, based on the forecaster's knowledge and past experience in similar stores.

The analog procedure has a major advantage in that it is easy to implement and reflects actual shopping patterns. It depends partly "on quantified experience and partly on subjective judgment."[5] Considerable judgment is required in selecting the analog store, and even then the forecast may need adjustment for differences between the analog store and the new outlet. The new store may, for example, have more aggressive competitors, so it may not achieve the same market penetration as the analog store.

The analyst can overcome this drawback by using more than one analog store. Instead of relying on only one store as the analog, the analyst can obtain patronage patterns from a number of similar stores. After making an initial series of forecasts based on the data for each analog store, these separate forecasts are then averaged to estimate the sales at the new site. Although averaging figures for a number of analog stores increases the cost of implementing the procedure, it reduces the possibility of error in the sales forecast due to the idiosyncrasies of a single store.

Regression Methods

Retail chains that operate many stores can apply the sales experience of all the existing outlets, instead of a single analog store, to forecast sales at a new location through regression analysis. **Regression methods** allow the analyst to systematically incorporate information from a number of existing stores in sales forecasts for new sites. Regression methods quantify the relationships between sales at different stores and the trade area, and store and site characteristics of the respective outlets. From this relationship, the analyst can calculate the expected sales at a new site. Because regression forecasting models require information from a large number of existing stores (at least 30 to 40), they are mainly used by retail chains that operate many outlets.

Regression forecasting systems are based on two major assumptions. First, they assume that the sales a store generates depend on the characteristics of the store, its site, and its trade area. The second assumption is that the relative impact of each of these factors on sales can be measured by a statistical procedure called regression analysis.

The Regression Model   To implement a regression procedure, one must first select a list of store, site, and trade area characteristics that might affect store sales. Since these characteristics explain the variation in sales among different stores, they are called **explanatory variables**. Store performance, on the other hand, is a **dependent variable** since its value depends on those of the explanatory variables.

In general, regression sales forecasting models have the following form:

$$Sales = b_0 + b_1X_1 + b_2X_2 + \ldots + b_nX_n$$

where,

$$b_0 = \text{the intercept term}$$
$$X_1, X_2, \ldots, X_n = \text{explanatory variables}$$
$$b_1, b_2, \ldots, b_n = \text{regression coefficients that measure the impact of each}$$
$$\text{explanatory variable on sales}$$

The regression model develops a quantitative relationship between the explanatory variables and the dependent variable, sales. The impact of each explanatory variable (the Xs) on sales is measured by the **regression coefficient** (the b value) associated with that variable. Larger numerical values of the coefficients indicate stronger impact on sales. The sign of the coefficient is important, too. A negative sign implies that a variable is inversely related to sales: as the value of the explanatory variable increases, sales drop. A positive coefficient, on the other hand, implies that sales increase as the value of the coefficient gets larger.

The explanatory variables included in a particular model depend on the type of retail store, but they must always include store, site, and trade area characteristics. Some typical store characteristics, for example, are the size of the store, the size of the frontage, and the number of employees. The importance of different site characteristics has been found to depend on whether the store is freestanding or located within a shopping center. Sales at freestanding sites have been found to be related to visibility, traffic flow, quality of access, and whether the site is at an intersection. Sales of stores within a shopping center, on the other hand, are typically related to the size of the shopping center, the quality of the anchor stores, and the proximity of the site to the anchor stores, entrances, exits, and highly trafficked areas such as the food court or center court.

The trade area characteristics that are typically related to store sales vary by the type of store. Convenience store sales, for example, may vary with trade area population and the number of competing stores. For a hardware store, on the other hand, such factors as the number of owner-occupied houses and average income in the area may be more important. Similarly, in forecasting sales at an automobile repair shop, the number of cars in the trade area would be a relevant characteristic. The number of teenagers and young adults in the trade area is likely to be strongly related to sales of athletic footwear and jean's stores.

Proper selection of explanatory variables is crucial in implementing a regression model and requires considerable experience and judgment. Analysts commonly start with a large number of variables that might affect store performance. As they develop the regression model they refine the list of explanatory variables with the help of information generated from the analysis. Exhibit 9.7 lists some of the store, site, and trade area characteristics commonly found to be related to sales.

Once the explanatory variables are selected, the next step is to collect information from stores already in operation. For each existing store, the analyst collects data on sales and all the explanatory variables. For example, if store size and trade area population are the two explanatory variables, then for each store informa-

Exhibit 9.7 *Some Store, Site, and Trade Area Characteristics Used in Regression Models*

Store Characteristics
Store size
Size of frontage
Number of employees
Level of advertising and promotion

Site Characteristics
The site characteristics used in regression models vary depending on whether the store is located in a mall or is freestanding.
Mall location
Size of mall
Number and type of anchor of the mall
Sales of the mall
Number of direct competitors within the mall
Proximity to main entrance, food court, or center court of mall
Freestanding site
Visibility
Traffic flow
Proximity to major roadway/intersection

Trade Area Characteristics
Total population and age composition
Household or per-capita income
Employment characteristics
Percent who own (rent) home
Average property value
Life style characteristics

tion on size and trade area population will be added to sales figures, and this data will be entered into the regression analysis. Irrespective of the type of store, however, sales are typically inversely related to the number of competing stores in the trade area.

An Example The steps in developing a regression model can be illustrated with a case study from a fast-food restaurant chain. The chain operates 50 outlets located mostly in freestanding sites in populated areas. The company wishes to develop a regression-based sales forecasting system to help it plan for new sites.

The first step is to identify the explanatory variables to include in the model. Based on past experience and some initial analysis, the firm has identified two variables: the size of the local population and the number of competing fast-food outlets within the trade area of each outlet. Customer-spotting analysis yields a typical trade area for a fast-food outlet of 1.5 miles in radius. Thus, the firm includes the population within 1.5 miles of the store and the number of competitive stores within the same area as explanatory variables in a regression model in order to forecast weekly sales.

As its next step, the firm collects information on weekly sales, population, and the number of competitors within 1.5 miles of each of its 50 existing outlets. These data are then subjected to regression analysis using a computerized statistical package, with the following results:

$$\text{Weekly sales} = 3{,}540 + 160 \times \text{Population (thousands)} \\ - 1{,}352 \times \text{Number of competitors}$$

To interpret the results, the values of the two regression coefficients should be examined first. The population variable has a coefficient of 160 and the competitive variable has a coefficient of –1,352. The positive number for the population coefficient implies that sales increase with trade area population. Outlets located in more densely populated areas can attract more customers and, therefore, generate more sales. The numerical value of the coefficient provides a quantitative measure of the impact of population size on sales, stating in this case that a gain of 1,000 people in the trade area increases weekly sales by $160, everything else remaining the same. Thus a restaurant with a trade area population of 40,000 would be expected to generate $1,600 more in weekly sales than an outlet with a trade area population of 30,000 people, if both of them faced the same competitive environment.

The coefficient associated with the second explanatory variable measures the impact of competition on sales. This coefficient has a negative sign, indicating that sales decline as the number of competitors in close proximity to the store increases. This is consistent with what one would expect intuitively. Everything else being the same, restaurants with fewer competitors nearby are likely to generate more sales than restaurants with more competitors. The numerical value of the coefficient measures the strength of the competitors' impact on restaurant sales. The presence of a competitor within the trade area decreases expected weekly sales by $1,352. Every time a competing outlet opens, weekly sales decrease by that amount.

Forecasting Sales at a New Outlet   The results of the regression analysis allow the managers of the fast-food restaurant chain to forecast the sales for any new outlet that they plan to open. To forecast the sales for a new site, they find the total population and number of competitors within a 1.5 mile radius of the proposed site. They can obtain data on competing stores from secondary sources or they can collect it by direct observation. As discussed earlier, data on population characteristics and competition can be obtained from various market research companies.

The site that the chain is presently considering has a population of 40,000 and one competing outlet within a 1.5-mile radius. The firm can calculate expected sales at this outlet as follows:

$$\text{Estimated weekly sales} = \$3{,}540 + (\$160 \times 40) - (\$1{,}352 \times 1)$$
$$= \$8{,}588$$

Given the trade area population of 40,000 and the presence of one competitor in the trade area, weekly sales of $8,588 would be consistent with the experience of the other restaurants in the chain. This forecast would, of course, change if the trade area population or the number of competitors in the area were to change. For example, two competing outlets instead of one would reduce the forecast to $7,236 ($8,588 – $1,352). Similarly, if population size increased by 5,000, expected weekly sales would increase by $800 ($160 × 5). As long as the firm knows the trade area population and the number of competing outlets, it can forecast the expected sales for any site.

With the help of its regression equation, the firm can forecast sales at a number of alternative sites based on the trade area characteristics of each. It can then rank the desirability of each site for opening new stores based on estimated sales potential. Exhibit 9.8 shows the forecasts for three sites. The sales forecasts vary considerably because of differences in population and number of competitors around each site. Although Site B has the lowest trade area population, the lack of competition makes its sales forecast the highest. Site C, on the other hand, loses the advantage of its large trade area population because of the high level of competitive activity in the area.

Retail chains are increasingly relying on regression models to forecast sales at alternative sites and to select one for opening a new outlet. (See Research Report: Forecasting Deposits at a Bank on page 307.) Although it may be costly to develop the system initially, once in place the regression model makes sales forecasting for many sites easy. For large retail chains that evaluate new sites almost continuously, this is a major advantage. Moreover, the regression model allows the firm to systematically incorporate experience from a large number of existing stores into sales forecasts for new stores.

Spatial Interaction Models

A third approach to retail sales forecasting is to use **spatial interaction models**. Spatial interaction models (or gravity models as they are sometimes called) are widely used to forecast sales of new outlets and to assess the impact of changes in retail environment on outlet performance.

Although spatial interaction models are similar to regression models in their intent to forecast sales of new outlets, there are two major differences. While regression models obtain a single forecast of sales for the store, spatial interaction models forecast the sales the store is expected to generate from different parts of the trade area. Sales estimates from different parts of the trade area are summed to obtain a store-wide figure. The second difference is that the spatial interaction models view trade areas to be probabilistic rather than deterministic. That is, it assumes that people may visit more than one store, but with different probabilities. In this

Exhibit 9.8   Regression Model Sales Forecast for Three Sites

Site	Trade Area Population	Number of Competitors	Forecast (sales/week)
A	40,000	1	$8,588
B	35,000	0	9,140
C	45,000	2	8,036

view the trade area is the *geographically delineated region containing potential customers who have a greater than zero probability of shopping at a particular store.*[6]

A popular spatial interaction model is the one proposed by David Huff (sometimes called the Huff model) to predict the trade areas of stores within metropolitan areas.[7] Huff argued that a store's ability to draw customers depends on its relative attraction. Therefore, to estimate its trade area and forecast sales, the attraction of the store to the customers in the area relative to all the other stores in the area must be measured. To forecast the sales of a supermarket, its attraction relative to all the other supermarkets in the area must be judged.

Measuring Store Attraction   The relative attraction of a store to a consumer, Huff argued, depends on two factors: (1) the size of the store and (2) distance. Large stores are more attractive than smaller stores and closer ones more attractive than distant ones. Huff's assumptions can be written more formally as:

$$A_{ij} = \frac{S_j^a}{D_{ij}^b}$$

where

A_{ij} = the attraction of Store *j* to Consumer *i*
S_j = the size of Store *j*
D_{ij} = the distance or travel time separating Consumer *i* from Store *j*
a = a parameter reflecting the consumer's sensitivity to store size
b = a parameter reflecting the consumer's sensitivity to distance or travel time

According to Huff's model, consumers trade off the disutility of traveling to a store with the benefits of larger size in forming their overall evaluations of store attraction. The attraction decreases as distance increases. This is consistent with the distance decay effect seen in customer origin maps. Larger size can, however, compensate the negative impact of distance.

Merchandise should be displayed in a way that is consistent with the expectations of its target customers. Supermarkets such as Food Lion arrange their products in a very functional manner consistent with high volume and customer convenience. Gucci displays its merchandise as single precious items so valuable they must be kept in glass cases.

Of the possible layouts for store interiors, the grid pattern is the most regimented. Discount and warehouse stores like Bradlee's and Costco use the grid pattern to increase space productivity and customer convenience. Department and apparel stores prefer the free-form layout because it encourages browsing and creates a more pleasant shopping atmosphere. J.C. Penney and Gold Coast use this type of layout to great advantage.

People must feel comfortable with a store's interior decor and ambiance before becoming regular customers. The cluttered surroundings of the Last Wound-up, an antique toy store, meets the expectations of its clientele. This type of atmosphere would be inappropriate at John Wanamaker's main store in Philadelphia where orderly and elegant surroundings are anticipated.

RESEARCH REPORT

Forecasting Deposits at a Bank

Sales forecasting is important not just for retail stores selling goods, but also for service outlets such as banks and hospitals. For example, banks need to forecast the amount of money they expect customers to deposit at different branches. Similarly, hospitals need to know how many patients will seek treatment at the hospital. The sales forecasting procedures described in this chapter serve these purposes, too.

An illustration of this type of forecasting is the regression model developed by Olsen and Lord. Based on three explanatory variables, the model predicts the amount of money deposited daily into checking accounts at branch offices of a retail bank in Charlotte, North Carolina. The first variable was the median household income within 1.5 miles of each branch, the branch's trade area. The second variable was the total square feet of retail space in the neighborhood of the branch. The final variable was the number of competing banks within the trade area.

Information from all the existing branches of the bank yielded the following regression equation:

$$\text{Daily checking account deposits (in units of \$1,000)} = -61.947 + 12.706 \times \text{Median income (units of \$1,000)} + 0.2365 \times \text{Retail square footage (in units of 1,000 sq. ft.)} - 8.669 \times \text{Number of competitors}$$

As one would expect, the coefficients for both median income and retail square feet have positive coefficients. Deposits increase as the household income and retailing activity in the trade area increase. Competition, on the other hand, has a negative impact. Each competitor in the trade area decreases expected daily deposits by $8,669.

The regression equation can forecast the daily checking account deposits at any branch. Suppose the median income of people residing with 1.5 miles of a proposed site is $12,000, and the same area has 340,000 square feet of retail space and four competitors. The expected daily deposits at this branch are:

$$\text{Daily checking account deposits (in units of \$1,000)} = -61.947 + 12.706 \times 12 + 0.2365 \times 340 - 8.669 \times 4 = 136.259$$

The bank can expect daily deposits at the branch of $136,259.

If no competitors were located in the site's trade area, deposits would increase. The forecast in this scenario would be:

$$\text{Daily checking account deposits (in units of \$1,000)} = -61.947 + 12.706 \times 12 + 0.2365 \times 340 - 8.669 \times 0 = 170.935$$

The branch could expect $170,935 in daily deposits into its checking accounts.

Source: L. M. Olsen and J. D. Lord, "Market Area Characteristics and Branch Bank Performance," *Journal of Bank Research* 10 (Summer 1981), pp. 102–110.

The values of parameters *a* and *b* reflect the importance consumers give to store size and distance in forming their overall evaluations of store attraction. Increases in the value of *b*, for example, reflect increasing importance given to distance. If the value of *b* is very large compared to *a*, consumers' evaluations depend almost entirely on distance, with little or no concern for store size. In this case, consumers will tend to patronize the closest store, as often occurs regarding convenience-oriented stores like 7-Eleven and supermarkets.

With the sizes and distances of all stores known, the analyst can calculate the relative drawing power of each. This drawing power determines the store's ability to attract customers and, consequently, the nature of its trade area. It is important to note that implicit in interaction models is the assumption that consumers shop at more than one store and that the probability that they will shop at a particular store depends on its relative attraction. For this reason, spatial interaction models are called probabilistic models.

To predict the likelihood of a consumer visiting a particular outlet, Huff followed a well-known axiom in psychology known as Luce's choice axiom.[8] He argued that the probability of a consumer visiting a particular store equals the ratio

Do consumers evaluate a convenience store like this 7-Eleven on its size and variety or on its proximity to them?

of the consumer's attraction for that store to the sum of the attraction of all competing stores of that type in the area. In other words:

$$P_{ij} = \frac{\text{Attraction of Store} = j}{\Sigma \text{ attraction of all stores} = \text{in the area}}$$

where P_{ij} is the probability of consumer i shopping at Store j and Σ is the Greek symbol that denotes summation. Since it has already been shown that the attraction of a store is given by S^a_j/D^b_{ij}, the probability of shopping at a particular store can be formally expressed as:

$$P_{ij} = \frac{(S^a_j / D^b_{ij})}{\displaystyle\sum_{j=1}^{n} (S^a_j / D^b_{ij})}$$

where

S_j = the size of Store j
D_{ij} = the distance or travel time between Consumer i and Store j
n = the number of competing stores in the area

The symbol Σ indicates summation. The denominator of the formula sums the attraction of all competing stores in the area.

An Illustration   Consider a person who has the opportunity to shop at three supermarkets. The sizes of the three supermarkets and their distances from the consumer's home are as follows:

Store	Distance (miles)	Size (square feet)
A	4	50,000
B	6	70,000
C	3	40,000

If $a = 1$ and $b = 2$, the relative attraction of each of the three stores to this individual are:

Attraction of Store A = $50,000/4^2 = 3,125$
Attraction of Store B = $70,000/6^2 = 1,944$
Attraction of Store C = $40,000/3^2 = 4,444$

The probability of this individual shopping at Store A is equal to the ratio of the attraction of Store A to the sum of the attraction of all the three stores. Or:

Probability of shopping at Store A = $3,125/(3,125 + 1,944 + 4,444) = 0.328$

The probability of the consumer shopping at the other two stores can be found similarly to be:

Probability of shopping at Store B = 1,944/(3,125 + 1,944 + 4,444) = 0.204
Probability of shopping at Store C = 4,444/(3,125 + 1,944 + 4,444) = 0.467

Note that the three probabilities sum to one (within rounding errors), as one would expect.

Parameters and Shopping Patterns   As is evident from the example above, the likelihood of the consumer patronizing a particular store depends on store size, distance, and the values of the two interaction parameters a and b. Since the values of the interaction parameters reflect the relative importance of store size and distance, any changes in these values shift the pattern of shopping. Consider what happens when the value of b changes from 2 to 3. As the value of b increases, distance has a greater impact on store choice and stores that are farther away lose some of their attractiveness to the customer.

For example, when $b = 3$ the attraction of Store A becomes 781.25 (50,000/4^3) compared with 3,125 (50,000/4^2) when $b = 2$. The attractions of Stores B and C also change to 324 and 1,481, respectively. Since a change in parameters changes the relative attractions of the stores, the consumer's likelihood of shopping at the three stores changes, too. These new probabilities are shown in Exhibit 9.9. The probability of shopping at Store C increases from 0.47 to 0.57, while the probability of shopping at the other two stores decreases. Store C, the nearest store, gains the most when the value of b increases.

A change in the value of a also affects shopping probabilities by changing the relative importance given to store size. For example, when $a = 2$ and $b = 2$, the share of the largest store, Store B, increases from 20 percent to 29 percent. Store C, on the other hand, loses because of its small size.

Determining Parameter Values   The sensitivity of shopping probabilities to the parameter values makes determining the parameter values that best fit the actual shopping patterns in the area a key issue in the application of this model. There are two ways in which the values of these parameters are determined in any par-

Exhibit 9.9 *Impact of Parameter Values on Shopping Probabilities in Three Scenarios*			
	Scenario 1 $a = 1, b = 2$	**Scenario 2** $a = 1, b = 3$	**Scenario 3** $a = 2, b = 2$
Store A	0.33	0.30	0.33
Store B	0.20	0.13	0.29
Store C	0.47	0.57	0.38

ticular application. First, in many industries certain norms have now been established for the parameters based on experience. It is common, therefore, in many applications to use a value of one for *a* and two for *b*. Adjustments are made to these numbers based on the local geography. In areas of low mobility, such as the core of urban areas, the value of *b* is increased to reflect a higher impact of distance. Conversely, the value of *b* may be decreased in areas where people are able to travel more easily.

The second approach to determining the parameter values is to survey shopping patterns in an area. Using statistical procedures similar to regression analysis, the parameter values that best describe the existing shopping pattern can be determined. Although this approach is favored on theoretical considerations, analysts rely on subjective estimates of parameter values in many applications because of the cost and time involved in conducting surveys and the complexity of the statistical procedure required to estimate parameter values from survey data.

Since its introduction to retailing literature in 1964, many empirical studies have supported the usefulness of the Huff model in predicting the trade areas and sales of individual outlets with reasonable accuracy. Over the years, a number of improvements have been suggested to the model. Many of these improvements have included factors besides store size and distance. These extended models have been used to forecast sales of shopping centers, supermarkets, convenience stores, branch banks, and hospitals, to name a few.[9] Conceptually, there is no restriction to the number of factors that can be included in the model to measure store attraction. Depending on the particular application, the retail analyst should include all factors that can influence consumer store choice behavior.[10]

Forecasting Sales with Spatial Interaction Model

The spatial interaction model is a very useful and common tool for forecasting sales at new sites. This section illustrates through a supermarket case study the use of spatial interaction models for developing sales forecasts. The study area is a town of about 50,000 people with six major supermarkets operated by three chains. One of the chains plans to open a new store.

Prior to opening the store, the chain's management would like to estimate the potential trade area of the store and forecast the sales they can expect at the proposed site. The managers must take the following steps to forecast sales using the Huff model:

1. Divide the market area into smaller customer zones or subareas. The subareas could be census districts, zip code areas or, simply a number of city blocks. In general, more compact trading areas should be divided into smaller subareas. Zip code areas are appropriate for analyzing trade areas of shopping centers since they attract customers from great distances. On the other hand, zip code areas are too large for supermarkets, which have small trade areas compared to

shopping centers. In this case, the total market area was divided into 29 subareas based on neighborhood characteristics and census information.

2. Determine the sizes of all competing stores in the area, in this case all supermarkets, including the proposed store.

3. Determine the distance or travel time between the center of each subarea and each store location.

4. Determine whether the parameters of the interaction model will be subjectively estimated or estimated by analyzing shopping patterns in the area. In this study the analyst subjectively estimated the values of a and b as 1.5 and 2.0, respectively, based on experiences from other studies of supermarkets.

5. If the parameters are to be estimated by statistical analysis of current shopping patterns, the managers should survey a sample of residents from each subarea. As its main purpose, the survey seeks to determine the frequency with which the residents at each subarea shop at each existing store. From this information, the firm can statistically determine the values of a and b that best describe the shopping behavior of the consumers in the area.

6. Once the parameter values are determined, the firm can calculate the probability of consumers in each subarea visiting the new store based on store size and distance. Exhibit 9.10 shows the predicted probability of shopping at the new store for each of the study's 29 subareas.

7. The next step is to predict the amount of sales that the new store can generate from each subarea. To calculate expected sales, the firm multiplies the shopping probability for a subarea by its population and the per-capita expenditure in retail stores (in this case supermarkets). Secondary sources provide both population and per-capita expenditure figures.

The sales from a subarea can be calculated as follows:

$$
\begin{aligned}
\text{Subarea } i \text{ sales } = \ & \text{Subarea } i \text{ shopping probability} \\
& \times \ \text{Subarea } i \text{ population} \\
& \times \ \text{Per-capita grocery expenditure}
\end{aligned}
$$

These calculations are shown in Exhibit 9.10. For example, the proposed store can expect weekly sales of $38,610 from Subarea 1. This forecast is obtained by multiplying the new store's share of trips from that subarea (0.75), the population of the zone (1,980), and a per-capita weekly grocery expenditure figure of $26. The per-capita expenditure figure came from a secondary source. In a similar manner, the expected sales from the other 28 subareas can be calculated as shown in the table. To arrive at a total sales forecast for the store, the firm sums the expected sales from all the subareas, giving $203,587 weekly.

The analyst can apply the sales forecasting procedure outlined above to a number of potential sites to compare their desirability for locating a new supermarket. As mentioned earlier, comparing the forecasts for different sites is important for making the final site-selection decision. Generating such sales forecasts, however,

Exhibit 9.10   *Sales Forecast for New Store*

Zone	Share of Trips from Zone	Population of Zone	Sales from Zone
1	75%	1,980	$ 38,610
2	65	1,150	19,435
3	20	1,025	5,330
4	79	830	17,048
5	31	1,570	12,654
6	0	1,460	0
7	60	1,630	25,428
8	6	2,900	4,524
9	20	2,810	14,612
10	10	2,320	6,032
11	0	2,910	0
12	3	3,040	2,371
13	1	3,440	894
14	3	2,190	1,708
15	1	2,260	588
16	36	1,300	12,168
17	21	1,540	8,408
18	1	1,660	432
19	2	2,320	1,206
20	4	1,980	2,059
21	2	2,100	1,092
22	1	2,020	525
23	32	2,450	20,384
24	5	1,940	2,522
25	5	1,340	1,742
26	3	1,472	1,148
27	3	1,360	1,061
28	3	1,620	1,264
29	1	1,310	341
Total			$203,587

requires extensive calculations. For this reason, analysts typically use computers to forecast sales with the Huff model.

The model is also useful for simulating the effects of changes in competitive strategy on store sales. For example, how would the sales of one store be affected if a competitor increased its size? How would the closure of a competing outlet affect sales? The Huff model can help firms answer these types of questions.

Summary

1. Trade area analysis and sales forecasting are important steps in developing retail location strategy and selecting sites for new outlets. The trade area is the geographic area from which the store draws its customers. The nature and size of the trade area determine, to a large extent, the size and composition of the store's customer base.

2. The size of the trade area depends on a number of factors including the type of goods the store sells, the size of the store, the store's marketing strategy, the type of location, the quality of available transportation, and the level of competition in the area. The shape of the trade area is determined by the transportation network, barriers to travel, and the locations of competitors' outlets.

3. The trade areas of existing stores can be determined by customer spotting, examining store records, and license plate surveys. They each determine the geographic origin of the customers who shop at the store. Typically, a store's ability to attract customers decreases with distance. This is called the distance decay effect.

4. Trade area information is useful for analyzing the demographic and socioeconomic characteristics of the store's customers. This is essential for streamlining merchandising and pricing policies and for effective response to customer needs. Trade area analysis is also important in formulating advertising and promotion strategies and in clarifying one's picture of the competitive environment.

5. Since the sales of a retail store depend to a large extent on its location, the firm must compare expected sales at a number of alternative sites prior to making a final site selection decision. Retailers commonly forecast sales by three methods: the analog method, the regression method, and the spatial interaction method. In the analog method the sales forecast is based on the performance of an analog store. Retail chains use regression models to use the sales experience of its many existing outlets to forecast sales at a new location. Spatial interaction models forecast sales generated from different parts of the store's trade area based on store size and distance. The forecasts from different subareas are combined to obtain a forecast for the store as a whole.

Key Concepts

Sales forecasts	Distance decay effect
Trade area	Analog method
Trade area estimation	Regression methods
Trade area size	Explanatory variables
Trade area shape	Dependent variable
Customer spotting	Regression coefficient
Customer origin map	Spatial interaction models

Discussion Questions

1. Why do retail stores have trade areas? Explain how store and site characteristics affect the size of a store's trade area.

2. Briefly discuss two methods for delineating a store's trade area.

3. What are some ways in which retail managers can use a customer origin map? Why do customer origin maps typically exhibit the distance decay effect?

4. What steps are involved in using the analog method to forecast sales for a new retail outlet?

5. A chain store has calibrated the following regression model for forecasting sales of individual outlets, based on experience from its existing outlets:

Sales ($000s) = 139.9 + 4.8 X (Population above 15 in thousands) + 14.5 (Average Family Income in $000s) − 52.6 X (Number of competing stores in market area)

The chain is planning to open new outlets in the following three sites:

Site	Popln. 15+ (000s)	Ave. Family Income ($000s)	Number of Competitors
A	105	32.8	1
B	122	29.4	3
C	156	28.1	2

Forecast the sales at each of these sites.

6. What steps are involved in using (a) the regression model, and (b) the Huff model to forecast sales of a new outlet?

7. The parameters *a* and *b* in the Huff model measure the relative influence of store size and distance on the perceived attractiveness of a store. What inference would you draw about consumer behavior if, for a group of consumers, the value of *a* were very large compared to *b*? What inferences would you draw if the weights were reversed?

8. The table below lists the distance and size of three typical stores at which Sue Collins shops. Using a Huff model with *a* = 1.5 and *b* = 2.0, (a) calculate the probability of her visiting each of the three stores. (b) How would this probability change if Store A increased its size by 50 percent? (c) How would the shopping pattern be affected if Store A closed down?

Store	Distance (miles)	Size (square feet)
A	2.8	65,000
B	4.8	80,000
C	2.0	40,000

Notes

1. "Selecting a Store Site, the Computer Way," *Chain Store Age Executive* (March 1981), p. 47.

2. William Applebaum, "Methods for Determining Store Trade Areas, Market Penetration and Potential Sales," *Journal of Marketing Research* 3, 1966, pp. 127–41.

3. For a review of multifacility location methods see Avijit Ghosh and Sara L. McLafferty, *Location Strategies for Retail and Service Firms* (Lexington, MA: D.C. Heath, 1987).

4. William Applebaum, "The Analogue Method for Estimating Potential Store Sales," in *Guide to Store Location Research*, ed. by C. Kornblau (Reading, MA: Addison-Wesley, 1968).

5. Applebaum, "Methods for Determining."

6. David L. Huff, "Defining and Estimating a Trading Area," *Journal of Marketing* (July 1964), pp. 34–38.

7. See David L. Huff, "A Probabilistic Analysis of Shopping Center Trade Areas," *Land Economics* 39 (1963), pp. 81–90; and David L. Huff, "Defining and Estimating a Trade Area," *Journal of Marketing* 28, 1964, pp. 34–38.

8. R. Luce, *Individual Choice Behavior* (New York: John Wiley and Sons, 1959).

9. See, for example, Arun Jain and Vijay Mahajan, "Evaluating the Competitive Environment in Retailing Using Multiplicative Competitive Interaction Models," in J. Sheth (ed.) *Research in Marketing* (Greenwich, CT: JAI Press, 1979); Avijit Ghosh, "Parameter Nonstationarity in Retail Choice Models," *Journal of Business Research* 12 (1984), pp. 425–36; S. T. Folland, "Predicting Hospital Market Shares," *Inquiry* 20 (1983), pp. 34–44; G.

E. Weisbrod, R. J. Parcells, and C. Kern, "A Disaggregate Model for Predicting Shopping Area Market Attraction," *Journal of Retailing* 60 (1984), pp. 65–83. For a review of these and other studies see A. Ghosh and S. McLafferty, *Location Stra-tegies for Retail and Service Firm.*

10. Masao Nakanishi and Lee G. Cooper, "Parameter Estimates for Multiplicative Competitive Interaction Models," *Journal of Marketing Research* 11 (1974), pp. 304–11.

PART III
Merchandise Management

At the heart of any retail store is the merchandise it sells. Retail managers must choose the merchandise with an eye towards the needs and expectations of the store's intended target. They must also manage merchandise investments by proper inventory control, vendor negotiations, merchandise performance evaluation, and pricing.

The five chapters in Part Three deal with various aspects of merchandise management. Chapter 10 discusses how merchandise decisions affect the overall image of the store and the key merchandise decisions that retail managers must make. Chapter 11 examines merchandise budgets and vendor negotiations, and Chapter 12 develops a framework for making pricing decisions for retail merchandise. Chapter 13 describes procedures for controlling merchandise inventories. Chapter 14 evaluates merchandise performance and describes some of the methods used to measure the performance of individual merchandise items.

CHAPTER 10
Developing Merchandise Strategy

Merchandise Drives The Gap's Success

The Gap, founded in 1969 by Donald Fisher, began as a blue-jeans and record store in San Francisco. Fisher felt there was a hole in the blue-jeans market, and wanted to create a store that offered jeans in a comprehensive array of sizes and provided customer service in terms of exchanges and selection. Once open, Fisher saw that he had read customer demand correctly, and the chain grew quickly, to over 200 outlets by 1976. Much of the growth was supported and pushed by heavy advertising, and by Fisher's careful site selection. However, by 1983 business for the chain slumped. The stores were cluttered, and the quality of the merchandise had declined. As proof, no Gap employee would be caught dead wearing any of the store's line. Fisher realized that while he was shrewd at selecting sites, constructing the stores and overseeing the manufacturing, he was no merchandiser, and the chain was beginning to suffer.

To counter these growing problems Mickey Drexler was hired away from Ann Taylor in 1983, where he had just finished a very successful turnaround of the chain. Drexler was hired as the merchandiser, and The Gap has had phenomenal success under his leadership. (Drexler is president, and oversees the design and merchandising aspects of the business, while Fisher is chairman, overseeing site selection, store construction, and apparel manufacturing.) Together, the two have created a chain that seems to be recession-proof and safe from the current trend of retailing retrenchment. This is due to the quality and value the chain offers, and also The Gap "image" that has been tended and perpetuated by the management style of Drexler.

Upon arrival at The Gap, Drexler commenced a total restructuring of the chain, from the design of the clothes and the stores, to the management philosophy and structure. First, he liquidated the existing merchandise, sending earnings down by 45 percent in 1984. Unperturbed, Drexler pushed forward with the single idea: *design clothes you would wear and the customer will follow.* Drexler boosted the quality substantially. The Gap designs its own clothes, chooses the materials, and monitors the manufacturing so closely that management can keep costs low and quality high. He then redesigned all the stores, so that customers can tell that the stores come from one mind: they are all white-walled, clean, and well-lit; they have wide aisles; and the clothes are easily accessible on low shelves and uncluttered racks. In addition, customers will always get the same product and service—in New York, in Arkansas, or in Europe—and *this is part of the appeal:* one product for all customers, a product that customers will know and trust *world-wide.* Finally, Drexler created The Gap label, which further reinforces The Gap "image." The firm grew to become the

After studying this chapter, the reader will be able to:
- *Understand how a firm's merchandising decisions are related to its marketing and financial goals.*
- *Describe the four important dimensions of merchandise policy.*
- *Describe the different variety and assortment policies followed by retailers.*
- *Understand the factors that affect a store's assortment of merchandise.*
- *Know how retailers use merchandise lists to plan assortments.*
- *Know how to evaluate new products and the sources for information on new products.*

second largest U.S. apparel brand by 1991. This merchandising strategy of look-alike stores selling good quality, reasonably priced basics that can fit into *everyone's* wardrobe eventually became the philosophy of the company, and with Drexler's leadership style and careful management formula of "good style, good quality, good value" as the catalyst, The Gap quickly became the retailing success of the 1980s.

One element behind The Gap's success is that the chain is not just its clothes; it is a whole concept: a carefully chosen network of sites; a well-tended vision of the stores where consumers can shop easily and quickly; sales supported by heavy advertising; and a high-tech distribution system that can ship to any of the 1,200 U.S. Gap stores in under 72

hours. The corporate culture fusses over *all* the details, from design issues to making GapKids child-safe, to ensuring that all the stores are kept clean and well stocked. This is not a hands-off management style. Drexler is involved in all aspects of The Gap's business, ensuring that his mantra "good style, good quality, good value" is adhered to. Drexler works on the design of each item and the color scheme of the line, stays involved with the advertising, and even determines how the clothes will be displayed at the stores. There is no personal expression at The Gap; there is Drexler's vision, period.

The Gap style is equally accepted by kids, teenagers, young-adults and greying baby-boomers. Customers always know what they will find in a Gap store: basic clothes, of good quality and good value—not the whole wardrobe, but the basic foundation. This kind of image has connected with consumers in a way that few consumer product companies have succeeded in doing; McDonald's and Coca-Cola are the rare examples. The formula's success is apparent as sales at The Gap and its sibling stores, GapKids and Banana Republic, rose 30 percent in 1990, and this in a period of recession and retailing retrenchment.

Sources: Barmash, Isadore: "Gap Finds Middle Road to Success," *The New York Times,* June 24, 1991, p. C1; Caminiti, Susan: "Reading the Customer Right," *Fortune,* December 2, 1991, p. 106; Mitchell, Russell: "The Gap: Can the Nation's Hottest Retailer Stay on Top?," *Business Week,* March 9, 1992, pp. 58–64.

Retailers commonly believe that the essence of retailing is merchandising. Although this may oversimplify the challenges of retail management, it does point to the central role of merchandising in retail organizations. The merchandise, the mix of products a store offers for sale, is the heart of the retail operation. A hallmark of a successful retail program is a merchandise selection that matches the tastes, preferences, and expectations of its target customers.

Merchandise decisions affect all aspects of retail operations. They affect the amount of funds the firm will have to invest to maintain merchandise inventory, along with the amount of space, labor, and equipment it will require for stock and display. The sales and margins generated by a store also depend on the merchandise. Finally, and most importantly, the merchandise selection determines the types of customers the store can attract. Of all the factors that influence a customer's decision to shop at a particular store, none is more important than the merchandise selection. The quality, price, and selectivity of merchandise strongly influences the consumer's perception of a store's image. The firm must fully integrate merchandising decisions with its overall marketing strategy and with the elements of the retail mix.

This chapter deals with merchandising strategy. The first section presents a framework for developing the overall merchandising strategy for a store and explains the relationship between a store's merchandise strategy and its marketing and financial goals. The second section focuses on the important elements of merchandising strategy and discusses four major aspects of merchandising strategy: (1) variety and assortment policy, (2) branding policy, (3) planning merchandise of assortments, and (4) new product decisions.

A FRAMEWORK FOR MERCHANDISING STRATEGY

The goal of **merchandising strategy** is to select the right mix of products or services to sell at the store. To develop the merchandise selection, the retailer must meet the four merchandise goals in the center of Exhibit 10.1. As indicated in that exhibit, to be "right," the merchandise selection must be consistent with the firm's marketing strategy and its financial goals.

Marketing Strategy and Merchandise Decisions

The store's merchandise is its primary means of satisfying customer needs. Therefore, a key element of a successful retail program is a merchandise mix that satisfies the tastes and preferences of the target market while being consistent with the store's position on the shopping opportunity line. A merchandise selection that ideally suits one retailer will not be ideal for another that follows a different marketing strategy. For example, to appeal to their target markets, stores such as I. Magnin, Neiman-Marcus, and Brooks Brothers, carry fashion-forward merchan-

Exhibit 10.1   Merchandise Planning Framework

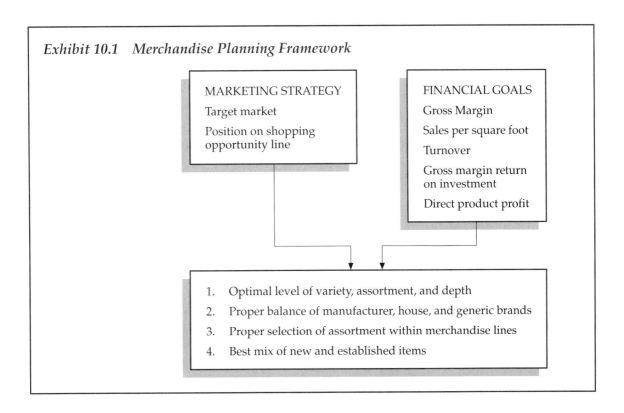

dise that reflect the latest styles and trends. Contrast this to the merchandise strategy of stores such as Sears and K mart. They tend to follow, rather than lead, fashion trends. Off-price apparel stores, on the other hand, often rely on closeout, and late-season merchandise to maintain their low prices.

Target Market and Merchandise Strategy   A store's merchandising strategy must reflect its marketing strategy. This is well illustrated by examining the merchandise selection of clothing specialty stores that cater to working women. During the last decade many stores have focussed on the clothing needs of working women, who now make up a large portion of the workforce. One example of such a store was Alcott and Andrews.

Alcott and Andrews was started by two department store executives who felt that the department stores did not adequately serve the needs of the professional woman. To meet the needs of this target market, they opened a chain called Alcott and Andrews that provided a complete assortment of work and leisure clothing for a wide spectrum of career women. The merchandise strategy emphasized classic and feminine work and leisure clothing rather than trendy styles. Casual dresses comprised only about 15 percent of the merchandise and occupied a section separate from the main selling area. Despite its marketing success, the chain ran into trouble after a few years due to inadequate financial management. Most observers, however, credit it with highly successful marketing and merchandising strategies. Michael Jeffries, president of Alcott and Andrews, once explained their success this way: "We are totally dedicated to our target customer. That is what separates us from the pack."[1]

As another example, reconsider the strategies of the toy retailers described in Chapter 5. The merchandising strategies of Toys R Us and F.A.O. Schwarz are quite different, even though they both sell toys. As discussed earlier, the marketing strategies of the two stores are quite different, and their merchandise selection reflects this difference. Toys R Us carries mostly branded toys that are typically heavily advertised by its manufacturers. Such a merchandise focus fits with the firm's goals of being the "toy supermarket" of the world. F.A.O. Schwarz, on the other hand, caters to customers who want novel, innovative toys. Some of its toys cost thousands of dollars and will never be found in Toys R Us.

Store Positioning and Merchandising Strategy

The store's position on the shopping opportunity line must also guide merchandise decisions. Stores differentiate themselves from their competitors based on the price and quality of the merchandise they carry, as comparing the price and quality of merchandise offered by traditional department stores, mass merchandisers, and discount stores makes clear. While all of these stores sell women's clothing, the particular brands and styles each sells are quite different, reflecting differences in the needs and expectations of their target markets. Each store concentrates on a specific price-quality range that suits the needs of its particular target market and that differentiates it from others. It would be inconsistent for K mart to offer ladies' dresses at $500, just as it would be for Jordan Marsh, Saks Fifth Avenue, or Neiman-Marcus to sell dresses for $14.99.

For another illustration of the impact of marketing strategy on merchandise selection, consider men's toiletries. Department stores, discount stores, drugstores, and supermarkets all sell after-shave lotions and colognes. Each type of store, however, typically sells quite different brands. Supermarkets usually sell a limited number of low-priced brands such as Brut 33, Mennen, and Old Spice. Drugstores, discount stores, and mass merchandise outlets also sell Old Spice. These stores also carry British Sterling, English Leather, Aqua Velva, and Brut (higher-priced than Brut 33), all of which cost more than the supermarket brands. Department stores carry a more exclusive array of brands, many of them associated with well-known designer names such as Ralph Lauren, Pierre Cardin, Armani, and so on. These products cost significantly more than the brands sold by the other types of stores.

A store's merchandise reflects its marketing strategy, and the merchandise selection has a profound influence on how consumers perceive the store's image. The retailer must therefore, carefully choose its merchandise to meet the expectations of its target market and to create the image for which it aims.

A store's merchandising strategy reflects its marketing strategy. F.A.O. Schwarz in New York is looking for customers who want innovative and unique toys and who may be willing to spend thousands of dollars for them.

Financial Goals and Merchandise Strategy

A store must also keep its merchandising decisions consistent with its financial goals; after all it is the sale of merchandise that creates the potential for profit. Merchandise decisions affect many aspects of the store's financial performance, including its sales and margins. The size of the merchandise selection determines the amount of funds the firm will have to invest in maintaining inventory and the amount of space, labor, and equipment it will need for stock and display. The store's profitability depends, to a large extent, on its merchandising policies.

Retailers use a number of different measures to monitor **merchandise performance**, three of the most common of which are shown in Exhibit 10.1. The first, *gross margin, shows the difference between the retail value of the merchandise and the cost of the goods.* Higher margins mean that more money is available to cover expenses and generate profits. Maintaining a healthy gross margin is a prime goal of merchandise managers.

The second common measure for judging merchandise performance is **sales per square foot**. Few retailers have enough space to stock all the items they would like to, so they must use the available space productively. Sales per square foot indicates the relationship of sales to the amount of space used to stock and display the merchandise. A higher sales per square foot indicates a more productive use of available space.

The third measure, **inventory (or stock) turnover**, measures how quickly the merchandise sells. *Turnover shows the relationship between the amount of merchandise the store sells and the amount it keeps in inventory.* The following expression is one way to measure merchandise turnover:

$$\text{Turnover} = \frac{\text{Net Sales}}{\text{Retail value of average inventory}}$$

Thus, higher turnover indicates a higher level of sales compared to the amount of money invested in inventory.

Retailers must continuously monitor merchandise sales and inventory in order to improve their financial performance. To do this, they should calculate two figures based on sales, margin, turnover, and cost information, called **gross margin return on investment (GMROI)** and the **direct product profit (DPP)**, for each item in the merchandise mix. GMROI measures the gross margins each item produces:

$$\text{GMROI} = \frac{\text{Gross margin}}{\text{Cost of average inventory}}$$

Retailers typically set GMROI targets for the entire store and for different merchandise classifications. From these guidelines, they formulate merchandise plans and evaluate the performance of merchandise items. Another criterion for this judgment, *DPP, measures the net income an item generates after accounting for all direct costs.*

The retailer must evaluate the profitability of each merchandise item separately based on these criteria in order to identify poor performers, eliminate them from the merchandise mix, and exploit to the fullest opportunities for improving the profitability of remaining items. Systematic procedures for monitoring and evaluating individual merchandise items are discussed in Chapter 13.

VARIETY, ASSORTMENT, AND DEPTH

Prior to discussing the four major elements of merchandising strategy identified in Exhibit 10.1, it is important to clarify some common terms.

Variety

Variety refers to the kinds of goods and services or merchandise lines a store carries. The cohesion of merchandise lines may be based on similarity of end use or customer group. Examples of merchandise lines are kitchen appliances, furniture, health and beauty aids, apparel, toys, and so on. For planning purposes, retailers usually divide the merchandise line into merchandise divisions. They can divide the apparel line, for example, into separate divisions based on sex or age—men, women, teens, children, infants. They can further subclassify the broad group of products classified as men's apparel into merchandise groups such as formal wear, shirts, sports clothes, and outerwear, for example (see Exhibit 10.2). Similarly, kitchen appliances may be subdivided into toaster, blender, food processor, and hand mixer groups, among others.

Assortment

Each merchandise group usually contains many brands, styles, colors, and sizes. *Assortment refers to the amount of selection in terms of these factors that the store offers within each product group.* Rarely can a store carry the entire spectrum of choices available within a merchandise group. The retailer must select the combination of brands and styles that is most appropriate for the store—not an easy task since the choice may be almost unlimited. Consider, as an example, men's shirts. No store could carry all the available brands, styles, colors, and sizes of shirts at all price points.

Retailers measure the range of merchandise assortment in **stock keeping units** or **SKUs**. *Each specific product item in a merchandise group that is distinguishable from all other items of that type represents one SKU.* For example, a blue, button-down Oxford, full sleeve, Arrow Dover shirt in a specific size constitutes an SKU. A store can stock quite a large number of SKUs within a product category because of the number of factors by which products can be distinguished. This is easily evident in the example shown below.

Shirt Department Stock

	3 brands of shorts	3
in	2 styles	× 2
in	4 sizes	× 4
in	4 colors	× 4
in	3 price points	× 3
Total SKUs		288

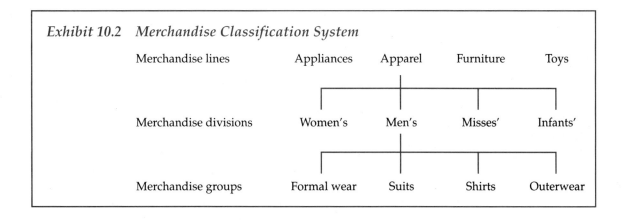

Exhibit 10.2   Merchandise Classification System

Merchandise lines	Appliances	Apparel	Furniture	Toys
Merchandise divisions	Women's	Men's	Misses'	Infants'
Merchandise groups	Formal wear	Suits	Shirts	Outerwear

STRATEGY IN ACTION

In Sourcing, the Accent Is Now on Global

U.S. retailers have long relied on foreign suppliers to fill some of their merchandise needs. For example, clothing marked "Made in India" is now common in U.S. department stores, specialty stores, and even mail-order catalogues. Retailers such as L.L. Bean, Macy's, The Gap, and Liz Claiborne source merchandise from India, buying clothing, accessories, and leathergoods. In recent years, Indian-made items have moved from low-end, low-quality goods to goods in the mid-price range.

For many years, sourcing from a foreign country necessitated working through in-country buying houses and purchasing agents. This meant that the U.S. retailers called, for example, an Indian buying agent and specified the items desired. However, the actual items to be purchased were left up to the agents, and the U.S. retailers simply had to hope for the best. Unfortunately, retailers often found the merchandise ordered to be far below the quality they sought, and the goods would often arrive behind schedule and in poor condition. Furthermore, U.S. retailers found that the agents dealt with so many clients that service and the merchandise quality ultimately suffered because the buying houses could not focus all their attentions and energies on any single client. Finally, agents charge a hefty commission. Such dissatisfactions have led many retailers to open their own buying offices in India and other foreign countries.

In 1988, J.C. Penney decided to run an Indian-goods promotion and ordered nearly $10 million worth of merchandise through their agent in India, only to find that the merchandise arrived late and in abysmal condition. Viewing the situation as the last straw in a series of poor relations with their agent, Penney decided to open up their own office in India to run the purchasing operations, wanting to ensure proper quality, service, and distribution for the nearly $50 million worth of merchandise they plan to source from India.

Another example is Quelle International, one of Europe's largest mail-order chains, which has been sourcing goods from India since the 1970s. The company was pleased with the quality of the goods they received and with the service their agent provided, but they found that their agent's commission was increasing, pushing Quelle's costs too high. In the face of rising costs, Quelle decided to open up their own office in India.

Chains including Macy's, Woolworth, Robinsons-May, and Pier 1, along with J.C. Penney, Quelle, and many others, have opened up their own offices in India. Not only have these companies significantly reduced their costs, but the companies are much more involved with the selection process. Retailers can work directly with Indian suppliers to find the items and the quality they want, and in many cases they can even work with the suppliers to develop specific product lines. U.S. and European retailers that have opened these offices are, across the board, more than satisfied with the results of being their own agents in India. Given this, U.S. customers are sure to see many more of the "Made in India" labels.

Source: Sanjit Singh, "Sourcing from Across the Seven Seas," *The Economic Times of New York*, January 2, 1993, p. 1.

To select the proper assortment, one cannot merely choose the number of SKUs to stock; the crucial task is to choose the particular brands, styles, fabrics, sizes, colors, and price ranges that best meet customer needs.

Depth

Merchandise **depth** is the *number of units of each SKU the store must keep in stock to meet expected demand.* Deciding on the appropriate depth is not an easy task. On one hand, the retailer would like to maintain a deep inventory so that no merchandise ever runs out of stock. Large inventories, however, result in greater interest costs and increased working capital. The costs of merchandise storage, handling, taxes, and insurance also increase with the level of inventory. Therefore, it is crucial to determine a level of stocks adequate to meet consumer demand that also controls the cost of maintaining inventory. Methods for determining optimal inventory policies are discussed in Chapter 13.

ELEMENTS OF MERCHANDISING STRATEGY

The multifaceted task of selecting the proper mix of merchandise requires consideration of many factors. As stated, the merchandise must meet the needs of the target market and also the financial goals of the retailer. In designing the merchandise strategy appropriate for any individual store, merchandise managers must address the four issues raised in Exhibit 10.1: (1) variety and assortment, (2) branding, (3) assortment policy, and (4) new products.

VARIETY AND ASSORTMENT

As one of its most important goals, a store's merchandise strategy must seek to properly balance the variety and assortment of its merchandise. The proper balance depends on the store's format, target market, and marketing strategy. Some firms, including variety stores, department stores, and mass merchandisers, create competitive advantage by offering a wide variety of goods to facilitate one-stop shopping. Customers expect to find a wide range of product lines at these stores. Specialty stores, on the other hand, stress assortment over variety. Each type of specialty store (electronics outlets, paint stores, liquor stores, apparel stores, and so forth) concentrates on only a few product categories. These stores create competitive advantage by the breadth of choice they offer within each category.

No single approach to variety and assortment suits all retailers. Each store must determine the balance between variety and assortment that is most consistent with its overall marketing strategy. Although each store follows a unique merchandising strategy, four general approaches can be identified based on relative emphasis on variety and assortment (see Exhibit 10.3).

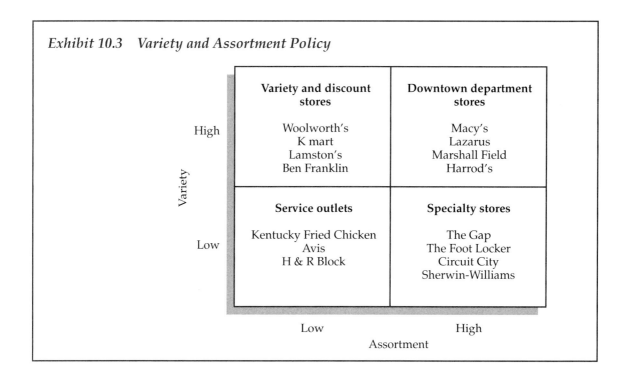

Exhibit 10.3   Variety and Assortment Policy

	Variety and discount stores	**Downtown department stores**
High	Woolworth's K mart Lamston's Ben Franklin	Macy's Lazarus Marshall Field Harrod's
Low	**Service outlets** Kentucky Fried Chicken Avis H & R Block	**Specialty stores** The Gap The Foot Locker Circuit City Sherwin-Williams
	Low	High

Variety (vertical axis label)

Assortment (horizontal axis label)

Low Variety–Low Assortment

The advertising slogan of Kentucky Fried Chicken, "We do chicken right," typifies its overall marketing strategy. The fast-food chain's menu features low variety (mostly chicken) and low assortment (limited types of preparation). The company has built its retail strategy around this limited merchandise selection.

Kentucky Fried Chicken is not alone in adopting this strategy. Most fast-food restaurants offer limited menu selections, although some have added breakfast items and salad bars to their menus in recent years. Service retailers typically follow this strategy, too. Car rental companies, tax preparation services, banks, and brokerage firms all concentrate on one or few services. Some newspaper vendors sell only one or two newspapers and neighborhood convenience and grocery stores also limit the variety and assortment of their products.

The advantage of the limited selection strategy is the opportunity it brings for specialization since the firm can concentrate its resources and skills on managing a few items. It also simplifies store operations, a great advantage to franchise operators who train and monitor many individual franchise owners. This strategy also limits the investment required to start and operate the business. Many small retailers, therefore, have limited variety and assortment.

This specialty store concentrates on one product category—books. Competitive advantage is created by the great breadth of choice it offers within that category.

Emphasis on Assortment

The merchandise strategy of Dunkin Donuts provides an interesting contrast to that of Kentucky Fried Chicken. Like Kentucky Fried Chicken, Dunkin Donuts specializes in a limited product line. Its main product is doughnuts, although some stores offer croissants, muffins, and soups, too. However, Dunkin Donuts sells 42 different kinds of doughnuts. The company then builds its advertising strategy around the themes of assortment and freshness. Similarly, Baskin Robbins stresses its wide assortment of 31 ice cream flavors.

Dunkin Donuts and Baskin Robbins are examples of retailers that emphasize assortment over variety in their merchandise selections. The merchandising strategies of many kinds of specialty stores—shoes, toys, jewelry, apparel, electronic goods, hardware—reflect this emphasis on wide assortments. They all specialize in a few merchandise lines, but offer large assortments of products within each line. The greatest advantage of specialization is the opportunity to develop a special market niche and a reputation of being a leader in a product line.

This strategy varies, of course, among specialty stores. In its purest form, the specialty store concentrates on a single product line. Ice cream stores and cookie shops (like David's Cookies and Mrs. Field's Cookies) are examples of this extreme specialization. Not all specialty stores, however, concentrate on a single product line. Electronics retailers usually carry a range of complementary product lines such as video equipment, audio components, personal computers, and calculators. Similarly, apparel stores carry different types of clothing items.

Emphasis on Variety

At the opposite extreme from the specialty store's strategy is the strategy adopted by variety stores. Variety stores such as Woolworth, Ben Franklin, and Lamstons, as well as some discount stores, offer a wide selection of product lines, but limit their assortments within each product line. The wide variety of products appeals to many customers who like the convenience of one-stop shopping. Most products carried by these stores fall into basic merchandise categories, in which consumers seldom have strong loyalty toward particular brands. This allows the stores to carry only a limited number of brands in each product line without losing potential customers.

The Balanced Strategy

Department stores and mass merchandisers take a fourth approach to merchandising: the balanced strategy. They balance the variety and assortment of their merchandise, rather than stressing one over the other. Like variety stores they sell a wide variety of merchandise in different product lines, but they also offer a large assortment within each product line. By balancing variety and assortment, department stores and mass merchandisers also facilitate one-stop shopping.

Department stores differ considerably in their merchandise selections. The variety of merchandise available at an outlet usually depends on its size, larger outlets generally offering greater varieties of merchandise. Large flagship stores, typically located in downtown areas of major cities, usually sell a large variety of products. Branch outlets of department store chains located in shopping malls are often much smaller than the downtown stores and offer relatively less variety.

The selection of merchandise within each product line at department stores and mass merchandisers can also vary. Consumers find much greater assortments in some merchandise categories than others, reflecting the store's merchandising emphasis. Typically, department stores offer their greatest assortments in apparel, cosmetics, and housewares, while the choice in cameras, electronic goods, and toys can be quite limited. Mass merchandise outlets such as Sears give considerable attention to small appliances, hardware, automotive products, and sporting goods in addition to apparel.

Exhibit 10.4 summarizes the advantages and disadvantages of each of these four strategies. In developing a strategy for its own store, the retailer must carefully evaluate these factors.

Exhibit 10.4 Alternative Variety and Assortment Policies

Policy	Advantages	Disadvantages
Low variety– low assortment	Specialist image Aimed at convenience customers Easiest to manage Small investment	Limited market Limited traffic
Emphasis on assortment	Specialist image Specialized personnel	Limited traffic Lack of variety may disappoint customers
Emphasis on variety	Broad market High traffic One-stop shopping	Weak image Less customer loyalty Many items turn over slowly
Balanced strategy	Broad market One-stop shopping No disappointed customers Strong customer loyalty Strong image	High inventory investment Difficult to manage Many items turn over slowly

Source: Reprinted with permission from Professor Ronald J. Dornoff, University of Cincinnati.

Changes in Variety and Assortment

The variety and assortment of a store's merchandise reflect the expectations of its target customers and their tastes, preferences, and shopping habits. Consumer behavior is not static, however. It changes with time, and retailers have to change their merchandise policies in order to respond to those changes. Consider the following examples:

- The three leading fast-food franchises, McDonald's, Burger King, and Wendy's, have added fresh salads to their menus.
- Many supermarkets have added fresh bakeries, delis, and salad bars.
- Convenience stores and supermarkets now rent video movies.

These are but a few examples of how retailers have modified their merchandising policies to respond to changing consumer preferences, expectations, and shopping habits.

Two apparently contradictory trends seem to be sweeping the retail industry. While some retailers are aggressively pursuing scrambled merchandising strategies and increasing the variety in their merchandise selections, others are specializing in limited variety. In some product categories, super specialty stores are beginning to focus on narrow varieties, but large assortments. For one example, the Athlete's Foot chain of shoe stores sells only athletic footwear and clothing. Victoria's Secret, a chain of high-quality women's lingerie outlets, is another example.

Scrambled Merchandising   Apart from adding fresh bakeries, delis, and salad bars, many large supermarkets also sell automotive products, health and beauty aids, and nonprescription drugs. Some have also added flowers, paperback books, and wristwatches to their product lines. It is estimated that a typical supermarket generates as much as 12 to 15 percent of sales from nonfood items. Drugstores, too, have expanded the variety of their merchandise. Some larger stores carry cameras, wristwatches, toys, and beverages in addition to health and beauty aids, infant care products, household goods, and drugs.

The two hottest trends in the retail industry are scrambled merchandising and super specialty stores. Foot Locker is a super specialty store that sells only athletic footwear, socks, and sports clothing.

The expansion of product variety in supermarkets and drugstores is an example of **scrambled merchandising**, a policy that increases variety by adding new product lines that are unrelated to existing merchandise. The expanded merchandise selection increases consumers' opportunities for one-stop shopping. By offering a wide selection of food, household products, and consumable general merchandise, supermarkets are structuring their policies to better meet the needs of today's fast-paced, time-pressed lifestyles. Scrambled merchandising also gives the retailer the opportunity to add high-margin items to the merchandise mix. Fresh bakery items, wristwatches, toys, and paperback books provide much greater gross margins to supermarket owners than typical grocery and produce items.

Scrambled merchandising has increased in recent years due to the introduction of many new products and services. Many different kinds of stores rent video movies, a service originally provided mainly by specialized outlets. As the popularity of VCRs increased, new types of retail outlets entered the business. Many supermarkets, drugstores, and convenience outlets now provide video rentals. The same pattern emerged when home computers became popular. Although initially sold only by specialist stores, now department stores, mass merchandisers, discount stores, bookstores, and electronics stores all compete for a piece of the home computer and software market.

Specialization   While drugstores and supermarkets increase variety, general merchandise stores seem to be tending toward specialization. Witness, for example, the phenomenal growth of The Limited, Benetton, The Gap (apparel), Toys R Us (toys and hobbies), and Circuit City (electronics). Each concentrates on limited variety, but wide assortment within a selected merchandise line.

Some reasons for the success of specialty stores in recent years include:

- Their ability to respond to the fragmentation of consumer markets by fashion attitudes, lifestyles, and purchase motivations.[2] As consumer markets become increasingly segmented, specialty stores are better able to meet the specific needs of individual segments.
- Their ability to combine dominant assortments of merchandise that attract shoppers within narrow segments.[3]
- They can provide well-informed salespeople, attentive point-of-sale service, quick checkout, and liberal return policies.
- Economies of scale give them competitive advantages over traditional department stores.

The success of specialty stores has put great competitive pressure on traditional department stores. Many department stores are responding to this challenge by improving service, developing unique merchandise, and, in general, refining market focus. In product categories such as toys and electronics, however, the success of specialty stores has forced many department stores to reduce emphasis on these departments; some have stopped selling the products altogether.

Balancing Variety, Assortment, and Depth

The proper balance among variety, assortment, and depth is crucial, and retailers must select it with considerable caution. The proper balance will depend on the operating policies of the store and its objectives. Decisions regarding variety, assortment, and depth are interrelated, since one can rarely be increased without sacrificing another.

The dilemma facing the managers of a variety store clearly illustrates the relationship among variety, assortment, and depth. The store carried a wide variety of products including housewares, gift items, small appliances, candies, and bath and kitchen fixtures. The managers recently considered adding a kitchen appliance department to the store. They realized that since the store could not expand in size, adding the new department would mean either eliminating an existing department or reducing the assortments in a number of departments. They feared, however, that reducing assortment or eliminating an existing department could decrease customer satisfaction and reduce sales in the long run. They had to trade off this potential loss against the desirability of opening the new department. Moreover, to fund the new merchandise from existing working capital, the store would have to reduce the depth of its inventory for some items, creating a risk of stockouts and reduced sales of those items.

A change in variety thus is likely to affect assortment, and depth, too, so decisions regarding them must be made jointly. Exhibit 10.5 illustrates the factors that tie these three dimensions of the merchandise selection together. Each store has a fixed amount of money available for investing in merchandise inventory. Increasing any one dimension inevitably means that merchandise selection must be curtailed in some other way to keep total investment under control. Each store also has a fixed amount of space. Thus, again, an increase in one merchandise dimension forces a reduction in the others. Variety, assortment, and depth decisions are also interrelated because they jointly affect the firm's financial performance.

BRAND POLICY

The second element of merchandise strategy is **brand policy**. Just as retailers must balance the variety and assortment of the merchandise, they must carefully determine the proper mix of manufacturer brands, house brands, and generic brands, since this decision, too, has a strong influence on store image.

Types of Brands

Manufacturer Brands   **Manufacturer brands** (also called national brands) are produced and distributed by manufacturers and are generally easily recognized

Exhibit 10.5 Merchandise Tradeoff Alternatives*

Key Constraint	Desired Action	Forced Trade-off Alternative
Fixed investment dollars	Expand variety	Reduce assortment, maintain depth for remaining assortment factors,
		or
		Maintain assortment, reduce depth supporting selected items
	Expand assortment for a product group	Reduce variety or depth
	Expand depth for a product item	Reduce variety or assortment
Fixed variety	Reduce total investment	Reduce assortment or depth
	Increase assortment for a product group	Increase investment or reduce depth
Fixed investment dollars and fixed	Increase assortment for a product group	Reduce depth
variety	Increase depth for a product item	Reduce assortment

*Not exhaustive, merely a sample.

Source: Danny Arnold, Louis Cappela, and Gary D. Smith, *Strategic Retail Management*, Reading, Mass.: Addison-Wesley, 1983, p. 335

by customers. Brands such as Heinz, Kraft, Nabisco, Del Monte, and Frito-Lay are examples of manufacturer brands in the food industry. IBM, Apple, Atari, Compaq, and Zenith are examples of manufacturer brands of personal computers.

Manufacturer brands also feature prominently in apparel lines. Botany 500 suits, Arrow or Van Heusen shirts, Levi's jeans, and DKNY, KIKIT, and Jones of New York dresses are some examples. In the apparel industry, the many manufacturer brands associated with names of fashion designers are called designer brands. Perry Ellis, Yves Saint Laurent, Norma Kamali, Liz Claiborne, and Pierre Cardin are some examples of designer brands of apparel. Consumers easily recognize manufacturer brands from extensive advertisement by manufacturers or their associations with famous fashion designers.

RESEARCH REPORT

The Link between Brand and Store Image

Each store has an image derived from the way consumers perceive it in their minds. Few would argue that store images exert a major influence on shopping behavior. Unfavorable images tend to adversely affect both patronage and purchase behavior, while favorable images are apt to improve such behavior.

The store's image, the total impression that consumers form about the store, depends on the types of products and the brands of those products that the store sells. There is a link, therefore, between brand image and store image. How, for example, is the image of J.C. Penney affected by the store's decision to carry the Halston line of designer apparel? Conversely, how might the image of a fashionable specialty store be affected if it stocked a brand with a low fashion image? A study published in the *Journal of Retailing* addressed these questions.

The study asked a group of shoppers first to evaluate two stores on an eight-item semantic differential scale (see Chapter 6 for a discussion of this instrument). One store was a specialty store with a very favorable image and the other a mass merchandiser with a relatively less favorable image.

Next, the shoppers used the same semantic differential scale to evaluate two brands of jeans: Calvin Klein and Lee. Calvin Klein's image was more favorable than Lee's.

In the final stage, the survey asked each shopper to evaluate two combinations of store and brand names. The first combination coupled the store with the more favorable image (the specialty store) with the less favorable brand (Lee), and the second combination included the less favorable store (the mass merchandiser) with the more favorable brand (Calvin Klein).

How does brand image affect store image? The Exhibit 10.a shows the answer. The first part of the exhibit shows the effect of combining a brand with a relatively low image with a high-image store. Notice that the combined image is somewhat less favorable than the image of the brand alone, and much less favorable than the store image.

The second part of the exhibit tells quite a different story. The low image of the store improves considerably when combined with the higher brand image.

These findings imply that a retailer might improve a less favorable image by carrying brand names that consumers view more favorably. A favorable retailer image, on the other hand, is likely to suffer damage if associated with a brand with a less positive image. This suggests that retailers should exercise caution in agreeing to carry a new brand.

Source: Jacob Jacoby and David Mazursky, "Linking Brand Name and Retailer Images: Do the Potential Risks Outweigh the Potential Benefits?" *Journal of Retailing* 60 (Summer 1984), pp. 105–122.

Exhibit 10.a   Brand and Store Image Evaluations: Jeans

a. High store, low brand

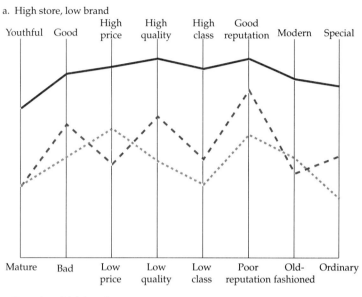

a. Low store, high brand

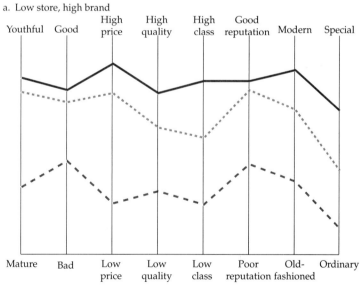

———— (a) High store alone; (b) High brand alone
– – – (a) Low brand alone; (b) Low store alone
······· (a & b) Brand-store combination (actual)

Private Label (House) Brands   Retail firms develop **private label** or **house brands** for sale only at their own stores. Although a manufacturer normally produces products that carry these brands for the retailer, the manufacturer's name is not identified on the product; instead the brands are identified either by the retailer's name or by distinctive names of their own. House brands are prominent in supermarkets, where many products carry the retailer's own brand name. Sainsbury, the British supermarket chain, launched its house brand of groceries as far back as 1869. In the United States, A&P was one of the first to introduce house brands. House brands are also important in apparel and department stores.

Sometimes house brands carry distinctive names of their own. Two well-known house brands with distinctive names are Kenmore appliances and Die Hard batteries, both of which are sold by Sears. Similarly, Eight O'Clock Coffee and Ann Page were house brands sold by A&P supermarkets.

Generic Brands   Supermarkets usually carry a third category of brands called **generic brands** (also called no-frill or no-name brands). Generics are not identified by any brand name and are normally sold in plain white packaging. Generics started appearing on supermarket shelves during the inflationary periods of the 1970s. Prices significantly below those of manufacturer brands were expected to make generics appeal to price-conscious consumers. They have not, however, become a significant factor in the grocery industry. Despite the fact that most grocery stores in the country carry generic products, they account for only a small percent of total grocery sales.[4]

Trend toward House Brands

As margins have tightened on many manufacturer brands, some supermarket chains have aggressively developed private labels to protect their margins and also to give customers a greater choice. Because of their size, large supermarkets can garner considerable economies of scale to package and distribute their own brands efficiently. For example, Albertson's, a 452-outlet chain, makes private labels available in all major product lines, and they account for approximately 20 percent of total sales.[5] According to one report, in 1992 private label goods accounted for 18.3 percent of all units sold and 14 percent of total dollar sales in grocery stores. On the average, the sales of private label goods grew twice as fast as manufacturer brands during 1992.[6]

There are a number of reasons for the recent growth of private label brands in supermarkets. The quality of many private-label brands has improved significantly overcoming consumer resistance to private-label products in general. This at a time when the recessionary economy prompted consumers to seek better value in their food purchases. During the 1980s, many food manufacturers increased their prices to keep their sales growing. This has prompted many consumers to switch to private labels. The share of private-label diapers, cold medications, and analgesics, for example, were around 13.0 percent of their total sales in 1992.[7] This is not to imply, however, that manufacturer brands are no longer important for supermarkets. They continue to dominate supermarket shelves because of their strong consumer images and easily identified quality.

In recent years, house brands of apparel have also become important. As department and apparel specialty stores rely less on manufacturer labels and more on promoting their own private labels. Private labels or house brands give the retailer greater control over the merchandise and more opportunity to develop exclusive images. While customers recognize manufacturer brands more easily, different types of competing retailers sell them. A brand sold by a department store may also be available from off-price retailers or mail-order catalogs at much lower prices. This decreases the exclusive image of the department store and its freedom to set its own prices. Moreover, the popularity of designer names can vary considerably over time as fashions change, forcing retailers to change suppliers every time a new designer label becomes popular. House brands give retailers more flexibility in dealing with changing trends and more control over prices. Finally, and perhaps most importantly, reliance on manufacturer labels decreases store loyalty, since they are available at many outlets. A private label, because it is sold exclusively by one store, builds consumer loyalty toward the store.

These problems with manufacturer brands have prompted many retailers to strengthen their private labels, and some already devote a large portion of their apparel merchandise to house brands. Nordstrom, for example, aims to carry 60 to 70 percent of all merchandise in private labels. Other department stores such as Dayton Hudson, Carter Hawley Hale, I. Magnin, and Macy's all have substantial private label programs. Specialty apparel chains such as The Gap and The Limited have also invested heavily in private labels.

Private label programs, however, are not so prominent in discount stores. Discount stores have to rely more on well-known manufacturer labels to attract their target customers. K mart, for example, de-emphasized its own apparel house brands and devoted more space to designer and manufacturer brands in order to create a more fashionable image.

The trend toward private brands is not universal, and some firms have actually reduced their emphasis on private brands in recent years. Sears, for example, has strengthened its representation of well-known manufacturer brands of appliances and electronics. Similarly, A&P has reduced the scope of its private brand program over the years and emphasized manufacturers' brands instead.

PLANNING MERCHANDISE ASSORTMENT

Once the retailer has decided on the proper balance between variety and assortment and the mix of brands, it must then select the assortment of merchandise within each line in terms of styles, brands, colors, sizes, and price ranges. As noted earlier, the almost unlimited choice makes this a difficult task. Two factors the retailer must specially consider in this respect are its desired fashion image and the spectrum of prices it wants to cover. Both will, of course, vary from store to store depending on target market and store image.

Fashion Orientation

Many retailers deal with **fashion merchandise**. That is, in addition to its functional properties, buyers also judge this merchandise in terms of its style. Fashion products are important to retailers, especially apparel stores, because they represent significant sales opportunities. Fashion merchandise helps to attract customers to the store and enhances store image. Moreover, fashion products generally yield high margins and greater-than-average profits since consumers are often relatively insensitive to price when buying them.

Because fashions can change quickly, retailing fashion merchandise is inherently risky. The highly uncertain life cycles of fashion products react to changes in cultural and social norms and to fashion trends. As one of its biggest challenges, the retailer of fashion products must anticipate general consumer acceptance of fashion trends and determine the amount of merchandise to keep in stock. The retailer must also judge whether its target market will follow the fashion trend.

Fashion merchandise can be classified into four categories: fads, best sellers, classics, and revivals. Exhibit 10.6 shows the life cycle characteristics of each of these fashion categories.

Fads   A fad displays rapid sales growth after introduction, but its life cycle is short and sales soon decline rapidly. Retailers gain little from repeat sales of fad products. The life cycle of a fad can range from a few weeks to several months depending on the product. Fads are common in the toy industry. Trivial Pursuit, Pictionary, Rubik's Cube, hand-held video games, and Trolls are some examples of fad products. Although fads have short life cycles, they usually generate a great deal of profit before they fade.

One problem in managing fad products is estimation of the depth of stock needed. Retailers would like to keep only limited stocks of fad items in order to minimize financial loss if the fad does not catch on. But if stocks are low and the fad does catch on, it may lose sales because of stockouts. This uncertainty makes fad products risky.

Best Sellers   A best seller is a fashion that is currently in its growth stage. These fashions enjoy wide recognition and acceptance by consumers. This category covers particular colors, styles or cuts, or designer merchandise that might be in vogue. Their wide consumer acceptance makes best sellers important sources of sales and profits for retailers. More importantly, retailers must stock best sellers to protect their fashion images and satisfy customer demand.

Classics   The third type of fashion merchandise, the classic, is an enduring style that remains popular with a sizable group of customers over a long period of time.

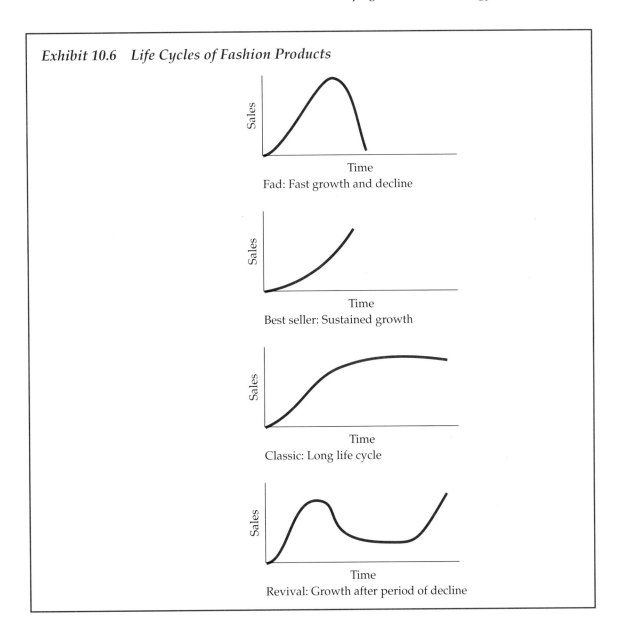

Exhibit 10.6   Life Cycles of Fashion Products

Fad: Fast growth and decline

Best seller: Sustained growth

Classic: Long life cycle

Revival: Growth after period of decline

In men's clothing, pin-striped suits, tweed jackets, and navy blue blazers are examples of classic styles that are always in fashion. Men's apparel stores always keep adequate assortments of these classic styles.

Revivals   The revival is an old fashion making a comeback. Although renewing a past success, the revival should be considered a new product. Retailers should first test the market by stocking small amounts before committing themselves heavily to revival merchandise.

Selecting the Appropriate Fashion Orientation   The fashion orientation of an apparel store's merchandise critically affects its image. For this reason, most apparel and department stores define their target markets in terms of customers' fashion orientations. Some stores carry the latest, most fashion-forward merchandise to attract fashion-conscious customers. Although these fashion-conscious customers are relatively insensitive to price, this type of merchandise brings considerable risk since it is not typically suitable for mass consumption.[8] Merchandise buyers at fashion-forward stores such as Neiman-Marcus, I. Magnin, Bergdorf Goodman, and The Limited must pick winners, and pick them early. Just as important is the ability to recognize mistakes quickly and take corrective actions.[9]

Most stores, on the other hand, prefer to follow fashions rather than lead them. Their customers have only moderate interest in fashion innovation and lag a little behind fashion trends. This strategy exposes the store to less risk since it can predict the demand for merchandise items with more confidence after trends become clear. However, this strategy brings fewer rewards, too, since customers who respond to it tend to be more price sensitive, typically reducing the store's margins.

Fashion Orientations of Customer Segments   The different fashion orientations of customers at different types of apparel stores is apparent in the results from the consumer survey reported in Exhibit 10.7.[10] The exhibit shows the fashion involvement of customers of four classes of stores selling men's apparel: (1) discount stores and mass merchandisers, (2) department stores, (3) mid-range fashion specialty stores, and (4) fashion-forward specialty stores. The survey interviewed nearly 2,400 male apparel shoppers in three North American cities. The survey results show significantly different fashion orientations among the four groups of shoppers. The customers of the specialty stores are the most fashion conscious and best informed about fashion trends. They read fashion news regularly and keep their wardrobes up-to-date with the latest fashion trends. Most discount-store shoppers, on the other hand, are either not interested in fashion or pay attention only to major fashion changes.

Customers perceive other differences besides fashion orientations among the four groups of stores, as highlighted in Exhibit 10.8. Most shoppers perceive discount stores to have the lowest prices, but the worst quality; the image of the high-fashion specialty store is diametrically opposite in these respects. The specialty stores are also perceived to have the most knowledgeable salespeople and the most exciting displays. Department stores' major strengths are their large assortments and overall value. The particular brands that a store carries also influence customer perception of the store's image (see Research Report: The Link between Brand and Store Image).

Exhibit 10.7 Fashion Orientations of Apparel Shoppers

Fashion interest: Reaction to Changing Fashions	Discounter/ Mass Merchandiser	Department Store	Midrange Fashion Specialty Chain	High- Fashion Specialty Chain	
Number of stores	3	9	10	7	
1. Read fashion news regularly and keep wardrobe up-to-date with fashion trends	0% ⎤	3% ⎤	1% ⎤	5% ⎤	
2. Keep informed of fashion changes, but do not always follow	⎬ 7%[a]	⎬ 19%[a]	⎬ 15%	⎬ 34%	
	7 ⎦	16 ⎦	14 ⎦	29 ⎦	
3. Check what is fashionable only if buying new clothes	20	25	25	26	
4. Only pay attention to major fashion changes	44	35	46	29	
5. Not at all interested in fashion	29	21	14	11	
Total	100%	100%	100%	100%	
Base	189	1,052	340	181	

[a] Among shoppers in the three cities who shopped at the nine department stores, 19 percent qualified as consumer fashion change agents; among those shoppers in the three cities who shopped at the three discounter/mass merchandisers, 7 percent qualified as consumer fashion change agents.

Source: Charles W. King and Lawrence J. Ring, "Market Positioning across Fashion Institutions: A Comparative Analysis of Store Types," *Journal of Retailing* Vol. 56, Spring 1980, p. 44. Reprinted with permission.

The Price Spectrum

Like fashion orientation, each store also has a **price spectrum** or price orientation. This, too, depends on the characteristics of the store's desired target market. A prestige-oriented specialty apparel store, for example, may sell ladies' dresses in the $100 to $250 range, while a mass merchandiser may focus on dresses in the $30 to $70 range. As discussed previously, the appropriate price range depends on the store's position on the shopping opportunity line and the image that it wishes to portray. A store is likely to confuse its image if it carries merchandise in too wide a price range.

Price Lining   Many apparel stores limit their prices to a few (often just three) price points to aid consumers' searches. This is known as **price lining**. An apparel store, for example, may carry blouses at three price points, low ($19.99), medium ($34.99), and high ($49.99). The store decides how many styles of blouses and how much stock to carry in each price category based on the pattern of past sales. In

Exhibit 10.8   Perceived Images of Types of Apparel Stores

Determinant of Patronage	Discounter/ Mass Merchandiser Average	Department Store Average	Midrange Fashion Specialty Chain Average	High- Fashion Specialty Chain Average
1. Easiest to get to from home	41%[a]	48%	32%	14%
2. Lowest prices	60	30	26	12
3. Highest quality	2	17	34	51
4. Best value for the money	47	54	50	43
5. Most knowledgeable, helpful salesclerks	21	38	50	65
6. Largest overall assortment/selection	27	43	33	20
7. Most exciting display	14	31	29	52
8. Best advertising	18	39	18	28
9. Best for conservative everyday men's wear	31	43	35	27
10. Best for current, up-to-date men's wear	21	29	31	63
11. Best for very latest, most fashionable men's wear	9	19	26	58

[a] On average, among respondents who "last shopped" at a discounter/mass merchandiser, 41 percent also said the discounter/mass merchandiser was the "easiest to get to from home," and 60 percent said the discounter/mass merchandiser had the "lowest prices."

Source: Adapted from Charles W. King and Lawrence J. Ring, "Market Positioning across Fashion Institutions: A Comparative Analysis of Store Types," *Journal of Retailing*, Vol. 56, Spring 1980, p. 50. Adapted with permission.

addition to price, the store must also carefully plan its distribution of sizes, styles, and colors. These, too, should closely follow demand patterns and customer preferences.

Merchandise Lists

To help them plan assortments within each merchandise line, retailers compile **merchandise lists**. Three common lists are: (1) basic stock list, (2) model stock list, and (3) never out list.

Basic Stock List   The basic stock list gives retailers a planning tool to determine their assortments of staple merchandise. Staple items are those that always stay in demand, requiring stores to remain well-stocked with them. For example, a supermarket must always carry Coca-Cola, Pepsi, and other popular brands of soft drinks. Similarly, socks and briefs are basic to any men's wear department. The basic stock list specifies in a standardized form the stock keeping units (SKUs) of staple items in the merchandise mix. The basic stock list also includes information on the minimum stock, expected sales, and frequency of reorders for each item. Often the names or identification numbers of the manufacturers and suppliers also appear.

The basic stock list simplifies the process of maintaining adequate inventories of basic products. Retailers who do not maintain formal stock lists often neglect maintenance of adequate stocks of their basic merchandise and experience frequent stockouts of these items. Stockouts of staple merchandise seriously harm the store's image since consumers are likely to form poor opinions of a store that runs out of staple items. Customers who cannot find aspirin at a drugstore, pens at a stationery store, or socks at a department store are unlikely to return to those stores in the future.

Model Stock List   The model stock list helps retailers plan their offerings of fashion merchandise. Fashion merchandise raises planning difficulties because of the changing demand for fashion goods. Since the demand for particular styles, colors, or brands can change over time, the model stock list is much more general than the basic stock list. For example, in developing the model stock list for a men's shirt department, the guidelines may state type of shirt (casual, dress), type of collars, sizes, type of fabrics, and prices. The model stock list simply specifies how the total stock of merchandise should be allocated among the different classifications in order to properly balance the assortment.

Never Out List   Some merchandise items are always in high demand. The retailer must take special measures to ensure that these stocks are always available. The never out list includes best-selling items of which the retailer cannot afford to run out. Most retailers set rigid standards to maintain inventory of best sellers to avoid stockouts, since failure to meet consumer demand for best sellers inevitably results in loss. Consumers typically find the product at another store rather than waiting for the stock to be replenished. Never out lists are commonly used for book departments, key seasonal items, and rapidly selling fashion merchandise. The list is updated frequently to delete items no longer in high demand and to add new ones.

NEW PRODUCT DECISIONS

The fourth element of effective merchandising strategy is a proper balance between new and established products. A retailer's merchandise mix comprises thousands of different items. A typical supermarket, for example, stocks about 20,000 items,

ENTREPRENEURIAL EDGE

Shopping for Office Supplies Supermarket Style

In 1985, Tom Sternberg launched Staples, the first deep-discount office supplies superstore, and single-handedly spawned an industry that now totals over $1 billion in retail sales. Staples operates 68 stores (in the Northeast and California), each averaging 16,500 square feet, selling office supplies from paper clips to desks. The company has annual sales totalling over $300 million, and even though Sternberg virtually created the industry and opened the door to scores of competitors, Staples remains adept at fending off even the most serious of competitors and staying atop its own industry.

The notion of shopping for office supplies as one would shop for food was a completely new idea in 1985. The brightly lit stores are similar to warehouse clubs in appearance and offer over 5,000 items usually priced as much as 50 percent below list price. Sternberg works with three basic tenets: cut costs, buy in volume, and slash selling prices. This novel approach to selling office supplies has taken the business community by storm—it makes shopping for office supplies easier and cheaper—and customers keep coming back.

Initially, customers were wary about shopping for office supplies in this kind of setting. The stores are vast spaces with the merchandise stacked in crates, like a warehouse, and the customers are greeted with the sight of rows of shopping carts, like a supermarket. It took customers some time to get accustomed to Staple's concept. However, Sternberg, who had a highly successful career in the supermarket industry before opening Staples, knew how to reach the consumer, and through a combination of aggressive promotion and clever advertising he managed to build up a loyal customer base.

Other retailers have now followed the one-stop shopping concept for office supplies. For example, Texas-based BizMart, has grown into a 45-store chain since its founding in 1988, with each store over 22,000 square feet. Its owner likes to think of BizMart as the Toys R Us of the office supply industry. In BizMart's area of operations, most office supply stores average a 2,000 item inventory, while BizMart offers close to 7,000 items in its stores. As customers realize the value of these stores and seek out this shopping format for their office supplies, most warehouse-style office supply stores are certain to open.

Source: "Retailing's Entrepreneurs of the Year," *Chain Store Age Executive*, December 1990, p. 28–38.

and a large supermarket can have many more. Some of these items are staples like milk and ketchup; others are new products such as microwave popcorn, low-calorie beef, and gourmet cat food. Similarly, department stores carry classic designs, but they don't ignore fashion trends. Despite the inherent risk, retailers have to carry some new products to satisfy the needs of their customers and project progressive images.

Manufacturers and their representatives continually approach retailers to sell the hundreds of new products they introduce into the market each year. For example, over 12,000 new grocery items were introduced in 1989 alone.[11] Before agreeing to sell new products, retailers must evaluate them in detail, a complicated job requiring consideration of a wide variety of factors.

The situation facing Mr. Victor Bruno, the merchandise manager of a supermarket chain headquartered at Jacksonville, Florida, is quite typical. The chain operates 22 stores in seven Florida cities. A salesperson from a national manufacturer recently approached Mr. Bruno regarding a new line of ready-to-drink iced coffees. The drinks were available in special asceptic packages that are now widely used for fruit juices and drinks because they do not require refrigeration. The manufacturer's new product line consists of four varieties of coffee, each in caffeinated and decaffeinated forms: (1) with milk and sugar, (2) without sugar, (3) without milk, (4) without milk and sugar. Should Mr. Bruno agree to stock the new drinks in his stores?

Factors Affecting New Product Introduction Decisions

Mr. Bruno must consider a number of different factors in deciding whether or not to carry the new item. These factors can be grouped into four categories: (1) demand factors, (2) balance with existing merchandise, (3) financial criteria, and (4) level of manufacturer support for the new product.

Demand Factors   First, Mr. Bruno has to consider the potential demand for product. He must seek answers to questions such as:

- Will my customers buy the product? This is a prime consideration in any merchandising decision. The new product is bound to fail if the store's customers do not demand it.
- What is the current stage of the product's life cycle? The stage of the product's life cycle will determine future demand for the product.

Balance with Existing Merchandise   A favorable demand environment is a primary requisite for successful merchandising. In addition, Mr. Bruno must examine how the new product will affect the balance of his existing merchandise:

- Will the new product complement the store's existing merchandise or compete with it?

Complementary products are typically used together. Photographic film and cameras are examples of two perfectly complementary products, as are flashlights and batteries. Perfect complements must always be used together—one cannot function without the other.

One product can also be an indirect complement of another. Most fast-food restaurants sell beverages along with food. Customers typically purchase indirect complements like beverages and fast-foods together, although they can be consumed separately. By carrying complementary products, retailers can increase consumer convenience, thus allowing them to buy both products at the same time.

Financial Criteria   Mr. Bruno must also consider how the new product will affect the store's financial goals. For example, he must determine:

- How much margin will the new product generate?
- How quickly will the merchandise turn over?
- How much space will the new product occupy?
- Will the store have to drop some other merchandise to provide space for the iced coffees?

Level of Manufacturer Support   The decision to carry a new product also hinges on the policies of manufacturers and wholesalers:

- What is the manufacturer's track record in introducing new products?
- How well do consumers know the manufacturer's name?
- Will the manufacturer support the new product with adequate advertising and promotion?
- Do the results of consumer research support the new product introduction?

Proper market research reduces (but never eliminates) the risk that the product will fail. Retailers more willingly introduce new products in their stores if the product is supported by good research and successful test market experiments. In a test market experiment, a new product is first introduced in a few retail outlets to judge consumer reactions.

If Mr. Bruno decides to carry the product, he must consider a further set of issues to develop a coherent policy for the product:

- Should all 22 stores stock the new product or only selected stores?
- Should the chain carry all eight items in the product line?
- Should the chain shelve the iced coffees with dairy products or with other packaged juices and drinks?
- How much space should stores devote to the product?
- Should they carry the product year round or only during the summer?
- How many boxes of each type of iced coffee should be kept in stock?

The questions facing Mr. Bruno illustrate the complexity in evaluating new merchandise items. As the most important criterion, new products should be consis-

This retail salesperson at Nordstrom is a valuable source of information on consumer concerns and preferences.

tent with the overall merchandising strategy and satisfy the needs and expectations of the firm's target market. For example, a few years ago, one leading department store on the East Coast decided to carry KIKIT and Basco brand clothes in its men's department. Both brands were considered to be fashion leaders, trendy, and somewhat more costly than brands such as Izod and Liz Claiborne. The typical customer of this store, however, was not highly fashion-forward; rather, its customers tended toward conservative tastes and bought mostly moderately priced clothes. Very few of the store's customers bought the new lines, and it dropped them after a year. While KIKIT and Basco are popular brands at many department stores, in this case they matched neither the expectations of the store's target customer, nor its overall merchandise strategy.

Retailers need to base their merchandising decisions on some idea of consumer demand for different items. Past sales records reliably guide decisions for staple items with consistent demand patterns. New items, of course, lack any past sales records, so the retailer must rely on various internal and external sources to gather information on new products and services. Some of the major sources of **new product information** are shown in Exhibit 10.9 and described in the next section.

Exhibit 10.9   Sources of Information for New Products

Internal Sources
- Sales Personnel
- Want Slips
- Resident Buying Offices
- In-Store Experiment

External Sources
- Competitor Surveys
- Consumer Surveys
- Focus Groups
- Manufacturers' Representatives and Brokers
- Trade Shows
- Trade and Fashion Publications

Internal Sources of New Merchandise Information

Sales Personnel   Retail salespeople come in direct contact with customers which makes them a good source of information on consumer preferences. Sales personnel can tell management which merchandise items are selling and which are not and can provide information on new merchandise items that the store should stock. Most consumers direct inquiries about new merchandise to the store's sales personnel. If the store does not carry merchandise for which consumers ask, the sales personnel should record and report that information to the management.

Want Slips   The want slip provides a formal procedure for sales personnel to record consumer inquiries. Every time a consumer asks for merchandise the store does not stock or that is temporarily out of stock, the sales person notes it on a want slip. The slip must describe the merchandise in detail, noting brand, color, size, style, and so forth, to provide adequate guidance to merchandise buyers.

Resident Buying Offices   The resident buying office is another important source of merchandise information. Most department stores maintain resident buying offices in such major market centers as New York, Chicago, and Los Angeles, and sometimes even in major foreign markets such as Paris, London, and Milan. A resident buying office helps store buyers identify potential suppliers and keep in touch with the latest merchandise trends.[12] Small retailers who cannot afford to maintain buying offices of their own use independent buying offices. As the name suggests, independent buying offices are not associated with a particular store, but perform buying office tasks for many retailers in exchange for fees.

In-Store Experiment   The demand for new products is always uncertain. Although consumer surveys and secondary sources can provide good indications of demand, a retailer can never be sure how well the merchandise will sell in the store. In-store experiments or tests invaluably aid judgments about demand for new items. These experiments offer a limited supply of new merchandise to customers, then observe how they react to the initial offering. Similarly, a chain store can conduct in-store experiments by first carrying new merchandise in a few outlets instead of all of them. Not all products, of course, will gain consumer acceptance. By carrying only a small amount of the merchandise, or by restricting it to just a few outlets, the retailer limits financial loss in case the product doesn't catch on.

Most retailers conduct in-store experiments in some form or another, but often improperly. A proper in-store experiment must simulate the conditions in which the store ultimately expects to sell the merchandise. The merchandise must benefit from proper advertisement and promotion during the test period. Sales personnel must give it adequate attention, and its displays must attract customer attention. Unless the experiment is conducted properly, the results cannot be used with confidence.

External Sources of New Merchandise Information

Competitor Surveys   Competitors' merchandise provides an excellent source of product information for retailers. Astute retailers regularly survey the merchandise offerings of other stores through comparison shopping programs. Trained observers regularly visit both competing and noncompeting stores to note their merchandise offerings and prices. They also observe the characteristics of the customers patronizing each store and the in-store displays and promotions in each. Retailers can augment information from comparison shopping by comparing advertisements run by different stores. This often reveals information on new products that other retailers are featuring. Although competitor surveys are an important source of information, retailers should not simply imitate the merchandising strategies of competitors, since other stores may have different target markets.

Consumer Surveys   To keep abreast of fashion trends, many apparel and department stores conduct fashion counts. Trained surveyors "located in areas of heavy customer traffic tabulate the clothing worn by passersby according to color, style, pattern, material, and so forth."[13] The fashion count provides an overall picture of current trends and styles against which retailers can compare their merchandise assortments to remain up-to-date.

Focus Groups   The focus group is another technique for obtaining information from consumers. A focus group session gathers a small group of people who are representative of the store's target market to discuss styles, fashions, colors, and other merchandise features. The group may also be asked to discuss the store's branding policy, prices, in-store displays, and any other aspect of the store's operation. Focus group discussions are usually informal, requiring participants to fill out no questionnaires, and are led by a moderator who directs the discussion to the relevant areas. Focus group discussions have an advantage over individual interviews in that the group setting fosters interaction and uncovers ideas that probably would not emerge in other types of consumer surveys, such as individual interviews.[14]

Manufacturers' Representatives and Brokers   One of the most direct sources of information about products are manufacturers and their brokers. Most manufacturers deploy their own sales forces or independent brokers to call on retail buyers with information about existing and new products. Wholesalers, too, are an excellent source of product information. For example, wholesalers can provide information on sales of a new brand in other areas or how many other outlets in the area carry the new brand.

Trade Shows   A trade show gives a retailer an excellent opportunity to learn about new products. At a trade show manufacturers exhibit their merchandise to retailers and wholesalers, offering the retailer the opportunity to compare their merchandise and marketing programs. Trade shows feature almost all merchandise categories. In the apparel industry, for example, merchandise buyers travel to New York, Los Angeles, Dallas, and Chicago a few times each year to attend trade shows and find out about the latest fashions and trends. Similarly, housewares buyers learn about new products at the annual housewares show held in Chicago.

Trade and Fashion Publications   Trade publications and fashion magazines are important sources of merchandise information for retailers. For example, *Women's Wear Daily* (WWD) is invaluable for women's and children's clothing buyers and the *Daily News Record* (DNR) is required reading for all men's wear buyers. Similarly, publications such as the *Progressive Grocer, Convenience Store Merchandiser, Chain Store Age Executive, Hardware Retailer*, and *American Druggist* provide information to different types of retailers. Trade publications give information on new merchandise and new management trends, along with useful advertisements by manufacturers. For fashion products, magazines such as *Vogue, Glamour*, and *Gentlemen's Quarterly* also help retailers keep abreast of current trends in consumer tastes and preferences.

Research Service Firms   A number of research service firms provide periodic reports on merchandise trends. Based on information from both domestic and foreign markets, the reports provide information on the popularity of different brands and styles, and trends in advertising, display, and prices. Buyers of fashion products refer to these reports quite extensively when planning their merchandise assortment.

Summary

1. Merchandise decisions affect and are also affected by both the marketing and financial aspects of retail operations. Merchandise decisions must be guided by the store's target market and its position on the shopping opportunity line. The store's merchandise policy affects the amount of funds the firm will have to invest in inventory; the amount of space, labor, and equipment it will require for stock and display; and the types of customers it can attract.

2. Four important dimensions of merchandise policy are (a) balance between variety and assortment of merchandise; (b) balance between manufacturers' brands, house brands, and generic products (in the case of supermarkets); (c) selection of assortment within merchandise lines; and (d) balance between established and new merchandise items.

3. Retailers combine variety and assortment in one of four possible ways: (a) low variety–low assortment, (b) emphasis on assortment, (c) emphasis on variety, (d) balance between variety and assortment. Two apparently contradictory trends are affecting variety and assortment. Supermarkets and drugstores are increasing their varieties through scrambled merchandising, while in the general-merchandise field, specialty stores are growing in importance. In branding, many apparel stores are carrying more house or store brands.

4. The retailer must select the assortment of merchandise to carry within each line. Two factors it must consider in this respect are its desired fashion image and the spectrum of prices to cover. Fashion merchandise can be classified into four categories: (a) fads, (b) best sellers, (c) classics, and (d) revivals. Each has a life cycle of its own.

5. To plan their merchandise mixes, retailers maintain different types of merchandise lists. Three common ones are (a) basic stock list, (b) model stock list, and (c) never out list.

6. Every year thousands of new products enter the market. Retailers must evaluate these new items carefully before deciding to sell them, and consider the market environment for these products: their profit potentials, trade policies of the manufacturers, and their relationship to existing products. Retailers have to rely on both internal and external sources for information on new merchandise. Sales personnel, want slips, resident buying offices, and in-store experiments are four internal sources. External sources include competitor and consumer surveys, vendors, trade shows, trade and fashion publications, and research service firms.

Key Concepts

Merchandising strategy	Gross margin return on investment (GMROI)
Merchandise performance	Direct product profit (DPP)
Gross margin	Variety
Sales per square foot	Assortment
Inventory (or stock) turnover	Stock keeping units (SKUs)

Depth
Scrambled merchandising
Brand policy
Manufacturer brands
Private label (house) brands
Generic brands

Fashion merchandise
Price spectrum
Price lining
Merchandise lists
Complementary products
New product information

Discussion Questions

1. Select two local retailers and discuss how their merchandise policies reflect their marketing strategies.
2. Define the terms *variety*, *assortment*, and *depth*. How are variety and assortment policies interrelated?
3. What is an SKU? How does one SKU differ from another?
4. State the advantages and disadvantages of each of the four variety-assortment policies. Give examples of local retailers who follow each of the four strategies.
5. You are the merchandise manager for the housewares department of a department store. Last week a manufacturer's representative informed you about a new type of ice-cream maker the firm would soon introduce into the market. Prepare a list of questions you would ask the representative before agreeing to carry the product. Also indicate how the answers to those questions might affect your decision.
6. Define a (a) basic stock list, (b) model stock list, and (c) never out list. What type of merchandise do each of these lists cover?
7. Describe the sources of new merchandise information.
8. Explain the following terms: (a) classic, (b) fad, (c) want slip, (d) best seller, and (e) price lining.

Notes

1. David Moin, "A High-Yield Strategy for Career RTW," *Women's Wear Daily*, April 16, 1984, p. 4.
2. Walter K. Levy, "Department Stores—the Next Generation: Form and Rationale," *Retailing Issues Letter* 1, no. 1 (1987).
3. Ibid.
4. See, for example, "No Frills Products Decline in Popularity," *Wall Street Journal*, November 15, 1984, p. 34; and Martha R. McEnally and Jon M. Hawes, "The Market for Generic Brand Grocery Products: A Review and Extension," *Journal of Marketing* 48 (Winter 1984), pp. 75–83.
5. *Albertson's Financial Highlights 1986*, Albertson's Inc., Boise, Idaho.
6. Kathleen Deveny, "More Shoppers Bypass Big-Name Brands and Steer Carts to Private-Label Products," *Wall Street Journal*, October 20, 1992, pp. B1 and B9.
7. Ibid.
8. Ronald D. Shipp, *Retail Merchandising* (Boston: Houghton Mifflin, 1985), p. 11.
9. Ibid.
10. Charles W. King and Lawrence J. Ring, "Market Positioning Across Retail Fashion Institutions: A Comparative Analysis of Store Types," *Journal of Retailing* 56 (Spring 1980), pp. 37–55.

11. Edward W. McLaughlin and Vithala R. Rao, *Decision Criteria for New Product Acceptance and Success* (New York: Quorom Books, 1991).

12. Ralph F. Shipp, *Retail Merchandising* (Boston: Houghton Mifflin, 1985), p. 11.

13. Ibid. p. 290.

14. Bobby Calder, "Focus Groups and the Nature of Qualitative Market Research," *Journal of Marketing Research*, August 1977, pp. 353–64.

CHAPTER 11
Implementing Merchandise Strategy

One Day in the Life of a Retail Buyer

A day in the life of a retail buyer is both hectic and exciting. For Wade Danis, assistant buyer at Macy's, the day starts early. Wade is the buyer for men's outerwear and beachwear, and he is responsible for 46 Macy's stores in New York, New Jersey, Pennsylvania, and Maryland. An average day for Wade begins at 8:00 A.M. with a visit to a vendor to see the upcoming line of clothing the vendor has to offer. Over coffee and donuts, Wade is shown the entire new line, the different display options, and the selection combinations the vendor hopes to sell to Macy's. Wade discusses the prices and lead-times involved with a possible order. By 10:00 A.M., Wade is at his desk in Macy's, and the first order of business is to check over the numbers (sales, returns, and so on) from his area during the previous day. He then compiles these figures into a report for the head buyer of the department as well as the merchandise administrator for his area and the senior vice-president in charge of the department.

By 11:00 the reports are completed. Wade begins the long, and very important task, of writing out purchase orders. These orders contain all the merchandise order information—the color, style, size, and price—and to which stores each portion is to be shipped.

Wade must order in bulk for all 46 of his stores. Sixty to seventy percent of merchandise ordered is standard from store to store. Based on previous years' sales, there are certain "core items" that all the stores will always have in stock. For Wade's area, this might be denim jackets and down parkas in the fall and winter, and standard bathing trunks in the spring and summer. However, there are roughly 30 percent of the orders that will be considered "fringe items," that is, items that sell only in certain stores. For example, flashy men's bikini trunks sell in the urban stores, while more teenage trunks are sold in the suburban stores. When he has completed this task, Wade must then contact all the vendors and shippers involved in the order to set delivery times and define an inventory flow that will allow the stock to move smoothly between Macy's warehouses.

Another part of Wade's usual morning routine is general trouble-shooting. Wade must track late orders and shipments and call the vendors or shippers to determine where late inventory is within the shipping process. Or, if a sale is coming up and the catalogues haven't arrived, Wade must track them down in order to ensure that they will be in the stores on the day of the sale to entice shoppers to buy. Or perhaps the problem is in the store, where a scheduled display cannot be completed because some of the merchandise

After studying this chapter, the reader will be able to:
- *Understand the organization of merchandise management functions.*
- *Explain the tasks of retail merchandising personnel.*
- *Describe the advantages and disadvantages of centralized buying.*
- *Forecast merchandise sales, prepare monthly sales estimates, and plan stock levels.*
- *Plan monthly purchases and calculate open-to-buy (OTB).*
- *Know the factors that should be considered in selecting vendors and understand how buying terms affect cost of goods.*

has not arrived; for that problem, Wade must check through the store inventory, the stockroom inventory, and even call vendors and shippers until he locates the necessary items.

Just before lunch, Wade visits the advertising office, to check on an upcoming advertisement featuring items from his department. When Macy's plans advertisements, catalogues, or brochures, management decides how much space each department will be allotted in the publication, and then it is up to the buyers or the assistant buyers to choose which items will be featured in the allotted space. For example, if Wade's area has a summer spread upcoming, Wade must be sure that the right swimsuits and beachwear are featured, in the colors and styles the department wishes to promote.

Finally, Wade checks all the journal entries for his department's merchandise to verify that all the inventory was logged correctly: in and out of the main warehouse, to and from each store, and in and out of each store's department. This last bit of in-office work is key, to make sure that everything is where it is supposed to be and can be tracked at all times.

Wade spends the afternoon visiting stores within his region, to ensure that the merchandising for each store is going according to plan. Each store in his region is graded, A through D, depending on the sales volume at that outlet. "A" stores are visited at least once a week, while "D" stores are visited once a month. Typically, Wade will drive from the New York City store to visit some of the other big stores in the area. He wants to make sure that his department is merchandised correctly in these stores. On arriving at a store, he checks over displays and in-store stockrooms. On the selling floor, Wade checks to see that all the styles are on display, that the department is filled in (meaning that there are no unnecessary gaps in the display areas), that the actual displays are set up properly, that the area is visually appealing, and that the sales associates are knowledgeable and are giving the right product information to the customers. He might also devise a "floor move," in which all the merchandise is rearranged in order to look more appealing to customers, or any other action that will help to get the "look" of the department just right.

At 6:00 P.M., Wade is back at the New York City store, to finalize the details of a large order with a vendor. Negotiations have been going on for a few weeks over a large order of raincoats for the upcoming season. Certain issues such as getting return privileges for items that may not sell, getting the vendor to split markdown costs on items that must be reduced in order to sell, or having the vendors provide fixtures for floor displays, have already been settled. A number of issues, however, still need to be worked out. Some of the issues to be determined at the upcoming final meeting include delivery dates and adjustments to the order quantity. The vendor is also negotiating to have one of its items featured in a Macy's publication or advertisement. Wade mulled over these matters as he headed home that evening.

Source: Sophie Henderson: Interview with Wade Danis, formerly assistant buyer for men's outerwear and beachwear at Macy's Herald Square store, August 1992.

The previous chapter outlined the various factors that retail managers must consider in developing the overall merchandising strategy for the firm, but even the best developed strategies will fail if improperly implemented and managed. Thus, this chapter will focus on implementing merchandise strategy and Chapter 12 will focus on pricing merchandise.

The chapter is divided into three sections. The first discusses how firms organize the merchandise management function. Merchandise planning and budgeting are discussed next. The final section considers vendor selection and negotiations.

ORGANIZATION FOR MERCHANDISE MANAGEMENT

Whether a store is small or big, independent or part of a chain, the merchandising function—forecasting, budgeting, vendor selection, vendor negotiations, ordering and pricing—is always important. The goal of merchandise management is to implement the firm's overall merchandise strategy in the most profitable manner.

Merchandising Functions

To implement this goal, firms first establish the **merchandising organization**. The organization identifies the store personnel responsible for merchandising decisions and clarifies the authority of personnel at each level of the organization. The organizational structures can vary considerably from one store to another depending on the size and the type of store.

A small store, for example, may not have a formalized merchandise department; the owner or some other senior employee may be responsible for all merchandising activities along with other store management responsibilities. Large stores, on the other hand, tend to have separate departments with distinct sets of employees who are responsible for all the merchandising activities for the store.

Merchandise Buyers   Exhibit 11.1 shows the typical organization of the merchandise department in large retail firms. The person with the most direct responsibility for implementing the merchandise strategy is the **merchandise buyer**, or, more simply, the buyer. The buyer is often aided by associate or assistant buyers. A buyer in a small store typically purchases a broad variety of products spanning many merchandise lines. Large department stores, on the other hand, typically employ many buyers, each of whom specializes in one or a few related merchandise lines. While specialization increases costs, it increases the buyer's knowledge of changing market conditions, consumer trends, and prices.

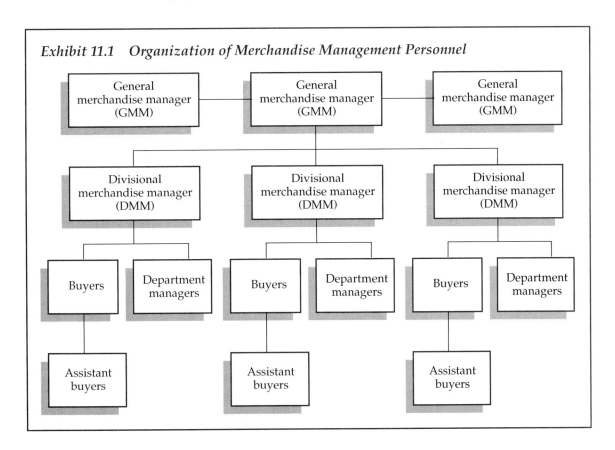

Exhibit 11.1   Organization of Merchandise Management Personnel

At large firms or small stores, buyers commonly have a number of distinct responsibilities:

1. To develop merchandise budgets to determine dollar inventory investments.
2. To convert the dollar inventory levels into specific unit plans detailing the number and specific assortments of merchandise to be purchased.
3. To evaluate alternative sources of supply and select vendors for each type of merchandise.
4. To negotiate with the vendor and obtain the merchandise.
5. To work with department managers and other store personnel to develop pricing and advertising plans.
6. To monitor sales trends and adjust buying plans, if necessary.

Tasks of Buyers   Buyers play the crucial role of translating the retail firm's marketing strategy into tangible merchandise assortments. In this process, they balance the needs of target customers with the profit potential of merchandise items. The buyer must decide which items to buy and how to display and promote them. Ultimately, the buyer answers for the profitability of these items.

The buyer's task is often complicated by long lead times between their orders for an item and its actual arrival at the store. A department store buyer typically orders merchandise four to five months before its selling season. This makes development of proper merchandise budgets (discussed later in this chapter) a critical part of the buyer's job.

Merchandise Managers   While the buyer in a small store may report to the owner directly, as shown in Exhibit 11.1, buyers in large stores typically report to divisional **merchandise managers**, or DMMs, each of whom supervises the activities of a number of buyers and is responsible for the performance of a distinct group of merchandise. A department store, for example, may have separate DMMs for women's wear, housewares, furniture, men's wear, and so on. Similarly, supermarket chains typically have separate merchandise managers for groceries, meat, produce, and health and beauty aids.

At a really large store, general merchandise managers, or GMMs, may comprise yet another level in the organizational hierarchy. These managers usually hold the rank of vice-president, and each typically supervises three to five DMMs. Usually GMMs are not directly involved with day-to-day merchandising activities; rather, they develop the store's seasonal and annual merchandise budgets and monitor merchandising activities to ensure achievement of overall performance goals.

Department Managers   At one time, when most retail firms operated just one or two stores, the buyer could directly supervise both the purchase and the selling of the merchandise. In fact, the buyer was responsible for all merchandising activities related to the products under his or her authority. As stores got larger and

One important function of this beverage department manager at Safeway is to control the merchandise inventory.

added branches at other locations, however, the buyer could no longer oversee the merchandising activities at all the outlets. **Department managers** and assistants took over the actual handling and selling of merchandise in each store.

While department managers perform tasks integral to the merchandise management function, their role differs substantially from that of merchandise managers and buyers. They do not deal with vendors or purchase merchandise. Instead they are responsible for all activities involved in selling certain merchandise items. Note from Exhibit 11.1 that, like buyers, department managers usually specialize along merchandise lines and report to DMMs.

Department managers perform four central tasks:

1. They work with buyers to develop the merchandise assortment. As part of the "front line" that comes in regular contact with customers, the department manager develops a good feel for the styles, colors, and brands consumers' demand.
2. They lead, motivate, and manage sales personnel in serving customers.[1] Service and personal selling are two important ways in which stores create value for customers. Department managers play a critical role in supervising these activities.

RESEARCH REPORT

Retail Buyers' Salability Judgments

Decisions concerning salability of merchandise are critical to successful retail buying. A good buyer must skillfully judge the salability of merchandise based on product characteristics and vendor policies. Product characteristics include such factors as brand name, style, color, durability, country of origin, and previous sales history. Vendor policies are factors such as potential markup, advertising support, and promotional allowances provided by the vendor.

In a recent study, two professors from the University of Maryland assessed the relative importance of various product and vendor characteristics to department store buyers to judge the salability of fashion merchandise. The study asked 18 buyers and 20 assistant buyers from a major New York department store to assess the salability of misses' blouses. Each participant played the role of the store's buyer of misses' blouses, to consider descriptions of 16 buying scenarios, each described in terms of eight factors:

- Fiber content (100 percent cotton versus 65 percent cotton and 35 percent polyester)
- Cut (full versus narrow)
- Color range (wide versus narrow)
- Brand (national versus private label)
- Country of origin (from U.S. versus oriental manufacturers)
- Potential markup (50 percent versus 60 percent)
- Previous sales history (reasonably vigorous versus sold extremely vigorous)
- Advertising allowance (large versus small)

Based on the participant's response to the 16 scenarios, the researchers rated the relative importance of each of the eight factors in their salability judgments. For both groups, previous sales history was the most important criterion in judging merchandise salability. The groups differed, however, on the level of importance given to other criteria. For example, compared with assistant buyers, buyers gave much more importance to markup potential; they judged it to be almost as important as past sales. Advertising allowance, on the other hand, had a much greater impact on the judgments of assistant buyers than those of buyers.

Source: Richard Ettenson and Janet Wagner, "Retailer Buyers' Salability Judgments: A Comparison of Information Use across Three Levels of Experience," *Journal of Retailing* 62 (Spring 1986), pp. 41–63.

3. They supervise and coordinate merchandise displays, in-store advertising, and other point-of-purchase materials.
4. They control merchandise inventory. Department managers receive all merchandise, check the merchandise against purchase orders, return damaged and soiled merchandise, and monitor merchandise availability and sales trends.

Retail Buyers as Social Gatekeepers

The merchandise buyer plays a pivotal role in implementing the firm's merchandise strategy. Not only do they help plan and monitor merchandise inventory, but they also represent both the store and the consumer in the market for merchandise.[2] They act as the consumers' purchasing agent when they choose from among the many available items only those that best fulfill the needs of the store's target market. For this reason, retail buyers (as well as merchandise managers directly involved in buying) are often described as social gatekeepers.[3]

The term gatekeeper refers to a person who has the authority to decide which items will enter or not enter a particular channel.[4] Retail buyers are gatekeepers of products entering the retail marketplace. They examine the thousands of products available from suppliers and select the few that the store will offer for sale. In essence, consumers can choose from only the reduced set of products that buyers preselected for them.[5] An item that buyers reject has little chance of being exposed to consumers.

In deciding which products to pass through the retail gate, buyers must always keep in mind the needs and preferences of the store's target market. If they open the gate to products that the target market does not desire, the store's sales, profits, and image suffer.

Centralization of Merchandising Functions

Retail chains that sell similar merchandise at hundreds of outlets generally centralize the responsibility for selecting and purchasing the merchandise for all outlets in a central buying office. These decisions are seldom made at individual stores. Managers at the central office plan what to buy, evaluate alternative sources of supply, select the best sources, price the goods, decide how much to buy, and allocate specified amounts to individual stores.[6] The central office regularly monitors sales records of individual stores, usually through a computer system, and replenishes their stocks as necessary. The central office also plans store displays, advertising, special sales events, and sometimes even window displays. Individual store managers have very little responsibility for merchandising in such firms; instead they concentrate on store operations only.

Centralized merchandising like this is common among apparel, food, shoes, hardware, and drug chains. Highly specialized buyers in the central offices of these chains each have responsibility for selected merchandise items. An apparel chain, for example, may assign one central buyer to specialize in tee shirts and another in moderately priced women's dresses. Similarly, one central buyer of a supermarket chain may be responsible for buying health and beauty aids for all outlets. Many chains typically operate central warehouses or a number of regional warehouses that receive all merchandise orders placed by central buying offices. Warehouse personnel inspect the quality of the merchandise and check each shipment before

The owners of The Heritage Shop in Boston design their own store displays. If this were an individual store in a retail chain, however, the store displays would be designed by the central office and would be uniform throughout the chain.

sending products to stores. In some cases, however, manufacturers ship merchandise directly to stores in order to reduce handling and transportation costs.

The growth of electronic communications systems and computerized record keeping have expanded the scope for centralized buying and merchandise control. Many, if not most, stores are now equipped with electronic point-of-sale (POS) terminals that automatically update inventory records at every sale. The system then electronically transmits data to the central office, usually at the end of each day. Central office personnel thus have access to up-to-date information on sales and stock by SKU and by outlet. Based on these records, central staff send replenishment schedules for each store to the distribution center, which ships products to the store using the most efficient means of transportation available.

Advantages of Centralization   Centralizing all merchandising activities in a single office brings a number of benefits:

• The central office can coordinate merchandising activities of individual outlets so that all stores project a uniform image for the chain.

- Consolidation also gives the firm greater bargaining power in negotiating discounts and other terms and conditions with vendors.
- Because central buyers specialize in specific types of merchandise, they become more skilled and knowledgeable than individual store buyers who deal with a wide variety of products.
- Central buying offices can develop private label merchandise more easily than individual store buyers.
- Centralization allows the firm more economies in warehousing and transportation.
- Central control makes inventory management more efficient, since a single system manages sales and stock at all outlets. For example, if an item is not selling well in one outlet, the central office can redirect some of the stock intended for that store to stores experiencing better than expected sales.

Disadvantages of Centralization   Despite its many advantages, not all firms centralize their merchandising activities because of two potential problems: (1) ineffective adaptation to local merchandise needs and (2) the possibility of friction between buying and selling personnel.

Firms that have outlets spread over a wide geographical area, especially those that specialize in fashion merchandise, often find centralization difficult because they cannot adapt the merchandise to local needs and wants. A central buyer who buys for an entire chain, may not be able to respond effectively to regional differences in merchandise needs. When merchandise requirements vary significantly from one store to another, a more decentralized organization may be needed, even at the cost of the efficiencies of centralized purchasing.

For another potential problem of centralization, separating the merchandising function from the individual store can create friction between central buyers and store sales personnel. For example, if a particular item does not sell as well as expected, the central buyer who purchased the item may blame inadequate sales support provided by store personnel. Store personnel, on the other hand, often contend that ineffective buying makes their selling efforts ineffective.

Partial Centralization   To gain some of the economies associated with centralization, and yet maintain a degree of flexibility, a number of chains give individual store managers some latitude in selecting merchandise for their stores, but direct all purchases through a central office. One common example of **partial centralization** is the central distribution system.[7]

In a central distribution system, central buyers purchase all merchandise, and vendors ship it to the chain's distribution center. Individual store managers requisition goods from the distribution center as needed. They can determine how much of each item to stock in their stores, even skipping some items altogether. Some chains give individual store managers further latitude to buy some items from local sources.

STRATEGY IN ACTION

Federated Centralizes Buying for Its Department Stores

For many years, centralized buying has been the domain of specialty retailers, mass merchandisers, and discounters. Department stores, eager to cater to local tastes, delegated buying to each individual department. This created a huge number of vendors for each store, as well as multiple vendors within each department. At Federated, the table linens section of the housewares department bought from three suppliers alone: one for the napkins, one for the tablecloths, and yet another for the placemats. This meant that product diversity was broad, but also that costs were high. But now many department stores, burdened with huge debt loads, are finding that one way to cut costs and streamline operations is to turn to centralized buying.

Specialty stores, like The Gap, Neiman-Marcus, and Saks Fifth Avenue, have long relied on centralized buying in order to maintain uniformity and consistency in their outlets. Using centralized buying ensures that customers across the country will find the same items and styles in all stores. Customers feel secure at stores with such consistency, knowing that they will never be surprised when they walk through the doors. In addition, this ensures that when their customers travel, they will shop at familiar stores if they need an extra item or an addition to their suitcase. Stores with multiple locations often prefer centralized buying because there are fewer inventory lists and orders to maintain. Centralized buying can also lead to better deals from suppliers because of the increased volume of purchase. Imagine the negotiation power Wal-Mart has over its supplier when buying for all 1,600-plus outlets at once.

Central distribution brings economies because the buyers concentrate the purchases of the entire chain. The individual store manager, on the other hand, has some flexibility in adapting to local conditions by selecting items that best suit the store. The store manager also has flexibility in deciding the amount of stock of each item to carry.

Conclusions   Because centralized buying can substantially reduce procurement costs, few stores can ignore it. Competitive pressures of cost control and the wider availability of computerized merchandise information systems have expanded the use of central buying. Central buying programs succeed depending to a large extent on how well the central buyers anticipate the merchandise requirements of consumers spanning a wide geographical area. As one major disadvantage, central buying reduces flexibility in responding to local demand patterns. Partially centralized organizations delegate some responsibility to individual store managers, allowing them to adapt centrally purchased merchandise to local conditions.

Federated Department stores, owners of Bloomingdale's, Abraham & Strauss, Burdines, Stern's, Rich's, Jordan Marsh and more, made the decision to begin centralized buying in mid-1990. It is estimated that the new centralized buying strategy will save the company millions of dollars and enable the stores to lower prices on selected items. Although this will ultimately reduce the autonomy of the company's nine chains, it will allow a commonality of merchandise in the stores that will help them make the stores more efficient in the long run. Federated has set up nine task forces, each with up to ten buyers and executives from the different chains, to buy for specific merchandise categories for all 260 stores. These teams will focus on the core items, roughly 70 percent of all items, and will leave a percentage of items to be bought individually by stores.

But customers shouldn't be wary; the rise in centralized buying by no means signals the end to the boutique style store, with one location and unique items. Rather, it signals that the larger the chain the more likely it will be to use centralized buying, for simplicity, savings, and consistency. Still, there will remain a percentage of all chains' inventory that will be bought outside the centralized buying function, focusing on local and specialty items. So while much of a chain's inventory will be similar store to store, some items will always vary region to region.

Source: Isadore Barmash: "Federated's New Buying Strategy," *The New York Times*, July 4, 1990, pp. 43, 45.

PLANNING INVESTMENT: THE MERCHANDISE BUDGET

The **merchandise budget**, one of the primary tools for planning and managing merchandise investments, specifies the planned level of sales, inventory, and purchases during a time period, for the entire store and for individual departments within it. Retailers need to carefully plan, review, and control the millions, often hundreds of millions, of dollars they invest in merchandise inventories. The merchandise budget provides "a clear cut plan for merchandise operations during a specific time period based upon careful study of existing needs and foreseeable conditions."[8] The budget states a course of action to satisfy the needs of the target market and also meet the firm's financial targets and objectives. Many executives and buyers typically combine to purchase merchandise for a store. The merchandise budget coordinates their individual activities and assigns responsibilities to each. Only through proper coordination and monitoring of the activities of individual buyers can the store reach its financial and operational goals.

The Budgeting Process

In developing the budget, a retailer judges how changes in external factors (such as the national and local economies, the level of competition, and trade area population) and in internal factors (such as the addition and deletion of merchandise lines, levels of promotion and advertising, and development of new merchandise sources) are likely to affect future sales. The budget also provides information on past plans and actual results on which the retailer can base future goals. Thus the process of developing a budget is in itself a valuable exercise, because it requires a thorough evaluation of past results and future trends. It forces managers to base purchase decisions on facts and figures rather than on guesswork and hunches.

Selecting the Budget Period   Many stores develop merchandise budgets for six-month periods, although this varies considerably. Most department and specialty apparel stores develop two 6-month budgets corresponding to the two distinct selling seasons: spring–summer and fall–winter. The spring season starts in February and the fall season in August. As shown in the retail calendar in Exhibit 11.2, the selling seasons do not always start on the same day of the year; also the calendar breaks the season into cycles of 4-5-4 week periods instead of calendar months. Organizing the retail calendar this way ensures comparability of figures from one period to another.

Selecting the Budget Unit   Before initiating the budgeting process, the firm must select the appropriate budget units, that is, the merchandise categories or classifications for which to develop separate budgets. Most stores are organized around different merchandise departments and merchandise classifications within each department; the firm must develop separate budgets for each merchandise classification to properly plan the amount of each type of merchandise to purchase.

As an example, consider a home improvement center that has six departments: lawn and garden, housewares, paint, sporting goods, hardware, and major appliances. Each department carries different classifications of related goods. The sporting goods department, for example, is classified into four groups: tennis equipment, ski equipment, camping equipment, and toys. The firm needs separate budgets for each merchandise classification since each serves as a basic control unit for merchandise management. Typically, buyers' responsibilities parallel this merchandise classification system. The home improvement center, for example, is likely to have separate buyers for each of its six departments. A large chain may assign specialized buyers in each department to handle individual classifications.

Steps in the Merchandise Budgeting Process   The sequential merchandise budgeting process comprises five important steps, as shown in Exhibit 11.3. The process starts with the forecast of expected sales for the entire store and the merchandise classifications for which separate budgets will be developed. The annual or seasonal forecast then serves as the basis for projecting monthly sales. Next, the

Exhibit 11.2   *Retail Calendar*

Fiscal 4-5-4 Calendar   53 Weeks   1993

FEBRUARY – 4 WEEKS

WEEK	SUN	MON	TUE	WED	THU	FRI	SAT
1	29	30	31	1	2	3	4
2	5	6	7	8	9	10	11
3	12	13	14	15	16	17	18
4	19	20	21	22	23	24	25

MARCH – 5 WEEKS

WEEK	SUN	MON	TUE	WED	THU	FRI	SAT
1	26	27	28	1	2	3	4
2	5	6	7	8	9	10	11
3	12	13	14	15	16	17	18
4	19	20	21	22	23	24	25
5	26	27	28	29	30	31	1

APRIL – 4 WEEKS

WEEK	SUN	MON	TUE	WED	THU	FRI	SAT
1	2	3	4	5	6	7	8
2	9	10	11	12	13	14	15
3	16	17	18	19	20	21	22
4	23	24	25	26	27	28	29

MAY – 4 WEEKS

WEEK	SUN	MON	TUE	WED	THU	FRI	SAT
1	30	1	2	3	4	5	6
2	7	8	9	10	11	12	13
3	14	15	16	17	18	19	20
4	21	22	23	24	25	26	27

JUNE – 5 WEEKS

WEEK	SUN	MON	TUE	WED	THU	FRI	SAT
1	28	29	30	31	1	2	3
2	4	5	6	7	8	9	10
3	11	12	13	14	15	16	17
4	18	19	20	21	22	23	24
5	25	26	27	28	29	30	1

JULY – 4 WEEKS

WEEK	SUN	MON	TUE	WED	THU	FRI	SAT
1	2	3	4	5	6	7	8
2	9	10	11	12	13	14	15
3	16	17	18	19	20	21	22
4	23	24	25	26	27	28	29

AUGUST – 4 WEEKS

WEEK	SUN	MON	TUE	WED	THU	FRI	SAT
1	30	31	1	2	3	4	5
2	6	7	8	9	10	11	12
3	13	14	15	16	17	18	19
4	20	21	22	23	24	25	26

SEPTEMBER – 5 WEEKS

WEEK	SUN	MON	TUE	WED	THU	FRI	SAT
1	27	28	29	30	31	1	2
2	3	4	5	6	7	8	9
3	10	11	12	13	14	15	16
4	17	18	19	20	21	22	23
5	24	25	26	27	28	29	30

OCTOBER – 4 WEEKS

WEEK	SUN	MON	TUE	WED	THU	FRI	SAT
1	1	2	3	4	5	6	7
2	8	9	10	11	12	13	14
3	15	16	17	18	19	20	21
4	22	23	24	25	26	27	28

NOVEMBER – 4 WEEKS

WEEK	SUN	MON	TUE	WED	THU	FRI	SAT
1	29	30	31	1	2	3	4
2	5	6	7	8	9	10	11
3	12	13	14	15	16	17	18
4	19	20	21	22	23	24	25

DECEMBER – 5 WEEKS

WEEK	SUN	MON	TUE	WED	THU	FRI	SAT
1	26	27	28	29	30	1	2
2	3	4	5	6	7	8	9
3	10	11	12	13	14	15	16
4	17	18	19	20	21	22	23
5	24	25	26	27	28	29	30

JANUARY – 5 WEEKS

WEEK	SUN	MON	TUE	WED	THU	FRI	SAT
1	31	1	2	3	4	5	6
2	7	8	9	10	11	12	13
3	14	15	16	17	18	19	20
4	21	22	23	24	25	26	27
5	28	29	30	31	1	2	3

Fiscal 4-5-4 Calendar   52 Weeks   1994

FEBRUARY – 4 WEEKS

WEEK	SUN	MON	TUE	WED	THU	FRI	SAT
1	4	5	6	7	8	9	10
2	11	12	13	14	15	16	17
3	18	19	20	21	22	23	24
4	25	26	27	28	1	2	3

MARCH – 5 WEEKS

WEEK	SUN	MON	TUE	WED	THU	FRI	SAT
1	4	5	6	7	8	9	10
2	11	12	13	14	15	16	17
3	18	19	20	21	22	23	24
4	25	26	27	28	29	30	31
5	1	2	3	4	5	6	7

APRIL – 4 WEEKS

WEEK	SUN	MON	TUE	WED	THU	FRI	SAT
1	8	9	10	11	12	13	14
2	15	16	17	18	19	20	21
3	22	23	24	25	26	27	28
4	29	30	1	2	3	4	5

MAY – 4 WEEKS

WEEK	SUN	MON	TUE	WED	THU	FRI	SAT
1	6	7	8	9	10	11	12
2	13	14	15	16	17	18	19
3	20	21	22	23	24	25	26
4	27	28	29	30	31	1	2

JUNE – 5 WEEKS

WEEK	SUN	MON	TUE	WED	THU	FRI	SAT
1	3	4	5	6	7	8	9
2	10	11	12	13	14	15	16
3	17	18	19	20	21	22	23
4	24	25	26	27	28	29	30
5	1	2	3	4	5	6	7

JULY – 4 WEEKS

WEEK	SUN	MON	TUE	WED	THU	FRI	SAT
1	8	9	10	11	12	13	14
2	15	16	17	18	19	20	21
3	22	23	24	25	26	27	28
4	29	30	31	1	2	3	4

AUGUST – 4 WEEKS

WEEK	SUN	MON	TUE	WED	THU	FRI	SAT
1	5	6	7	8	9	10	11
2	12	13	14	15	16	17	18
3	19	20	21	22	23	24	25
4	26	27	28	29	30	31	1

SEPTEMBER – 5 WEEKS

WEEK	SUN	MON	TUE	WED	THU	FRI	SAT
1	2	3	4	5	6	7	8
2	9	10	11	12	13	14	15
3	16	17	18	19	20	21	22
4	23	24	25	26	27	28	29
5	30	1	2	3	4	5	6

OCTOBER – 4 WEEKS

WEEK	SUN	MON	TUE	WED	THU	FRI	SAT
1	7	8	9	10	11	12	13
2	14	15	16	17	18	19	20
3	21	22	23	24	25	26	27
4	28	29	30	31	1	2	3

NOVEMBER – 4 WEEKS

WEEK	SUN	MON	TUE	WED	THU	FRI	SAT
1	4	5	6	7	8	9	10
2	11	12	13	14	15	16	17
3	18	19	20	21	22	23	24
4	25	26	27	28	29	30	1

DECEMBER – 5 WEEKS

WEEK	SUN	MON	TUE	WED	THU	FRI	SAT
1	2	3	4	5	6	7	8
2	9	10	11	12	13	14	15
3	16	17	18	19	20	21	22
4	23	24	25	26	27	28	29
5	30	31	1	2	3	4	5

JANUARY – 4 WEEKS

WEEK	SUN	MON	TUE	WED	THU	FRI	SAT
1	6	7	8	9	10	11	12
2	13	14	15	16	17	18	19
3	20	21	22	23	24	25	26
4	27	28	29	30	31	1	2

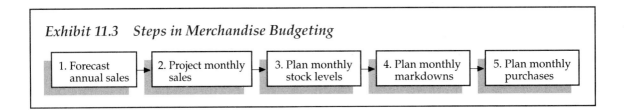

Exhibit 11.3   Steps in Merchandise Budgeting

1. Forecast annual sales → 2. Project monthly sales → 3. Plan monthly stock levels → 4. Plan monthly markdowns → 5. Plan monthly purchases

firm plans the levels of inventory and markdowns. The final step is to determine the dollar amount of merchandise to purchase.

Sales Forecasting

Sales forecasting, projecting sales for a future time period, is one of the most important elements of the merchandise budgeting process since an inaccurate forecast would introduce errors into each subsequent step in the process. Sales forecasting is both an art and a science: Forecasts must be based on proper analysis of available information as well as the forecaster's and other managers' judgments about future conditions.

Firms can forecast retail sales in either units or retail dollars, but the latter is customary. As a result, the forecast must take the rate of inflation into account. Even without any change in unit demand, sales figures will change from one period to another depending on inflation. Retail sales typically increase during periods of high inflation because of rising prices.

Sales forecasting normally progresses through three basic steps, as shown in Exhibit 11.4. The process starts with past sales, carefully analyzing historic trends in sales for each merchandise classification. Prior to arriving at the final forecast, the firm must adjust trend projections for anticipated changes in overall economic conditions that may affect consumer demand for the product. Finally, adjustments need to be made for changes in the marketing environment. Changes in the store's or its competitors' marketing strategies will also affect sales.

Measuring Past Trends   Three approaches are common for projecting future trends based on past sales. The simplest approach is to assume that the sales will increase (or decrease) by the same amount as the preceding year. Thus, if 1991 sales were 9 percent higher than 1990 sales, then the firm projects 1992 sales to be 9 percent more than the 1991 level. The second approach is to compute a moving average. Consider, for example, that sales of a product category increased by 7 percent, 8 percent, and 9 percent during 1989, 1990, and 1991, respectively. A three-year moving average would forecast 1992 sales to be 8 percent [(7 + 8 + 9)/3] above the 1991 figure. Similarly, the 1993 forecast would be based on the average increase in 1990, 1991, and 1992.

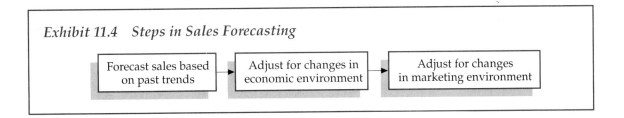

Exhibit 11.4 *Steps in Sales Forecasting*

The third approach is trend extrapolation, which projects future sales based on the trend in past sales. In the previous example, note that sales increased at an increasing rate in each of the three years. If this increasing trend continues, next year's sales increase should be even higher than last year's. By extrapolating the trend of rising sales over three years, projected 1993 sales should be 10 percent higher than 1992 sales. Although trend extrapolation is quite simple in this case, it can become a difficult manual operation when the number of data points becomes large and sales fluctuate widely from year to year. Easy-to-use statistical computer software simplifies trend extrapolation.

Although they provide a convenient starting point, past sales figures indicate what has already happened, not what will happen in the future; the firm must adjust forecasts based on past trends to reflect anticipated changes in both the economic and the marketing environments.

Adjusting for Economic Changes   Even a trend that is clearly discernible from past data must be adjusted for changes in the economic climate. In the previous example, sales may not increase by 10 percent if the economy slows down or the rate of unemployment increases. On the other hand, sales may increase more strongly if disposable income increases substantially or inflation is high. The firm must adjust the base trend after reviewing potential changes in external factors that affect retail sales.

A number of secondary sources forecast economic trends. Business publications such as *Business Week* and *The Wall Street Journal* regularly report forecasts of gross national product, disposable income, total retail sales, unemployment, and other economic indicators. Forecasts for specific geographic regions and states are also available from secondary sources for the benefit of regional and local chains.

A retailer with outlets in just one or two cities should consider economic forecasts for those specific cities rather than relying on national or regional trends. All Chambers of Commerce, local banks, newspapers, utilities, and real estate firms can supply local market information. For another useful source, *Sales and Marketing Management* magazine publishes the "Survey of Buying Power" annually; it provides data on retail sales by merchandise categories for states, counties, SMSAs, and all cities of more than 25,000 people, as discussed in Chapter 8.

Adjusting for Marketing Environment Changes   The marketing environment changes every time the firm or one of its competitors changes its marketing strategy. The firm must analyze the impact of such changes in marketing policies on future sales. Some examples of factors that may affect sales include:

- Addition of new merchandise lines.
- Changes in advertising and promotion policies.
- Expansion of store hours, particularly evening and weekend openings.
- Expansion of parking facilities and improvements in road conditions near the store.
- Upgrading of store interiors and improvements in customer service.

The most difficult part of sales forecasting is anticipating changes in competitors' marketing strategies during the forecast period, since such changes may be secret until actually implemented. It is important for the forecaster to keep abreast of competitive changes.

In summary, firms forecast annual sales for merchandise categories by adjusting their sales from the previous year to reflect projected economic conditions in the area and changes in the marketing environment. Deciding on the proper adjustment factors calls for considerable judgment, experience, and skill. The forecast should benefit from the opinions of professional forecasters as well as store managers and buyers.

Monthly Sales Estimates

The annual sales forecast estimates how much the store will sell over the entire year. To plan monthly inventory and purchases, however, the firm must allocate the annual sales projection to monthly sales estimates. Each month's share of annual sales can vary considerably because of pronounced seasonality in nonfood retail sales. For example, apparel sales peak during the months of November and December due to Christmas and decline during January and February. The monthly sales pattern also reflects the timing of storewide promotions. For example, sales of children's clothing and accessories (such as socks and shoes) are high in August and September, because of the many back-to-school sales during those months.

The monthly sales projection must be based on past seasonal patterns. Historical sales data are broken down to show each month's share of annual sales. Multiplying the annual (or seasonal) forecast by the appropriate percentage yields projected monthly sales. As an illustration consider the case of Ralph's Clothing Store. This family-owned store sells moderately priced ladies' casual apparel in a midwestern town. Last year the store had sales of $2.2 million, but the owners expect sales to reach $2.5 million in the coming year because of inflation, introduction of new merchandise, and improved advertising.

To project monthly sales for the coming year, the managers first inspected the sales pattern for the previous three years. Based on an average of the past three

Managers at apparel stores like Saks Fifth Avenue know that their monthly sales estimates will be highest during the Christmas shopping season, the months of November and December.

years, they calculated each month's share of annual sales. These appear in Exhibit 11.5 in the column labeled "Month's Share of Annual Sales." As one would expect for a store selling clothes, December accounts for the highest level of sales, 19.4 percent. January and March, the leanest months, supply only 5.4 percent and 5.2 percent of sales, respectively.

Adjustments to Monthly Sales   The monthly distribution of sales shown in Exhibit 11.5 needs refinement and adjustment before it is used to project sales for future time periods. First some adjustment may be necessary to account for the timing of Easter holidays. Since many stores run special promotions at Easter, the timing of this holiday can shift monthly sales patterns. The timing of other special promotional events may also make adjustments necessary. For example, February is a relatively busy month at Ralph's compared to other stores because of its annual Presidents' day sale. The timing of white sales and storewide clearances, too, affect the distribution of sales during the year. If the timing of these events changes in the future, the firm should adjust the distribution of sales as well. As shown in the "Adjusted Monthly Shares" column of Exhibit 11.5, Ralph's managers expect

Exhibit 11.5   Monthly Sales Projections: Ralph's Clothing Store

Month	Month's Share of Annual Sales	Adjusted Monthly Shares	Monthly Sales
February	6.6	6.2	$155,000
March	5.2	5.6	140,000
April	8.2	8.2	205,000
May	7.0	7.0	175,000
June	6.6	6.6	165,000
July	7.0	7.0	175,000
August	8.0	8.0	200,000
September	8.0	8.0	200,000
October	8.6	8.6	215,000
November	10.0	10.0	250,000
December	19.4	19.4	485,000
January	5.4	5.4	135,000
	100.0	100.0	$2,500,000

February sales to drop and March sales to rise because of the discontinuation of the Presidents' Day sales.

With the percentage distribution of sales by month determined, it is a relatively easy matter to project expected sales during each month. The firm allocates its projected annual sales figure among the months based on the percentage of sales it expects during that month. Ralph's owners project sales for the month of February to be 6.2 percent of the year's total of $2.5 million, or $155,000; they can calculate sales for the other months similarly, as shown in Exhibit 11.5.

Stock Planning

An old retailing adage warns that empty shelves don't sell. To achieve its planned monthly sales, Ralph's will have to invest funds and stock the store with merchandise. **Stock planning** is one of the most important elements of the merchandise budget. The store must, on the one hand, maintain complete assortments to satisfy customer demand satisfactorily and avoid stockouts. On the other hand, however, it must control the amount it invests to meet financial goals and objectives.

The first step in planning the stock level is to set the target **stock to sales ratio**, which measures the total amount of inventory investment relative to the level of expected sales. For example, if a store with projected sales of $200,000 has $600,000 worth of stock on hand, its stock to sales ratio is 3. The stock to sales ratio measures the level of inventory investments required to generate each dollar of sales. Lower stock to sales ratios indicate more productive investments. A low stock to sales ratio can, however, lead to inadequate assortments and frequent out-of-stock conditions, damaging sales. Each store must set a target stock to sales ratio that optimally trades off these conflicting concerns.

Suppose that the managers of Ralph's Clothing Store have set a target stock to sales ratio of 4.4 for the spring–summer season, which lasts from February to July. They project average monthly sales during these six months of $169,167 (see the monthly sales figures in Exhibit 11.5). The store should, therefore, maintain an average stock worth $744,335 ($169,167 × 4.4) for the season. Things are not that simple in practice, though, because, as seen in Exhibit 11.5, sales vary considerably from month to month during the season. The firm must adjust its stock level each month to reflect those variations.

It can take four approaches to planning monthly stock levels: (1) the basic stock method, (2) the percentage variation method, (3) the monthly stock to sales method, and (4) the week's supply method.

Basic Stock Method   This simplest of the four methods calculates the planned stock for any month by adjusting the average stock depending on the monthly fluctuations in sales. The amount of stock at the beginning of any month (B.O.M. inventory) is calculated as follows:

$$\text{B.O.M Inventory} = \text{Average stock level} \\ + \text{Planned sales for month} \\ - \text{Average monthly sales}$$

The average stock level is based on the store's target sales to stock ratio and its planned sales for the season. As shown earlier, the target average stock level for the season for Ralph's Clothing Store is $744,335 and its average monthly sales for the season is $169,167. The store calculates its February B.O.M. inventory as follows:

$$\text{B.O.M. inventory (February)} = \$744{,}335 + \$155{,}000 - \$169{,}167 \\ = \$730{,}168$$

Similarly, planned stock for the beginning of March is:

$$\text{B.O.M. inventory (March)} = \$744{,}335 + \$140{,}000 - \$169{,}167 \\ = \$715{,}168$$

Percentage Variation Method   As in the basic stock method, this method starts to calculate monthly stock by increasing or decreasing the planned average inventory for the season based on the ratio of that month's planned sales to the average monthly sales:

$$\text{B.O.M. Inventory} = \text{Average stock level} \times 0.5 \left[1 + \frac{\text{Projected sales for month}}{\text{Projected average monthly sales}}\right]$$

The planned February and March stock for Ralph's Clothing Store according to the percentage variation method is as follows:

$$\text{B.O.M. inventory (February)} = \$744,335 \times 0.5 \,[1 + \$155,000/\$169,167]$$
$$= \$713,168$$
$$\text{B.O.M. inventory (March)} = \$744,335 \times 0.5 \,[1 + \$140,000/\$169,167]$$
$$= \$680,168$$

Monthly Stock to Sales Method   In the two methods described previously, the firm first determines an average stock level based on the seasonal stock to sales target and then adjusts this average based on the planned sales for the month. One alternative to those methods that is especially popular with department and apparel stores is to set a separate stock to sales target for each month. For example, if Ralph's Clothing Store sets a target February stock to sales ratio of 4.8, management can calculate the stock level for that month simply by multiplying planned sales for the month ($155,000) by 4.8, giving $744,000. A stock to sales target of 4.6 would give a planned stock level of $713,000 ($155,000 × 4.6). Similar calculations provide the stock levels for the other months, once the firm sets target stock to sales ratios for those months.

Figures published by trade associations, government agencies, and business publications help firms set monthly stock to sales targets. The *Survey of Current Business* publishes sales and inventory data for different types of businesses. Changes in retail inventory levels are published by the Department of Commerce and reported by various publications. Trade associations publish specific industry figures. Exhibit 11.6 shows the monthly stock to sales ratios for specialty stores and department stores with annual sales between $10 and $50 million that is published by the National Retail Federation.

The stock to sales ratio varies from month to month. Note, for example, the low stock to sales ratio for both specialty and department stores in December, the highest selling month for both types of stores. On the other hand, beginning-of-month stock to sales ratios are high for low-selling months.

Why does stock to sales ratio fall during months with high sales and rise during months with low sales? Firms must maintain some degree of uniformity in their stock levels. Even when sales are low, they must keep adequate stock on the shelves, fearing that lower stocks might lower sales even more. During brisk selling periods, a relatively lower stock to sales ratio still assures a large supply of stock because total sales are high.

To use the stock-to-sales method the manager must first set the monthly stock-to-sales ratios. On the basis of its past experience, the managers of Ralph's Clothing Store set the following stock to sales targets for each of the six months in the budget period: February 4.8, March 4.8, April 3.8, May 4.2, June 4.8, and July 4.2. Exhibit 11.7 shows the firm's planned B.O.M. stock for each of the six months and for the month of August. Since the store operates continuously, it plans a B.O.M. stock for August too, even though the current budget period ends with July. The

Exhibit 11.6   Stock-to-Sales Ratios for Department and Specialty Stores

Month	Department Stores (annual sales between $100–$300 million)	Specialty Stores (annual sales between $20–$100 million)
February	6.45	4.80
March	4.10	4.10
April	4.57	3.24
May	5.63	4.30
June	4.91	4.17
July	6.21	3.23
August	5.31	3.67
September	4.55	4.51
October	4.63	4.14
November	4.30	4.34
December	2.41	3.11
January	6.62	4.32

Source: Merchandise and Operating Results of Department and Specialty Stores in 1990, National Retail Federation, New York, 1991.

August figure links the budget for the first half of the year with that for the second half.

The firm calculates its B.O.M. inventory for each month by multiplying the target stock to sales ratio with the projected sales for the month. February's projected sales of $155,000 and stock to sales ratio of 4.8 result in a target B.O.M. stock of $744,000. Similarly, multiplying planned March sales of $140,000 by that month's stock to sales target of 4.8 gives a planned stock level of $672,000.

Week's Supply Method   While the first three methods just discussed plan stock levels by the month, the fourth method is a weekly plan. It sets the planned stock at any point in time equal to the projected sales for a predetermined number of weeks.

To implement the week's supply method, the retailer must first determine the number of weeks of sales to maintain in stock, and then forecast sales for those weeks. For example, if a firm's target is to keep enough stock to cover six weeks of sales, then on February 1 it should have on hand what it expects to sell between then and March 15. The retailer cannot, however, wait six weeks to adjust the stock; it must adjust stock levels periodically in a rolling or moving fashion. A firm that adjusts stocks every two weeks would set its stock on February 15 equal to its cumulative sales for six weeks from that date, and so on.

One disadvantage of the week's supply method is that stock fluctuates in direct proportion to changes in sales. If a firm projects sales during a certain period as

---

Exhibit 11.7   B.O.M. Stock: Ralph's Clothing Store

Month	Planned Sales	B.O.M. Stock/Sales	B.O.M. Stock
February	155,000	4.8	744,000
March	140,000	4.8	672,000
April	205,000	3.8	779,000
May	175,000	4.2	735,000
June	165,000	4.8	792,000
July	175,000	4.2	735,000
August	—	—	735,000

---

twice those of another, stock for that period will be double the stock for the other. This leads to extreme fluctuations in the stock level, with very high stocks during high selling periods and low stocks during low selling periods. As discussed earlier, this is not a very desirable situation. The week's supply method is used, therefore, mostly by supermarkets and convenience stores since they have relatively steady sales throughout the year.

Each of the four methods for calculating beginning stock levels is helpful to retailers. The retailer must choose the one that best suits its needs, given its level of fluctuation in sales. Irrespective of which method a firm actually uses, it is important to realize that all provide guideposts and targets to aid planning. None is the final word.

The final stock figure must be based on the retailer's judgment, since none of the methods considers such factors as the speed with which inventory can be replenished, savings from buying larger quantities, potential scarcity of merchandise, and expected price increases. All of these factors will influence the retailer's determination of the final stock level. Moreover, since the B.O.M. stock level is based on the projected sales for the month, any change in the sales forecast will automatically change the level of stock. Retailers must, therefore, carefully monitor actual sales to check the accuracy of the forecasts.

Reduction Planning

In the next step in planning the budget, **reduction planning**, the buyer considers potential reductions to the value of the stock. Markdowns, stock shortages, and employee discounts can all reduce stock values. That is, they all represent depreciations of the value of the inventory.

Suppose, for example, that of $150,000 worth of merchandise in stock, a store loses $2,000 worth of merchandise due to theft or other causes. The loss reduces the value of the stock to $148,000. Similarly, promotional price reductions or markdowns reduce the retail value of merchandise. For example, consider a store that has 100 sweaters in stock priced at $50 each. The retail value of this stock is $5,000 ($50 × 100). How would reducing the price of the sweaters to $30 each affect the value of the stock? The value is reduced by $2,000 ($20 × 100), that is, by the total amount of the markdown. For a third source, reductions include any loss of inventory due to shoplifting or employee theft. Since markdowns and discounts are a normal part of retail operations, and firms do suffer thefts and losses, the merchandise budget must reflect their impact on the stock value.

To incorporate markdowns into the budget, the firm must project the monthly distribution of their total dollar amount. It is important first to examine the store's previous experience and industry trends. Exhibit 11.8 shows monthly markdowns for specialty stores and department stores with annual sales between $10 and $50 million. Note the high rate of markdowns in January and July. Apparel stores clear out old inventory during these two months in anticipation of merchandise for the new season.

For some years, the managers of Ralph's Clothing Store have been trying to reduce their use of markdowns. They have set a target of a maximum of 25 percent in January and July and 15 percent in all other months. In addition, they expect employee discounts and stock shortages (due to theft and loss) to equal 3 percent of each month's sales. Exhibit 11.9 shows the planned monthly reduction for Ralph's.

Exhibit 11.8   *Monthly Markdowns as Percentage of Net Sales for Department and Specialty Stores*

Month	Department Stores (annual sales between $100–$300 million)	Specialty Stores (annual sales between $20–$100 million)
February	26.90	43.07
March	13.74	25.83
April	14.09	20.00
May	10.84	21.18
June	17.10	25.78
July	26.38	39.45
August	29.40	31.14
September	19.68	25.96
October	17.94	27.48
November	16.27	26.21
December	20.15	29.38
January	50.10	42.75

Source: Merchandise and Operating Results of Department and Specialty Stores in 1990, National Retail Federation, New York, 1991.

Exhibit 11.9   Monthly Reductions: Ralph's Clothing Store

Month	Planned Sales	Planned Markdown	Planned Discounts	Total Reductions
February	155,000	23,250	4,650	27,900
March	140,000	21,000	4,200	25,200
April	205,000	30,750	6,150	36,900
May	175,000	26,250	5,250	31,500
June	165,000	24,750	4,950	29,700
July	175,000	43,750	5,250	49,000
August	200,000	30,000	6,000	36,000
September	200,000	30,000	6,000	36,000
October	215,000	32,250	6,450	38,700
November	250,000	37,500	7,500	45,000
December	485,000	72,750	14,550	87,300
January	135,000	33,750	4,050	37,800

Should Firms Plan Markdowns?   Opinions differ among retailers as to whether they should plan markdowns and reductions. Some argue that firms should treat markdowns as aberrations from normal conditions and not plan for them in advance. According to these critics, managers may use the entire amount of planned markdown even when it is not necessary, if the budget makes provisions for it. This may increase the store's reliance on markdowns and increase the difficulty of controlling shortages.

These arguments have considerable merit. Managers should resort to markdowns only after carefully considering all relevant factors. Even so, they are inevitable and it is helpful in the long run to include them in the budget. A store manager should not, however, think of them as targets to meet, but as guidelines for planning and controlling stock value. Firms should encourage and reward managers for "beating" the budget for markdowns.

Purchase Planning

In the final step of the budgeting process, purchase planning, the firm decides the amount of stock to purchase each month. From monthly sales, stock, and reduction projections, the firm can easily calculate monthly purchases.

Consider, for example, the situation confronting the buyer at Ralph's Clothing Store. At the beginning of March, the store projects stocks worth $672,000 (see Exhibit 11.7), it plans sales for the month of $140,000, and it plans B.O.M. stock for April (or for the end of March) of $779,000.

Markdowns must be incorporated into the budget. Winter clothing clearances typically take place in January in anticipation of the new spring and summer lines.

How much merchandise should the buyer purchase for March? To obtain the answer first note that the B.O.M. inventory for April exceeds the March B.O.M. inventory by $107,000 ($779,000 – $672,000). Even if the store does not sell a single item during March, the buyer must purchase $107,000 worth of merchandise to reach the planned B.O.M. inventory for April. Since, however, the firm expects March sales to total $140,000, the buyer must purchase $247,000 ($107,000 + $140,000) worth of merchandise all together. In general:

$$\text{Initial planned purchase} = \begin{array}{l} \text{Planned E.O.M. Stock} \\ - \text{ Planned B.O.M. Stock} \\ + \text{ Planned sales} \end{array}$$

Effect of Reductions on Planned Purchase   How do reductions affect the planned purchase amount? If the store lost $2,000 worth of merchandise due to theft or other causes during March, the value of its stock would decline by that amount. Therefore, to maintain the planned stock value at the beginning of April, the store would have to buy $2,000 worth of additional merchandise. A markdown would have a similar effect, since a markdown, too, would reduce the retail value of the inventory. Thus, the firm must increase its initial planned purchase amounts by the reductions it anticipates in stock value due to markdowns, shortages, and employee discounts. In other words:

$$\text{Initial planned purchase} = \text{Planned E.O.M. Stock}$$
$$- \text{Planned B.O.M. Stock}$$
$$+ \text{Planned sales}$$
$$+ \text{Planned reductions}$$

Since the firm anticipates total reductions during March of $25,200 (see Exhibit 11.9), its **planned purchase** for the month is:

$$\$779,000 - \$672,000 + \$140,000 + \$25,200 = \$272,200$$

Converting to Cost Base   The planned purchase figure of $272,200 shows the retail value of the merchandise Ralph's should buy during March. This is not the actual amount of money the firm should spend for merchandise. To calculate that amount, the firm must convert its planned purchase amounts from retail value to cost base. To do this, it multiplies the retail value by the **cost complement**, the ratio of the cost of goods to sales revenues. For example, a retailer that pays $5,000 for merchandise it sells for $10,000, has a cost complement of 50 percent.

Based on historical cost and revenue figures, Ralph's managers have established their average cost complement at 60 percent. Their planned purchase for March at cost is, therefore, $163,320 ($272,200 × 0.60). They must budget this amount of money for purchases during the month. Exhibit 11.10 shows monthly planned purchase amounts at both retail and cost for Ralph's Clothing Store.

Budget Tracking Form   Exhibit 11.11 illustrates the kind of form firms typically use to prepare and track budgets. The form provides space for each component of the budget, including sales, stock, reductions, and purchases at retail and at cost.

Exhibit 11.10   *Monthly Purchase Plan: Ralph's Clothing Store*

	February	March	April	May	June	July	Total
1. B.O.M. stock	744,000	672,000	779,000	735,000	792,000	735,000	—
2. E.O.M. stock	672,000	779,000	735,000	792,000	735,000	735,000	—
3. Sales	155,000	140,000	205,000	175,000	165,000	175,000	1,015,000
4. Reductions	27,900	25,200	36,900	31,500	29,700	49,000	2,000,200
5. Purchases (at retail)	110,900	272,200	197,900	263,500	137,700	224,000	1,215,200
6. Purchases (at cost)	66,540	163,320	118,740	158,100	82,620	134,400	729,120
7. Initial markup	44,360	108,880	79,160	105,400	55,080	89,600	486,080

Notes: Items 1, 2, and 3 come from Exhibit 11.7. Item 4 comes from Exhibit 11.9. Item 5 = 2 + 3 + 4 − 1. Item 6 = 5 × 0.60. Item 7 = 5 × 0.4. Cost complement = 0.60.

Exhibit 11.11 Six-Month Merchandise Budget Form

Six-Month Merchandise Plan (Budget)

- Total Store
- Department _____ Department no. _____
- Classification _____ Classification no. _____

• Spring 19	Feb.	Mar.	Apr.	May	June	July	Total
• Fall 19	Aug.	Sept.	Oct.	Nov.	Dec.	Jan.	
Net sales							
Last year							
Plan							
Revision							
Actual							
Beginning-of-month stock (at retail)							(End-of-season stock)
Last year							
Plan							
Revision							
Actual							
Markdowns + Shortages + Discounts							
Last year							
Plan							
Revision							
Actual							
Purchases (at retail)							
Last year							
Plan							
Revision							
Actual							
Purchases (at cost)							
Last year							
Plan							
Revision							
Actual							

Source: Fig. 12.1, "Six Month Merchandise Budget Form" from *Retailing: New Perspectives*, p. 329 by Dorothy Rogers and Mercia Grassi, copyright © 1988 by The Dryden Press, a division of Holt, Rinehart and Winston, Inc., reprinted by permission of the publisher.

In addition to recording the planned figures, the budget form also indicates the corresponding figures from the previous year and allows space for recording the actual performance.

Open to Buy (OTB)

Open to buy is a budgeting tool by which retailers commonly regulate and coordinate the timing of purchases. It helps them monitor the buyers' actual purchase commitments in relation to planned amounts. OTB specifies how much of an item to buy for delivery during a specific time period to avoid exceeding planned purchase amounts for that period. Simply stated, the amount of open to buy equals the difference between the planned purchase amount during a time period and the amount of merchandise already received together with the amount on order for delivery during the period.

To illustrate open to buy, suppose that a retailer's budget lists the following figures, all expressed at retail value:

Planned B.O.M. inventory—February	$30,000
Planned E.O.M. inventory—February	33,000
Planned sales—February	16,000
Planned reduction—February	1,500
Merchandise on order for February delivery	6,000
Merchandise on hand for February	5,000

On January 1 the buyer reviews the store's budget and purchase plans in order to calculate open to buy for February. The first step is to compute planned purchases for February. The procedure described previously gives a February planned purchase figure of:

Planned purchase = E.O.M. inventory – B.O.M. inventory + Planned sales
+ Planned reductions
= $33,000 – $30,000 + $16,000 + $1,500
= $20,500

This is the total amount that the firm must buy for delivery during the month of February. The store has, however, already ordered some merchandise for February delivery, some of which it has already received. The buyer must deduct these amounts from the planned purchase figure to determine how much of February purchases remain uncommitted. In addition, the buyer must also consider any stock that the firm needs to return to the vendor (RTV). Suppose that the store must return $5,000 worth of merchandise to the vendor because of defects. This, in effect, reduces the value of the current stock by $5,000 and, therefore, increases the open to buy amount. In other words:

Open to buy = Planned purchases for month
– Merchandise received already
– Merchandise on order for delivery during month
+ Return to vendor

The store's open to buy for February is:

$$\text{Open to buy (February)} = \$20,500 - \$5,000 - \$6,000 + \$5,000$$
$$= \$14,500$$

This is the budgeted amount of merchandise that remains open to buy for February. Note, however, that this figure, like the planned purchase figure, is expressed in retail dollars, so it does not represent the amount of money the buyer can actually commit to new orders. To determine that amount, the buyer must multiply open to buy at retail by the cost complement to calculate open to buy at cost:

$$\text{Open to buy (at cost)} = \text{Open to buy (at retail)} \times \text{Cost complement}$$

If the store has a cost complement of 0.50 (50 percent), its open to buy at cost is:

$$\text{Open to buy (at cost)} = \$14,500 \times 0.50 = \$7,250$$

Buyers often have to place orders for retail merchandise many months prior to actual need. Thus, they have to base open to buy calculations on planned inventory and sales figures. As actual sales information becomes available, they may need to revise planned figures, which may also require a revision in the open to buy amount.

Suppose, for example, that on January 20 the store's managers find that sales are exceeding expectations; that is, sales for the first 20 days of the month already equal planned sales for the entire month. They expect sales during the rest of the month to total $2,200. Further, based on the January sales experience, the managers have raised the February sales projection to $19,500. What impact does this have on February OTB?

With January sales expected to be $2,200 above previous estimates, the February B.O.M. inventory will fall short of the budget amount to $27,800 (30,000 – 2,200). Thus, the planned purchase for February should increase. The increased sales expected during February will also increase planned purchases for the month. The new planned purchase figure can be calculated as follows:

$$
\begin{aligned}
\text{Planned purchase} &= \text{E.O.M. inventory} - \text{B.O.M. inventory} + \text{Planned sales} \\
&\quad + \text{Planned reductions} \\
&= \$33,000 - \$27,800 + \$19,500 + \$1,500 \\
&= \$26,200
\end{aligned}
$$

The revised OTB calculation for February looks like this:

$$
\begin{aligned}
\text{Open to buy} &= \text{Planned purchases for month} \\
&\quad - \text{Merchandise received already} \\
&\quad - \text{Merchandise on order for delivery during month} \\
&\quad + \text{Returns to vendor}
\end{aligned}
$$

or:

$$\text{Open to buy (February)} = \$26,200 - \$5,000 - \$6,000 + \$5,000$$
$$= \$20,200$$

The revised OTB at retail exceeds the original amount by $5,700, the exact amount by which the revised planned purchase exceeds the original estimate. Any change in the planned purchase amount due to revisions of planned inventory, sales, or markdown levels will affect open to buy levels. It is important, therefore, that retailers periodically revise open to buy figures with the most up-to-date sales and inventory information.

Buyers typically resist fully committing their entire open to buy amounts; they like to have at least some funds available at all times. This gives them flexibility in responding to unexpected changes in customers' merchandise preference, introduction of new products, or special limited-time discounts offered by manufacturers. Vendors' special price concessions or other discounts can be an important source of additional margin and profit for the store. In addition, buyers should keep some amount of open to buy available for reordering fast-selling items. A buyer without any open to buy may have to pass up unique buying opportunities or seek special authorization from senior merchandise managers to deviate from the budget.

VENDOR SELECTION

The merchandise budget details the amounts of merchandise the firm must acquire to achieve its planned level of sales. Once the budget is specified, as the next step in the merchandising process, the firm must procure the merchandise from suppliers or vendors to create a balanced assortment. Success in merchandising depends critically on the buyer's ability to identify potential sources of supply, evaluate alternative vendors, and negotiate purchase agreements with them. This section of the chapter discusses **vendor selection** and the process of negotiation between buyers and suppliers.

Evaluating Alternative Sources of Supply

Typically many sources or vendors can provide buyers with merchandise. Some manufacture the products themselves, and others are wholesalers and distributors that represent producers. Many retailers concentrate their purchases of a particular merchandise item from a few vendors, although some buy from many vendors based on the best opportunity at any given point in time.

Concentration of purchases with a few vendors has a number of advantages. First, it fosters a long-term cooperative relationship between a retailer and its suppliers. Such cooperation can lead to a more active retailer-supplier interaction in the design of new products and marketing programs. Further, vendors are likely to favor their established customers in distributing a limited supply of popular items. Concentration of suppliers can also lead to cost savings due to quantity discounts and better inventory management.

Whether a retailer seeks to deal with a few or many suppliers, it must carefully research the strengths and weaknesses of all prospective vendors before selecting any. Several factors are important.

Reputation of Supplier   A survey found that buyers from department stores and mass merchandisers consider supplier reputation (along with supplier cooperation) to be the most important criterion in vendor selection.[9]

Brand Names and Images of Items   The suitability of a supply source depends on whether its merchandise is appropriate for the store's target customers. The image of the brand must be consistent with the store's merchandise strategy. For example, some vendors enhance the prestige images of their products by limiting distribution to selected stores. High-end stores often favor these vendors.

Price and Payment Terms   Wholesale prices can vary, even for similar merchandise. Firms must carefully compare the list prices, quantity discount schedules, and payment terms of different suppliers.

Reliability of Vendors   Buyers attach crucial importance to a vendor's service standards. For example, does the vendor deliver on promised dates? How accurately are orders filled? Are bills correct?

Promotional Programs   Retailers prefer vendors that provide promotional assistance, such as cooperative advertising dollars, point-of-purchase displays, and product demonstrations, to those that do not support retailer selling efforts.

Support Programs   In addition to promotional support, vendors can support the retailer's program in many ways. Some vendors, for example, may preticket items, arrange modular displays, provide specially packaged items, and even produce items in certain colors at a retailer's request.

Decision Matrix Approach to Supplier Selection

Although buyers typically select vendors by evaluating alternative sources of supply subjectively based on the criteria listed above, they can employ a more systematic procedure for vendor selection called the decision matrix approach.[10] The decision matrix approach involves the following steps:

1. List the factors to be considered in evaluating vendors. This list of factors will resemble the one that appears above, but may change from one situation to another depending on the type of merchandise.
2. Assess the importance of each of the factors identified in Step 1 and assign each factor an importance weight measured on a five or ten point scale, with larger numbers denoting greater importance. The importance weights will change for each application because of differing needs for different types of merchandise.

STRATEGY IN ACTION

Retailers Gain Power

Power retailers, huge mass-merchants such as Wal-Mart and Toys R Us, have gained such importance in their markets that they can now virtually tell their manufacturers what to make. These giants are using highly refined inventory management, carefully designed selections, and competitive pricing to crowd out the weaker players in their industries, and as they do, manufacturers rush to ensure that these stores will keep selling their products. And what do the giants want? They want to specify what goods are made, in what colors and sizes, and the size and timing of the shipments. In short, they want to run the show.

And why should manufacturers play along? Take the example of Wal-Mart, America's leading retailer. Industry analysts estimate that Wal-Mart will grow by a whopping 25 percent in 1993, when retailers as a whole will be lucky to grow by a mere 4 percent, and sales are expected to climb to $55 billion for the year. This means that while

many a store will be closing their doors because they cannot compete with the giants, which can offer everyday low prices on a whole variety of items, manufacturers will be scrambling to make sure they have contracts with the super-retailers.

These power retailers are beginning to demand customized products and packages, computer link-ups for faster stock replenishment, and special delivery schedules. They know what sells in their stores, and they want the manufacturer to make it for them, and at the best price possible. During product development, manufacturers consult with the retailers about style, color, warranties, components, and all the other specifications. Once the product is available, retailers want to be electronically linked with the manufacturer to ensure that they keep the products in stock. Wal-Mart is on-line with more than half of their 5,000 suppliers and K mart with more than three-quarters. The goal for both parties is to increase sales, cut

For a staple merchandise, for example, supplier reliability is likely to be much more important than promotional support, whereas for a new item promotional support may be the most important criterion.

3. Assign a score to each potential supplier on each criterion listed in Step 1 based on an evaluation of the vendor's program. As with importance weights, retailers typically use a five- or ten-point scale for this purpose.
4. Compute a weighted average score for each supplier by multiplying each criterion score by the importance weight for that criterion and summing.
5. Rank suppliers according to their scores.

Exhibit 11.12 illustrates each of these five steps.

The decision matrix approach has the advantage that it bases the decision on quantitative assessments of the relative abilities of individual vendors to meet ex-

lead times, reduce costs, keep inventories lean and manageable, and eliminate errors in specifications or delivery schedules.

This forces the manufacturers themselves to be more competitive. Many manufacturers are unable to keep up with the pace of a 1,600-outlet Wal-Mart, especially when large retailers insist on purchasing multiple lines from the same manufacturer. This means that only the manufacturing giants can keep pace, a Unilever, a P&G, or a Rubbermaid. And Wal-Mart keeps them on their toes. For example, Wal-Mart insisted that Totes, a manufacturer, put the price stickers on the products—a task that had always been assigned to personnel. Most manufacturers will find that they have to tailor some or all of their products, packages, and services in some way to please their large clients.

On the downside, these retailing giants are squeezing out not just their competition, but their competition's manufacturers. In the toy industry, Toys R Us controls 20 percent of the market, and five chains control over half the market. This concentration reduces the variety of toys brought to market, and thus the number of manufacturers involved. In the early 1980s, no one toy manufacturer controlled more than 5 percent of the market, now there are only six manufacturers that control the market. This much more efficient production offers price reductions to the customers and cost savings to the retailer, but there will be fewer new products brought to market in the long run.

But not to worry, if you want a product badly enough, just be sure to let Wal-Mart know, and if you are not alone, your product may appear on the shelf some day soon.

Source: Zachery Schiller and Wendy Zellner, "Clout!: More and More, Retail Giants Rule the Marketplace," *Business Week*, December 21, 1992, pp. 66–73; Brent H. Felger, "Retailers Grab Power, Control Marketplace," *Marketing News*, January 16, 1989, p. 1.

plicitly defined criteria. As shown in Exhibit 11.12, this yields a summary measure of the relative strengths and weaknesses of each potential supplier. The quantitative approach eliminates reliance on ad hoc, subjective judgments and forces decision makers to gather complete information prior to making final supplier selections.

Negotiating with Vendors

One of the important yardsticks by which firms evaluate the performance of retail buyers is the amount of profit the store earns from selling the merchandise they buy. Buyers must, therefore, negotiate the best deal they can with each vendor to improve their profits. Three factors are especially important in **vendor**

Exhibit 11.12   Decision Matrix for Vendor Selection

		Supplier			
Criterion	Weight	A	B	C	D
Reputation	4	7	5	6	3
Cooperation	3	5	5	6	9
Brand image	3	9	6	7	5
Price/payment terms	4	7	6	5	8
Reliability	5	6	6	7	7
Promotion	3	5	7	7	6
Support programs	5	6	7	6	8
Weighted score		173	163	169	179
Rank		2	4	3	1

negotiations: (1) discounts, (2) shipping charges, and (3) promotional allowances. Each of these factors affects the final cost of goods to the retailer.

Discounts   The Robinson-Patman Act requires that vendors charge the same price to all retailers for goods of like grade and quality. Vendors therefore maintain list prices that apply uniformly to all retailers. The list price, however, is far from firm since the vendor can offer various types of discounts. The types and amounts of a retailer's discounts depend on the terms and conditions under which it actually purchases the goods. A price discount is legal as long as the purchase quantity, buying method (payment timing, for example), or timing of the purchase reduces the vendor's cost of doing business. Moreover, the vendor must offer the discounts to all retailers who meet the same terms and conditions.

Quantity discounts   For one common form of discounting, vendors offer **quantity discounts** to bulk purchasers. Since large orders reduce the vendor's handling, billing, transportation, and inventory costs, it can legally pass these cost savings on to retailers in the form of discounts from list prices. Quantity discounts reduce the retailer's cost of goods and allow it to lower price without sacrificing profitability.

Although quantity discounts reduce costs significantly for retailers, bulk buying has its risks, too. As the most significant risk, the retailer might not sell all the merchandise at the originally intended price, thus, forcing it to mark the price down as the end of the season approaches. Bulk buying also increases the cost of storing the merchandise and ties up scarce financial resources. Therefore, the retailer must carefully evaluate the potential savings of quantity discounts in light of the increased risks and costs.

Seasonal discounts   For another form of price reduction, manufacturers of seasonal products offer discounts to increase sales during off seasons and to even out production schedules. A toy manufacturer, for example, will grant a discount to a retailer who takes delivery during spring or summer instead of fall, just prior to the Christmas season. Like quantity discounts, seasonal discounts shift the burden of inventory risks from the manufacturer to the retailer, reducing the supplier's cost.

Vendors of fashion merchandise give another type of seasonal discount. Since fashions change from season to season, vendors often find themselves burdened with excess supply at the ends of selling seasons. Retailers willing to purchase end-of-season merchandise can often negotiate substantial discounts.Vendors also give discounts for buying lines that are to be discontinued. Buyers from off-price apparel stores take advantage of such discounts to reduce their cost of goods.

Cash discounts   Vendors offer **cash discounts** to encourage prompt payment by retailers. Suppliers often permit retailers to deduct a certain percentage from the net invoice amount, that is, the net amount of the order less all quantity and seasonal discounts, if they pay within a specified time period. Early payment by retailers benefits suppliers since it reduces their cash flow requirements.

The actual amount of a cash discount depends on the discount rate and dating term negotiated by the buyer. **Discount rate** refers to the applicable percentage discount and the **dating term** refers to the amount of time the retailer has to qualify for the discount. For example, the notation "2/10 net 30" on a $50,000 invoice means that if the retailer pays the bill within 10 days from the date of the invoice it can take a discount of 2 percent. A retailer that does not pay the bill within 10 days can take no cash discounts and must pay $50,000 within 30 days. Interest charges may accrue if the bill is unpaid after 30 days.

The discount rate and the dating term determine the actual amount of cash discount a retailer receives. The discount rate typically varies between 1 and 8 percent depending on the kind of merchandise, but the most common rate is 2 percent. Dating terms, too, can vary considerably, and buyers must negotiate the most favorable terms they can.

Dating terms can generally be divided into two categories: immediate and future. An immediate dating requires payment of the invoice either prior to delivery or immediately upon delivery (that is, cash on delivery, or C.O.D.). A future dating gives the retailer some interval of time between the invoice date and payment due date. Longer intervals give the retailer greater advantage since it can maintain merchandise inventory without tying up its finances. Exhibit 11.13 describes a number of common dating terms.

Anticipation   Cash discounts encourage retailers to pay within specified time periods to reduce the cost of the invoice. But what happens when the retailer pays

Exhibit 11.13   *Common Payment Dating Terms*

Ordinary: 2/10/N30
The retailer can take a 2-percent discount on any invoice it pays within 10 days, or it can pay the full invoice amount within 30 days.

E.O.M.: 8/10 E.O.M.
The retailer can take an 8-percent discount if it pays within 10 days after the last day of the month in which billed. For example, for a bill dated March 5, the discount period expires on April 10.

R.O.G.: 2/10/N30 R.O.G.
In this variation on ordinary dating, the discount time clock starts from the day the retailer receives the goods, not from the date of the invoice.

AS OF: 2/10/N30 as of September 1
In this second variation on ordinary dating, the discount time clock starts on the date indicated, irrespective of when the retailer receives the shipment or invoice.

C.O.D.
Full payment is due on delivery. This is also called *cash and carry*.

before the expiration of the cash discount period? Should it receive a further discount? Suppose, for example, a retailer that can take a 2-percent discount for paying within 10 days actually pays in 2 days. In many cases such early payment can entitle retailers to additional discounts over and above negotiated cash discounts. This form of discounting, known as **anticipation**, would allow the retailer that paid the invoice in 2 days instead of 10 to deduct 8 days of anticipation at an agreed-upon daily discount rate.

Large retailers, especially those with surplus cash, generally negotiate favorable anticipation terms to further reduce their cost of goods. A store cannot automatically claim an anticipation discount when it pays its bill early. Anticipation is a matter of negotiation between the retailer and the supplier. For this reason, some critics argue that anticipation should be deemed illegal since small retailers typically do not receive its benefits.

Shipping Charges   A retailer that pays the cost of shipping merchandise from the vendor adds that cost to its cost of goods. Thus, buyers must always negotiate to reduce **shipping charges**. Three factors are important in negotiating shipping terms: (1) who pays for transportation costs? (2) who will actually bear the shipping charges? and (3) when does title to the goods change hands?

Note that someone other than the party that actually pays for transportation may ultimately bear that cost. For example, the vendor may pay for transportation, but add the cost to the retailer's invoice.

The vendor of this Bart Simpson merchandise may well have offered a promotional allowance to the retailer in exchange for this prominent store display.

The question of when legal title to the goods passes from the vendor to the retailer is also important in negotiating shipping terms. When the title passes to the retailer, it becomes responsible for any loss or damage to the merchandise. If the retailer assumes title before the vendor ships the merchandise, it is responsible for any damage or loss during shipment and, therefore, has to pay for insurance during transit.

Promotional Allowances   Suppliers offer various **promotional allowances** to encourage retailers to market their products. Buyers must actively negotiate for these allowances since they, too, reduce the retailer's cost. One common type of promotional allowance, the cooperative advertising, or "co-op" program, offers the retailer an allowance to underwrite all or a part of the cost of retailer advertising featuring the vendor's product, generally within certain prescribed limits. Cooperative advertising benefits both the retailer and the vendor, stretching the retailer's advertising budget and promoting the vendor's product and increasing its sales. Details of how a co-op program is implemented are discussed in Chapter 16.

Some vendors also offer promotional allowances to retailers who demonstrate their products in the store or give them prominent positions in store displays. Housewares manufacturers, for example, often pay retailers allowances for demonstrating new products to customers or featuring them in the stores. The allowance may be set as a fixed percentage of the retailer's purchases from the vendor, or it may be a negotiated lump sum. Although vendors intend to pay the allowance only to retailers who actually demonstrate or promote the product, some buyers may be able to negotiate for the allowance without actually doing so. This, in effect, reduces the cost of the goods to the retailer, increasing its margin.

Suppliers offer a variety of other kinds of promotions, especially in the food industry. Food manufacturers, for example, give off-invoice allowances to supermarkets, which entitle them to deduct fixed percentages from total invoice amounts. Food manufacturers periodically give other kinds of trade discounts, often expecting that supermarkets will reduce shelf prices, making their products more competitive. However, only a small portion of these trade discounts actually reach ultimate consumers.

Conclusions

Vendor negotiation is an important element of the retail buyer's job. Whatever skill and experience a buyer has in selecting merchandise, "unless she or he learns how to negotiate with the vendors, the store's profit potential may not be fully realized."[11] Astute buyers can substantially reduce the cost of goods by negotiating favorable terms and conditions.

For example, off-price retail stores such as Marshall's, T.J. Maxx, Hit or Miss, Syms, Pic-A-Dilly, J. Brannam, and T. H. Mandy can sell branded apparel at 20 to 40 percent less than department stores, because their buyers negotiate substantial discounts from vendors. Typically, buyers for off-price stores will get as much as 30 to 40 percent off the vendor's quoted price by purchasing late in the season. They also buy irregular, surplus, and close-out merchandise at prices significantly less than list prices. In addition, off-price retailers earn cash discounts by paying their invoices promptly. They pass these savings along to customers in the form of lowered prices. Although their prices are lower than department stores, off-price retailers still maintain healthy profit margins because of lower cost of goods.

Summary

1. Large retail firms typically have a formalized merchandising department responsible for implementing their merchandise strategies. The person most directly responsible for

implementing a store's merchandise strategy is the merchandise buyer. Divisional merchandise managers and general merchandise managers supervise the activities of buyers. Department managers link buying and selling operations.

2. The buyers, along with merchandise managers, develop merchandise budgets to determine dollar inventory investments, convert dollar inventory levels into specific assortment plans, evaluate and select alternative sources of supply, negotiate with vendors, work with department managers to develop marketing plans, and monitor sales trends.

3. Large stores often centralize their buying operations to realize economies of scale. However, centralization may result in friction between the buying and selling arms of the store and reduce the firm's ability to adapt to local needs. Central distribution systems allow central buying, but give local managers some latitude in tailoring merchandise to local needs.

4. The merchandise budget specifies a plan for merchandise investments for a specific time period. The budget process comprises five steps: (a) forecasting annual sales, (b) projecting monthly sales, (c) stock planning, (d) reduction planning, and (e) purchase planning. The budget specifies the amount of merchandise to purchase each month.

5. From the budget figures, buyers calculate not only the amount of merchandise to buy each month, but they can also compute open to buy (OTB), the amount of money available for buying merchandise at any point in time. Any changes in monthly sales forecast, in markdowns, and in other reductions from planned levels will change purchase plans and OTB.

6. Whether a retailer deals with a few or many suppliers, it must carefully evaluate the strengths and weaknesses of each to guide vendor selection. Some of the criteria to consider include: (a) reputation and cooperation of suppliers, (b) brand names and images of items, (c) prices and payment terms, (d) reliability of vendors, (e) promotional programs, and (f) other support programs.

7. The retailer's profits depend on the buyer's ability to negotiate with each vendor the best purchase terms possible. Three factors are especially important in negotiations between buyers and vendors: (a) discounts, (b) shipping charges, and (c) promotional allowances. Quantity discounts, seasonal discounts, and cash discounts are the three common forms of discounting.

Key Concepts

Merchandising organization	Planned purchase
Merchandise buyer	Cost complement
Merchandise managers	Open to buy
Department managers	Vendor selection
Centralized merchandising	Vendor negotiations
Partial centralization	Quantity discounts
Merchandise budget	Cash discounts
Sales forecasting	Dating term
Stock planning	Anticipation
Stock to sales ratio	Shipping charges
Reduction planning	Promotional allowances

Discussion Questions

1. What are the responsibilities of a merchandise buyer and a department manager?
2. Explain why merchandise buyers (and merchandise managers) are often referred to as social gatekeepers.
3. Why do many chain stores centralize their merchandising functions? What are some potential drawbacks of centralization?
4. What is a merchandise budget? What are the steps in developing a merchandise budget?
5. Explain the term open to buy (OTB). How do buyers use OTB to control merchandise investments?
6. Consider the monthly sales estimates and the planned reductions for Ralph's Clothing Store shown in Exhibits 11.5 and 11.9, respectively. Calculate the monthly planned purchases for the store using first the basic stock method and then the percentage variation method. (Assume a target stock to sales ratio of 4.4.)
7. Last year a hardware store had net sales of $560,000 and a stock turnover rate (at retail) of 6.0. It projects that sales will increase by 5 percent next year. How much inventory must the store maintain to achieve a planned stock turnover rate of 6.4?
8. Alpha Beta, a small campus bookstore, has the following plans for the month of April: Sales of $70,000, B.O.M. stock worth $200,000, E.O.M. stock worth $195,000, planned reductions of $2,500, and an average cost complement of 60 percent. Calculate the store's planned purchases for the month at retail and at cost.

9. Based on the following information from the merchandise budget for men's accessories in a department store as of April 1, calculate OTB as of that date.

Planned monthly sales	$62,000
B.O.M. inventory	75,000
E.O.M. inventory	80,000
April merchandise already received	45,000
April merchandise on order	18,000
Planned reductions	12,500

Based on the following additional information, obtained on April 10, calculate OTB as of that date.

Actual April sales to date	15,000
Actual reductions to date	5,500
Merchandise to be returned to vendor	4,000
Orders placed since April 1	8,000

10. Explain the steps in using the decision matrix approach to vendor (supplier) selection.
11. Explain these terms: (a) quantity discount, (b) dating term, (c) discount rate, and (d) promotional allowance.

Notes

1. Robert F. Lusch, M*anagement of Retail Enterprises* (Boston: Kent Publishing, 1982), p. 394.
2. Richard Ettenson and Janet Wagner, "Retail Buyers' Salability Judgments: A Comparison of Information Across Three Levels of Experience," *Journal of Retailing* 62 (Spring 1986), pp. 41–63.
3. See Elizabeth C. Hirschman and Ronald W. Stampfl, "Roles of Retailing in the Diffusion of Popular Culture: Microperspectives," *Journal of Retailing* 56 (Spring 1980), pp. 16–36; and Edwin J. Gross, "Bureaucracy, the 'Gatekeeper' Concept, and Consumer Innovation," *Journal of Retailing* 43 (Spring 1967), pp. 9–16.

4. See Gross, "Bureaucracy," p. 12.
5. Hirschman and Stampfl. "Roles of Retailing."
6. Karen R. Gillespie and Joseph C. Hecht, *Retail Business Management* (New York: McGraw Hill, 1977), p. 138.
7. Ibid, p. 139.
8. Delhart J. Duncan and Stanley C. Hollander, *Modern Retail Management* (Homewood, IL: Richard D. Irwin, 1977), p. 263.
9. Elizabeth Hirschman and David Mazursky, "A Trans-Organizational Investigation of Retail Buyers' Criteria and Information Sources," New York University, School of Business, Working Paper.
10. John S. Berens, "A Decision Matrix Approach to Supplier Selection," *Journal of Retailing* 47 (Winter 1971), p. 52.
11. Gillespie and Hecht, *Retail Business Management.*

CHAPTER 12
Planning for Effective Pricing

Retailers Respond to Value Shopping Trend with Deep Discounting

The recession in the United States during the late 1980s and early 1990s created a new kind of consumer—the value shopper. Even consumers who could afford to pay full price on expensive items began to look for good deals on their purchases. Finding the off-price retailer became a necessity for many, and the "in thing" to do for others. Once the domain of clothing retailers, deep discounting spread to everything from supermarkets to bookstores, from cosmetics to prescription drugs. To remain a competitive retailer, prices had to be low. *Haute couture* designers began offering casual (read less expensive) clothes: Donna Karan with her DKNY line and Armani with his Armani Exchange outlets; gourmet food stores began offering "value items" on staples such as soup or flour, while still selling expensive fresh produce and meats; and even the cosmetics industry got into the fray by keeping booths in expensive department stores and simultaneously selling their items to discounters.

Costco Wholesale Retail Corp. is a perfect example of a store responding to the change in consumer behavior by offering just what consumers want at prices they can afford.

Costco has a wide assortment of products, selling everything from car tires to fresh produce, all at discount prices. For a low annual membership fee ($30 in 1990), customers can visit Costco as often as they wish. The strategy behind the store is to offer the basics, like toilet paper and soap, but keep customers enticed with a certain number of fancier items, like steaks and fresh fruit from around the world. Shoppers can purchase items for their home and auto, all at 50 to 70 percent less than regular retail prices. Costco has also been successful in beating out its heavy competition by attracting more affluent value-shoppers with items beyond the mundane: a customer can buy the weekly groceries, *plus* that baby grand piano they've been yearning for. Such "impulse" items include the latest best sellers, Ralph Lauren suits or Dom Perignon champagne. These items have helped to boost margins, with profits rising at an anticipated 63 percent between 1991 and 1993. Sales also continue to rise, from $40 million per warehouse in 1987 to $75 million in 1991, or $5.3 billion in 1991 overall.

Deep discount drugstores are another fast-growing area in the discount retail industry. Price Less, a California-based chain, has opened four new stores in the last two years. While this seems to be a cautious expansion

After studying this chapter, the reader will be able to:
- *Describe the role of price in retail strategy and the factors that affect retail price.*
- *Calculate initial and maintained markup.*
- *Discuss the relationship among price, demand, and revenue.*
- *Describe the factors that affect consumer price sensitivity.*
- *Plan and control retail markdowns.*
- *Describe the major federal and state laws that affect retail pricing practices.*
- *Understand the use of in-store experiments to assess the impacts of price changes on sales (see Appendix).*

according to general industry standards, owner George Jeffers believes that it is crucial to choose sites carefully in his business. For many years, the public has had the impression that discount stores should be only for low income shoppers, and although that is changing, Jeffers believes that some of his customers still have to get over the stigma of shopping in discount stores. He chooses the sites by the income level of the area, but also by the customer demographics: areas where there are many young families and where K mart and Wal-Mart are neighbors.

Price Less's pricing policy often leaves customers with more choices than in the average drug store. Price Less buys in bulk from manufacturers and distributors, but sometimes the prices for the same item will vary from purchase to purchase, resulting in the same items on the shelf with different prices. Instead of changing the prices, Price Less employees simply encourage the customer to buy the less expensive item. This strategy keeps customers coming back, because they feel that they can always find a bargain. Markup is traditionally only 20 percent, giving the chain an average of 16 percent gross margin, which means that Price Less continues to make money while customers continue to find great deals.

Cosmetics were a late entrant into the realm of discount stores. So much of the cosmetics industry depends on its image, that for years manufacturers resisted the sales to be gained from discounting. But now, with chains like Miami-based Perfumania and Maryland-based Cosmetic Center, Inc., even the big names are joining the trend. While many of the major firms in the industry, Estée Lauder, Elizabeth Arden, Chanel, and Christian Dior, keep their cosmetics counters in fancy department stores—for their image and for their very affluent customers—the shelves of discounters are lined with their products, too. Cosmetic Center sold $88 million in discounted perfumes, cosmetics, shampoos, and soaps in fiscal 1991, and Perfumania sold $85 million.

With discounts of 20 percent to more than 60 percent off suggested retail prices on numerous items, consumers are rushing to this new breed of discounter. The cosmetics industry waited for a long time to join the ranks of discounters for a number of reasons, the most obvious of which is that there was al-

ways a choice for cosmetics consumers. If the consumer was unwilling to pay $18 to $20 a tube for designer lipstick, the local drugstore had lesser-quality brands for $4 to $5, and for years that choice was enough for the consumer. But the cosmetics industry can no longer afford to pass over the growing number of affluent consumers who can get their clothes, electronics equipment, and food at discount prices, and now expect discounts on their cosmetics, too.

Sources: Dori Jones: "Corn Flakes, Aisle 1, Cadillacs, Aisle 12," *Business Week*, April 29, 1991, p. 68–69; Debra Chanil: "The Right Price at Price Less," *Discount Merchandiser*, January 1992, pp. 30–31; Gretchen Morgenson: "Save $35 on Chanel," *Forbes*, March 16, 1992, pp. 70–71.

Retailers create utility for their customers by offering the right merchandise, designing the proper shopping atmosphere, making shopping convenient, and providing information and service. Price is what customers pay for that utility. As discussed in Chapter 1, utility and price jointly determine the value consumers perceive. The retailer that provides more utility for a certain price creates more value and attracts consumers. If price exceeds utility, there is no potential for exchange; consumers may forego the purchase or patronize a different retailer that offers a better value. Through the pricing decision, the retailer translates some of the value it creates into profits for the firm (see Exhibit 12.1).

Exhibit 12.1 shows how retail prices relate to costs, on the one hand, and consumer utility on the other. The difference between the retail price of a merchandise item and its cost to the retailer is the **margin**. Part of the margin covers the selling, general, and administrative (SGA) expenses, and the remainder is the retailer's profit. One way to increase retail profits, therefore, is to reduce SGA expenses, and all retailers try to do this as far as possible. They must exercise caution, however, since too heavy an emphasis on cost control can reduce consumer utility. Cutbacks in customer service or advertising may cost a retailer customers and sales.

As an alternative approach to increasing profits, a retailer can seek to increase consumer utility by improving merchandise quality, providing better service, running better advertising, and so on. Although these methods may increase costs, they also enhance consumer utility, allowing the retailer to increase price without

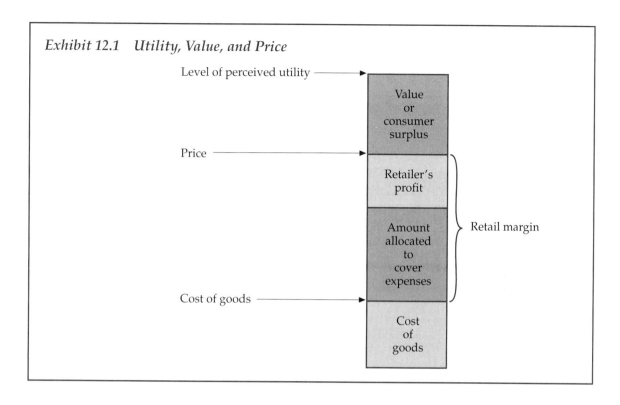

Exhibit 12.1   Utility, Value, and Price

decreasing value. In reality, firms must work toward both of these goals simultaneously, increasing utility in the most cost effective way.

Price determines the amount of profit a retailer can earn. This is clearly seen from the following profit equation:

$$\text{Profit} = \text{Sales revenue} - \text{Cost of goods sold} - \text{SGA expenses}$$

Price influences each of the three elements of the profit equation. It affects the quantity sold and therefore sales revenue and cost of goods sold. Price can also affect SGA expenses through the quantity sold figure. The retailer must always consider the relationships between price and quantity sold and between quantity sold and costs in setting merchandise price.

A FRAMEWORK FOR EFFECTIVE PRICING

The many factors that firms must consider make the pricing decision quite complex. Moreover, although a store must price each of the thousands of items it sells individually, it must blend these separate decisions with its overall marketing strategy. This combination determines whether the firm achieves its long-run financial and marketing goals. This interdependence makes a proper framework essential for effective pricing decisions. Such a framework assures that the firm considers all the relevant factors in pricing merchandise items.

Since retail stores carry thousands of different items, many individuals may share responsibility for making pricing decisions. Most large retail organizations make the pricing decision in two stages. Top corporate managers first set the firm's overall pricing policy and then department managers, merchandise managers, or store managers price individual merchandise items in accordance with this policy. Coordination between the two levels of decision makers is necessary to ensure achievement of long-term goals.

Exhibit 12.2 shows the steps in the pricing process. Like all marketing mix decisions, price decisions start with consideration of the store's overall marketing strategy, which provides guidelines for developing pricing policy. The firm must undertake cost and demand analysis to set profit goals for the store and assess the sensitivity of demand to price. While these analyses are the basis for price decisions, the firm must also study the merchandise environment before setting final prices of merchandise items. In the last step, the price-making process adjusts prices through markdowns. Subsequent sections of this chapter discuss each of these five steps in detail. The chapter ends by discussing some important legal issues related to pricing and the role of in-store experiments to determine price sensitivity.

The Role of Price in Retail Strategy

Since price is an important element of the retail mix, pricing policies must support the overall retail marketing strategy. Earlier chapters have stressed that all retail

---

Exhibit 12.2 *Framework for Making Pricing Decisions*

Step	Task
Define overall pricing strategy	Review marketing strategy and position on shopping opportunity line
Set markup goal	Conduct cost analysis
Determine consumer sensitivity to price	Analyze demand
Set retail price	Review: Merchandising objectives Competitive environment Supplier relationships
Adjust final price	Markdown merchandise and organize promotions

mix elements must match the expectations of the store's target consumers. Different consumer segments expect different things of retail stores and their willingness to pay also differs. The type of merchandise a store carries and the prices it charges must reflect those expectations. Otherwise the store's image will be confused and it will fail to attract customers.

A store's position on the shopping opportunity line shows the influence of consumer expectations on pricing decisions. Compare, for example, a discount store and an upscale department store. Exhibit 12.3 shows the relative positions of two stores on the shopping opportunity line. The discount store appears in the lower left part of the line, while the department store is positioned in the upper right. As discussed in earlier chapters the positions of the two stores reflect their marketing strategies and target markets. The discount store appeals to price-sensitive customers in search of basic merchandise, while the department store's customers seek fashion, quality, and personal service. Differences in the two customer groups' shopping expectations would lead one to expect the department store to have generally higher prices than the discount store.

Firms cannot make pricing decisions in isolation from other retail mix decisions. To justify its higher prices, department stores must carry fashionable, high-quality merchandise and create the posh shopping atmosphere that the customers it wants to attract expect. Compare, for example, the spartan interiors of discount stores,

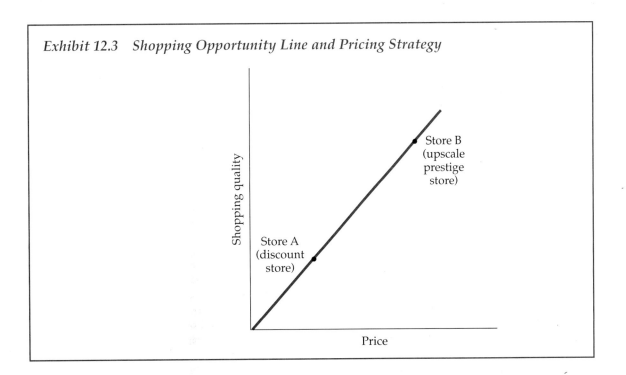

Exhibit 12.3   Shopping Opportunity Line and Pricing Strategy

ENTREPRENEURIAL EDGE

The Children's Bookshoppe Caters to Baby Boomlet

The latest spurt in the U.S. birthrate has added to the popularity of one type of specialty bookstore: the children's bookstore. Children's bookstores led the publishing industry in sales dollars throughout the latter half of the 1980s. According to the Dessauer Report in *Publishers Weekly*, sales of juvenile paperbound books recorded huge increases during this period. Such results are perhaps not surprising considering that the parents of many of these babies are ambitious, college-educated baby boomers who want to see their children succeed.

One store benefitting from this demographic trend is The Children's Bookshoppe in Newport Beach, California. Owner Sara Brant says that atmosphere is the key to success for her business. "We believe in fresh flowers," she says, "and we spend a lot of money to prepare and present a beautiful 'house' for our books." The Children's Bookshoppe features an open play area that includes a riding horse and a child's rocking chair.

A major draw is the story hour. "Children are on a waiting list a mile long to attend," says Brant. "We read stories and poetry and sing songs." She limits the group to 12 to 15 children, a comfortable number to gather round the storyteller during each session.

Brant has run The Children's Bookshoppe for 16 years. Her success is derived in part from her prior background: 31 years as an elementary school reading specialist. Brant believes that her background certainly is a bonus because she developed an interest and love for children's books. Her goal is to place quality books in the hands of children.

For other people interested in starting their own retail business, Brant has the following advice: The foremost requirement is to be enthusiastic about the work. Those wanting to open bookstores should be excited and interested in learning about and selecting books.

Source: Kevin McLaughlin, "The Little Bookstore that Could," *Entrepreneur*, January 1989, pp. 66–70.

---

such as K mart, Target, and Wal-Mart, with the glittering displays at department stores like Emporium, Dillard's, and Hudson's. Similarly, service, location, and promotion strategies must also harmonize with a store's price structure and other retail mix elements. Only in this way can the firm avoid evoking conflicting feelings in the customer.

The firm cannot ignore the actions of direct competitors either. Since increasing similarity between the marketing strategies of two stores increases competition between them, retail managers must pay special attention to prices charged by other stores that are positioned near it on the shopping opportunity line. These stores are likely to compete very intensely for similar customers, and price will play a critical role in determining consumer patronage. To improve its competitive position within the strategic group, a store might follow a price leadership strategy and attempt to become the low-price supplier. Such a store would need to keep its prices low in order to create a competitive advantage. Other stores may choose to differentiate on the basis of customer service or a spatial monopoly. Differentiation reduces the level of price competition, although it cannot eliminate it altogether. (See Chapter 2.)

A comparison of two New Jersey liquor retailers illustrates the impact of marketing strategy on pricing policy. Until 1980, the New Jersey state government controlled liquor prices, requiring all liquor retailers within its jurisdiction to maintain a legislated minimum margin. When the state lifted price controls, many liquor retailers slashed prices to increase sales. A store in Clifton, for example, doubled its sales from $1 million to $2 million by cutting prices. It earned about the same profit, however, since the price cut reduced the gross margin percentage (return on sales) to nearly half the previous state-mandated level.

Not all retailers relied on price to attract customers, though. Some retained their old prices but created competitive advantages by providing high levels of service. The Watchung Liquor Store in Montclair, New Jersey, provided free delivery, opened charge accounts, and offered advice on wine purchases and party planning. These services induced the store's customers to pay its higher prices. The store maintained a gross margin of about 24 percent, which is nearly double that of the Clifton store.[1]

The key issue in setting prices, therefore, is consistency with overall marketing strategy. The firm must carefully consider the expectations of its target consumers and their willingness to pay. In this way, it can keep its pricing policy consistent with all other retail mix elements and with its strategy for competing with other firms.

PLANNING MARKUPS AND MARGINS

The pricing policy specifies the role of price in the firm's marketing strategy. As the next step in the pricing process, the firm conducts cost analysis and sets markup goals.

Chapter 7 discussed the costs incurred by retail stores. Recall that the cost of goods is the total cost of obtaining merchandise from suppliers. Often this is simply called **merchandise cost**. Since the difference between price and merchandise cost determines the margin on the product, the firm has to first compute merchandise cost before determining the price. The firm includes in merchandise cost the supplier's price for the item and transportation charges paid by the retailer. It also adds other direct charges such as excise duties or customs fees (for imported merchandise) to merchandise cost. On the other hand, it deducts any trade or quantity discounts. The firm groups other operating expenses such as payroll, rent, utilities, advertising, and so forth, under SGA expenses as shown in the income statement of Alpine Ski Shop in Chapter 7 (Exhibit 7.1).

To understand the relationship between cost and retail price, it is first necessary to understand certain common terms discussed below.

Original Retail and Sales Retail

The term **original retail** designates the price at which a seller "first" offers an item for sale. Most retailers, however, sell some amount of merchandise below original prices; that is, they sell it "on sale." These markdowns on original prices reduce the original retail value of the inventory since the retailer does not get the original price for it. As mentioned in Chapter 11, employee discounts and stock shortages also reduce original retail. A distinction must, therefore, be made between original retail and the revenue that the retailer actually earns.

The revenue that the retailer actually earns from selling the item is called **sales retail** or **net sales**. Note that sales retail or net sales never exceeds original retail.

Consider the following example. At the start of a season, a department store puts a $25 price on a sweater. This is the sweater's original retail price. After selling 200 of these sweaters within the first month, the retailer still had another 100 in stock. In order to hasten the sale of the remaining stock, the store reduced the price to $19.99 and sold the entire lot in the next two weeks. For these 100 sweaters, the sales retail, $19.99, falls short of the original retail price.

The cumulative original retail value for the entire stock of 300 sweaters comes to $7,500 ($25 × 300), but the actual sales retail for the stock reaches only $6,999 [($25 × 200) + ($19.99 × 100)]. This cumulative sales retail (or net sales) is thus $501 less than the cumulative original retail. Original retail and sales retail figures are often expressed as averages. The average original retail is, of course, the original price of each sweater, $25. However the average sales retail is $23.33 ($6,999/300).

Initial Markup

The **initial markup** is the difference between the original retail value of an item and its cost. If the retailer bought the sweaters for $12 each and set an original price of $25, the initial markup equals $13. This gives an initial markup on the entire consignment of 300 sweaters of $3,900 [300 × ($25 − $12)]. Some retailers call initial markup *markon*, but the term *markup* is preferred and used in this text.

Maintained Markup (or Margin)

Since sales retail typically comes in below original retail, the retailer actually makes less than $3,900 from selling the 300 sweaters. If, as discussed earlier, it sells 100 of the sweaters at $19.99 each, the maintained markup or the difference between actual revenue and merchandise cost for the consignment is $3,399:

$$\text{Maintained markup} = \text{Sales retail (Net sales)} - \text{Merchandise cost}$$
$$= \$6,999 - \$3,600$$
$$= \$3,399$$

Retailers often use the terms *maintained markup* and *margin* synonymously. In this text, the term **maintained markup** will be used to refer to an individual merchandise item, while *margin* will be used to refer to the cumulative maintained markup of an entire store or a department within a store.

Markup Percentages

Retailers customarily express markup as a percentage of either retail price or cost. One can, for example, calculate **markup on retail (MUPR)** as follows:

$$\text{Markup percentage on retail (MUPR)} = (\text{Markup} / \text{Sales revenue}) \times 100$$

When a store sells sweaters it bought at $25 for $45 each, its markup is $20 ($45 – $25). The markup percentage on retail (MUPR) is:

$$[(\$45 - \$25) / \$45] \times 100 = 44\%$$

Similarly, when a store has revenues of $68,000 and a cost of goods (merchandise cost) figure of $40,000, its markup percentage on retail is:

$$[(\$68,000 - \$40,000) / \$68,000] \times 100 = 41.18\%$$

Retailers can also express markup as a percentage of the cost of goods with **markup on cost (MUPC)** figures:

$$\text{Markup percentage on cost (MUPC)} = (\text{Markup}/\text{Cost}) \times 100$$

Expressed as a percentage of cost of goods, the markup on sweaters is ($20/$25) × 100 or 80 percent. The markup of $20 represents a 44-percent markup on retail and an 80-percent markup on cost.

Many small retailers set prices of individual merchandise items based on markup percentage on cost. The retailer adds a fixed markup percentage to the cost of the good to arrive at the price. Suppose a retailer buys 100 packets of envelopes at 48 cents each and wants to gain a 50-percent markup on cost. It can calculate the retail price that achieves this markup goal as follows:

$$\text{Retail price} = \text{Cost} + \text{Dollar markup}$$

where,

$$\text{Dollar markup} = \text{Cost} \times (\text{MUPC}/100)$$

Substituting the second equation into the first gives:

$$\text{Retail price} = \text{Cost} (1 + \text{MUPC}/100)$$

The following calculation yields the retail price for each packet of envelopes:

$$\text{Retail price} = \$0.48(1 + 50/100) = \$0.72$$

Many retailers favor this method of price determination, called **cost plus pricing**, because the calculation is easy to apply to a large number of items. Many hardware stores, grocers, and drugstores price individual items by adding a standard markup percentage to their cost. They face a problem, however, in determining the appropriate markup. Moreover, different merchandise categories may require different markup levels since one markup percentage is seldom appropriate for all items. The cost plus method does, however, provide a starting point. Retail managers can then adjust final prices depending on demand conditions, special sales, and the competitive environment.

A large and increasing number of retailers prefer to express markup as a percentage of retail price (MUPR) to gain the advantage of comparability. Since retailers typically express most financial data (for example, net and gross profit margins and return on sales) as percentages of sales revenue, it is helpful to calculate markup percentage in the same way. For these reasons, firms should calculate markup percentages based on retail price. The cost basis is discussed here for illustrative purposes only and to show the mathematical relationship between the two measures.

Note that MUPR closely resembles the gross profit margin or return on sales (ROS) ratio discussed in Chapter 7. However, the terms *return on sales* or *gross profit margin* customarily refer to the performance of the store as a whole, whereas retailers can calculate markups for the store, a department within the store, a merchandise classification within the department, or even an individual piece of merchandise.

The two methods for calculating markup percentages need not cause great concern, because if one is known, the other can be calculated. The relationship between the two ways of calculating markup can be seen in the following:

$$\text{MUPR} = [\text{MUPC}/(100 + \text{MUPC})] \times 100$$
$$\text{MUPC} = [\text{MUPR}/(100 - \text{MUPR})] \times 100$$

As an illustration, recall the example in which a department store bought sweaters at $25 each and sold them at $45 each, giving an MUPR of 44 percent. What is MUPC?

$$\text{MUPC} = [(44/(100 - 44)] \times 100 = 80\%$$

Note that this matches the value of MUPC calculated earlier.

It is also possible to derive an MUPR value from a known MUPC value. For example, if MUPC is known to be 80 percent, what is MUPR?

$$\text{MUPR} = [(80/(100 + 80)] \times 100 = 44.4\%$$

Consider some other examples. If MUPR is 5 percent, what is MUPC?

$$\text{MUPC} = [5/(100 - 5)] \times 100 = 5.3\%$$

If MUPR is 10 percent, what is MUPC?

$$\text{MUPC} = [10/(100 - 10)] \times 100 = 11.1\%$$

The two formulae allow retailers to convert any MUPR value to MUPC and vice versa, as shown in Exhibit 12.4. Note that while MUPC can exceed 100 percent, MUPR must always be less than 100 percent, since the markup cannot be greater than sales revenue.

Markup Goals

Retail pricing decisions rely heavily on the markup concept. The ultimate profitability of the store depends on the amount of markup it generates relative to merchandise and operating costs. Consider for example, a store with annual sales of $200,000 and operating expenses of $60,000 a year. To avoid any loss, the store must have a maintained markup of at least $60,000 to cover all expenses. However, a markup of $60,000 does not generate any profit. If the firm's profit goal for the year is $10,000 (5 percent of expected sales), then the maintained markup must be $70,000 ($60,000 + $10,000). As discussed earlier, to achieve a maintained markup of $70,000, the firm's initial markup must exceed its maintained markup by the amount of total reductions from original retail.

Exhibit 12.4   Markup Conversion Table

Markup on Retail (MUPR)	Markup on Cost (MUPC)
5.0%	5.3%
10.0	11.1
20.0	25.0
30.0	42.8
35.0	53.8
40.0	66.6
45.0	81.8
50.0	100.0
55.0	122.2
60.0	150.0
65.0	185.7
70.0	233.3
80.0	400.0
90.0	900.0

To meet profitability goals, retail firms set **markup goals** for the store, individual departments within the store, and individual merchandise classifications to guide them in setting prices. Although the price set for a particular merchandise item may vary from the overall goals, aggregate markups must relate pricing decisions to overall profit goals.

Initial Markup Percentage (IMUP)   Consider again the previous example in which a store set a profit goal of $10,000 and expected net sales of $200,000. It expected total SGA expenses of $60,000. With the profit goal, anticipated sales, and SGA expenses established, the firm then must estimate reductions, the loss in the original retail value of the merchandise due to markdowns, employee discounts, and shortages. Suppose that the firm expects total reductions of $10,000 (5 percent of net sales). Its initial markup then is:

$$\text{Initial markup} = \text{Expenses} + \text{Profits} + \text{Reductions}$$
$$= \$60,000 + \$10,000 + \$10,000$$
$$= \$80,000$$

To compare results among merchandise departments and stores, firms customarily express initial markup as a percentage of original retail:

Initial markup percentage (IMUP) = (Initial markup / Original retail) × 100

Since original retail is the sum of net sales and total reductions, and initial markup is the sum of profit, expenses, and reductions, IMUP can also be expressed as follows:

$$\text{IMUP} = \frac{\text{Expenses} + \text{Profit} + \text{Reduction}}{\text{Net sales} + \text{Reductions}} \times 100$$

Applying these formulae, the retailer can calculate initial markup as shown below:

$$\text{IMUP} = \frac{\$60,000 + \$10,000 + \$10,000}{\$200,000 + \$10,000} \times 100 = 38.1\%$$

Given its expected sales, expenses, and reductions, the store must have an aggregate initial markup of 38.1 percent to meet its profit goal.

Maintained Markup Percentage (MMUP)   An aggregate IMUP of 38.1 percent, however, does not mean that the store will actually generate this level of margin. Reductions will hold the maintained markup below 38 percent. The retailer can calculate the maintained markup and the maintained markup percentage (MMUP) with formulae similar to those for initial markup and IMUP:

$$\text{Maintained markup} = \text{Expenses} + \text{Profit}$$
$$\text{MMUP} = [(\text{Expenses} + \text{Profit}) / \text{Net sales}] \times 100$$
$$= [(\$60,000 + \$10,000) / \$200,000] \times 100$$
$$= 35.0\%$$

That is, if IMUP is 38.1 percent and reductions are $10,000, the store will maintain a markup of 35 percent.

Exhibit 12.5 further illustrates the relationship between initial and maintained markup percentages. Note that initial markup can never be less than maintained markup, and the two match exactly when no reductions bring the original retail price down. Retailers calculate initial markup based on anticipated figures to help them set prices. While they can also calculate MMUP based on anticipated figures, they cannot calculate the actual maintained markup until they sell all affected merchandise because they can never know exact net sales until the sales have actually taken place. MMUP is very useful to monitor the store's actual margin at the end of any accounting period.

The initial and maintained markup percentages contribute important information for price determination. They indicate the margin the store must generate to meet its overall financial goals and serve as guidelines for determining prices of individual items. Retailers should never, however, automatically apply them to determine prices of all items in a store. Markups for individual items will vary depending on demand, competitive conditions, consumer price sensitivity, and the marketing environment.

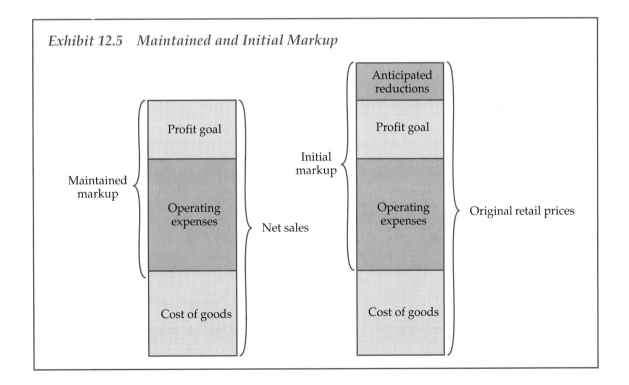

Exhibit 12.5   Maintained and Initial Markup

STRATEGY IN ACTION

47th Street Photo: Competing on the Basis of Price

It started about 20 years ago in a small second floor room on Manhattan's West 47th Street. But the steep climb on narrow stairs did not deter customers from flocking to the store to find the best prices on cameras, audio equipment, and other electronic goods. Today the four 47th Street Photo outlets sell more than $100 million of electronic goods annually and attract customers from all over the world. The spartan interiors of the small, cluttered stores contain the state of the art in discount retailing.

The marketing strategy of 47th Street Photo follows a simple philosophy—to sell quality branded electronic merchandise at the lowest price possible, ensuring profits by controlling costs and generating high sales volume. The stores carry a huge inventory of cameras, computers and software, calculators, VCRs, stereos, typewriters, telephones, and telephone answering machines. The key to the firm's low costs is smart, opportunistic buying of branded goods in high volume. For example, when the high value of the dollar made electronic goods cheaper in foreign markets, 47th Street Photo bought aggressively from the "grey market" to keep costs down. A grey market product is one that is intended for foreign markets, but diverted to the United States because its price is lower than what a U.S. retailer would have to pay for it directly from the manufacturer. Recently the Supreme Court confirmed the legality of

---

DEMAND ANALYSIS: PRICE VERSUS QUANTITY

The relationships among price, quantity, and revenue fundamentally affect the prices of individual merchandise items. Retailers must continually reconsider whether they should increase, decrease, or hold stable the prices of products. For most products, a lower unit price increases sales of the product, but this does not always increase total revenue. Sales revenue will increase only if the increase in quantity compensates for the drop in price. This depends on the sensitivity of consumer demand to price.

Demand Curve

To judge the sensitivity of consumer demand to price, retailers look to the demand curve. A **demand curve** shows the number of units of a product or service demanded by all potential buyers at different price levels. Consider, for example, the demand curve for Good *A*. The total demand for this product is 2,900 units, if the price is $50 per unit. But demand drops to 2,525 when price is $75 per unit. If

such buying practices despite protests from manufacturers.

Compared to department stores that sell electronic goods, 47th Street Photo provides its customers few services, fewer frills, and no ambience. The salespeople are efficient and well-informed, but have little time for those who are not sure of what they want. In-store product demonstrations and prolonged conversations with salespeople are discouraged and a sizable line typically waits at the check-out counter. But the customer can expect to pay a significantly lower price than a department store would charge.

To maintain its high sales volume, the store relies on mail-order and telephone sales in addition to in store sales. The store's advertisements listing prices of hundreds of products appear regularly in *The New York Times*, *The Wall Street Journal*, and many computer, photography, and audio magazines. Despite its provincial name, the store sells to the entire country. Over the years it has gained a reputation as a trustworthy store that stands behind the merchandise it sells.

Overall, 47th Street Photo has put together all the elements necessary to gain a cost advantage over its competitors and passes the benefits along to consumers in the form of lower prices—that is the secret of its success.

the price was $200 per unit, demand would drop to only 400 units. Note that this demand curve represents the total market demand at various prices. That is, it is the sum of each individual's demand curve for the product.[2]

The precise shape and slope of the demand curve is determined by a number of factors. The demand curve for some goods may be steeply sloped, as is the case for Good *A* in Exhibit 12.6. Compare, for example, the two demand curves shown in the exhibit; they are quite typical for consumer products. Both demand curves slope downward, that is, as unit price increases, the number of units demanded decreases. The numerical relationship between price and quantity, however, differs for the two cases. The demand for Good *A* is more sensitive to price than the demand for Good *B*. This means that an equal change in the prices of both products will affect the demand for Good *A* much more than that for Good *B*. Such differences can arise because of the nature of the product or service. Typically, the more important the product to the customers and the fewer substitutes for it, the less sensitive is demand to price.

The demand curve summarizes the relationship between price and quantity demanded, everything else being constant. The shape of the demand curve can

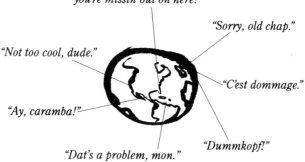

Competition among commercial airlines is so keen that when a company like Northwest Airlines offers a 35% reduction in air fares, the demand becomes intense. What
would the demand curve look like for this industry?

Exhibit 12.6 **Downward-Sloping Demand Curves**

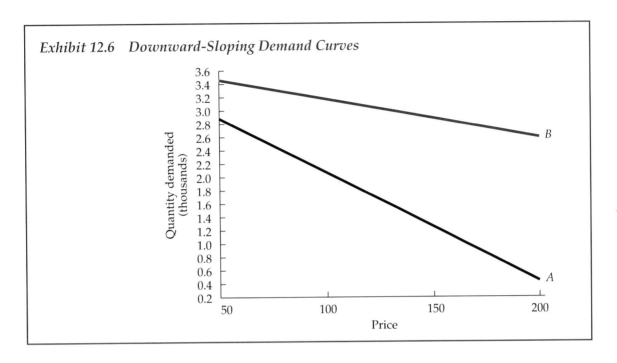

shift, however, due to changes in consumer income levels, tastes, and the competitive environment for the product. According to demand curve D_2 in Exhibit 12.7, for example, 2,900 units are demanded when the price is $50. This demand level is determined partly by consumer income (that is, their ability to spend), partly by consumer tastes (that is, by how much they value this type of product compared to others), and partly by the competitive environment (that is, by the price and quality of direct substitutes). A change in any of these factors will shift the demand curve to the right or left as shown in Exhibit 12.7.

When income increases, for example, the demand curve shifts to the right (see curve D_3). This means that consumers demand more units of the merchandise at the same price. While they originally demanded 2,900 units at $50 each (see curve D_2), the shift reflects an increase in demand at the same price to 3,150 units. This type of demand shift can result from product improvements, increased advertising, better service, reduced competition, or greater product awareness. An increase in the level of consumer incomes can also shift demand curves to the right. However, if incomes drop or the product value diminishes, demand will be lower for a given price, causing a leftward shift in the demand curve (see curve D_1). Leftward shifts often result from the introduction of new substitutes, increased marketing for substitute products, or a general drop in the income level.

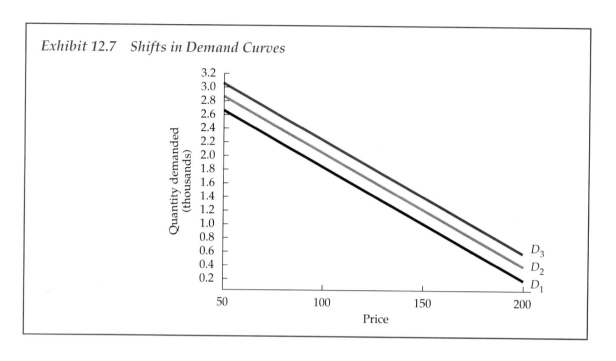

Exhibit 12.7   Shifts in Demand Curves

Demand, Price, and Revenue

The shape of the demand curve determines the amount of revenue generated at different price levels. Total revenue is the money received from selling a particular item of merchandise, that is:

Total revenue = Unit price × Number of units sold

Exhibit 12.8 shows the total revenue at different price levels for the demand curve D_2. Consumers demand a total of 2,900 units at a price of $50, generating total revenue of $145,000 (2,900 × $50). If price increases to $75, demand decreases to 2,525 units, but total revenue increases to $189,375. Total revenue is higher at a price of $100 a unit, but decreases thereafter.

Exhibit 12.8 also shows the **marginal revenue (MR)**, which is the change in total revenue that results from a change in price from one level to another. For example, changing price from $50 to $75 a unit yields marginal revenue of $44,375. This is the additional revenue the firm gains by raising price. It gains marginal revenue of $20,625 by raising the price from $75 to $100 a unit. It is important to note that marginal revenues can be negative. A price increase from $125 to $150 yields a marginal revenue of –$21,875. This means that demand drops so far that even the higher price cannot compensate for the lower margin and hence total revenue decreases.

Exhibit 12.8 *Total and Marginal Revenue at Different Price Levels for Demand Curve*

D_2

Price	Quantity	Total Revenue	Marginal Revenue
$50	2,900	$145,000	—
75	2,525	189,375	$44,375
100	2,100	210,000	20,625
125	1,675	209,375	–625
150	1,250	187,500	–21,875
175	825	144,375	–43,125
200	400	80,000	–64,375

Information on total and marginal revenues at different price levels helps retailers set prices, since it shows how a change in price will affect revenue. It is evident from Exhibit 12.8, for example, that prices of $125 or $150 will yield negative marginal revenue. Although per-unit revenue is lower at $100 a unit, this price maximizes total revenue.

This does not mean, however, that firms should always choose the revenue-maximizing price. If suppliers can provide only 1,250 units of the item, the firm should set the price at $150. Alternatively, it could set prices below $100 and sacrifice some present revenues in order to gain customer loyalty or increase store traffic and increase future revenues and profits.

Price Elasticity of Demand

The **price elasticity** of demand measures the sensitivity of demand to price changes as the percentage change in quantity demanded relative to the percentage change in price. That is:

$$\text{Elasticity} = \frac{\text{Percent Change in Demand}}{\text{Percent Change in Price}}$$

To compute price elasticity, demand is measured in number of units sold. Because demand typically increases with lower prices, price elasticity is usually negative; it is customary, however, to express elasticity as an absolute number without the sign. An elasticity of 1.5 means that a 10-percent reduction in price increases demand by 15 percent.

With regard to price elasticity, demand can be characterized in one of three ways: (1) elastic demand; (2) inelastic demand; and (3) unitary elasticity of demand. Elastic demand indicates that the absolute value of price elasticity exceeds 1; that is, any percentage decrease in price causes demand to increase by a greater percentage. When demand is elastic, total revenue increases if price decreases, but falls if it increases. Curve D_2 in Exhibit 12.8 depicts elastic demand at a price of $150 a unit.

Inelastic demand, the opposite of elastic demand, indicates an absolute value of price elasticity less than 1; that is, a percentage change in price results in a smaller percentage change in demand. In this case, total revenue increases when price rises and falls when price falls. In Exhibit 12.8, the curve D_2 is inelastic at $75 a unit.

Unitary demand elasticity indicates that a percentage change in price results in exactly the same percentage change in quantity demanded; that is, the absolute value of price elasticity exactly equals 1. A small change in price will not affect total revenue significantly in this case.

Factors that Affect Price Sensitivity

The demand curve graphically portrays the relationship between price and quantity, and the elasticity value provides a summary measure of that relationship. The shape of the demand curve and the elasticity value depend on how consumers react to changes in price. Different products have different demand curves and different elasticities because consumer price sensitivity varies from one product to another. To determine merchandise price, retailers need to understand what determines consumer price sensitivity. Six general factors affect price sensitivity: (1) uniqueness of the merchandise, (2) total purchase amount, (3) scope for comparison shopping, (4) the price–quality effect, (5) the price-ending effect, and (6) the context effect. Each of these factors affect in some manner the role of price in consumer purchase decisions.

Uniqueness of Merchandise   Consumers' sensitivity to price depends on their perception of the uniqueness of the merchandise. In general, consumers show less sensitivity to the price of more unique merchandise, that is, merchandise that is better differentiated from potential substitutes. Firms can differentiate products based on unique functional qualities (such as durability), styling, and fashionability. Other bases for differentiation include the reputation of the manufacturer and the brand name. Many computer buyers, for example, are willing to pay more for IBM computers despite the availability of cheaper alternatives that provide equal functional benefits.

Total Purchase Amount   Price sensitivity also depends on the amount of the purchase.[3] Observers have noted, for example, that consumers engage in more comparison shopping and display more price sensitivity when buying large appliances like refrigerators than when buying toasters and irons.[4] Small items such as gum and candy tend to have very low price sensitivities because consumers often buy them on impulse. The low total dollar amounts of these purchases do not inspire much interest in prices in consumers.

Scope for Comparison Shopping   The shape of the demand curve depends not only on the characteristics of the product, but also on the retail environment. Consider, for example, a convenience store in an airport and one near a popular intersection with many stores nearby. The lack of alternatives makes consumers less sensitive to price when buying from an airport store. When consumers have easy access to alternative shopping opportunities, they typically engage in comparison shopping to search for the best alternative. Similarly, when they can find the same brand of merchandise at many retail stores, consumers compare prices closely before purchasing. For this reason branded products sold at supermarkets and drugstores tend to create extreme price sensitivity when a number of these stores cluster together. A geographically isolated store (that is, one with a spatial monopoly) affords customers less opportunity to compare prices.

The level of comparison shopping depends not just on the existence of alternatives, but also on the level of consumer awareness of alternatives.[5] As consumers become more aware of substitutes, they are more likely to engage in comparison shopping. Restaurants and stores located near popular tourist areas, for example, can often charge higher prices because the transient tourists are usually unaware of alternative stores and, therefore, cannot engage in comparison shopping.

The Price–Quality Effect   Whirlpool Corporation once offered an extra supply of 18,000 vacuum cleaners to retailers at a substantially lower price than normal. Both K mart and Western Auto bought some of the vacuum cleaners from Whirlpool. K mart priced them at $29 each, but stopped stocking them because consumers showed little interest. Western Auto, on the other hand, quickly sold the entire lot at $49 each.[6] The law that demand increases as price falls apparently failed. It failed because consumers associated price with quality. This demonstrates the **price–quality effect**. Customers at K mart took the unusually low price of $29 as an indicator of low quality. They did not feel confident buying a vacuum cleaner at that price.

This relationship between price and perceived quality may slow demand for certain items when price falls below an acceptable range. Researchers have found that in many situations "price is not inversely related to quantity demanded"[7] because of the negative image created by low price.

The association between price and perceived quality is especially strong for products like perfume, jewelry, crystal, upscale apparel, and certain liquors that appeal more to image concerns than to function concerns. Since buyers cannot objectively judge the quality of these products easily, they tend to rely on price as a signal of quality. This is particularly true when consumers have little information beyond price about the relative characteristics of different brands.

High prices often create an image of exclusivity and prestige by limiting the size of the market. Consider, for example, a Rolex President watch. Although some people would buy a Rolex President watch if they could find one for $250 instead of the usual price of nearly $8,000, the total demand for these watches would probably fall if the normal price declined to that level. At $250, the watch would lose its prestige image.

STRATEGY IN ACTION

Take Care of Your Customers and They Will Take Care of You

Home Depot, the Atlanta-based building supplies and home improvement products retailer, has grown into a powerful chain in its industry in just over a decade by offering high-quality products and innovative service. Started in 1978, Home Depot now owns and operates over 182 stores nationwide, and plans to raise that number to over 500 by 1996. Sales continue to grow with no sign of slowing down.

There are many reasons for Home Depot's success including its merchandising and service strategy. The stores stock a wide variety of products needed for home building and repair, and do-it-yourself improvement projects. Yet despite the wide variety, stores manage to keep their inventory costs down by using rapid ordering systems that synchronize supply with demand. Home Depot's employees are considered to be the best in the industry. They are highly knowledgeable about the products they sell and about home repairs in general. Many of the store employees are erstwhile home builders and tradespeople themselves.

This solid product and service strategy is further augmented by the corporate mission of working with the community. According to many observers, one way that the chain attracts and retains customers is through its solid record of corporate social responsibility to the communities in which it operates. For example, in the wake of Hurricane Andrew in August 1992, Home Depot reopened its stores in Southern Florida as soon as the wind stopped blowing in order to help the ravaged Floridians begin to rebuild their homes. Many other retailers reopened much later and raised their prices considerably.

Just as hardware stores will often double the price of snow shovels after a big winter storm, many stores in Hurricane Andrew's path raised their prices for items such as emergency generators and water pumps, selling them for three and four times their normal price. The corporate officers of Home Depot, however, insisted that stores in Southern Florida forgo the standard profit on items rather than benefit from the tragedy surrounding them in South Florida. Company headquarters acted rapidly to see

The Price-Ending Effect   Why do retailers commonly set prices at numbers like $1.99, $9.99, $199, or $495, rather than $2, $10, $200, and $500? It is not clear how retailers discovered this **price-ending effect**, but some evidence suggests that this sort of pricing can increase demand for a product substantially. For example, a study conducted in a supermarket found that sales of margarine reacted significantly to prices ending with a 9. In one case, a reduction in price from 71 cents to 69 cents nearly doubled weekly unit sales from 9,120 units to 17,814 units. In a second case, a reduction from 63 cents to 59 cents resulted in a 75-percent increase in unit sales, from 8,283 units to 14,567 units a week.[8]

that damaged stores were provided with tents out of which to operate, and that prices were instantly lowered across many product categories. Plywood was determined to be the most valuable item in stock, and other stores in the chain rushed to send their inventories to the South Florida locations. Home Depot believes that the move to help Floridians cope with the hurricane was the right one, both ethically and for its business in the long run, and probably no one in Florida will forget what Home Depot did for them in their time of need.

Home Depot has also developed a "green" program to help customers choose products that are environmentally friendly. Planned for over two years, the campaign debuted during the Rio summit in 1992, when customers thoughts were focused on the environment. The first stage of the campaign was a print campaign for in-store displays that suggests products in the store that can save energy and protect the environment. Management believes that a "green" program of this nature in all the stores will help customers chose the products that best

serve their needs while still helping the environment. Furthermore, as "green shopping" can often be difficult, management sought to make shopping easier for consumers by trying to remove some of the guess work. Shopping for environmentally safe products can be confusing for consumers because of the possible dual effects of some products. For example, florescent light bulbs are more energy efficient, but they contain mercury which can leak into landfills when the light bulbs are discarded and can potentially taint the water supply. The company identified 70 products in their green program, and the campaign has remained a successful feature in Home Depot stores. Customers find the print campaign to be honest and straightforward, and that it does not lead to any confusion over products, a problem that many consumers have experienced with "green labeling."

Sources: Adam Bryant: "Making hardware environmentally friendly," *The New York Times*, June 4, 1992, and Steve Lohr, "Lessons from a Hurricane: It Pays Not to Gouge," *The New York Times*, September 22, 1992, pp. D1, D5.

Although other studies have not found such drastic effects, retailers favor odd prices in the belief that consumers find a price like $19.95 more acceptable than $20.00, despite the negligible difference between them. For one possible explanation, people may tend to mentally process price information from left to right, truncating the information rather than rounding it to the nearest whole number. Thus, they perceive "59" as 50 and "19.95" as 19.00 rather than 20.00.

Compare the two sets of prices shown below.[9] The numbers in the left-hand column show the original prices of two brands of margarine and those in the right-hand column show reduced sale prices for the same brands.

	Original Price	Sale Price
Brand A	$0.89	$0.75
Brand B	$0.93	$0.79

For which pair is the lower price more of a bargain? Most people will select Brand B, even though the absolute difference in price is the same in both cases and the percentage change is higher for Brand A. Consumers might think that Brand B represents a better bargain if they did not actually calculate the difference in price, rather than simply approximating it by looking only at the left-most digit. This makes the difference for Brand A seem to be 10 cents (80 – 70) while the difference for Brand B is 20 cents (90 – 70).

The Context Effect   Consumer sensitivity to price can change significantly depending on the context in which a product is sold. Supermarkets can sell dried fruits as ingredients for cakes and in the baking-needs section or packaged as nutritious snacks and displayed together with other health foods. Basically the same product sells for a much higher price when packaged as a snack, and consumers are less sensitive to its price. The reason is the **context effect**: when a store sells dried fruits alongside other snacks, the prices of those snacks influence consumer perceptions of the fair or appropriate price of dried fruits.

A recent study also found that the type of outlet that sells a product can influence consumers' perceptions of the appropriate price.[10] This study asked respondents to imagine that they were lying on a beach on a hot day and longing for a nice cold bottle of their favorite beer. It then asked the respondents to state the maximum price they would be willing to pay for the bottle of beer if a companion offered to go and get it for them. The study presented two scenarios. In the first, the nearest retail outlet was a bar in a resort hotel; in the second, the nearest outlet was a small, local grocery store.

The maximum price respondents were willing to pay differed dramatically for the two scenarios. Half of the respondents were willing to pay a hotel up to $2.65 for the beer. In the second scenario, half of the respondents would pay only $1.50. Since the person consuming the beer would not physically enter either the hotel or the grocery store, one might suppose that the respondents would have been willing to pay the same amount irrespective of the outlet. The fact that the maximum prices people were willing to pay differed so significantly reflects the context effect. The respondents' past experiences of prices at resort hotels and local grocery stores influenced their responses.

Past prices also influence consumers' perceptions of price. Examine, for example, the results of a pricing study shown in Exhibit 12.9. This study sold five products in two sets of stores. One set (the control group) sold the products at their regular prices throughout the experiment. The stores in the experimental group initially charged a low price and then increased it to the regular level.

As one might expect, sales started out higher in the experimental stores because of the lower price. However, after the initial period, the sales at the control stores

Exhibit 12.9   Effect of Past Prices on Later Sales

		Weekly Average Unit Sales	
Product	Store Type[a]	Initial	Final
Mouthwash	Experimental	300	365
	Control	270	375
Toothpaste	Experimental	1,280	1,010
	Control	860	1,050
Aluminum foil	Experimental	4,110	3,275
	Control	2,950	3,395
Light bulbs	Experimental	7,350	5,270
	Control	5,100	5,285
Cookies	Experimental	21,925	22,590
	Control	21,725	23,225

[a] Experimental stores began with a low price, then raised it to the regular price. Control stores charged the regular price in all periods.

Source: Albert J. Della Bitta and Kent Monroe, "The Influence of Adaptation Levels on Subjective Price Perceptions," in *Advances in Customer Research*, ed. by Peter Wright and Scott Ward, 1973 Proceedings of the Association for Consumer Research, vol. 1 (Urbana, IL: ACR, 1974), pp. 359–369.

were higher for all five products, even though both groups of stores had the same price. Note, too, that in the control stores the sales of all five products increased with time. In the experimental stores, sales dropped for three of the five products. Even in the two cases in which sales increased (mouthwash and cookies), the increases in the experimental stores failed to keep pace with those in the control stores.

The initial lower price at the experimental stores probably made consumers more sensitive to price when it rose to its regular level. Another possible explanation is stockpiling. At the lower price, people bought more than they actually consumed and stored the rest for future use. Their demand, therefore, was lower in the subsequent period. Chapter 17 discusses the impact of price on stockpiling behavior.

SETTING THE RETAIL PRICE

While cost and demand analysis are the foundations of all pricing decisions, the retailer must analyze the merchandise environment of each item in detail before setting a final price. Three factors influence this decision especially strongly: (1) merchandise objectives, (2) competitive environment, and (3) supplier relationships.

Consumer sensitivity to price can change significantly depending on the context in which a product is sold. This vacationer is willing to pay considerably more for the cold drink on this cruise ship than she would be from her local grocery store.

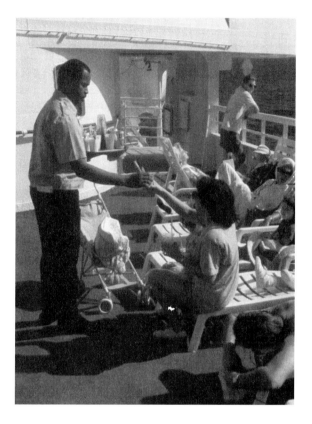

Merchandise Objectives

Although all merchandise must generate profit in the long run, stores often sacrifice the profitability of individual items in order to fulfill their overall objectives. For example, retailers often price selected merchandise lower than demand and cost conditions would warrant in order to build store traffic or generate market share. This is known as loss-leader pricing.

Loss-Leader Pricing   Retailers offer loss-leader items at lower prices than their normal prices, sacrificing some amount of profit that the items could have generated. Despite the word *loss*, the item's price need not fall below its cost. Retailers practice **loss-leader pricing** because they believe that lower prices attract customers who buy other merchandise besides the reduced item. This strategy builds store traffic and increases sales of other merchandise, which more than offsets the lower margin on the reduced-price items.

For another reason, retailers practice loss-leader pricing to create overall images of low prices. Since retail stores carry thousands of individual items, it is difficult for consumers to compare the prices of all items at different outlets systematically. Rather, consumers tend to form price images of stores based on the prices of a limited selection of merchandise items. The prices of milk, eggs, laundry detergent, coffee, and cereals, for example, strongly influence consumers' price images of supermarkets. By reducing markup on these products below average, a supermarket manager can create a favorable price image for the store and build loyalty among price-sensitive customers.

Supermarkets use loss-leader pricing heavily. Studies have found that consumers buy more than 60 percent of grocery items on impulse.[11] This means that a low price on a few key items will likely boost sales and profits for the entire store as customers buy impulse products at full price along with the items with reduced prices.

An extreme form of loss-leader pricing sets the price of the item below even its cost. Although retailers occasionally price goods below cost, this practice is often viewed as unethical. In some cases, it is even illegal. Critics argue that loss-leader pricing unfairly damages small retailers who cannot compete with large outlets, especially chain stores. For this reason a number of state laws prohibit sales below cost. These laws are discussed in more detail later in this chapter along with other legislation affecting price decisions.

Price Lining   Another merchandising objective, **price lining**, also affects the prices of individual items. Retail stores, especially apparel stores, often carry the same type of merchandise at different price points. A men's wear retailer, for example, will carry shirts of different styles and fabrics that it buys from suppliers at varying prices. Typically, however, it will group shirts at one of three distinct price levels (for example, $15.99, $19.99, and $24.99). This practice is known as price lining. By grouping all shirts at three price points, the retailer can appeal to customer groups with varying incomes and tastes, while at the same time keeping down administrative costs. Price lining also simplifies the consumers' buying task, since they have to compare only a limited number of price points.

In order to clearly demarcate price points, retailers consolidate merchandise from different suppliers and sell it at the same price, even if the suppliers charge different prices. For example, a retailer may obtain shirts from two suppliers at $10 and $12 each, respectively. If it applied a standard markup of 40 percent, it would price the two shirts at $14.00 and $16.80. However, to keep price points consistent, it may price both shirts at $15.99, setting different percentage markups on the two shirts.

Competitive Environment

Retailers can make no pricing decision without considering the competitive environment. Unless a retailer exclusively distributes a product, other retailers in the market area will probably duplicate its merchandise to some degree. Competitors can upset the best-laid pricing plan by changing their own prices, thereby manipulating what consumers are willing to pay. For example, a retailer that prices a loss-leader item 15 percent below normal in order to increase market share may not benefit if competitors reduce their prices, too. At times, in order to maintain its market share, a retailer may find itself forced to match price changes initiated by competitors. Retailers need to monitor the price at which a product sells at competitive outlets in order to make their own price decisions.

As explained in earlier chapters, similar stores located close together are likely to find that price is an important basis for competition. As the stores become more similar, consumers become more sensitive to price and, therefore, the potential for price competition increases. Vigorous price competition forces managers to evaluate the role of price in their own and also in their competitors' marketing strategies. Managers must determine competitors' likely pricing strategies and their likely reactions to any price changes. In many cases, a price cut initiated by one firm is quickly matched by competitors, with devastating effects on profitability of all firms. Such price wars frequently take place in gasoline, airline, and car rental industries.

Increasingly, retailers are relying on price cuts to build competitive advantage, vainly hoping that competitors will not retaliate to maintain their own competitive positions. Unfortunately, as competitors vie to become the lowest-priced retailer, the general profitability of the industry declines, to the detriment of all firms.[12] Such competition can benefit an industry only if price reductions increase the total level of demand for a product and, therefore, the sales and profits of all retailers increase. This, however, is an exception rather than the rule.

A low-price strategy can benefit an individual firm if it has a cost advantage over competitors. Recognizing their disadvantage, competitors will hesitate to engage in a price war. Discount electronics stores such as 47th Street Photo can set prices lower than many of their competitors because of economies of scale and low operating costs. (See Chapter 2 for a discussion of 47th Street Photo's marketing strategy.) These firms can initiate aggressive price cuts to build volume, which, in turn, creates further economies of scale.

Low-price strategies also brought success to off-price apparel chains (for example, T.J. Maxx, Hit or Miss, Marshalls) during the first half of the 1980s. Compared to department stores and other specialty apparel stores, off-price stores reduced costs through opportunistic buying, locating at low-rent sites, reducing personal service, and minimizing expenditures on advertising and store interiors.

Price, of course, is not the only competitive weapon available to retailers. As discussed in Chapter 2, many retailers successfully reduce the importance of price by differentiating themselves with unique merchandise, superior service, or accessible locations. A store that increases its differentiation from its competitors also increases its latitude to set its own prices.

Supplier Relationships

Price also depends on a retailer's relationship with its suppliers and the suppliers' goals and objectives. Suppliers may object, for example, when a retailer consistently picks one of its brands as a lead item and sells it at a low price. Manufacturers spend considerable money and effort to develop favorable images for their brands. Aggressive price cutting by retailers can diminish that image and restrain the brand's long-term sales. Although suppliers cannot control the prices retailers charge customers, channel relationships become highly confrontational if a retailer consistently undermines the supplier's policies. Often suppliers try to deny offending retailers' access to supply.

In one incident, Kids R Us, the children's apparel chain operated by Toys R Us, charged that General Mills had illegally tried to stop the chain from selling Izod shirts because of the low-price policy of Kids R Us. General Mills, which owned Izod, resented the chain's low-price policy since it undermined the exclusive image of Izod shirts. General Mills also feared that the low prices would make the Izod shirt unattractive to department stores, who are its major customers.

ADJUSTING PRICES THROUGH MARKDOWNS

The discussion of the markup concept at the beginning of this chapter noted that in order to maintain a desired markup level, retailers have to start with a higher initial markup to allow for anticipated reductions in the retail value of the merchandise. The most important source of reductions, **markdowns**, reduce the prices of items from their original levels.

In an ideal world, retailers could measure demand accurately and buy exactly the amount of merchandise they could sell at the profit-maximizing price, leaving little need for markdowns. In the real world, markdowns inevitably result from the risk of holding inventory in uncertain demand conditions. For example, at the beginning of the season an apparel retailer has to buy clothes in a variety of styles, colors, and fabrics, without knowing the precise demand for each item. It will acquire much more of some items than it needs because of fashion changes or slowdowns in the economy. The retailer must markdown slow moving items in order to adjust inventory levels to demand conditions.

Exhibit 12.10 shows typical markdowns for different categories of merchandise carried by department stores. Note that markdowns affect prices of clothing items most because frequent fashion changes make accurate demand predictions difficult. Moreover, stores must clear inventory of fashion apparel at the end of each selling season to make room for new merchandise. Markdowns increase sales because more people are willing to buy products at lower prices.

Retailers must carefully plan and implement markdown policies. Since a markdown decreases markup without reducing cost, it lowers net profits. Retailers lose millions of dollars in potential profits every year because of markdowns. For some merchandise lines, the dollar amount of reductions can even exceed their total gross margins! Just as retailers are relying more and more on price as a competitive tool, they are using more markdowns, too. A markdown indirectly reduces price without decreasing the general price level.

Exhibit 12.10   Markdowns and Initial Markups for Selected Merchandise Categories in Department Stores

Department	Markdowns as Percent of Sales		Initial Markup	
	1990	1989	1990	1989
Female apparel	38.5	30.8	53.2	53.3
Infants and children's clothing	31.4	26.4	52.1	52.4
Men's and boys' apparel	30.3	25.7	53.5	53.2
Footwear	31.9	23.3	51.0	52.0
Leisure and home electronics	19.3	13.5	45.9	47.3
Home furnishings	20.5	16.7	48.4	47.0

Source: Merchandise and Operating Results of Department and Specialty Stores in 1991, New York: National Retail Federation, 1991.

Markdown Calculations

Like markups, retailers can calculate markdowns either in total dollars or as percentages. For the purpose of planning markdowns and evaluating merchandise performance, retailers express markdowns as percentages of net sales:

$$\text{Markdown percentage (of net sales)} = \frac{\text{Dollar amount of net markdown}}{\text{Net sales}} \times 100$$

For example, suppose that a store bought 100 sweaters at the beginning of a season and sold 80 percent of the stock at its original price of $50 each. The store then reduced the prices of the remaining sweaters to $30 and sold them all. What is the markdown percentage?

Since it sold 80 sweaters at $50 each and 20 at $30 each, its net sales revenue is $4,600. The dollar markdown amount is $400, since it marked 20 sweaters down by $20 each. Thus:

$$\text{Markdown percentage} = (\$400/\$4{,}600) \times 100 = 8.69\%$$

For the purpose of advertising the price reduction to consumers, however, retailers compute markdowns based on original retail prices:

$$\text{Markdown percent (off original retail)} = \frac{\text{Dollar price reduction per unit}}{\text{Original price per unit}} \times 100$$

$$= (\$20/\$50) \times 100 = 40\%$$

The store's advertisement will announce a 40 percent price reduction on the sweater, since that is how much customers who buy on sale will actually save compared with the original price.

Controlling Markdowns

Markdowns make up for the lack of synchronization between inventory and demand. Although perfect synchronization is impossible, retailers should periodically review their merchandise plans to avoid excessive overbuying. Overzealous merchandise buyers may undermine a store's merchandise plan by purchasing certain items far in excess of planned amounts.

Sometimes retailers must mark down merchandise that is damaged during storage and transit. It may need to improve merchandise handling and storage procedures to remedy that situation.

Excessive markdowns also sometimes indicate lack of adequate merchandise support. Retailers can stimulate demand by improving merchandise displays and advertising and increasing selling effort. They must fully explore the potential for increasing sales through such activities before resorting to markdowns. Some retailers encourage salespeople to actively sell slow-moving items by paying them special bonuses for selling these items. This practice can, however, tarnish store image if salespeople push too hard to sell customers merchandise they do not want.

As a final alternative for controlling markdowns, retailers can transfer some of the risks of holding inventory to suppliers. Often suppliers are willing to take back unsold merchandise that is selling well in other parts of the country or in other types of retail stores. Many suppliers are willing to cooperate with retailers who are steady customers in order to foster a mutually beneficial long-term relationship.

If retailers can better synchronize their merchandise inventories with changing customer tastes and preference, they can reduce their need for markdowns. Examination of Benetton's operations illustrates how retailers can use new production and communications technologies to improve synchronization. A communication network links all Benetton outlets and manufacturing plants. The plants produce garments in undyed fibers, delaying coloration until the last moment. Based on information on "hot" selling colors and styles gathered every day from individual stores through the network, each store's shipment is specially selected to appeal to the preferences of its customers. Benetton's computer-assisted design and manufacturing (CAD/CAM) technology is an essential part of the system since it cuts down the lead time between receipt and delivery of an order.[13]

Timing and Sizes of Markdowns

Since retailers cannot avoid some amount of markdowns, they must properly plan and execute them. The success of a markdown policy depends crucially on the timing and the sizes of the price reductions. They must choose between taking markdowns early in the season or taking them later, near or at the end of the season. Factors such as store image, the nature of the merchandise, and the type of store influence markdown timing.

Early Markdowns   Many retailers, especially department and discount stores, take markdowns early in the season for the following reasons:

* Taking markdowns early, while some demand remains for the item, increases the probability that the merchandise will sell.
* A smaller price reduction is usually sufficient to spur sales if the retailer takes the markdown early.
* Early markdowns free shelf space and capital tied up in slow-moving merchandise.
* Early markdowns provide insurance that if sales don't increase, time remains to take more drastic markdowns at the end of the season.

This retailer had to consider how much of a markdown would be sufficient to bring customers into the store while at the same time not significantly cutting into his profit.

Late Markdowns   Although early markdowns seem to be gaining in popularity, many specialty stores and exclusive, prestige outlets prefer to delay markdowns until the end of the selling season. These stores prefer late markdowns for the following reasons:

- Limiting markdowns to the end of the selling season upholds the store's image by differentiating its regular patrons from price-sensitive customers who shop the store only during seasonal markdown periods.[14]
- Frequent early markdowns can undermine consumer confidence in the store's regular prices.

By concentrating all markdowns at the end of the season, the store can organize special sales events to attract large numbers of price-conscious shoppers.

Sizes of Markdowns   The size of a markdown depends on the amount and salability of excess inventory in hand. Since retailers take markdowns to spur sales and decrease inventory levels, the size of the markdown must be large enough to spark consumer interest in the merchandise. At the same time the dollar amount of the markdown must not be so great as to significantly erode profits.

THE LEGAL ENVIRONMENT OF PRICING

A number of federal and state laws affect retail pricing practices. The following discussion focuses on three major areas: (1) price fixing, (2) price maintenance, and (3) price discrimination.

Horizontal Price Fixing

Can the managers of two competing supermarket chains jointly decide what prices to charge or what specials to offer? Absolutely not. This would be a case of horizontal **price fixing**. Section 1 of the Sherman Antitrust Act and the Federal Trade Commission Act prohibit any type of collusion among people or firms to fix prices. "Under no circumstances may competitors form any agreement concerning prices to be charged for products."[15]

In one incident, the managers of three local supermarket chains met surreptitiously in parking lots once every week to decide on which items they would promote as specials and the prices they would charge for those specials. All three then promoted the same specials at the same prices. Their secret collusion was exposed and the supermarkets were fined a total of $1.7 million. The court fined the managers, gave them suspended jail sentences, and placed them on probation.[16]

Vertical Price Fixing

What power does a manufacturer have to determine the prices at which retailers sell its product? The repeal of the **resale price maintenance** (fair trade) law in 1976 stripped manufacturers and wholesalers of any legal power to determine prices once they pass title to retailers.

Until 1975, the congress exempted retail price maintenance by manufacturers from federal antitrust laws. In states that had passed fair trade laws, manufacturers could specify the prices at which retailers sold their products.[17] Fair trade laws were motivated by the belief that manufacturers had the right to protect the images of their brands from indiscriminate price cutting by retailers. The law also protected small, independent retailers from direct price competition by large chains. Indeed, the lobbying efforts of independent retailers accounted for a major part of the support for fair trade laws.[18]

Since fair trade laws reduced retailers' freedom to set their own prices, many consumer groups and retailers (specially discount chains) considered them anticompetitive. Many states began to repeal fair trade laws in the 1970s, and the final blow came with the passage of the Consumer Goods Pricing Act by Congress in 1975, which essentially prohibited fair trade practices.

Without fair trade laws, manufacturers have difficulty maintaining resale prices unless they start their own retail stores. They have to rely on market power and persuasion to convince retailers that widespread price cutting will, in the long run, hurt both the manufacturer and the retailer. Intense price competition among retailers and the dominance of mass merchandisers and discount stores erode manufacturers' power to set retail prices. As one alternative, they can sell merchandise on a commission basis and not give title to the retailer. This means, however, that the manufacturer assumes the risk of excess inventory and inventory damage.

Some manufacturers and wholesalers have tried to coerce retailers to keep them from selling their product below the desired price. For example, Fortunoff filed suit against the North American Watch Company, which distributes Piaget, Movado, and Concord watches, accusing the wholesaler of refusing to sell to it and other discount stores. The suit also alleged that the exclusive jewelry store, Tiffany, conspired with the wholesaler to fix prices.[19] The conflict between Kids R Us and General Mills mentioned earlier is another example of a manufacturer refusing to sell to price discounters. Also, as mentioned in Chapter 4, the Panasonic Corporation agreed to pay $16 million to consumers after the state of New York charged it with fixing retail prices.

In May 1988, the U.S. Supreme Court issued a ruling in the *Business Electronics Corporation* v. *Sharp Electronics Corporation* case that is starting to have a significant impact on retail pricing decisions. The court's decision could make it easier for manufacturers to stop supplying price-cutting retailers in order to protect other retailers. Prior to this decision, courts generally held that any action by manufacturers that directly or indirectly curbed a retailer's freedom in setting its own price was a per se violation of the Sherman Act. A per se violation is automatically considered illegal since it is presumed anticompetitive.

In the 1988 decision, a majority of the justices agreed that it may be reasonable in certain situations for manufacturers to curb price-cutting retailers to protect other retailers from intense price competition. Often, especially in the electronics industry, two types of retailers sell the same good, one charging a higher price and promoting the product, maintaining good displays, providing customer service, and repair facilities; while the other offers minimal or no service, but charges a lower price. The Supreme Court's ruling allows manufacturers to discontinue supply to this second group of price-cutting retailers in order to protect the first group of retailers from price competition. Such protection may be warranted because of the higher costs of promotion, service, and so on. In the long run, according to the court, such curbs may increase competition among different brands and benefit consumers.[20]

Sales-below-Cost Laws

Sales-below-cost laws prohibit retailers from setting prices below the cost of the item or below cost plus some designated minimum markup. About 20 states have such laws, although some are repealing them. In some instances the law applies only to specified lines of trade such as liquor or groceries. Some laws specify the factors included in retailer's cost while others define the retailer's cost as the sum of the delivered cost of the item plus a stated percent markup at retail.[21]

These statutes intend to reduce price competition by making it illegal to price below cost. This prevents large, well-financed retailers from "predatory" pricing to drive small retailers out of business. Critics of the laws argue, however, that they merely protect inefficient retailers and hurt consumers by reducing price competition. For these reasons, many states are repealing sales-below-cost laws and, where they exist, enforcement is often lax. Retail managers must, however, familiarize themselves with the details of any sales-below-cost laws that apply in the states in which they operate.

Price Discrimination

Price discrimination occurs when a supplier sells the same item to different retailers at different prices. It is not illegal for retailers to discriminate in price among consumers, although few actually do so, as long as such discrimination does not violate a person's civil rights. It is a different matter, however, when a manufacturer or a wholesaler discriminates in price among retailers. The Robinson-Patman Act prohibits manufacturers from either directly or indirectly discriminating in price between different retailers (or wholesalers) purchasing items of like grade and quality. Like the laws preventing price maintenance, this law seeks to protect small retailers from large chains who, because of their greater bargaining power, may obtain discounts from manufacturers far more than cost savings would justify. The Robinson-Patman Act also prohibits manufacturers from discriminating in the promotional allowances they give to retailers.

In three types of situations, manufacturers can legally charge different prices: (1) cost justification, (2) quantity discounts, (3) good faith defenses.

Cost Justification   Price differences are legal differences if cost of manufacture, delivery, or distribution justify them. The burden of proof of cost difference, however, is on the seller.[22]

Quantity Discounts   The laws do allow for quantity discounts to large retailers, as long as the discount does not exceed the actual cost savings of selling to those who buy in large quantities. Also the schedule of discounts should not be designed to exclude all but the very large retailers.

Good Faith Defense   A manufacturer can charge lower prices to one retailer than others in order to meet the low price of a competitor. For example, a firm that sells to retail stores in California and New York initially charges retailers in both states $10 per item. After some time, a new competitor enters the California market charging $8 for the same item. In this situation, the original seller can lower the price to its California customers to $8 per item while still charging $10 in New York.

Such a price differential is justified by the good faith defense argument that without the lower price, the firm would lose its California customers. Note, however, that the argument cannot justify a price below $8. The firm can match its competitor's price, but not undercut it.

Summary

1. Price and perceived utility jointly determine the value of merchandise to consumers. As utility increases compared to price, so do value and the chance consumers will buy the product. Through the pricing decision, the retailer translates some of the value it creates into profits. The many factors that retailers have to consider in setting final prices complicate the pricing decision. The firm's overall marketing strategy, demand and cost factors, merchandise objectives, competitive and supplier environments, and anticipated markdowns are some factors that affect retail prices.

2. Retailers must base all price decisions on cost and demand analysis. Cost analysis is essential for setting an overall markup target to ensure achievement of the firm's financial goals. Markup is the difference between the retailer's selling price for an item and its cost for the item. The markup level that the retailer must maintain in order to cover expenses and meet profit goals is called maintained markup. When first sold, an item will typically have a markup greater than the maintained markup to account for future reductions in retail value. This is the initial markup.

3. The demand curve shows the number of units of a product that customers demand at different price levels. Typically, demand curves slope downward; that is, the number of units consumers demand decreases as price increases. The price elasticity of demand

measures the sensitivity of demand to price changes as the percentage change in quantity consumers demand relative to the percentage change in price. Price elasticity can be characterized in three ways: (a) elastic demand, (b) inelastic demand, (c) unitary demand.

4. Six factors affect price sensitivity: (a) uniqueness of the merchandise, (b) the total purchase amount, (c) the scope for comparison shopping, (d) the price–quality effect, (e) the price-ending effect, and (f) the context effect.

5. Markdowns adjust the retail price by reducing it from its original level. Holding inventory in uncertain demand conditions makes markdowns inevitable. The impact of a markdown depends crucially on its timing and size. Retailers can take markdowns early in the season or near the end of the season. Firms should carefully plan and implement markdowns since they decrease margin without reducing cost.

6. A number of federal and state laws affect retail pricing decisions. Three major areas of concern are: (a) collusion among retailers to fix prices, (b) the extent to which manufacturers can control retail prices, and (c) price discrimination by manufacturers selling products of like grade and quality to different retailers at different prices.

Key Concepts

Margin	Price elasticity
Merchandise cost	Price–quality effect
Original retail	Price-ending effect
Sales retail (net sales)	Context effect
Initial markup	Loss leader pricing
Maintained markup	Price lining
Markup on retail (MUPR)	Markdowns
Markup on cost (MUPC)	Price fixing
Cost plus pricing	Resale price maintenance
Markup goals	Sales-below-cost laws
Demand curve	Price discrimination
Price sensitivity	Price experiments
Marginal revenue	

Discussion Questions

1. "The best way to price a product is to add a fixed markup to the cost of the good." Comment on this statement.

2. How are markup percentage on retail (MUPR) and markup percentage on cost (MUPC) calculated? If the MUPR of an item is 60 percent, what is the equivalent MUPC? Explain why MUPR never exceeds 100 percent.

3. Explain the term *price elasticity*. By how much will the demand for an item change when its price falls by 10 percent, if its price elasticity is 1.8?

4. Explain the terms *initial markup* and *maintained markup*. How are these terms calculated? When do original and maintained markups equal each other?

5. Why are some markdowns inevitable in retail stores? Why and how should firms control markdowns?

6. What are the advantages and disadvantages of taking a markdown early in the season versus taking it late?

7. Explain these terms: (a) loss-leader pricing, (b) price lining, and (c) horizontal price fixing.

8. Should manufacturers be allowed to dictate the price at which retailers can sell their products? What is your opinion and what is the general opinion of the U.S. courts?

9. Explain the term *price discrimination*. Under what conditions can a manufacturer or a wholesaler legally sell the same item at different prices to different retailers?

10. A retailer is contemplating decreasing the price of an item by 10 percent and advertising the price cut in the local newspaper. Design an experiment to monitor the effects of the price cut and advertising. Explain how you would analyze the results of the experiment.

Notes

1. Sanford L. Jacobs, "Deregulation Forces Owners of Liquor Stores to Adjust," *The Wall Street Journal,* March 16, 1981, p. 25.

2. Walter Nicholson, *Intermediate Microeconomics and Its Application*, Chicago: Dryden Press, 1990, p. 118.

3. Thomas T. Nagle, *The Strategy and Tactics of Pricing* (Englewood Cliffs, N.J.: Prentice-Hall, 1987), p. 62.

4. See William P. Dommermuth, "The Shopping Matrix and Marketing Strategy," *Journal of Marketing Research* 2 (May 1965), pp. 128–132; and Louis P. Bucklin, "Testing Propensities to Shop," *Journal of Marketing* 30 (Winter 1966), pp. 22–27.

5. Nagle, *The Strategy and Tactics*, p. 60.

6. E. Berkowitz, R. Kerin and K. Rudelius, *Marketing* (St.Louis, MO: Times Mirror/ Mosby, 1986).

7. Brian Sternthal and C. Samuel Craig, *Consumer Behavior: An Information Processing Perspective* (Englewood Cliffs, N.J.: Prentice-Hall, 1982), p. 298.

8. Nagle, *Strategy and Tactics*, p. 249.

9. This example is from Nagle, *Strategy and Tactics*.

10. Richard Thaler, "Mental Accounting and Consumer Choice," *Marketing Science* 4 (Summer 1985), pp. 195–214.

11. POPAI Supermarket Consumer Buying Habits Study (Englewood Cliffs, N.J.: Point of Purchase Institute, 1987).

12. Avijit Ghosh, "Customer Service: Key to Successful Retailing," *Channels of Communication*, Winter 1988, p. 1.

13. See Andrea Lee, "Being Everywhere," *The New Yorker*, November 10, 1986.

14. Ernest H. Risch, *Retail Merchandising* (New York: Merrill Publishing, 1987), p. 242.

15. Douglas J. Bowersox, M. Bixby Cooper, Douglas M. Lambert, and Donald A. Taylor, *Management in Marketing Channels*, (New York: McGraw Hill, 1980), p. 141.

16. Michael J. Duggan, "*United States* vs. *First National Supermarkets*," *Journal of Marketing* 47 (Fall 1983), pp. 127–128.

17. Louis W. Stern and Adel I. El-Ansary, *Marketing Channels* (Englewood Cliffs, N.J.: Prentice-Hall 1978), p. 375.

18. J. C. Palamountain, Jr., *Politics of Distribution* (Cambridge, MA.: Harvard University Press, 1955).

19. "Fortunoff Files Suit Against Watch Firms, Charges Price Fixing," *The Wall Street Journal*, May 3, 1984, p. 14.

20. See "High Court Backs Discounter Curbs by Manufacturers," *New York Times*, May 3 1988, p. A1; and Patrick J. Kauffman, "Dealer Termination and Resale Price Maintenance: Implications of the *Business Electronics Case* and the Proposed Amendment to the Sherman Act," *Journal of Retailing* 64 (Summer 1988), pp. 113–124.

21. Willard F. Mueller and Thomas W. Paterson, "Effectiveness of State Sales Below Cost Laws: Evidence from the Grocery Trade," *Journal of Retailing* 62 (Summer 1986), p. 167.

22. Stern and El-Ansary, *Marketing Channels*.

23. Nagle, *Strategy and Tactics*, p. 265.

Appendix to Chapter 12

Measuring Price Sensitivity

Although retail managers' experience gives them considerable insight into consumer demand factors, numerical estimates of price sensitivity can improve the effectiveness of pricing decisions. As one author stated, "The more precisely a firm can pinpoint the effect price has on sales, the more it can make price adjustments with confidence."[23] As one way to obtain numerical estimates of price sensitivity, firms can conduct price experiments. In a **price experiment**, a retailer systematically varies the price of an item and observes the impact of the price change on quantity demanded.

In the simplest type of experiment, the retailer initiates a price change and then observes how sales change from their base level. For example, a store that typically sells 100 light bulbs per week can reduce its price by 10 percent and monitor the effect of that price change on sales, noting, perhaps, that weekly sales increased by 25 percent after the price reduction. This simple test of price sensitivity has a serious drawback: the retailer cannot say with confidence that the price decrease caused the sales increase as opposed to changes in other external factors.

The addition of a control store can reduce this problem and increase confidence in the experiment. To establish the control, the retailer has to find another store closely resembling the one that will implement the price change. The control store must be similar in size, trade area characteristics, store atmosphere, level of service, and so forth. Also the historical sales levels in the control and in the experimental store should show similar patterns of variation. For example, if the experimental store had seen weekly sales of the item increase at a rate of 5 percent a year, the control store should have shown a similar increase. After choosing the control store, the retailer changes the price at the experimental store and monitors sales at both the control and the experimental store.

Exhibit 12A.1 presents an example of results from such an experiment. Consider again that the price reduction increases sales in the experimental store by 25 percent compared with the base level. Sales at the control store also increased by 10 percent, even though price remained constant at this store. This indicates that factors other than price are causing some change in sales. Since these factors could have affected sales at the experimental store, too, the firm cannot attribute all of the 25-percent increase in sales to price reduction. To adjust for these other factors, the firm must subtract the change in sales at the control store from the sales increase in the experimental store. The net effect of the price change, therefore, is 15 percent (25 − 10).

Experiments give retail managers a simple, yet versatile tool. They must, however, be properly designed to yield valid results. The design of the experiment described in the previous paragraph is known as the before–after with control

Exhibit 12A.1   Results from a Pricing Experiment

	Weekly Base Sales	Sales during Promotion	Percentage Increase
Experimental store	100	125	25
Control store	120	132	10
Sales increase due to promotion			15

design, since it measures sales both before and after the price change and compares results with a control store to estimate the effect of nonprice factors on sales. Although, in the extreme, a firm could conduct the experiment with only one experimental and one control store, adding more stores increases accuracy. With just one store in each group, the results may not be generalizable. Factors peculiar to the market area in which the experiment is conducted could bias the results. Large chains should use a number of experimental and control stores and obtain a more representative sample of their outlets.

Retailers can conduct experiments to study other aspects of their operations besides pricing decisions. Similar experimental designs can test how promotions, changes in advertising, point-of-purchase displays, and shelf positions affect sales. In-store experiments can also test how two different marketing variables jointly affect sales, as illustrated by the following example.

A supermarket chain wished to test the possible sales effect of decreasing the price of a frequently purchased convenience food item by 10 percent. It also sought information on how advertising the item in the local media would affect sales. This resulted in three experimental conditions:

1. Price reduction with advertising
2. Price reduction without advertising
3. Present price with advertising

The firm added a fourth group as a control:

4. Present price without advertising

The chain randomly selected 24 outlets in four cities and assigned six outlets to each group. Exhibit 12A.2 shows the effects of price and advertising on sales. The table takes the control group's sales (without price change or advertising) as a base, and expresses the sales of all the other groups in relation to that base. A value of 108, therefore, means that the experimental group generated sales 8 percent higher than the control stores.

The results show that both price and advertising affected sales. Price reductions of 10 percent without advertising increased sales by 14 percent, and advertising without price reductions increased sales by 8 percent. Price reductions together with advertising increased sales by 35 percent. The interaction of price reductions

Exhibit 12A.2 Sales in Four Experimental Conditions

	No Advertising	Advertising
Present price	100 (control group)	108
Reduced price	114	135

and advertising improved sales far more than the combined effect of reducing price or increasing advertising separately. The interaction of the two marketing variables creates synergy for the store.

While price reductions and advertising significantly improved sales, one cannot, based on these results, say that the chain should implement these changes. The ultimate test is profitability. The amount of sales increase may not compensate for the loss in margin due to the price reduction and the cost of advertising.

Another issue is the long-term impact of the change. The firm must monitor sales for a long period after the experiment to make sure they do not later drop below the base level.

Retail experiments are becoming easier to conduct in supermarkets because many stores are equipped with scanners and more products now carry universal product codes (UPC). Scanners allow firms to easily monitor the sales of each individual item. Since these systems collect sales data continuously, they can track merchandise movement by day of the week or even by hour of the day. These data can then be related to changes in price or other marketing variables.

CHAPTER 13
Inventory Valuation and Control

Lands' End Reorganizes to Improve Inventory Management

Inventory is a key asset for retailers—without it consumers would have nothing to buy—and controlling inventory is critical for smooth retail operations. Inventory management entails making sure that items are kept in stock; ensuring a smooth flow of merchandise items by timing deliveries properly; tracking inventory between warehouse, stockroom, and display areas; handling returns when necessary; and processing orders promptly to keep inventory in stock. Managing and controlling inventory is a huge job, because when the customer wants an item, a retailer can lose the sale if the item is out of stock.

Inventory management process for direct mail retailers can be more difficult than for an in-store retailer for two basic reasons. First, publishing a catalogue creates longer lead-times, making it difficult for direct mail retailers to react to sudden changes in consumer demand. Second, out-of-stocks are far more damaging to a direct mail retailer: when customers want to purchase via catalogue, they request *specific items*, and will not be able to make the purchase in the case of out-of-stock items. In an in-store retail situation, out-of-stock items are removed from display, and customers do not know what items they are being denied. However, if direct mail customers find that the items they want are out of stock on more than one occasion, they could stop ordering from that catalogue, and the company could begin to lose sales.

Lands' End is a perfect example of a direct mail retailer that let inventory problems almost foul up its business. During 1990, Lands' End earning suffered from two major inventory-related problems: lost sales from customers unwilling to wait for delivery, and high shipping and handling costs due to a high ratio of out-of-stocks. Lands' End follows a policy of charging customers a single shipping fee for an order, even if the order involves more than one item. During 1990, Lands' End was often forced to send large orders to customers in multiple shipments because not all items were available at the same time, and the company had to bear the additional shipping costs. Lands' End had a great number of out-of-stocks because it poorly anticipated customer demand, poorly managed the available inventory, and inadequately controlled the flow of incoming inventory from their suppliers.

During the late 1980s, Lands' End built a technology-driven company that is nearly unrivaled in sophistication. Through technology, Lands' End simplified the shipping pro-

After studying this chapter, the reader will be able to:

- *Explain why retailers need to control inventory.*
- *Understand how inaccurate inventory valuation affects profit calculations.*
- *Know how to implement the cost and retail methods of inventory valuation.*
- *Understand the importance of shrinkage control programs.*
- *Determine order quantities and safety stock for staple merchandise.*
- *Use management information systems for controlling fashion and seasonal merchandise.*
- *Understand how the wide availability of computers and advances in communication technology are improving inventory management.*

cess for customers and improved the terms of ordering and returning items. They also linked their merchandise information systems with their shippers for more speedy delivery and pick-up. However, Lands' End entered 1990 with a weakening demand picture as the United States slumped into recession, and bloated inventories of unsold merchandise from the previous year. Lands' End sought to counter these problems by aggressively liquidating its stocks through promotions and introducing new products within existing lines (for example, straight collar shirts were added to the historically success-

ful button-down line) as well as new lines entirely (such as children's clothing and home accessories). The new product push was extremely successful, with a very strong recovery in customer demand and increased ordering of existing products. In fact, the company could hardly keep up with customer demand, and the fulfillment rate on the new lines was poor. This led to lost sales from customers unwilling to wait for delivery and increased shipping costs for the company, all due to poor inventory management.

Lands' End handled this problem with major changes in their inventory management. First, Lands' End changed the organizational chart within the merchandising and inventory management functions, adding more focus to each function. Historically, Lands' End's buyers were organized by product line (men's, women's, and children's pants or sweaters, and so on), but in order to bring more focus to the product, buyers were reorganized into more specific areas like men's pants or women's sweaters. This was also intended to reduce the number of compromises made in the way inventory was acquired and sold. Very often, buyers were forced into purchasing contracts in which they took on certain items that they did not want in order to secure a desired volume on items they did want. This resulted in excess inventories in areas in which the company did not specialize. For example, in order to secure enough men's button down shirts to meet demand, a buyer might have agreed to include boy's dress shirts in the order, even though it is not a fast-moving item for the company.

Land's End then changed the inventory management area so that it mirrored the buying function, with staff responsible for tracking specific areas of inventory rather than entire lines. In this fashion, inventory managers could be more in tune with the buying process of their area, as there was a single buyer and inventory manager for each area. Previously, one buyer might have handled the inventory for more than one inventory manager, and vice versa, which complicated the communications between the two functions. With the new organizational chart, the inventory managers deal with one buyer only, and the buyers with just the one inventory manager. The pair can follow the movement of their specific area much more carefully, and see that items are kept in stock and are easily trackable.

Source: *Land's End Company Report*, prepared by D. O'Neill for William Blair & Company; June 10, 1991.

Regardless of their size or the type of merchandise they sell, all retail firms must accurately value their stock or inventory. An accurate inventory valuation is necessary to control monetary investment in inventory. It is also necessary for measuring inventory productivity as well as for calculating gross margin and profits. An incorrect inventory valuation will distort all performance figures and render the best-laid merchandise budgets and plans useless.

Merchandise inventories represent a major portion of the retailer's asset base. Exhibit 13.1, for example, shows the composition of current assets of three leading retail firms. Although the three firms operate different types of retail stores, in each case inventories represent the bulk of their current assets. To improve asset turnover and overall financial performance, retail firms must, therefore, carefully manage and control how much they invest in inventories.

This chapter explains the process of inventory valuation and control. Since inventories represent both dollar investments and physical entities, firms must control them in terms of both dollars and units. The chapter is similarly divided into two sections. The first focuses on inventory valuation or **dollar control**, discussing the methods by which firms determine dollar values of inventories and the ways in which they control the funds they invest in inventories to reach financial goals. The second section of the chapter focuses on unit or **inventory control**, answering such questions as: How many units of an item should a firm keep in stock? How often should a firm reorder an item? How many items should it order at a time?

INVENTORY VALUATION

To control and regulate the amount of money a store and its departments invest in inventory, managers must appraise the value of the inventory accurately. An ef-

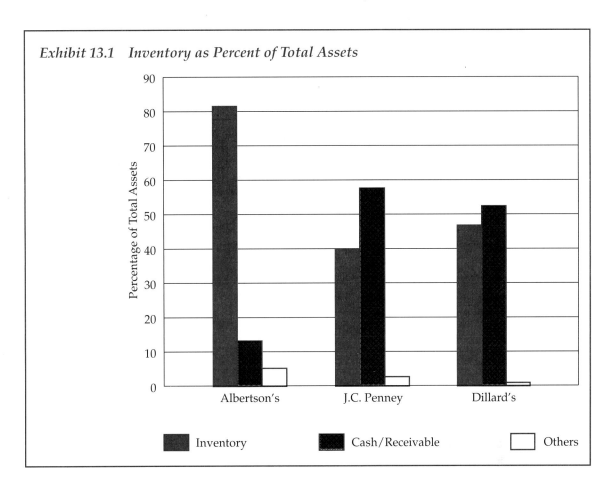

Exhibit 13.1 Inventory as Percent of Total Assets

fective valuation method (also called a dollar control system) provides up-to-date information on (1) the dollar value of the merchandise the firm sells, (2) the dollar value of the merchandise it has on hand, and (3) the amount of gross margins and profits it generates during any period. The firm must continuously update this information so that it can determine the monetary value of its inventory at any point in time.

Inventory Value and Profit

On December 7, 1992, the stock price of Eagle Hardware and Garden fell from $33.375 to as low as $19.50. The precipitous drop was a direct result of the company's announcement that it had overvalued its inventory by $2.4 million. This meant that the gross margins and profits reported by the company earlier were overstated. As Eagle Hardware's experience demonstrates, a firm must value the amount of inventory it has on hand accurately, since inaccuracies in inventory valuation distort profit calculations. As an illustration of how inventory valuation affects the firm's gross margin and profitability, consider the abbreviated income statement shown in Exhibit 13.2.

Recall from the discussion in previous chapters that gross margin is the difference between net sales and cost of goods sold. To calculate the cost of goods sold, the firm must accurately determine the value of its **beginning inventory**, its **closing inventory**, and its **purchases** during the period. The store began the month with inventory worth $230,000 and purchased another $150,000 worth of merchandise during the month, as shown in Exhibit 13.2. Thus, the value of the **total merchandise available** during the period was $380,000. The inventory at the end of the month was $220,000. The difference between the total merchandise available and the closing inventory is the cost of goods sold during the period. This means that the **cost of goods sold (COGS)** during the month was $160,000 ($380,000 − $220,000). The gross margin earned during the month is computed by subtracting cost of goods sold from net sales. This results, in this case, in a gross margin of $65,000 ($225,000 − $160,000). To compute net profit, the firm subtracts total SGA expenses of $35,000 from this gross margin. The store thus earned a profit of $30,000 before taxes.

Suppose now that the firm inaccurately valued its ending inventory at $225,000 instead of $220,000. What impact would this inaccuracy have on the store's profits? Exhibit 13.3 answers this question. *Overstating the value of ending inventory decreases the cost of goods, and increases gross margins.* Profits, too, become inflated by the same amount. By overstating the value of the ending inventory by $5,000, the firm increases its profit by $5,000. If, on the other hand, it understated ending inventory by 5,000, profits would decrease by that amount, as shown in the last column of Exhibit 13.3.

Any inaccuracy in the value of the ending inventory directly affects the firm's profits. Since the ending inventory from one period becomes the beginning inven-

---

Exhibit 13.2   *Abbreviated Income Statement for XYZ Co., January 1993*

Net sales		$225,000
Opening inventory	$230,000	
Purchases	150,000	
Total merchandise available	380,000	
Ending inventory	220,000	
Cost of goods sold		160,000
Gross margin		65,000
SGA expenses		35,000
Profit		$30,000

Exhibit 13.3   *Impact of Inaccurate Inventory Valuation on Store Profit*

	Inventory valued at $225,000	Inventory valued at $215,000
Net sales	$225,000	$225,000
Opening inventory	230,000	230,000
Purchases	150,000	150,000
Total merchandise available	380,000	380,000
Ending inventory	225,000	215,000
Cost of goods sold	155,000	165,000
Gross margin	70,000	60,000
SGA expenses	35,000	35,000
Profit	$35,000	$25,000

tory for the next period, the inaccuracy will also distort the profit figure for that period. Overstated profits can cost the firm additional taxes on "paper profits" that it does not actually earn and give managers a false sense of well-being that the firm does not deserve. Understated profits can reduce investor confidence and limit the firm's future growth.

Exhibit 13.3 demonstrates the importance of correct inventory valuation. Procedures for computing inventory value are discussed in the next section. Like most measures, retailers can value inventory at cost or at retail. The aims in both cases are to determine the value of the inventory at hand and compute cost of goods, but they involve very different accounting and record-keeping procedures.

Cost Method of Inventory Valuation

Retailers have employed the **cost method of inventory valuation** for a long time. Historically, when customers commonly bargained with retailers, the retail price of an item could not be determined before the sale became final; retailers thus valued their inventories at cost. Many small retailers, especially those selling few merchandise items, still use the cost method because of its simplicity and lighter record-keeping burden compared to the retail method.

Cost Method Based on Physical Counts   As Exhibit 13.2 showed, three pieces of information are essential for computing the cost of goods sold during any time period: (1) beginning inventory, (2) purchases, and (3) ending inventory. In the cost method, the retailer records the cost of each item it purchases, either on the price tag attached to the item (using a code that customers cannot easily decipher)

Many small retailers use the cost method of inventory valuation. This rug merchant uses the method because it is simple to understand and record.

or on the containers and racks that store the merchandise. They also record the cost of each purchase in a ledger, which shows the total purchases at any point in time.

To calculate the cost of inventory at the end of a period, the retailer physically checks each piece of merchandise in the store and the stock rooms. This determines the cost of each item, and the firm can calculate the total value of ending inventory by summing the values of the items. For its beginning inventory, it simply takes the ending inventory from the previous period. It obtains total purchases during the period from the purchase ledger. It then calculates the cost of goods sold based on the following relationship:

$$\text{Cost of goods sold} = \text{Beginning inventory (at cost)} - \text{Ending inventory (at cost)} + \text{Cost of purchases} + \text{Inbound freight}$$

The retailer adds inbound freight to the cost of goods sold, if it pays freight.

Cost Method with Book Inventory

The procedure described above requires a physical check of all inventories to calculate the value of the ending inventory. Most retailers find this a time-consuming and arduous task because they have thousands of items in stock. Since most retailers conduct physical inventory checks only once or twice a year, they cannot calculate profits and gross margins frequently because computing the true cost of goods sold during a period requires a physical inventory. One way to get around this problem is to maintain a **book inventory system** on a cost basis. A book (or perpetual) inventory system determines the cost value of the inventory at hand at any point in time by recording the cost of each purchase and the cost of each merchandise item sold.

To maintain an accurate book inventory, store personnel must record the original cost of each item as each sale takes place. To allow calculation of the cost of each transaction, the merchandise cost is recorded in a coded form on the price tag. At the point of sale, store personnel detach the section of the price tag with the cost code. At the end of each day, or week, the retailer decodes accumulated tags and computes the total cost of all items sold. In an alternative procedure, sales personnel can record the SKU number of each item they sell and then look up the cost of each in a master file. In either case, the retailer can calculate the cost value of the inventory at any point in time from the record of purchases and sales, as shown below:

Date	Inventory (at cost)	Purchases (at cost)	Cost of Sales
1/1	$5,000	---	$300
1/2	4,700	$1,000	500
1/3	5,200	---	300
1/4	4,900	---	600
1/5	4,300	750	350
1/6	4,700	---	400
1/7	4,300	---	---

In the illustration, the book or perpetual inventory (column 2) reflects the cost value of the inventory at any point in time.

Book inventory often differs from the actual value of physical inventory. Such discrepancies can arise from two sources: (1) inventory shrinkage or overage, and (2) market value of the physical inventory dropping below its original cost.

Shrinkage and Overage The book inventory value typically exceeds the physical inventory value because of **retail shrinkage**. Inventory shrinkage (or shortages) results from employee theft, shoplifting, physical loss, or spoilage. All stores suffer some amount of inventory shrinkage. This reduces the value of the inventory, since stolen or lost materials are no longer available for sale. In calculating the cost of

STRATEGY IN ACTION

Crime Prevention Reduces Shrinkage at Saks

When shrinkage or inventory loss occurs, there are two possible reasons: shoplifters or employee theft. Retailers, small and large alike, have long fought shrinkage and are always trying to invent more effective ways to stop theft by shoplifters and employees. Although easier said than done, one retailers has found a way to prevent such losses and is seeing solid results from its shrinkage control efforts.

Saks Fifth Avenue, the 48-store, fashion specialty company, has seen its shrinkage drop from 2.8 percent to about 2 percent in the past five years as the result of an ongoing rigorous deterrence program. The key to its success is consistency—keeping the program active and obvious at all times. Saks' management believes that an intermittent program would not offer a solution, and that the store's unremitting program keeps both shoplifters and employees on their toes. In the beginning Saks determined that simply trying to apprehend every shoplifter who walked through their doors was next to impossible and that rather than spending time catching them, understanding *how* and *why* the thieves committed their crimes would be much more beneficial. In this vein, the company set up an employee awareness program aimed at deterrence, and the program has worked successfully, keeping shrinkage to 1.8 to 2 percent of sales since its inception.

The key to the Saks crime prevention program is to involve every employee. Saks began by running a contest to solicit loss-prevention artwork from the staff, which was aimed at simply creating awareness that thefts occur and that the company was well aware of it. In the end, the contest proved so successful that many of the submissions have actually been turned into posters,

ending inventory, retailers must make an allowance for shrinkage, typically around 2 percent of net sales.

When book inventory exceeds physical inventory, the difference is called **overage**. An overage results from errors in physical inventories or in maintaining book inventory figures.

Drop in Market Value   Book value may also differ from the value of the actual physical inventory due to drops in market value of inventory. Suppose, for example, that a retailer bought an item for $5, but can now sell it for only $2.50 because it is no longer in season. The retailer should reduce the item's book value to $2.50 despite its $5 cost. Similarly, a retailer may have to sell some damaged or obsolete items below cost. It would be incorrect to value such items at their original cost because that would overstate the true value of inventory and profits for the period. For this reason, firms always value in-

which are prominently displayed in all staff areas. At closing time, the sales staff locks doors, tallies sales, and closes registers, followed by a sweep of the premises by security. When any procedure is forgotten, security leaves a brightly colored helium balloon that will be visible to everyone the following morning.

Sophisticated computer software has also helped in combatting employee theft. Point-of-sale systems now no longer just monitor sales at a given register, but they keep track of when cash drawers are opened and closed and if the inventory logs are accessed at unauthorized points. And on the flip-side, when advances are made to combat loss-prevention in any department, announcements are made at staff meetings, and incentives such as cash bonuses and gift certificates are offered as encouragement to keep up the good work.

Technology has been important in combatting shoplifting. Saks has installed both visible and invisible video cameras all over the stores. The most visible ones are planted right at the entrances, giving potential thieves a glimpse of the security system even before they enter the store. Also helpful are the electronic tags attached to the merchandise, which sound alarms if they are removed or tampered with or if an item is taken outside. Electronic tags have grown more sophisticated and invisible, fooling many a shoplifter. In addition, each tag at Saks is coded, so that security knows where the item was placed, indicating a prime spot for a video camera to be installed when a loss occurs from that spot.

Source: "Case Study: Saks Fifth Avenue," *Chain Store Age Executive*, January 1991, Section 2, pp. 38–39.

ventories by the **conservative rule**; that is, they always value inventories at the lower of market value or cost.

Because the cost method using book inventory requires coding and decoding the cost of each item, it serves only relatively small stores that stock few items or stores that have few transactions of large unit-value items. Auto dealers, furniture retailers, furriers, and jewelry stores are some examples of retail stores that use the cost method of valuation.

Retail Method of Inventory Valuation

The **retail method of inventory valuation** allows the retailer to estimate the cost value of closing inventory and the cost of goods sold without taking a physical inventory and without recording the cost of each item sold during the period. To determine the cost of ending inventory, the retailer: (1) determines the retail value of the inventory; (2) calculates the cost complement from the average relationship between cost and retail value of the merchandise it sells during the period; and (3) multiplies the retail value of the ending inventory by the cost complement to get the cost value of the inventory.

The retail method uses a book or perpetual system, so firms can calculate gross margin and profit at any point in time without conducting physical inventories. They must still take physical inventories once or twice a year to verify the accuracy of the book inventory and to determine the amount of shrinkage. However, a physical inventory count under the retail method is much simpler than under the cost method, because the firm must check only the retail price and not the original cost of each item.

Large retailers, especially those selling multiple categories of merchandise, strongly prefer the retail method. The concept of the retail method is consistent with the practice of relating all retail operating measures to retail price rather than to cost. Since retail planning goals and operating targets (planned sales, gross margin, return on sales, sales per square foot, and so on) are expressed at retail value, it is convenient and practical to value inventory at retail rather than at cost.

Implementing the Retail Method

Retailers must follow a number of different steps to calculate cost of goods and profits by the retail method:

1. Determine the retail and cost value of the beginning (opening) inventory and total purchases during the period.
2. Determine the ending (closing) inventory at retail.
3. Calculate the cost complement.
4. Determine the ending (closing) inventory at cost.
5. Calculate cost of goods sold and profit.

Step 1   In the first step, the retail method computes the cost and retail value of the beginning inventory and the goods purchased during the period. The retail and cost value of the beginning inventory, that is the ending inventory from the previous period, comes from the accounting records of the preceding period. As in the cost method, the retailer must keep a record of all purchases during the period. In the retail method, however, store personnel record the retail value of the purchases (that is, their selling prices) along with cost. The sum of the total purchases and the beginning inventory gives the total merchandise available during the period.

To illustrate the retail method, consider the following information obtained from the accounting records of ABC Store, a small electronics outlet:

ABC Store: January 1992

	Cost	Retail
Opening Inventory	$60,000	$90,000
Purchases	120,000	180,000
Inbound freight	5,000	---
Additional markup	---	2,500
Total Merchandise Available	$185,000	$272,500

As noted earlier, the ending inventory from December becomes the beginning inventory for January. The retailer adds the cost and retail values of all purchases it makes during the period to this beginning inventory figure. To find the cost value of purchases, it simply adds the invoice or wholesale costs of all items it receives during the month plus inbound freight costs. It adds inbound freight charges to the cost because this represents an expense it incurred in acquiring the merchandise from the wholesaler or supplier.

In the retail method, the retail price of each item purchased during the period is recorded along with its cost. These are all added together to give the retail value of purchases during the period. Occasionally, this figure will need adjustment if the price of an item increases from its original level. The firm must increase retail value of its merchandise by the amount of the price increase. The total merchandise available at retail is then calculated as follows:

Total merchandise available (at cost = Cost value of beginning inventory
+ Net purchases (at cost)
+ Inbound freight
Total merchandise available (at retail) = Retail value of beginning inventory
+ Net purchases (at retail)
+ Additional markup.

Step 2   In the second step, the retail method calculates the retail value of the ending inventory. Ordinarily, the ending inventory can be found by simply subtracting total retail sales during the period from total available merchandise. In practice, reductions due to markdowns, theft, and loss complicate things a bit. To calculate the retail value of ending inventory, the retailer computes total deductions for the month and then subtracts this figure from the total merchandise available.

Total deduction = Net sales + Markdown + Other reductions

Ending inventory (at retail) = Total merchandise available – Total deduction

To calculate total deductions, the retailer must keep complete records of all markdowns it takes and all discounts it gives to employees. Keeping track of all markdowns can become complicated because merchandise that is marked down for a temporary promotion may be reassigned the original price. In addition, the calculation requires an estimate of the amount of inventory shrinkage due to loss and theft. Adding total reductions for the period to the net sales figure yields the total deduction amount.

Returning to the ABC Stores example in Step 1, consider the following additional information:

- Net sales for the month totaled $100,000.
- The store recorded total markdowns of $4,000 during the month, but canceled $300 worth of these markdowns.
- Employee discounts during the month totaled $150.
- Based on its past experience, the store estimates 2 percent of sales for shrinkage due to employee theft, shoplifting, and lost and damaged items.

The store can calculate total deductions for the month as follows:

Net sales	$100,000
+ Original markdowns	4,000
– Markdown cancellations	300
+ Employee discounts	150
+ Allowance for shrinkage	2,000
Total deductions	105,850

With total deductions calculated, the store can calculate the retail value of its inventory accurately by subtracting this figure from the total merchandise available during the month:

$$\text{Ending inventory (at retail)} = \$272,500 - \$105,850$$
$$= \$166,650$$

Step 3   As the next step in the retail method, the retailer calculates its average cost complement of the total merchandise available during the period by dividing the cost value of the total merchandise available by the corresponding retail value:

$$\text{Cost complement} = \$185,000/\$272,500 = 0.68$$

This means that 68 cents of each sales dollar represents the cost of the good, while the remaining 32 cents is the gross margin. The retailer determines the cost and retail value of merchandise available in Step 1.

Step 4   To calculate the cost value of the ending inventory, the retailer multiplies the ending inventory at retail by the cost complement:

$$\text{Ending inventory (at cost)} = \text{Ending inventory (at retail)} \times \text{Cost complement}$$
$$= \$166,650 \times 0.68$$
$$= \$113,322$$

This gives a conservative estimate of the inventory value since it always represents the lower of cost or market value. If an item's market value (that is, its current retail price) is lower than the cost, the item will automatically be valued at this lower figure because total deductions include the amount of markdown on the item. This built-in conservatism is an important advantage of the retail method.

Step 5   In the final step in the retail method, the retailer calculates the cost of goods sold and the profits for the period based on an abbreviated income statement as follows:

ABC Stores: Abbreviated Monthly Income Statement

Net sales	**$100,000**
Total merchandise available (at cost)	$185,000
Ending inventory (at cost)	$113,322
Cost of goods sold	71,678
Gross margin	28,322
SGA expenses	20,000
Profits (before taxes)	8,322

Note that the firm must maintain a record of all sales during the period to compute net sales. Most stores today use electronic point-of-sale terminals that automatically record and total all sales. Recall that firms must deduct the retail value of all merchandise returned by customers from the total sales figure to obtain net sales. It can determine SGA (operating) expenses from its expense records. When calculating profits for individual departments, firms must allocate storewide SGA expenses among their departments based either on size or level of sales.

Adjustments to Income Statements   Firms must sometimes make two types of adjustments to abbreviated income statements. For the first, they must include cash discounts they earn for timely payment to suppliers, and for the second, they must account for workroom costs. As discussed in Chapter 11, suppliers typically give retailers discounts from invoice amounts, if they pay invoices promptly. When they first receive shipments, retailers calculate the cost of the merchandise based on total invoice amounts, making no allowance for potential discounts. At the end of the period, they deduct the total cash discounts they earn during the period from the cost of goods sold to generate an adjusted cost of goods figure called the net cost of goods.

At most department and specialty apparel stores, customers can have clothes they buy altered for better fit. Stores should add the cost of providing such services (usually called workroom costs) to the cost of their merchandise. However, since they do not know the real cost until the sale actually takes place, stores add no workroom costs to the cost of merchandise when they first receive it. Like cash discounts, stores make adjustments for workroom costs only at the ends of periods. Since workroom costs represent expenses incurred by the retailer, it adds the expenses for the period to the cost of goods sold. If it charges customers for some alterations, it should deduct these credits from the total costs and add only the net expenses to the cost of goods sold.

Advantages of the Retail Method

The retail method grows naturally out of the philosophy that retailers should focus on retail value rather than costs. Compared to the cost method some advantages of the retail method include:

1. The book inventory system allows firms to calculate gross margins and profit at any time without conducting physical inventories.
2. It values inventory conservatively, assigning the lower of cost or market value. (This is also true of the cost method with book inventory.)
3. The retail method, because of the perpetual system, provides an up-to-date estimate of the amount of inventory on hand at any time. This is important not only for merchandise planning, but also for determining insurance needs. In case of theft or fire, the book inventory shows the amount of merchandise in stock at the time for the purpose of insurance claims.
4. A physical inventory under the retail system is much simpler than that under the cost method, because it requires only current retail prices (which are readily available on price tags) and not the costs of items.

These advantages and the fact that it focuses the retailer's attention on the retail value of merchandise rather than cost make the retail method generally preferable.

Limitations of the Retail Method

One reason all firms don't use the retail method is its burden of record-keeping. It requires firms to maintain accurate records of all sales, markups, markdowns, markdown cancellations, employee discounts, purchases, freight costs, returns by customers, and returns to vendors. Prior to the wide use of computers in retail stores, such extensive record-keeping required a lot of time and effort. The growing use of electronic point-of-sale (POS) terminals and computerized stock records is easing this burden. Nonetheless, many small retailers, especially those with relatively few stocks and transactions, continue to use the cost method.

Some critics complain about inaccuracies in the retail method since the cost value figure for the ending inventory is based on the "average" cost complement. This assumes that the composition of the ending inventory resembles the composition of the total merchandise available during the period. It is hard to check this assumption when a store sells many different types of merchandise.

Although the averaging process does limit the retail method, retailers can overcome the problem by maintaining separate records for different merchandise classifications. Instead of maintaining a single system for an entire store or even an entire department, a retailer can keep separate records for groups of similar merchandise. Again, computerized information and accounting systems have simplified such detailed record-keeping, giving the retailer a detailed picture of the performance of different merchandise classifications.

Despite its versatility the retail method does not suit all cases. The method will not work in situations where the retailer transforms the good before selling it. A restaurant, for example, cannot use the retail method since it has no real basis for assigning retail value to the food and supplies it buys. Other service retailers such as automobile and appliance repair shops, carpet cleaners, and tailors, have to use the cost method for the same reason. Service departments within department stores

This high-volume grocery store has computerized its stock records, thereby easing the burden of record-keeping required by the retail method of inventory valuation.

(such as custom drapery departments) use the cost method, even if other departments in the store use the retail method.

Retail Shrinkage

Over the years, retailers have worried about shrinkage in inventory value due to theft and loss. It is estimated that loss from shrinkage may reach 3 to 4 percent of sales, and that employee theft and shoplifting together represent at least 2 percent of annual sales. Although the problems of shoplifting have received much publicity, employee theft actually costs firms more. According to one survey,[2] retailers attribute 43 percent of shortages to employee theft and 30 percent to shoplifting; the rest is due to record-keeping errors and theft by suppliers (see Exhibit 13.4). Any shortage is a significant loss to the retailer since it directly affects profitability.

To examine the impact of inventory shortages on profit, consider again the case of ABC Store. Shrinkage at this store has historically equaled 2 percent of sales.

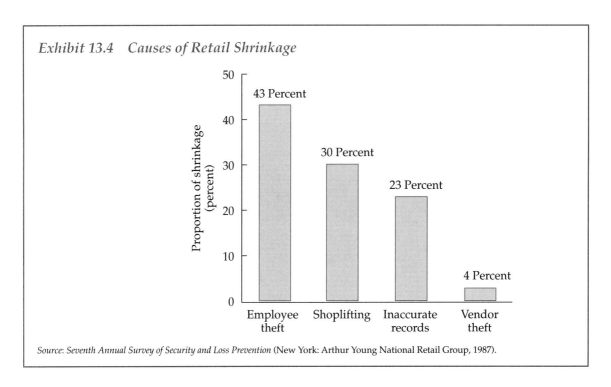

Exhibit 13.4   Causes of Retail Shrinkage

Source: *Seventh Annual Survey of Security and Loss Prevention* (New York: Arthur Young National Retail Group, 1987).

How would its profits change if it eliminated the shrinkage? As shown earlier, in January the store had sales of $100,000 and profit of $13,822. Total shrinkage for the month cost $2,000 (2 percent of sales). By eliminating shrinkage, the store could increase ending inventory by $2,000, decreasing cost of goods sold by the same amount. This would boost both gross margin and profits by $2,000, resulting in a 14.5 percent increase in profits. In other words, *every dollar of shortage represents a dollar of lost profit*! And total retail shrinkage in the United States may cost as much as $50 billion a year!

Controlling Shortages   Stores probably cannot eliminate shortages completely, but they must control these losses as much as possible. Retailers implement different types of shrinkage control programs to curb shortages. As perhaps the most visible part of retail shrinkage control programs, stores can attach electronic security tags to merchandise or install other electronic article surveillance (EAS) systems as clothing stores commonly do. Retailers have tightened security at stores and are aggressively prosecuting apprehended shoplifters to deter others from engaging in such behavior.

Shrinkage control is not, however, just a matter of deterring shoplifters: Employee theft accounts for most retail shrinkage. Shrinkage control, therefore, calls for making employees aware of the need for continuous monitoring. Over 75 per-

The procedures in this 15-page booklet given to Virginia Specialty Stores' employees are designed to reduce employee theft.

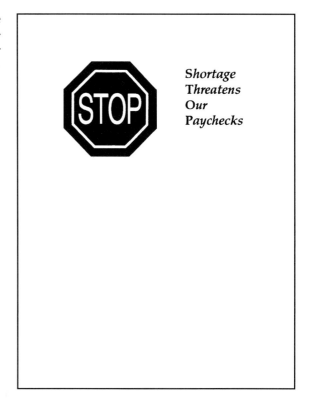

Shortage Threatens Our Paychecks

cent of retailers now operate shrinkage awareness programs which, through periodic meetings, newsletters, and poster campaigns, seek to reduce theft and shoplifting.[3]

The program initiated by Virginia Specialty Stores (VSS), a chain of 115 women's apparel stores, is a typical example.[4] The chain's shrinkage control effort centers on its highly visible S.T.O.P. program, which stands for "Shortages Threaten Our Paychecks." Every employee receives a personal copy of a 15-page handbook that presents the program. The chain requires all employees to review the handbook together with their supervisors and to sign agreements to "faithfully abide by the policies and procedures that it establishes, understanding this to be a condition of employment."[5] In addition, the firm encourages employees to apprehend shoplifters and offers them rewards of $100 for information leading to the apprehension of a thief (either shoplifter or fellow employee).

To control internal theft, VSS avoids temporary help, even in peak seasons, and publicizes apprehension of an employee for theft. The firm will dismiss an employee who knows of theft by fellow workers and does not report it. Each store names one employee Security Manager of the Month and makes him or her

ENTREPRENEURIAL EDGE

Controlling an Inventory of Biographies

In New York City's West Greenwich Village is a specialty store that not only specializes in books, but in one kind of book: biographies. The Biography Bookshop, owned by Carolyn Epstein and Charles Mullen, carries an inventory of about 10,000 titles, each of which is a biography, autobiography, memoirs or collection of letters. Because the popularity of specific titles varies relatively unpredictably, the store's merchandise is in effect a type of fashion good.

At this stage in the store's life, the owners try to control inventory by attuning themselves to what customers like to read and keeping a personal watch over how various titles perform. Because the store is

small (with only 400 square feet of selling space) and publishers offer so many choices, space is a primary concern in deciding how many of each title to order. Epstein and Mullen test the demand for their selections by ordering only one copy of most titles. With this method, they find surprises such as the popularity of a biography of the founder of aikido (a Japanese self-defense technique). This flexible approach works for the Biography Bookshop because the book business allows small, frequent orders and because the owners maintain a sense of what customers want.

Selecting and ordering inventory is a relatively complex task at the Biography Book-

responsible for monitoring security at that store. The overall program has been highly effective in reducing shrinkage and involving employees in this effort.

INVENTORY PLANNING AND CONTROL

Since inventories represent both dollar investments and physical entities, valuation is just one part of inventory management. The other is inventory planning and control. *Inventory control plans specify the number of units of each item to be stocked, that is, the store's depth of each item.* Only by properly controlling the physical stock of each item can the firm maintain total dollar investments at the planned level. Failure to control physical inventory inevitably reduces inventory productivity and harms financial performance.

Inventory control systems help the retailer decide for each item of merchandise (SKU) carried in the store (1) when to reorder it, if at all, and (2) how much to reorder. Simple as these decisions may sound, they require analysis of many factors such as past sales trends, price, seasonality, future demand projections, vendor lead times, and so forth. Moreover, the best approach to making these decisions depends on the product's status as a staple good with a predictable demand pattern, a fashion good, or a seasonal item.

store. To provide their wide selection of titles, Epstein and Mullen must search through the catalogs of many publishers, each of which may publish only a few biographies in a given season. Says Mullen, "We probably deal with more publishers than B. Dalton. Who goes entirely through a Cambridge University Press catalog? If I find one or two books, it's worth it."

Complicating the job of selecting inventory is the fact that the store's customers are more interested in finding an unusual life story than in picking up the latest best seller. (The store didn't sell a single copy of *Vanna Speaks*.) This means not only that Epstein and Mullen must keep abreast of the latest new titles, but they must order many backlist titles (those that the publisher introduced in the past, but still carries) and remainders (books that publishers are no longer producing).

Epstein plans to develop a basic backlist for the store, showing titles they frequently reorder. The store could then order 7 to 10 copies at a time, rather than purchasing single copies. Epstein hopes that this list can eventually develop into a data base for computerized inventory control.

Source: Allene Symons, "The Business of Selling Biography," *Publishers Weekly*, January 15, 1988, pp. 62–63.

Inventory Costs and Trade-offs

Inventory control seeks to minimize the total cost of maintaining inventory while adequately meeting forecasted demand. Three types of costs affect the optimal inventory policy: (1) the cost of holding inventory, (2) the cost of ordering, and (3) stockout costs. Exhibit 13.5 shows the sources of these costs. Inventory decisions become difficult because these costs conflict with each other, and firms must trade one off against the others to determine the best policy.

Holding Costs   Firms incur **holding costs** in two major categories. First, the opportunity cost of dollar investments in inventory equals, at a minimum, the interest payment on the working capital required to finance the inventory; opportunity cost could be greater if the firm needs capital for other parts of the business. The second category of holding costs includes the costs of physical storage, taxes, insurance, and the risk of spoilage. Both these categories rise in magnitude as the level of inventory in the store (or in the retailer's warehouse) increases.

Ordering Costs   **Ordering costs** include all costs associated with order placement, transportation, receiving, and handling. The costs of order placement and receiving depend on the firm's order processing system. They will be low for regular, frequent reorders of standardized products and high for special orders. Trans-

---

Exhibit 13.5   Sources of Inventory Costs

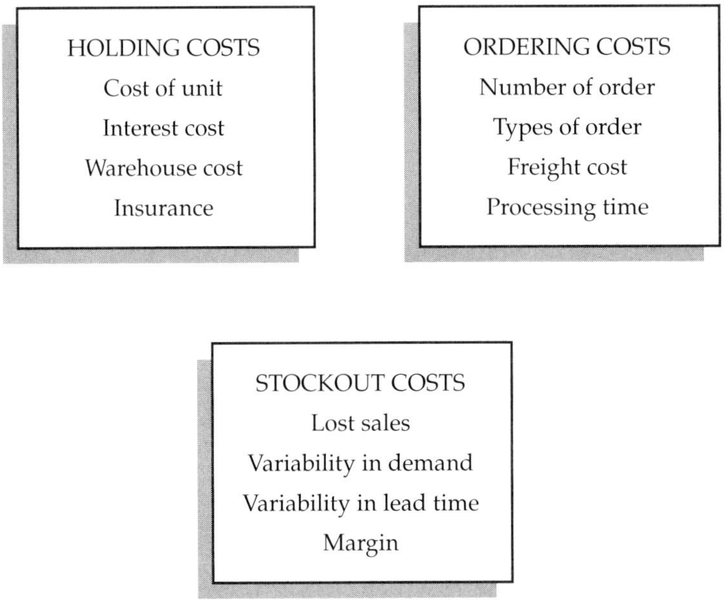

HOLDING COSTS
Cost of unit
Interest cost
Warehouse cost
Insurance

ORDERING COSTS
Number of order
Types of order
Freight cost
Processing time

STOCKOUT COSTS
Lost sales
Variability in demand
Variability in lead time
Margin

---

portation costs increase when a firm orders an item in many small installments, since bulk shipments reduce the per-unit costs of transportation. For both special orders and regular orders, procurement costs increase directly with the number of orders.

Stockout Costs   A **stockout** occurs when the store does not have an item demanded by a customer in inventory. Stockouts result in financial losses, since they represent a lost opportunity to gain additional revenues and margins. For many items, customers will simply fill their need at another store rather than wait for a store to restock an item. Stockouts can have long-term effects, too, if customers stop patronizing a store because of frequent disappointments.

The Trade-off   As stated earlier, inventory control seeks to minimize the total cost of the inventory system. Inventory decisions become difficult when the costs conflict with each other, and the firm must trade one off against another to determine the best policy.

Ideally, one would like to maintain only the minimum inventory possible to reduce holding costs, since these costs increase with the depth of the inventory. Reducing depth can increase risk, however, since the possibility of stockouts increases as units in stock decline. In addition, this would require more frequent reorders, increasing ordering costs. Thus, while reducing average inventory can decrease holding costs, it can increase both procurement costs and stockout costs (see Exhibit 13.6). This conflict between holding costs on the one hand and procurement and stockout costs on the other hand, complicates inventory decisions. The optimal inventory policy trades off these costs to minimize the total cost of the whole system. For example, in some cases the firm may be able to reduce the cost of stockouts by using overnight deliveries to satisfy customer needs.

Types of Products

The particular procedure by which a firm implements its inventory policy depends on the nature of its product. For the purpose of inventory control, products can be categorized into three broad groups: (1) staple merchandise, (2) fashion goods, and (3) seasonal items.

1. **Staple merchandise** is characterized by relatively steady demand pattern that the firm can predict fairly accurately. Grocery products such as detergents,

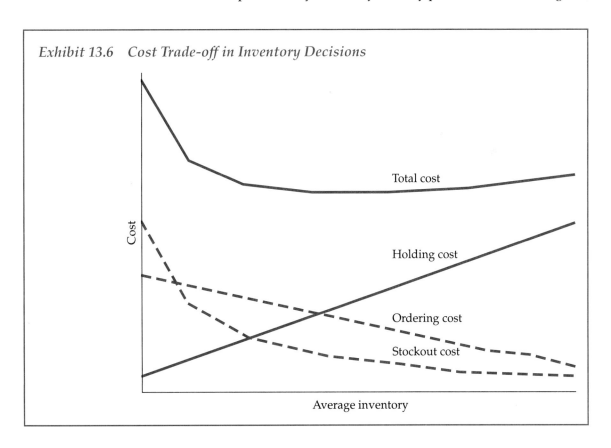

Exhibit 13.6   Cost Trade-off in Inventory Decisions

toothpaste, soft drinks, and canned tuna are some examples of staple merchandise. Socks, briefs, and other accessories are examples of staple merchandise at department and apparel stores.

2. Typically, a retailer has to order **fashion goods** long before the actual selling season based on the firm's expectation of how well the items will sell. If an item sells much better than expected, the retailer would ideally like to reorder the item to get more supplies. Unfortunately, in many cases such reorders in the middle of the season are not feasible, and the company loses potential sales. On the other hand, if sales turned out to be lower than expected, the retailer may have to markdown the price of a slow-selling item to spur consumer interest. Thus, retailers have to closely monitor sales trends of fashion goods.

3. Christmas cards and Easter eggs are examples of **seasonal goods**. Sales of these items are concentrated during particular periods of the year, usually related to holidays or climatic patterns. Iced tea mixes and hot dogs, for example, sell well during the summer months. (More hot dogs are probably consumed on July 4

Sandals are in much higher demand in the summer than they are in the winter months and thus are considered "seasonal" items.

than on any other day of the year.) Similarly, sales of many gifts and novelties peak around Christmas and Mother's Day.

Inventory Control for Staple Merchandise

If firms could predict demand perfectly, monitor merchandise inventories continuously, and take delivery on all orders overnight, inventory control would be relatively simple. Every evening prior to closing the store, the retailer (or a computer) could order the next day's requirements of each item. This may indeed occur in the near future; for the present, however, inventory control, even for staple goods, remains somewhat more complex.

The present reality differs from the ideal scenario in three important ways. First, the time between placement of an order and its delivery, called the **lead time**, usually spans days—often weeks—rather than hours. Second, firms do not typically review merchandise inventories every day, although the standard **review period** (the number of days between reorder decisions) is getting shorter. Third, firms can never predict demand with certainty, so they must maintain a **safety stock** to cover variations in demand. The reorder point model provides a procedure for dealing with these concerns systematically.

The Reorder Point Model

Firms implement the **reorder point model** in three basic steps:

1. Determine the review period and lead time for the item.
2. Calculate the maximum inventory for the item.
3. Review current inventory status and determine order quantity.

Determine Review Period and Lead Time   As the first step in applying the reorder point model, firms determine the review period and the lead time for each item. As stated earlier, the review period specifies the frequency with which firms check stocks and place new orders. For example, if the review period is ten days, then the firm will place new orders at ten-day intervals. Review periods tend to be short for perishable items; supermarkets typically review their inventories of produce daily, whereas they may review grocery items once or twice a week. The review period for major appliances, on the other hand, may be as long as a month because frequent reorder of bulky items increases per-unit transport costs.

Lead time is the time between order placement and delivery. Suppose, for example, that a retail store places an order with a vendor on the first of the month and that this merchandise is physically received by the store on the 10th of the month. The lead time for the merchandise is then ten days. Lead time depends on vendor policies and the typical mode of transportation for the products. With the increasing automation of inventory review and ordering procedures, both review periods and lead times are getting shorter.

Calculate Maximum Inventory   After establishing the review period and the lead time for each item, the retailer calculates the maximum inventory required for each. To find maximum inventory, the retailer sums the expected unit sales during the review period and the expected sales during the lead time. For example, assume that the review period is ten days and the lead time is seven days for an item the firm expects to sell at ten units a day. The maximum inventory for the item is then:

$$\text{Maximum inventory} = (\text{Review time} \times \text{Daily demand}) + (\text{Lead time} \times \text{Daily demand})$$
$$= (10 \times 10) + (7 \times 10) = 170 \text{ units}$$

Review Current Inventory Status and Determine Order Quantity   At each review period, the retailer first determines its current stock of each item. By a simple rule, the reorder point model then determines the amount of stock to reorder: the number of units ordered equals the difference between the maximum inventory and the current inventory level:

$$\text{Order quantity} = \text{Maximum inventory} - \text{Current inventory}$$

As an example, if the firm currently has inventory of 100 units and maximum inventory is 170 units, then it should order 70 additional units to bring the inventory back to the maximum level (see Exhibit 13.7).

The following examples show the logic of this decision rule. As before, let the lead time and review periods be seven days and ten days, respectively, and let the maximum inventory point be 170 units. Suppose that a review finds inventory on hand of 160 units. If the manager were to wait until the next review period to place an order, the inventory would fall to 60 units because the next review period would be ten days away and daily demand is ten units [$60 = 160 - (10 \times 10)$]. Even if the manager places a new order at the next review, the store will run out of stock for a day since the order will take seven days to reach the store, requiring 70 units to satisfy demand during that time.

Consider another example. Suppose now that inspection revealed current inventory of 100 units. The reorder point rule suggests that the store order 70 new units. What would be the consequence of ordering less than 70 units, for example, 60 units? The store would review inventory status again in ten days, during which time it would sell all 100 units currently in stock (since it sells ten units each day). This would leave an inventory level at the time of the next review of 60 units (the number of new units ordered). However much the store ordered at the next review, it would not receive the merchandise for seven days. Since its inventory of 60 units would last six days only, the store would run out of stock for a day. Note that if the store ordered 80 units instead of 70, it would end up with ten units more than it required. Only when it orders 70 units do supply and demand balance perfectly.

Perpetual Review   In the reorder point model just described, the firm reviews inventory on a fixed interval, the review period. This situation is typically called the fixed order interval situation. In some cases, however, firms may evaluate stocks daily or even continuously. These are called **perpetual review** situations. Com-

Exhibit 13.7 Reorder Point Model

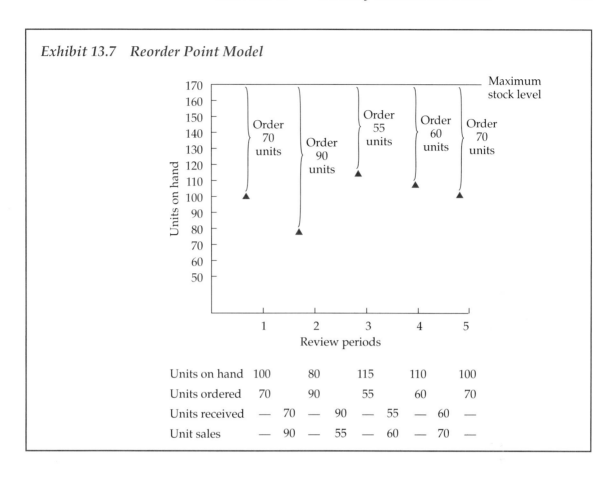

Units on hand	100		80		115		110		100
Units ordered	70		90		55		60		70
Units received	—	70	—	90	—	55	—	60	—
Unit sales	—	90	—	55	—	60	—	70	—

puterized inventory control systems typically perform perpetual review, monitoring actual stock continuously and placing orders whenever the sum of the units on hand and units on order reaches a minimum level determined by the total expected demand during the lead time. Thus if the lead time is seven days and the firm expects demand of ten units per day, the minimum level is 70 units. The store should always have at least 70 units on hand or on order.

Reorder Point with Uncertain Demand: The Need for Safety Stocks

The reorder point calculations above presume that the firm can accurately predict demand during the buying period, the sum of the lead time and the review period. Inaccurate demand predictions make stockouts likely, since the store may not have adequate stocks to meet customer demand. Consider the following scenario related to the earlier example: a review found 170 units of an item in stock, so the store placed no new order, since the stock was not less than the reorder point. During the next ten days, however, the store actually sold 15 units a day instead of ten, so the next review found the stock level down to 20 units [170 − (15 × 10)]. Since the store would not receive any new order for another seven days, it would be without adequate stock for most of the week (see Exhibit 13.8A). The store could also face stockouts if demand ran at ten units a day as expected, but the lead time took longer than seven days (see Exhibit 13.8B). In practice, however, variation in demand poses a much greater problem than variation in lead time. Since stores can rarely predict demand with complete certainty, they must maintain some safety stock to reduce the possibility of stockouts.

Consider the pattern of the firm's demand experience from previous buying periods in Exhibit 13.9. On average, demand during each 17-day buying period is 170 units, but it varies considerably around that average exceeding 170 units in some buying periods and falling short of the average in others. Therefore, a reorder point of 170 units would allow substantial stockouts during periods in which actual demand exceeds the average, costing the store in lost sales and deterioration in customer service. To maintain adequate customer service, the store requires some safety stock over and above the reorder point of 170 units.

Keeping a large enough safety stock can eliminate the possibility of stockout completely, but the cost of such a policy can be prohibitive. The store should, therefore, seek to maintain adequate service at a reasonable cost to the firm. It must consider two factors in determining appropriate safety stock in uncertain demand conditions: (1) variability in demand, and (2) desired service level.

Variability in Demand   The probability distribution of demand gives information on how demand varies over time. While demand patterns differ for different products, many follow the well-known bell-shaped curve associated with the normal probability distribution. This case appears in Exhibit 13.9.

The shape of the normal distribution curve, and therefore the variability of demand, can be measured by standard deviation (σ). Standard deviation, which in Exhibit 13.9 equals 15, measures the probability of different levels of demand occurring. Exhibit 13.9 shows that an inventory of 170 units is likely to leave the store out of stock 50 percent of the time. Adding 15 units of inventory, one standard deviation, to the stock would reduce the probability of stockout from 50 to 16 percent. In other words, the **service level** would increase from 50 percent to 84 percent. *The service level is the probability that the item will be in stock when a customer asks for it.* With 185 units in stock, there is an 84 percent probability that any customer coming into the store will be able to find the item, and 14 percent will find it out-of-stock. Another 15 units reduce stockout probability to 2.5 percent and service level to 97.5 percent. This is because 97.5 percent of the area under the normal curve lies to the left of the point that is 2.0 standard deviations above the mean.

Determining Desired Service Levels   Firms cannot practically eliminate stockouts altogether, since the costs of maintaining large safety stocks usually far outweigh the marginal revenue gained by selling the last item. Thus, as they do in determining optimal reorder points, firms must make certain trade-offs in

Eye-catching visual displays play a very important role in catching the attention of the customer and in creating an appealing and interesting store atmosphere.

Display designers, like this young man at the A&S outlet in Paramus, New Jersey, must create attractive and appealing window dressings, in-store displays and merchandise arrangements. All these things must be consistant in theme and design in order to present the store at its very best.

Visual atmosphere can be as elaborate as the one created in the Far East Plaza in Singapore or as folksy as the surroundings of the Stockbridge General Store in Massachusetts. The key is knowing what will draw the attention of the target customer.

Exhibit 13.8   Stockout Due to Variability in Demand and Lead Time

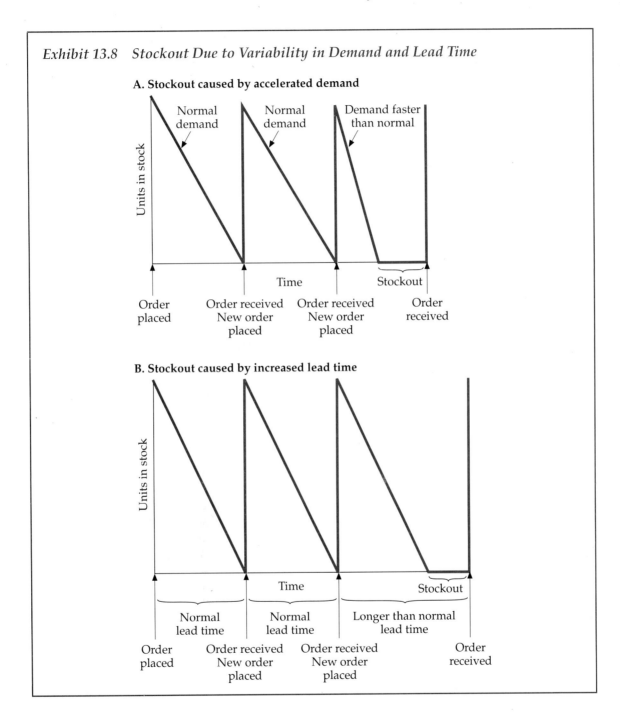

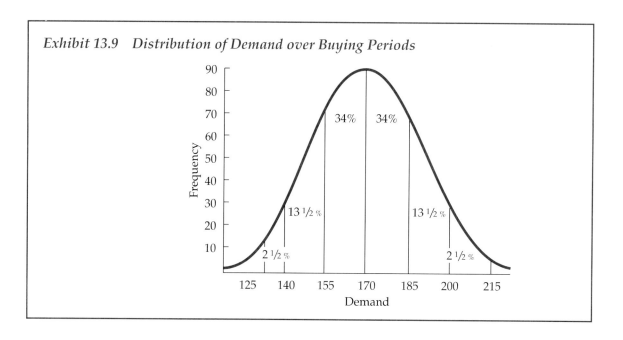

Exhibit 13.9   Distribution of Demand over Buying Periods

determining the desired service level. They must balance the cost of holding an additional unit with the marginal revenue it provides by increasing the service level. Based on this trade-off, the retailer must decide on an acceptable service level and then calculate the amount of safety stock appropriate to the service level.

The marginal revenue the firm gains from increasing its service level depends on the short-run and long-run costs of stockouts. In the short run, stockouts represent a lost sales opportunity. Studies have shown that many customers who do not find the staple merchandise they want in their regular stores are likely to buy it from others (see Exhibit 13.10). Thus, the firm loses the gross margin it could have earned from the item during a stockout. Stockouts have a long-term effect too, because frequent stockouts tarnish a store's image and reduce customer patronage.

As mentioned earlier, however, increasing the safety stock increases inventory holding costs. Moreover, for perishable products, unsold products that cannot be salvaged impose a severe penalty. The firm must carefully balance the potential revenues and costs of different service levels to determine its optimal level.

Calculating Safety Stock Level   With its target service level set, the firm determines the standard deviation of its demand distribution and then computes the level of safety stock required to achieve the target service level from statistical tables showing the area under the normal curve. A firm that sets a target service level of 95 percent must keep safety stock of 1.64 times the standard deviation of demand because 95 percent of the area under the normal curve lies to the left of the point that is 1.64 standard deviations above the mean. It can be seen from Exhibit 13.11 that the firm would have to keep 25 (1.64 × 15) units.

Exhibit 13.10 *Behavior of Shoppers during Stockouts*

Action Taken	Number	Percentage
Bought same brand, different size	21	4.8
Bought different brand	22	5.0
Bought different product	54	12.4
Postponed purchase until next visit to same store	48	11.1
Decided not to buy	81	18.7
Searched in other stores	208	47.9
Total	434	100.0

Source: Philip B. Schary and Martin Christopher, "The Anatomy of a Stock-out," *Journal of Retailing* V55 (Summer1979), p. 66.

Standard tables that typically appear in statistics texts can provide the area under the normal curve at various distances from the mean. The table in Exhibit 13.11 indicates the levels of safety stock required to maintain some selected service levels.

Fashion Goods

Controlling stocks of fashion goods requires more effort monitoring sales and stocks than determining reorder points and reorder quantities. As discussed in the previous chapter, the firm allocates a budget before the start of the season to purchase fashion goods based on projected sales, markdowns, and stock to sales ratios. It orders the bulk of the stock in advance of the selling season, although actual shipments may

---

Exhibit 13.11 *Service Level and Safety Stocks with Normal Demand Distribution*

Service Level	Safety[a] Stock	Probability of Stockout
50.0	0.00	50.0
60.0	0.26	40.0
70.0	0.53	30.0
75.0	0.68	25.0
80.0	0.84	20.0
84.0	1.00	16.0
90.0	1.28	10.0
95.0	1.64	5.0
97.5	2.00	2.5

[a] To obtain required safety stock multiply by standard deviation.

spread throughout the season. When it places the initial order, its open to buy commitment for the item diminishes by the amount ordered, and the remaining open to buy amount remains available for fill-in reorders, if necessary.

Proper control of fashion goods inventory requires an effective **merchandise information system** that provides up-to-date information on sales of different brands, styles, colors, and so on. Small and large retailers alike are increasingly using software packages that analyze information gathered by electronic point-of-sale terminals to improve their management of fashion goods inventory. Exhibit 13.12 shows one section of an inventory report generated for an apparel store by an inventory management system developed by WDC Systems, a supplier of software for the retail industry.

The report highlights sales performance of an entire department in terms of both unit sales and retail dollars. It shows the department's week-to-date sales, sales during the last four weeks, stocks on hand, and stocks on order. It breaks down the information on total sales into three categories based on price status: (1) regularly priced merchandise, (2) promotionally priced merchandise (items with temporarily reduced prices), and (3) permanently marked down merchandise.

Exhibit 13.12   *Merchandise Inventory Report for Apparel Store*

		Unit Analysis			
		Week-to-Date Sales	4-Week Sales	On Hand	On Order
Total	Total	1,282	5,084	14,171	10,690
department	Regular	689	2,683	8,203	7,167
	Promotional	103	743	794	2,106
	Marked down	490	1,658	5,174	1,417
Total fast	Total	225	620	487	278
	Regular	152	427	392	237
	Promotional	10	17	19	3
	Marked down	63	176	76	38
Total slow	Total	45	230	2,379	1,456
	Regular	22	105	1,276	1,142
	Promotional	15	61	165	26
	Marked down	8	64	938	288
Total no sales	Total	0	153	4,251	1,266
	Regular	0	102	2,550	1,266
	Promotional	0	12	57	0
	Marked down	0	39	1,644	0

Altogether, this department carried 409 merchandise items. Of these 409 items, 165 (or 40 percent) were marked down permanently; the prices of 8 items (2 percent) were temporarily reduced; and 236 (58 percent) carried regular prices. The report also classifies the 1,282 units sold during the week into these categories. Just over 50 percent (689 units) of the units sold during the week was regularly priced merchandise. Eight percent (103 units) of the units was promotionally priced merchandise, and the rest was purchased at permanently marked down prices.

The lower part of the report provides analysis of the several categories of sales and stocks. It presents this analysis separately for three categories of merchandise. The first is *fast sellers*. These are items that sold very well during the week. Next are *slow sellers*, items with significant below-average sales. The final category, *total no sales*, comprise styles that have not sold at all during the week. The report shows that 16 of the department's 409 styles qualified as fast sellers. These 16 styles represented 18 percent of the department's sales during the previous seven days, 12 percent of its previous four-week sales total, 3 percent of its current inventory, and 3 percent of the merchandise on order.

Of the department's 409 styles, 67 were slow sellers, accounting for only 3 percent of total sales during the previous seven days and 4 percent of sales during

	Percentage Analysis			Style Analysis	
Week-to-Date Sales	4-Week Sales	On Hand	On Order	Number of Styles	Percentage of Total
100	100	100	100	409	100
53	53	58	67	236	58
9	15	6	20	8	2
38	33	37	13	165	40
18	12	3	3	16	4
12	8	3	2	11	3
1	0	0	0	1	0
5	3	1	0	4	1
3	4	17	14	67	16
2	2	9	11	44	11
1	1	1	0	1	0
1	1	7	3	22	5
0	3	30	12	115	28
0	2	18	12	65	16
0	0	0	0	1	0
0	1	12	0	49	12

the previous four weeks. These slow-selling styles comprise 17 percent of the department's current inventory and 4 percent of its merchandise on order.

The final section is the disaster area! It shows that 28 percent of the items carried by the department, 30 percent of its current inventory, did not sell a single unit during the past seven days. Sales for the previous four weeks totaled 153 units, just 3 percent of the total sales during that period. Note, too, that these 115 nonselling styles represent as much as 12 percent of the merchandise on order.

Merchandise reports like that in Exhibit 13.12 give stores invaluable tools for managing fashion goods. They provide the information necessary to balance inventory with sales and determine which items to mark down and which to reorder. Managers of this department should be concerned that they have generated no sales in the previous week for 115 items, or 30 percent of the current inventory. Moreover, they have 1,266 units of these nonselling items on order for future delivery. The managers should explore the possibility of canceling or postponing those orders and also consider marking down the prices of some items in order to increase sales and reduce inventory levels.

On the other hand, they should watch closely the inventory of each of the fast selling items to reduce the possibility of stockouts. The information system can also provide a detailed report of the inventory status of each of these 16 fast sellers.

With the basic information system in place, managers can summarize data in different ways to identify profit opportunities and problem areas more easily. They can analyze sales and inventory information for all items that share a similar characteristic—grouping items, for example, according to classification (sweaters versus coats versus jackets), price range, color, style, vendor, silhouette (V-neck versus crew neck versus cardigan sweaters), fabric (synthetic versus wool versus cotton), and so forth. They can also create categories by combining characteristics—for example, examining sales and stocks of sweaters or sports jackets under $100. In fact, once the system is in place, it can summarize the information in any form and level of detail necessary to support profitable merchandising decisions.

Today's highly competitive and continuously changing retail environment makes computerized merchandise information systems essential for controlling fashion goods stock. As stores handle larger numbers of merchandise items, their needs for proper information systems increase. At one time only large stores could afford computerized information systems, but many systems now run on personal computers and cost as little as $5,000. According to one report, retailers who invest in these systems can reduce their inventory investment in the range of 15 to 30 percent and control their markdowns much more effectively.[6]

Seasonal Goods

Seasonal goods generate high demand during specific periods of the year, requiring stores to keep them in stock during that period. Stockouts of seasonal goods result in lost revenues because customers are likely to purchase from another store rather than wait for the store to restock the item. However, unsold inventory at the end of the season brings its own cost because a store must either keep it in stock until the next season or sell it at sharply reduced prices. Sales on calendars around the middle of February and annual sales on Christmas cards and decorations just after the holiday are two examples.

One challenge of controlling seasonal goods inventories is to estimate demand properly. For some items retailers can estimate demand from past sales. The demand for novelties and new gift items, however, is extremely difficult to predict because of the lack of past histories. Retailers have to base forecasts for such products on their subjective judgments and experience with similar products. While some may favor stocking new items conservatively to test the waters, this can result in high potential losses if the product becomes popular and the supplier cannot accept reorders for the season.

Like fashion goods, stores must monitor stocks of seasonal goods to identify slow and fast sellers. Managers must compare the sales of seasonal items with target or expected sales at a given point into the season. Suppose that, based on past experience, a store expects to sell 50 percent of its stock of a certain gift item within a month of stocking it, but finds that it has actually sold only 20 percent of its stock by that time. The store may need to mark down the price of this item or to promote it more energetically to completely sell it out by the end of the season. However, if actual sales exceed the target, the store may need to reorder the item to assure adequate supply.

New Technology and Stock Control

The entry of computers into retail stores and advances in communication technologies are profoundly affecting retailers' management of total inventories in addition to systems for fashion goods discussed earlier. Large chains such as Wal-Mart, K mart, and J.C. Penney have linked all their stores with regional and national headquarters and to central warehouses through satellite communication systems. Although smaller chains may not be able to afford their own satellite channels, individual stores can send information to warehouses over high-speed data transmission lines.

Direct communication links between stores and warehouses speeds up ordering and improves accuracy. Store personnel can type an order into a computer and instantaneously transmit it either to the chain's warehouse or to a supplier. In some even more automated systems, special computer programs automatically check a store's inventory records, determine if inventory on hand is below the reorder point, and then electronically place an order, if necessary.

Direct electronic communication links between retailers and suppliers promises to be one of the most important breakthroughs in inventory management. Direct links with suppliers will reduce lead times and therefore stock needs at the store. Electronic transmission speeds up the ordering process and can save significantly on labor cost for large chains that place millions of orders every year. The store can also program computer software to check for inaccuracies in orders and verify delivery

RETAIL RESEARCH REPORT

Electronic Data Interchange (EDI) Increases Inventory Productivity

EDI, electronic data interchange, is becoming the method for speeding the flow of information and merchandise through the retail pipeline. EDI is included in the growing bevy of "quick response" technologies, systems that aid the flow of inventory information between the retailer and the supplier, so that restocking of inventory happens quickly and effectively at a cost saving for the retailers. EDI can help retailers increase sales and reduce inventory carrying costs, as well as reduce the clerical and administrative costs associated with the inventory management function. Given these benefits, it is no surprise that many retailers are requiring that their suppliers use EDI.

According to a 1991 survey, general merchandise retailers can save as much as 0.14 percent of annual sales by using EDI. While other quick response technologies can offer higher annual savings, EDI has been taken up by many retailers because the benefits derived from the system are felt much faster

and there is less investment—both time and capital—involved with EDI. Furthermore, EDI has far less impact on the management structure than other systems, which means that it can be integrated quickly and without much fuss, while offering fast results.

To implement EDI, retailers need the EDI "architecture" of hardware, application and transaction software, communication vehicles, and an organization to manage the process. There are three applications involved with EDI, all aimed at simplifying the inventory management process for both retailers and their suppliers. First, there is the purchase order management application, which is the source by which electronic purchase orders, change notices, cancellation documents and receival information are all conveyed from retailer to vendor. Then, there is the receiving application, which receives the advance shipping notices from vendors, and the invoice processing application, which matches the invoices and gen-

dates. If it finds that a supplier is out of stock, the retailer can modify or cancel an order on the spot. A manual system loses valuable time before the retailer learns whether the supplier can fulfill the order.

Widespread adoption of **electronic data interchange (EDI)** between retailers and suppliers hinges on the development of a common system similar to the Universal Product Code (UPC) system in the supermarket industry for identifying general merchandise items. Every packaged item sold at supermarkets carries a unique product code (the barcode) printed on its package. Optical scanners can read product codes, speeding up the checkout process and allowing computers to maintain inventory records automatically. More importantly, retailers can precisely identify the brands and sizes of the items they wish to order with the appropriate UPC code. No widely accepted product code system is yet available for nonsupermarket products. A consortium of general merchandise retailers, their suppliers, and com-

erates payment. Finally, the merchandise information system provides SKU levels, sales, and inventory information to vendors so that inventory can be restocked faster and more efficiently.

Because suppliers deal with multiple retailers, another feature of EDI is the communications standards that are incorporated into the system to allow proprietary communications between one retailer and one vendor, and vice versa. The standards require that all electronic documents—purchase orders, invoices, receipts, and so on—are grouped together into an electronic envelope that specifies the source and the destination addresses. These envelopes, or files, can be opened only with a security code, defined by the retailer and passed to the vendor. Codes can be changed at any time, and retailers are informed if a certain code is "locked" or is in use by another retailer.

Information flows between the retailer's point-of-purchase station, the inventory management and accounting stations, the retailer's financial institution, the vendor, and shippers. It is an efficient method for dealing with all aspects of inventory management.

With such a system, much of the clerical work long associated with the buying and inventory management functions is reduced. Buyers have their time freed up to more closely monitor customer buying patterns; inventory managers have quick access to all information in terms of tracking and controlling inventory; and suppliers are kept informed so that they can fill orders more efficiently. The businesses that use EDI are able to generate more sales, less inventory costs, and more savings overall.

Source: "EDI and Quick Response—Easy Money," *Chain Store Age Executive*, March 1991, p. 20B.

puter firms is actively supporting the development of a commonly accepted product code system to hasten the spread of EDI systems among general merchandise retailers.

Summary

1. An important element of merchandise management is the control of merchandise inventory. Merchandise inventories represent a major component of the assets of retail firms. Dollar inventory control systems control and regulate the amount of money firms invest in inventory, and stock control procedures monitor the number of units of items in stock.
2. An effective dollar control system provides up-to-date information on (a) the dollar value of the merchandise a firm sells, (b) the dollar value of the merchandise it has in stock, and (c) the gross margins and profits it generates during any period. As an essential

feature, a dollar control system must value inventory at the end of an accounting period. Inaccurate valuation of inventories distorts firms' true profits.

3. The cost method values inventory at actual cost or current retail price (whichever is lower); the retail method values inventory at current retail selling prices. The cost method is the older of the two methods and some retailers still use it, although most prefer the retail method. The retail method is a book inventory system that allows the retailer to estimate the cost value of ending inventory without counting physical inventory and without having to record the cost of each item sold. It bases the cost of ending inventory on the average relationship between the cost and retail price of all items sold during the period.

4. Every year retailers lose billions of dollars in profit because of shrinkage. Shrinkage is a reduction in inventory value due to employee theft, shoplifting, or damaged or lost merchandise. It is estimated that employee theft and shoplifting account for 2 percent of annual sales. Retailers have implemented active shrinkage control programs to curb shortages.

5. In addition to controlling dollar investments, inventory control procedures must control stock, that is plan the depth of each item. To control stocks of staple merchandise, firms seek to minimize the total cost of holding inventory subject to forecasted demand conditions. They must consider several costs, including (a) holding costs, (b) costs of ordering, and (c) stockout costs. Uncertain demand requires firms to maintain safety stocks over and above regular inventory to reduce the probability of stockouts. Levels of safety stock depend on the variability in demand and the target customer service level.

6. Controlling stocks of fashion and seasonal goods must emphasize monitoring sales and stocks rather than determining order quantities and safety stocks. Proper control of fashion and seasonal stocks requires an effective merchandise information system that provides up-to-date information on sales and stocks of different brands, styles, colors, for example. Timely sales and stock information helps firms identify profit opportunities as well as problem areas.

7. Wider availability of computers and advances in communication technologies are profoundly affecting retailers' management of inventories. Direct electronic links between retailers and suppliers can reduce lead times and the number of units stores must keep in stock. Electronic order transmission also quickens order processing and reduces inaccuracies. The development of a commonly accepted product code (similar to the Universal Product Code in the supermarket industry) will hasten the use of electronic data interchange (EDI) by general merchandise retailers.

Key Concepts

Dollar control	Conservative rule
Inventory control	Retail method of inventory valuation
Beginning inventory	Holding costs
Closing inventory	Ordering costs
Purchases	Stockout
Total merchandise available	Staple merchandise
Cost of goods sold (COGS)	Fashion goods
Cost method of inventory valuation	Seasonal goods
Book inventory system	Lead time
Retail shrinkage	Review period
Overage	Safety stock

Reorder point model
Perpetual review
Service level

Merchandise information systems
Electronic Data Interchange (EDI)

Discussion Questions

1. Explain, with examples, how an inaccurate valuation of ending inventory affects the retailer's profit for the period.
2. What are the steps in implementing the cost method of inventory valuation using a book inventory system? Which stores are likely to prefer the cost method of inventory valuation over the retail method? Why?
3. What are the steps in implementing the retail method of inventory valuation? What are its advantages compared to the cost method?
4. Consider the following information obtained from the accounting records for ABC Stores for the month of June 1988:
   (a) It had B.O.M. inventory worth $100,000 at cost and $150,000 at retail.
   (b) It made purchases during the month worth $100,000 at cost and $150,000 at retail.
   (c) It paid freight charges of $7,000.
   (d) It had net sales of $120,000 at retail.
   (e) Its total markdowns came to $5,000.
   (f) It gave employee discounts of $150.
   (g) Its shrinkage allowance is $2,400.
   Calculate the retail and cost values of ABC Stores' ending inventory.
5. What does the term *retail shrinkage* mean? How does shrinkage affect retail profits?
6. What three sources of costs must be taken into account to determine optimal inventory policy? Explain how these costs arise and their relationship to average inventory size.
7. Explain the following terms: (a) lead time, (b) review period, (c) reorder point, and (d) order quantity.
8. An item has a lead time of five days and a review period of five days. If its average daily demand is five units, specify its reorder point. If the store has 25 units on hand, how many units should it order? How many units should it order if it has 60 units on hand?
9. Why must stores maintain safety stocks? What factors determine the optimal level of safety stock? Discuss how these factors influence the level of safety stocks?
10. The Xenon Supermarket reviews its stock of canned tuna every seven days. The lead time for the delivery of tuna to the store is five days. The average demand for canned tuna during the buying period is 70 units and the standard deviation is 15 units. How much stock should the store keep to ensure a 95 percent service level?

Notes

1. Ernest H. Risch, *Retail Merchandising* (Columbus, OH: Merril, 1987), p. 373.
2. *Annual Survey of Security and Loss Prevention* (New York: Arthur Young, National Retail Group, 1986).
3. Ibid.
4. This example is from *Peter Berlin Report on Shrinkage Control*, executive edition (Jericho, NY: February 1987).
5. Ibid.
6. Christine Adamec, "Retailers Streamline as Operations Grow," *In Business*, March–April 1987, p. 42.

CHAPTER 14
Evaluating Merchandise Performance

Merchandise Tracking

The Metropolitan Museum of Art in New York City is fast becoming a leader in specialty retailing, with ten satellite stores in over five states selling art objects and gifts. The Met earned $75 million in revenues from its stores in 1990, making them one of the Museum's most critical assets for generating revenue. To help the stores keep track of their valuable inventory, the Museum recently installed a PC-based retail management system, the Atrium 9000, and this retail management solution is critical to the stores' success. Atrium 9000 is intended for specialty retail outlets and provides full sales transaction processing, credit/check authorization, manager workstation functions and a whole variety of communications for the stores.

The stores sell reproductions of the Museum's masterpieces, books, sculpture, jewelry, prints, posters, and souvenir merchandise. The Met began opening satellite stores in the early 1980s, to help boost their fund-raising efforts. As the stores grew in sales, it became obvious that a better system for tracking merchandise and processing transactions was necessary. Atrium 9000 was customized for the stores by the Museum's management information system (MIS) staff for the specific kinds of transaction sets, tax tables, fees, and menus needed. Now, sales associates simply key in the stock keeping unit (SKU) number of the object being sold, and the system not only provides the proper price and tax, but it processes the data into the inventory logs, so that the store managers will know what inventory is low and when to order. All ten stores are linked, so that reordering can be done for all the stores at the same time, simplifying the process. While MIS standards are believed to be lower in not-for-profit organizations like the Met, Atrium 9000 is setting new standards.

Another example of merchandise tracking is the very sophisticated system used by the 101-specialty store chain Designs Exclusively for Levi Strauss & Co. The Massachusetts-based retailer has only one vendor, Levi Strauss & Co., who is an industry leader in the use of EDI (electronic data interchange), a "quick response" merchandise tracking system for retailers. Designs and Levi work their unique quick response arrangement with Levi's retail-to-vendor management information system, Model Stock Management, linked together with Levi's own "LeviLink."

The inventory quantities, or model stock levels, by style, size, and color, for each outlet of Designs are keyed into the system. Each

After studying this chapter, the reader will be able to:

- *Understand the importance of evaluating merchandise performance.*
- *Describe the factors that affect merchandise performance.*
- *Measure stock turnover and set stock turnover goals.*
- *Identify ways to improve stock turnover rates.*
- *Calculate gross margin return on investment and evaluate merchandise based on GMROI.*
- *Compute direct product profit (DPP) of individual merchandise items.*
- *Understand the relationship between the performance of individual merchandise items and the store's overall financial health*

outlet of Designs sends Levi a sales data file each week; Levi matches those figures against the model stock level for that outlet and sends a stock replenishment directly to the store. In this way, unwarranted paperwork has been cut out of the actual ordering process, and Designs estimates that lead time for orders has been reduced to a week to ten days. The model stock levels are changed when necessary, with changing seasons or changing customer demand, directly from the stores. Sales people who no longer need to spend time writing orders and counting merchandise can now spend more time with the customers and follow changing consumer patterns more closely. Buyers and merchandising staff have additional time to more carefully monitor sales reports and detect changing customer trends. The model stock levels are constantly being reassessed to make sure that both the buyers and the merchandisers are following sales trends correctly. But even with all the adjusting that does have to be done, Levi's Model Stock Management System saves Designs (and all of their retailers) a great deal of time. Designs is a perfect example: the chain can support $120 million in sales annually with a merchandising and buying staff of fewer than ten people.

The Model Stock Management System also provides Designs with other inventory management benefits. For one, the stores are rarely out of stock on any merchandise because Levi usually sends replacement stock on an item before it is even sold out. Also, because of the more accurate inventory control, inventory in units is 10 to 15 percent lower than it was prior to going on-line with Levi. Furthermore, Designs receives invoices from Levi electronically, so that before the order arrives, the stores know exactly what is coming, and when it should arrive. When the shipment arrives, store personnel keys in an "input document" that comes from Levi, and the system then matches it with the original invoice, logging merchandise into the store. Even the billing and payment is done through the system: once the input document is keyed in and matches with the original invoice, the data is transmitted to the accounts payable system, which automatically prepares a check the following month for Levi. And, because all the Design stores are linked with the system, it can also act as electronic mail for staff, sending notice of price changes or other information. The system takes care of all the details: tracking inventory in the stores, ordering, logging merchandise in and out of the stores, billing, and even payment. The system simplifies the inventory management problem for both retailer and supplier, allowing each company to streamline its operations and creating great cost savings for both.

Sources: "Museum Gets Artsy with POS"; *Chain Store Age Executive*, June, 1991, pp. 44–45; "Chain's One and Only Vendor Makes Quick Response Easy"; *Chain Store Age Executive*, March 1991, pp. 18B–19B (part of a special section "Quick Response: The Path to Better Customer Service").

Merchandise is the engine that drives the retail machine. Like all engines, its performance must be continuously monitored, controlled, and fine-tuned. A retail store sells thousands, often hundreds of thousands, of merchandise items. It is unlikely that each of them will contribute equally to profitability; in fact, some may not generate any profits at all. Retail managers must continuously evaluate the performance of merchandise lines and individual items to decide whether to keep an item in stock, how much stock to keep, and what price to charge. Only by continuously asking these questions can retailers improve their financial results.

This chapter discusses the methods used to measure and monitor merchandise performance. It starts by discussing the concept of stock turnover, which, together with gross margin, allows firms to compute gross margin return on investment (GMROI). Next, it presents a second, related measure called direct product profit (DPP). Computers have made the task of monitoring and controlling merchandise inventory more manageable in recent years. This chapter presents an example of how computerized information systems help managers make merchandise decisions.

MEASURES OF MERCHANDISE PERFORMANCE

If a store sells twice as many of one merchandise item as another, is its performance twice as good? Although firms must generate sales to earn profits, and increasing sales is an important goal for most retailers, it is not the final objective. The overall goal must be to increase sales while also ensuring higher profits. A product that generates higher sales does not necessarily generate higher profits, because the margin on the two items may differ. Margin, as mentioned in earlier chapters, is the difference between an item's price and its cost to the retailer. Margin is an important measure of **merchandise performance**, since it indicates the extent to which the item can contribute toward meeting the firm's operating expenses and profit goals.

To illustrate how margins and dollar sales influence merchandise performance, consider the sales and inventory data for two brands of televisions shown in Exhibit 14.1. Two hundred and fifty units of both items were sold during the period. The cost of goods sold were also the same. The store paid $190 for each unit, irrespective of brand. But Brand A's average selling price was $250, while Brand B sold at $271, on an average. Because of its higher selling price, Brand B had a **gross margin** of 30 percent (that is, the item cost the retailer 70 percent of its price), while Brand A had a gross margin of 24 percent. Thus, although both brands cost the retailer the same amount and both had the same unit sales, the store made more money from selling Brand B than from selling Brand A. For the year, Brand B contributed $20,357 toward expenses and profits, while Brand A contributed $15,000. Does this imply that the retailer should prefer Brand B over Brand A?

While an item must have a positive margin to be profitable, a higher margin does not necessarily mean greater profitability. To measure profitability, one must also consider how many resources were used to generate the margin. This is obtained from information on inventory turnover, which must be used along with margin to measure merchandise performance. Inventory or stock turnover measures the relationship between the sales and margin of a merchandise item and the amount of resources necessary to generate sales and margins. Note, for example, that the store kept an average of only 40 units of Brand A in stock, while the average stock for Brand B was 60 units. Since the unit costs of both brands were the same, this means that the store invested 50 percent more funds to sell Brand B than it did to sell Brand A. Firms must consider this difference too in evaluating the relative performance of the two brands. Only by combining information on turnover and margin can the firm properly assess the relative performance of different merchandise items.

Exhibit 14.1 Sales, Costs, and margins for Two Brands of Televisions

	Brand A	Brand B
1. Number of units sold	250	250
2. Cost of each unit	$190	$190
3. Cost of goods sold	$47,500	$47,500
4. Original unit retail value	$275	$300
5. Average selling price	$250	$271
6. Average number of units in stock	40	60
7. Net sales revenue	$62,500	$67,857
8. Gross margin percent	24%	30%
9. Total gross margin	$15,000	$20,357

STOCK TURNOVER

One of the crucial tasks of merchandise management is to maintain a healthy balance between inventory investment and sales. Stock turnover measures this relationship by indicating the speed with which the merchandise moves into and out of the store. (This chapter uses the terms inventory and stock interchangeably.)

Measuring Stock Turnover

Firms can measure stock turnover in terms of physical units of merchandise, dollar cost of inventory, or retail value of inventory. Whatever the basis for the measurement, **stock turnover** *is defined as the number of times the firm sells and replaces its* **average inventory** *during a given time period.* In other words, it measures how productively the resources invested in inventories generate sales. For example, expressing stock turnover based on physical units gives this formula:

$$\text{Stock turnover} = \frac{\text{Number of units sold}}{\text{Average number of units stocked}}$$

The following two expressions measure turnover based on cost of goods and retail value of inventory:

$$\text{Stock turnover} = \frac{\text{Cost of goods sold}}{\text{Cost of average inventory}}$$

and

$$\text{Stock turnover} = \frac{\text{Net sales}}{\text{Retail value of average inventory}}$$

Yet another measure of stock turnover is the sales by stock ratio:

$$\text{Sales by stock} = \frac{\text{Net sales}}{\text{Cost of average inventory}}$$

This figure measures sales in retail value and inventory investments at cost. The appendix to the chapter describes the procedure for calculating average inventory.

As illustrations, consider again the information for Brands A and B from Exhibit 14.1. The respective stock turnover calculations for the two brands look like this:

Brand A
Stock turnover (in units) = 250/40 = 6.25
Stock turnover (at cost) = $47,500/$7,600 = 6.25

To obtain the $7,600 figure, which is the cost of average inventory, one multiplies the cost of each unit ($190) by the average number of units in stock (40).

Stock turnover (at retail) = $62,500/$11,000 = 5.68

The $11,000 figure comes from multiplying the original retail value per unit ($275) by the average number of units (40).

$$\text{Sales to stock} = \$62,500 / \$7,600 = 8.22$$

Brand B

$$\text{Stock turnover (in units)} = 250 / 60 = 4.17$$
$$\text{Stock turnover (at cost)} = \$47,500 / \$11,400 = 4.17$$
$$\text{Stock turnover (at retail)} = \$67,857 / \$18,000 = 3.77$$
$$\text{Sales to stock} = \$67,857 / \$11,400 = 5.95$$

Note that both brands' stock turnover at cost figures match their stock turnover in units, while stock turnover at retail falls below these figures. This is the result of reductions in the retail value of merchandise due to markdowns and employee discounts. Reductions to original retail value make stock turnover lower measured at retail rather than at cost. Note from Exhibit 14.1 that the store had originally intended to sell each unit of Brand A at $275, but that the average selling price came to only $250 each ($62,500/250). This is because the store marked some of the units down from the original price during a special sale and it sold a few to

Electronics stores strive to increase stock turnover in order to increase their return on assets.

employees at a discount. As discussed in the previous chapter, markdowns and discounts reduce the retail value of the merchandise.

The same was true for Brand B. The firm intended to sell these items at $300 a unit, but its actual average selling price was only $271 per unit. The difference between the original intended selling price and the actual selling price typically reduces stock turnover at retail below stock turnover at cost. The two figures match when no markdowns or other types of discounts lower actual price from the originally intended level. Since most retail firms now maintain inventory records at retail value, they should compute stock turnovers on the retail basis, too; this allows easy comparability with other retail performance measures, which are typically calculated at retail value.

Irrespective of the particular method by which firms calculate it, the turnover measure is not a dollar or percentage figures, but simply a ratio. Higher ratios indicate faster merchandise turnover; that is, the firm is generating sales with less inventory. The stock turnover ratio, therefore, measures the productivity of the inventory. Compare, for example, the stock turnover of the two brands of televisions calculated earlier. Although Brand B generated more revenue, its stock turnover was lower than that of Brand A. This tells the firm that the money it invested in maintaining the inventory for Brand A worked more productively than that it invested in Brand B. Retailers always strive to increase stock turnover since it increases the firm's return on assets and return on net worth.

Setting Turnover Goals

Since stock turnover rate has a great impact on the financial performance of the firm, it is one of the criteria by which retailers judge merchandise performance. They typically calculate stock turnover rates for each merchandise item (SKU) and then compute aggregate turnover figures for merchandise classifications, departments within the store, and the store as a whole.

No single level of turnover suits all kinds of stores, however, or even all departments within a single store. What constitutes a good turnover rate depends on the type of store and the type of merchandise. Some merchandise turns over quickly while others turn over much more slowly. Jewelry stores, for example, could never achieve the rate of turnover that supermarkets commonly obtain. Similarly, the turnover rates for various departments within a department store vary considerably. Because turnover rates vary for different types of merchandise, firms must set separate **turnover goals** for each department and evaluate merchandise performance against these goals. Only stores that sell a single type of merchandise can rely on a single store-wide turnover target.

Firms can compare departmental turnover figures to two types of standards. First, the firm should always compare current performance to past experience. Historical comparisons can highlight declining trends that may call for corrective action. Looking at the trends also helps the firm set goals for future years.

As a second standard, firms can compare themselves to the current performance of competitors. Although turnover figures of specific competitors may not be available, various trade associations provide industry wide figures. For example, the National Retail Federation (NRF) publishes stock turnover statistics for department and specialty stores annually, as shown in Exhibit 14.2. In setting the stock turnover goal for a department, a department store manager can compare the firm's performance against the median turnover rate achieved by all other department stores. To make the comparisons more meaningful, separate figures are available for different sizes of department stores. In general, larger department stores have higher turnover rates than smaller ones, reflecting their greater economies of scale.

The NRF also publishes turnover rates for narrower merchandise classifications. For the men's clothing category, for example, it provides separate turnover rates for coats, suits and formal wear, casual wear, shirts, sweaters, and so on. Turnover can vary considerably among these narrower merchandise classifications (see Exhibit 14.3A). Thus, a store should set a separate turnover goal for each classification rather than a single goal for all of men's clothing. Exhibit 14.3B shows stock turnover of some health and beauty aid items sold in drugstores.

Benefits of High Turnover

High turnover rates reflect more productive use of resources through the maintenance of good merchandise balance. Retailers derive several benefits from high turnover rates:

1. They lower operating costs relative to sales. A faster turnover reduces the average level of inventory relative to sales, which reduces insurance, interest, and storage costs. It also helps firms save on the cost of space, since less inventory

---

Exhibit 14.2   **Median Stock Turns (at Retail) for Selected Merchandise Categories in Department Stores**

Department	Stock Turnover	
	1990	**1989**
Female apparel	2.9	3.1
Men's and boys' apparel and accessories	2.3	2.2
Infant's and children's clothing and accessories	2.9	2.8
Footwear	1.7	1.6
Cosmetics and drugs	2.3	2.1
Home furnishings	1.5	1.7

Source: *Merchandising Operating Results of Department and Specialty Stores 1991*, National Retail Federation, New York, 1991.

Exhibit 14.3A   Variation in Stock Turnover Rates within Female Apparel Department

Classification	Stock Turnover
Female apparel—Summary	2.9
Coats	3.2
Suits	2.9
Dresses	3.2
Sportswear	3.1
Intimate daywear	2.0
Intimate nightwear	3.2
Loungewear and robes	3.2
Furs	1.2

Source: *Merchandise Operating Results of Department and Specialty Stores 1991*, National Retail Federation, New York 1991.

---

occupies less space. Lower inventory levels also reduce the need for working capital since less money is tied up in inventory.

2. Higher turnover can increase sales. Quicker turnover creates more opportunities to bring in fresh, new merchandise to replace old stock. New items can stimulate customer interest and also excite the salespeople to push the merchandise.

3. Higher stock turnover can reduce the need for markdowns.

4. Faster turnover also reduces merchandise spoilage; this is especially important for supermarkets with their large stocks of perishable products.

5. Faster turnover provides more opportunities to take advantage of special buying situations. More frequent buying cycles allow buyers to benefit more from

---

Exhibit 14.3B   Stock Turnover of Health and Beauty Aids in Drugstores

Item	Stock Turnover
All HBA items	4.3
Men's toiletries	4.1
Skin-care items	4.1
Hair-care items	4.1
Oral hygiene items	4.9
Color cosmetics	2.9
Cold/cough medicines	4.4
Analgesics	4.5
Paper goods	7.2

Source: *1986 Nielsen Review of Retail Drug Store Trends*, (Northbrook, IL: Neilsen Marketing Research, 1987).

special trade promotions and other favorable buying situations. By buying frequently, the retailer can also respond promptly to demand for new items and styles.

6. Higher stock turnover increases the firm's return on assets and return on net worth.

Ways to Increase Stock Turnover

Since it is so important for firms to maintain healthy turnover rates, they must take corrective steps if they find unsatisfactory turnover rates for departments or merchandise items. Inspection of the formula for stock turnover shows that the turnover rate can increase only if the ratio of average inventory to sales increases. This may be achieved by decreasing stocks without losing sales or by increasing sales without increasing inventory investment, or both in tandem.

For example, if current sales in a department were $240,000 with average retail value of stock of $60,000, turnover would be 4.0. A sales increase of 10 percent while maintaining the current level of inventory increases turnover to 4.40. Even if a firm had to increase inventory 5 percent to increase sales by 10 percent, stock turnover would still increase to 4.19. Similarly, a 10 percent reduction in inventory from the current level of $60,000 without any drop in sales would increase the stock turnover rate from 4.00 to 4.44.

The particular avenue a firm chooses for improving stock turnover depends on the circumstances of each situation, but it is always a very critical decision. A firm should adopt a strategy for improving turnover rates only if it boosts profits. They must not sacrifice overall profits and merchandise selection in the quest for higher turnover.

Improving the Timing of Purchases   Firms can lower inventory without affecting merchandise selection through improved timing of purchases. Synchronizing buying schedules more closely with demand patterns can improve turnover without affecting profitability. This is especially important for seasonal goods. Firms often buy and stock seasonal goods too far in advance of appropriate selling periods, leaving the goods sitting on the shelves for a long time before they sell. The early arrival of new stock also increases pressure to clear existing stock through markdowns.

Reducing Markdowns   Firms can also seek to control markdowns to improve turnover rates. Although they cannot avoid some markdowns, they can increase turnover by controlling the amount of markdowns. Better advertising, display, in-store promotion, and personal selling can decrease the need for markdowns. Firms that operate multiple outlets can often decrease the need for markdowns by shifting goods among the stores to take advantage of local demands. The following experience of a small discount clothing chain illustrates the potential benefit of this policy.

Effective personal selling can decrease the need for a store to markdown merchandise. By answering his customers' questions about surfboards, this salesman is increasing his chances for a sale.

The chain operates seven stores in a northeastern city. It had given individual store managers the authority to mark down slow-selling items at their stores. A review of store procedures found that store managers often marked down items that were in short supply at the chain's other outlets. This prompted the company to require store managers first to consult with the main office prior to marking down any item, except for planned chainwide promotional events. The main office tried to shift the merchandise to another branch that could sell it at the regular price. The chain permitted markdowns only if no other branch of the chain wanted that merchandise. Total markdowns fell and turnover increased significantly due to this policy.

Controlling Depth   Another key to improved turnover is the proper amount of each SKU to stock. An inventory control method that properly matches the level of inventory with fluctuations in the level of demand (such as the reorder point model discussed in the previous chapter) is a key ingredient in determining optimal inventory levels.

A Cautionary Note

Although retailers should always strive to improve turnover, they should do so cautiously. High turnover can adversely affect financial performance if it reduces merchandising standards. Firms should never sacrifice the ideal stock balance—the balance between variety and assortment—in their efforts to increase turnover. Limiting variety or assortment in the quest for rapid stock turnover may lead to customer disappointment with the merchandise selection and they may stop patronizing the store. This will ultimately damage sales and financial performance.

Increasing stock turnover by reducing the depth of the stock instead of variety or assortment may also be dangerous. This would leave the store with fewer units of each SKU on hand at any given time. A significant reduction in stock depth can create frequent stock outs resulting again in lost sales. Out of stock situations can seriously reduce sales of basic stock items that the customer can easily buy from a competitor. Instead of waiting for the store to restock the item, customers will simply go to another store. If this occurs frequently, some customers may stop patronizing the store altogether.

The pursuit of higher turnover by lowering average inventory can sometimes actually increase costs because of inefficiencies in frequent reorders of smaller amounts of merchandise. Per-unit shipping costs are usually higher for goods shipped in smaller lots, more paperwork increases ordering costs, and receiving and handling costs are higher, too. The store may also miss out on opportunities for quantity discounts when it buys small amounts of merchandise.

GROSS MARGIN RETURN ON INVESTMENT (GMROI)

As mentioned at the beginning of the chapter, information on stock turnover and gross margin must be considered together to obtain a comprehensive measure of the productivity of resources invested in inventory. Consider the experiences of three hardware stores that sold flashlights.

On January 1, Store A purchased 100 flashlights from a wholesaler at $1.50 each. It displayed the flashlights for sale at $3.00 each, selling the last one just before the store closed on December 31.

Store B also bought 100 flashlights on January 1 at $1.50 each, but sold the entire lot by June 30 at $3.00 each. It then received a new shipment of 100 flashlights on July 1 and sold out the second lot on December 31.

Like the other two stores, Store C had started the year with 100 flashlights that it had purchased at $1.50 each, but it sold them at $3.75 a piece. By closing time on December 31, it had sold only 80 of the 100 units.

What returns did the three stores get from the monies they invested in flashlight inventory? On December 31, Store A completely depleted the stock of 100

STRATEGY IN ACTION

Target Gets by with Less Inventory

Using techniques that would have astounded inventory managers even ten years ago, Target, one of the nation's leading mass-merchandisers, has greatly reduced costs while increasing sales. Since the late-1980s, Target has managed to carry less inventory while keeping an average of 99 percent of products on display at all times. For a chain that handles upward of 65,000 items—when variations in size and color are taken into account—keeping 99 percent of its offerings visible at all times is no small feat.

Target has succeeded in lowering the percentage of stock that the average store has in the stockroom rather than on display in recent years. In 1989, at least 50 percent of stock was in the stockroom while in 1992 that figure had dropped to 30 percent. Does this mean that customers won't find what they are looking for? Not in the least. It does, however, mean that last minute clearance sales are fewer at Target, but with its every-day low prices, this doesn't faze many Target customers. The company has cut inventory by roughly $800,000 per store, or $400 million overall, and management intends to increase that number.

Target's first efforts to increase efficiency and save money began in the early 1980s. Faced with higher costs for sales and administrative functions than its largest competitors, Target set out to reduce costs and increase efficiency, without sacrificing product quality or in-store service so that it could effectively compete with Wal-Mart and K mart. Target focused on two areas: scanner technology linked to computers, which allowed instant data processing, and a new teamwork orientation between previously separate functions (such as purchasing and distribution) and also between the stores and their vendors.

The new technology has steadily made it easier and less expensive to keep track of

flashlights it bought from the wholesaler on January 1. Thus, its average inventory for the year was 50 units (see Exhibit 14.4). The value of this inventory was $75.00 (50 x $1.50). This $75 investment earned the firm revenues of $300 (100 units x $3/unit) and gross margins of $150. The firm's gross margin of $150 on its investment of $75 gave it a gross margin return of 200 percent on the merchandise investment.

As shown in Exhibit 14.4, Store B also had an average inventory of 50 flashlights, so its investment in flashlight inventory was also $75.00. Unlike Store A, however, Store B sold 200 flashlights generating $600 of revenues and $300 of gross margins. The gross margin return on its investments was thus 400 percent.

Store C maintained an average inventory of 60 units, so its inventory investment was $90.00. Since the store sold only 80 units during the year, its gross mar-

the location, price, and amount of all items that Target stocks. Like most major retailers, Target uses scanners at checkout points which save time and offer an exact accounting of all items sold. But Target also uses portable scanners with radio transmitters to connect with the store's computers. Shop-floor employees use the hand-held scanners to check on items on the shelf. A display instantly tells them how much of the item is available in inventory and precisely where it is located in the stockroom. The same scanner can also tell the employee if the item is on-order. Given that so much of an employee's time was previously spent tracking down items, counting inventory, and reordering, the scanners save countless hours of useless searching. Each employee is responsible for a specific section of items, which are checked upon arrival and then again at multiple times during a shift. In this way, Target can carry less inventory and restock efficiently as items run low.

While this new technology allows for greater savings and efficiencies than ever before at Target, it also requires much more communication between the stores and their vendors, hence the need for increased teamwork from many areas. The vendors are now as much a part of the inventory management team as are the store managers, but in the newly established environment of teamwork, the suppliers want to keep their goods on the shelves as much as Target wants to ensure accurate inventory management. Now that all parties feel involved and responsible, customers will find better prices and constant supplies of the inventory they seek.

Source: Barnaby J. Feder, "A Store Unfazed by a Few Empty Shelves," *The New York Times*, December 23, 1992, pp. D1, D2.

gins from flashlights totaled $180.00 (80 x $2.25). Store C, therefore, earned a gross margin return on investment of 200 percent, the same as Store A.

Measured by the criterion of gross margin return on investment, Store B performed the best of the three stores, and Stores A and C performed equally well. Store A and Store B both made the same unit margin on flashlights, but Store B generated higher returns because of its greater stock turnover. Although both stores made $1.50 from each flashlight, the higher turnover at Store B increased its return on inventory investment.

But how did Store C get the same return as Store A despite its lower sales? The answer is in its greater unit margin. Although Store C had a lower inventory turnover, it generated gross margins of $2.25 on each sale compared to $1.50 at Store A. The higher margin compensated for the lower inventory turnover.

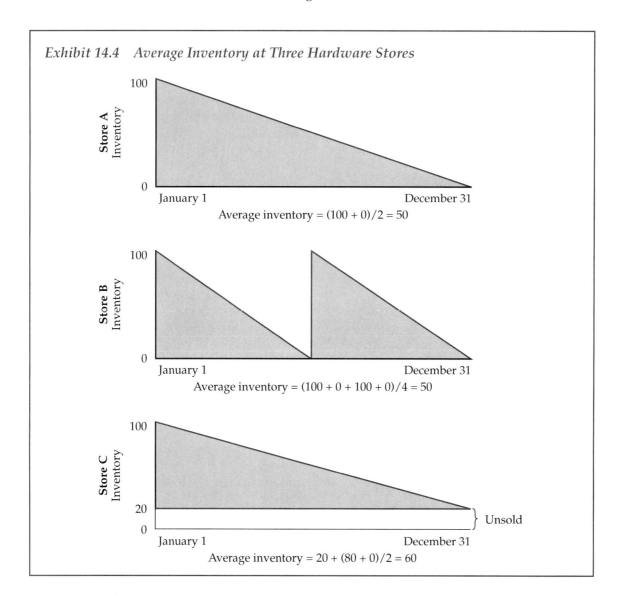

Exhibit 14.4   Average Inventory at Three Hardware Stores

Store A Inventory

January 1   December 31

Average inventory = (100 + 0)/2 = 50

Store B Inventory

January 1   December 31

Average inventory = (100 + 0 + 100 + 0)/4 = 50

Store C Inventory

January 1   December 31

Average inventory = 20 + (80 + 0)/2 = 60

Calculating GMROI

The experiences of the three hardware stores reveal the importance of both the gross margins a merchandise item generates and the dollar amount of inventory investment in it when evaluating merchandise performance. Together they yield the **gross margin return on investment (GMROI)**, an important yardstick for measuring merchandise performance. GMROI is formally defined as follows:

$$GMROI = \frac{\text{Total gross margin (dollars)}}{\text{Dollar cost of average inventory}} \times 100$$

GMROI directly measures the amount of total margins an inventory investment generates. A GMROI of 100 percent, for example, means that each dollar invested in a particular inventory item generates a dollar of margin. If GMROI is 200 percent, a dollar invested in inventory generates two dollars of margin. Thus, a higher GMROI indicates a more productive item than a lower GMROI.

GMROI is one of the most important measures by which firms monitor and evaluate the performance of merchandise items. GMROI evaluates merchandise performance from a return on investment perspective, just as ROA measures the return on total assets and RONW measures the return on net worth. GMROI measures the gross margin returned per dollar invested in specific merchandise inventories. It measures the productivity of assets invested in merchandise inventory.

There is another important similarity between ROA and GMROI. Recall from Chapter 7 that ROA expresses in a single ratio the relationship between a firm's return on sales (ROS) and asset turnover. Similarly, *GMROI combines gross margin percentages with **sales to stock ratios**,* as shown below:

$$GMROI = \text{Gross margin percent} \times \text{Sales to stock ratio} \times 100$$

or:

$$GMROI = \frac{\text{Gross margin}}{\text{Net sales}} \times \frac{\text{Net sales}}{\text{Average inventory (at cost)}} \times 100$$

The first expression measures gross margin in relation to sales and the second one indicates the amount of dollar sales generated by each dollar invested in inventory. Note that the numerator of the second expression is measured in retail dollars, while the denominator is measured at cost.

To further illustrate the calculation of GMROI, consider again the information shown in Exhibit 14.1. Based on that information, the GMROI figures for the two brands of televisions are:

$$GMROI \text{ (Brand A)} = \$15,000/\$62,500 \times \$62,500/\$7,600 \times 100$$
$$= 0.24 \times 8.22 \times 100$$
$$= 197\%$$
$$GMROI \text{ (Brand B)} = \$20,357/\$67,857 \times \$67,857/\$11,400 \times 100$$
$$= 0.30 \times 5.95 \times 100$$
$$= 178\%$$

Thus, every dollar invested in stock of Brand A generated a gross margin of $1.97, and every dollar invested in Brand B generated a margin of $1.78. The store's investments in Brand A stocks therefore generated gross margins more productively.

Since both margin and turnover rates affect GMROI, different combinations of margin and turnover can produce the same GMROI. Indeed, one value of this measure is the direct comparison it allows between the performances of merchandise with widely varying margin and turnover characteristics.

Consider the margins, sales to stock ratios, and resulting GMROIs for four merchandise items shown in Exhibit 14.5. Although each item has a different margin and sales to stock ratio, all have the same GMROI. The investments in the four inventories are, therefore, equally productive. It is important to note from this example that, while margin and turnover are important components of merchandise performance, neither by itself allows firms to evaluate merchandise decisions. The interrelationship between the two ratios provides critical insight. For this reason, the combination of margin and turnover information in GMROI is so widely used to compare the performance of different types of merchandise.

Because of intense price competition some products have low margins. Firms must manage inventory of those products carefully to ensure that high turnover compensates for the low margin. They may even lower price and sacrifice some margin, if this increases turnover enough to boost GMROI. Retail managers must trade off margin against turnover rather than look at them separately. GMROI's simultaneous attention to margin and turnover provides the basis for making such trade-offs.[1]

GMROI and Overall Profitability

Retail managers need to ask an important question: How does the store's GMROI affect its overall profitability, as measured by return on assets (ROA) or return on net worth (RONW)? To answer this question one must look at the relationship of GMROI to the various elements of the strategic profit model. Consider, for example, the financial information for Superior Department Store shown in Exhibit 14.6. In 1988, the firm achieved a RONW of 17.10 percent with the following figures:

$$\text{RONW} = \text{Net profit margin} \times \text{Asset turnover} \times \text{Leverage ratio}$$
$$17.10\% \quad = 3.94\% \qquad\qquad \times\ 2.17 \qquad\qquad \times\ 2.0$$

The firm can also calculate the overall GMROI from the information shown in the strategic profit model:

Exhibit 14.5   *Different Pathways to the Same GMROI*

Margin		Sales to Stock		GMROI
35%	×	3.14	=	180%
40	×	4.50	=	180
45	×	4.00	=	180
50	×	3.60	=	180

Exhibit 14.6   *Strategic Profit Model Data for Superior Department Store*

Sales	$1,824,000
Cost of goods sold / Sales	59.7%
Return on net worth	17.11%
Return on assets	8.55%
Net profit margin	3.94%
Asset turnover	2.17
Leverage	2.00

Calculations

Step 1

	Sales	$1,824,000
−	Cost of goods	− $1,088,576
=	Gross margin	= $735,424

	Wages and salaries	$304,000
+	Rent and occupancy	+ $182,400
+	Selling expenses	+ $102,500
+	General expenses	+ $74,700
=	Total expenses	= $663,600

	Gross margin	$735,424
−	Total expenses	$663,600
=	Net profit	$71,824

	Net profit	$71,824
÷	Sales	÷ $1,824,000
=	Net profit margin	= 3.94%

Step 2

	Inventory	$396,668
+	Accounts receivable	+ $167,000
+	Other current assets	+ $86,000
=	Total current assets	= $649,668

	Total current assets	$649,668
+	Fixed assets	+ $190,000
=	Total assets	= $839,668

	Sales	$1,824,000
÷	Total assets	÷ $839,668
=	Asset turnover	= 2.17

Step 3

	Accounts payable	$13,800
+	Notes payable	+ $53,000
+	Other current liabilities	+ $12,000
=	Total current liabilities	= $78,000

	Total current liabilities	$78,800
+	Long-term liabilities	+ $341,034
=	Total liabilities	= $419,834

	Total liabilities + Net worth	$419,834 + $419,834
÷	Net worth	÷ $419,834
=	Leverage	= 2.00

Step 4

	Net profit margin	3.94%
×	Asset turnover	× 2.17
=	Return on assets	= 8.55%

	Return on assets	8.55%
×	Leverage	× 2.00
=	Return on net worth	= 17.11%

$$\text{GMROI} = \frac{\text{Gross margin}}{\text{Net sales}} \times \frac{\text{Net sales}}{\text{Average inventory (at cost)}} \times 100$$

$$= \frac{\$735,426}{\$1,824,000} \times \frac{\$1,824,000}{\$396,668} \times 100 = 184\%$$

This performance did not satisfy Superior's managers. They wanted to increase RONW to at least 25 percent. They noted that in previous years, the store had maintained a gross margin around 42 percent and also that the current sales to stock ratio of 4.60 fell short of the target of 5.2. After discussing a number of proposals for improving performance, the managers resolved to strive to meet gross margin and sales to stock ratio goals for the next year.

How would the store's ROA and RONW change if it achieved its margin and sales to stock turnover targets the next year? To answer this question it is necessary to perform a what-if analysis like those in Chapter 7. The first step in performing such an analysis is to specify how the factors in the strategic profit model are expected to change in the future. Superior's managers anticipated, for example, that sales would increase by 10 percent and that all expenses other than rent would increase proportionately. They did not feel that they could improve the deployment of noninventory current assets or collection of accounts receivable, so these figures, too, would increase in proportion to sales. Finally, the store set a policy of maintaining a leverage ratio of 2.0.

Exhibit 14.7 shows Superior's projected financial model for the next year assuming that sales to stock ratio increases to 5.2 and margin improves to 42 percent. The 10 percent increase in sales and the improvement in the gross margin percentage boost total gross margin from $735,424 to $842,688. The model project's total expenses of $711,720, yielding a net profit of $130,568. Consequently the model projects that net profit margin will reach 6.53 percent.

The asset turnover component of the profit model also changes. Note that both accounts receivable and current assets increase by 10 percent because of the anticipated increase in sales while inventory investments decline. This is because the sales to stock ratio increases from 4.60 to 5.20. With projected sales of $2,006,400 and a sales to stock ratio of 5.20 the average inventory investment is $385,846 ($2,006,400/5.2), a 2.7 percent decline from the current level despite the increased sales. Total assets, therefore, increase by only a small amount to $854,146. In keeping with the store's financial policy, it would fund half of the new assets through new debts and half through owners' equity.

Projected sales of $2,006,400 and projected total assets of $854,146 yield a projected asset turnover in the new scenario of 2.35. With the net profit margin in this scenario of 6.53 percent, ROA increases to 15.35 percent and RONW to 30.70 percent. Thus, achieving margin and sales to stock targets will substantially improve Superior's performance, boosting its return on net worth by nearly 80 percent. The projected GMROI calculation gives:

Exhibit 14.7   Projected Strategic Profit Model for Superior Department Store

Sales	$2,006,400
Cost of goods sold / Sales	58.0%
Return on net worth	30.57%
Return on assets	15.29%
Net profit margin	6.51%
Asset turnover	2.35
Leverage	2.00

Calculations
Step 1

Sales	$2,006,400
− Cost of goods	− $1,163,712
= Gross margin	= $842,688
Wages and salaries	$334,400
+ Rent and occupancy	+ $182,400
+ Selling expenses	+ $112,750
+ General expenses	+ $82,570
= Total expenses	= $712,120
Gross margin	$842,688
− Total expenses	− $712,120
= Net profit	= $130,568
Net profit	$130,568
÷ Sales	÷ $2,006,400
= Net profit margin	= 6.51%

Step 2

Inventory	$385,846
+ Accounts receivable	+ $183,700
+ Other current assets	+ $94,600
= Total current assets	= $664,146
Total current assets	$664,146
+ Fixed assets	+ $190,000
= Total assets	= $854,146
Sales	$2,006,400
÷ Total assets	÷ $854,146
= Asset turnover	= 2.35

Step 3

Accounts payable	$15,180
+ Notes payable	+ $58,300
+ Other current liabilities	+ $12,559
= Total current liabilities	= $86,039
Total current liabilities	$86,039
+ Long-term liabilities	+ $341,034
= Total liabilities	= $427,073
Total liabilities + Net worth	$427,073 + $427,073
÷ Net worth	÷ $427,073
= Leverage	= 2.00

Step 4

Net profit margin	6.51%
× Asset turnover	× 2.35
= Return on assets	= 15.29%
Return on assets	15.29%
× Leverage	× 2.00
= Return on net worth	= 30.57%

$842,688/\$2,006,400 \times \$2,006,400/\$385,846 \times 100$
= 0.42 $\times$ 5.2 $\times$ 100
= 218%

Thus, if sales to stock ratio increases to 5.2 and gross margin increases to 42 percent, GMROI will increase by 18 percent along with the increase in return on net worth of nearly 80 percent. Superior could, of course, achieve the same financial results by increasing margins without affecting sales to stock ratio, or by increasing the ratio even further while sacrificing margin. The store's managers must decide which of these approaches is most feasible and take steps to implement it for the coming year.

Developing a Hierarchical Monitoring System

To improve GMROI, the managers of Superior Department Store have to identify the part of their operations where improvement would give the best overall results. They probably cannot increase GMROI to the same extent for all merchandise items. The opportunity to improve GMROI may be high for some items, while others may already be earning high GRMOIs. They must develop a separate target for each item depending on its characteristics, level of competition, and historical performance. To develop such targets, they must monitor the GMROI level of each department, each merchandise classification, and even for each merchandise item carried by the store in addition to looking at storewide figures.

As the initial step in such a **hierarchical monitoring system**, managers examine gross margins and inventory investments for the store as a whole and for its departments. Exhibit 14.8 shows such a breakdown for the Superior Department Store. It reveals considerable variation in GMROI across departments. The female apparel department generates the highest GMROI, while the GMROI for the recreational goods department is the lowest. The average storewide figure of 185 percent hides these significant differences among departments.

Which department should the store target for improvement? Before the managers can answer this question, they have to compare the figures in Exhibit 14.8 with previous results. Does the low GMROI in the recreational goods department depart from historical trends, or is it consistent with results from previous years? They should also compare departmental figures with results from similar departments in other department stores. A study published by the National Retail Federation found that recreational goods departments at better department stores typically achieve GMROI around 150 percent. Superior's departmental GMROI of 70 percent is surely below par and a prime candidate for improvement.

To improve their insight into the recreational goods department, the managers must analyze the performance of each merchandise classification within the department separately. Just as GMROI varies among departments within the store,

Exhibit 14.8 Superior Department Store Merchandise Performance Analysis

	Sales	Gross Margin	Gross Margin Percentage	Average Inventory at Cost	Sales to Stock	GMROI
Storewide	1,824,000	735,426	40.3%	396,668	4.60	185%
By department						
Female apparel	592,000	255,702	43.2%	82,675	7.16	309%
Female accessories	138,000	64,398	46.7	24,020	5.75	268
Men's and boys' apparel	312,000	129,952	41.7	62,115	5.02	209
Infants' and children's apparel	100,000	41,692	41.7	18,431	5.43	226
Shoes	94,000	38,974	41.5	26,774	3.51	146
Cosmetics and fragrances	124,000	48,360	39.0	32,240	3.85	150
Recreational goods	128,000	34,634	27.1	49,392	2.59	70
Home furnishings	310,000	113,624	36.7	97,551	3.18	116
All other merchandise	26,000	8,090	31.1	3,470	7.49	233
Recreational goods						
Audio-visual, musical	12,000	1,908	15.9%	6,360	1.89	30%
Home electronics	42,000	6,762	16.1	16,905	2.48	40
Toys, hobbies, games	12,000	4,056	33.8	3,687	3.25	110
Books, stamps, coins	4,000	1,208	30.2	1,510	2.65	80
Office equipment and stationery	24,000	9,984	41.6	5,873	4.09	170
Photographic equipment	10,000	1,660	16.6	3,320	3.01	50
Luggage	10,000	4,310	43.1	3,079	3.25	140
Sporting goods	12,000	3,912	32.6	7,824	1.53	50
All other recreation goods	2,000	834	41.7	834	2.40	100
Summary—Recreational goods	128,000	34,634	27.1%	49,392	2.59	70%
Female apparel department						
Women's coats	38,000	16,226	42.7%	4,917	7.73	330%
Women's suits	6,000	2,262	37.7	943	6.37	240
Furs	8,000	2,992	37.4	3,324	2.41	90
Women's dresses	64,000	25,408	39.7	8,761	7.30	290
Junior dresses	14,000	5,824	41.6	1,618	8.65	360
Women's sportswear	284,000	121,552	42.8	35,751	7.94	340
Junior sportswear	82,000	35,342	43.1	10,098	8.12	350
Intimate daywear	36,000	18,144	50.4	7,889	4.56	230
Intimate nightwear	24,000	11,496	47.9	3,285	7.31	350
Loungewear and robes	14,000	6,468	46.2	1,748	8.01	370
All other female apparel	22,000	9,988	45.4	4,343	5.07	230
Summary—Female apparel	592,000	255,702	43.2%	82,675	7.16	309%

In a large store it is important to evaluate the performance of the merchandise in each individual department. Why do female apparel departments like this one typically outperform such departments as recreational equipment?

each classification within a department will also perform at a different level. Audio-visual and musical merchandise at Superior, for example, have a GMROI of only 30 percent, and that for home electronics is just 40 percent. Office equipment and stationery goods, on the other hand, have a much higher GMROI. Similarly, even the vigorous performance of the female apparel department includes considerable variation among merchandise classifications. Furs, for example, have a GMROI of only 90 percent, while junior dresses have a GMROI of 360 percent.

Since departments and merchandise classifications within them perform at different levels, a firm needs a comprehensive merchandise reporting system to evaluate merchandise performance and set GMROI targets. This requires a hierarchical reporting system, like the one in Exhibit 14.8 "so it is possible to move from summarized reports to more detailed reports in an attempt to track down problems and develop solutions."[2]

A firm may need to break down the information shown in Exhibit 14.8 even further and look at the performance of each SKU within a classification to find those that don't contribute to its overall financial health. This helps the firm analyze the performance of each merchandise item, set goals for the future, and take actions to achieve those goals. Efficient hierarchical monitoring systems can employ personal computers and commercially available computer software.

GMROI: A Summary

GMROI is a simple, yet useful measure for evaluating merchandise performance. It highlights several important facts:

1. Firms should evaluate investments in merchandise inventory in terms of the returns from those investments.
2. Margin and turnover are the two paths to increased return on inventory investments.
3. Different merchandise items may provide the same returns on investment despite very different margin and turnover characteristics.

GMROI figures help firms perform several important tasks:

1. They facilitate ranking merchandise items based on return on investment. Such rankings help managers judge the relative performance of items within a merchandise class, concentrating on items with high ranks while carefully monitoring those with low ranks, possibly even discontinuing them.
2. They clarify decisions to allocate scarce financial resources and selling space among items. Few retailers can carry all available merchandise lines, and the decision to carry one may preclude stocking another. GMROI figures support such resource allocation decisions, since an item with a higher GMROI represents a better investment than one with a lower GMROI.
3. They link performance of individual merchandise items, merchandise classifications, entire departments, and finally the total store. It allows the manager to evaluate the effect of performance at one level on results at another level. The managers of Superior, for example, can calculate how the GMROI for the recreational goods department will change if it can increase GMROI for photographic equipment by 50 percent.

DIRECT PRODUCT PROFIT (DPP)

Although GMROI is widely used to measure merchandise performance, a number of retailers have begun adopting a method called **direct product profit (DPP)**.[3] Some managers worry that, since GMROI measures product performance based on gross margins, it can hide important differences in the cost of selling merchandise. For example, two products that have the same GMROI may require different expenditures for sales personnel or advertising. These cost differences make for different profitability between the two products. Similarly, terms of payment for the two

---

RESEARCH REPORT

Scanning Tells More Than Just the Price

Shopping in supermarkets is something most Americans do on a weekly basis. In fact, more shoppers pass through supermarkets than almost any other kind of store. But such shoppers are anonymous to the stores: while a supermarket keeps close track of the items its sells, it rarely knows to whom they are sold. Is it a wealthy customer? One who swears by fish on Fridays? One who will buy only a certain brand of toothpaste, or one who follows the sales? Supermarkets have not previously been able to track the individual preferences of their customers, and instead have had to rely on the general trends of items that sell or don't sell in order to know what to stock and how to keep the cash flowing. But new scanner technology is changing all of that, allowing stores to follow not just what sells but who buys.

The laser bar-code scanner and computer link-ups coupled with in-store customer cards are now making it possible for stores to build databases about each of their customers, and the new techniques come in a variety of forms. The earliest types of "supermarket micromarketing" were shoppers' clubs. Offered as incentives for more deals and better prices, regular customers use bar-coded cards which register all items purchased as well as identify the customer. Then, the stores and the product manufacturers monitor the sales, and offer coupons and other values for items regularly purchased. For example, if the customer has a cat, the cat food manufacturer could send direct mail coupons offering discounts, or if the customer switches brands, the same manufacturer could send coupons in the hope of regaining the customer.

Customers who regularly clip coupons find the micromarketing service helpful—now they don't need to bother clipping coupons—and manufacturers are finding less of a need to place coupon ads in local circulars. In fact, food suppliers have found that direct electronic micromarketing generates four to five times the sales as the free-standing coupons generate. Redemption of news-

goods may differ, one, perhaps, calling for payment within seven days, while the other allows a 30-day payment term. Thus, even if the average inventories of two goods are the same, the actual cost of maintaining the inventories would differ, since the retailer can eliminate the cost of holding inventory if it sells the merchandise before payment for it comes due.

To capture these differences in actual cost of selling different merchandise, it is necessary to modify the GMROI measure, shifting attention from gross margins to net margins and from average inventory investments to the actual cost of holding inventory. In other words, firms must focus their attention on the amount the item contributes directly toward the store's profits.

paper coupons averages 2.3 percent while the newer forms of direct mail coupons average 10 to 11 percent redemption.

But what about customers who already feel inundated with junk mail? For most electronic marketers, the pros outweigh the cons, and more direct mail is sure to arrive. But these new forms of marketing still have a long way to go before becoming smooth and unobtrusive. For instance, some supermarkets were using the information to track customers in general, not just their purchases. When customers stopped frequenting a store, the market would write to them, entreating them to return. Unfortunately, most customers felt this was too much an invasion of privacy, as if they were being watched too closely. That aspect of micromarketing has been dropped by supermarkets.

Other kinds of electronic marketing include on-site computers that generate coupons for competing products as purchases are made. Installed at the check-out counter, PepsiCo, for example, can pay to have a coupon generated each time a customer buys Coke. While these systems definitely help impulse purchases, they do little to monitor who buys what or why the customer chose one product over another. For more supermarkets and their suppliers, the real value of micromarketing is in knowing who shops and why they buy what they do. The downside of this is that an immense amount of data is generated, on a daily basis, leaving markets and the manufacturers multiple options. Should they target younger shoppers? Senior citizens? Shoppers with pets or ones with kids? The options are many. While it is sure to take markets time to determine what the best mode of electronic marketing will be for them, it is clear that some type of micromarketing is here to stay.

Source: N. R. Kleinfeld, "Targeting the Grocery Shopper," *The New York Times*, May 26, 1991.

The idea of evaluating merchandise based on direct product profitability is not new. It is reported that the concept of DPP was first presented at a comptroller's meeting of the National Association of Food Chains in 1959.[4] It was only in the late 1970s, however, that the use of DPP spread, especially in the supermarket industry. At this time many supermarkets installed optical scanners at checkout counters and the data generated by scanning systems could be used directly in DPP systems. The use of DPP in supermarkets was greatly facilitated by the introduction of a industry-wide standard for calculating DPP by the Food Marketing Institute in August 1985. This lead to the spread of DPP use among supermarkets, especially the large chains.[5]

By using optical scanners at the checkout counter, supermarkets can gather important data on individual products. This information can be used to calculate such things as the amount of profit each item contributes to the overall profits of the store.

Although food-industry managers have successfully used DPP for quite some time, only recently have other retailers started adopting this system. One reason for DPP's slow acceptance in the past was the difficulty of collecting and organizing all the data required to compute it. Ideally, a manager should include in DPP analysis all variable costs associated with handling a merchandise item from warehouse to the final sale. The cost of maintaining such data has been prohibitive in the past, but the increased use of computers at retail stores and distribution centers has changed this situation considerably in recent years. Many mass merchandise and department stores are developing DPP systems for their stores. As a group of authors recently noted, "ultimately most retailers and manufacturers may be forced to adopt DPP to remain competitive."[6]

Calculating DPP

DPP measures the profit a product generates by considering, in addition to the gross margin, all the **direct costs** associated with selling a product. Such direct product costs include warehouse costs, selling expenses, advertising and promotion expenses, inventory interest expenses, and so forth. By deducting these expenses from gross margin, one can measure how much a product directly contributes to profit. The example shown in Exhibit 14.9 illustrates how to calculate DPP.

The retailer buys the item at $10.00 and retails it at $14.99 a unit, generating a gross margin of $4.99 per unit. The retailer must adjust this gross margin figure to reflect two factors. First, the manufacturer offers a 2-percent discount off the invoice if the retailer pays within 10 days. Thus, the retailer can save 20 cents per item by paying the bill on time. Secondly, the manufacturer is currently offering a special 2.5-percent merchandise allowance to promote the product, effectively reducing the cost by 25 cents a unit. After adjustments, therefore, the gross margin comes to $5.44 per unit instead of $4.99.

To calculate the item's contribution to the store's profits, the retailer must subtract direct or variable costs associated with selling the item from its adjusted gross margin. Any expenditure that the firm can directly allocate to a merchandise item must be included under variable costs. Exhibit 14.9 shows some major sources of variable costs. Note that they include costs incurred at both the distribution center and the retail store, and that inventory expenses also fall into this category.

Exhibit 14.9   Computing DPP for a Merchandise Item

Retail price	$14.99	
Cost of goods	$10.00	
Gross margin		$4.99
Payment discounts earned	$0.20	
Merchandise allowances earned	$0.25	
Adjusted gross margin		$5.44
Warehouse expenses	$0.55	
Warehouse inventory expenses	$0.20	
Transportation to store	$0.15	
Retail store expenses	$1.10	
Promotion	$0.10	
Total direct costs		$2.25
DPP per item		$3.19
Unit sales per week	20	
DPP per week		$63.80

The difference between the adjusted gross margin and total direct cost gives the amount that the merchandise contributes directly to profit. The item in Exhibit 14.9 has direct costs of $2.25, which results in a per-unit DPP of $3.19. This means that every time the retailer sells one unit of this merchandise, it earns $3.19 to cover fixed costs.

The retailer also needs to know the total amount that the item contributes to profit in a given time period. An item's total contribution depends on its DPP per unit as well as the number of units sold during the time period. More sales, of course, increase an item's contribution, and for a given level of sales, contribution increases with higher per-unit DPP. The retailer sells 20 of the item shown in Exhibit 14.9 per week, resulting in a weekly profit contribution of $63.80 ($3.19 × 20). The retailer has this money available to pay for fixed expenses such as the cost of land and buildings, administrative expenses, and other overhead expenses that all merchandise items sold at the store share. A store makes a net profit only if the sum of the profit contributions of all items exceeds its fixed costs.

Factors that Affect DPP

Four factors affect DPP: (i) gross margin, (ii) turnover, (iii) payment terms and allowances, and (iv) warehouse, transportation, selling, and promotional expenses.

Although neither the gross margin percentage nor the sales to stock ratio appear directly in the formula for DPP, an item's DPP reflects both margin and turnover. As the item's gross margin increases, its DPP increases by the same amount, and when gross margin falls, DPP falls just as far. In Exhibit 14.9, for example, the gross margin is $4.99. If this increases by a dollar, DPP increases from $3.19 to $4.19. A reduction in gross margin by a dollar will decrease DPP by the same amount.

Turnover also affects DPP. Any change in turnover changes both warehouse and retail inventory expenses and, consequently, the item's DPP. High turnover allows firms to maintain less stock, reducing inventory expenses. A drop in turnover, on the other hand, increases inventory expenses. Thus, both margin and turnover affect DPP, as they do GMROI.

GMROI and DPP differ in that the latter changes with terms of payment and any allowances received from vendors. Retailers can increase item profitability by taking advantage of cash discounts offered by vendors for early payment. Vendor allowances for advertising, promotion, and demonstration also increase profits by subsidizing the retailer's cost. Merchandise buyers can significantly improve the profitability of the items they purchase by negotiating with vendors for the best purchase terms possible.

Reducing the costs of transporting merchandise from the manufacturer to the store and physical handling of the goods can also improve merchandise performance. As these costs climb higher, store's profits fall. An item's DPP reflects the cost of selling an item. Items such as cosmetics, cameras, and major appliances, for example, have high selling costs. This reduces the DPPs of these items. An item with a higher gross margin than another may actually have a lower DPP if its selling costs are higher.

Using DPP

Since DPP measures the profit potential of individual merchandise items, managers can use it just like GMROI for making merchandising decisions. It does, however, have certain advantages over GMROI.

For one major advantage, it gives a more accurate picture of merchandise profitability than GMROI, since it reflects to both gross margins and direct expenses. Thus it allows more meaningful comparison of merchandise items even if they require different amounts of selling effort or advertising expenses or have different payment terms. Managers can further simplify such comparisons by expressing DPP in terms of a common unit such as DPP per square foot of space needed to sell the item. When different products occupy different amounts of selling space, DPP per square foot helps managers compare them despite this difference. In drugstores, for example, items such as batteries and razor blades have a higher than average DPP per square foot, even though the DPP per unit is relatively low. Cigarettes, on the other hand, are high on both DPP per unit and DPP per square foot. Retailers can use graphical pictures like the merchandising performance chart shown in Exhibit 14.10.

In the supermarket industry, DPP is widely used for space planning. Supermarket managers can use DPP and shelf-space management software to manage return on investment on a category-by-category basis.[7] Retailers can categorize the products they carry based on DPP per unit and sales as shown in Exhibit 14.11. An item that has a high DPP per unit and also sells very well should be supported aggressively compared to one that has low DPP and sales. Items that sell well but have low DPP need special management attention. The store must either decrease the direct costs associated with selling the product or be able to increase the margin. Margin may be improved by negotiating a better price from the vendor, higher discounts from vendor, or better payment terms. Items with high DPP and low sales also need attention, but of a different kind. The retailer must explore ways to increase the demand for the product through advertising, better shelf placement, and sales support, for example. Alternatively, if demand is elastic, a slight reduction in price may spur sales and increase revenues. However, the retailer must ensure that these actions do not drive DPP to an unacceptable level.

DPP also supports cost-benefit analysis for decisions on alternative distribution arrangements. For example, suppose a manufacturer offers to ship merchandise directly to a store instead of sending it to the firm's warehouse. If the retailer were to choose the direct shipment option, it would lose a 25-cent per unit merchandise

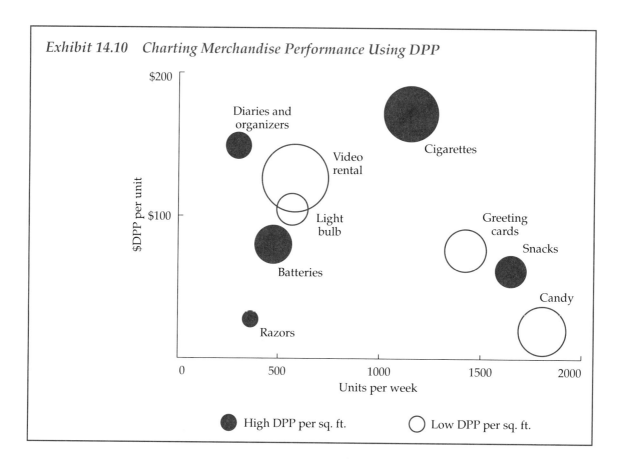

Exhibit 14.10   Charting Merchandise Performance Using DPP

allowance and also have to pay an additional charge of 30 cents per item. Although direct shipment would reduce gross margin, it could still benefit the retailer by reducing warehouse costs and eliminating the cost of shipping from warehouse to store. Large enough cost savings would compensate for the lower margin. Before responding to the manufacturer's offer, the retailer should work out the costs and benefits of store delivery versus warehouse delivery; one way to do this is to compute DPP in the new scenario as shown in Exhibit 14.12, and then compare it to the information in Exhibit 14.9.

The adjusted gross margin in the new scenario, $4.90, is 54 cents below the current level. The firm also projects that variable costs would change: the firm would incur no warehouse-related costs with direct shipment, but it expects handling costs in the store to increase by 20 cents a unit. As a result of these changes, per-unit DPP in the new scenario would be $3.35, an increase of 16 cents a unit. The weekly DPP, therefore, would increase by $3.20 ($0.16 × 20), if the manufacturer were to

Exhibit 14.11 DPP Decision Matrix

	Low Volume	High Volume
Low DPP per unit	Requires thorough investigation. If DPP or sales cannot be increased, consider discontinuation or reduced space.	Increase DPP by reducing direct costs and by negotiating better prices and discounts.
High DPP per unit	Increase sales by advertising and promotion support or price reduction.	Continue supporting these winners.

ship the product directly to the store. The retailer should, therefore, agree to the manufacturer's proposal.

Other Criteria for Judging Merchandise Performance

In the final analysis, all merchandise must contribute to the store's profits. GMROI and DPP measure the amount of profit that merchandise items generate directly. Some items, however, contribute indirectly rather than directly. For example, firms price loss leaders lower than their costs and the store's normal margins would warrant. Although these products sacrifice some amount of direct profits, they, too, contribute indirectly to profits by creating an overall image of low prices and by building **store traffic**. Customers attracted by the low prices of loss leaders are likely to buy other products as well at their normal prices. Thus, while loss leader items may not look attractive in terms of GMROI or DPP, firms should not eliminate them. Their ability to build store traffic compensates for their lack of direct profit generating power.

Summary

1. The profitability of a store depends on how well each merchandise item performs. Therefore, retail managers face a major task in evaluating the performance of individual merchandise items. They must monitor the profitability of each item and decide whether to keep it in stock or discontinue it.

Exhibit 14.12   DPP for Direct Shipment

Retail price	$14.99	
Cost of goods	10.30	
Gross margin		$ 4.69
Payment discounts earned	0.21	
Merchandise allowances earned	0.00	
Adjusted gross margin		4.90
Warehouse expenses	—	
Warehouse inventory expenses	—	
Transportation to store	—	
Retail store expenses	1.25	
Retail inventory expenses	0.20	
Promotion	0.10	
Total direct costs		1.55
DPP per item		3.35
Unit sales per week	20	
DPP per week		$67.00

2. As a crucial aspect of merchandise management, the manager must maintain a healthy balance between inventory investment and sales. The stock turnover ratio measures the relationship between inventory and sales. A higher stock turnover indicates that a firm generates sales with less inventory. High turnover rates benefit firms by reducing operating costs, increasing sales, limiting markdowns, and freeing up resources to allow it to take advantage of special buying situations.

   Margin, the difference between the price a store charges for an item and its cost for that item, also affects merchandise profitability. Items with higher margins contribute more toward meeting the firm's operating expenses and profit goals.

3. Because the turnover ratio indicates how fast merchandise is selling relative to the level of inventory, retailers use it to set goals. Each retailer must determine the turnover goal that is most appropriate for it, since turnover rates vary depending on target market, location, pricing policy, and so on. These goals also vary for departments and merchandise classifications within a department.

4. Firms can increase turnover rates by widening the difference between sales and inventory. One approach increases sales while keeping inventory steady or decreasing it. Alternatively, achieving the same sales with less inventory also improves turnover. Control of markdowns, improved timing of purchases, and proper selection of the amount of each SKU to stock all help firms improve turnover.

5. Gross margin return on investment (GMROI) is calculated by combining information on turnover with information on gross margins. GMROI indicates the return on each dollar invested in maintaining inventory. Since GMROI combines both margin and turnover,

many firms use it to compare the performance of different types of merchandise. They also set goals in terms of GMROI for merchandise departments and classifications and refer to it when developing plans for allocating resources among merchandise items.

6. A number of retailers have begun to measure merchandise performance in terms of DPP. DPP indicates the direct profit potential of merchandise items. It considers both the gross margin earned and the variable costs associated with selling the item. Variable costs include warehouse costs, transportation costs, handling costs, and selling costs at the retail store.

Key Concepts

Merchandise performance
Gross margin
Stock turnover
Average inventory
Turnover goals
Gross Margin Return on Investment (GMROI)

Sales to stock ratio
Hierarchical monitoring
DPP
Direct costs
Store traffic

Discussion Questions

1. A. If the cost value of average inventory is $28,000, and the cost of goods sold is $52,000, what is the stock turnover rate?

   B. If first quarter net sales are $80,000 and the average retail stock on hand is $60,000, what is the annual stock turnover?

   C. What is the stock turnover rate if the average inventory at cost is $50,000, net sales are $125,000, and the cost complement is 60 percent?

2. What aspect of merchandise performance does GMROI measure? Explain how stock turnover affects GMROI.

3. Compute GMROI and its two component ratios for the following three merchandise items and comment on the relative performance of the three items.

Item	Sales	Cost of Goods Sold	Average Inventory (at cost)
A	$150,000	$80,000	$35,000
B	160,000	115,000	30,000
C	200,000	108,000	55,000

4. Last year a hardware store had net sales of $560,000 and a stock turnover rate (at retail) of 6.0. Its manager projects that sales will increase by 5 percent next year. How much inventory (at retail) must the store maintain to achieve a planned stock turnover rate of 6.5?

5. The lawn furniture department of a home center store has a stock turnover of 2.4. How would you evaluate whether the department has done well or poorly?

6. The average GMROI at a department store is 180 percent and its return on assets is 15 percent. How will the store's return on assets (ROA) change if next year the store achieves a higher GMROI?

7. Consider the information given in Exhibit 14.1.

   A. Calculate the GMROI for Brand A if the average units in stock increased to 60.

   B. Calculate GMROI for Brand B if the average selling price increased by $6 per unit.

C. How would Brand B's GMROI change if the cost of each unit increased by $10?

Show all calculations clearly.

8. What is DPP? How does this measure differ from GMROI?

Notes

1. Alan D. Bates, *Retailing and Its Environment* (New York: Van Nostrand, 1979), p. 156.
2. Ibid. p. 149.
3. Harris Gordon, Daniel O'Connor, and John Phipps, "Direct Product Profit: Introducing a Comprehensive Measure of Retail Performance," *Retail Control* 54 (September 1986), pp. 36–43.
4. Steven Bliss and Chris Leamon, *Direct Product Profit*, Unpublished Report, New York University.
5. For an excellent discussion of DPP in the food industry see the three-part series,

"DPP: Putting It to Work," in *Supermarket News*, September 21, 1987; September 28, 1987; October 5, 1987.
6. Ibid.
7. D. Merrefield, "DPP Vastly Improves Space Management," *Supermarket News*, May 11, 1987.
8. Murray Krieger, *Practical Merchandising Math for Everyday Use* (New York: National Retail Merchants Association, 1980).

Appendix to Chapter 14

Calculating Average Inventory

To compute the turnover ratio one must accurately determine the average level of inventory investment. Firms use an average stock figure for this purpose because they often find it very difficult to know the exact value of the inventory at any given moment.[8] At one time, most retailers made a valuation of their inventory only once or twice a year and calculated average stock based on those figures. Computerized cash registers now automatically update inventory records without the need for physically counting stock, allowing firms to value their inventories more frequently. the following discussion assumes that a firm determines inventory value at least once a month. This would be true for most large retail firms and even for many small retail organizations.

The average inventory for any time period is the average of all the inventory valuations made during that period. For example, to calculate the average inventory for the months of June, July, and August, the manager averages the inventory levels at the beginning of June, July, and August and at the end of August. The manager can then calculate the average inventory for the three-month period of June, July, and August as follows:

Month	Retail Value of Inventory
B.O.M. June	$12,000
B.O.M. July	10,000
B.O.M. August	14,000
E.O.M. August	7,000
Total inventory	$43,000
Average inventory	$43,000/4 = $10,750

If the net sales during the three-month period were $12,000, then the turnover rate for this period would be 1.12. Firms commonly express stock turnover rates for years rather than for parts of the year, even when they base the calculation on information from a part of the year only. Since the turnover rate of 1.12 is based on three months, the turnover for the entire year is four times that number. Thus to convert a turnover figure for part of a year to an annual figure, multiply it by the number of such time periods in the year. If the turnover calculation were based on only two months of data, the annualized rate would be six times that amount.

By the procedure outlined above, a manager can calculate the average inventory for any time period and the annual turnover rate. Exhibit 14A.1 applies this procedure to calculate a turnover rate based on inventory information for six months. Notice two points about this procedure. The E.O.M inventory for any month is the B.O.M inventory for the next month. The average inventory in the previous example would not change if the E.O.M. inventory for August were replaced by B.O.M. inventory for September.

Exhibit 14A.1 Stock Turnover Based on Six-Month Inventory and Sales Figures

Inventory		Sales	
B.O.M. January	$ 40,000	January	$14,000
B.O.M. February	38,000	February	13,800
B.O.M. March	39,000	March	13,000
B.O.M. April	41,000	April	17,500
B.O.M. May	40,500	May	16,000
B.O.M. June	38,500	June	14,800
B.O.M. July	40,000		
Total	$277,000	Total	$89,100

Average inventory = $277,000/7
= $ 39,571

Six-month turnover = $89,100/$39,571
= 2.25

Annual turnover = 2.25 × 2 = 4.50

Note also that the number of inventory valuations included in the computation always exceeds the number of periods by one. Calculation of an average inventory for a three-month period requires four inventory valuations. To compute a four-month average requires five valuations.

PART IV
Supporting the Merchandise

Retailers augment the value of the merchandise that they sell by providing customers with information and service and by creating a pleasant atmosphere in which to shop. This section examines the different ways in which retailers support the merchandise by creating a favorable store image in the customer's mind.

Chapter 15 looks at how retailers enhance the value of their merchandise by creating a pleasant shopping atmosphere and by providing support services. It discusses the role of visual merchandising in making the shopping experience enjoyable and using retail space efficiently and effectively. Retailers communicate with their customers through media advertisements, in-store announcements, and direct mail. Each of these kinds of communication is discussed in Chapter 16. The chapter deals with such questions as: How to select target audiences? How to set communication objectives? How to monitor the impact of communications programs?

The focus of Chapter 17 is on personal selling and services retailing. The chapter starts by discussing the role of personal services in retailing and describing the steps in the personal selling process. Service retailing is now an important feature of the retailing scene. For this reason this chapter examines the characteristics that separate services from goods and discusses some important challenges in service retailing and how service firms can respond to these challenges.

515

CHAPTER 15
Creating Shopping Atmosphere

Sears Changes Store Design to Create New Image

During the 1980s, Sears, then America's largest retailer, experienced a sharp downturn in profits. Sales became sluggish, and the 864-store chain realized that some dramatic changes were in order if they were to save the empire. At that time, Sears was a traditional mass merchandiser, and its largest competitor was J.C. Penney. However, consumers were turning away from mass merchandisers, finding the offering too wide and jumbled, and the stores confusing and lacking cohesiveness between the disparate departments (auto parts to children's furniture). Furthermore, the quality of the offering was poor in relation to the prices charged. Given these choices at the mass merchandise stores, consumers opted to shop either at discount stores, where they could find brand names at discount prices, or at department stores, where the extra frills of customer service and elegant atmosphere warranted the higher prices demanded. While Sears was losing customers to both discounters and department stores, it was primarily discounters such as Wal-Mart and K mart that were eating away at Sears' customer base. Faced with this downturn, Sears decided to reposition itself to customers and to better position itself to compete head-on with these retailers.

Sears sought to bring back customers by tempting them with a new image and merchandise mix. Its positioning goal was a moderate department store—below Macy's or Nordstrom in price and selection and above the quality and selection of Wal-Mart and K mart, but matching their prices. This was no small task for the giant, as it meant a full revamping of its image across all 864 stores, and at the time, Sears had a limited cash flow available to complete this task.

The company's strategy was to improve store atmosphere by creating attractive settings in which to shop. Sears had been plagued with over-crowded, poorly lit stores that had messy and disorderly displays. The first step in remodeling the stores was to decide what lines of merchandise would be offered, and how the different departments could be combined into a cohesive whole. In the end, management redefined their merchandise into seven specialty businesses that could be united into one store by means of clever design elements. The seven "power-formats" are men's, women's, and children's apparel, home appliances and electronics, automotive supplies, home improvement products, and home furnishings. Sears main-

After studying this chapter, the reader will be able to:

- *Understand the facets of retail stores that affect shopping atmosphere.*
- *Describe the emotional responses retail store atmosphere evokes.*
- *Know the pros and cons of the different types of store layouts.*
- *Be able to allocate space to merchandise departments and locate them appropriately within the store.*
- *Understand the elements of visual merchandising.*
- *Evaluate the role of customer support services on the store's environment.*
- *Explain the different ways in which retailers can improve the quality of transactional services.*

tained that by positioning itself as a powerful specialty merchant in each of these businesses it would be better able to compete against Wal-Mart and K mart. After all, this sort of single-minded focus on sharply de-fined specialties is how Sears' strongest competitors got where they are, and ignoring this type of positioning is how Sears fell behind.

Sears believed that the heart of their success would be with increased apparel sales, by attracting new apparel shoppers and by reconverting existing Sears shoppers. Sears wanted to fill a mid-market niche. The company stated that the goal would be to present a wide variety of moderately priced fashion clothing that represents good value to the customer. Sears hired more experienced buyers to upgrade the lines and bring nationally recognized labels into Sears. Sears sought to help overcome the stigma that many people had about buying clothes at Sears, and the chain knew that this alteration would require not just a better merchandise mix, but also a new kind of store that would attract new customers and convince existing ones to buy apparel for the whole family at Sears. The strategy was to have the apparel lines be the keystone for the stores and have the other departments rotate around them.

The redesign efforts focused on the goal to have "high-speed" rather than "high-style" stores, where shoppers could shop quickly and efficiently. Striking a balance between comfort and formality, Sears added wide aisles and clear sight lines in order to give the store an open feeling and make it easier to shop. Good signage also enhanced the stores accessibility, and designers used a hanging signband with complete and clear information to replace the hanging signs and banners that many shoppers associated with Sears. The overall design emphasized Sears' specialty store positioning, with each department having its own individual identity through carpeting, wall treatments, and fixtures, while the whole store is unified through the repetition of similar materials and details. To that end, the women's apparel department looks unique, but blends with the other six departments, and vice versa.

The redesign has brought an organization and uniformity that was lacking in the chain before the remodeling began. All of the new design elements, from better lighting to wider aisles, were executed to make the store more customer friendly and thus easier to shop. Customer service also plays a key ele-

ment in the redesign, in an overall effort to make shopping as easy as possible at Sears.

Sears now needs to choose the right mix of its departments, or power formats, for each of its stores. Not all the stores are large enough to fit all seven departments comfortably, and at first Sears was keen on placing all of them in every store. In some stores, particularly in larger metropolitan areas, this meant that some departments had to be so small that only a few items could be displayed, and the area ending up looking like a cramped collection of unrelated pieces that did little to grab the customers' attention. The veteran retail analyst Walter Loeb, put it this way in an article in *Fortune*: "Sears has the right idea with its power formats. It's just the execution that needs a lot of work."

Sources: Susan Caminiti, "Sears' Need: More Speed," *Fortune,* July 15, 1991, pp. 81–89; and Marianne Wilson, "Sears Bets Its Future on Updated Design," *Chain Store Age Executive*, October 1991, pp. 64–66.

As the secret behind the phenomenal success of Bloomingdale's, the longtime jewel of Federated's retailing empire, many observers point to the synergy between its merchandise and its store atmosphere. At its flagship store on Manhattan's 59th Street, black marble, glittering mirrors, live models wearing fancy furs, sales assistants spraying exotic perfumes, and colorful ensemble displays all blend together to create a shopping atmosphere that gives true meaning to the often-repeated phrase "retailing as theater."

The glittering decor is part of a well-thought-out marketing strategy that supports a distinctive selection of merchandise gathered from all over the world, with an exciting shopping atmosphere and a high level of personal service to create a distinctive image in the consumer's mind. Bloomingdale's, or Bloomie's, as many fondly call it, prides itself on being like no other store in the world. The strategy not only creates excitement for the customers, but fills the store's coffers too: Bloomingdale's sales per square foot of floor space ranks among the highest in the nation.

Synergy between store atmosphere and merchandising philosophy is also the key to McDonald's success. Although formica and plastic replace mirrors and marble, the design of McDonald's outlets suit the expectations of its customers well. Big glass windows, bright colors, and cheerful, uniformed personnel create an image of efficiency as well as cleanliness. To appeal to families with children, many outlets provide toys and playgrounds for young customers. The outlets are specially designed to facilitate quick service to both in-store and drive-in customers.

As its central task, retailing facilitates the flow of merchandise from manufacturers to customers. The merchandise is often described as the "heart" of the retail exchange process. The retailer offers much more than a mere assortment of merchandise, however. Successful retailers facilitate the exchange process by creating a **shopping atmosphere** that enhances value for the store's target customers. The physical environment in which the store sells the merchandise is an integral part of the exchange process since, in making purchase decisions, consumers "respond to more than the tangible product or service that is being offered."[1] The aesthetics and ambience of the store, the way in which it displays merchandise, the personal service it provides and the efficiency with which transactions are completed, are all integral to the store's image. If the merchandise is the heart of the retailer's offer, the internal store environment is its soul.

PLANNING THE STORE ATMOSPHERE

Elements of Store Atmosphere

The various factors that affect store atmosphere fall into three broad groups:

1. The physical environment in the store, including its design, merchandise layout, and display.
2. The store's support services, including acceptance of credit cards, gift wrapping, law-away plans, and return policies.
3. The efficiency of checkout and other services necessary to complete retail transactions.

This chapter discusses each of these three facets of store atmosphere. It must be stressed, however, that in the final analysis, it is the interaction of these three components that creates an image in the mind of the customer. Thus, planning each of the components well is not enough, the store must properly blend them together. Moreover, they must be consistent with the store's overall marketing strategy. As always, the critical factor is consistency with the expectations of the target market. As two examples, consider again the strategies of F.A.O. Schwarz and Toys R Us described earlier in Chapter 5. Recall the boutique style ensemble displays of novel and unique toys at F.A.O. Schwarz and the regimented supermarket style aisles of Toys R Us. Although the shopping atmosphere of these two stores is distinctly different, in each case it matches the expectations of their target markets (see Chapter 5 for a more detailed description of the marketing strategies of these two stores).

STRATEGY IN ACTION

Ambience Sells the Merchandise

The Carnival, the Indiana-based shoe and fashion accessory chain, reaches its audience with a rather unusual principle: offer crazy deals and customers will flock to the store. By creating an exciting and ever-changing shopping environment, the Carnival has become a multimillion dollar shoe and accessories empire that looks as much like a circus as it does a retail venture. Started in 1978 by David Russel, the company now boasts 35 stores and sells an estimated $100 million worth of shoes and accessories in a most unusual way. Russel began his career in foot apparel with Kinney shoes, where he worked for 20 years. Restless with the conventional way of selling the merchandise and sure that there was another, more exciting and unusual way to sell shoes, Russel launched his own venture, Shoe Biz. From Shoe Biz, Russel built a shoe and fashion accessory empire, one that is as outrageous as it is successful. Vowing that his goal was to put the fun back into retail, Russel built The Carnival with a combination of hard work, determination, and a wee bit of eccentricity.

The stores get their name from the environment created at each location. Flashing lights and banners adorn the facades, and loud music greets customers at the door. There is a ring-master, equipped with a microphone, announcing discounts and customer contests. Such activities as a free pair of shoes to the customer who can hula-hoop the longest are announced frequently, and the action never stops. This kind of carnival atmosphere even extends to selling: customers can haggle over prices, and salespeople have been known to follow people out of the stores offering further deals to secure the sales, and when shoppers arrive in the parking lot, there is someone with a bullhorn shouting out the deals to be found inside. Shopping for shoes is a rather mundane activity, like going to the supermarket or brushing your teeth. But Russel wanted to

The store's ambience and internal design must reflect the changing attitudes of customers. This realization led the venerable Endicott Johnson chain of stores to change the design of its Father and Son outlets. The new design, which is being tested in 13 of the chain's 185 outlets, is a marked departure from the past. The store is now visually separated into formal and casual areas, with athletic footwear located in between to act as a transition. This, according to the designer, reflects the store's philosophy that there is a "father" and "son" in every man, but it is divided by attitude not by age. The new design is consistent with the increased role of life styles over age in shaping customer attitudes and preferences. According to store managers, the new design has been successful in attracting customers who formerly didn't view Father and Son as their type of store.[2]

offer a little more pizzazz, and make this most ordinary task more fun.

Although Russel isn't the first retailer to use the shopping-as-entertainment theme to attract customers, he has clearly given the idea new meaning. Anything goes at The Carnival, as long as it creates a fun atmosphere for the customers. A customer who arrives at the store to purchase a hairbrush or a handbag might be confronted with a contest for a pair of shoes. Once he or she has won the shoes, the shopping spirit picks up. The customer can barter for the best deal on new socks, include shoelaces in the purchase, and leave with much more than intended. On the way to the car, barkers hawking more deals entice customers to buy *just one more* pair of socks, and therein lies the secret of The Carnival: generating impulse purchases.

But Russel is also a keen merchandiser, and the success of the chain is due as much to his merchandising strategy as to the zany atmosphere. Russel employs volume buying and no-frills displays to cut costs, and he uses over 500 vendors to insure a huge selection at the stores. The Carnival is legendary for its selection and good prices, and this keeps customers coming back. Warehouse techniques for displays keep overhead low, and the stores are packed with discounted items and a wide selection. The stores average 12,000 square feet, which is not huge compared with a mass merchandiser, but given that the product category is limited—only shoes and accessories—this is a lot of space. Moreover, Russel is deeply committed to the stores, and has even been known to make announcements over the microphone himself. Given this, it is no wonder that The Carnival continues to be such a success.

Source: "Retailing's Entrepreneurs of the Year," *Chain Store Age Executive*, December 1990, pp. 28–38.

Designing the Physical Environment

A retail store is more than just bricks and mortar, it is the package in which a store displays its merchandise.[3] Just as a product's package must attract and entice customers, the store's design must attract shoppers and project the desired retail image. The retailer must carefully blend all the features of the store's physical environment to create the appropriate retail atmosphere.

Retail atmosphere *is the psychological effect or feeling created by a store's design and its physical surroundings.* Whether consciously planned or not, the store's physical environment evokes certain feelings. Music or lighting may make a store appear cheerful or its colors may make it seem depressing. Similarly, the video displays commonly used nowadays in many stores evoke positive feelings in the minds of shoppers. These emotional reactions, in turn, influence consumer attitude toward the store and their behavior within it including:[4]

- Shopping in the store with enjoyment.
- Spending time browsing and exploring the store's offering.
- Willingly talking with sales personnel.
- Spending more money, perhaps, than originally planned.
- Returning to the store.

Retailers fully recognize the impact of the physical environment on customer behavior. To create the desired ambience, they design stores to produce specific emotional effects in buyers, effects that ultimately influence consumer behavior.[5] Both the exterior and interior design of the store are important in evoking the desired emotional effect.

Traditionally, the exterior design of the store served as the major form of communication between retailers and their potential customers. The frontage and windows identified the type and quality of the store and created the initial impression in the customer's mind. However, with more and more stores located in shopping malls, it is the interior rather than the exterior of the store that shapes consumer attitudes toward it. To create the proper in-store atmosphere, retailers must appeal to customers' sensory perceptions of sight, sound, scent, taste, and touch. While each of these individual sensory appeals is important in itself, the truly important concern is the total effect created by the combination of all five sensory appeals.[6]

Finding the right combination is not easy, since research has provided few systematic generalizable findings. For example, although it is known that background music affects the behavior of shoppers, the precise nature of its impact is difficult to predict. Similarly, finding the right combination of color and lighting requires experimentation and experience.

Psychology of Retail Atmosphere[7]

The Stimulus-Organism-Response (SOR) paradigm proposed by environmental psychologists helps explain the effects of store atmosphere on shopping behavior. The SOR model has three components: a set of stimuli, a set of responses or outcomes, and a set of variables that mediate between stimuli and outcomes (see Exhibit 15.1). In the retail store context, the different facets of the store's design and layout such as exterior and interior designs, merchandise presentation, colors, lighting, music, and so on, make up the stimulus set. Shoppers' responses to these stimuli can be characterized as **approach behaviors** or **avoidance behaviors**. Approach and avoidance behaviors are described in retail stores in four ways:

1. A desire to stay in (approach) or leave (avoidance) the store.

Exhibit 15.1   Three Components of the SOR Model

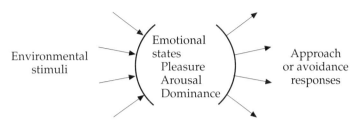

Environmental stimuli → Emotional states Pleasure Arousal Dominance → Approach or avoidance responses

Source: Robert J. Donovan and John R. Rossiter, "Store Atmosphere: An Environmental Psychology Approach," *Journal of Retailing* 58 (Spring 1982), p. 42.

2. A desire to explore and interact with the shopping environment (approach) or a tendency to ignore it (avoidance).
3. A desire to communicate with others in the store (approach) or to ignore the attempts of sales personnel to communicate with customers (avoidance).
4. A feeling of satisfaction (approach) or disappointment (avoidance) with the shopping experience.

Three basic emotional states of the shopper mediate between stimuli and responses:

Pleasure	————————	Displeasure
Arousal	————————	Nonarousal
Dominance	————————	Submissiveness

The pleasure–displeasure state determines the degree to which the shopper feels good, joyful, happy, or satisfied in the store. The second state determines the degree to which the shopper feels excited and stimulated. The third determines the extent to which the shopper feels in control of, or free to act in, the store environment. Stronger feelings of pleasure and arousal make the shopper's attitude toward the store more positive. On the other hand, an atmosphere that creates a submissive emotional state leads to avoidance behavior.

Retailers can affect the emotional responses of shoppers by designing their stores to provide sensory cues. For example, to create an atmosphere that is attractive to their predominantly teenage target market, stores such as CODA and Urban Outfitters play popular rock music and use bright, vibrant colors, flashing neon lights, and even video displays to create the desired atmosphere. Contrast this with the internal environment of most jewelry stores. That environment creates a very different shopping atmosphere with soft lighting, pastel colors, and carpeting. Smell, too, can create emotional responses. The aromas of fresh coffee and fresh bread cause many passersby to pause at a restaurant or bakery. Some stores are known to use fragrances to evoke feelings of freshness and cheerfulness.

The Key: Individuality

No ideal atmosphere is appropriate for all stores. Each must find the combination of sensory cues that best evokes the desired emotional states and most clearly projects its intended image. Just as any other retail decision, decisions on store atmosphere must start with analysis of the needs and preferences of the store's target market. Stores such as Tiffany's, Bergdorf Goodman, Saks Fifth Avenue, and Neiman-Marcus appeal to their exclusive, high-income clienteles with gracious and elegant interior designs. Contrast these with the spartan interiors of most discount stores and supermarkets. They project images of shopping efficiency that match the expectations of their target markets. Neither Tiffany's nor K mart's design, on the other hand, would be appropriate for the teenage and young adult customers of The Gap, The Limited, or Foot Locker.

IN-STORE DESIGN

Store layout, that is, the spatial relationship among merchandise departments and the overall organization of retail selling space, has an important influence on a store's internal environment. Just as colors and lighting affect store atmosphere, so do layout and display.

Retailers should design layouts to create a pleasant ambience, to encourage customer traffic, and to use store space productively. The interior design and layout of the store has a significant influence on the retailer's ability to generate sales. A number of studies have shown that in many merchandise categories customers are increasingly making purchase decisions after entering the store. This is especially true in supermarkets where, it is estimated that over half of the purchase decisions are made after the customer is in the store.[8] Studies have shown that while most customers plan the general categories of products they wish to purchase prior to coming to the store, increasingly they are making decisions regarding the specific merchandise they will buy only after they are in the store.[9] A store's interior design and merchandise layout, therefore, can have a significant impact on consumer purchases.

Retail space is scarce. The high cost of retail real estate has forced retailers to use available space as efficiently as they can to justify its cost. For example, if a store increases the size of one department, it will probably have to reduce another to compensate. Moreover, all parts of the store are not equally valuable. Many customers will see merchandise displayed near the entrance and miss items placed near the back wall. By what criteria should the retailer allocate space to different departments? Which merchandise departments should occupy the preferred locations? These are some of the questions that must be addressed in designing the internal layout of the store.

A systematic approach to designing store layout involves five different steps:

1. Planning the general layout of the store.
2. Classifying merchandise into related categories or departments.
3. Allocating selling space for departments.
4. Locating departments.
5. Arranging merchandise within departments.

Planning the General Layout

As one of its first decisions in designing the store interior, a retailer has to plan the general arrangement of space, or the store layout. In making this decision, the retailer has to consider a number of factors. One important factor is the need to use all space productively. Another is to guide the traffic flow within the store. The layout should direct customers throughout the store to facilitate planned purchases and also stimulate unplanned and impulse purchases. At the same time the layout must ensure that customers can move among the different parts of the store easily to find the merchandise they need. Finally, the retailer must be concerned about the overall aesthetics of the layout and its impact on the store's image.

There are four broad categories of layouts considered by retailers: (i) grid, (ii) free flow, (iii) loop, and (iv) boutique.

Grid Pattern   As shown in Exhibit 15.2, the grid pattern arranges shelves and aisles parallel to one another. The aisles all measure equally across their widths and secondary aisles, if any, run perpendicular to the main aisles. Typically, the checkout counters are concentrated on one end of the store near the exit and entrance. The grid pattern is common in supermarkets, drugstores, hardware stores, and other convenience-oriented stores.

Grid layouts have a number of advantages. They reduce facility cost and simplify security. They also maximize selling space because the regular arrangement displays the greatest amount of merchandise for any given amount of space. A grid pattern helps regular customers develop routine patterns of movement through the store so they can shop quickly. Some critics argue, however, that the regularity of the grid pattern rushes the shopper and discourages impulse buying.

Free-Flow Pattern   In contrast to the regularity of the grid pattern, the free-flow pattern avoids uniformity (see Exhibit 15.3). It arranges merchandise into a series of geometrical patterns that allows free movement of customer traffic. Low displays make the entire selling floor visible from any one point in the store.

Free-flow arrangements encourage customer browsing and allow more creativity in visual display. They encourage impulse purchases and **cross selling** across departments. A customer walking into the store to shop at one department sees merchandise in a number of other departments, too. This encourages unplanned purchases and increases the amount of money the customer spends at the store. Another advantage of the free-flow pattern is flexibility. Stores can expand or

Exhibit 15.2   Grid Pattern

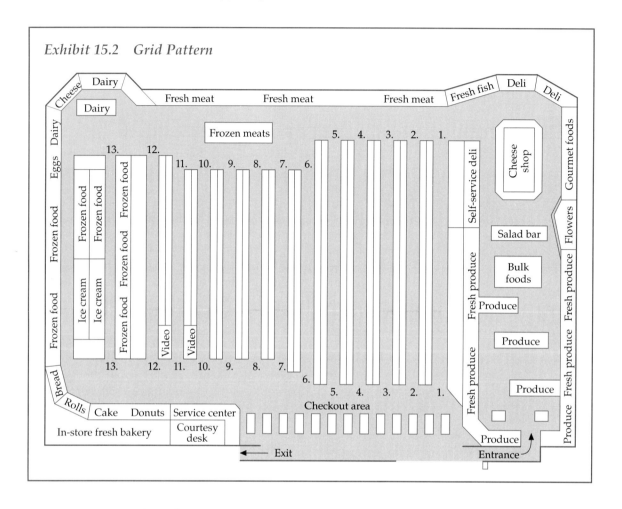

reduce the sizes of individual departments as the need arises without disrupting the overall pattern.

Free-flow patterns do, however, reduce the efficiency of space usage and increase the cost of maintenance. Specialty stores, department stores, and boutiques typically arrange departments in free-flow patterns.

Loop Pattern   The loop pattern resembles the free-flow pattern in its lack of regimentation. The loop pattern features a race-track-shaped pathway that runs around the shopping floor. All departments have frontage onto this loop, which channels the flow of shoppers through the entire store, exposing them to all the departments. This encourages browsing and impulse buying at many departments.

Boutiques   The boutique, a relatively new innovation in store layouts, has grown out of the popularity of designer names. Boutiques are essentially separate

Exhibit 15.3   Free Flow Pattern

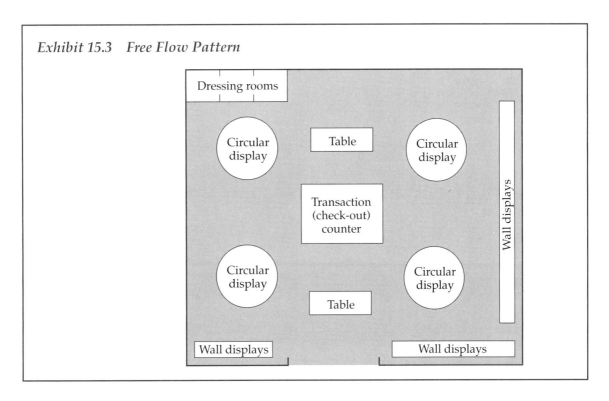

stores within the main store featuring merchandise from a single designer or aimed at a specific life style segment. For example, the Polo Club at Bloomingdale's features merchandise designed exclusively by Ralph Lauren. Similarly, many department stores maintain a separate department devoted to merchandise for the professional women.

In recent years, retailers have begun to combine features from the four basic patterns to improve the flow of customer traffic and to increase visual impact. Many supermarkets, for example, have broken from the tradition of grid patterns and introduced a combination of grid and free-flow patterns. They organize special sections featuring such items as cheese, baked goods, and fresh fish in separate areas to break the monotony of parallel aisles. This separation gives these departments special prominence in the store and helps to attract customers.

Moreover, since these departments generally have high margins, supermarket managers give them prime locations in the store.

Designing the most appropriate store layout requires considerable experience and expertise since it depends on the type of merchandise sold, the size of the store, and its physical configuration. Retailers commonly seek the help of experts and consultants who specialize in store interior design. In the final analysis, all store layouts must be judged in terms of ease of customer traffic flow, space productivity, and overall aesthetics.

Toys R Us lays out its stores in a grid pattern. This maximizes the selling space and makes it easy for the customers to find the toys they wish to purchase.

In the final analysis, the design must make a statement that helps the store stand out in the consumers' minds, while, at the same time, making efficient use of space and allowing customers to shop at ease. One example of successful blending of these three design criteria is Nike Town in Portland, Oregon. This futuristic-looking store with 15,000 square feet of selling space is to serve as the prototype of outlets Nike plans to open throughout the world. The design concept incorporates themes of sports, fitness, and entertainment while emphasizing the breadth of Nike's product line. Shoppers enter the store through an entry pavilion that brings them to a central square. The square is organized into free-standing boutiques, each emphasizing apparel and shoes related to a particular sport. The sports theme is augmented by sculptures of athletic superstars hanging from a black ceiling.[10]

Departmentalization

Retail stores sell thousands of merchandise items. To facilitate customer shopping, retailers must group these items into meaningful clusters based on compatibility as perceived by customers. This **departmentalization** forms the basis for organizing the store layout and deciding on the physical locations of merchandise items.

NIKE TOWN Chicago is a sports and fitness store that houses a full array of Nike products representing 20 different sports. The uniqueness of the design helps the store to stand out in the consumers' minds.

Retailers commonly group merchandise based on several criteria.

Similarity of Merchandise   Department stores, for example, group furniture, shoes, and housewares together in separate departments. Similarly, supermarkets put produce in one section, meat in another, and so on.

Customer Segment   Stores selling apparel for a broad target market typically display men's, women's, and children's clothing in separate departments. Also, stores organize their merchandise presentations according to life styles. The most prominent of these life style presentations target working women and provide appropriate apparel and accessories.

Price Range   Retailers typically organize apparel into three price ranges: budget, moderate, and better. Similarly, electronics stores typically cluster audio components together according to their prices.

Designer Name   In another recent phenomenon, stores often display merchandise supplied by the same designer together. For example, a department store may fill a Bill Blass department with items that carry that designer's name.

STRATEGY IN ACTION

Ikea—Designed for Shopping

Ikea, the Swedish home furnishings chain started in 1958, has grown to 90 stores located across 22 countries in just three decades. The chain even managed to double its sales—to $3.2 billion—between 1987 and 1981, despite recession in the United States and a difficult economy across Europe. How does Ikea do it? There are two main reasons: (1) Ikea offers *value* in terms of price, style, information accessibility, and shopping format, and eliminating any part of the business that does not offer the consumer value; and (2) the store layout has been carefully designed to ensure that the majority of shoppers actually purchase items. Founder Ingvar Kamprad perceived that what home furnishings consumers really need when shopping is information and time to browse, not aggressive salespeople and cramped showrooms. This simple concept of direct value and relaxed

shopping format has proved successful for Ikea across the globe.

The Ikea stores are all alike, featuring three main parts: showroom, "marketplace," and warehouse. The festively decorated showroom displays furniture in real-life setups so consumers can compare the different items. Shoppers can see if the chairs and the sofa they were interested in really go together, or if, perhaps, another item would be better suited. Customers are welcome to move items around, creating their own displays, in order to examine the merchandise, and no salesclerks will be hovering, offering opinions or asking them to replace the items moved. One level below the furniture showroom, the marketplace is filled with linens, glassware, lamps, and other housewares at deep discounts. Marketplace is set up with items for each room of the house grouped together, so that customers are able to envi-

Usage Occasion   Apparel stores commonly divide clothes into separate categories depending on whether they are appropriate for casual or formal occasions.

Retailers organize their merchandise into departments based on one or more of these five criteria, among others. These are meant to serve as examples and not as an exhaustive list. In fact, one can define departments on any basis as long as the organization is meaningful to customers. This may mean in some instances the use of multiple criteria arranged in a hierarchical fashion as shown in Exhibit 15.4.

Allocating Selling Space for Departments

As mentioned earlier, retail space is a scarce commodity. Allocating more space for one department inevitably reduces the allocation for another. Retailers must carefully plan **space allocation** for different merchandise departments in light of

sion one room at a time and what merchandise is lacking from their homes. Having just visited the showroom, the empty sofa stands out in the mind's eye, and the throw cushions found in marketplace seem the perfect accompaniment. Again, customers are left to browse, and fill their shopping carts at their leisure. Few customers make it out of marketplace without an item in hand. Finally, there is the huge warehouse space, where the furniture, which comes in kits, and is neatly stacked on open shelves so that the customers themselves can locate a particular kit, determine the right color, and move onto the next item.

Shoppers move through the carefully designed store layout looking at the merchandise, checking product specifications (size, price, weight, and so on) with the help of in-store posters and signage, and make purchase decisions without the help (or inter-

ference) of salespeople. The stores have a single entrance, which leads into the showroom, *one* door leading from the showroom into the marketplace, and *one* door leading from the marketplace into the warehouse, so that customers are obliged to follow the intended route through the stores. Furthermore, there is only one exit, positioned *after* the cashier stations, so that customers cannot slip out before seeing the entire store and all the merchandise. Thus, even if customers have preselected an item, they must pass through all three areas before paying or exiting the store. In this fashion, a trip to Ikea for one item usually ends up becoming a shopping spree. For Ikea, it is this kind of self-service, without the frills but with good quality and good prices, that keeps customers coming back.

Sources: Bill Saporito: "Ikea's Got 'Em Lining Up," *Fortune*, March 11, 1991, p. 52; Ravi Sarathy, Associate Professor, Northeastern University, Case study: "Ikea," 1989.

---

the departments' relative salability and profitability. Retailers commonly perform space allocation in one of two ways: (1) the sales per square foot method, and (2) the model stock method.

Sales per Square Foot Method   Retailers can determine the amount of space a department needs by relating the planned total sales for that department to its expected sales per square foot. Consider, for example, that an apparel store anticipates annual sales for its shirt department of $200,000. This forecast is based on past sales after considering anticipated changes in the economy, competition, price, and the firm's own marketing strategy. (See Chapter 11 for a discussion of merchandise sales forecasting.)

To determine the amount of space the shirt department requires, the store has to estimate the sales productivity of space allocated to it. Based on prior experience, the store expects to sell $170 worth of shirts annually per square foot

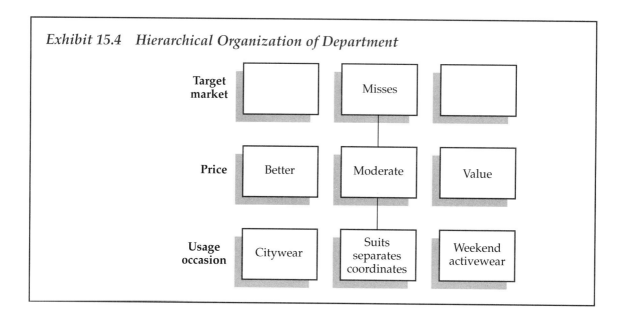

Exhibit 15.4   Hierarchical Organization of Department

of selling space. Since it plans annual sales for the department of $200,000, it can determine the space to allocate to that department by dividing that number by the anticipated sales per square foot. In other words:

$$\text{Required space (square feet)} = \frac{\text{Planned sales}}{\text{Target sales per square foot}}$$

$$= 200,000/170 = 1,176.5 \text{ square feet.}$$

Although this method is simple, firms must apply it with care. They must estimate accurately both planned sales and expected sales per square foot. New stores which lack any historical basis for estimating these figures have to rely on industrywide trends published by trade organizations. The National Retail Federation publishes the sales per square foot data for departments within department stores (see Exhibit 15.5). Similar data for other kinds of stores are also available from various trade publications.

Even a well-established store should take extreme care in estimating space productivity. Although past performance provides a basis for estimating future performance, firms must adjust past data for anticipated future conditions. A general price increase affects dollar sales per square foot, boosting sales volume even while unit sales hold constant. The retailer must also consider how well the department used its space in previous years. If it used space inefficiently in the past, productivity could improve in the future.

Model Stock Method   To determine departmental space allocations, the model stock method (also called the buildup approach) begins with the model or ideal

Exhibit 15.5 Space Productivity in Department Stores

	Sales per Square Foot	
Department	1989	1990
Female apparel	164	130
Men's and boys' apparel	185	178
Infants and children	111	104
Cosmetics and drugs	116	104
Home electronics	126	100
Home furnishings	78	84

Source: *Merchandising and Operating Results of Department and Specialty Stores in 1991*, New York: National Retail Federation, 1991.

stock plan for the department. Recall from Chapter 10 that the model stock plan provides a detailed breakdown of the merchandise selection in terms of styles, brand names, price ranges, and so forth, and specifies the number of units of each item to keep in stock. In essence, it specifies the total amount of merchandise a department must display and stock.

The retailer can calculate departmental space requirements by estimating the amount of space required to display and stock all the merchandise in the department's model stock plan. This involves five steps:

1. Determine how many of each item to display and to keep in reserve in the store.
2. Decide on the most appropriate way to display the merchandise and to store the reserve stock.
3. Calculate how many racks, shelves, bins, and so on are needed to display items and to store reserve stock.
4. Based on the calculations in Step 3, estimate the amount of selling space required for the department.
5. Determine the amount of nonselling space required (payment counters, for example) and add to the total of the figure from Step 4.

These steps bring the retailer to an estimate of the space requirements for each department in the store. If the total space requirement for all departments exceeds the selling space available at the store, the retailer must trim the model stock plans for all or some of the departments by reducing the merchandise assortment. It should not cram the store with excess merchandise. Overcrowding reduces the aesthetic appeal of stores and creates customer traffic flow problems.

Reallocating Space

Retail managers must frequently decide how to reallocate space among departments. Although at first glance this seems like a simple decision, in reality it is not. Suppose that the men's wear department of a store currently generates $170 per square foot and the shoe department generates $130 per square foot. Should the men's wear department take over some space from the shoe department in order to improve the combined results?

A number of factors affect the answer to this question. The most important consideration is the impact of space reallocation on the productivity of the men's wear department. If the reallocation adds 25 percent more space to that department, its sales must increase by 25 percent to maintain its present sales per square foot. One must, therefore, ask whether the men's wear department could increase its sales by that amount. If the department already has a large share of the total men's wear sales in the market, it may be difficult to increase sales any further. One must also consider how space reduction will affect the shoe department. Will shoe sales drop off drastically without adequate space for display of the model stock?

Yet another factor to be considered is gross margin. While the men's wear department generates $30 more sales per square foot than the shoe department, the two departments may earn different gross margins per square foot. Suppose, for example, that average margin on men's wear is 33 percent and the average margin on shoes is 50 percent. This means that each square foot of space in the men's wear department currently generates $56.10 ($170 × 0.33) in gross margins, but each square foot in the shoe department generates $65.00 ($130 × 0.50). Thus, compared to men's wear, the space devoted to shoes actually generates more funds to cover the store's operating costs.

This demonstrates the difficulty of comparing space productivity across departments. Instead, the firm should compare the performance of each department with similar departments in other stores and with performance in previous years. Chain stores, for example, commonly compare the performance of the same departments in the different stores operated by the firm. Even in this case, space productivity will vary depending on such factors as the location of the store, its total sales volume, and the level of competition in the area.

Locating Departments

After allocating space to each department, the retailer must select locations for the departments within the store. The organization of merchandise departments creates an ambience that becomes a part of the store's image. A women's fashion store, for example, puts cosmetics and jewelry departments in prominent locations on the main floor to stamp its personality. Discount department stores, on the other hand, may not have any permanent department along the main aisle near the store entrance. The merchandise in this location may change from week to week depending on what is on sale.[11] The spatial relationship among the locations of the different departments should be guided by the following principles:

Relate Value of Item to Value of Space   Parts of retail stores differ according to **value of space** because some locations attract more customer traffic than others. Merchandise displayed in the high-value locations has greater potential to generate sales because these locations offer more exposure to customers. In multistory department stores, the highest value area is the main floor; on the main floor, the best locations lie between the entrances and escalators or elevators to upper floors. Space value declines as one moves to the higher floors because customer traffic thins out with vertical distance.

Within each higher floor or basement space, value depends on access to escalators or elevators. Less accessible areas have less customer traffic and, therefore, less valuable space. The same pattern of space value is evident in single-floor stores: the space near the front entrance is the most valuable and space value declines with distance from the front entrance.

Relate Merchandise Characteristic to Traffic Flow The pattern of customer flow through the store determines, to a large extent, the productivity of retail space. For example, 50 percent of all supermarket profit comes from the top 33 percent of space in terms of traffic flow. The next 33 percent of profit comes from the middle third of space, while the 33 percent of space with the least traffic count generates only 17 percent of the store's profit.[12]

The characteristics of merchandise dictate where it should be located. Impulse items that consumers buy on the spur-of-the-moment rather than by prior plan must be located in high-traffic areas for maximum customer exposure. For this reason supermarkets locate candies, small novelties, and magazines near checkout counters. Staple items, on the other hand, are often placed in locations near the back or side walls.

Place Complementary Merchandise Together Since consumers often shop for more than one type of good at a time, retailers must facilitate cross selling by placing related departments near each other. Thus, stores locate handbags and gloves adjacent to each other, and they locate floor coverings, draperies, and slipcovers together. In a department store socks and shoes and shirts and ties should be located adjacent to each other to encourage cross selling.

Match Seasonal Demand Patterns Firms plan department locations to accommodate seasonal sales patterns. For example, they usually place toys next to a department whose sales peak in summer. They can then expand the toy department in winter when toy sales are high by allocating some of the space from the other department, since its sales decline during winter. During summer and spring, when toy sales are low, the firm can reallocate space to the other department to accommodate its increased need.

Arranging Merchandise within Departments

Retailers arrange items within each department in much the same way that they determine locations of departments. The only difference is the scale. The most salable items and those with the highest gross margins occupy the most prominent locations within the department. The scarcity of space means that each displayed item must generate an adequate margin to justify its location. Placing related items together encourages cross selling. The firm must also consider traffic flow, space value, and merchandise compatibility.

Most nonfood outlets arrange merchandise informally within departments. Supermarkets and drugstores are an exception because the large number of items they carry in a limited amount of space necessitates a more systematic approach. Moreover, experience has shown that in these outlets the location of an item within the department can significantly affect its sale. For example, moving an item from the bottom shelf to an eye-level shelf, or shifting from the middle of an aisle to the end of the aisle could increase sales by as much as 50 to 60 percent (in some cases even more). Determining proper shelf positions, called **shelf merchandising**, is crucial at these outlets.

To ensure proper **shelf merchandising** in all their outlets, supermarket and drugstore chains (along with some discount stores) use **planograms** to control the location of each item. *A planogram shows in a detailed schematic plan the amount of space allocated to and the arrangement of each item within a department.* The corporate merchandising department at the chain's headquarters designs the planogram and sends it to the managers of all outlets. In this way the seasoned judgment and skill of merchandisers and display experts at the corporate headquarters can benefit each store. Since the planogram specifies in detail the relative shelf position of each item and the number of items to stock, it ensures standardization of merchandise and display across the chain's outlets, which helps to project a consistent image.

A number of factors influence the designing of the planogram. Most important, of course, are the gross margin, DPP, and salability of each item. High-profit items receive more prominence to encourage their sales. The planogram must also allow for the bulk and size of different packages. When the same item comes in different sizes, the lower shelves hold larger packages and the higher ones hold smaller sizes. Moreover, the planogram must carefully balance the overall mix of items to fit consumer needs and preferences. Finally, the display must visually appeal to customers. Computerized shelf merchandising systems are now commonly used for designing planograms. These allow planners to simulate the expected space productivity and the visual impact of different merchandise arrangements prior to implementing them in the store.

Visual Merchandising   The retail store is often compared to a theater. Like a theater it must grab the attention of its audience and convey to them a sense of what it has to offer. The visual presentation of merchandise is an important part of the store's overall ambience. It must present merchandise visually in a way that relates to customer life styles and expectations. Retailers are acutely aware of the importance of visual merchandising techniques to create an attractive shopping atmosphere. They search continuously for new and innovative merchandising presentation formats.

This store display has been designed to capture the attention of kids, the ultimate consumers of the toys being displayed.

Visual merchandising is an integral part of the total store design. It interacts with the store layout and particularly with the arrangement of individual items within the department. The properly designed combination encourages customers to spend more time at the store, exposing them to more merchandise items. As its main objective, visual merchandising seeks to convert those who pass by an item from mere browsers to actual buyers.

Displays take many shapes and forms and they change continuously to maintain customer interest. While each display should be distinctive, to be effective, all must:[13]

- Arouse the attention and interest of shoppers.
- Match the image the retailer wants to project.
- Present a simple message that the shopper can quickly understand. Studies have shown that shoppers typically pass by a display in 10 seconds or less. A complex message has little chance of being understood in so short a time.

Choosing Items to Display   The merchandise is the centerpiece of all displays. Whether the displays appear in windows, at the store entrance, or inside the store it should emphasize the merchandise that the store is trying to sell. Therefore, the selection of merchandise to include in a display is an important strategic issue. A number of factors have to be considered in this regard.

Visual displays can effectively announce the arrival of new merchandise at the store. Displays of new items are likely to attract shoppers' attention. Items that are likely to generate **impulse purchases** are also good candidates for display since the special attention given to them is likely to increase their sales. Supermarkets, for example, typically display candy and magazines near check-out counters for this purpose. Bookstores, on the other hand, prominently display current best sellers since they are frequently sought by customers. For the greatest impact, displays should be coordinated with merchandise featured in media advertising. This creates a synergy that exceeds the impact of display and advertising separately.

CUSTOMER SUPPORT SERVICES

Customer **support services** give retailers another important means through which to enhance the value of their offerings to customers and influence their behavior within the store. Examples of such support services include acceptance of credit cards, check cashing, delivery, and gift wrapping. These services are intended to support the sale of merchandise and are not consumed by themselves. They do, however, influence the store's atmosphere and consumer behavior.

There is almost no limit to the kinds of services a retailer can offer, but they all fall into one or more of the following categories:

1. *Services that directly increase the utility of a merchandise item.* Consider, for example, alteration services at a clothing store. A retailer that does not offer such service can lose sales. For the same reason, furniture and major appliance retailers typically offer installation services.
2. *Services that directly facilitate the retail exchange process.* For example, retailers grant credit, accept third-party credit cards (for example, Visa, MasterCard, American Express) and personal checks, and deliver merchandise to make shopping easier for customers. Many such services are essential to consummating retail exchanges. Most car dealers, for example, arrange credit for their customers, and furniture stores routinely deliver their products. Their customers would be reluctant to buy from them if these services were not provided.
3. A third category of services is designed to make shopping more comfortable and pleasant for customers. Examples include the provisions for restroom facilities, sitting areas, and water fountains. Managers at Ikea, the European furniture chain that now has a significant presence in the United States, have put considerable thought into designing support services. Realizing that most of their customers are parents with young children and that furniture shopping is often time-consuming, the stores are equipped with supervised playrooms where parents can leave young children while they shop for furniture. The stores also have restaurants and rest areas for customers. The restaurants serve baby food and

gladly warm up milk bottles for children. Ikea's support services are uniformly praised by its customers.

4. Some services are designed to create demand for particular lines of merchandise. Bridal registries, cooking demonstrations, beauty counseling, and interior decorating advice are some examples.

5. A fifth category of services provide merchandise information to consumers. For example, people with questions about home improvement can call the Channel Home Center for free advice. Rickels, another home center chain, publishes booklets covering home improvement topics for distribution to customers.

6. Finally, retailers can perform after-sale services to ensure customer satisfaction after completion of the transaction. These include repairs and servicing of appliances and handling of merchandise returns and exchanges.

Service Cost

To control the cost of support services, many stores impose fees for some of their services. Furniture delivery is one example. While most furniture retailers offer delivery services, few offer them free. Most charge graduated fees depending on distance and bulk. Some stores charge graduated fees for gift wrapping and alterations, too. The fees offset, at least partially, the cost of providing the service.

Some argue, too, that this is a more equitable policy since those who use the service bear its costs. Free delivery, for example, would force all customers to pay more since the retailer would have to pass on the cost of delivery to customers via higher prices. Thus, customers who did not utilize the delivery service would bear part of the cost and subsidize those who have merchandise delivered. Charging a fee for the service, therefore, indirectly segments customers so that only those who use a specific service bear its cost. Of course, retailers should charge no fee for services that benefit most of their customers (for example, parking) or that build their own positive images (for example, offering product information).

Some support services not only pay for themselves, but actually generate profits for the store. For example, retailers started offering their own credit cards as conveniences to their customers and as a means of building customer loyalty. Today store credit cards are integral parts of the service strategies of many firms. An estimated 40 million individuals have Sears credit cards and they collectively charge more than $15 billion to their accounts each year.

The growing importance of credit sales has prompted stores increasingly to view credit card services as profit centers rather than merely support services. Dayton Hudson, for example, treats credit card operations as a profit center, requiring it to generate the same return on investment as any other part of the firm. To calculate the revenue generated by its credit department, the firm estimates the incremental sales that result from the availability of credit and the revenue generated from interest payments. The profits generated in this way often exceed the profitability of some merchandise departments in the store.

Responding to Changing Customer Needs

Retail services can take a variety of forms, and the list of services changes continuously in response to changing consumer needs. In major urban areas, many supermarkets offer delivery services and even accept phone orders to suit the needs of busy dual-career households. They also offer ready-to-eat meals, salad bars, and fresh baked items. They stay open late at night and for extended hours during weekends. Many offer the convenience of automatic cash machines to save the customer a trip to the bank. As customer lifestyles change, the stores have to change the type of support services they provide to meet customer expectations.

As retail competition intensifies, customer service is becoming an increasingly important weapon in the retailer's competitive arsenal. In fact, numerous studies have established that customer service is a critical factor that affects where people choose to shop. The retailer can maximize the effectiveness of its support services by ensuring that they support its overall marketing effort. They must fulfill the needs of its target market and match its image. Services must also be cost effective. As noted earlier, some services carry fees to cover costs, while others are offered free of charge. Retailers must periodically review the costs and benefits of all services along with their contributions to store image.

A long line can be quite irritating for customers. What could this bakery do to reduce waiting time?

RETAIL TRANSACTION SERVICES

A store's atmosphere also depends on how efficiently the store allows customers to complete their transactions. Anyone who has stood in lines at banks, airports and retail checkout counters has experienced the frustration of dealing with inefficient transaction services. **Waiting lines** at retail stores are by no means a new phenomenon, but two causes have increased their significance. First, in an effort to control costs, retailers have generally reduced the number of shop floor employees. Moreover, many employees lack proper training and motivation. As a result customers spend more and more time waiting in lines. Second, in today's time-pressed society, customers are no longer willing to spend scarce time waiting in lines. People simply don't have time to wait. Thus, while lines keep getting longer, customers become less tolerant of them.

Increasing Transaction Efficiency

Realizing that long waiting lines lead to customer complaints and ultimately to lost sales, many retailers are trying to improve the quality of their **transaction services**—that is, such services as checkout, bagging, wrapping, check cashing, and so on, that are necessary to complete the retail transaction after the customer has selected the merchandise—make the transaction services more efficient. Indeed, some retailers have tried to differentiate themselves from competitors based on how quickly they complete sales transactions. One prime example is Caldor, a discount store chain. In early 1990 the chain embarked on a mission to improve the quality of the transaction service at its outlets. Video cameras were installed at ceilings over checkout counters to record how customers went through the checkout routine. A group of business school students analyzed the videos to measure the amount of time customers were spending in line and to catalog the activities of customers and employees during the checkout process. The students discovered that the checkout process was slowed significantly because cashiers took a lot of time bagging the merchandise. Because of the design of the checkout counter, cashiers had poor maneuverability within the checkout space. Conversations with employees and customers confirmed these findings.

In 1991 Caldor renovated the checkout areas in a number of its outlets. These stores were equipped with new checkout stands especially designed for the chain. The new stands gave the cashiers more flexibility in movement. In addition, the cashier could face the customer throughout the checkout and bagging process. The new design also made it easier for customers to get merchandise out of the cart to the checkout stand. According to store managers, the new checkout stand has increased the rate of customers moving through the lines an average of 10 to 15 percent.[14]

Transaction efficiency is also important for service retailers such as banks, hotels, airlines, and restaurants. Chemical Bank, for example, introduced a novel

ENTREPRENEURIAL EDGE

At Gadzooks, the Teenager Rules

In 1983, in Texas, during one of the worst state-wide recessions ever, Larry Titus and Jerry Szczepanski decided to leave their successful tee-shirt business to launch a new venture. Risky? It's hard to describe just *how risky* this new venture was. What's more, the pair decided to enter the ever fickle and highly difficult teenage apparel and accessories market. Crazy? Maybe, but nine years and 46 stores later, the company—Gadzooks—is thriving, with an estimated $17 million in annual sales. Titus and Szczepanski have managed to roll out the stores into the South, Southwest and Midwest, and they have their sights on both the East and the West Coast.

Titus and Szczepanski met in college and joined forces in 1976 to launch Tee-Shirts Plus in Texas. In seven years, the small operation was franchised into a chain of 296 stores. Pleased with their success, and ready for the next challenge, the pair decided to launch Gadzooks.

When asked why they chose recession-deep 1983 to launch the store, the partners answer that their experience in the tee-shirt business taught them that teenagers spend money regardless of the economy. As anyone who has ever been a teenager knows, peer-pressure is the ultimate decision maker and powerful buying incentive for teenagers. Furthermore, the partners were hoping that the soft economy would help them start the business with limited funds. They were right, because of the dismal retail climate, mall developers were desperate to rent space. In this environment, Titus and Szczepanski were able to secure prime mall space, with minimal cash, for their first store.

Gadzooks is specifically designed for teens, which is one element to the stores' success. The interiors, filled with trendy fashions, loud music, and bright colors create the kind of fun and fast-paced shopping environment that their customers demand. Both partners know that there is no fooling

program to reduce customer frustration with long lines. In some of its business branches, the bank instituted its 5-4-7 program under which any customer who has to wait for more than seven minutes receives a $5 gift from the bank. According to the bank, customers have responded to the program very positively.[15] Customers no longer feel that the bank is completely indifferent toward them but recognize that it is making some effort to improve service. The program seems also to have increased employee productivity, forcing the bank to pay out much less than it had anticipated. The program demonstrates bank management's commitment to improving customer service and provides a clear standard for bank employees.

Efficient transaction service is an integral part of the benefit offered by any fast-food restaurant. If service at fast-food restaurants is not quick, customers will have little reason to choose them over conventional restaurants. Realizing the impor-

a teenager, in fact there is hardly a more de-termined consumer group; they know ex-actly what is in style and what they want to buy, and no amount of in-store marketing, advertising, or luck will persuade them to do otherwise. Armed with this knowledge, Gadzooks owners listen carefully to their customers. Not only does Szczepanski seek out the opinions and advice of his two teen-age sons, but the company relies on exten-sive market research studies, updated con-tinuously, to sound out teenagers and their shopping preferences. Another key to the success of Gadzooks is the partners' ability to stay on top of the rapidly changing trends in the teen market. The partners' world-wide travels and efficient use of the market re-search data, keep Gadzooks stocked with the latest items.

Finally, the partners follow an un-wavering rule: the customer rules, even when the customer is a demanding teenager. Shoppers are given all the leeway and lati-tude they want in Gadzooks, unlike other stores where salesclerks follow teenagers to keep an eye on them. Teenagers are fickle customers; they try on every item they can fit into the dressing room, often leaving the clothes in a heap and not buying anything. But the usual policies of clothes shopping are waived in Gadzooks: kids can try on as much as they want and buy all or none of it, and they are always welcome to return; neatness has no bearing; and all customers, whether dressed in ripped jeans or in tee-shirts, are treated as real customers.

Titus and Szczepanski have done well, and despite a capricious market and poor retail climate, they remain optimistic about expansion.

Source: "Retailing's Entrepreneurs of the Year," *Chain Store Age Executive,* December 1990, pp. 28–38.

tance of efficient service to their marketing strategies, fast-food restaurants pay considerable attention to maintaining and improving service standards. Wendy's, for example, serves drive-in customers within 30 seconds of placing their order. To maintain this standard, the chain rigorously trains and supervises its employ-ees. At each store, electronic timers beep 30 seconds after an order is placed. The buzzer both motivates and monitors. It continually reinforces the service standard and allows the store to monitor performance at all times.

Reducing Waiting Times

To reduce customer **waiting time**, retailers are exploring a number of ways to im-prove transaction efficiency. These include: (1) improvements in technology, (2) increasing training of checkout personnel, and (3) better workforce scheduling.

Improved Technology   More and more stores are adopting hand-held and fixed scanner technology to increase the speed of transactions at checkout counters. According to the Food Marketing Institute (FMI), for example, over 80 percent of all chain supermarket stores and over 60 percent of all independent supermarket outlets now scan all merchandise passing through the register.[16] Scanners eliminate the need for the cashier to read and key in the price of each item. This speeds up the checkout process and also eliminates mistakes by the cashier. Equally important, scanners allow stores to automatically update prices without physically changing the price tag on each item. They also allow the store to automatically update inventory and accounting records at the end of each day. Banks, too, are automating transaction services to increase efficiency. They are relying on automatic teller machines to reduce the number of customers requiring teller service. In addition, banks have increased teller efficiency with fast, computerized systems for recording customer deposits and withdrawals.

Increased Training of Checkout Personnel   Lines at many stores move slowly because supervisors have to authorize all payments made by personal checks and credit cards. Each time a customer offers such a payment, the line stops while the sales clerk locates a supervisor. Retailers can eliminate this step by adequately training checkout personnel to deal with credit card and check payments.

Better Workforce Scheduling   To shorten waiting times, retailers are paying closer attention to workforce scheduling. The level of activity in a store varies throughout the day and the week. By shifting employees among departments, reassigning lunch and break periods, and rescheduling working hours for part-time employees, retailers can better synchronize workforce availability with demand patterns.

Involving the Customer in the Transaction Process   Another way to increase efficiency of transaction services is to involve the customer directly in it. The automatic teller machines (ATM) used by banks is one good example. Similarly, customers at fast-food restaurants typically have to collect their own utensils and napkins. Some supermarkets are experimenting with self-checkouts by customers using scanner-equipped checkout counters. Three supermarket chains—Kroger, Safeway, and Dominick's—have introduced self-scanning automated checkouts in some of their stores. Customers in these stores can scan their own purchases and then take the receipt to a centralized cash counter.[17] The self-scanner design ensures that all items are scanned properly before they can be removed from the store. These self-checkout stands are designed to appeal to customers who want to save time. Because of lower labor cost the stores are able to keep more checkout counters operating at busy times. The verdict on these self-checkouts is, however, still mixed. Some customers feel that they actually slow the transaction process instead of speeding it up. Moreover, such involvement in the transaction process may be viewed as a drop in service quality by customers and have a negative impact on store image.

Summary

1. Retailers facilitate the exchange process by creating a shopping atmosphere that enhances the value of their offer to their target markets. The retail atmosphere is affected by (a) the in-store environment, (b) support services, and (c) transaction services.

2. Retail atmosphere is the psychological effect or feeling created by a store's design and physical surroundings. These emotional reactions influence the behavior of consumers within the store. The influence of retail atmosphere on shopping behavior can be understood using the Stimulus-Organism-Response (SOR) paradigm proposed by environmental psychologists. Shoppers' responses to the store take the form of either approach or avoidance behavior, and affect their desire to stay in the store, explore the merchandise, and communicate with store personnel, and their overall feeling of satisfaction.

3. The retailer must design in-store layouts to create a pleasant ambience, encourage customer traffic, and use store space efficiently. This involves five steps: (a) planning the general layout, (b) classifying merchandise into departments, (c) determining space allocation for each department, (d) deciding the location of each department, and (e) arranging the merchandise within each department.
   Retailers favor four basic layout arrangements: grid, freeflow, loop, and boutique. In a grid, a regular pattern of shelves and aisles lie parallel to each other. The other three less regimented layouts encourage browsing by customers.

4. Since retail stores sell thousands of items, they must organize them into departments based on such criteria as type of merchandise, customer segment, price, designer name, and usage occasion. Retailers commonly determine the amount of space to allocate to each department in two ways: (a) the sales per square foot method and (b) the model stock method. The locations of departments within the store depend on merchandise characteristics, traffic flow patterns, seasonality, and merchandise compatibility. These same factors influence the arrangement of merchandise within each department.

5. Retailers are paying increased attention to visual merchandising techniques to create attractive shopping environments. The merchandise must be presented visually in a way that relates to customer life styles, attracts their attention, and arouses their interest. It must please aesthetic senses while encouraging impulse purchases.

6. By providing customer services that support merchandise sales, a retailer significantly enhances the value of its offering to customers. Support services increase the utility of merchandise items, increase demand, facilitate retail transactions, provide information to customers, and make the shopping environment more pleasant and comfortable. Stores' service policies differ widely depending on the expectations of their target consumers.

7. A store's atmosphere is also affected by the quality of the transactional services. Consumers express considerable dissatisfaction with the quality of transaction services at many stores. In response, retailers are attempting to smooth service procedures and reduce waiting times through: (a) improved technology, (b) increased training of checkout personnel, and (c) better workload scheduling.

Key Concepts

Retail atmosphere
Approach behavior
Avoidance behavior
Store layout

Cross selling
Departmentalization
Space allocation
Value of space

Shelf merchandising

Planogram

Visual merchandising

Impulse purchases

Support services

Service cost

Transaction services

Transaction efficiency

Waiting lines

Waiting time

Discussion Questions

1. What are the elements of a store's atmosphere? Explain how the Stimulus-Organism-Response (SOR) paradigm helps in understanding the effects of store atmosphere on shopping behavior.

2. Describe and comment on the relative advantages and disadvantages of the common layout arrangements for retail stores.

3. In what ways can a department store group merchandise items into departments?

4. Explain with examples how to allocate space among departments by the sales per square foot method and the model stock method.

5. The toy department in a particular department store achieves only 5 percent of the store's sales, while misses' blouses generates 15 percent of sales. Should the store reallocate the space devoted to toys to misses' blouses? Explain your answer.

6. The Xenon department store is opening a new outlet in Alpha Town. What factors must Xenon's managers consider in determining the locations of departments in the store? Explain how these factors would affect the locations of the furniture department, the cosmetics department, and a department that carries accessories to go with business clothing for women.

7. What does the term visual merchandising mean? What are the goals of visual merchandising? Which items should visual displays feature prominently?

8. Stores provide various support services to facilitate shopping. Explain, with examples, how support services augment the retailer's offer.

9. Visit a discount store and a supermarket in your area. Write a short report on the quality of the transaction services you observe at these stores. Suggest ways in which you think these stores can improve their transaction services.

10. You are the owner of a sportswear shop located in a shopping mall. The store has five departments that total 1,000 square feet of selling space. In addition, 250 square feet are devoted to nonselling uses. The store pays a monthly rent of $3,000. Based on the data shown below, comment on the relative space productivity in each of the five departments.

Department	Selling space (sq. ft.)	Annual Sales	Gross margin (percent)
Accessories	90	$45,000	54
Active sportswear	225	250,000	38
Blouses and sweaters	200	234,000	42
Slacks and shirts	130	125,000	46
Outerwear	355	360,000	40

How would your conclusions change if 30 square feet of space was moved from the slacks and skirts department to the outerwear department, but no change in sales occurred?

Notes

1. Philip Kotler, "Atmospherics as a Marketing Tool," *Journal of Retailing*, 49 (Winter 1974), p. 48.

2. Based on "Updated Image for Faher and Son," *Chain Store Age Executive*, September 1991.

3. Robert F. Lusch, *Management of Retail Enterprises* (Boston: Kent Publishing, 1982), p. 456.

4. Robert J. Donovan and John R. Rossiter, "Store Atmosphere: An Environmental Psychology Approach," *Journal of Retailing*, 58 (Spring 1982), p. 56.

5. Kotler, "Atmospherics," p. 54

6. Alan D. Bates, *Retailing and Its Environment* (New York: Van Nostrand, 1979), p. 128.

7. This section is based on Donovan and Rossiter, *Store Atmosphere*, op. cit.

8. "Pilot Study Finds Product Choice Is Made in the Store," *Marketing News*, August 6, 1982.

9. Cathy J. Cobb and Wayne D. Hoyer, "Planned versus Unplanned Purchase Behavior," *Journal of Retailing* (Winter 1986), pp. 384–409.

10. This description is based on "Nike Town Goes Back to the Future," *Chain Store Age Executive*, February 1991, p. 82.

11. Karen R. Gillespie and Joseph C. Hecht, *Retail Business Management* (New York: McGraw Hill, 1977), p. 240.

12. Robert F. Lusch and Patrick Dunne, *Retail Marketing* (Cincinnati, OH: SouthWestern Publishing, 1990), p. 484.

13. William R. Davidson, Daniel J. Sweeney, and Ronald W. Stampfl, *Retailing Management* (New York: John Wiley and Sons, 1984), p. 222.

14. "Checkstand Pushes Caldor's Productivity," *Chain Store Age Executive*, February 1991. See also "Checkstands Boost Supermarket Profits," *Chain Store Age Executive*, December 1991, p. 14B; and N. R. Kleinfield, "Controlling Killer Queues," *New York Times*, September 25, 1988, p. F1.

15. N. R. Kleinfield, "Controlling Killer Queues," *New York Times*, September 25, 1988, p. F1.

16. Quoted in "Checkstand Boosts Supermarket Profits," *Chain Store Age Executive*, December 1991, p. 14B.

17. Ibid.

CHAPTER 16
Communicating with Customers

Video Walls Provide Stores in Mall with New Advertising Medium

Like all advertisers, retailers constantly search for new advertising medium to increase the effectiveness of their ads. Video Walls, first introduced in the Galleria Mall in White Plains, New York, is the latest result of this search. The walls consist of video monitors stacked together, usually four monitors by four. Retailers can purchase 30-second or 60-second spots, which run on a regular schedule during shopping hours, for a monthly fee. Strategically placed in areas where shoppers sit, like a food court or a resting area with benches, these ads reach customers who are actually in the mall and have the opportunity to immediately purchase most of the items that are advertised. This was a revolutionary form for point-of-purchase advertising to take, and one that has proved very successful for the retailers involved. People tend to sit in the food courts or rest in the bench areas for at least 15 minutes, so the video walls have an optimal location as well as an attentive audience. The screens are typically owned and operated by outside companies, like Cleveland-based Creative Production Services and New York-based ADmotion Company, or by some large developers, like JMB Properties Co., a real estate management firm that operates about 40 malls.

The walls consist of multiple screens, and retailers can use both straight advertising and creative programming during their spots. For example, a store can place its logo in the center screen, and surround it with shots of the latest items. Or, a retailer can choose to screen a regular commercial, shown on all 16 monitors simultaneously, for maximum viewer impact. Both national and local retailers can place ads in the walls, but the majority of ads are sponsored by retailers who have stores located in the mall itself. The attraction for retailers is the immediate response that they can receive from the ads: they are reaching a public who is on the premises, and usually, already in the mood for shopping. The ads can help shoppers to decide about a purchase they have already been considering, or they can help to stimulate impulse purchases. At the very least, it creates awareness of the retailer, for the customer's future visits to the mall.

From the retailer's perspective, an important feature of the walls is that the ads can provide information for shoppers about cur-

After studying this chapter, the reader will be able to:
- *Understand how communication facilitates retail exchange.*
- *Describe the steps in developing an advertising plan.*
- *Explain the importance of defining an advertising campaign's communication objectives.*
- *Know how to evaluate alternative media for retail advertising and determine advertising budgets.*
- *Design studies to measure advertising effectiveness.*
- *Explain how point-of-purchase advertising increases sales.*
- *Describe the types of lists and list targeting criteria used by direct retailers.*
- *Be familiar with the major legal issues relating to retail advertising.*

rent sales and promotions. In this way, the walls provide a value-added service for shoppers, and it provides a valuable merchandising tool for the retailers. The programs are updated monthly, allowing retailers to change the items featured in their spots and to include information about special sales and promotions. Thus, the walls can respond to seasonal fluctuations and changes in consumer trends, and keep shoppers informed about on-site mall activities. The companies that own and operate the walls

also try to add some features to the programming to keep the variety high for viewers, varying the ratio of features to ads month to month. Feature topics range from fitness and beauty ideas to home decorating and fashion trends. Often the companies will have local celebrities host the features, with bold graphics and original music as the backdrop. Periodic updating of the programs and changes in the ads keep the repeat shopper from growing bored with viewing the walls.

One drawback of the walls, however, is their high cost. While many mall developers are interested in including a wall in their mall, they are reticent about the price. The hardware alone can run $60,000 to $100,000, and then there are the added costs of production and software programming for the walls with each monthly change. To lower the financial burden the high cost places on the retailers, the developing companies typically give some video wall time to national advertisers. A number of auto manufacturers and other consumer goods companies include spots in the video walls to bolster their national advertising even though they do not have actual outlets in the malls. While the main function of the walls is to stimulate point-of-purchase sales, national advertisers feel that the video walls provide a novel and interesting way to complement their ads in other vehicles, such as television or print. It is the companies that operate the walls that contract with the national advertisers, and then use their fees to offset the prices for the mall developers and local retailers.

The video walls provide a significant way for stores in the malls to enhance their merchandising methods. While the ads work especially well for small, specialty retailers who do not advertise elsewhere and who traditionally relied on foot-traffic for their sales, the walls stimulate purchases for all the advertisers. Before the New York-based ADmotion company first launched their services nationally, they did a test run in the Galleria Mall in White Plains. When they installed a wall in the mall they also surveyed customers to determine the impact of the ads on actual shopping behavior. They found that 13 percent of the respondents had made a purchase as a result of the video wall, which was enough to demonstrate that the medium was well worth the cost.

Sources: Aimee L. Stern: "Video Ads Reach Local Malls," *Adweek's Marketing Week,* March 13, 1989, p. 4; "Video Advertising Goes to the Wall," *Chain Store Age Executive,* November, 1989, pp. 104–105.

Success in today's competitive retail environment calls for more than just choosing the right location, merchandise, and price. To attract shoppers, a retailer must inform them of the store's location, the types of merchandise it carries, the store's atmosphere, and the services it provides. It must also persuade consumers that the store can fulfill their shopping expectations and provide them with superior value relative to its competitors. Thus, retailers must design effective **communication programs** to provide information to customers and persuade them to shop at their stores.

Communication between retailers and their customers takes place both inside and outside the store. External communication takes place through **advertising** in such varied media as magazines, newspapers, radio, television, outdoor displays, direct mail, transit cards (signs on buses and subways), flyers, and posters. Advertisements can achieve a variety of **communication goals**, including enhancing consumers' responses to the store's offerings by giving them reasons to patronize the store, demonstrating how the store fulfills customer expectations, and providing information about the store's merchandising, pricing, and service policies.[1] In this era of time-pressed customers, an advertising program must be effective to communicate its message and draw customers into the store. As one noted industry observer noted, "For many [retailers], the lack of an effective advertising program accelerated their disappearance from their customers' mental shopping list. . . ."[2]

Direct response or direct retailers communicate directly with customers using mail or TV. The catalog is the direct retailers' store in print. It must display the merchandise, persuade the customer, and close the sale. Direct response advertising on TV, too, must also both inform and sell.

Advertising can draw customers into the store, but the communication process cannot stop there. In fact, the most direct communication takes place within the store through retail salespeople. The store's sales personnel can directly enhance value by helping customers find desired merchandise, speeding up the transaction, and increasing shopping convenience. Retail salespeople can influence the consumer's attitude toward the store by making retail transactions more efficient and the entire shopping experience more pleasant for the customer.

The remainder of this chapter focuses on nonpersonal communication between retailers and their customers through mass media or direct advertising. The chapter presents a framework for developing retail advertising strategy and discusses implementation of the steps in an advertising program. Mass-media advertising is discussed first, followed by point-of-purchase and direct-response advertising. The chapter ends with a discussion of some important legal issues relating to retail advertising. The objective is to provide an overall appreciation of the role of advertising in retail communication programs and the strategic issues related to designing effective advertising strategies.

DEVELOPING ADVERTISING STRATEGY

Almost all large and medium-sized retailers today rely on some form of mass-media advertising. The dollar amounts they spend on advertising increase every year. For example, in 1987 McDonald's spent nearly $700 million on advertising, and Burger King, its major competitor, spent approximately $270 million. Sears spent nearly $1 billion on advertising in 1987. One reason for the popularity of advertising is its ability to reach a large number of potential customers in a cost-effective manner. An advertisement in any prime-time network television program, for example, reaches millions of people. Similarly, an advertisement in a major urban newspaper can reach a large portion of shoppers in that city. Exhibit 16.1 shows the top 10 retail advertisers and their 1991 expenditures.

Advertising and Marketing Strategy

Designing the proper advertising strategy is an important task for retailers, since its advertisements communicate its marketing strategy to potential customers. Most retailers are so acutely aware of the importance of advertising "that they need to be told little about *why* they must advertise. They are keenly interested, however, in knowing *how* they should advertise."[3] Successful advertising is based on careful planning that considers the store's intended target market and the message that it wishes to communicate to that target market.

Even the most attractive advertisement will have little effect unless it reaches the intended audience and provides the message that the retailer wants to convey.

Exhibit 16.1   Top 10 Retail Advertisers, 1991

Retailer	1991 Advertising Expenditure (in millions of dollars)
Sears, Roebuck	1,179
McDonald's	745
K mart	527
J.C. Penney	363
May Department Stores	277
Dayton Hudson	226
Federated Department Stores	223
American Stores	202
Wal-Mart	190
Wendy's	124

Source: Copyright © 1992 by the *Advertising Age.* Reprinted by permission of Crain Communications, Inc.

Although advertising is often labeled "mass" communication, in practice every advertisement is directed at a specific target audience. A retailer must direct its advertising program to the specific target market it wants to attract to the store. As discussed in earlier chapters, the target market decision emerges from market segmentation to form the foundation for the store's overall marketing strategy. A firm that knows more about its target market's demographic characteristics, lifestyles, values, purchase motivations, and media habits can more easily make advertising decisions.[4]

Hierarchy of Advertising Effects

Advertising affects consumers' behavior by communicating key information to them and influencing their attitudes toward a store. Communication researchers generally suggest that advertising affects consumer behavior through successive stages, each moving the customer progressively toward the final purchase step. Typical of these hierarchical models is one called DAGMAR (Defining Advertising Goals for Measured Advertising Results).[5] As illustrated in Exhibit 16.2, the DAGMAR model conceives the role of advertising as moving consumers from complete unawareness about the store to a decision to buy at the store through the intermediate steps of awareness, comprehension, and conviction.

As its first task, then, advertising must inform potential customers of the store's existence and move them from unawareness to awareness. Next, advertising must provide information about the merchandise that the store carries, the services it

Exhibit 16.2   Hierarchy of Communication Effects

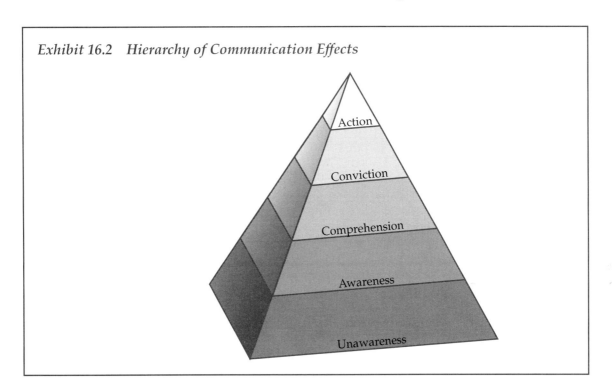

provides, the prices it charges, and so on. This moves consumers to a stage of comprehension. Advertising moves the consumers to conviction by building favorable attitudes toward the store. The final stage is one of action—shopping at the store. Advertising's role, however, does not stop once the consumer is in the store. Instore, or point-of-purchase (POP) advertising tries to convert shoppers into buyers by drawing their attention to specific merchandise items.

Types of Retail Advertising

Compared to typical manufacturing firms, the retailer faces a special challenge in planning its advertising. Manufacturers can wait for results over a longer term than retailers. Retail advertising must not only convey a positive image to reinforce the store's long-term competitive position, but it must also increase immediate sales by attracting customers into the store. To achieve their short- and long-term goals, retailers rely on three types of advertising: (1) institutional advertising, (2) product advertising, and (3) promotional advertising.

Institutional Advertising   Institutional advertising emphasizes the store's differential advantage and reinforces its positive image. Such advertising may stress

STRATEGY IN ACTION

"The United Colors of Benetton" Campaign

In the mid-1980s, Benetton Group, the Italian clothing manufacturer and retailer, launched an advertising campaign that changed the face of advertising. Called "The United Colors of Benetton," it was the first retail advertising campaign to deal with social issues on a global scale. While many other companies have followed suit, linking their products to social and environmental causes in an effort to woo the socially conscious consumer, no other campaign has quite had the effect of Benetton's. The campaign, which has generated both criticism and praise, in a veritable media frenzy, focuses on themes of racial harmony, religious tolerance, and environmental issues. In the long-run, the media attention that the campaign has garnered has succeeded in turning the company into a powerful and global brand.

The campaign's advertisements have included a black woman breast-feeding a white baby, a nun and a priest kissing, a newborn, blood-smeared baby, an array of multicolored condoms, interracial couples, homosexual couples, AIDS victims, and torture and abuse victims. The company has turned the controversy over these advertisements into a spectacularly successful marketing strategy by talking about the importance of bringing these issues into the social consciousness. For example, the AIDS advertisement showed an image of a dying man surrounded by his family. Some AIDS groups spoke out harshly against the advertisement, saying the ad capitalized on people's pain; but other groups praised it, believing that this advertisement, as well as the whole series, brings this important issue and many others into the mainstream consciousness. The company held press conferences about the necessity for people all over the world to be aware of the AIDS crisis.

The company has been highly criticized about some of the advertisements, and some have even been banned in different countries. But the company has contended throughout that the images are designed to

the store's wide merchandise selection or its quality and fashion leadership. It may also draw attention to the store's convenient location, long operating hours, or delivery service. The overall objective is to inform customers of the reasons for shopping at the store.

Product Advertising   Another form of retail advertising informs customers of the availability of specific merchandise items and their features. Product advertisements typically promote new, innovative merchandise or merchandise with well-known brand names. Some product advertisements feature the store's private-label brand.

raise social consciousness. The social issues campaign took off with speed with a six-part series featuring the dying AIDS patient, the shrouded corpse of a mafia hit surrounded by grieving relatives, and refugees clambering aboard a ship. The mafia advertisement will be run only in Italy, as Benetton feels that the impact of the issues will only truly be felt and understood in Italy, but the six others in the series will run worldwide, all as part of Benetton's $60 million campaign designed to raise awareness of social issues, and—of course—Benetton's attention to them.

Complaints abound that companies like Benetton that use such persuasive and controversial campaigns are not showing the advertisements because they care about the causes, but because they know that attention to these issues will help sell their products (for example, Spike Lee selling Nike sneakers, Esprit's campaign about how teenagers feel about racism, and many others). But such companies believe that by associating themselves with what they think their customers value helps sales immensely. The company's point of view is that the campaigns make the customers feel as though they are helping: if they buy a product from a company that espouses racial harmony, they may feel that they too are espousing the same theme.

For Benetton, the campaign coincided with a huge rise in sales. Sales in 1991 rose 12 percent, to $2.1 billion. Although it's impossible to trace the effectiveness of the campaign, it seems clear that the series of ads are having some effect on consumers—either by the advertisements themselves, or by all the media attention to them—both pro and con.

Sources: Bruce Horovitz: "Can Ads Help Cure Social Ills?," *Los Angeles Times*, June 2, 1992, p. D1; Gary Levin: "Benetton Brouhaha," *Advertising Age*, February 17, 1992, p. 62(1); "More Controversy, Please, We're Italian," *The Economist*, February 19, 1992, p. 70(1).

Since product advertisements featuring manufacturer brands benefit both the retailer and the manufacturer, the two often share the cost of such advertisements. Many manufacturers offer retailers an allowance to subsidize part of the cost of retailer advertising that features the manufacturer's brand. Called *cooperative advertising* or *co-op programs*, such allowances are a major source of funding for many retail advertising budgets. Cooperative advertising programs are discussed in more detail later in the chapter.

Promotional Advertising   Promotional advertising, often described as the bread and butter of retail advertising, seeks to promote immediate sales of specific mer-

Since this ad benefits both Amalfi shoes and the Bullock's department stores, they may well have shared in the cost of the adver-tising.

chandise items. Its primary purpose is to increase sales in the short run. Promotional advertising may feature regular price lines or it may inform potential customers of temporary price reductions on selected merchandise. These could be temporary price reductions on specific items or seasonal storewide sales such as Labor Day sales.

Stores typically engage in all three types of advertising. They must, then, achieve a proper balance between all three types of advertisements. Some retailers concentrate heavily on promotional advertising to achieve short-term sales goals; but without clearly defined images they become too dependent on promotions to generate sales. For this reason, many retailers have been shifting resources to institutional advertising campaigns. Moreover, retailers must design even promotional advertisements with an eye toward enhancing the store's image instead of focusing exclusively on price.

THE ADVERTISING PROCESS

The retailer must carefully manage advertising to produce its intended impact. The following steps are important in developing an effective advertising campaign:

1. Set advertising goals.
2. Define the communication objectives.
3. Develop creative strategy.
4. Develop the media plan.
5. Determine the advertising budget.
6. Evaluate the impact of advertising.

The various steps in developing an advertising campaign are discussed briefly in the next three sections. The intent, however, is not to provide an exhaustive discussion of each step. The focus is mainly on defining the goals and objectives of retail advertising campaigns and on methods for evaluating their impacts. Some terminology and concepts used in media scheduling and in setting advertising budgets are also discussed.

DEFINING ADVERTISING GOALS AND OBJECTIVES

Setting Advertising Goals

As its long-run objective, all advertising seeks to increase sales and profits. Since, however, a retailer advertises for a variety of purposes, it must clearly define the specific operational goals of each advertising campaign.

Operational goals are the specific and measurable end results a firm expects from advertising. It must set operational goals for specific time periods and for specific campaigns, in terms that allow quantitative measurement. Some examples of operational goals follow:

- A supermarket wanted to increase the sale of produce by 10 percent over the previous year by December 31.
- A discount store with four outlets in Anytown wanted to increase its share of appliance sales in Anytown by two percentage points by the end of the year.
- A drugstore wanted to increase the number of prescriptions it filled during the second half of 1993 by 10 percent over the number it filled during the first six months of that year.
- A department store wanted by the end of the year to achieve a 40-percent first mention among 35- to 39-year-old female heads-of-households with family incomes above $30,000 when asked the question, "At which store in town would you shop for an evening dress?"
- An off-price apparel store wanted to achieve a 10-percent increase in the number of annual transactions by the end of the year.
- A direct mail retailer wanted to increase the response to its Christmas catalog by 15 percent.

Note that each firm expresses its operational goal in terms of specific criteria that it can measure such as market share, the number of customers, or number of transactions. Each also states a definite time frame within which to achieve the goal. Note, too, that each criterion is a stepping stone toward increased sales and profits.

DEFINING COMMUNICATION OBJECTIVES

To achieve its operational goals, advertising must communicate the benefits of shopping at the store to the target audience. Therefore, the firm must translate operational goals into specific communication objectives, that is, the specific messages or key facts that the advertising must convey. For example, to achieve its goal of increasing market share of the appliance department, a discount store might set the following communication objective:

• To inform residents of Anytown that the store carries a wide variety and selection of appliances at reasonable prices.

Similarly, a department store might set the following communication objective:

• To convince target consumers that the store carries a wide selection of up-to-date, fashion-forward women's clothing.

Effective advertising campaigns must be based on (1) the image that the retailer seeks and (2) the perceived image of the store in consumers' minds. The following example of a men's clothing store illustrates how these two factors influence communication objectives.

The store carried a wide selection of well-known branded apparel at moderate prices and competed with five other stores in the area. In order to understand how potential shoppers perceived the stores in the area, the store's managers commissioned a retail image study. Using multidimensional scaling, the study generated the perceptual map shown in Exhibit 16.3. (See Chapter 6 for details on development of perceptual maps.)

The perceptual map raised the managers' concerns that the store's perceived image (labeled C in the map) differed sharply from what they had intended. Consumers perceived the store to have somewhat high prices with a relatively poor selection. In reality the store offered one of the widest selections among the five stores and its prices were generally lower than those of Stores D and E.

Based on the study results, the managers decided to undertake an advertising campaign to change the store's perceived image. As its overall goal, the campaign intended to change consumers' perception of the store from a high-priced one to a moderately priced one and from a store with a relatively narrow selection to one with a wider selection. The perceptual map in Exhibit 16.3 shows the position the store wanted to reach as C ′.

The advertising campaign included both promotional and institutional advertisements. Promotional advertisements stressed the store's competitive prices and institutional ads stressed its wide selection. The store also ran a few product advertisements in cooperation with leading apparel manufacturers. The managers decided to run the campaign for the fall–winter season and reevaluate consumer perceptions after the campaign. The results of this evaluation are described later in the chapter.

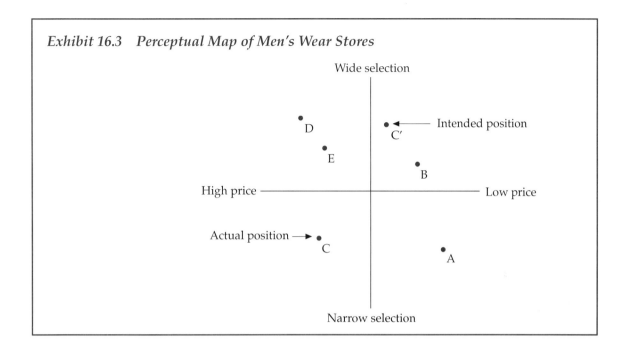

Exhibit 16.3 *Perceptual Map of Men's Wear Stores*

By looking at current consumer perceptions and its intended image, the apparel retailer clearly defined the key information to convey to consumers, leading to clearly defined communication objectives. Unfortunately, many retailers do not give adequate attention to the communication objectives of their advertisements, resulting in advertisements with unclear messages that confuse rather than sharpen the stores' images. Also, some firms define advertising goals simply as increasing sales. Although this is indeed the long-term goal of all advertising, no campaign can reach it without a clearly defined message.

MEDIA FOR RETAIL ADVERTISING

To have its effect, an advertisement must reach the intended target audience. Retailers can reach target audiences through a variety of media including newspapers, television, magazines, transit cards, direct mail, billboards, flyers, and even skywriting. Most retailers have traditionally preferred newspapers, although television, radio, and direct mail are becoming increasingly popular media for retail advertising.

The **media selection** is a two-step process. The first step is to choose the media to carry the message. Media planners consider the characteristics of different media and the habits of the intended target audience in their selection of the appropriate mix of media. The second step in the media selection process is to choose the specific vehicles within each medium through which to deliver the intended message to the target audience. In selecting the specific mix of vehicles, the media planner must consider costs, audience characteristics, and the potential duplication of audience among vehicles.

The major media for retail advertising—newspapers, television, radio, outdoor signs and direct mail—all have their own strengths and weaknesses. The suitability of a medium for advertising depends on its ability to reach specific well-defined target audiences at reasonable cost. A retailer specializing in sporting equipment, for example, will want to advertise in magazines such as *Sports Illustrated* or during broadcasts of sports events. For the same reason, a women's clothing store may advertise in such magazines as *Mademoiselle* and *Ms.*

Media costs depend primarily on the size and demographic characteristics of its audience. Media costs need to be considered both in absolute and relative terms. The relative cost is determined by dividing the absolute cost by the number of people reached. The *absolute* cost of a 30-second commercial during the Super Bowl, for example, is nearly one million dollars, whereas a 30-second spot on a local radio station may cost only a few hundred dollars. But the *relative* cost of the Super Bowl ad is likely to be low because of the large number of people who watch the telecast. For comparison purposes, relative costs are expressed as CPM, or cost per thousand viewers. (The M represents the Roman symbol for 1,000.)

Comparison of Major Media

Newspapers   The selective coverage of newspapers makes them extremely popular as a retail advertising medium. The circulation area of a local newspaper is likely to closely match the trade area of a major store located in the same city. By advertising in the local paper the retailer can be assured of reaching nearly all its potential customers. This is especially true for large department stores and mass merchandisers who appeal to broad groups of consumers. Retail chains that operate multiple outlets in the same city also favor newspapers, because a single advertisement can reach customers of all their stores. A small, independent store with a local market area, on the other hand, would waste resources it spent advertising in large city newspapers with wide geographic circulation.

Another advantage of newspapers is their immediate impact. Many believe that consumers in the final stages of purchase decisions read newspaper advertisements most closely.[6] An ad in the newspaper can, therefore, sway the customer to patronize one store instead of a competitor.

The editorial policies and organization of newspapers enhance the impact of newspaper advertising. For example, many newspapers feature special sections on fashion and home decorating. Apparel stores and furniture outlets advertise heavily in these sections since the readers are likely to be very receptive to their advertisements.

One disadvantage of newspapers is their frequently poor reproduction quality of pictures. Limits on use of color can be especially bothersome when a strong visual impact is desired. To overcome this weakness many newspapers are upgrading their paper stock to better reproduce color.

Television   Very few retail store advertisements appeared on television before around 1975, but the popularity of this medium has grown substantially since that time.[7] The greatest advantage of television compared to other media is its visual impact. The combination of video and audio and the use of motion and color opens up many creative opportunities for merchandise presentation that no other medium can match.[8] Television also allows a clear demonstration of store ambience and in-store display.

Just as the geographic coverage areas of local newspapers match retail trade areas, the viewing areas of local television stations match the trade area of local stores quite well. A commercial broadcast by a local television station is likely to reach its entire metropolitan area.

One problem of television is that many small retailers cannot afford its frequently high absolute cost. Large retailers, however, find television advertising very effective in terms of cost per viewer, since large audiences watch television programs. Only a few retailers who operate nationwide networks of outlets, such as K mart, J.C. Penney, McDonald's, Burger King, Radio Shack, and Sears, can take full advantage of the cost effectiveness of national television, although smaller chains and regional companies generally use spot television to advertise in selected metropolitan markets.

Radio   Radio is quite attractive as an advertising medium due to its selectivity. The wide variety of available radio formats allows advertisers to target their messages to specific audiences without wasting the message on those who are not part of their target markets. A sporting goods store, for example, can use radio stations that cover local sporting events. Similarly, to reach a teenage audience, retailers can advertise on rock stations that attract teenage listeners. However, retailers that appeal to broad target markets often view the extreme selectivity of radio as a disadvantage rather than an advantage. Because numerous radio stations broadcast in large urban areas, an advertisement in any one station will reach only a small fraction of the total population. The retailer must use several stations in conjunction to reach a significant portion of the population.

Another virtue of radio is flexibility. Once the retailer has decided on a message, it can be aired on short notice. The message can be changed at the last minute to take advantage of weather conditions or to announce a special sale. Finally, the relatively low cost of radio advertisements makes them affordable for even small retailers.

Outdoor Advertising   Many retailers favor outdoor advertising media, such as billboards, signs, and transit cards because of their low cost. Another advantage is their immediate impact from locations near the stores that sponsor them or along highways and major traffic arteries. Because of their strategic locations they can direct potential shoppers directly to the store. Advertisements for motels and fast-food restaurants along major interstate highways illustrate this immediate impact well; motorists often rely on these advertisements to decide where to eat and stay during a trip.

One constraint in designing outdoor advertisements is the length of the message. Typically the communication objective is simply to make viewers aware about the store. Some critics argue that outdoor advertisements, especially those within urban areas, do not reach many different people, but rather the same group of people over and over again. This reduces the effectiveness of the ads after a short initial period.

Direct Mail   The popularity of direct mail as an advertising medium has grown tremendously in recent years. Through direct mail, retailers can communicate their intended messages directly to their target audiences giving them great selectivity. They do this by creating a mailing list of the names and addresses of potential customers, who are then sent the ad. Many retailers use the name and addresses of their existing customers to create mailing lists. Alternatively, they can purchase mailing lists from list brokers who compile them from various sources. Mailing lists and other aspects of direct mail advertising are discussed in more detail later in the chapter.

Implementing the Media Mix

After selecting the mix of media for an advertising campaign, the media planner must choose the specific vehicle within each medium that can deliver the desired message to the target market in the most cost effective manner. Selecting specific media vehicles requires detailed analysis of their relative cost and coverage. Typically, retailers seek the help of professional media planners or advertising agencies to select the most desirable set of media vehicles.

Identifying the Best Media Mix

A number of different mathematical models have been developed to identify the best mix of media vehicles.[9] The concept of reach, frequency, and Gross Rating Points (GRPs) of media schedules underlie these models. A media schedule is the set of specific media vehicles (TV, radio, magazines, newspapers, and so on) that will be used for a particular advertising campaign.

Reach   Reach measures the number or percentage of target audience (persons or households) exposed to a particular media schedule at least once during a specified time period (usually four weeks).

The retailing industry has been undergoing constant change in the last one hundred years. New retail institutions continually emerge to challenge established ways of doing things. The great open-air markets of the eighteenth century marked by hustle-and-bustle and much social interchange are a long way from the 1990's where the shopper can stay at home and order items directly off a television screen.

Until the turn of the century rural general stores were the source for all types of goods, from sewing needles to farm implements. As the population migrated from the country to the city, the focus of retailing shifted as well. Today, shopping malls with expensive luxury goods flourish in urban areas such as this mall on Rodeo Drive in Beverly Hills.

© Jerry Cooke/Photo Researchers
© Spencer Grant/Photo Researchers

The small town mainstreet was pre-eminent in American retailing until the 1950's. Locally-owned and one-of-a-kind stores met the needs of the small community. Today, nation-wide franchise stores, like Avis rental car agencies, offer the same convenience, speed and predictability whether the customer is in Washington, D.C. or Juneau, Alaska.

The large department stores, once the mainstay of central business districts and suburban shopping malls, have lost market share to mail-order catalogs where the customer can make selections, order over the telephone using a credit card and never leave the comfort of home.

Frequency **Frequency** measures the number of times within the specified time period that a person or household will, on average, be exposed to the media schedule.

The hypothetical example in Exhibit 16.4 clarifies the concepts of reach and frequency. The exhibit shows the television viewing habits of eight individuals (A through H), who have a choice among ten television shows. Suppose that these eight individuals comprise the total market, and that the retailer can advertise on any one or a combination of the ten programs. The exhibit shows that different sets of these eight people watch each program. For example, Individuals A and B watch Program 1, while Individuals E, F, A, and B watch Program 2. A commercial aired during this program can reach these four people.

Note that reach always measures potential exposure rather than actual exposure since no one can guarantee that a person watching the program will actually watch the ad, too. Similarly, the reach of magazines or newspapers is determined by the number of individuals who subscribe to or buy them. There is no guarantee that these individuals actually read all the advertisements on their pages.

What will be the total reach and frequency of a media schedule that includes an ad during Programs 1, 2, 3, 4, and 5? The reach will be eight (or 100 percent) since all eight individuals can see the ad at least once. Each person will view the advertisement with different frequency, however. Three individuals (D, G, and H) will be exposed to the ad only once, Persons A, C, and E will be exposed twice, Person F will get three exposures, and Person B can see it four times. One can, therefore, calculate the average frequency of exposures for this media schedule by noting that a total of 16 exposures are distributed among eight people. That is:

Exhibit 16.4 **Reach and Frequency of TV Programs**

Households	1	2	3	4	5	6	7	8	9	10
A	x	x				x	x		x	x
B	x	x	x		x			x	x	
C				x	x		x	x		
D				x		x	x	x	x	
E		x	x			x	x	x		
F		x	x		x	x	x		x	
G					x					
H			x							

TV programs

$$\text{Average frequency} = \text{Total impressions}/\text{Number reached} = 16/8 = 2$$

What reach and frequency numbers would result from choosing the other five programs, instead? The reach of this schedule is only 6 (or 75 percent) since Individuals G and H do not watch any of the five programs. Total impressions are 18. These figures give an average frequency of 3 (18/6). This means that this media schedule would expose fewer people to the ad with greater frequency.

Gross Rating Points (GRP)   Reach and frequency measure two aspects of the effectiveness of media schedules. Combining these concepts gives a measure of the total impact of the media schedule, that is, its **gross rating points**. This is computed by multiplying reach by frequency:

$$\text{GRP} = \text{Reach} \times \text{Frequency}$$

For example, a media schedule that reaches 75 percent of the target audience with an average frequency of 2 has a GRP of 150 (75×2). A different media schedule may achieve the same GRP by reaching 50 percent of the audience with an average frequency of 3. Note that reach is always expressed as a percentage when calculating GRP.

The main task of media planning, therefore, is to choose the schedule that combines reach and frequency in the most cost effective manner. Typically, given a specified budget, firms can increase reach only by sacrificing frequency and vice versa. The retailer must determine the relative importance to place on reach and frequency before making the media selection decision. In advertising a one-time special sale, for example, the firm must reach as much of the target audience as possible without concern for high frequency. Frequency is important, however, for an institutional campaign designed to reposition the store in the minds of selected consumers, since each succeeding advertisement strengthens the impact of initial exposures. Some argue, however, that the marginal impacts of additional exposures decline after an individual has seen an advertisement three or four times.[10]

ADVERTISING BUDGETS

Determining How Much to Spend

Various factors determine the total amount of money that a store should spend on advertising and how that amount should be allocated over time. First of all, the size of the total **advertising budget** will depend on sales. Higher sales generally mean larger budgets. Therefore, firms customarily express advertising expenditures as percentages of sales generated by the store, yielding a figure known as the **advertising-to-sales ratio**.

Unfortunately, no rule states the correct advertising-to-sales ratio for retail organizations. Some fast-food restaurants, for example, tend to spend as much as

10 percent of their sales on advertising, while supermarkets typically spend less than 1 percent of their sales on advertising. The appropriate advertising-to-sales ratio depends on the type of store, its age, the nature of its trade area, and its competitive environment.

In highly competitive environments, a store that appeals to a broad target market needs to advertise to hold on to its customers and win new ones. This is one reason why fast-food chains tend to advertise heavily. Supermarkets, discount chains, and electronic specialty stores, too, advertise heavily due to high levels of competition. Stores that serve narrow target markets, on the other hand, rely less heavily on mass-media advertising and, therefore, have smaller budgets. New stores spend relatively more money on advertising than older stores in order to establish themselves in the market place.

Although advertising budgets are typically determined by industry-accepted rules of thumb, a more systematic approach is advisable. One such approach is the **objective and task method**. This calls for the firm to first clearly specify the objectives of the advertising campaign. The tasks to be performed to achieve the objectives are then determined. This calls for specifying the number of ads to be run, the media in which they will be placed, and the target reach and frequency. The tasks then determine the costs of implementing the campaign.

Cooperative Advertising

Retailers can often augment their advertising budgets by taking advantage of cooperative advertising programs sponsored by manufacturers of their merchandise. **Cooperative advertising** emerged around the turn of this century, and was based on the simple concept that a manufacturer would sell more merchandise if retailers who carried its product advertised it locally. All co-op programs today are based on the same concept. If the retailer advertises an item or promotes it in any way, both the manufacturer and the retailer benefit from the increased sales. Manufacturers, therefore, encourage retailers to advertise their products by underwriting a part or all of the cost of the retailer's advertising featuring the manufacturer's products, generally within certain limits.

While all co-op programs share costs between manufacturers and retailers, they do this in many ways. Some manufacturers pay 100 percent of the retailer's cost, whereas others may pay as little as 20 percent; although 50 percent reimbursement is quite typical. The reimbursement rate depends on a number of factors, including industry practices, the level of national advertising sponsored by the manufacturer, the level of competition among manufacturers, and the retailer's bargaining power.

The typical co-op program, called vertical co-op, offers the retailer an allowance (also known as accrual), which is a fixed percentage (commonly 5 percent) of the retailer's dollar purchases from the manufacturer. These programs commonly offer 5 percent. Upon proof that the advertisement ran and featured the manufacturer's brand, the program reimburses the retailer for all qualified costs, up to the amount of the earned allowance. Generally, the manufacturer imposes certain stipulations about the media in which the ad may appear and the time period during which the ad must run.

In another form of cooperative agreement, the vertical and horizontal co-op, a group of retailers pool together their co-op accruals from a common manufacturer or supplier. Each retailer then adds its proportionate share of advertising dollars to this pool to create a joint fund. By pooling their resources, small retailers can create advertising programs that have much more impact than they could afford alone. Often, this is the only way small retailers can afford to advertise in costly media such as television and magazines.

Although cooperative advertising programs benefit retailers, since the manufacturer's funds stretch the retailer's budget, retailers often fail to take full advantage of available co-op funds. Still, co-op monies fund a large portion of retail advertising. It is estimated, for example, that co-op allowances pay for 50 percent of all newspaper advertising by department stores and this figure may be as high as 75 percent for food stores and electronics outlets. On the other hand, co-op funds account for only about one-third of all newspaper advertising by furniture stores and discount outlets.[11]

Despite the fact that cooperative advertising programs give valuable subsidies to retailers, considerable controversy surrounds its role and use. Much of the controversy grows from the struggle between manufacturers and retailers for control of co-op programs. Manufacturers typically want to control how the advertising looks, its message, the prominence it gives to the manufacturer's brand name, the time when the ad appears, and the medium in which it appears. Retailers, of course, view this as an incursion into their decision-making territory. This frequently raises conflicts between retailers and manufacturers.[12]

Some manufacturers provide retailers with designs and formats for co-op ads. Often these manufacturer-designed formats give little prominence to the retailer, focusing instead on the manufacturer's name with the retailer's name added almost as an afterthought. Manufacturer-supplied cooperative television advertisements often give even less prominence to the retailer. They usually feature "an extended product discussion followed by a trailer that says `available at,' followed by the name of the store, or worse yet, a long list of stores."[13] Because of this, many retailers resist participating in co-op programs that restrict their freedom in designing the advertisements.

Despite their limitations, retailers have stepped up their use of co-op funds to augment their advertising budget. Some retailers have created special co-op departments whose task it is to identify available cooperative advertising funds and coordinate the available programs to fit with the store's overall advertising campaign. It is expected that in the future both retailers and manufacturers will pay more attention to increasing the effectiveness of co-op advertising.

Scheduling Advertising Expenditures over Time

After determining the total advertising appropriation, the retailer must allocate it over seasons, months, and weeks based on the expected pattern of sales during the year. They should allocate their advertising appropriations for the year in approximate relation to the percentage of their annual sales volume they expect during individual months. Low-volume months should receive slightly more than proportional amounts and the high-volume months should receive slightly less than proportional amounts.[14]

Exhibit 16.5 shows the relationship between monthly sales and monthly advertising levels for a retail store. Note that the proportion of annual advertising budget allocated to months with average sales closely follows the month's share of

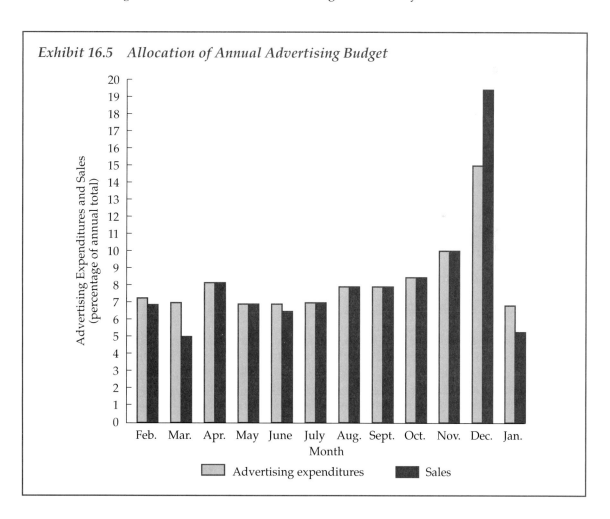

Exhibit 16.5   Allocation of Annual Advertising Budget

STRATEGY IN ACTION

Good Social Policy Is Also Good Business

In 1991, Nordstrom, Inc., the Seattle-based department store chain, began to use disabled models in their advertising. The action was prompted by the passage of the Americans with Disabilities Act which was set to go into effect in January 1992. Provisions of the Act required that retailers not discriminate against the disabled in any way, from hiring and firing, to merchandise presentation and showcasing. The Act also requires that all public spaces be rendered accessible. As very few retailers were reaching out to the disabled—through their advertising or their accessibility—Nordstrom took the opportunity to gain competitive advantage by tapping into the disabled market before their competitors. The company soon found out, however, that these moves would provide more than just a surge in business, but could also act positively on both customer perceptions and employee morale.

When Nordstrom began using disabled models in their summer 1991 catalogue, let-

ters of praise began pouring into the company from all over the country, from disabled people, from civil rights groups, and from Nordstrom's own customers. Furthermore, Nordstrom employees spoke up about the advertisements, saying that they were proud to work for a company that supported the disabled. The first models were chosen from a school for disabled children in Seattle, and included a child in a wheelchair, one on crutches, and one with Down's syndrome. The company continued the use of disabled models in subsequent catalogues and advertisements, and the retailer continues to receive letters of praise.

There are over 43 million disabled Americans, constituting a strong customer base that previously has had a limited range of choices in retailers. These 43 million Americans are fast becoming a solid customer base for Nordstrom, and for many other stores that have chosen to target this consumer segment with advertisements or charitable

annual sales. Low-selling months such as January and March, however, have slightly more than their proportional share. The budget for December is lower than the month's proportion of sales because of the high sales during that month. This type of adjustment assures that the store maintains an adequate level of advertising, even during low-volume months. Moreover, strict proportional allocation could also result in excessive advertising in months when demand is already high.

Special sale events such as White Sales and Easter Sales also affect retailers' allocation schemes, since the dates of these may vary from year to year. Retailers commonly allocate a separate advertising budget for each promotional event and then add this to the month's total.

works. Some companies use the disabled models in conjunction with the charities that the company supports: for example, Eddie Bauer works closely with the Easter Seals campaign each year, and Kids R Us is associated with the Institute for Child Development at the Hackensack Medical Center. These companies have found that working with the disabled community is a way to build up their customer base, and is also a form of corporate philanthropy that the employees, management, and the customers all praise.

For Nordstrom, the difference in sales since the addition of disabled models into their advertising and the reconfiguration of the stores for accessibility has been great. Many disabled activist groups have singled out Nordstrom for their efforts, which has helped to cultivate customers. Furthermore, praise from other customers about how the stores treat the disabled has also boosted sales. And, finally, the positive press that the

company has received has also helped to attract new customers.

During the late 1980s, while other department store chains were retrenching and down-scaling, Nordstrom flourished. The success of the company is attributed to its superior customer service which is fostered by an aggressive sales motivation program. Its renowned customer service policy drew customers away from other stores, and the quality of the products kept customers coming back. This latest venture by Nordstrom, to reach out to the millions of disabled consumers, has once again proven that the company is able to carefully analyze its consumer base and provide just what the customers want.

Sources: Candy Sagon: "Retailers Reach the Disabled," *The Washington Post*, December 19, 1991, p. B10; "Retailers Find a Market in the Disabled," *The New York Times*, August 6, 1992, p. C3.

MEASURING ADVERTISING EFFECTIVENESS

The venerable retailer John Wanamaker once said that half of all advertising is wasted, but no one knows which half that is. Advertising may not achieve the expected results for many reasons. Often advertising is ineffective because the retailer aims it at the wrong target market, selects the wrong media, or communicates an inappropriate message. It is important, therefore, that the retailer monitor its advertising to measure its impact.

Considerable controversy surrounds the **evaluation of advertising results**. Much of this controversy stems from disagreement regarding the appropriate criteria by which to judge advertising performance. Some argue that the principal purpose

This Welcome Home ad is offering a special two-for-one price on its afghans during the Christmas season. Separate advertising budgets are commonly set up for promotions like these.

From now through Christmas buy one all-cotton, all-American afghan for $19⁹⁹ and receive the second for half the price. Only at Welcome Home.

WELCOME H·O·M·E

A World of Affordable Treasures for Your Home
Over 100 locations throughout the USA. Call 1-800-348-4088 for the location nearest you.
In Northern California and Nevada, we are known as Home Again.

of advertising is to stimulate sales and profits, so these are the most appropriate criteria for measuring advertising effectiveness. However, others argue that while advertising must surely improve long-run profitability, measuring short-run sales results is misleading. The more appropriate short-run measure, they suggest, is the effect of advertising on consumer attitudes and beliefs.

No side is clearly right or wrong in this division of opinion.[15] Retailers cannot justify advertising that does not result in profitable sales, but advertising is also a communication tool intended to influence consumer attitudes toward the store. Indeed, only by performing its communication task can advertising influence sales. Thus, retailers must measure advertising effectiveness in more than one way depending on the nature of the advertisement and the objectives of the campaign.

Evaluation by Sales

The easiest way for a retailer to judge the sales impact of advertising is to monitor sales before, during, and after the advertising campaign. To preclude the possibility of other factors biasing the results, a proper controlled experimental procedure must be followed. Retailers can adapt the before and after with control design for pricing experiments described in Chapter 12 to measure advertising effectiveness.

In this case, they judge the impact of advertising by measuring sales both before and after running the advertising and then computing the difference. This type of sales monitoring is relatively easy in stores equipped with optical scanners because these systems automatically maintain detailed records of sales of all items. A supermarket, for example, can evaluate the impact of advertising a special sale on coffee by comparing coffee sales before and after it placed the advertisement, controlling for any other changes likely to affect the sales pattern.

Although scanner data can easily show the sales impact of advertising, the retailer needs more detailed information to identify the sources of incremental sales. For example, it must determine whether incremental sales result from increased purchases by regular customers or whether the advertising drew customers who did not typically shop at the store. In the latter case, the customers are also likely to buy other, nonadvertised items, thus increasing their sales, too. Therefore, an advertisement featuring one product can actually increase the sales of other products, if it draws new customers into the store. Moreover, some of these customers may switch their loyalty and become regular customers of the store.

To get a more detailed picture of the impact of advertising, retailers should augment the analysis of scanner data with **exit interviews**. In an exit interview, the retailer asks a randomly chosen group of customers a series of short questions as they leave the store. It may ask them whether they saw the ad prior to coming to the store, whether they would have bought the item if it were not advertised, whether they regularly shop at the store, and what other items they bought. Answers to such questions give a more detailed picture of the impact of advertising.

Evaluating Institutional Advertising

As mentioned earlier, not all advertising is designed to have an immediate impact on sales. Institutional advertising, for example, seeks to influence consumer attitudes and achieve a favorable long-term image for the store. Firms cannot judge the effectiveness of such advertising by monitoring sales, rather, this requires monitoring the store's image.

Consider, for example, the results of a store image study shown in Exhibit 16.6. The top half of the exhibit shows the average responses by potential customers to a set of semantic differential scales describing two stores. (See Chapter 6 for a discussion of how semantic differential scales measure retail images.) The managers of Store A were concerned by the results since their image was inferior to that of Store B on all dimensions. They undertook a complete review of the store and embarked on a new marketing strategy. As part of this strategy, they designed a series of advertisements to change customer attitudes toward the store. The advertisements carried pictures of the redesigned store interiors, announced the addition of new, higher-quality merchandise, and stressed that prices remained moderate.

Six months into the new campaign, they conducted another customer survey to judge its impact using the same set of semantic differential scales. The results of

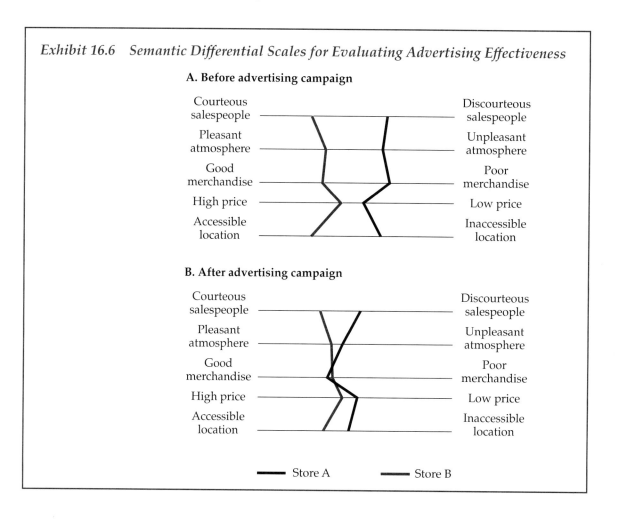

Exhibit 16.6   Semantic Differential Scales for Evaluating Advertising Effectiveness

A. Before advertising campaign

Courteous salespeople		Discourteous salespeople
Pleasant atmosphere		Unpleasant atmosphere
Good merchandise		Poor merchandise
High price		Low price
Accessible location		Inaccessible location

B. After advertising campaign

Courteous salespeople		Discourteous salespeople
Pleasant atmosphere		Unpleasant atmosphere
Good merchandise		Poor merchandise
High price		Low price
Accessible location		Inaccessible location

——— Store A   ——— Store B

this survey appear in the bottom half of the exhibit. The advertising campaign altered consumer perceptions on every dimension. It brought its most significant improvements in consumer perceptions of store atmosphere, merchandise quality, and prices, the three attributes stressed in the campaign. It is interesting that consumers came to view the store as more accessible although it did not change its location. This is a kind of halo effect: consumers perceive the store to be more accessible because their overall attitude toward it has improved.

Before–after monitoring of image is not limited to studies using semantic differential scales. Perceptual maps based on multidimensional scaling (see Chapter 6) can also help retailers monitor changes in consumer perceptions of store image. Exhibit 16.7 illustrates this evaluation procedure. The top half of the exhibit reproduces the perceptual map seen earlier in Exhibit 16.3, which was part of a study commissioned by the managers of Store C to plan their advertising campaign. Based on the study, the firm initiated a campaign to reposition its image with shoppers

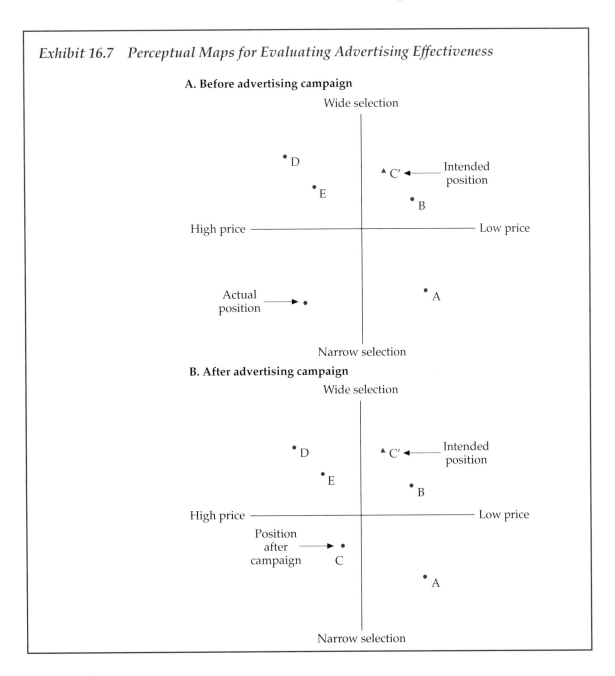

Exhibit 16.7 Perceptual Maps for Evaluating Advertising Effectiveness

A. Before advertising campaign

Wide selection

D

E

▲ C' ◄——— Intended position

B

High price ———————————————— Low price

Actual position ——→ •

A

Narrow selection

B. After advertising campaign

Wide selection

D

E

▲ C' ◄——— Intended position

B

High price ———————————————— Low price

Position after ——→ •
campaign   C

A

Narrow selection

as closer to Stores A and B in price, but offering a better selection. The managers repeated the study after running the new advertising campaign. The result from that study appears in the bottom part of the exhibit. The advertising campaign partially fulfilled its objectives. Consumer perceptions of the store's price and

---

RESEARCH REPORT

Blue Lights and Red Dots

"Attention K mart shoppers," starts the familiar in-store announcement of another blue light special. K mart's blue light special is one of the longest running in-store advertising campaigns in retailing. The revolving blue light attracts bargain-hunting K mart shoppers like a magnet draws iron filings. At the Grand Union supermarket chain, shoppers look for red dots on small cards placed alongside the week's special buys, finding, for example, a can of tuna fish for 79 cents instead of the regular price of 99 cents, 20 cents off the price of a quart of orange juice, or a special sale on chicken wings.

How well do such point-of-purchase advertisements work? To answer this question two researchers monitored sales of a brand of instant coffee for four weeks in four supermarkets. The researchers wanted specifically to discover whether (1) point-of-purchase advertising is more effective than a 20 percent price reduction in increasing sales, and (2) combining POP advertising with price reduction results in even greater sales than the two separately. As POP advertising, the researchers placed 5 × 7 inch shelf talkers that showed the item's brand name, price, size, and a small picture of the package.

Over the course of a month the study exposed shoppers at the test store to four different experimental conditions: (1) regular price without shelf talker, (2) 20-percent price reduction without shelf talker, (3) regular price with shelf talker, and (4) price re-

---

selection had changed as a result of the advertising, but the perceived image was still not the one that the firm desired. Since the change moved its image in the desired direction, the firm decided to continue the campaign for another year.

Measurement of advertising effectiveness is essential. Firms must evaluate each advertising campaign's fulfillment of its goals and objectives. This means, of course, that the firm must clearly define the goal of each campaign before initiating it. Unfortunately, many firms fail in this important step. They do not define their goals clearly and therefore cannot measure the impact of their advertising accurately.

POINT OF PURCHASE (POP) ADVERTISING

Advertisements in newspapers and on radio and television programs draw shoppers into the store. Inside the store **point-of-purchase (POP)** announcements draw shoppers' attention to specific merchandise items. This point-of-purchase (POP) advertising located adjacent to the merchandise display has been found to have a

duction with shelf talker. It rotated the four experimental conditions every day in each of the four stores. After a month, the researchers compared the sales under each condition. Their results are summarized in the exhibit.

Average Weekly Sales under Four Experimental Conditions

	Regular Price	Reduced Price
No Shelf Talker	100	216
Shelf Talker	250	625

Note: All sales figures are indexed to the no shelf talker–regular price condition.

The results confirmed the belief that a 20-percent price reduction increased weekly sales significantly. Sales increased even more, however, when a shelf talker supplemented the price cut. Even without a price reduction, a shelf talker doubled sales compared to the base level without price reduction or advertisement. Sales increased the most when advertising and price reduction were combined. In this condition, sales increased five-fold compared to the base level. Furthermore, the impact far exceeded the sum of the impacts of reducing price or advertising separately. The combination of price reduction and advertising creates a synergy that far outweighs the impact of each individually.

Source: Arch G. Woodside and Gerald L. Waddle, "Sales Effect of In-Store Advertising," *Journal of Advertising Research*, June 1975, pp. 29–34.

significant impact on sales. POP advertising closes the gap between the mass media advertising and final sales.

POP announcements can range from simple handwritten signs announcing special prices to sophisticated electronic broadcasts and point-of-purchase video and audio programs. One hardware chain, for example, recorded a 300-percent increase in sales of electric bulbs after it featured the item in a video display.

Radio, too, is becoming an important medium for POP advertising. For example, WA&P Radio is featured in more than a thousand A&P outlets. WA&P Radio pipes commercials mixed with music into the stores. Every hour it plays ten minutes of commercials sponsored by manufacturers and two minutes of commercials sponsored by A&P for its own private-label brands. According to POP Radio and Muzak, A&P's partners in this venture, the commercials increase sales an average of 20 percent within a month, with some brands' sales increasing as much as 50 percent within the same period.[16] A number of other supermarket and drugstore chains have now adopted in-store radio announcements. While the use of video and audio POP advertising is increasing, the most common type of POP advertisements are still shelf-talkers, the small signs placed on supermarket shelves.

What better place to advertise new cars than along a busy street?

The importance of POP advertising to product manufacturers and retailers is increasing for three important reasons:[17]

- POP is cost effective. The cost of reaching 1,000 adults through a 30-second network television advertisement can reach $12, while the cost per thousand for a POP sign may be less than 50 cents.
- POP programs can reduce the workload for retail salespeople by providing shoppers with needed product information.

One way POP advertising increases sales is by drawing shoppers' attention to specific items. The special attention given to the item sets it apart from other, similar goods. By stressing the special features or advantages of a product (which may or may not include a special price), POP announcements allow consumers to quickly determine the product's value and help them decide whether to purchase it.

Perhaps the most important impact of POP advertising is its encouragement of impulse purchasing. Shoppers may not have planned to buy a product before entering the store, but a POP advertisement can draw their attention to it and encourage them to consider buying it then and there.

POP announcements effectively supplement and reinforce promotional advertising. Sales of marked-down items increase significantly when a POP advertisement publicizes the price reduction. It helps shoppers find the advertised merchandise quickly and reinforces their decision to buy it.[18]

The advantage of POP announcements have made retailers increasingly receptive to manufacturers' POP programs. Even firms that traditionally discouraged manufacturer promotions in their stores (such as K mart) are now using manufacturer-provided POP materials.[19] However, in the proliferation of manufacturers' POP programs, retailers must carefully select the programs they will support. POP programs must not be allowed to distort the store's image or inhibit the store's ambience.

DIRECT RETAILING

Direct retailing, or **direct response retailing**, as it is sometimes called, is one of the fastest growing areas of retailing. Most people regularly receive catalogs, flyers, and free samples by mail from such firms as Sears, L. L. Bean, Lands' End, American Express, American Airlines, Time-Life Books, Spiegel, Gulf Oil, Williams Sonoma, and others. These are all examples of direct retailing. *Direct retailing is defined as product and service offers through one or more media to solicit direct responses from present or prospective customers by mail or telephone.* Exhibit 16.8 lists some of the leading general merchandise direct retail companies.

Confusion often arises between direct retailing and mail-order retailing. In the past, the terms *direct mail* or *mail order* typically described all direct response retailing. The growth of television shopping programs as a form of direct retailing has outdated such a nomenclature. Direct mail describes only that part of direct retailing that solicits purchases through the mail. However, since direct mail currently dominates direct retailing, some still use the terms synonymously. This section focuses on direct retailing through mail offers.

Direct retailers share many problems and challenges with store retailers. They have to choose the right target markets, select the right merchandise, control inventory levels, and evaluate merchandise profitability just like store retailers. What makes them unique, however, is the manner in which they reach their customers. Instead of building stores and making shoppers come to them, they sell to customers directly at their homes. They achieve this by describing products through the mail or on the telephone. People who wish to make a purchase can order through the mail, or by telephone or a computer terminal and pay with a credit card.

The Growth of Direct Retailing

Convenience is the most important reason people buy from direct retailers. Direct buying obviates the necessity of a trip to the store and thus eliminates the

Exhibit 16.8   *Leading General Merchandise Direct Retailers*

Company	1991 Sales ($Millions)
Stores with Mail-Order Business	
Sears, Roebuck	3,445.3
J.C. Penney	3,169.8
May Department Stores	677.8
R.H. Macy	553.6
Victoria's Secret (The Limited)	527.5
Direct Retailing Only	
Primerica (Fingerhut)	1,674.6
Otto Versand (Spiegel)	1,383.4
Home Shopping Network	1,078.5
QVC Network	921.8
Lands' End	648.8
Hanover Direct	623.6
Bass Pro Shops	560.0
L.L. Bean	525.9

Note: Total for Sears, J.C. Penney, and Primerica include insurance sales.

Source: "Mail Order Top 250+," *Direct Marketing*, July 1992, p. 19–37.

time and cost of travel. Also, many direct retailers sell items that are not available at stores. Two of the pioneers of direct retailing—Sears, Roebuck and Montgomery Ward, for example—used their catalogs to reach consumers in rural areas who did not have easy access to stores that carried the variety of products that were available through the catalogs. Even today, specialty direct retailers typically offer wide varieties of novel merchandise that are not easily available from stores everywhere. One example, Williams Sonoma, specializes in kitchen appliances, utensils, and gadgets. Suppliers make many items in its catalog especially for the firm and do not make them available in stores (except at a few Williams Sonoma outlets in major cities). Consumers often cite price as another reason for buying direct. Often a product available at a store is also available from a direct retailer at a lower price.

During the last decade, general merchandise sales through direct response is estimated to have grown at a rate of about 14 percent annually. While the growth rate has slowed somewhat, sales by direct retailers is growing faster than store-based sales. A number of reasons are driving this phenomenal growth. For one reason, the general growth in consumer education and income means that individuals have more disposable income to spend. Direct retailers have responded to this growing affluence by providing luxury items rather than basic requirements of life. As discussed in Chapter 4, disposable incomes have risen as a consequence of more women joining the work force. With more and more women working, shopping time has become scarce. This has expanded the potential scope of direct retailing.

Advances in communication technology have also contributed to the growth of direct retailing. On the one hand, technology has given rise to newer forms of direct response retailing such as in-home television shopping and videotex (see Chapter 4). At the same time, innovations in WATS telephone service (toll-free 800 numbers) have resulted in tremendous changes in mail-order retailing. Customers can now make toll-free calls, instead of mailing in order forms, reducing the waiting period. Armed with a computer, the order-taker can immediately check the inventory of the item and advise the customer of a delivery date.

The growth of direct retailing has also been fueled by the proliferation of credit cards. Before credit cards, the direct retailer would first receive the customer's check and then have the funds transferred to its account before shipping the order. Alternatively, it would offer credit on its own and assume the associated risk of bad debts. The credit card provides a quick and efficient means of transferring funds from customer to the retailer, with relatively little risk to the retailer (but the retailer has to pay a fee for the service).

Target Marketing

As their biggest advantage, direct mail or telephone retailers can direct their messages to good prospects. Consider, for example, a firm that sells clothes for newborn infants. Although the firm could advertise in local newspapers throughout the country or on national television, such an advertising campaign would be inefficient, reaching only a few parents with new babies along with many others who would not be likely to buy what the firm has to offer. Moreover, the ad would not reach all of the firm's target customers. Mass media advertising favors wide coverage over selectivity, resulting in wastage when the advertised product or service is intended for a narrowly defined target audience.

Instead of mass media advertising, the retailer could use direct mail. By contacting all the hospitals in the country, it could create a list of all parents with newborn children and mail information directly to them. The list targets the information to prospective customers only and avoids any wastage. Similarly, an electronics retailer can send out its catalog of products to people who have bought similar items in the past and are known to purchase heavily through mail order. A credit card company can create a list of all female college seniors living in a particular state and send credit card applications to all or some of them. Each firm directs its offer to likely customers of the advertised products or services.

The key to success in direct retailing is list creation and management. This involves acquiring the names and addresses of prospective customers, updating the list periodically, and estimating the potential profitability of each customer.

Types of Lists

A list is a record of names and addresses of people who share some characteristic that makes them likely targets for a retailer's goods or services. Direct marketers use three types of lists: (1) compiled lists, (2) vertical lists, and (3) internal lists.

Compiled Lists   Firms generate these lists from secondary sources such as vehicle registrations, telephone directories, credit references, and so on. The greatest advantage of compiled lists is their easy availability and wide geographical coverage. However, they are typically too general, requiring the retailer to select within the list based on other information. For example, after obtaining a list of all car owners in an area, a retailer may select the names and addresses of people who own station wagons in order to reach families with young children. Similarly, a retailer with a high-income target market may select only those individuals who own luxury cars.

Vertical or Qualified Lists   These lists include people who share some characteristic that uniquely qualifies them as prospective customers. A retailer of tennis equipment, for example, may compile the names and addresses of all subscribers to a tennis magazine. Similarly, a retailer wanting to sell stereo equipment by mail, can obtain a list of people who have previously bought electronic goods through mail order.

Internal Lists   Retailers also maintain internal lists of existing customers. The greatest advantage of the internal list is the established relationship between these customers and the retailer. Another advantage is that firms typically have more information on their own customers than just their names and addresses. A good internal list will contain such information as how much each customer has purchased in the past and the date of his or her last purchase. This information helps define the target market very specifically. Moreover, since the firm compiles these lists itself, it incurs no direct cost or fee. Internal lists have a disadvantage however, since they reach only the firm's existing customers and do not generate new ones. Many department stores sell their products by mail as well as at the store (see Exhibit 16.8). Typically, they send catalogs to people on an internal list of all customers who have charge accounts with the store. In some cases, firms augment internal lists with compiled and vertical lists.

Firms also acquire the customer lists of other companies. A new mail-order firm, for example, can send its catalogs to customers of other mail-order retailers selling similar types of products. These are often known as **affinity lists**. Affinity lists are expensive, and their owners often require users to pay royalties on sales the lists generate.

List Duplication   Most retailers create lists from more than one source. They frequently obtain the same name from more than one source list. For example, the name of an individual who subscribes to two tennis magazines will appear twice on a list created from the subscription lists of both magazines. A procedure called **merge-purge** handles this duplication. A computer merges the individual lists into a master list, then eliminates all duplicated names from this master list.

Increasing List Productivity

Firms send out billions of mail offers annually. Of this vast number, it is estimated that only about 2 percent generate any response from customers. This means that although direct marketing reduces wastage compared with mass media advertising, it still suffers from considerable inefficiency. All direct retailers, therefore, strive to improve the productivity of their mailing by sending offers only to customers with the greatest likelihood of buying, a process called **list targeting**.

In list targeting, firms seek to screen all the names in a list and rank them according to each individual's propensity to buy the products and services offered. It can then send the message only to individuals it believes have high propensities to buy. This reduces wasted mailings and increases the **response rate**. Consider for example, a retailer that has compiled a list of one million names and addresses of potential customers. Based on experience, it expects a response rate from this list of 2 percent; that is, if it mails the advertisement to all one million addresses on the list, only 20,000 (1,000,000 x 0.02) people will actually buy the product. The gross margin generated from these 20,000 orders must cover the cost of mailing to all one million names on the list.

Ideally, of course, the retailer would like to first identify the 20,000 people who would buy the product and mail the offer to them specifically, generating a response rate of 100 percent and no wastage. In practice, however, this is not possible since it learns the names of the 20,000 buyers only when they order. Only by sending the mailing to every name on the list and tracking their responses can the retailer identify the 20,000 customers. The retailer can, however, increase the response rate from 2 percent, if it eliminates from the list the names of people who have very low propensity to buy. Conversely, it can do the same thing by identifying the names of people who have a greater than average propensity to buy. This is the objective of list targeting.

The graph shown in Exhibit 16.9 illustrates the rationale for list targeting. The horizontal axis of the graph reflects the universe of names in a mailing list and the vertical axis, the total number of customers in the list. The diagonal line, which makes 45-degree angles with the axes, shows the response performance of an untargeted list. Suppose, for example, that the retailer randomly chose 50 percent of the names in the list and mailed an offer to each of them; the retailer could expect to reach 50 percent of the buyers in the list. Similarly, an offer mailed to 75 percent of the names chosen randomly would reach 75 percent of the ultimate buyers.

The second line on the graph illustrates the effect of targeting on list efficiency. Proper targeting covers a higher percentage of buyers with fewer mailings. In Curve

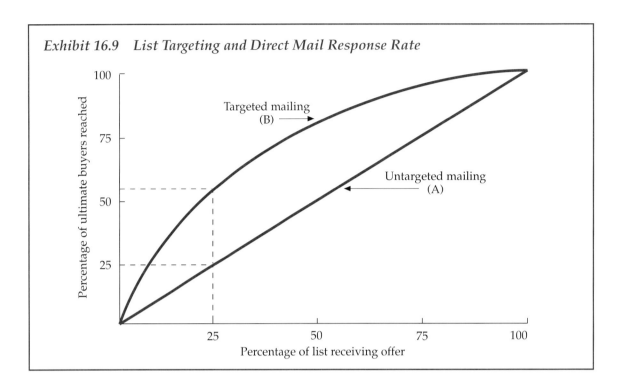

Exhibit 16.9   List Targeting and Direct Mail Response Rate

B, the firm reaches over 50 percent of the ultimate buyers by mailing to only 25 percent of the list. The increased efficiency in Curve B represents the impact of targeting. Because the firm generates no efficiency when it selects names randomly from a list, the response rate is likely to be low. By first ranking the names according to propensity to purchase, it can target the mail to better prospects and increase the response rate.

List Screening   Ranking individuals according to their propensity to buy requires more information than just their names and addresses. The retailer must add other information to the data file containing the list in a process referred to as **data overlaying**. For example, overlaying the demographic and socioeconomic characteristics of each individual on the list lets the retailer screen individuals based on their similarity to its intended target market for the product. People who more closely resemble the retailer's target market are more likely to become customers. A retailer selling a high-priced item, for example, can screen the names on the list by income.

RFM Criteria   Firms also screen names on a list by past purchase behavior, commonly using the RFM criterion. The R stands for recency—how recently the person has made a mail-order purchase. The F stands for frequency—how frequently the person buys through mail order. The M stands for money—the monetary value of the person's mail-order purchases.

One way firms can score each name on the list based on recency, frequency, and money (RFM) is to assign points or weights to each of the three factors. They assign a person who has made a mail-order purchase within the last three months a higher score than one whose most recent purchase was six months ago. Similarly, they assign a higher score to those who have spent more compared to those who have spent less. A higher cumulative score indicates greater likelihood that the person will buy. Exhibit 16.10 shows an example of an RFM scoring system.

After computing RFM scores, the firm can rank the names on the list according to their scores, then mail the offer to the names at the top of the list, that is, to people who are most likely to buy. This way the firm can increase its response rate and generate more sales with fewer mailings.

Considered in another way, the firm can acquire more customers with a fixed budget by concentrating on the "top of the list." For example, if the firm with one million names has a budget large enough to mail only 500,000 offers, it can acquire only 50 percent of the customers on the list by random selection. By ranking

---

Exhibit 16.10 **Example of RFM Scoring**

Recency		*Points*
Customer ordered _____ months ago.	3	25
	6	20
	12	15
	18	10
	more than 18	0
Frequency		
Customer ordered on the average once every _____ months.	1	50
	2	40
	3	30
	4–8	20
	8–12	10
	more than 12	0
Money		
Size of average order was _____.	more than $300	25
	$250–$299	20
	$150–$249	15
	$75–$149	13
	$50–$74	12
	$25–$49	11
	$10–$24	10
	less than $10	5

the names according to RFM criteria and then sending the offer to the top half of the list, it can acquire more customers with the same budget.

Exhibit 16.11 illustrates the impact of list targeting on the profitability of mail-order campaigns by showing costs and revenues under two mailing schemes. The first scenario assumes that the firm sends the mail offer to all one million names on a list. This mailing generates 20,000 orders representing a 2 percent response rate. Each order represents sales of $60, resulting in total revenues of $1.2 million. In the second scenario, the firm sends the mail offer to only the top half of the list ranked according to the RFM criteria. The targeted list gives a response rate of 3 percent instead of 2 percent and generates 15,000 orders (3 percent of 500,000). The firm acquires 75 percent of the customers by mailing to only 50 percent of the list. It generates total revenue of $900,000, $300,000 less than the previous case, but costs in the second case are considerably lower, since the firm prints and mails fewer offers. Pretax profits in the second scenario are $82,000, compared with only $20,000 in the first scenario.

Other Criteria for List Targeting   RFM is not the only method for list targeting. Other factors such as an individual's media habits, psychographic characteristics, geographic location, and so on, can also figure in the estimate of the propensity for purchasing products through mail order. Essentially, the firm seeks to determine the factors that best differentiate between buyers and nonbuyers. Statistical techniques such as regression analysis often serve this purpose.

Exhibit 16.11   *List Targeting and Direct Mail Profitability*

	Untargeted Mailing	Targeted Mailing
Number of offers mailed	1,000,000	500,000
Orders	20,000	15,000
Response rate (%)	2.0[a]	3.0[b]
Average order value	$60	$60
Sales revenue	$1,200,000	$900,000
Cost of goods	540,000	405,000
Variable operating expense	108,000	81,000
Mailing cost as $400/1,000	400,000	200,000
Gross margin	152,000	214,000
Overhead	132,000	132,000
Pretax profit	20,000	82,000

[a] Based on industry average.
[b] At 75 percent of total achievable response.

Source: Computer Daily, 7620 Little River Turnpike, Annandale, Virginia 22003.

LEGAL ISSUES IN RETAIL ADVERTISING

Great Savings! Best Deal in Town! Lowest Prices Ever! These headlines appear in many retail advertisements. Many consumers, however, do not believe these claims. They complain that retail advertising is often deceptive and misleading. Consumers most commonly complain about bait-and-switch offers, unsubstantiated claims, "free" offers that require a purchase, and exaggerated price claims.[20] As a result, regulatory agencies such as the Federal Trade Commission (FTC) and organizations such as the Better Business Bureau actively police retail advertisements. Like pricing, the advertising practices of retailers are subject to a number of legal restrictions. These regulations fall into two major categories: (1) restrictions on deceptive advertising messages and (2) restrictions on bait and switch.

Deceptive Advertising

An advertising message must represent facts and cannot mislead consumers. This principle guides the Federal Trade Commission, the government agency in charge of regulating advertising. The FTC issues cease-and-desist orders if it finds advertising false or misleading.

Most retail advertisements make true statements, but some firms willfully mislead consumers with **deceptive advertising**. The area of greatest concern is the accuracy of "sale" prices or reductions announced in promotional advertisements. According to the FTC guidelines, a retailer may announce price savings or reductions by comparing the promotional price to either the price at which the retailer sold the item previously, or to the current price of identical merchandise at other stores.

When a retailer announces a 25-percent price reduction, the promotional price should be at least 25 percent less than the price at which the retailer sold the item immediately preceding the sale, on a regular basis, and for a substantial period of time. This means that a retailer cannot advertise a product at a 25-percent discount unless it offered the item at the higher price for a sufficiently long period of time.

Sometimes ads compare prices to suggested retail prices to imply a savings. This is deceptive if representative principal retailers in the market area did not actually sell the product at the suggested price prior to the sale. Under pressure from consumer groups, regulatory agencies have been scrutinizing retail advertising closely and requiring stores to document their price claims. Policing of smaller retailers, however, is still lax, and some continue to make deceptive price claims in their advertisements.

Bait and Switch   A retailer advertises a special sale on a VCR for $189 in the local newspaper. Attracted by this special price, a potential customer goes to the store to buy the VCR. Once the customer enters the store, however, the salesperson claims that the model is sold out and is uncertain when a new shipment will arrive. The salesperson then derides the advertised model and encourages the customer to buy a higher-priced one.

Such a scene is enacted too often, according to many consumer advocates and regulatory agencies. This store has engaged in **bait and switch**. It used the advertisement as bait to draw potential customers into the store and then tried to switch them from the advertised item to a higher-priced model. The primary purpose of the advertisement was not to sell the advertised item but to attract into the store persons interested in buying VCRs to try to persuade them, typically through high-pressure selling techniques, to purchase a higher-priced model. Bait-and-switch advertising is illegal because it is deceptive.

Many retailers have answered charges of running bait-and-switch advertising. In a much publicized case, Sears agreed to an FTC desist order and stopped using advertisements that were considered misleading.[21] It can be quite difficult, however, to differentiate between willful bait and switch and legitimate trading up. In trading up, a time-honored and widely accepted retail selling practice, the retailer provides customers with information on models covering an entire price range and genuinely convinces them that a higher-priced model suits their needs better and provides better value. Honest trading up is a good sales technique because it matches a customer's needs with product features. The line between trading up and bait and switch is thin, however, and many retailers who face charges of bait and switch claim that they were engaging in legal trading up.

Since their intentions may be difficult to judge, retailers should follow strict guidelines to avoid charges of deceptive advertising. They must not:

1. Refuse to demonstrate an advertised item.
2. Disparage an advertised item.
3. Refuse to give rain checks and ensure delivery within a reasonable period of time.
4. Knowingly demonstrate a defective sample of an advertised model.
5. Penalize salespersons for selling an advertised item.

Regulatory scrutiny of retail advertising is increasing, especially for large firms. To avoid legal problems, retailers must maintain adequate records to substantiate claims in their advertisements and stock adequate quantities of advertised items. Unfortunately, a few retailers mislead customers with false advertising. Such unethical practices, even if they are rare, hurt the entire retail industry by lowering the credibility of all retail advertising.

Summary

1. Communication programs contribute to the overall marketing effort by informing potential customers of the store's features and how it can fulfill their shopping expectations. Communication programs seek to persuade potential customers to visit the store

by influencing their perceptions and attitudes. As another task, communication reminds consumers of the store and reinforces its image.

2. Retailers develop effective advertising campaigns in five steps: (a) set the advertising goal, (b) define the communication objectives, (c) develop creative strategy; (d) develop the media plan, (e) determine the advertising budget, and (f) evaluate the impact of the advertising campaign.

3. To achieve its goals, advertising must communicate the benefits of shopping at the store to the target audience. Each advertising campaign must, therefore, have specific communication objectives, that is, a specific message or set of key facts.

4. Retailers can reach their target audiences through a variety of media. Most retailers have traditionally preferred to advertise in newspapers although this trend is changing; the popularity of television, radio, and direct mail are increasing. To decide what medium to use, media planners consider the characteristics of each in terms of selectivity, flexibility, and cost. With the mix of media chosen, the media planner must choose the specific vehicles within each medium that can deliver the desired message to the target market in the most cost effective manner. The total allocation for advertising typically depends on the type of store, its age, the nature of its trade area, and its competitive environment.

5. Retailers measure the effectiveness of advertising by tracking how well the campaign fulfills its objectives. They must monitor the impact of advertising on sales and profits as well as on consumer attitudes and beliefs. Typically, they undertake consumer surveys both before and after an advertising campaign to assess its impact. Exit interviews also help them monitor the effect of advertising.

6. The use of point-of-purchase (POP) advertising is increasing in retail stores because of its impact on sales. POP announcements can range from simple handwritten signs to sophisticated electronic broadcasts and POP audio and video systems. POP advertising encourages impulse purchases by customers. In conjunction with other kinds of media advertising or sales promotion, POP advertising can increase sales substantially.

7. Direct mail advertising allows the retailer to direct its offer to people who have a high propensity to purchase the product. To accomplish this, it creates lists of names and addresses of potential customers. Direct retailers use three types of lists: (a) compiled lists, (b) vertical lists, and (c) internal lists. To improve the productivity of their mailings, direct retailers spend a great deal of effort to improve list targeting. The objective of list targeting is to screen all names in a list and rank them according to each individual's propensity to buy the products and services offered. Sending the offer only to those who are the most likely to buy increases the response rate from the mailing. The RFM criteria provide firms with one way to target a list.

8. It is illegal to willfully mislead consumers with deceptive advertising. The retailer must be able to substantiate all claims made in an advertisement. The area of greatest concern is the accuracy of "sale" prices or reductions announced in promotional advertising. Another area of concern is "bait and switch." In this practice, which is illegal, a retailer advertises the sale of a particular model of a product at a low price. Once customers come into the store, however, the retailer resists selling the model and pushes a different (typically higher priced) model instead. Thus, the primary purpose of the advertisement is not to sell the advertised model but as a bait to draw potential customers into the store to persuade them to purchase a higher-priced product. Bait and switch advertising is illegal because it is deceptive.

Key Concepts

Communication	Point-of-purchase (POP) advertising
Advertising	Direct retailing or direct response retailing
Communication goals	Target marketing
Institutional advertising	List targeting
Promotional advertising	Compiled lists
Media selection	Vertical lists
Reach	Internal lists
Frequency	Affinity lists
Gross rating points	List productivity
Advertising budget	Response rate
Advertising-to-sales ratio	Data overlaying
Objective and task method	RFM criteria
Cooperative advertising	Deceptive advertising
Evaluation of advertising results	Bait and switch
Exit interviews	

Discussion Questions

1. Why do well-established companies like McDonald's and Sears need to advertise?

2. What objectives must a communication program fulfill?

3. How does advertising affect consumer behavior?

4. Briefly describe the steps in the advertising management process.

5. A manager of Xenon Stores stated that the firm's advertising objective was to "improve our image in order to increase sales." What is wrong with stating the advertising objective in this way? Give an example of a well-stated advertising objective.

6. By what criteria would you judge the suitability of different media for a retail advertisement? Using these criteria, compare radio, newspapers, and television as potential advertising vehicles for a regional supermarket chain.

7. Explain the terms (a) reach, (b) frequency, and (c) GRP.

8. A new hardware store will open in your town shortly. Write a short report advising the management of the store on how much should be spent on advertising.

9. Pay a visit to the local supermarket and note the types of in-store point-of-purchase (POP) advertising there. Why is the importance of POP advertising increasing?

10. What factors have nurtured the growth of direct retailing?

11. Explain the following terms: (a) compiled lists, (b) affinity lists, (c) vertical or qualified lists, (d) internal lists, and (e) merge-purge.

12. What is the purpose of list targeting? Explain how the RFM criteria help retailers screen lists for targeting.

13. Explain how bait-and-switch advertising works. What guidelines should a retailer set to avoid accusations of bait-and-switch tactics?

Notes

1. This definition is adapted from Philip Kotler, *Marketing Management* (Englewood Cliffs, NJ: Prentice-Hall 1991), p. 570.

2. Kenneth A. Banks, "Does Anybody See Ads," *Retailing Issues Letter*, 4(6), November 1992.

3. Charles M. Edwards and Carl F. Lebowitz, *Retail Advertising and Sales Promotion* (Englewood Cliffs, NJ: Prentice-Hall, 1980), p. 3.

4. Eric N. Berkowitz, Roger A. Kerin, and William Rudelius, *Marketing* (St. Louis, MO: Time Mirror/Mosby, 1986), p. 462.

5. Raymond H. Cooley, *Defining Advertising Goals for Measured Advertising Results* (New York: Association of National Advertisers, 1962), pp. 33–45.

6. Raymond A. Marquardt, James C. Makens, and Robert G. Roe, *Retail Management* (Hinsdale, IL: Dryden Press, 1975), p. 247.

7. Alan D. Bates, *Retailing and Its Environment* (New York: Van Nostrand, 1979), p. 208.

8. Ibid.

9. For a review of some of these models see Roland T. Rust, *Advertising Media Models* (Lexington, MA: D.C. Heath, 1986).

10. Michael Naples, *Effective Frequency: The Relationship Between Frequency and Advertising Effectiveness* (New York: Association of National Advertisers).

11. William L. McGee, *Building Store Traffic with Broadcast Advertising* (San Francisco: Broadcast Marketing Company, 1988), p. 170.

12. See Robert F. Young and Stephen A. Greyser, *Managing Cooperative Advertising: A Strategic Approach* (Lexington, MA: Lexington Books).

13. Bates, *Retailing and Its Environment*, p. 214.

14. Edwards and Lebowitz, *Retail Advertising*.

15. Martin L. Bell and Julian W. Vincze, *Managerial Marketing* (New York: Elsevier, 1988), p. 533.

16. Marianne Meyer, "Attention Shoppers," *Marketing and Media Decisions*, May 1988, pp. 67–70.

17. See John A. Quelch and Kristina Cannon-Bonventre, "Better Marketing at the Point of Purchase," *Harvard Business Review* 61 (November–December 1983), pp. 163–69. Also see various issues of POPAI News published by Point of Purchase Advertising Institute.

18. Howard Stumpf and John M. Kawula, "Point of Purchase Advertising," in *Handbook of Sales Promotion* ed. by Stanley Ulanoff (New York: McGraw Hill, 1985), p. 145.

19. Quelch and Cannon-Bonventre, "Better Marketing."

20. Bates, *Retailing and Its Environment*, p. 150.

21. "Sears Dishonest Ad Draws Ire of FTC," *Chain Store Age Executive*, April 1979, p. 43.

CHAPTER 17
Managing Retail Service

Full-Service Retailers

As the customer of the 1990s grows more demanding, many retailers are adding new elements of service to their business to keep customers coming back. American consumers have more choices than ever in terms of retail outlets, and the nature of retail competition has changed in the face of the increased number of outlets selling similar products. No retailer can be sure that last year's customer base will return for products alone: today's consumers have a wide array of choice among outlets for purchasing items, and in many cases it will be an element of service that will bring customers back year after year. Service can take on many different aspects in the retailing industry: it can be the one-on-one personalized service accorded to customers at luxury outlets, or it can be a wide selection of products with deeply discounted prices. Two examples of service, which differ greatly, but have each ensured success for the retailers implementing the programs, come from Marriott, the full-service hotel chain, and Ikea, the warehouse-style discount furniture chain.

At Marriott, the basic rule of business is to give customers top quality at a fair price. Easier said than done in a turbulent economy, but Marriott has taken great pains to redefine each of its operational functions in order to ensure the highest quality possible for its guests. Many of the different management teams work together to ensure that quality is at its highest across all the hotel services. One example of this idea is clear from the cooperation among Marriott's operations and its procurement, distribution, and quality control staff. Working together, these departments guarantee that the Marriott chefs will have the ingredients they need to serve high-quality meals at competitive prices.

This kind of process begins at the operating unit level where the chefs and the food and beverage staffs will determine menus based on their research of customer dining trends. The procurement staff then reviews the ingredient specifications with suppliers, using the company's enormous buying power to establish agreements that adhere to Marriott's price and quality standards. Quality control staff then has final inspection on all ingredients as they are shipped to the hotels. The Marriott chefs know that once the ingredients reach their kitchens, they are of the highest quality and freshness for the meals they will prepare. It is this kind of team effort across all the operations that provide the highest standards for all Marriott guests.

In addition, Marriott has a wide range of hotels to meet the needs of all kinds of travelers, from convention centers, to a moderately priced chain, to resort hotels. All travelers, both business and leisure, can find a Marriott hotel suited to their needs. There are

After studying this chapter, the reader will be able to:
- *Understand the role of personal services in retailing.*
- *Describe the steps in the personal selling process.*
- *Recruit, train, and motivate salespeople.*
- *Explain the characteristics that separate services from goods.*
- *Discuss some important challenges in service retailing and how service firms respond to them.*
- *Understand how consumers evaluate service quality.*

hotels for the business traveler with suites equipped with conference rooms, and resorts that look out over manicured links for the avid golfer on holiday.

Furthermore, each of the hotel chains are implementing new incentive programs to entice clients. At the family and economy hotels, Marriott sponsors programs to attract families with children, like the "Kids eat free vacation plan" in which for families of four, children under twelve eat free. Also for vacationers, Marriott offers "Rain Cheque" in some of its Florida locations, a program under which travelers will be reimbursed for their lodgings fees if it rains, and many travelers have flocked to these sites for "satisfaction guaranteed or your money back" vacations. Marriott's full-service hotel group has instituted an ambitious quality improvement program. New features include the establishment of a guest relations manager at many hotels, an enhanced frequent-stay program called "The Honored Guest," implementation of division-wide guest response systems, and satisfaction guaranteed on certain service offerings. Marriott continues to support service quality and efficiency through technological development, such as a computerized reservation system which has greater compatibility with some airlines' systems. Marriott is also securing agreements with airlines and car rental agencies to offer competitively priced packages for their guests, to simplify vacation and business trip planning.

At Ikea, the notion of service is quite different. Service at this chain is aimed at keeping customers on the store premises until they are able to make a purchase decision.

Customers are drawn to the stores by the lure of good quality merchandise at low prices, and Ikea wants to ensure that customers do not give up on the often tiring and frustrating task of furniture shopping because of tired and hungry children or a lack of information. Ikea's success stems in part from the company's idolization of the customer. Buying furniture can be a shopping nightmare, but Ikea's flair for service, especially to young couples with children attempts to make the experience as simple as possible. Ikea's key marketing and selling tool is its catalog, which contains all the product specifications—size, price, weight, and colors. The catalogs take the place of salespeople and not only cut costs for Ikea, but allow the customer the time and freedom to shop and make their own purchase decisions unimpeded by salespeople. The stores also feature day-care and changing areas for children, and inexpensive restaurants serving traditional Swedish food. The changing rooms have free diapers and other amenities,

and clerks at the restaurants will warm baby food at no extra charge. Furthermore, the restaurants sell baby food, and the day-care centers will allow customers to leave the children for a full shopping day—at no charge. Thus, customers can take the kids with them through the store and to the snack areas, or they can leave them in supervised play areas. These extras aim to keep customers in the store and offer them the time, space, and freedom to make up their minds.

Sources: 1990 Marriott Corporation Annual Report; Bill Saporito: "Ikea's Got 'Em Lining Up," *Fortune*, March 11, 1991, p. 52; Ravi Sarathy, Associate Professor, Northeastern University, Case study: "Ikea," 1989.

Survey any group of shoppers across the country about their biggest complaints against retail stores, and the low level of **personal service** is likely to top the list. Shoppers seem unanimously dissatisfied with the personal service they receive at retail stores, despite a number of notable exceptions. According to many shoppers, retail salespeople and other personal service employees are often inadequately trained and not motivated to help the customers. Many retail managers, too, agree that improving the level of personal service at the retail store continues to be one of the greatest challenges they face.

Personal service is especially important for retailers who sell services instead of tangible products. Hotels, motels, real estate brokers, travel agents, dry cleaners, beauty salons, and banks, for example, are all engaged in retailing, since they serve the needs of individual consumers. The service sector has grown phenomenally since the 1940s, and firms such as Avis, Hertz, Century 21, McDonald's, Pizza Hut, Holiday Inn, and H&R Block, to name just a few, now form an integral part of the retail industry.

This chapter is divided into two major sections. The first section discusses the importance of personal selling in the retailers's marketing strategy and describes the different steps in the selling process. Issues in recruiting, training, compensating, and motivating the sales personnel are also discussed. The second section of the chapter focusses on the unique characteristics of service retailing. Although service retailers face many of the same problems and challenges that confront goods retailers, some unique characteristics do require special attention. Consumers perceive buying services as different from buying goods. Service retailers must understand how to adapt traditional retailing principles to this form of retailing.

RETAIL PERSONAL SELLING

In today's highly competitive environment, the quality of **personal selling** and customer service is an important way in which retailers differentiate themselves. Two often-cited examples are Nordstrom and Wal-Mart. Shoppers at Nordstrom receive a high level of personal attention from Nordstrom's well-trained salespeople. The salespeople actively help customers find the merchandise they want and complete the retail transaction smoothly. In this way, they augment the "value" customers receive at the store. Because of the self-selection environment, customers at Wal-Mart require less individual attention, yet the level of service at the store is excellent. Each customer is greeted at the store and shop-floor employees are always willing to help locate merchandise and provide other relevant information to customers.

All retail employees who come in contact with customers—cashiers, stockpersons or salespeople—are a vital part of the retailer's marketing strategy. These frontline people play four major roles in the retailer's marketing effort:

- They are the most direct means by which retailers communicate with their customers. Thus, they facilitate the exchange process by providing information to shoppers and matching the retailer's offering to consumers' needs.
- The quality, ability, and cooperation of shop-floor employees have a major influence on how customers perceive a store. By providing adequate services through well-trained employees, retailers can positively influence consumer attitudes toward their stores.
- They increase sales by turning browsers into buyers and by building long-term relationships with customers.
- They have direct responsibility for managing the shop floor: speeding up transactions, handling customer complaints, accepting returns, and even watching for shoplifters.

The importance of each of these four roles varies, of course, among stores. Supermarkets and discount stores, for example, stress self-service and self-selection by customers so their shop-floor employees mainly manage retail transactions and direct customers to merchandise sections. Specialty stores, department stores, and jewelry stores, on the other hand, place much more emphasis on the selling function. At these stores, salespeople actively interact with customers to communicate merchandise information and persuade them to buy at the store.

This does not imply, however, that personal service is any less important in stores that encourage self-service. Even in a self-service environment, customers must have adequate information and the retail transaction process must proceed smoothly. An efficient transaction process is a basic service required of all stores, irrespective of the merchandise they sell and the customers they attract.

Personal selling involves the two-way flow of communication between retail employees and their customers. Unfortunately, many people have misconceptions about the selling process and the role of personal selling in the marketing

Dorris, Wal-Mart's People Greeter at the Santee, California store, plays a key role in how customers perceive the store.

strategy.[1] Some view personal selling as the use of high-pressure sales techniques to induce customers to buy without regard to their long-term satisfaction. On the contrary, the true role of retail selling is to facilitate customer decision-making by providing relevant information about products and store policies and to make shopping a pleasant experience. The ultimate aim is to build a strong relationship with customers.

To fulfill their role, sales personnel must perform the following tasks:

- Provide information that helps customers better define their shopping needs.
- Explain features of different products.
- Provide information on new merchandise, fashion trends, and innovations.
- Help customers compare the relative merits of merchandise items and demonstrate the products, if necessary.
- Assist customers in finding merchandise that best fits their needs.
- Draw attention to support services (such as delivery, gift wrapping, and layaway plans) that may influence the customer's decision to purchase.
- Speed up the retail transaction process.

The Personal Selling Process

Selling is a complex task. To help understand the different actions and tasks involved, the selling process is best viewed as comprising a sequence of steps.[2] Exhibit 17.1 presents the five steps in the retail selling process: (1) approaching the customer, (2) determining customer needs, (3) presenting merchandise, (4) closing the sale, and (5) follow-up. Note, however, that not all actual salespeople strictly follow this sequence of steps. The salesperson is likely to move back and forth between the different steps, or revisit earlier steps, as the selling process unfolds.[3] But it is necessary to perform the tasks associated with each of the five steps in almost all selling situations.

Approaching the Customer

One major difference between retail selling and other forms of selling is that retail salespeople do not have to search for their customers. Rather, they rely on the other elements of the retailer's marketing strategy to bring prospective customers into the store. For this reason many observers compare the retail salesperson's task to that of a "host receiving a guest."[4] If a courteous greeting makes the customer feel welcome, the selling process gets off to a good start. Neglecting customers or

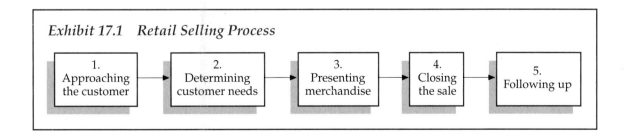

Exhibit 17.1   Retail Selling Process

1. Approaching the customer → 2. Determining customer needs → 3. Presenting merchandise → 4. Closing the sale → 5. Following up

STRATEGY IN ACTION

Wal-Mart, America's Number 1 Retailer, for Customers and the Community

One of the most talked about retail firms in the United States today is Wal-Mart. Wal-Mart is a national discount chain offering a wide variety of merchandise to the consumer. The company runs over 1,600 stores and price clubs (1,627 discount department stores, 184 wholesale clubs, and 4 hypermarkets), each with an average of 36 departments, from family apparel and health and beauty aids to automotive, lawn, and craft supplies. Some stores even have a pharmacy and a snack bar, automotive supply and service centers, and photo and vision centers for improved customer convenience. Sam and Bud Walton, cofounders of the company, opened the first Wal-Mart store in 1962 in Rogers, Arkansas. In 1991 it surpassed Sears & Roebuck to become the world's largest retailer.

According to management, the secret to Wal-Mart's success is in the company's adherence and strict attention to three basic principles, which have led the company since its inception in 1962 and will continue to guide the retail giant into the next century. The first principle is the concept of providing value and service for customers, always and at every location. Sam Walton believed that the key to providing value and service to his customers begins with a friendly atmosphere, a clean environment, and an overall pleasant shopping experience. For Wal-Mart, this means being dedicated to providing high quality merchandise at the lowest price possible, *every day*. To demonstrate the company's confidence in their products, Wal-Mart has instituted a "Satisfaction Guaranteed" refund and exchange policy. Management believes that the customer is not just always right, but is the real boss.

The second principle involves the partnership between management and sales associates.

Sam Walton had a philosophy that all staff should be partners and share in the profits. This has created a family-like working environment which fosters teamwork

approaching them with indifference can lose sales. Unfortunately, few retailers seem to give adequate importance to this step of the selling process.

The salesperson's opening remark when approaching the customer often critically affects the development of the interaction between the customer and the salesperson. Too often salespeople approach customers with such phrases as "May I help you?" or "Do you need help?" These opening approaches usually elicit responses like "No, thank you" or "Just looking." The salesperson cannot then continue the approach without appearing aggressive and pushy.

The ideal approach allows the salesperson to initiate a conversation with the customer and discover his or her needs. For example, the salesperson in a clothing store may approach a browsing customer by asking "What size were you looking

among staff members. Individual efforts and contributions to the teams are welcomed and rewarded, but it is the teams that dictate most operations. Sam Walton believed that by creating a family-like atmosphere for the employees, the employees would take care of Wal-Mart. All company employees, from salesclerks to management, have a share in the company stock, and thus share in profits at each year's end. By making everybody a partner, everybody works toward the same goal: success for Wal-Mart.

Finally, the third principle is based on a commitment to the communities in which the stores are located. Wal-Mart strives to be a good corporate neighbor, and each local store seeks to become an active part of the local community. Store employees try to work with other local merchants to create a solid retail trade center for the community, and in this way a long-term partnership with the stores and their customers is fostered. Employees are expected to volunteer in their communities, in whatever charity they

choose, from working with the homeless or infirm to working in the schools or churches. In this fashion, the Wal-Mart stores gives back to the communities that support them.

Another driving force for the company is its everyday low prices policy. Wal-Mart frowns on specials and gimmicks to entice customers to buy and instead offers good deals every day on all items. Because of Wal-Mart's huge merchandise volume and its low operating costs (the stores are run as veritable no-frills warehouses), the stores are able to offer most merchandise at far below the regular retail price without having to rely on special deals.

This good value and service for its customers and communities keeps the checkout lines long at Wal Mart, and it is no wonder that the company has grown into America's number one retailer.

Sources: Vertanig G. Vartan, "Many Bullish on Wal-Mart," *New York Times*, June 10, 1987; and Wal-Mart, Inc., press release: "Facts about Wal-Mart Stores, Inc." Bentonville, AR, March 1992.

for?" "Have you seen these new styles?" or "Did you have something special in mind?" All these phrases offer assistance to the customer without the customer asking for it. At the same time, the answers help the salesperson get a better idea of the customer's needs and shopping expectations. The manner in which the salesperson approaches the customer is as important as the particular approach he or she uses.[5]

Determining Customer's Need

To sell effectively, a salesperson must understand the customer's need and find the merchandise that best satisfies that need. Thus, the salesperson must learn as

To make the sale this bicycle salesman will have to be adept at answering customer questions about his merchandise. He must also strive to understand the customer's need and be able to handle any of the customer's objections.

much as possible about the customer's needs, budget for the purchase, and so on. Only then can the salesperson complete the exchange process by finding the merchandise that best matches what the customer wants. Because such a variety of people shop at retail stores, determining the customer's need can be one of the most difficult steps in retail selling.[6]

Some customers walk into a store with a clear idea of what product they need and even the brand they want. Some, however, may know what product they want to buy, but not the brand. Yet others may want something, but not know precisely what. For example, a person shopping for a gift for a friend's birthday may walk into the store without any clear idea of what to buy. The salesperson must first determine broadly the customer's need and then decide what information will be relevant in helping the customer define the need more precisely.

Selling is an act of communication. It is not always an easy matter to judge what a customer wants or needs in a product merely by observation. For this reason, good salespeople must be expert listeners rather than just talkers. The basis for effective selling is listening to customers to ascertain their needs and identify the criteria by which they will select merchandise. Only then can the salesperson find a product that will satisfy the customer.

Presenting the Merchandise

With knowledge of the customer's needs, the salesperson can start **presenting the merchandise** to the customer. The salesperson should present merchandise that reflects what he or she believes will best suit the customer.[7] Presentation involves more than just physical demonstration of products. It includes three distinct tasks: (1) providing customers information about merchandise, (2) refining the salesperson's understanding of the customer's need, and (3) handling customer objections.

Providing Merchandise Information   As an essential part of presentation, the salesperson must show the customer merchandise items and explain how they fit his or her needs. An effective salesperson must have a thorough knowledge of the merchandise that the store carries. The salesperson must answer questions about the relative advantages and benefits of different products and explain why some cost more than others. Lack of product knowledge is one of the most commonly cited complaints against retail sales personnel. Moreover, many salespeople learn the technical features of products, but fail to relate those features to the benefits sought by customers. A salesperson gains little, for example, from reciting lists of optical properties of lenses and f-values to an unsophisticated camera buyer. The salesperson must explain to the customer how and why those features result in better pictures.

Refine Understanding of Customer Needs   While presenting merchandise, the salesperson must pay close attention to how the customer responds to each item. Responses such as: "This is my favorite color, but I don't like the style" or "That shoe is beautiful, but it won't be comfortable. I have to stay on my feet eight hours a day" provide important clues for the salesperson. The responses clarify the precise benefits the customer wants and the criteria by which the customer will judge the suitability of merchandise items. Presentation is thus an interactive, dynamic process through which the salesperson identifies the specific merchandise item that best meets the customer's need.

Handling Customer Objections   To make a sale, the salesperson must overcome any customer objections to the merchandise being presented. Customers often say things like, "I think that brand is over-priced," or "I have never heard of this brand." Inexperienced salespeople tend to feel that customers raise objections because they do not really want to buy, but are just browsing. This is not necessarily the case. "Customers who do not want to buy, or who do not see what they want, leave; they do not stand around to discuss the matter."[8] Objections do not signal a lack of interest, only that the customer is still actively considering all the alternatives.

Salespeople can effectively handle objections by anticipating them. Salespeople can diffuse potential objections by addressing them during the course of the presentation. For example, when demonstrating a brand that carries a higher price than the customer seems willing to pay, the salesperson should describe the unique benefits of the brand: "This air conditioner costs a bit more, but it is more energy efficient, so you will save on your electricity bill," or, "This brand is backed up by a three-year warranty." This way the salesperson addresses the source of the customer's objection even before the customer has a chance to raise the objection.

Closing the Sale

The sale is the ultimate objective of selling. Once all customer objections have been handled, the salesperson must attempt to **close the sale** by asking for an order. According to a number of studies, sales personnel are often reluctant to ask for an order and close the sale.[9]   Retail salespeople commonly try to close sales with such statements as: "Shall I wrap this up for you?" "Will this be cash or charge?" "Would you like it delivered?" The question prompts the customer to make the final selection and commit on the decision to buy. Exhibit 17.2 illustrates a number of common closing techniques.

The most important decision in closing is timing. The salesperson can lose the sale by attempting the close too quickly or too late. Attempting to close too early may make the customer resentful of being pushed by the salesperson. On the other

---

Exhibit 17.2   *Closing the Sale: Some Common Approaches*

The Summary Close	The salesperson summarizes all the benefits of a product.
The Balance Sheet Close	In this more formal version of summarization close, the salesperson writes down the reasons for buying the product on a sheet of paper.
The Continuous Yes Close	The salesperson asks a series of questions, each worded in such a way that the customer will answer "yes." The final question asks the customer to buy.
The Assumptive Close	The salesperson acts as if the customer has already agreed to buy. For instance, the salesperson can close by saying, "I will write the order up for you."
The Standing-Room-Only Close	The salesperson tries to get the customer to buy immediately instead of postponing, saying, for instance, "The sale ends today, you will have to pay more if you wait until tomorrow."

hand, stores often lose sales when they delay the close too long and the customer postpones the decision to buy.

In deciding when to close, the salesperson must consider each shopper individually. No single rule can cover all of them. As mentioned earlier, some customers walk into the store with a relatively clear idea of their needs, and they may well be ready to close early. Some, on the other hand, may require more time to make their decision and would not like to be rushed to a close. The salesperson must judge a customer's readiness before attempting to close the sale.

Often customers themselves provide verbal and nonverbal cues suggesting the best time for the salesperson to initiate a close. For example, a customer often starts asking questions about delivery and warranty conditions instead of the product per se when he or she is ready to buy. Similarly, when the customer examines the same product repeatedly, the salesperson should move to close the sale.

Follow-up

The selling process does not stop with the closing of the sale. Good salespeople follow up on their sales to make sure that customers are completely satisfied. Two types of **follow-up** are necessary in retail selling. First, some follow-up is necessary before the customer leaves the store. In many stores, salespeople do not process orders themselves. Upon closing the sale, the customer takes the merchandise to a cash station and pays for it there. The salespeople must follow up on their sales and ensure that the transaction proceeds smoothly. Many a sale collapses between the close and the payment counter.

The salesperson's interaction with the customer must not end when the customer leaves the store. Good salespeople always follow up on their sales by contacting customers later. A car salesperson, for example, may call up new car buyers a few days after the sale to inquire how the car is running. Though this type of after-sales follow-up is only possible for big ticket items, it is extremely effective in building long-term relationships with customers. Follow-up increases the customer's satisfaction with the product as well as the store.

One hallmark of successful selling is building a long-term relationship with the customer. The follow-up is essential to build these long-term relationships, because it increases customer loyalty and provides an opportunity for new sales. For example, salespeople at Nordstrom maintain records on each of their customers, noting their names and addresses, the sizes of clothes they wear, the colors and styles they prefer, and the clothes they have purchased in the past. The salesperson inspects the records regularly to identify any new merchandise that would be especially appropriate for a specific customer. The salesperson then sends the customer a postcard with information about the new merchandise and an invitation to visit the store. This builds a lasting relationship between the customer and the salesperson, improving the chance that the customer will ask for the salesperson by name when he or she next comes into the store. This is why a famous salesperson

When this couple started asking about warranty and delivery, the appliance sales-man knew they were ready to buy.

once defined successful selling this way: "Selling merchandise that won't come back to customers who will."[10] The follow-up is an essential step to such long-term success.

Suggestion Selling and Trading Up

The total sales that the store achieves at the end of any day depends on the average dollar amount of each sales transaction and the number of transactions completed during the day:

Total sales = Average revenue per transaction × Number of transactions

Therefore, to increase sales, the store must increase the number of transactions by attracting more customers or increasing the amount customers spend at the store. Suggestion selling and trading up are two ways in which salespeople try to increase average transaction size.

Suggestion Selling   Suggestion selling increases transaction size by **cross selling** related items to the same customer. In the time between closing a sale and ringing it up, a salesperson has the opportunity to suggest merchandise that is related to the article the customer has just bought. For example, the salesperson might suggest some socks to go with a pair of new shoes, film for a new camera, or a bottle of wine with dinner. Such suggestions are often effective, because the buyer is already in a positive frame of mind.[11] Unfortunately, many salespeople lose the opportunity for suggestion selling because they neglect to ask or make the suggestion improperly. Consider two customers who have both just purchased new suits. Before ringing up the sale, the salesperson attending to the first customer asks: "Will there be anything else?" The second salesperson, on the other hand says: "Let me show you some ties to match that suit." The second customer is much more likely to buy some ties along with the suit.

Trading Up   Trading up is another technique for increasing the sizes of transactions. In trading up, the salesperson tries to sell a better-quality and higher-priced product than the one the customer originally intended to buy. After first showing items within the price range requested by the customer, a good salesperson will also show higher-priced alternatives, explaining their relative advantages over the lower-priced brands. The customer then has the opportunity to consider the cost and benefits of all the alternatives and reassess his or her need. Often customers choose an item that costs more than they had originally contemplated spending once they become aware of its additional benefits.

Trading up is a time-honored sales technique for increasing transaction size. It should, however, result from a genuine re-evaluation of needs and expectations by the customer and not from aggressive or deceptive selling on the part of the salesperson.

MANAGING THE SALES FORCE

Like all other business functions the selling function, too, must be managed with diligence. Implementing a sales program involves recruitment, training, motivating, and directing the behavior of the sales personnel.[12] The recruitment of good salespeople is the foundation of all effective sales programs. The manager must find salespeople and then train them in selling skills and product knowledge. The manager must also motivate them to perform effectively and create a working environment that encourages them to continue their employment with the firm. A number of important issues related to training, motivating, and compensating retail sales personnel are discussed in this section.

Training Salespeople

As they search for ways to improve their productivity and gain competitive advantage, many retailers are increasing their emphasis on proper sales training for their employees. Training in proper selling techniques can greatly enhance the effectiveness of retail sales personnel. The increasing complexity of the retail environment, the need to improve service quality, and the installation of complex automated transaction systems has increased the need for formal training for sales personnel.[13]

Sales training programs typically include both formal training sessions in a classroom setting and on-the-job training for new recruits.

Formal Training Sessions   Many stores train recruits in formal "classroom" training sessions to provide product knowledge and instruction in selling skills. These sessions also acquaint new salespeople with company policies on complaints, returns, and exchanges. Sales training programs can use a variety of teaching methods ranging from lectures, printed reading material, video, and case discussion. Recently some companies have been experimenting with the use of interactive video that combines personal computer and a laser videodisc to simulate different sales situations.[14]

Another training method is **role playing**, where one recruit plays the role of a salesperson while another plays the role of a customer. The class then discusses the salesperson's performance and offers suggestions for improvement. Some critics argue, however, that role playing and the critical appraisal that often follow can be highly stressful for a new recruit and can have negative results.[15] Demonstration of selling techniques by established, successful salespeople is another highly effective training method. Such demonstrations are both informative and inspirational for new employees.

Effective training programs combine training methods to reinforce learning during the sessions. J.C. Penney, for example, uses motivational lectures, video demonstrations, and role playing to train new salespeople. Prior to the training session, each employee receives detailed information on the store's products. Macy's training program is similar, but it supplements other instructional methods with case discussions.[16]

Training sessions provide an excellent forum for the store's senior managers to demonstrate their commitment to selling as an essential store service and to stress the pivotal role salespeople play in retail stores. For years, Stanley Marcus, the venerable chief executive of Neiman-Marcus during the store's prime, personally joined in to train salespeople before they were allowed onto the shop floor. Marcus' involvement didn't stop with the training program. He oversaw salespeople's performance on a regular basis, and remained personally available to assist a salesperson in closing a sale, irrespective of whether the sale was for $10 or $10,000.[17]

On-the-Job Training   On-the-job training is the most direct form of training in which the new recruit attends to customers under the supervision of a superior. The process gives new employees first-hand knowledge of the sales process, along with experience in dealing with customers. On the negative side, however, inadequately prepared recruits may lose sales opportunities.

In many stores, new recruits learn about the merchandise they sell on the job. This creates customer resentment and dissatisfaction with the store. Since product knowledge is an essential prerequisite to selling, it must come before on-the-job training.

Sales coaches, experienced salespeople who act as trainees' coaches, can increase the effectiveness of on-the-job training. Initially the trainee simply watches the coach and learns by observation. With time, the trainee takes a more active role under the supervision of the coach. At the end of each day, or more frequently if possible, the coach and the trainee meet to discuss each sale and draw lessons from the experience.

Motivating the Sales Force[18]

It is widely accepted that salespeople need motivation to be effective. However, there is no universally accepted definition of *motivation*. In the context of sales force management, it is useful to define **motivation** as the *"amount of effort the salesperson desires to expend on each activity or task associated with the job."*[19] The framework developed in **expectancy theory** is helpful in understanding the motivational process.

Expectancy theory   As shown in Exhibit 17.3, expectancy theory links (1) a salesperson's effort with performance; and (2) performance with rewards. The first link is mediated by the salesperson's *expectancy*, which is the person's estimate of how performance is affected by effort. Thus a salesperson may expect that there is a 50 percent chance that he or she can increase sales by 5 percent by improving the initial approach. In motivating the sales force, managers must ensure that salespeople have accurate perceptions of the relationship between the effort put into improving the different stages of the selling process and ultimate performance. Inaccurate perceptions are likely to lead to misallocation of effort. It is often the case that salespeople put too much effort in activities that have little impact on

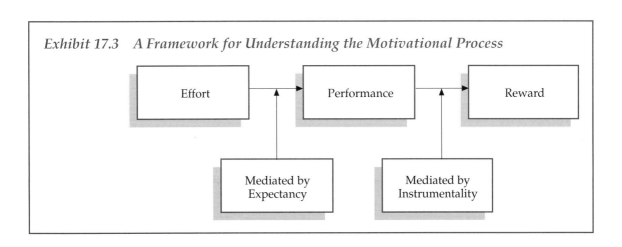

Exhibit 17.3   A Framework for Understanding the Motivational Process

performance. It is because of this that, according to some observers, the challenge is to get salespeople to "work smarter rather than harder."[20]

The link between performance and reward is mediated by **instrumentalities**. These are the salesperson's perception of how improvement in performance will lead to greater rewards. The greater the perceived link the more willing the salesperson is to spend more effort in improving performance. As with expectations, the sales manager must ensure that the salesperson's perceptions of the link between performance and reward are accurate. Misperceptions may lead to disillusion when the reward is not forthcoming at the expected level or lack of effort if the link is perceived to be too weak. Both will ultimately lead to loss of motivation and dissatisfaction with the job.

Role Conflict and Ambiguity   Many researchers have found that retail salespeople tend to suffer from role conflict and ambiguity. Role conflict occurs when a person experiences incompatible job demands or expectations. Role ambiguity occurs when the salesperson has inadequate knowledge or information about how to perform a job effectively. Role conflict and ambiguity reduce a salesperson's motivation to perform and increase his or her propensity to leave the job. To reduce role conflict, the company must make its expectations of its salespeople clear. To reduce ambiguity, it must train them properly in all aspects of their jobs.

Rewards and Incentives

A salesperson's motivation also depends on rewards and incentives. A study comparing rewards given by companies to salespeople found that they preferred financial rewards. Opportunities for growth, sense of accomplishment, promotion, respect from peers, and job security were then mentioned in that order.[21] This finding has been supported by a number of other studies, although some studies have found nonfinancial rewards to be preferred more to higher pay.[22]

Most retail salespeople are paid a straight salary, typically on an hourly basis. In recent years, however, many retailers have begun to restructure their payment systems. A number of stores, for example, have been moving from straight salaries to **commission systems**. Commission selling lost popularity in the 1960s as stores stressed self-service and reduced the role of personal selling in order to cut costs. Today, more and more stores are reverting to the commission system, joining such well-known retailers as Nordstrom and Neiman-Marcus, which have used their commission systems with great success.

Commissions can significantly improve motivation. One employee at a Parisian store in Alabama, which introduced its commission system in 1979, says it aptly: "There's no question the customer gets better service with it (commission). You help her and she helps you."[23] A senior manager at Sears expressed similar sentiments after the store recently began paying salespeople on a commission system, "It's amazing what a 1, 2, or 3 percent commission will do. We are experiencing an upsurge in caring for customers."[24]

Commission systems can be structured in a variety of ways. Sales employees at Bloomingdale's designer shoe department, for example, get a 10-percent commission on each sale, but no salary.[25] This is an example of a straight commission system. Of all available payment systems, straight commission provides the greatest incentive to salespeople: the more they sell, the greater their rewards. Straight commission also adds to the employer's flexibility since it ties expenses to sales productivity.[26]

In contrast to their counterparts at Bloomingdale's, shoe salespeople at Sears get a commission of only 3 percent, but also earn salaries.[27] Salary plus commission has both advantages and disadvantages. It assures the salesperson of a minimum level of compensation even when sales are low. Since, however, the commission rate is usually lower than that in a straight commission system, it may not motivate salespeople as well.

Whether by itself or in conjunction with a minimum salary, the commission system does have certain disadvantages.[28] First, it can create rivalry, and even animosity, among salespeople competing for the same customer. Second, some employees experience a fall in total compensation when a store switches from straight salary to a full or partial commission system. Some of them may leave as a result. At the Seattle department store, Frederick & Nelson, for example, employee turnover increased threefold when the store switched to a commission system in 1987. A third drawback is the potential impact on customer service. It has been observed that when commissions are linked to sales performance, salespeople may ignore customer service activities that do not result in immediate sales.

These problems can be overcome, at least partially, however, by properly designing the commission system. The group bonus system, for example, can encourage more teamwork among salespeople. In a group bonus scheme, a salesperson receives a guaranteed salary, which the firm supplements with a year-end bonus. The amount of the bonus depends on the total sales the department generates. From a pool for the entire department, amounts are allocated to individual employees depending on their seniority and hours worked. In Nordstrom's group bonus scheme, the size of the departmental pool depends on the amount by which the department's sales exceed a specified target. Similarly, Dayton Hudson offers a combination of straight salary and bonus. The amount of the bonus is linked to the departments' ability to meet or exceed specified service standards.

Postscript: Scope for Differentiation through Personal Service

Writers have concentrated recently on the decline in the number and quality of retail shop-floor employees, including both cashiers and sales personnel. Not only have firms deployed fewer such personnel, but they have provided less training and developed less skill. A vicious cycle seems to be driving the quality of retail

ENTREPRENEURIAL EDGE

Dial 1-800-FLOWERS

When James McCann bought the rights to 1-800-FLOWERS, the toll-free telephone number for ordering and sending flowers worldwide, he felt it was a sure bet for success. While it had not been a prosperous business under previous owners—losing upwards of $400,000 a month—McCann believed that he had the skills and experience in the retail flower industry that it would take to turn the business around. And McCann has shown that he was more than correct: purchased in 1986, 800-Flowers now does an estimated $20 million in annual sales, and shows no signs of wilting.

800-Flowers works on a single premise: receive and send orders for the freshest flowers to and from anywhere in the world, 24 hours a day. Simple? Not at all. To perform such a task, 800-Flowers relies on a complex operating system, including a computer system which connects the business to all existing wire services for flowers internationally, as well as to its own network of over 10,000 flower shops throughout the world. Because McCann has been in the business for so long, he knows where the most reliable, high-quality flower shops are, and he never stops updating or verifying his list. Furthermore, McCann has developed an in-house software program that automatically sends and tracks orders. In this kind of business, such systems are imperative for promoting the overall image of the business as one that maintains a high level of customer service and satisfaction. The bottom line of the business is to get the freshest possible flowers anywhere in the world, under any conditions, at any time of the day or night.

To keep customers satisfied and reassured, 800-Flowers tracks the order at all points along the way to ensure that it reaches its destination properly. For example, if you lived in Bozeman, Montana, a small city almost at the Canadian border, where could

personal services down. In order to control costs, retailers pay relatively low wages to their shop-floor employees. As a result, they attract low-quality employees who have poor attitudes toward their jobs and little motivation to perform well. This tends to continue the low-wage cycle.

The impact of this cycle is evident almost everywhere. Almost everybody has experienced long lines at checkout counters staffed by inadequately trained, often discourteous, retail employees. Customers can recite one horror story after another. Most establishments take customers for granted and treat them with indifference. Most retailers themselves agree that the level of personal service in the industry is dismal, and many have plans (at least on paper) to improve service.

However, in spite of good intentions, little seems to have changed. Retailers need to realize that differentiation through personal service can increase revenues by

you find fresh lilies in February? You probably couldn't find such flowers, but James McCann could. Or what if you needed to send a dozen orchids, rare and delicate flowers, to Athens, Greece, and it was 8:00 P.M. here and 3:00 A.M. there? 800-Flowers would find a way, and the orchids would arrive, undamaged, and smelling sweet. And if you needed to know the status of your order, at any point between placing the order and its arrival at the destination, 800-Flowers would be able to tell you the exact situation.

800-Flowers has built itself a solid reputation for high service levels and fresh flowers, and more and more people are becoming customers because they trust the company's reputation. The idea of ordering flowers by phone has only recently taken off. While FTD has had this type of service for many years, sales were flat initially. Buying flowers is something that most customers would prefer to do in person where they can choose the freshest flowers, arrange the bouquets, or at least see the flowers, themselves. McCann had to overcome customer concern about his ability to guarantee his product. But now complaints are rare, and if one arrives, McCann will go out of his way to correct the situation by sending a second order free of charge, or even sending a bouquet to the person who placed the order. Customer satisfaction has grown, and continues to soar. He attributes his success in winning over customers to his consistently fresh flowers and solid service, and clearly 800-Flowers smells sweet, not just for McCann, but for his customers too.

Sources: "Retailing's Entrepreneurs of the Year," *Chain Store Age Executive*, December 1990, pp. 28–38, and James McCann's talk to students at New York University.

attracting more customers, increasing customer satisfaction, and increasing average transaction size. It also reduces reliance on low price as a competitive weapon. It is no coincidence that stores like Nordstrom and Parisian, which are known for the quality of their personal service, are among the industry leaders in sales per square foot.

Improved personal service comes from more than just increased spending; it comes from managerial commitment to a service philosophy that permeates all levels of the organization. Unless this strategic beacon guides the firm, it is not likely to achieve service differentiation however much money it spends. Attentive personal service requires dedication on the part of shop-floor employees and continuous motivation from senior management. As Bruce Nordstrom, co-chairman of Nordstrom puts it, "You've got to work on it every day."

SERVICE RETAILING

Services are not tangible objects. They are essentially intangible activities, deeds, or acts that one party can offer to perform for another. Ownership of no physical product changes hands during a service transaction. Large firms such as airlines, car rental agencies, and banks, to name just a few, can perform services, as can individuals such as hairstylists, baby sitters, and cleaners.

The Characteristics of Services

To appreciate the differences between services and goods retailing, one must first understand the four characteristics shown in Exhibit 17.4 that make services different from goods.[29]

Intangibility   As mentioned earlier, goods and services differ fundamentally in tangibility. Since services are actions performed by a provider for a consumer, that cannot be "seen, felt, tasted, or touched in the same manner in which goods can be sensed."[30] Consumers can only fully understand a service by experiencing (consuming) it. This experiential nature of services means that they cannot be transported, stocked, packaged, or displayed. It also means that they cannot easily be

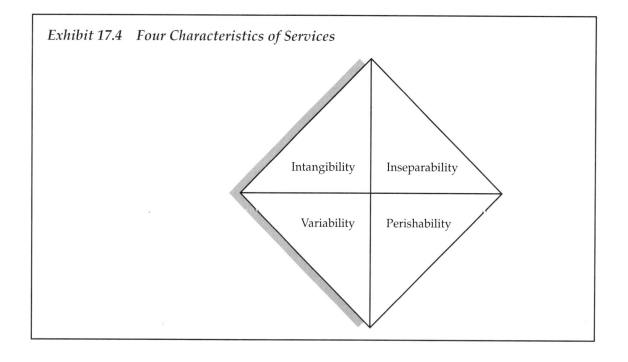

Exhibit 17.4   Four Characteristics of Services

Rental car agencies have only the intangible of service to sell. Therefore the competition is intense to provide the easiest and fastest service possible.

standardized, presenting difficulties in measuring capacity levels and productivity and in maintaining consistent service quality.

Production and Consumption at the Same Time and Place   The production or creation of most service offerings directly involves the customer. This gives rise to the second important difference between goods and services retailing, the **inseparability of production and consumption of services**. Unlike goods—which manufacturers typically produce—after which other firms stock and sell them to final consumers, firms sell services and then they are produced and consumed at the same time.[31] For many services, like beauty salons, nursing homes, and taxis, the consumer must be present during the production of the service itself. Other services such as lawn care, tax preparation, or financial services do not necessarily require the customer to be physically present. Nevertheless, these services too are produced and consumed at the same time.

Variable Quality   Service standards vary widely depending on who provides the service and when it is provided. Not all car rental agencies or airlines, for example, provide the same level of service. The quality of the same service provider can also vary from one customer to another depending on the employee who provides the service and the load on the system at the time. Service quality tends to deteriorate drastically if too many customers demand service at the same time.

Perishability   Since services are produced and consumed at the same time, they cannot be stored. An airplane cannot take more passengers than its capacity because it flew half empty the previous day. Similarly, a hotel cannot store and sell an empty room another day. Conversely, when demand exceeds capacity, customers face disappointment, since no inventory is available for backup. Product retailers can match supply and demand through careful inventory planning; service retailers do not have that opportunity.

The Services Challenge   The four characteristics of services mentioned in Exhibit 17.4 create unique management challenges for service retailers that differ substantially from the problems facing goods retailers. Service retailing requires special strategies for dealing with these problems, because experience in goods retailing does not translate to services.

For example, the intangibility of services presents a problem to the retailer that must communicate to consumers just what it offers for purchase. Consumers have difficulty assessing whether or not the firm offers what they want. Consider, for example, cruise ships or resort hotels; customers cannot judge the firm's offering without really experiencing it themselves.

As a consequence, potential customers attach great importance to physical evidence surrounding the service for clues to the desirability of the service itself. Many customers look for tangible cues to service quality such as the professionalism of the sales agent, the ambience of the office, or the quality of printed brochures. Potential customers use these tangible cues to assess a firms' ability to deliver quality service and to judge whether the service will meet their expectations.

The intangibility of services also raises problems in communicating the benefits of the service to consumers. Firms can display and demonstrate goods, but they can only describe services. Thus, word-of-mouth communication from past users becomes especially important in services. Positive recommendations from past users influence consumer decisions significantly, since they reduce the uncertainty and risk of purchasing the service.[32]

The potential variability of service quality creates special problems for services with high customer contact such as cruise ships, airlines, restaurants, and hotels. Since customers come into contact with more than one employee, firms must maintain consistency of behavior across employees. The rude behavior of a single crew member can easily mar a positive image of an entire cruise line. Similarly, an inefficient waiter or waitress can negatively affect a restaurant's image.

Since services cannot be stored, service managers face a difficult task in coordinating supply and demand. The demand for rooms at resort hotels varies seasonally, peaking during vacation periods and languishing during the rest of the year. Hotels that serve business travelers, on the other hand, often have high de-

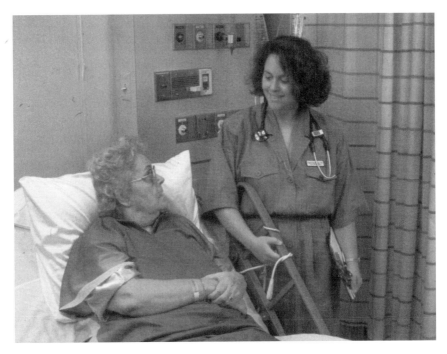

Professional services provided by people such as doctors are highly intangible.

mand during weekdays and low demand during the weekends. This affects the capacity they should maintain and how they manage demand during peak periods. If the hotel maintains enough rooms to meet all demand during peak periods, most of them are likely to be empty during slow periods. Reducing the number of rooms, on the other hand, forces the hotel to turn away customers when demand is high.

Classification of Services[33]

A number of authors have noted the difficulty of generalizing about service firms because services vary so much. The basic differences between products and services identified in the previous section provide one basis for classifying services, though (see Exhibit 17.5). The classification schemes allow one to note commonalities among different types of service providers and identify competitive strategies for each.

One can classify services by degrees of tangibility. Professional services provided by accountants, doctors, lawyers, interior designers, and management consultants are highly intangible, whereas the services provided by car rental, television repair, and tuxedo rental services are quite tangible. Such services as hotels,

---

Exhibit 17.5   Classifying Services

Tangibility

Low ——————————————————————————————————— **High**

Doctors   Hotels   Banks   TV Repair

Lawyers   Airlines   Tuxedo rental

Degree of customer contact

Low ——————————————————————————————————— **High**

Laundromats   Hotels   Doctors

Automated car washes   Airlines   Beauty

Movie theaters   parlors

---

motels, airlines, restaurants, and banks lie somewhere between these extremes. These services have both tangible and intangible aspects, but often those aspects are difficult to separate from one another.

One can also classify services by degrees of customer contact. Professional services require extensive customer contact. Airlines and hotels also require customer contact, but not as much as professional services. Contrast these services with automatic car washes, coin-operated parking garages, or movie theaters which involve only minimal contact between the customer and the service provider.

MANAGING SERVICE STRATEGIES

Since services differ from goods, service retailers face different challenges in developing successful strategies. This section discusses four of the most important concerns in service retailing and describes how some service providers have responded to them. These are (1) matching supply and demand, (2) managing quality, (3) training and evaluating personnel, and (4) pricing.

Matching Supply and Demand

Since firms cannot maintain inventories of services, they frequently experience periods when demand exceeds capacity and other periods when demand falls short of capacity. Exhibit 17.6 shows the nature of the problem in the pattern of demand for a hotel. The exhibit shows significant peaks and valleys in the demand pattern. Demand is high during weekdays, since the hotel caters mostly to business travelers, and falls off during weekends. The capacity of the hotel (the number of rooms), however, is fixed. The managers of the hotel face a major question, therefore, in deciding what capacity to maintain and how to synchronize demand with capacity.

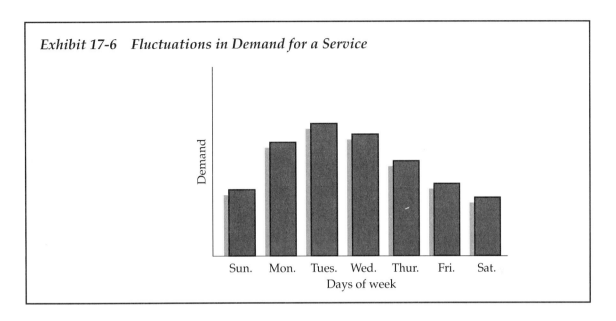

Exhibit 17-6   Fluctuations in Demand for a Service

Exhibit 17.7 illustrates the implications of two levels of capacity. In the top panel, capacity equals the average demand during the week. This level of capacity brings significant space problems during the busy parts of the week, and excess capacity during the weekend. In the bottom panel, capacity can accommodate peak load demand. While the hotel significantly increases its ability to fulfill demand during busy weekdays, its occupancy rate (the percentage of total rooms that are occupied) falls drastically during the weekend. Moreover, building the additional capacity adds significantly to costs.

How many rooms should the hotel build? Determining optimal capacity requires careful consideration of costs and revenues. First, the firm must calculate the cost of building and maintaining additional rooms. Then it must estimate the incremental margin or contribution that it can generate from the additional rooms. It must then balance the cost of new rooms with their potential revenues to determine the optimal size.

Whatever the optimal size, the hotel will be full some times and have excess capacity other times. This means that during busy periods, the hotel will lose potential revenue by turning away potential customers and during the lean periods it will have unoccupied rooms. Moreover, fluctuations in demand also complicate management of the service process. The quality of the services often falls during peak demand levels. The hotel's kitchen may not provide room service as rapidly as desired and check-in and check-out services are likely to be delayed. Service quality may fall even during periods of very low demand, when employees become bored and lose interest in service quality. Researchers have found that many service facilities operate most effectively at around 75 percent of capacity.[34]

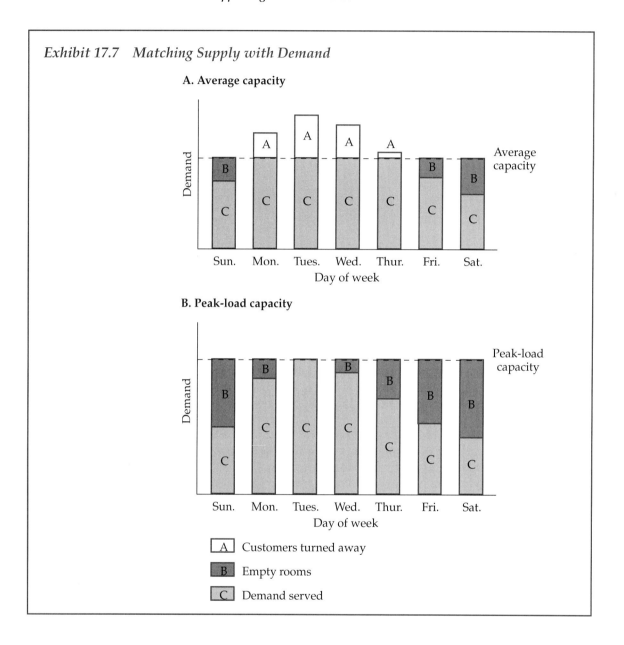

Exhibit 17.7   Matching Supply with Demand

A. Average capacity

B. Peak-load capacity

A   Customers turned away

B   Empty rooms

C   Demand served

Service managers adopt various strategies to synchronize demand and capacity. These strategies fall into two classes: those that influence demand and those that influence supply.

Demand Management   Such services as hotels and airlines that need to build a fixed level of capacity before offering their services attempt to synchronize demand and supply by managing demand through pricing and promotional policies. For example, to increase demand during slow weekend periods a hotel catering typically to business people can have special packages for tourists. Even if the rate is lower than the normal weekday rate, this reduces the potential loss, since it generates incremental revenues that exceed direct costs. Moreover, creating demand during slow periods raises the level of service quality and improves employee morale.

Many service providers try to manage demand through pricing policies. Resort hotels charge more during peak seasons than during off-peak seasons, many movie theaters charge less for matinee shows than for evening shows, and some hospitals even charge less for rooms during weekends. Similarly, many utilities charge higher rates during summer months when demand is high to encourage economy.

The pricing policies of telephone companies provide a good illustration of management of service demand through variable pricing. Long distance telephone lines are busiest during business hours from 8 A.M. to 5 P.M., whereas demand falls off during evenings, late nights, and weekends. To shift some daytime calls to other times, the telephone companies charge lower rates during off-peak hours. The rates are highest during the day, 35 percent lower between 5 P.M. and 11 P.M., and 60 percent lower after 11 P.M. and on weekends and holidays. This structure reflects the company's effort to shift demand from peak to off-peak periods.

Another way to manage demand is to involve the customer in the service delivery process. For one example, banks encourage customers to use ATMs (automatic teller machines) for routine transactions to reduce the demand for human teller services. This allows the tellers to concentrate on more complicated transactions. Moreover, since ATMs usually provide service 24 hours a day, they reduce the concentration of demand during regular banking hours. ATMs have succeeded because they offer convenience to customers, who can withdraw cash at any time.

Firms have also found **reservation systems** to be effective tools for managing demand. Customers benefit from reservations in two ways. First, the reservation ensures that they will get service whatever the demand for the facility. Second, the advance notice helps the service provider to maintain service quality. In some sense, a reservation system indirectly inventories service demand and manages demand to fit supply.

Supply-Side Management   Even with proper management of demand, service firms experience periods of high and low usage. Several supply-side strategies can help them match demand and supply:

- Hiring part-time or temporary employees to work during peak demand periods or letting regular employees work overtime.
- Postponing nonessential tasks during peak periods. A doctor's aide directly assists physicians during busy periods, but does necessary paperwork during off-peak periods.
- Conducting routine maintenance activities during off-peak periods. Cruise ships and airlines can undergo repainting and remodeling when demand is low.

STRATEGY IN ACTION

Service Can Kill—the Competition

Success in the retail environment of the 1990s has been a difficult task for many stores. The stores that have had success have often focused on a very simple, but crucial, marketing strategy: they anticipate and prepare for future trends in their field, and step up to those new challenges by recognizing and meeting the needs of their customers in innovative ways.

For example, in the automotive aftermarket services and supplies market, customers are often at the mercy of their mechanics, in terms of price, availability, and service. Because the field is so small and the work so specialized, some companies in the industry have been able to exact huge fees for poor service. In the mid-1980s, Pep Boys—Manny, Moe, and Jack recognized that what their customers truly valued were time and convenience, as well as good value and high quality service in the industry. The company realized that few of its competitors were changing their operations to suit customers, and Pep Boys stepped up to the challenge. The company began to offer hours that were more convenient for their working customers, as well as services beyond the usual quick tune-up and lube, and resulted in more customers. The company continues to grow because of this new level of customer service designed specifically to meet the needs of their busy, urban customers who are a time-pressed and a convenience and quality oriented public. Furthermore, in trying to raise the standards of automotive supply quality, Pep Boys has begun to offer national brands to its product line and has added a lifetime guarantee to its parts liabilities. All of this has done wonders to raise consumer perceptions in the industry, and Pep Boys is causing their competition to carefully rethink how they do business.

In fact, it might be said that Pep Boys is *killing* its competition. CEO Mitchell

• Shifting resources among service sites. A firm that operates a large, geographically dispersed network of service facilities can match demand and supply by shifting resources from one area to another. In summer, when tourist traffic in Florida slows, car rental agencies move some cars from Florida to places with high summer demand. For many years, Pan American Airways leased some of its aircraft to National Airlines during the winter season. National needed extra capacity to service the peak demand for its flights to Florida during the winter, while Pan American experienced relatively low demand for its transatlantic flights.[35]

Managing Service Encounter Quality

Perhaps the greatest challenge in service retailing is quality control. The inseparability of production and consumption keeps personal interaction between the cus-

Leibovitz takes a dim view to peaceful competition, and each time Pep Boys forces another automotive supply chain to abandon a location—and there have been many—Leibovitz gloats. He takes a snapshot of the abandoned location, and adds it to his collection. He videotapes himself burning anything with the rival corporate logo, and shows the video to his 14,500 employees. Peaceful? Not at all, rather, Leibovitz has a killer instinct and a good head for business. Leibovitz believes that the $125 billion automotive aftermarket industry is facing serious consolidation now, and only the cream of the crop will survive. Thus, he demands that all his locations be top-notch, which to him means offering superior selection, price, and service. Alone among its major competitors, Pep Boys offers unique and superior service in the industry: it installs what it sells (if the customer doesn't want to), keeps long hours, offers multiple technicians at every

site so the wait is minimal—no appointment needed—and most of all, Pep Boys offers a wider selection of automotive parts than do its major rivals, and at better prices. Furthermore, Pep Boys was recently noted for its low parts and service prices versus brand name dealers—as much as 50 percent less expensive in many cases.

This successful retailer has found that identifying the service attributes that are more important to customers as well as developing new ways to offer superior service will be critical to real success in the 1990s. And, as Pep Boys' sales continue to grow, and its competition to struggle, it is clear that its methods are on target.

Sources: "Four of the Trendsetters: Innovative Service Is a Common Goal" (Pep Boys—Manny, Moe, and Jack, Land's End, Inc., Home Depot, Inc., and Wal-Mart Stores, Inc.), in "Toward 2000," *Chain Store Age Executive*, Jan. 1990, p. 33; Alex Taylor III, "How to Murder the Competition," *Fortune*, February 22, 1993, pp. 98–100.

tomer and service provider at the heart of many services.[36] Services that require the customer's presence and involvement in the service production process cannot totally separate service personnel from customers. As one group of authors put it:

> In a service business, you're dealing with something that is primarily delivered by people—to people. Your people are as much of your product in the consumer's mind as any other attribute of that service.[37]

The Service Encounter   Since services themselves are intangible, few customers separate their evaluation of service quality per se from their feelings toward service personnel. In fact, customers typically evaluate high-contact services predominantly by the quality of the service encounter, that is, their personal interaction with service personnel.

Consider the bank as an example. Customers can evaluate a bank's service based on such factors as the rates of interest on its savings and checking accounts, the range of financial services it provides, and the accuracy of its statements. But when banks ask customers to rate the quality of their service, customers typically consider factors related to the service encounter: how long they had to stand in line, or the professionalism, friendliness, courtesy, knowledge, and other characteristics of the teller. Moreover, since firms can rarely protect service characteristics through patents or copyrights, competitors can very easily imitate them. Most banks in an area offer the same interest rates and range of services. The service encounter, therefore, determines consumer evaluations of service quality.

Quality of Service Encounters   Customer satisfaction with a service encounter depends on the congruence between the quality customers expect and the perceived quality of the actual service encounter (see Exhibit 17.8). Thus, customers evaluate service encounters in relative rather than absolute terms, by reference to an internal standard called the comparison level. "The comparison level is the quality of outcomes the person expects or believes that he or she deserves in a particular interaction."[38] Encounters that compare better to the comparison level better satisfy customers. Conversely, customers become dissatisfied when actual outcomes fall below comparison levels. Too long a wait at a fast-food restaurant, for instance,

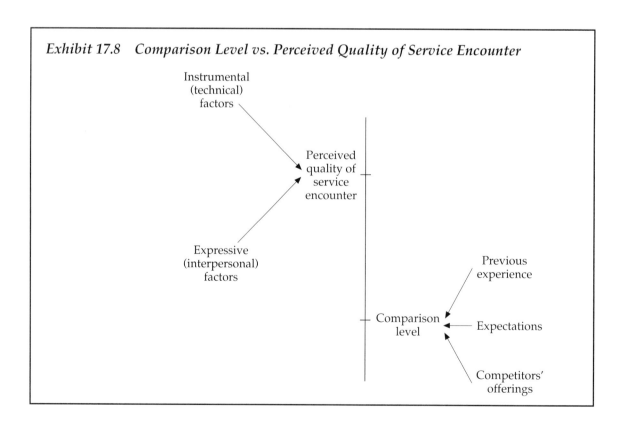

Exhibit 17.8   *Comparison Level vs. Perceived Quality of Service Encounter*

Instrumental (technical) factors

Perceived quality of service encounter

Expressive (interpersonal) factors

Previous experience

Comparison level

Expectations

Competitors' offerings

would alienate customers since they expect swift service. On the other hand, patients would become dissatisfied if a physician were to spend less time with them than they deemed appropriate.

A number of factors influence comparison levels or customer expectations. These include the customer's previous experience in similar service encounters, cultural expectations, and promises communicated through advertising and word of mouth. Comparison levels also change with the general level of service provision. A higher general level of service in an industry raises customers' comparison levels. The existence of comparison levels implies that levels of satisfaction may differ among individuals and over time, even when the quality of service does not fluctuate.

As shown in Exhibit 17.8, the perceived quality of a service encounter results from two evaluations by customers. First, they rate the instrumental or technical part of the encounter (for example, the actual haircut at a salon, the ride in an airplane, the accuracy of a bank teller). Second, they consider the expressive or interpersonal component of the encounter (for example, the chit chat with the barber, the helpfulness of the flight attendants, the friendliness of the bank employees). Researchers have found that the typical service customer does not consider good instrumental performance by itself to ensure a high-quality service encounter.[39] In fact, satisfied customers more frequently mention interpersonal or expressive attributes of service providers as reasons for their satisfaction. This suggests that interpersonal quality is more important to a customer's perception of a service encounter than technical quality, as long as technical quality does not fall below an acceptable minimum. Thus, through expressive or interpersonal quality, a service firm can create differential advantage, assuming it provides technically adequate service.

Customization of Services   Service retailers must resolve the dilemma of how to provide efficient technical services at some acceptable level of quality while still customizing the service to some extent to meet each customer's unique expectations. Equally important, they must find a way to maintain consistent quality over time and across customers.

Customers of low-contact services (such as movie theaters and mass transportation) generally expect efficiency and consistency; they feel little need for customization. When customers expect a predictable, standardized level of service, customization does not necessarily increase customer satisfaction. In fact, it may make customers uncertain of the quality of service to expect.

Extensive customer involvement in high-contact service encounters does, however, allow for customization, where it is appropriate. Many advisors recommend that firms provide high-contact professional services in two stages in order to reduce the customer's uncertainty about the service outcome.[40] In the first stage, the firm diagnoses the customer's problem. In the second, it implements a proposed solution to the problem. This gives customers a better idea of what to expect during the service process and a chance to withdraw from the encounter, if they so desire.

Successful service firms achieve consistently high quality by developing explicit procedural guidelines and carefully training their employees, by using technology, and by creating a work environment that stresses the importance of quality. McDonald's, for example, invests heavily to provide detailed training to franchisees in all aspects of the fast-food business. The firm provides specific operational guidelines for such procedures as how long and at what temperature to cook french fries and how to assemble hamburgers. The guidelines assure consistent quality.

Training and Evaluating Service Personnel

The critical importance of the service encounter to customers' perceptions of service quality forces service firms to pay special attention to **training service personnel**. Effectively trained and motivated employees are the only long-term answer to the quality problem. In service firms, the employees themselves are an element of the retail mix. Thus, customer contact personnel need training in basic marketing skills to understand the effects of their attitudes and behavior (verbal and nonverbal) on the quality of the service encounter. In addition, they need training in the operational skills necessary to provide the service efficiently.

Walt Disney Enterprises and Marriott Hotels are well-known for consistently high quality. The secret to their success is the importance they give to employee training and motivation. Both train each employee thoroughly for his or her job through lectures, simulations, and role playing. Disney executives spend a week each year behind the ticket counter or refreshment stand to inspect operational procedures and demonstrate to employees the firm's commitment to service quality.[41]

Marriott's management sets detailed standards for every aspect of operations, including the tasks of the bellman. The firm has designed a booklet entitled "The Marriott Bellman" to convince bellmen of their importance to the overall image of the hotel.[42] While bellmen may be among the lowest-paid employees of the hotel, guests typically come into contact with them more often than any other hotel employee. Thus, they heavily influence the customer's overall perception of the quality of the hotel. They must, therefore, be properly trained in interacting with the guests and giving them information about the hotel's services.

Evaluating Service Personnel   To ensure consistent service quality, a firm needs to create an atmosphere and a personnel management system that encourage and reward employees for their efforts toward customer satisfaction. Unfortunately, firms often **evaluate service personnel** based on operational criteria rather than on customer relations criteria. For example, an airline reservation person or hotel manager may be held accountable more for paperwork errors than for the goodwill they generate with customers. Firms continue to measure employee performance by operational criteria because they are easier to measure. The quality of an employee's performance during a service encounter, on the other hand, can be difficult to judge.

To evaluate service employees, some firms use company shoppers, or mystery shoppers, as they are sometimes called. These employees of the firm (or some organization hired for this purpose) pose as customers in order to evaluate the quality of service employees. A number of hotels and airlines use mystery shoppers. In addition to evaluating service employees, programs of this nature help firms identify needed improvements in their total service delivery systems.

Customer surveys are another way to evaluate employees and the overall delivery system. These surveys ask recent customers of the service to evaluate its quality and their own satisfaction. Ford Motor Company, for example, surveys new car buyers regarding the dealer's services. The company evaluates dealer performance based on these surveys. Similarly, many hotels ask guests to complete survey forms prior to checking out. These responses help them monitor service quality and customer satisfaction.

Creating a Service Atmosphere   No amount of training and evaluation will produce success, however, if the firm lacks a leader who champions the service cause. Behind every high-quality service provider lie "one or more store leaders coaching, praising, and modeling service excellence."[43] These leaders set high standards and demonstrate the firm's unremitting commitment to high levels of service for its customers.

Two essential ingredients for creating a good service atmosphere are (1) a strategy for effectively communicating to all employees the importance of quality and (2) a commitment on the part of the management to work together to achieve service standards. The top management of Delta Airlines, a firm known for its service, meets all employees in groups of about 25 at least once every 18 months. Bill Marriott, Jr., spends considerable time visiting the hotels that bear his family name and talking to employees. In addition, the company conducts an annual attitude survey of its employees and reports back to them about actions taken as a result of the survey within two weeks.[44] Similarly, the direct involvements of Bruce Nordstrom and Sam Walton were critical in setting the high service standards at Nordstrom and Wal-Mart, respectively.

Pricing Services

Pricing is another issue that requires the special attention of service firms. In goods retailing, the cost of a good to the retailer provides an important benchmark in setting prices. Service retailers have no such benchmark, however. The true cost of providing a service to a particular customer is often difficult to ascertain, especially when the firm provides many different services to a heterogeneous set of customers. It is difficult, for example, for a bank to estimate the cost of providing

STRATEGY IN ACTION

Did Sears Commit Fraud?

When consumer complaints against Sears Auto Repair centers shop up 50 percent in one year in California, the state's Department of Consumer Affairs launched an 18-month undercover investigation. In June 1992, the department charged Sears, Roebuck & Co. with defrauding customers in 72 outlets by performing unnecessary repairs. On average, customers were overcharged by $235. Drawn into the repair centers by advertisements offering brake jobs for $48 to $58, customers were then told that calipers, shock absorbers, coil springs, idler arms, and master cylinders needed to be repaired or replaced. During the undercover investigation, even cars in good working order, with as little as 20 miles on them, were slated as needing repair.

According to the Department of Consumer Affairs, investigators found that repair center workers were bound to "incentive" programs that fostered the fraudulent claims. Employees were instructed to sell a certain number of repairs or services during every eight-hour work shift, including a specific number of brake jobs and alignments. The workers felt pressured to sell the right number of parts for each hour worked, and told investigators that if they failed to meet these figures they risked being moved to another department or having their hours docked.

checking account services to an individual customer, since the same set of company resources provides checking accounts, savings accounts, money market accounts, certificates of deposit, and so forth. Moreover, not all customers use the same set of services with similar intensity.

Many service companies set prices based on existing competitors' prices, a practice often called competitive pricing. A new movie theater, for example, will charge the same amount as its direct competitors. A firm must, however, carefully define the set of competitors for this purpose. A movie theater that shows mainly second-run films cannot charge as much as one that shows only first-run movies.

Demand-oriented pricing is also common among service firms. As mentioned earlier, many service companies charge different prices during different seasons, or different days of the week, or at different times of day to reflect the pattern of demand for the service.

Some service firms use a **two-part pricing** scheme. As the first component, all customers pay a fixed fee, irrespective of the amount of service they use. The second part of the fee varies depending on the customer's use of the service. Consider, for example, how banks typically price NOW accounts. Every customer pays a fixed fee and can write a specified number of checks each month. Customers

The California Department of Consumer Affairs concluded that it was the commission structures that led to the fraud. Employees were pressured to sell, and management created quotas that were difficult to attain during a typical shift, without such actions.

Consumer Affairs departments in other states, fearing similar practices across the country, began to check the Sears centers in their states. Only New Jersey has filed a claim against Sears, citing overcharging in at least six auto repair centers. Consumers across the country are outraged, feeling that the company slogan "Where America Shops," founded on the trust that Sears had built up with its customers, rings false. To counter the growing storm, Sears moved quickly to change the pay structure at its centers. By the end of June, less than three weeks after the original charges were filed, the company announced that the old incentive programs would be replaced with a new payment structure intended to reward employees for high customer-satisfaction levels, eliminating most goals for specific products.

Source: Lawrence M. Fisher: "Sears Auto Centers Halt Commissions after Flap," *The New York Times*, June 23, 1992, pp. D1, D2.

who write more checks have to pay an additional fee for each check in excess of the specified maximum. Many amusement parks also use two-part pricing. Every customer pays a fixed fee to enter the park, which also entitles them to a fixed number of rides and games. Those who want additional rides have to buy special tickets.

Like variable pricing schemes, two-part pricing allows firms to charge different prices to different user segments. Heavy users pay more, while light users pay less. If all users pay a common fixed price, light users indirectly subsidize heavy users. For example, a single fee for all NOW account holders would penalize those who write only a few checks, since the single price would have to be higher than the first part of the two-part price. This could deter light users from patronizing the service.

The profitability of a service firm is very sensitive to its fixed expenses. The majority of a service firm's costs are fixed rather than variable. Additional sales, therefore, contribute directly toward increasing the firm's profits. (As discussed in Chapter 7, this is true for goods retailing too, although not to the same extent.) Consider, for example, an airline or a hotel. Once the airline undertakes a flight, the variable cost of flying additional passengers is negligible. Its four major cost elements—fuel, employee time, airport fees, and depreciation of the airplane—remain fixed and do not increase with additional passengers. The same is true for a hotel. The only additional cost of an extra guest is the cost of laundering sheets and towels and the cost of electricity. These costs are negligible compared to the typical price of a hotel room. This often prompts hotels and airlines to give price discounts to attract additional customers.

Because of the extreme sensitivity of service profitability to service use, service managers must carefully assess the sensitivity of demand and revenue to price. The appendix to this chapter illustrates a marketing research technique called *trade-off analysis* to estimate this relationship.

Summary

1. Quality of personal service has a major influence on how consumers perceive a store. When they come into contact with customers, all retail employees become a vital part of the retailer's marketing strategy. They are the means through which retailers communicate directly with their customers. Their ability and cooperation influence how customers perceive the store. They must also speed up retail transactions and handle complaints. The quality of transaction service and personal selling will ultimately affect the store's long-term success.

2. Personal selling involves two-way communication between retail employees and their customers to facilitate consumer decision-making by providing relevant information about products and services and by making shopping a pleasant experience. The personal selling proceeds through a sequence of five steps: (a) approaching the customer, (b) determining customer needs, (c) presenting merchandise, (d) closing the sale, and (e) follow-up. Suggestion selling and trading up are two ways in which salespeople try to increase average transaction size.

3. As retailers search for ways to improve their productivity and gain competitive advantage, they increasingly emphasize proper sales training for store personnel. Trainees typically participate in both on-the-job training and formal, classroom training sessions. Classroom sessions may consist of lectures, video presentations, role playing, and demonstrations.

    To motivate salespeople, retailers must reduce role conflict and ambiguity by making the company's expectations clear to salespeople and properly training them in all aspects of their jobs. Adequate rewards and incentives can also increase motivation. Paying a commission on sales instead of, or in addition to, a salary is one way in which retailers can motivate salespeople to become more productive.

4. Although many people associate retailing with the selling of products only, service retailers are important, too. The service sector has grown phenomenally since the 1940s and has become an integral part of the retail industry. Four important characteristics differentiate services from goods: (a) intangibility, (b) inseparability of production and consumption, (c) variability in service standards, and (d) perishability. Services can be classified by degrees of tangibility and levels of customer contact.

5. Four of the most important challenges to managers of service firms are: (a) matching supply and demand, (b) managing the quality of the service encounter, (c) training and motivating service employees, and (d) pricing services. One way service firms synchro-

NOW AVAILABLE AT THE ATHLETE'S FOOT.
Before you hit the hardcourt, hit The Athlete's Foot and get the new Air Raid II by NIKE®. Its durable, high-traction outsole is specially designed for outdoor use. And it's just one of the hot, new shoes available at the store that always carries the latest technology and styles. So pave your way to The Athlete's Foot for the new Air Raid II. And get ready to tear up your opponent. Instead of your shoes.

Nobody Knows The Athlete's Foot
Like The Athlete's Foot.

Much of the communication between retailers and their customers takes place outside the store through advertising. Joint magazine print ads have become common because the retailers can share the expense of the advertising with manufacturers. News-paper ads are still the most popular with retailers such as J.C. Penney.

Courtesy Fitzgerald & Co.
Courtesy J.C. Penney

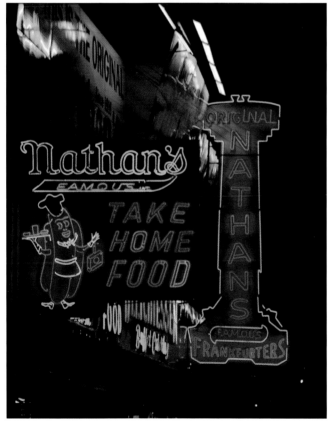

Outdoor signs can be quite theatrical and memorable thereby creating name recognition with the public.

Flyers with coupons attached are used to good advantage by producers of food and drug products. This is also an effective way of introducing a new product. Student Works Painting left this door hanger advertisement at each home in their targeted area. This is a cost efficient way of getting the most from your advertising dollar since the ad reached only people living in houses.

Courtesy Student Works Painting
© 1991, A.H. Robins Company

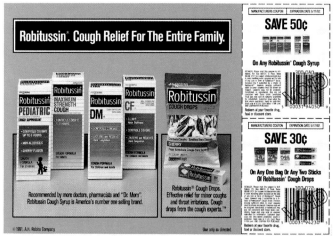

nize demand and supply is by variable pricing. They also use reservation systems and involve the customer in the service delivery process, for two other ways. Supply-side strategies also help firms match supply and demand.

6. Since services are intangible, customers generally evaluate them predominantly by the quality of the service encounter, that is, their personal interaction with service personnel. Customer satisfaction with a service encounter depends on the match between the quality they expect (the comparison level) and their perception of the quality of the actual service encounter. Given the critical importance of the service encounter to customer satisfaction, the service firm must pay special attention to training its service personnel. It must also create an organizational philosophy and a personnel management system that encourage and reward employees for their effort toward customer satisfaction.

Key Concepts

Personal service

Personal selling

Approaching the customer

Determining customer need

Presenting the merchandise

Closing the sale

Follow-up

Suggestion selling

Cross selling

Trading up

Formal training sessions

Role playing

On-the-job training

Sales coaches

Motivation

Expectancy theory

Instrumentalities

Role conflict

Role ambiguity

Commission systems

Intangibility

Inseparability of service production and consumption

Variable service quality

Perishability

Classification of services

Reservation systems

Service encounters

Quality of service

Customization of service

Training service personnel

Evaluating service personnel

Service atmosphere

Two-part pricing

Discussion Questions

1. Explain how retail personal services affect consumer behavior.

2. What role does personal selling play in retail stores? How do retail salespeople fulfill this role?

3. Explain the steps in the retail selling process.

4. Explain the terms *trading up* and *suggestion selling.* Do you feel trading up is an unethical practice?

5. You have been hired by a small specialty electronics chain to help it set up a train-ing program for new salespeople. Write a short report outlining the type of training program you would recommend.

6. Many retailers are instituting commission compensation systems for their sales employees. What are the advantages and disadvantages of a commission system compared to straight salary? How do firms typically structure commission systems?

7. Explain the characteristics that differentiate services from goods. Point out some

managerial problems that arise from these characteristics.

8. It is often said that one of the greatest challenges of service retailing is matching supply and demand. Using an airline as an example, discuss some ways in which service retailers try to match supply and demand.

9. What does the term service encounter mean? What factors affect a consumer's evaluation of the quality of a service encounter?

10. Compared to goods retailing, what special factors affect prices of services? What is two-part pricing?

Notes

1. Gilbert A. Churchill, Jr., Neil M. Ford, and Orville C. Walker, Jr. *Sales Force Management*, Homewood, IL: Irwin, 1993, p. 10.
2. Douglas J. Darymple and William L. Cron, *Sales Management*, New York: John Wiley, 1992, p. 43.
3. Ibid., p. 43.
4. Frederick A. Russell, Frank H. Beach, and Richard H. Buskirk, *Textbook of Salesmanship* (New York: McGraw Hill, 1978), p. 381.
5. Raymond A. Marquardt, James C. Makens, and Robert G. Roe, *Retail Management*, Hinsdale, IL: Dryden Press, 1975, p. 282.
6. David L. Kurtz, H. Robert Dodge, and Jay E. Klompmaker, *Professional Selling* (Plano, Texas: Business Publications, 1976), p. 274.
7. Raymond A. Marquardt, James C. Makens, and Robert G. Roe, *Retail Management*, Hinsdale, IL: Dryden Press, 1975, p. 283.
8. Ibid., p. 274.
9. See, Richard R. Still, Edward W. Cundiff, and Norman Govoni, *Sales Management: Decisions, Policies and Cases* (Englewood Cliffs, NJ: Prentice-Hall, 1976), p. 303.
10. Karen R. Gillespie and Joseph C. Hecht, *Retail Business Management* (New York: McGraw Hill, 1977), p. 323.
11. Ronald B. Marks, *Personal Selling* (Boston: Allyn and Bacon, 1975), p. 385.
12. Gilbert A. Churchill, Jr., Neil M. Ford, and Orville C. Walker, Jr., *Sales Force Management*, Homewood, IL: Irwin, 1993, p. 14.
13. Arthur J. Rawls, "Training Programs Must Reflect Today's Environment," *Chain Store Age Executive*, June 1989, pp. 60–63.
14. Warren S. Martin and Ben H. Collins, "Sales Technology Applications: Interactive Video Technology in Sales Training: A Case Study," *Journal of Personal Selling and Sales Management* 11 (Summer 1991), pp. 62–68.
15. Jack Falvey, "Forget the Sharks: Swim With Your Salespeople," *Sales and Marketing Management*, November 1980, p. 8.
16. "A New Realistic Approach to Training Retail Sales Personnel," *Retail Week*, September 1, 1981, pp. 15–21.
17. Stanley J. Marcus, *Minding the Store* (Boston: Little Brown, 1974).
18. This section is adapted from Churchill, Ford, and Walker, *Sales Force Management*, pp. 541–47.
19. Churchill, Ford, and Walker, *Sales Management*, p. 541.
20. Barton A. Weitz, Harish Sujan, and Mita Sujan, "Knowledge, Motivation and Adaptive Behavior: A Framework for Improving Selling Effectiveness," *Journal of Marketing*, October 1986, pp. 174–91.
21. Gilbert A. Churchill, Jr., Neil M. Ford, and Orville C. Walker, Jr., "Personal Characteristics of Salespeople and the Attractiveness of Alternate Rewards," *Journal of Business Research* 7 (1979), pp. 25–50.

22. See, for example, Thomas N. Ingram and Danny N. Bellenger, "Personal and Organizational Variables: Their Relative Effect on Valences of Industrial Salespeople," *Journal of Marketing Research,* May 1983, pp. 198–205 and Neil M. Ford, Orville C. Walker, Jr., and Gilbert A. Churchill, Jr., "Differences in Attractiveness of Alternative Rewards among Industrial Salespeople: Additional Evidence," *Journal of Business Research*, April 1985, pp. 123–38. Unfortunately, most studies on salesperson motivation have been conducted among industrial salespeople.

23. "With Commission System Selling Has Its Own Rewards," *Chain Store Age Executive*, March 1984, pp. 29–30.

24. Leonard Sloane, "Stores Offer Staff Incentives as Sales Commissions Return," *New York Times*, August 6, 1988, p. 33.

25. Ibid.

26. Dorothy S. Rogers and Mercia T. Grassi, *Retailing* (Hinsdale, IL: Dryden Press, 1988), p. 489.

27. Sloane, "Stores Offer."

28. The examples cited in this and the next paragraph are based on Amy Dunkin, "Now Salespeople Really Must Sell for Their Supper," *Business Week*, July 31, 1989, pp. 50–52 and Francine Schwardel, "Chain Finds Incentives a Hard Sell," *The Wall Street Journal*, July 5, 1990, pp. B1, B4.

29. For a review of the literature, see Valarie A. Zeithaml, A. Parasuraman, and Leonard L. Berry, "Problems and Strategies in Services Marketing," *Journal of Marketing* 49 (Spring 1985), pp. 33–46; Leonard L. Berry, "Big Ideas in Services Marketing," *Journal of Consumer Marketing*, Spring 1986, pp. 47–51; and John E. Bateson, *Managing Services Marketing Text and Readings* (Hinsdale, IL: Dryden Press, 1989). The discussion of service retailing has benefited greatly from an unpublished paper, *Marketing and the Service Sector,* by Gina Colarelli O'Connor.

30. Zeithaml, et al., "Problems and Strategies, p. 33.

31. William J. Regan, "The Service Revolution," *Journal of Marketing* 27 (July 1963), pp. 57–62.

32. Duane L. Davis, Joseph P. Guiltinan, and Wesley H. Jones, "Service Characteristics, Consumer Search, and the Classification of Retail Services," *Journal of Retailing* 55 (Fall 1979), pp. 3–21. See also Christopher H. Lovelock, *Services Marketing* (Englewood Cliffs, NJ: Prentice-Hall, 1991), especially Chapter 4.

33. This section is based on Christopher H. Loverock, "Classifying Services to Gain Strategic Marketing Insights," *Journal of Marketing* 47 (Summer 1983), pp. 9–20.

34. See John E. G. Bateson, "Why We Need Service Marketing," in Conceptual and Theoretical Foundations in Marketing, ed. by O. C. Ferrel, S. W. Brown, and C. W. Lamb, Jr., (Chicago: American Marketing Association, 1977), pp. 131–46; and Christopher H. Lovelock, "Classifying Services to Gain Strategic Marketing Insights," *Journal of Marketing* 47 (Summer 1983), pp. 9–20.

35. James L. Heskett, *Managing in the Service Economy* (Cambridge, MA: Harvard Business School Press, 1986), p. 38.

36. W. Earl Sasser, Jr., "Match Supply and Demand in the Service Industries," *Harvard Business Review* 54 (November–December 1976), pp. 133–40.

37. Heskett, *Service Economy*, p. 62.

38. John A. Czepiel, Michael R. Solomon, Carol F. Surprenant, and Evelyn G. Gutman, "Service Encounters: An Overview," in *The Service Encounter*, ed. by John A. Czepiel, Michael R. Solomon, and Carol F. Surprenant (Lexington, MA: D. C. Heath, 1985), p. 3.

39. J. Richard McCallum and Wayne Harrison, "Interdependence in the Service Encounter," in *The Service Encounter*, ed. by Czepiel, et al., pp. 35–48.

40. J. E. Swan and L. J. Coombs, "Product Performance and Consumer Satisfaction: A New Concept," *Journal of Marketing* 40 (April 1976), pp. 26–32.

41. Lovelock, "Classifying Services," p. 10.

42. Heskett, *Service Economy*.

43. Ibid.

44. Leonard L. Berry, "Delivering Excellent Service in Retailing," *Retailing Issues Letter* 1 (April 1988), Arthur Andersen and Co.

45. Heskett, *Service Economy*, p. 128.

APPENDIX TO CHAPTER 17

Measuring Price Sensitivity through Trade-off Analysis

Trade-off or conjoint analysis is a market research technique by which service firms commonly measure consumers' sensitivity to price and to other attributes. Trade-off analysis provides an estimate of how many consumers are likely to use a service at various prices and also how other service attributes affect demand.

To illustrate trade-off analysis, consider the following example: Fix-It Corporation plans to offer repair services to personal computer owners in a city in the Northeast. To utilize the service, computer owners will have to buy annual repair contracts from the firm for a fixed fee. The repair contracts entitle the customers to call the company any time their computers break down. The company then sends a technician to the person's home within four hours and repairs the computer without further charge.

The company has estimated that it will incur fixed costs of $4 million per year and variable costs of $40 per contract. It has also estimated that 2 million personal computer owners live in the city. The managers wonder how much they should charge for the service. They realize that the likelihood of a customer buying a repair contract will depend greatly on its annual price.

To judge customer sensitivity to price, the company commissioned a survey of 1,000 personal computer owners. The first part of the survey questionnaire's two parts explained the proposed service concept. The second posed three trade-off questions that asked the respondents whether they would sign up for the service given three alternative price schedules: $50 per year, $75 per year, and $100 per year.

The company found that 14 percent of the computer owners are likely to sign up at a fee of $50 per year, but only 11 percent of the owners said they would use the service at an annual fee of $75. A $100 a year fee would reduce consumer response even further, attracting only 4 percent of the respondents. Which price should the firm charge?

Exhibit 17A.1   *Profits for Fix-It Corporation at Three Price Levels*

Price ($) (1)	Margin per Customer ($) (2)	Percentage of Owners Likely to Sign Up (3)	Total Number of Computer Owners (4)	Expected Number of Customers (5)	Total Margin ($) (6)	Fixed Costs ($) (7)	Expected Profit ($) (8)
$50	$10	14	2 million	0.28 million	$2.8 million	$4 million	– $1.2 million
75	35	11	2 million	0.22 million	7.7 million	4 million	3.7 million
100	60	4	2 million	0.08 million	4.8 million	4 million	0.8 million

(2) = Price – 40
(5) = (3) × (4)
(6) = (5) × (2)
(8) = (6) – (7)

The firm can determine its optimal price by calculating the amount of profit it would earn at each of the three price levels, and selecting the one that maximizes expected profits. These calculations are shown in Exhibit 17A.1. The best price, $75 a year, would yield a profit of $3.7 million a year. Although more customers would sign up at a price of $50, the increase does not compensate for the lower margin per contract. The firm would actually incur a loss at this price, despite attracting 60,000 more customers. Margins would improve at a price of $100 a year, but the firm could expect only 80,000 customers to sign up at this price, reducing total revenue significantly. The $75 price represents the best trade-off between the extra customers attracted by a lower price and the increased margin from a higher price.

Trade-off analysis also helps firms judge customer sensitivity to other service attributes. For example, Fix-It Corporation can find out how many more customers are likely to sign up if it reduces the response time from four hours to two hours. By trade-off analysis, the firm can also identify customer segments with different price sensitivities and different preferences for service attributes. It is possible, for example, that small businesses and professionals are less price sensitive than other personal computer owners, but they prefer a two-hour response time. The company could accommodate these differences in a dual-pricing system, charging a higher price for those who want a response within two hours and a lower price for a four-hour response. Because it can help managers answer important strategic questions in designing service attributes, the use of trade-off analysis is growing rapidly.

CASES

Video Case
Wal-Mart Stores, Inc.

The day in the summer of 1964 when Sam Walton opened his second store in the small town of Harrison, Arkansas, was a hot one. The temperature in the parking lot reached 115 degrees. In fact, it was so hot that some of the truckload of watermelons stacked in front of the store began to pop, creating a huge mess. The mess continued inside. "It was just terrible," recalls one long-time Walton associate.

From this less than impressive beginning has sprung one of the most talked about business enterprises of the 1980s and America's most admired retail firm—Wal-Mart Stores. In 1992 Wal-Mart generated more than $55 billion in sales, which was 25 percent higher than the previous year. Only the retail giant Sears has more sales than Wal-Mart, but the gap is closing fast. With its impressive growth, Wal-Mart is soon expected to become America's largest retail firm.

The story of Wal-Mart's emergence as the premier retailer in the United States is legendary. After graduating from the University of Missouri in 1940, Sam Walton joined J.C. Penney as a trainee. His stint at Penney was cut short, however, by World War II. On returning from the war, Sam Walton opened a Ben Franklin outlet in Arkansas and soon became the company's largest franchisee with 14 outlets. But Walton, who was an astute observer of retail trends, quickly realized that the wheel of retailing was turning. It was the early 1960s and K mart outlets were opening in suburbs across America. Walton approached the management of Ben Franklin with the idea of opening discount stores in rural markets, but the company turned down his proposal.

After this rejection, Walton, and his brother James "Bud" Walton, founded Wal-Mart. Going against the conventional wisdom that discount stores were suited only to metropolitan areas or large towns, the brothers opened the first Wal-Mart store in 1962 in the small town of Rogers, Arkansas. Two years later, they opened the next Wal-Mart store in Harrison, Arkansas, and by the end of the decade the Walton brothers operated 18 Wal-Mart stores in Arkansas, Missouri, Kansas, and Oklahoma.

In October 1970, the company went public and started an expansion program that is still continuing. By the end of 1979, 276 Wal-Mart stores were open in 11 states. Sales increased from $44 million in 1970 to $1.248 billion in 1979. By the end of 1988, sales had reached $20 billion from just over 1,200 stores in 26 states. Over the last five years sales have increased by over 240 percent.

What impresses observers about Wal-Mart is not just growth in sales, but that profits and sales have increased in tandem. Wal-Mart stores have one of the highest profit margins among all discount and general merchandise retailers. Profits for 1992 were nearly $2 billion, a 24 percent increase from the previous year. Since it went public in 1970, Wal-Mart's shares have strongly appreciated in value. A $1,000 investment in the company in 1970 is now worth more than a half of a million dollars. Stock analysts throughout the country are unanimous in praising Wal-Mart. Fantastic" is the verdict of one analyst. Others call it America's best-managed firm.

CUSTOMER FOCUS

Wal-Mart outlets are designed to offer one-stop family shopping in 36 departments including family apparel, health and beauty aids, household needs, electronics, toys, fabrics and crafts, automotive supplies, lawn and patio furniture, jewelry, and shoes. In addition, some stores have pharmacies, tire, battery and automotive centers, garden centers, or snack bars.

From the beginning, the company has focused on small town and rural markets ignored by large, national chains. Although it does have outlets in Dallas, Houston, St. Louis, and Kansas City, most stores are located in towns of 5,000 to 25,000 people in the Midwest and sunbelt states. Stores range in size from 29,000 square feet to more than 80,000 square feet, depending on the size of the market.

Wal-Mart's strategy is to offer quality name-brand merchandise at low prices every day rather than just during sales. Wal-Mart strives to provide customers with a clean, pleasant, and friendly shopping atmosphere. Its satisfaction-guaranteed policy allows customers to return any merchandise bought from the store for a refund without any questions being asked. As Sam Walton put it: The customer is the boss.

Customers walking into a Wal-Mart store are welcomed by a "people greeter"—an employee whose task it is to personally welcome each customer entering the store. The idea was first suggested by a store employee and with Sam Walton's encouragement the idea became an integral part of the company's philosophy of "aggressive hospitality." The aggressive hospitality motto was proposed by Sam Walton in a chat with store managers broadcast over the firm's satellite network. He suggested that sales associates should look approaching customers in the eye, greet them, and offer to help. This simple gesture, Walton suggested, works magic on the customers and differentiates Wal-Mart from other retailers. At the end of the broadcast, listeners raised their right hand and pledged in the name of Sam Walton to smile at all customers, look them in the eye, and offer greetings.

MERCHANDISE MANAGEMENT

The company's six-channel satellite system links each store to its headquarters in Bentonville, Arkansas. The system continuously tracks sales of items at each outlet, approves credit in five seconds, and links each store to the company's regional distribution network. Wal-Mart's distribution system is state-of-the-art in computerized inventory control and management. Faced with a lack of reliable independent distributors and wholesalers in small town markets, Wal-Mart was forced to develop its own distribution system for moving goods efficiently from a variety of manufacturers to its network of outlets.

Under the leadership of David Glass and Don Soderquist, the current chief executive and chief operating officers, respectively, Wal-Mart pioneered the application of modern communication technology to manage and control inventory. By the mid-1970s, all Wal-Mart stores were equipped with computers and scanners. The computers and satellite channels provide a vital communication link between stores, distribution centers, and headquarters. This link and the capability to electronically interchange data (EDI) with vendors are the backbone of the inventory management system. The system cuts the length of the typical order cycle to only 36 hours. Each order goes through a sequence of five steps:

1. Optical scanners at the checkout counter track sales of all items and monitor inventory at the store.
2. When the stock of an item reaches a predetermined minimum point, an order is transmitted electronically to a computer at headquarters in Bentonville.

3. Orders from different stores are consolidated and again electronically transmitted to the manufacturer. The manufacturer then schedules shipment to Wal-Mart distribution centers.

4. Shipments are received at the distribution center and labels are affixed to each box indicating the location of the store where it is to be shipped. Optical scanners read the bar codes on the labels, automatically directing the box to the proper truck bay.

5. When full, the truck is dispatched to the store.

The communication system is a valuable asset for the firm's buyers and merchandise managers, too. With the help of computer terminals, buyers located at Bentonville can get immediate information on how any item is selling at each store. Based on this data they can adjust their purchase plans for each item. By keeping a constant tab on store sales, buyers can better synchronize their purchases with demand. It also gives them information that is useful in negotiating and dealing with vendors. The satellite channels have also been a direct means for the headquarters staff to communicate with the far-flung network of outlets. Merchandise managers, for example, continuously monitor prices at competing stores, especially at K mart outlets. Often prices have to be changed in light of this information. In urgent cases, the information is broadcast from Bentonville to all the stores instantaneously.

CORPORATE CULTURE

Not all of Wal-Mart's success can be attributed to computer and communication hardware. Wal-Mart's corporate culture—the set of values that everybody in the firm shares—has played a big part, too. Wal-Mart's culture stresses the involvement of all employees in managerial decision-making. This culture shows through in the attitudes of top level managers, and all employees are encouraged to get involved in managing the company. All employees at Wal-Mart are known as "associates" and are treated as partners. Most employees, for example, have access to company records that only top managers of most companies are privileged to see.

To motivate its employees, the company instituted a broad-based profit sharing plan that includes even hourly workers at stores and distribution centers. Each store is given a profit goal, and if the store exceeds this goal, all employees get a share of the additional profit. Employees also earn a bonus if the store reduces shrinkage or holds it below a set target. As a result, Wal-Mart's shrinkage is estimated to be 50 percent below the industry average.

Another part of the company philosophy is hands-on management. Sam Walton visited each Wal-Mart outlet at least once a year. Many senior managers spend half their time flying around the country in one of the firm's 11 turboprops visiting stores. When at Bentonville, they pore over reams of computer outputs tracking store sales and cost data.

DIVERSIFICATION

During the 1980s, Wal-Mart diversified into a number of new ventures. In 1983 Wal-Mart opened the first Sam's Wholesale Club in Oklahoma City. Today, the chain has more than 100 of these outlets throughout the country. Wholesale clubs are low margin, high volume cash and carry operations geared mainly toward small business customers who pay an annual membership fee to shop. Dot Discount Drugstores and Helen's Arts and Crafts stores are two more divisions. In 1987 the company also started a chain of superstores called Hypermarkets USA. Hypermarkets, a concept popular in Europe, offer a full line of groceries and general merchandise in huge five-acre stores. The first Hypermarket outlet opened in Garland, Texas, and two more outlets have been added since. One diversification venture, a do-it-yourself building supply chain, failed.

3. Discuss Wal-Mart's corporate culture and comment on how this culture impacts its performance.
4. How has Wal-Mart maintained its growth over the years?

Assignments

1. Describe how Wal-Mart's marketing strategy enhances value to customers and differentiates it from competitors.
2. What role does technology play in Wal-Mart's success?

Sources: Based on John Huey, "Wal-Mart: Will It Take Over the World?" *Fortune*, January 30, 1989, pp. 52–61; George Waldon, "Bargains and Billionaires," *Spirit*, November 1988, p. 34; Vertanig G. Vartan, "Many Bullish on Wal-Mart," *New York Times*, June 10, 1987; and company Annual Reports and Fact Sheets. Fortune's Service 500, *Fortune*, May 31, 1993.

Case 1
Sylvia's Dream

"Opening a retail store has always been my dream," said Sylvia Thornton. As a child, I used to make believe that I ran a store. One day it would be a supermarket, another day a clothing store or a bookstore. While my friends played with their doll houses, I played with my make-believe stores."

The days of make believe were now over for Sylvia. Soon she would be graduating from college and embarking on her professional career, but the dream of running a store had not died. Although she had job offers from two companies, Sylvia wanted to open her own bookstore instead. Only three bookstores served Silvertown, where she lived. Two of them, outlets of large national chains, were located in a mall. The other was the campus bookstore at the university. Personally, Sylvia did not care for either the chain stores or the campus store very

much. "My store will be unique," she told her friends. "Being independent, I can focus on the needs of the local customers much better," she argued.

She planned to open the store in a small shopping complex near the university campus. According to Sylvia, this would enable her to attract students as well as many parents and tourists who visit the campus. Sylvia's intention was to make the store distinctive through a high level of personal service. In speaking with friends, Sylvia had noted that many were dissatisfied with the personal service they received at either the chain stores or the campus bookstore. The employees at these stores were frequently uninformed about books in general and not very helpful to customers.

Another common complaint was other stores' limited selections of special-interest and professional books. The chain stores carried mainly popular novels and how-to books, while the campus bookstore sold only textbooks.

To transform her plan into reality, Sylvia intended to apply for a loan from the local bank. The application form called for a detailed report on the store's proposed marketing strategy, listing three specific questions:

1. What is the store's intended target market?
2. How will the store create value for its customers?
3. How will the store differentiate itself from its competitors?

Assignments

1. Assume the role of Sylvia Thornton and answer the bank's questions based on the information given in the case and your own experience and knowledge of bookstores and consumer behavior.
2. Discuss the major decisions that Sylvia Thornton will have to make once the loan is approved.

Case 2
Joanna's Place

As she sat at her desk in the tiny office behind the store, Joanna Price looked across her desk at the calendar. Exactly three years had passed since she had inherited Joanna's Place from her parents. The store, which opened about 10 years earlier, sold fashionable, ready-to-wear women's apparel. It attracted a small, but loyal group of customers with its service and fashionable merchandise. Although it was one of the area's smallest ready-to-wear apparel stores, Joanna's parents were happy with the steady profits that it generated.

Joanna's Place is located in Greenville (population 98,000) along with four other stores that sell women's apparel. The largest is Cody's, a branch of a regional department store chain. Another competitor, The Woman's Shop, is a branch of a specialty apparel chain headquartered in Columbus, Ohio. Local residents own the other two stores, which are about the same size as Joanna's Place. One of them, Ms., opened about three years earlier, while the Fashion Store had been a Greenville landmark for over 15 years. All five stores are located within a few blocks of each other in Greenville's central shopping district.

On taking over the store three years earlier, Joanna had initiated a number of changes. In an effort to attract more customers and increase sales, she had added a number of new lines of merchandise in the mid- to low-priced range. She also opened a discount section that sold closeout merchandise at bargain prices. Unfortunately, sales did not increase as much as expected. The changes did not attract many new customers and many of the store's regular customers seemed to have stopped coming. The twin burdens of high inventory costs and low sales forced Joanna to reduce the number of salespeople and cut down on advertising.

The turn of events worried Joanna. She realized that something had to be done to reverse the trend. Two months earlier she had hired David Bass, a recent marketing graduate, to help her develop a strategic plan for the store. David had done extensive research on the store, its competitors, and its customers. As part of his research, David conducted a survey of 400 women between the ages of 25 and 45 to determine their opinions about women's apparel stores in Greenville. On the table before Joanna lay the folder containing a summary of David's findings. Apprehensively, she opened the folder and reviewed the two summary tables David had prepared.

Exhibit 1 showed how respondents evaluated Joanna's Place and each of the four competitors in terms of six attributes. Results of a preliminary focus group interview with 10 women had indicated that these store attributes generally affected selection of an outlet for clothing purchases. The table measured these beliefs on a 7-point scale. For the first five attributes, a low score on the scale indicated dissatisfaction with the store on that attribute, while a high score indicated satisfaction. For example, a high score on the first attribute would indicate that customers believed the store had good quality merchandise. The interpretation of the price attribute, however, needs special mention. A high score on this attribute indicated that respondents believed prices to be high, while a low score indicated an impression of low prices.

Exhibit 2 shows the differences in relative importance of different store attributes to two groups of respondents: (a) those who mentioned that they currently plan to shop at Joanna's Place and (b) women who said they used to shop there in the past, but plan to do so no longer. This table also measured the importance of each store attribute on a 7-point scale, with a low score indicating less importance.

Assignments

1. From the information in the case, prepare a strategic group map of women's apparel stores in Greenville.
2. What problems inhibit Joanna's current strategy?
3. What advice would you give to Joanna Price?

EXHIBIT 1   *Consumer Evaluation of Greenville Stores*

Characteristic	Joanna's Place	The Woman's Store	Fashion Store	Ms.	Cody's
Quality of merchandise	4.8	6.4	6.1	4.0	6.6
Selection (assortment)	4.4	6.5	6.5	5.0	5.7
Quality of sales personnel	4.2	5.5	6.4	3.8	6.7
Liberal return policy	5.6	6.5	6.0	5.8	6.5
Up-to-date fashions	5.5	5.8	6.4	4.5	6.7
Prices	6.2	6.0	5.4	4.5	6.7

EXHIBIT 2   *A Comparison of Current and Past Patrons*

Characteristic	Current	Past
Quality of merchandise	5.5	6.8
Selection (assortment)	6.0	6.2
Quality of sales personnel	5.2	6.0
Liberal return policy	4.8	5.0
Up-to-date fashions	5.0	6.0
Prices	6.5	5.7

Case 3
Sandwiches Etc.

Sandwiches Etc. runs a chain of franchised sandwich shops in the Southwest. In 1986 Carol Smith, owner of the Sandwiches Etc. franchising company, opened the first store in Denver. The store sold six types of sandwiches, three salads, and a variety of bottled and canned drinks. Its proximity to many commercial buildings quickly made the store a popular lunch spot for office workers. In 1987, the first full year of store operations, sales exceeded $225,000. Encouraged by her success, Carol opened a second store about 15 blocks from the existing one, near another office complex. Sales in the second store also exceeded her expectations.

Encouraged by the success of her two stores, Carol wanted to venture into other cities in Colorado and some neighboring states. At about this time, Carol met with Eugene Smith, president of the local Chamber of Commerce. Eugene suggested that Carol look into the possibility of franchising the operation, since she would have difficulty raising enough capital to expand on her own.

By the end of 1987, Carol had entered into a number of franchise agreements and 27 franchised Sandwiches Etc. outlets were open in Colorado, New Mexico, and California. Tony Smith operated 15 of the franchised outlets under a master franchise agreement with Carol. Individual franchisees operated the remaining stores. A franchisee paid Carol a one-time initiation fee of $40,000 and an annual franchise fee equaling 4 percent of sales. In addition, franchisees contributed 1.5 percent of their sales to a common advertising fund which covered the cost of all local and regional advertising. Carol bore the cost of developing advertising and promotional materials. In addition, Carol trained store managers and provided new product ideas.

As part of the same franchise system, each outlet had a similar look both inside and outside. Carol personally visited each store at least once every four months. Supervising the franchise stores kept her so busy that her sister had taken over the day-to-day management of the two Denver stores.

Carol had been pleased with the franchise agreement at the beginning. Trouble started to brew, however, in 1992. Faced with increases in the cost of supplies as well as rising rents in many cities, some franchisees became lax in quality control. Carol's policy stated that stores make sandwiches only with fresh bread supplied each morning. Carol had personally selected the local bakeries that supplied each store and checked their quality carefully. On a recent visit to a California store, she had found that the franchisee had shifted to a different bakery that supplied only two days a week. Enraged at this violation of standards, Carol had confronted the manager and without mincing words made it clear that the practice had to stop.

On returning home from the trip, Carol wrote a letter to each franchisee reiterating the need to maintain quality. She asked that the other franchisees join her in condemning the offending California outlet. The response to her letter was surprising and quite disturbing.

A number of the franchisees, including Tony Smith, supported the California franchisee and stated that they had similar plans of their own.

"While our revenues are satisfactory, our profits are inadequate," wrote one franchisee. "We must cut our costs to increase profits," he added. Some franchisees also complained of the required contribution to the advertising fund, suggesting that Carol rather than the individual franchisees should bear advertising costs. Of all the letters, Tony Smith's was the most disturbing to Carol. He mentioned plans to sell pizza, beer, and other snacks from his outlets. "I must seek all avenues for improving profits," he wrote.

Carol feared chaos if she allowed franchisees to go their own ways. In her view, a franchise must have a uniform image and all outlets must sell the same products. Carol felt that her venture was in trouble and wondered what to do.

Assignments

1. What options does Carol Smith have?
2. How could she best deal with the situation?

Case 4
Get Well Pharmacy

Get Well Pharmacy, owned and operated by Douglas Bass, is situated on the Upper West Side of Manhattan. A registered pharmacist, Douglas has operated the store at the same location for over 20 years. In an area where stores seem to come and go, Get Well has been a familiar landmark. It has a loyal following among local residents, especially senior citizens. As a business venture, Get Well has been a suc-cess. The store has generated a moderate, but steady increase in profits except for the last two years.

While happy with his past performance, Douglas is concerned about the future. His Upper West Side neighborhood is changing rapidly. Since 1985 a number of new high-rise apartment buildings have been built, two of them within five blocks of Get Well. Many old houses have been remodeled and converted to luxury apartments. This has produced a steady change in the age distribution of the area's population. The number of households headed by young working couples has risen. Many of these families have young children, typically less than five years old. On the other hand, the number of people aged 65 or older has dropped.

The change in demographic composition has brought a change in competition, too. Last year two new outlets of drugstore chains opened in the area. Just six months ago the local supermarket, located in the same block as Get Well, expanded its health and beauty aid (HBA) department and added a number of popular over-the-counter (OTC) medicines to its merchandise assortment. (OTC medicines can be purchased without doctors' prescriptions.)

Since the new drugstores and the supermarket are part of large regional chains, they enjoy considerable economies of scale in supplies and advertising. The supermarket chain, for example, spends well over $1 million to advertise in the New York City area. While most of the supermarket ads feature produce and grocery items, they periodically include HBA and OTC products. Moreover, any advertising by the chain increases consumer awareness and drawing power of the local supermarket. In contrast, advertising for Get Well is limited to a quarter-page listing in the Yellow Pages and occasional small ads in the *Westsider*, a local weekly newspaper with limited circulation.

By pooling their purchases, outlets in a chain can obtain merchandise more cheaply than independent stores. Get Well's prices for comparable HBA products were generally 5 to 10 percent higher than the chain outlets. For example, Get Well sold a pack of disposable diapers for $23.99, while the chain stores charged $21.99. While the same situation generally holds for OTC products, Douglas has followed a policy of matching chain store prices for some of the most popular items such as Dimetapp and Tylenol.

However, the chain stores' frequent special discounts often undercut his efforts to match their prices. Just last week, for example, one of the chain drugstores was selling Tylenol at 20 percent off its regular price.

Most of the products at Get Well are also available at one of the three chain stores. Despite this similarity in merchandise assortment, a major difference separates Get Well from the chain stores. Nearly 60 percent of Get Well's revenue comes from filling prescriptions, while prescription sales account for only 30 percent of total sales at the chain drugstores. The supermarket did not have a prescription service. Get Well's prescription service is well-known for good service and the ability to fill almost any prescription. The chain drugstores often lacked needed medicine and made customers wait several hours before filling prescriptions. Get Well customers often have their doctors phone in prescriptions so that they will be ready when the customers arrive at the pharmacy. Get Well also provides free delivery of medicine for senior citizens and for anybody whose purchases exceed $25. It provides other services like monthly billing and computerized records for filing insurance claims.

Despite increasing competition, Douglas is not yet ready to quit. He has reviewed the situation thoroughly and has concluded that he can continue to operate his store profitably if he can reorient its strategy to meet the challenges of the new environment.

Assignments

1. Discuss how the changing demographic composition has affected Get Well.
2. How should Get Well reorient its strategy to respond to the changing demographic environment?
3. How can Douglas successfully compete against the chain stores?

Case 5
Magnum Retail Corporation (MRC)

MRC is a large, diversified retail company with sales exceeding $9 billion headquartered in Madison, Wisconsin. MRC has located outlets in all but five of the 50 U.S. states and in three Canadian provinces. The original company began in the early 1900s to operate full-line department stores in Madison, Minneapolis, and Detroit. MRC continued to concentrate its business on department stores until the early 1970s. Since that time, however, the company has diversified into a number of other retail businesses and expanded its network of outlets. Currently, MRC groups its businesses into four major divisions: (a) department stores, (b) discount stores, (c) specialty stores, and (d) off-price apparel outlets.

Peter Taylor, MRC's chief financial officer, joined the firm in 1980 as manager of its department store outlet in Denver. He rose quickly through the corporate ranks and became Chief Financial Officer in 1990.

Every year the top managers of MRC met for a planning session to discuss the corporation's long-range goals and evaluate the performance of its divisions. The next planning meeting was scheduled to take place within a month. Customarily, the meeting opened with a few words from the CEO and then the financial officer presented an appraisal of each division's performance and a set of recommendations for the future. Further discussion then centered on this report.

In preparing for the meeting, Peter asked his staff to prepare a series of tables summarizing the performance of the four divisions over the previous three years. He received the tables the previous evening. As he studied the tables, he wondered what he should say at the meeting.

Assignments

1. Prepare a growth-gain matrix for MRC for the period 1990 to 1992.
2. Prepare a short report on the performance of MRC's four divisions.

EXHIBIT 1   Sales and Profits by Business Segment (millions of dollars)

Segment	1990		1991		1992	
	Sales	Profits	Sales	Profits	Sales	Profits
Discount stores	3,550	236	3,931	278	4,345	311
Specialty stores	2,141	223	2,527	245	2,862	160
Department stores	1,548	107	1,450	121	1,458	166
Off-price apparel stores	280	20	349	20	376	2

EXHIBIT 2   Assets and Capital Expenditures by Business Segment (millions of dollars)

Segment	1990		1991		1992	
	Assets	Expenditures	Assets	Expenditures	Assets	Expenditures
Discount stores	1,374	110	1,519	138	2,178	598
Specialty stores	1,329	165	1,615	177	1,817	243
Department stores	727	33	738	37	739	31
Off-price apparel stores	151	25	210	42	318	49

EXHIBIT 3   Industry Growth by Business Segment, Sales Growth 1990–1992[a]

Department stores	3.2%
Discount stores	15.6%
Specialty stores	6.2%
Off-price apparel stores	16.1%

[a]Average growth in geographic markets in which MRC businesses compete.

Case 6
The Saratoga

Saratoga is the largest store in Green City. The Silverstein brothers, Jeff and Moe, opened the original Saratoga store in 1912 as a women's clothing store. The Saratoga had, however, expanded several times by adding new lines of merchandise. Presently the store sells men's, women's, and children's clothing; cosmetics; and home furnishings. It is estimated that the store accounted for about 17 percent of total sales of clothing and home furnishings in the Green City metropolitan area.

Green City is a major town in southwestern Ohio with population of about 1.5 million. The Green City area grew rapidly during the 1960s because of economic expansion in the region. New businesses attracted a large number of blue- and white-collar workers, giving The Saratoga the opportunity to increase its sales. Although regional growth had attracted new competitors, too, timely expansions had maintained The Saratoga's position as Green City's premier retailer. The Saratoga now operates three stores in the Green City metropolitan area:

• The flagship downtown store, which has been extensively remodeled on a number of occasions since its opening in 1912, most recently in 1978. The downtown store occupies a five-story building: the selling area fills the bottom three floors, and the top two floors house executive offices.

- The store in Green City's first major suburban mall, which opened in 1969. As the major retailer in the area, The Saratoga moved in as an anchor tenant with 200,000 square feet of multilevel space.
- A 180,000-square-foot store opened in 1972 to anchor a mall in a secondary shopping district in the northern part of Green City. This store replaced a 155,000-square-foot store the firm had opened five miles away in 1967.

The retail environment in Green City resembles those of most metropolitan areas. Besides The Saratoga, two other department stores serve the area, both branches of large regional chains. Green City is also home to a Sears, a J.C. Penney, and two K mart outlets. In addition, three major local discount stores sell clothes and home furnishings. In 1983, two off-price clothing stores opened in Green City, one operated by T.J. Maxx and the other by Marshall's. A number of clothing specialty stores also compete in the area including a Limited and a Gap. Rumors predict that Green City's first Benetton outlet will open within six months.

Michael Silverstein, grandson of Jeff Silverstein, joined The Saratoga in 1988. After spending four years in various merchandising and operating positions, he became Executive Vice President of Planning in 1992. His main responsibility was to coordinate the store's strategic planning process and evaluate the operating performance of its departments.

While he had participated in planning meetings in the past, Michael knew that this year was going to be different. He felt all eyes on him. The planning meeting had been scheduled for April 1, which meant that he had to circulate his initial report within a week.

To prepare for his task, Michael had commissioned a series of studies to provide data on which to base his recommendations. As he looked through the study report, three tables looked particularly important to him. The first two reported The Saratoga's share of market sales in the Green City area by age and income categories. The third table showed The Saratoga's share of market sales for five merchandise categories: women's apparel, men's apparel, infant's and children's apparel, cosmetics, and home furnishings. These five categories together accounted for over 75 percent of The Saratoga's total sales. Each table provided data for the current year as well as the two preceding years.

Assignments

1. What do the data in the three tables imply for The Saratoga?
2. What should Michael Silverstein recommend to the planning group?

EXHIBIT 1   Market Share by Age Classification

Age Group	1990	1991	1992
Under 25	16%	15%	12%
25–34	17%	17%	13%
35–44	15%	13%	13%
45–54	16%	18%	19%
Over 54	18%	18%	20%

EXHIBIT 2   *Market Share by Income Classification*

Income Group	1990	1991	1992
Under $15,000	11%	10%	9%
$15,000–$24,999	13%	13%	12%
$25,000–$34,999	19%	20%	22%
Over $35,000	23%	22%	23%

EXHIBIT 3   *Market Share by Merchandise Category*

Merchandise	1990	1991	1992
Women's apparel	19%	20%	21%
Teen's apparel	20%	18%	16%
Men's apparel	22%	19%	18%
Infants' and children's apparel	18%	17%	15%
Cosmetics	23%	22%	20%
Home furnishings	14%	15%	17%

Case 7
Alpine Ski Shop

From its location in a town in New England, the Alpine Ski Shop sells ski equipment, camping and hiking gear, athletic shoes, and outdoor clothing. Two friends who had just graduated from the local university with degrees in marketing and retailing opened the store in 1975. After an initial period of uncertainty, the store has recorded increasing sales and profits each year since 1982. The latest income statement and balance sheet for Alpine Ski Shop appear in Exhibits 7.1 and 7.2, respectively, in Chapter 7.

Alpine's two owners are currently considering a plan to expand by renting a vacant storefront adjacent to the existing store. They expect the cost of expansion to total $37,000. After a number of planning meetings, the two owners have concluded that if they expand:

- Net sales will increase by $80,000 a year.
- Wages and salaries will increase by $5,000 a year.
- Rents and occupancy costs will increase by $12,000 a year.
- Advertising and promotion will increase by $4,000 a year.

- Costs of goods sold will consume 63 percent of sales.
- Inventory investment will increase by $30,000.
- Fixed assets will increase by $7,000.
- They can obtain a bank loan at 10 percent annual interest.

The one issue on which the two owners disagree is the amount of the bank loan. One owner wants to take out a new loan for $20,000, but the other would like to fund the expansion completely through their own funds.

To decide on the best funding option and to evaluate the financial consequences of their expansion plan, the owners approached Bruce Harris, a principal of Strategic Planning Consultants with considerable experience in financial planning for retail firms. He suggested that Alpine conduct a what-if analysis using the Strategic Profit Model (SPM). Specifically, he recommended that the store calculate the expected return on net worth (RONW) under two new scenarios, one in which the owners fund all of the $37,000 needed for expansion, and another in which they take out a $20,000 loan from the bank. He further recommended that, as a contingency, the owners should also evaluate how the store's RONW would be affected if the expansion increased sales by $75,000 instead of $80,000. He suggested they compare the results of these analyses to the store's current RONW to decide on the desirability of expansion and the best way to fund the expansion.

Assignments

Using the information in the case and in Exhibits 7.1 and 7.2, calculate the expected return on net worth for Alpine Ski Shop in the following four scenarios:

1. Sales increase by $80,000 and the firm obtains a bank loan for $20,000.
2. Sales increase by $80,000 and it obtains no bank loan.
3. Sales increase by $75,000 and it obtains a bank loan for $20,000.
4. Sales increase by $75,000 and it obtains no bank loan.

Compare the results from the four scenarios with the current RONW and recommend a course of action for the owners. Calculate RONW using the SPM framework presented in Chapter 7.

Case 8
City Drugstores, Inc.

Michael James is Vice-President of City Drugstores, a privately owned pharmacy chain in Fairfax, Virginia. Recently, Michael had commissioned a feasibility study for a new site location. He, however, has mixed feelings about the location, believing there are better opportunities elsewhere. There, also, is some difference of opinion with his father, Morton James, who is President.

Up to this point, little market research has been used for store locations. Typically, in the past, Michael's father would locate a store near a major supermarket chain or within a university town. Michael strongly believes market analysis must replace this outdated type of location analysis. Therefore, Michael and his father have agreed that before a decision would be made on the proposed site, research would be done.

Over the years, City Drugstore has grown from a local chain in Fairfax to a profitable corporation with 62 stores located in central cities throughout the state of Virginia. This expansion was due to a combination of acquisitions, mergers, and new-store construction.

City Drugstore enjoys a good reputation because of its convenient location, competitive prices, and brand product line. Like many drugstore chains, City Drugstore has four core departments. The most profitable is prescription drugs, followed by over-the-counter drugs (OTC), cosmetics, and toiletries. A medium-size City Drugstore must register approximately three quarters of a million dollars in sales to break even. A profitable store will produce $150 in annual sales per square foot of selling space, with prescription drugs the most instrumental product line in generating volume.

THE PROPOSED LOCATION

Michael's father has asked him to consider a site near the local university, a state-supported institution with 15,000 students and located in Fairfax. Morton James was a graduate from the Pharmacy School in 1949. Recently, a fellow graduate, who is owner of Paramount Pharmacy and wishes to retire, offered to sell James his drugstore.

Paramount Pharmacy is both adjacent to and within one block of the university's three student residence halls and is located on the corner of a busy one-way street heading to the downtown business district. If this site was purchased, the Paramount Pharmacy would be razed and a modern City Drugstore built in its place. Estimated construction costs are $950,000 and other capital needs (assets) would amount to $475,000.

Annual fixed costs for operating a new drugstore are $160,000, with cost of goods expected to be 67 percent of sales and other variable costs estimated at 5 percent of sales.

Paramount Pharmacy attracts a small but loyal group of low- to middle-income customers and some university students and faculty. The Paramount Pharmacy, however, has not been very profitable nor competitive in recent years despite being the only drugstore within the immediate area. For example, Paramount has not taken advantage of university health service contracts (based on bidding) for prescription drugs to a local pharmacy. Often these contracts include prescriptions for several hundred students during the academic year.

Upon Michael James' urging, marketing faculty at the university were contacted for the study. It was agreed that a telephone survey of a representative sample of 200 residents living within census tracts surrounding the present Paramount Pharmacy and university fringe would be questioned. In addition, a survey was mailed to 250 college students living in the nearby dorms.

An estimate was to be made of the traffic flow past the planned store and the proportion of customers it could attract from this traffic. A rough guesstimate was also to be provided on walk-in traffic from other students, faculty, and staff. With this information, annual sales potential for the proposed site could be estimated.

The Jameses must make a decision within 30 days whether to buy out Paramount Pharmacy and build one of their own drugstores. Michael has reviewed the data that the researchers collected and needs to make a recommendation to his father.

RESEARCH FINDINGS

A summary of responses to some key questions in the resident survey are presented in Exhibit 1.

EXHIBIT 1 Do You Buy Prescription Drugs?

N = 201

	Number	Percentage
Yes	134	67
No	67	33

Where Do You Buy Prescription Drugs?

N = 174

	Number	Percentage
People's Drug	46	34
City Drug	37	28
Paramount	19	14
Revco	19	14
Other	53	40

Scores do not add up to 100 percent due to multiple responses.

Buying Frequency and Expenditures on Drugstore Items

N = 179

	Expenditures				
Frequency	Under $3	$3–$5	$5–$15	>$15[a]	Total
Daily	2	1	1	2	6
Twice per week	3	3	2	3	11
Once per week	9	8	19	2	38
Twice per month	7	10	14	9	40
Once per month	12	9	17	19	57
Other[b]	5	11	6	5	27
Total	38	42	59	40	179

[a]Assume none over $25.
[b]Assume once per six months on the average.

Would You Shop at a Modern Drugstore?

N = 196

	Number	Percentage
Yes	107	55
No	52	27
Don't know	37	18

Would You Shop at a City Drugstore?

N = 196

	Number	Percentage
Yes	156	84
No	15	8
Don't know	15	8

Why Would You Shop at a City Drugstore?

	Number	Percentage
Close and convenient	142	71
Cheaper prices	52	26
Better products	21	11
Already loyal to City Drug	28	14
Loyal to Paramount	8	4
Other	20	10

Scores do not add up to 100 percent due to multiple responses.

The data in Exhibit 1 are responses from households represented by randomly selected adults (18 years and older). The expenditure data tabulated represents individual purchases and has to be converted to household expenditure by multiplying it by the average number of (adult) spenders, i.e., 1.18. Average overall household size amounts to 2.27. Hint for estimating expenditures: try to substitute average dollar amounts for the tabulated ranges.

According to the latest U.S. Census data, the people (individuals) living in the target area number 2,949. Unfortunately, this data is four years old. The city's Planning Department has estimated that this mostly low-income population has been declining at an approximate rate of 1 percent per annum. According to the survey, the average household spends approximately 65 percent of all its drugstore purchases at one store (average purchase ratio).

In the student survey, on-campus dormitory students, as a whole, appear to have little store preference when buying prescription drugs. Approximately, 28 percent of the respondents didn't purchase prescription drugs. When buying health and beauty aid items, however, a significant number of respondents shop near campus.

Better than half of the students surveyed buy something at a drugstore at least twice a week. Over one-third buy at least once a month. This indicates a sizable number of students who are frequent purchasers of drugstore products. In fact, on their last visit to a drugstore, these students spent approximately $5 on the average.

When asked if they would shop at a modern drugstore at the Paramount site, half the dormitory student respondents were not sure, implying price, product offerings, and distance as factors to their decision to shop. If the drugstore were City Drug, almost two-thirds would shop there, with about one-third undecided.

Based on the survey data, the dormitory students' total monthly per capita expenditure in drugstores is estimated at $21.80 during the regular academic year. (Actual stay is 7.5 months due to Christmas and other holidays.) Average purchase ratio was found to be 60 percent while 62 percent of the students indicated they would shop at the new drugstore.

According to university records, the Fall and Spring dormitory population is 2,232 (all singles). During the three summer months, approximately 20 percent of this number attends school while staying in these dorms and spending approximately the same (per capita) monthly amount in drugstores. Some decline in student population, including dormitories, is expected during the next 10 years.

Traffic flow past the new store is estimated at 5,000 per day, for approximately 300 days per year (allowing for Sundays, holidays, and bad weather). This figure includes a roughly 20-percent duplication of the student population above. It is estimated that 5 percent of this traffic results in actual store visits and purchases, the latter averaging $5 per trip.

Based on a very limited survey and some rough estimates, walk-ins representing faculty, staff, and other students, are expected to spend roughly $30,000 per annum on drugstores in the vicinity of the intended new store.

Discussion Questions

1. Estimate the market potential for all drugstore sales in the area and using this figure as a base, also estimate the sales potential for the new City Drugstore.
2. Determine the expected profitability of the proposed store.
3. What are the main arguments for and against locating a City Drugstore on the intended site?
4. Based on your answers to the questions above, what should Michael James do? Why?

Source: Reprinted with permission from Dr. Michael W. Little and Dr. Heiko de B. Wijnholds, Virginia Commonwealth University.

Case 9
Xenon Supermarkets

At nearly 5 o'clock on a Friday evening Frank Green, Director of Real Estate Operations of Xenon Supermarkets, was getting ready to head for home. Before packing his briefcase, Frank sat down, as he always did on Friday afternoons, to check his calendar for the coming week. The big event the following week was a meeting on Project Argon. The management committee was to meet on Monday afternoon to discuss plans for new store locations in Argon City. At a meeting three months earlier, the management committee had accepted Frank's recommendation that the firm expand into the Argon City market. Expansion had been planned for the coming spring. Monday's meeting was scheduled to discuss and decide on specific sites in Argon for opening new stores. As the Director of Real Estate Operations, Frank was expected to recommend new store locations and also justify his choice to other members of the management committee.

COMPANY BACKGROUND

Headquartered in Chicago, Xenon Supermarkets was one of the fastest-growing supermarket chains in the Midwest. Although it operated five stores in Chicago, most Xenon stores were located in small- or medium-sized towns with populations of 50,000 to 100,000 people. Xenon stores served a number of such towns in the midwestern states of Iowa, Illinois, and Indiana. About seven years earlier, the company had consciously chosen the strategy of entering smaller towns often neglected by big supermarket chains. Once a particular market was chosen for expansion, the company usually built two or

three stores within two years. This resulted in increased market presence and name recognition as well as efficiencies in advertising and distribution. The strategy had proved to be highly successful in the past. In each of the previous five years, the company had entered three new towns, opening a total of seven stores each year. Argon City is one of the two markets Xenon planned to enter the following year. Frank realized that as soon as the Argon project was completed he would have to start work on the next project.

THE SITE-SELECTION DECISION

Frank approached the site-selection decision in three distinct stages. First, he chose a market for expansion (supermarket executives often use the term market in a geographic sense to mean a town or city). Factors such as population size, income, spending patterns on food, and existing competition were all important considerations in this decision.

Having chosen a market, the next step involved gathering information on potential sites for Xenon stores. Typically, Frank would spend a week to 10 days in the market talking to real estate agents and city officials and generally trying to get a feel for the market. Real estate agents provided information on available lots and the potential for new lots becoming available. Since most cities had their own zoning laws and city codes, Frank always met with city officials to learn about them.

As one outcome of these investigations, he developed a list of feasible sites for new stores. He considered a site to be feasible if it was available with at least a 10-year lease and was large enough to accommodate a 50,000-square-foot store along with parking space for 30 cars. In addition, the sites had to be easily accessible to shoppers and in a part of town with commercial zoning.

The third step involved choosing the actual sites for store construction. The best two or three sites (depending on the number of stores to be constructed) would be chosen from the list of feasible sites. He tried, of course, to find the sites most accessible to customers since these sites offered the highest potential sales. Some companies add a further step to the process. After choosing the sites, they make decisions regarding the sizes of the stores and their designs and layouts. Like some other chain stores, Xenon's policy has been to use the same design and layout pattern for its stores. Similarly, Xenon stores were always 50,000 square feet in size, had ample parking space, and were usually located at intersections of streets to allow easy access to shoppers.

ARGON CITY

Xenon had completed the first decision stage for Argon City about three months earlier. The management committee had approved Frank's choice of Argon City as the next expansion market in a lengthy Monday afternoon meeting during which he had presented detailed information about Argon City. Argon City had a year-round population of about 62,000 people, having grown steadily during the previous five years.

Argon City was home to Argon University and the seat of the Argon county government. Argon University had an enrollment of 18,000 students, and employed 8,000 of the town's population as faculty or staff. In addition, businesses that catered to the university community employed a large number of people. A meat packing factory, a furniture manufacturing plant, and a large textbook printing press were also located in or near the town. A sizable number of Argon residents also worked in a number of manufacturing plants located in an industrial complex about 30 miles north of town.

The presence of a large academic institution and an unusually large number of manufacturing and service-related jobs had attracted Frank's attention. His assistant had also informed him that in comparison to similar-sized towns in the area, Argon residents had a higher median household income and a lower unemployment rate. Further, despite fears to the contrary, both university enrollment and local employment had continued to grow modestly each year. Two years earlier the city council had initiated an ambitious redevelopment and infrastructure improvement project for Argon City. The project, which was expected to be completed in another two years, promised to further improve the quality of life and the city's attractiveness to the local population. In talking to various people, Frank expected that Argon's population would continue to grow in the future. A number of new housing developments starts in the city supported this conclusion.

Perhaps what had attracted Frank to Argon City most was the fact that none of the major national or regional supermarket chains had yet entered this market. Two local supermarkets and a number of small neighborhood stores currently served the town. During his stay in Argon City, Frank had heard a number of people complain about the lack of good grocery stores and supermarkets. He realized the lack of strong competition provided Xenon with a unique opportunity. He knew from previous experience that local supermarkets couldn't compete effectively with Xenon. Because of its size, it could obtain goods at cheaper prices than local stores. Larger size also resulted in greater economies in transportation, warehousing, and management in general. This was especially true because Argon City stores could share some costs with Xenon stores in two nearby towns.

THE SUPERMARKET CONSUMER

As the Real Estate Director of Xenon, Frank had gathered considerable information about the supermarket consumer. He knew, for example, that most consumers considered distance the primary factor in choosing between alternative supermarkets because of the similarity of competing grocery stores in terms of price and merchandise assortments. Small neighborhood mom-and-pop type stores were an exception to this rule. Consumers often bypassed these stores due to their small assortments and generally higher prices. In fact, according to a study published in a marketing journal, people visited those stores mainly for "filler" trips to buy one or two items. The study, which was conducted in towns similar to Argon City, also revealed that most consumers drove to supermarkets, and that typically 95 percent of a store's customers resided within a 3/4-mile radius of the store.

THE ARGON PLAN

Based on his visits to Argon City and his meetings with real estate agents and city officials, Mr. Green had listed 12 feasible sites for opening new stores. The sites were marked on a large map of the town which hung on his office wall. A copy of the map is shown in Exhibit 1. For planning purposes, he had divided the city into 48 zones. Each zone represented a $1/2 \times 1/2$ mile area. Since customers typically traveled no more than 3/4 mile to a grocery store, Frank estimated that a store located at a site in any zone would draw customers from the immediately neighboring zones in all directions. One of his assistants had spent considerable time looking through the city records and census reports to determine the approximate number of people residing in each

of the 48 zones. These figures appear on the map as relative populations, with a score of 1 representing a population of 300 people. Thus, a zone with a relative population score of 4 has approximately 1,200 people, while one with a score of 0.5 has 150. The population count did not include students living in the university dormitories. On the basis of the information gathered, Frank had chosen two potential sites for new stores.

THREAT OF COMPETITIVE ENTRY

A rumor Frank had heard from a Xenon executive in the accounting department complicated matters, however. A food distributor, who also did business with a number of Xenon's competitors, had mentioned to this executive that the Helium Corporation was also planning to open stores in Argon City. Helium Corporation, which was based in St. Louis, Missouri, was a major competitor to Xenon. Helium supermarkets were usually similar in size to Xenon's, if not slightly larger, and posed direct competitive threats. Competition between the two chains had been intense for the previous few years and a number of towns in the Midwest had stores belonging to both chains. Frank's experience was that when both Helium and Xenon stores were located in the same market, prices tended to be generally similar, since each store usually matched the other's price.

While the news of Helium's plans had surprised Xenon management, the decision to enter Argon City remained unchanged. It still planned to open two stores in the following two years. The company was ready to start constructing the first store in three to four months. It expected that Helium would open its first store some time immediately following the first store opening by Xenon. Frank expected that Helium, too, would ultimately locate two stores in Argon City. He realized that in choosing the

EXHIBIT 1   *Schematic Map of Study Area*

4	5		1		3				
7	3		1	1	3.5 (1)				
	3 (2)	7.5	1	6 (3)	3	2	1.5 (4)	2	
	8	12	6	6.5	6.5	7	7		
1	3.5	2.5	4 (5)	3.5	6.5	7 (6)	7 (7)	6.8	7
1	3.5	2.5	2 (8)	1 (9)	8	7 (10)	5 (11)	4	4.5
					8	3	3.5 (12)	1.5	

7	Relative population of zone

(1)	Feasible site no. 1

two locations for Xenon Supermarkets, he must anticipate where Helium would locate its stores. This was no easy matter since the number of possible construction scenarios was large. He was confident, however, that he had correctly identified the 12 feasible sites available in Argon City. Thus both chains would have to limit their location choices to these 12 sites.

Pondering over the problem, Frank remembered a note one of his assistants had prepared for him once. The note showed the pattern of consumer travel when two similar supermarkets located at neighboring sites. Searching through his files, he found a set of diagrams that had accompanied the note (see Exhibit 2). He put the diagrams in his Argon Project file as he got ready to leave for home. As he gathered his papers on Project Argon, Frank realized that a working weekend lay before him.

Assignment

1. Describe the procedure that Frank Green should use to select the best site for the new store.

2. Estimate the market share of a new store at Site 6, if no new competitors entered the market.

3. By how much would the market share estimated in the previous question be reduced, if a new competitor located at Site 9?

4. Which site would you choose for Xenon's new store: (a) if no new competitor was expected to enter, or (b) if Helium Corporation also opened a store in Argon City?

EXHIBIT 2   *Supermarket Travel Pattern*

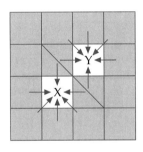 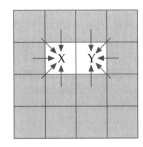

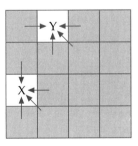 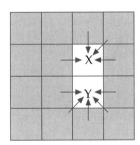

The arrows indicate the pattern of consumer travel when two competing stores are located in close proximity to each other.

Case 10
The Eating Place

Hooray! Hooray! Pamela Smith shouted in joy. She had just completed the profit and loss statement for the second year of operation of The Eating Place. Barely breaking even in the first year, the store had earned a net profit before taxes of $32,500 in the second. She was thrilled.

When she started The Eating Place two years earlier, her family had advised against her resigning her position with a nationally known book publisher. Her father had remarked, "Running a restaurant is risky business. It's too competitive to make a living." But running her own business had been Pamela's dream, and she had started The Eating Place despite her family's protests. Although in its first year it had not done very well, she had not given up hope, and now the sun was shining bright. She was eager to call her parents and let them know the good news.

The Eating Place was located in Sunnyville, near the campus of Sunnyville State University. The store sold sandwiches and beverages for take-out customers. Although The Eating Place was open from 9 A.M. to 6 P.M., nearly 70 percent of sales came between 11 A.M. and 3 P.M., when students and faculty picked up sandwiches for lunch. Over the year, the store had earned a strong reputation among a loyal group of customers for its fresh sandwiches and hearty soups.

Happy as she was with the previous year's performance, Pamela Smith had no intention of becoming complacent. "I must keep growing," she said to herself. With her feet back on solid ground, she looked forward to the future with excitement. Within three weeks, Pamela had developed two possible strategies for expansion.

The first expansion strategy was to serve muffins for breakfast. This would bring in more traffic during the morning hours when sales were low. A number of newspaper and magazine articles had indicated the growing popularity of muffins, especially oatmeal and bran muffins, as breakfast items among young adults since they had a healthier image than croissants and doughnuts. According to some sources, oatmeal and bran help to reduce cholesterol levels.

Pamela could buy muffins in bulk from a local bakery at $4 a dozen. She estimated that she could sell each muffin for $0.60, giving her a 45-percent gross margin on each muffin. Alternatively, she could make the muffins herself. According to her calculations, it would cost 20 cents to bake each muffin from scratch. While this represented a substantial savings from the bakery price, The Eating Place lacked an oven large enough to bake muffins efficiently. A restaurant equipment dealer had quoted a price of $6,500 for a new oven, plus $500 for delivery and installation.

Ms. Smith had discussed her idea with some of her regular customers. One of them, a marketing student at the university, had helped her design a short questionnaire, which she had given to customers over a period of two weeks. Based on responses to that questionnaire, she estimated she could generate weekly muffin sales of 500 units. She worried, though, that a number of people had also indicated that they would buy fewer sandwiches if muffins were available. Sandwich sales could fall by as much as $200 a week if she introduced muffins.

EXHIBIT 1   *Operating Statement for Year Ending October 31, 1988*

Sales		
Sandwiches	$196,560	
Beverages	40,320	
Other items	15,120	
Total		$252,000
Cost of goods sold		
Sandwiches	78,120	
Beverages	7,560	
Paper products	10,080	
Miscellaneous items	5,040	
Total		100,800
Gross margin		$151,200
Other expenses		
Labor	68,440	
Rent	24,000	
Cleaning supplies	8,500	
Utilities	5,600	
Insurance and licenses	6,000	
Depreciation	5,000	
Miscellaneous expenses	1,160	
Total expenses		118,700
Net profit before taxes		$ 32,500

As a second strategy, she considered a special promotion to attract more customers. Currently, the store attracted about 280 customers a day whose checks averaged $4 each. The store was open on weekdays only for 45 weeks a year. Pamela considered advertising in the campus newspaper and distributing flyers to students and faculty in order to attract more customers. The plan called for six quarter-page advertisements in the campus newspaper at a cost of $75 each. She estimated that printing and distributing flyers would cost $400.

Pamela wondered what she should do. While she was happy with the store's performance to date, she was eager to expand even further.

Assignments

1. Should The Eating Place sell muffins?
2. Should it buy the muffins from the local bakery or make them in the store?
3. Assuming that customers continue to spend $4, on the average, how many more customers must the store attract to justify the contemplated advertising plan?

Case 11
Stuyvesant's Department Store

Stuyvesant's Department Store, a full-line department store located in a medium-sized New England town, had annual sales of $7.8 million last year. In business for over 40 years, the store has a strong reputation among middle- and upper-income shoppers in the region.

Each September the managers of Stuyvesant's six major departments prepared merchandise plans and budgets for the next fiscal year starting February 1. Peter Lynch, the manager of the men's apparel department, was reviewing the reports and memos he had put together for this purpose.

The first report from the local Chamber of Commerce projected moderate growth (between 4 and 5 percent) in retail sales in the area, mainly due to inflation. The report did not project any significant population growth in the area, nor did it expect any real growth in purchasing power. Peter's folder also contained a memo from the company president stating that the store expected sales overall to grow by about 5.5 percent next year. The memo also mentioned that each department must ensure that its markdowns did not exceed previous year's levels.

Men's apparel sales at Stuyvesant totaled $670,000 the previous year, up by nearly 10 percent over the year before. Peter was proud of his department's performance, since storewide sales had increased by only 5 percent during the same period. Especially gratifying was the fact that the department achieved the sales increase without sacrificing margin. The cost complement for the

---

EXHIBIT 1   *Average Monthly Sales, Markdowns, and Stock-to-Sales Ratio, 1990–1992*

Month	Sales[a]	Monthly Markdown[b]	Stock-to-Sales Ratio
February	5.8	14.0	6.7
March	7.4	7.8	6.2
April	7.8	8.2	6.0
May	6.7	9.5	6.5
June	7.8	15.9	6.0
July	7.3	18.1	6.2
August	6.7	12.0	6.5
September	8.8	7.6	5.6
October	8.2	7.9	5.8
November	11.0	7.9	5.2
December	16.9	13.8	3.5
January	5.6	31.8	8.1

[a]Percentage of annual sales.
[b]Percentage of monthly sales.

department was 50 percent. Prior to Peter's appointment, the men's department at Stuyvesant had been languishing. The store had given much more attention to women's clothing and furnishings, by far the two largest departments in the store. Peter had, however, turned things around substantially with intelligent buying, timely sales promotions, and attentive customer service. He was confident that the increase in men's department sales would again exceed the storewide level, although he doubted it would achieve a 10-percent increase again.

The file also contained a report prepared by Peter's assistant showing the average monthly distribution of sales, markdowns, and stock-to-sales ratio for the previous three years. Peter had compared these figures with those for similar-sized department stores supplied by a national trade organization. Markdown and stock levels at Stuyvesant seemed to be in line with those of men's apparel departments in similar-sized department stores. Stock-to-sales figures were based on B.O.M. inventory. Historically, the store had always set aside 2 percent of sales for stock shortages and employee discounts.

Peter knew that the time had come to prepare the following year's budget,. He expected to have $300,000 worth of inventory at the end of January and wanted to end at the same level the following January. He also wanted to maintain the department's current margin.

Assignment

Prepare a budget for the men's department for the next year showing the monthly planned sales, B.O.M. and E.O.M. stocks, reductions, and purchases. (See Exhibit 11.10 in Chapter 11.)

Case 12
Martin's

Susan Smith was worried. She had just received a phone call from Bill Hanson, merchandise manager of Martin's. Jeffrey Martin, the owner and CEO of Martin's, had asked to see Bill and Susan the first thing the next morning. Susan had been fearing such a call for some time. Two years earlier she had been promoted from assistant buyer to buyer for cosmetics at Martin's. Since she took over, cosmetics sales had been flat, with no immediate sign of reversal.

Four years earlier, just after graduating with a retailing degree from the local university, Susan had joined Martin's as assistant buyer of cosmetics. She fondly remembered those days. She had been euphoric when Bill Hanson had called her with the offer, and so had her parents. The Smiths were long-time residents of Capital City, where Martin's was located. They had shopped their since their own childhoods and Susan's grandmother had even worked there for a short while as a sales associate. Susan's father described Martin's as the centerpiece of Capital City's shopping scene. It was the town's only full-line department store, and its 1988 storewide sales had exceeded $4 million. Cosmetics sales that year had been $160,000.

When Susan joined as assistant buyer in 1988, she worked with Lisa Sullivan who was then the store's cosmetics buyer. Susan had learned a lot from Lisa, a 15-year veteran of the cosmetics department at Martin's, and they had worked well together as a team. Susan quickly picked up techniques of inventory control and ordering procedures, freeing Lisa from day-to-day buying operations.

In 1990, Lisa Sullivan retired from Martin's to spend more time with her family and Susan was promoted to buyer for cosmetics, the youngest person ever to hold that position. As she sat in her small office in the store, she fondly remembered working with Lisa Sullivan and wondered whether she should call her for some advice, or even just to chat about things. After all, Lisa had initiated her into the trade, introducing her to suppliers and teaching her about all the brands, whose names—Revlon, Estee Lauder, Lancome, Elizabeth Arden, Clinique—had become so familiar. Instead, she took out a piece of paper and doodled, wondering what she was going to tell Jeffrey Martin the following day.

Although Martin's was the only department store in Capital City, it was not the only outlet for cosmetics. Within a mile of Martin's location, three other stores sold cosmetics and related products: Dart, an outlet of a nationwide discount chain, and two drugstores, both outlets of national drug chains. Of course, none had the selection nor the atmosphere of Martin's, nor did their customers receive the personal attention and service that Martin's would provide.

In a survey conducted in 1991, Capital City shoppers had rated Martin's highest in terms of service, assortment, and knowledgeable sales personnel; the cosmetics department had received special mention for its beauty counselling service, which was available for a modest fee. On the other hand, many respondents had indicated that they bought cosmetics at discount stores and drugstores because of lower prices.

Susan had done some checking of her own. She had visited each of the three competing outlets and carefully noted their prices, display, and personnel. All three stores provided minimal sales help and arranged displays in simple racks or on counter tops. The stores carried many of the same brands available at Martin's. Susan estimated that about 50 percent of the merchandise was common. The competitors, of course, did not offer many of the up-scale brands sold at Martin's, but Martin's priced shared brands such as Revlon and Elizabeth Arden at least 15 percent higher. Reviewing her sales records closely, Susan had found that these were precisely the brands that were slipping at Martin's; the exclusive brands were holding their own.

Susan wondered what she should tell Jeffrey Martin the next morning. She had thought of a number of possible strategies, but since each seemed to have its own pros and cons, it was hard to decide which to choose.

One possibility, for example, was to reduce the prices of all nonexclusive brands to match competitors' prices. Such a move would significantly lower her department's margins, though. Currently, the department had an average gross margin of 46 percent, and Susan was certain that Jeffrey Martin wouldn't allow the average margin to drop below 42 percent. Her competitors had one advantage, she realized, in their much lower overhead, which allowed them to get by with smaller margins. The competitors had very low selling costs, too, while Susan's department bore the cost of four sales associates.

Susan had even considered the possibility of dropping all cosmetics lines that were available at discount outlets and drugstores. Martin's could then concentrate only on brands that it sold exclusively and stop worrying about competitors undercutting its prices. This would mean cutting the size of the department in half, which might risk Martin's image as a store with a wide assortment.

A third alternative, suggested by the shoe department buyer, was to increase the department's advertising and promotion budget by $5,000 to attract more customers.

Finally, Susan wondered whether she should provide free beauty counselling to all customers. Currently, the store collected nearly $8,000 annually in fees from beauty counselling. Providing free counselling would mean doubling the hours of the two part-time beauty counsellors at an estimated cost of $4,000 a year.

Assignment

Discuss the pros and cons of each alternative.

Case 13
The Computer Store

The Computer Store's outlet at Silver City was the latest addition to its network of retail computer outlets. Headquartered in Phoenix, Arizona, The Computer Store sells personal computers, software, computer-related books, and supplies to small businesses located in the suburbs of metropolitan areas in the Southwest. With its January 1, 1992 inauguration of the Silver City store, the chain opened its 23rd outlet in just three years. On April 15, the store's manager, Mr. Dobbs, received a letter from the chief financial officer at Phoenix asking him to prepare an income statement for the first four months of operations ending on April 30.

At the end of business on April 30, Mr. Dobbs conducted a physical inventory of each of the store's five departments and found the retail value of the inventory to be $250,000. On January 1 the store had started with inventory totaling $133,000 at cost and $242,000 at retail. Exhibit 1 presents other relevant data on purchases, sales, and markdowns. During the four months,

---

EXHIBIT 1   *Revenue, Purchases, and Markdowns, January–April, 1992*

	January	February	March	April
Purchases (at cost)	10,000	10,000	12,500	15,000
Inbound freight	600	500	650	650
Retail value of purchases	19,000	19,000	21,500	28,000
Net sales (retail)	14,000	17,000	18,000	22,000
Total markdowns[a]	2,000	1,600	800	1,200
Employee discounts	—	300	—	250

[a]Adjusted for markdown cancellations.

the store had spent $6,000 for advertising, $1,400 for utilities, $12,800 for wages and fringe benefits, and paid rents totaling $8,000. In addition, it spent $5,000 on other miscellaneous expenses. As he scanned these figures, Mr. Dobbs wondered whether the first four months had been profitable.

Assignment

Prepare the store's income statement for the period January 1 to April 30, 1992.

Case 14
The General Store

"There aren't too many stores like ours around any more," said Tom Haas, owner of The General Store in Yulan, New York. "When I was young each town had its own general store, but now most of them are gone, victims to chain hardware stores and DIY (Do It Yourself) stores." Tom was having a cup of coffee at Cindy's, a popular local gathering spot, with Harry Carson, the sales representative from Craftsperson Inc., a tool manufacturer located in Binghamton, New York. Tom continued, "We can't compete with the chain stores on price, but people still come to our store because it is convenient. I am right here in town. The nearest DIY center is at Monticello—that's 20 miles on winding roads. You need a tool, a few nails, rubber hose for watering the garden, electric bulbs, you don't want to drive 20 miles. My customers come from all over the area. They come from Yulan, Eldred, Tusten, Highland, Sohola [small towns within 10 miles of Yulan]."

Although small, The General Store was well-managed. Two years ago, at the urging of his son and partner Jeff, Tom Haas instituted a computerized merchandise information system. For this purpose, they organized all merchandise items in the store into four departments: hardware, plumbing, small appliances, and miscellaneous. They numbered these departments 1, 2, 3, and 4, respectively. They then divided each department into separate classifications based on analysis of all SKUs within the department. The hardware department, for example, includes three classes: nuts and bolts (110); tools such as pliers, screwdrivers, etc. (120); and saws (130). They further divided these classifications into finer classifications and assigned them four-digit numbers. One four-digit class within classification 120, for example, was classification 1200, adjustable pliers. The store carried six types of adjustable pliers denoted by the five-digit numbers 12001, 12002, 12003, 12004, 12005, and 12006. Exhibit 1 summarizes the store's hierarchical classification system.

The information system could generate a number of different reports. These reports could reflect different levels of aggregation as desired. At the most aggregate level, the system could provide sales, gross margin, inventory turnover, and other performance indicators for the entire store at any time. It could also provide reports for each two-digit, three-digit, or four-digit clas-

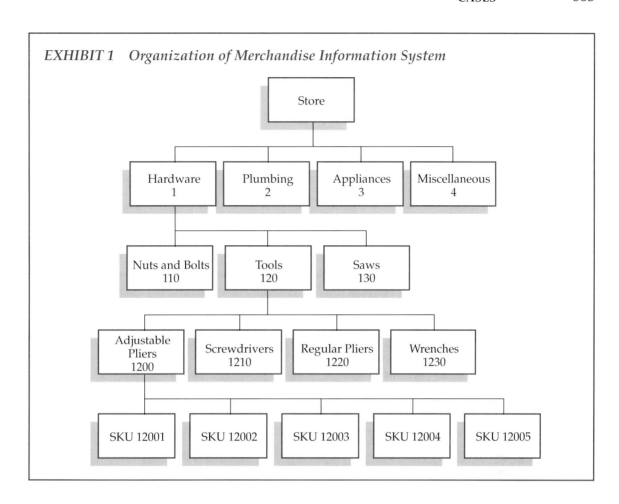

EXHIBIT 1   *Organization of Merchandise Information System*

sification. Exhibit 2 shows a report for classification 1200, which Tom Haas was studying when Harry Carson walked into his office. Harry wanted to sell him a new brand of adjustable pliers and invited him to Cindy's to talk.

"We have the best deal on pliers," said Harry, as he pulled out a sample and a fact sheet from his briefcase. Tom was quite impressed with the quality of the tool, but was concerned about devoting more shelf space to pliers. "The only way I can stock this is by dropping item 12004," he said to Mr. Carson. "They are too similar, it wouldn't make sense to keep both on a crowded shelf." Harry argued that the new brand gave the store a better deal, but Tom wanted to make his own decision. "It's time to evaluate all the items in this group," he said. "Call me in a week and I will have an answer for you."

On returning to the store, Tom started closely examining the performance report for classification 1200. The following notes aid interpretation of the report in Exhibit 2:

- Item 12001 sold at an average retail price of $6.99.
- The store sold 1,465 units in the previous year.

EXHIBIT 2   *The General Store Merchandise Report: Classification 1200*

	12001	12002	12003	12004	12005	12006
Retail price	6.99	5.79	19.99	5.99	10.99	12.99
Unit sales	1,465	1,885	720	2,210	1,420	1,610
Sales	$10,240	$10,914	$14,392	$13,238	$15,606	$20,914
Gross margin	23.8%	24.2%	28.6%	23.6%	25.2%	27.0%
Gross margin	$2,437	$2,641	$4,116	$3,124	$3,932	$5,647
Inventory turnover	4.1	3.9	3.2	3.6	4.9	3.8
Cash discount	78	124	205	152	0	0
Promotional allowance	400	0	750	0	1,000	0

- Item 12001 generated $10,240 in dollar sales volume during the previous year.
- The gross margin percent for previous 12-month period is 23.8 percent.
- The item generated $2,437 in dollar gross margin for the previous year.
- Inventory turnover of 4.1 is obtained by dividing sales at cost by average inventory at cost.

- Cash discounts received for timely payment amounted to $78.
- The store received a promotional allowance from the manufacturer of $400.

In addition to the information in the report, Tom had obtained two other pieces of information that he considered important. The store had recently taken a bank loan at 15-percent annual

---

EXHIBIT 3   *Craftsperson Inc.*
Binghamton, New York

To: Tom Haas

From: Harry Carson

I wanted to draw your attention to a new line of adjustable pliers soon to be introduced by Craftsperson Inc. The first item to be introduced is the 8-inch adjustable pliers with rubber protected handles. The pliers are priced at $4.50 and we recommend that you sell them at $6.50 each. Although the item resembles the Eagle brand (your stock 12004) in looks and features, we believe that the Craftsperson brand is more durable. We encourage you to carry this item at The General Store, and we are sure that your customers will appreciate the product.

   We estimate that a store like yours is likely to sell 1,400 units a year and achieve a turnover of around 3.8. We realize that it is costly for retailers to carry new items; to partially offset this cost, Craftsperson will pay a $250 slotting fee to The General Store. In addition, we offer a promotional allowance equaling 3 percent of your purchases. We also offer a 2-percent cash discount for on-time payment. Craftsperson is committed to serving your customers' needs and also increasing your store's profits.

interest to cover increased working capital needs. The previous year, Jeff Haas argued that in evaluating merchandise performance, they should also consider relative selling expenses. According to him, they should allocate $4,000 to classification 1200 as selling expenses. Discussions with the store's three salespeople and with Jeff led Tom to estimate that 40 percent of the sales effort in this classification went toward Item 12003, since customers typically had many questions about this item; 20 percent went to

12005, 15 percent to 12002, 10 percent each to 12001 and 12006, and 5 percent to 12004.

Assignments

1. Calculate the profitability of each SKU in classification 1200.
2. Should the store drop Item 12004 or 12001 in favor of the new line?

Case 15
Turnpike Station

The Turnpike Station is one of at least four gasoline stations located along the stretch of Corallville Avenue that feeds into Interstate 80 near Iowa City. Being near a major interstate highway, the stations serve local motorists as well as highway travelers. Their close proximity keeps the gas stations highly competitive and they engage in frequent price wars. Sylvia and Stan, the husband-and-wife team that manages Turnpike Station, were discussing changes in gasoline retailing since they opened the station 14 years earlier.

Gasoline retailing in the United States has changed dramatically since the early 1980s. Consumer demand for gasoline has been flat because of conservation and more fuel efficient automobiles. At the same time, new, low-price gasoline chains have posed a serious challenge to better-established firms such as Texaco and Gulf. Faced with increasing competition in a shrinking market and fluctuations in oil prices, retail gasoline chains have been forced to control costs wherever possible.

One cost that has come under increased scrutiny is the cost of credit card sales. In the 1970s, most retail gas companies aggressively marketed their own credit cards to millions of gasoline consumers. Credit cards tended to create some brand loyalty in an industry with a core product that is difficult to differentiate. The cost of credit cards can be substantial, though, in some cases as much as 9 cents per gallon of gasoline purchased. Until a few years ago, most companies typically charged the same prices for purchases on credit as for cash purchases. Still, only one-third of gasoline buyers regularly used credit cards.

A number of proposals have been suggested to control credit sale costs:

- Make credit card holders pay annual fees, like those holders of bank cards and American Express cards pay, to cover the cost of credit card sales. Some feared, however, that most credit card holders would cancel their cards rather than pay annual fees.

- Charge customers using credit cards higher prices than customers who pay cash to cover the higher cost of credit sales.
- Eliminate credit sales altogether. Firms could pass on their savings from the elimination of credit sales partially or wholly to customers in the form of lower prices.
- Aggressively push credit card sales without surcharges to differentiate the firm from competitors.
- Encourage the use of debit cards. A debit card looks like a credit card, but it operates quite differently. Instead of granting the customer credit, the card allows a retailer to transfer payment from the customer's checking account to its own. Since the account is debited immediately, the retailer does not have to bear the cost of credit. Gasoline companies could either issue their own debit cards or accept debit cards issued by third parties.

Assignments

1. Describe the pros and cons of each proposal.
2. What additional information do managers need to compare each alternative? Clearly discuss the market research procedure that should be used to collect this information.
3. How can the owners of Turnpike Station differentiate their station from competitors?

Case 16
The Pizza Parlor

Inspired by the success of Thomas Monaghan, Charles Lazarus, Sam Walton, and Gary Comer, among others, an increasing number of college graduates are choosing not to work for existing firms, instead becoming entrepreneurs and managing their own businesses. Jim Mercer is one of them. Two years ago, after he graduated with a business degree from a midwestern university, Jim turned down job offers from various organizations, and instead opened a pizza parlor in Super Town.

The prospect of managing his own business had always excited Jim, but he also knew that opening a new business entails considerable risk. It is estimated that, of the thousands of new businesses started each year, about 30 percent survive less than a year and nearly half fail within two years. To increase the odds of success, Jim had spent considerable time preparing a good business plan for his new venture.

Ultimately, he was able to get a $20,000 loan from a local bank to set up The Pizza Parlor in a neighborhood center just east of Super Town's central business district. The center had eight stores anchored by a supermarket and a drugstore. Jim Mercer defined his market as young adults in the age group 15 to 35, but he placed special emphasis on high school and college students. To differentiate The Pizza Parlor from the three other pizza stores within three miles of its site, Jim created a sporting atmosphere in his store to benefit from the recent popularity of sports bars. The Pizza Parlor had one large-screen, projection television and five 21-inch television monitors throughout the eating area. Patrons could watch televised broadcasts of sporting events as they ate their pizza.

Jim's strategy seemed to have worked. The previous year the store had sales of $85,000. The current year's trend seemed to indicate a 10- to 15-percent growth in sales. Although Jim was happy with his present performance, he was scheduled to meet with the manager of a local advertising agency the following week to plan a new advertising campaign to attract more customers. Prior to that meeting he had to decide on the goals of the campaign and its overall ob-jectives. As he thought about the meeting, Jim browsed through the summary results of a consumer survey the agency had undertaken for him recently (see Exhibit 1).

Assignments

1. Suggest a set of goals for The Pizza Parlor's advertising campaign. Give reasons why you chose these goals.
2. Describe how you would test the campaign's effectiveness.

EXHIBIT 1 Retail Research and Advertising, Inc. Super Town

Jim Mercer
The Pizza Parlor

Dear Mr. Mercer:

In preparation for our meeting next week, I have put together some information on the Super Town market and The Pizza Parlor consumer. Most of this information comes from a telephone survey of 500 Super Town residents conducted last month, supplemented with information from various secondary sources and syndicated research reports.

1. The Pizza Parlor Consumer

Eighty-five percent of The Pizza Parlor's customers reside within three miles of the store. Fifty percent of them are between 15 and 24 years of age, 30 percent are between the ages of 25 and 34, and the rest are 35 years or older. The average check per party is $12 and the average size of each party is three.

2. The Super Town Market

It is estimated that about 20,000 people reside within three miles of The Pizza Parlor's site. The age distribution of these 20,000 people is as follows: 11 percent are younger than 15 years; 19 percent are between 15 and 24 years; 29 percent are between 25 and 34 years; 22 percent are between 35 and 54; the rest are older than 54 years.

3. Eating Habits of Super Town Residents

I present the following results from the consumer survey separately for three age groups: 15 to 24 years old, 25 to 34 years old, and 35 to 54 years old.

15–24 Years   Of the respondents in this age group, 80 percent ate out at least once during the 30 days preceding the survey. Of those who had eaten out, 40 percent had eaten at a pizza restaurant during the same period, and 40 percent of the respondents in this age group were aware of The Pizza Parlor. Of the respondents who were aware of The Pizza Parlor, 30 percent had eaten there once during the preceding 90 days, 18 percent had been there twice, 9 percent three times, and 3 percent four times. Of the respondents who had eaten at The Pizza Parlor at least once, 81 percent rated it as excellent or very good.

25–34 Years   Of respondents in this age group, 70 percent ate out at least once during the 30 days preceding the survey. Of those who had eaten out, 25 percent had eaten at a pizza restaurant during the same period. Of the respondents in this age group, 35 percent were aware of The Pizza Parlor, and 30 percent of these people had eaten there once during the previous 90 days, 12 percent had been there twice, 5 percent three times, and 2 percent four times. Of the respondents who had eaten at The Pizza Parlor at least once, 41 percent rated it as excellent or very good.

35–54 Years   Of respondents in this age group, 40 percent ate out at least once during the 30 days preceding the survey. Of those who had eaten out, 10 percent had eaten at a pizza restaurant during the same period. Of this age group, 15 percent were aware of The Pizza Parlor. Of these respondents, 25 percent had eaten there once during the previous 90 days, 10 percent had been there twice, and 2 percent three times. Only 11 percent of the respondents who had eaten at The Pizza Parlor at least once rated it as excellent or very good.

Case 17
Winterthur Department Store

Harvey Morris, the president of Winterthur Stores, believed strongly in the power of personal selling. According to him, the only way department stores can successfully compete with specialty stores is by providing high-quality service to their customers. This attitude led him always to take a personal interest in hiring, training, and evaluating Winterthur sales associates. He knew that, in the final analysis, what counted was whether customers left the store with a positive impression. A positive impression would bring them back to the store, maybe with their friends.

All sales associates at Winterthur participated in a two-day training session before their assignment to the shop floor. The first day's session, conducted by a sales consulting firm, dealt with various selling techniques. The second day's session was conducted by the store's senior merchandise managers, who described the store's organization and its policies and also provided information on products. The session traditionally ended with a short speech by Harvey Morris.

Harvey was a hands-on manager. Every day he spent an hour or so walking the shop floor inspecting displays, talking to customers, and observing salespeople. He also employed an outside agency that sent mystery shoppers whose reports helped the store evaluate sales personnel. Representatives of this agency, posing as potential customers, visited the store each quarter. The agency provided verbatim reports of these visits, which Mr. Morris used to evaluate the performance of each salesperson.

He picked up the reports on three recently hired salespeople: Christine Molloy, a sales associate in the sweater department, Jack Sessions of the electronics department, and Marilyn Peterson from the women's apparel department.

Christine Molloy

Christine: (approaching customer) Can I help you?

Customer: I am just looking. Thank you.

Christine: O.K.

Christine leaves and starts chatting with a cashier. After about five minutes, customer approaches Christine.

Customer: Do you have any cardigans in lamb's wool?

Christine: Yes, I think they are in one of the racks at the back.

Christine continues to chat with the cashier.

Customer: I looked there and I didn't see any lamb's wool. Could it be somewhere else?

Christine: You must have missed it. It is supposed to be there.

The customer goes to the back of the department while Christine stays with the cashier. After a few minutes, the customer returns.

Customer: I still don't see any lamb's wool sweaters at the back. Could they be in any other place?

Christine: No, we keep all sweaters in this section. If there are no lamb's wool ones at the back, I guess we must be all sold out. We have a lot of other varieties you can choose from.

Customer: Well, I was particularly interested in lamb's wool. It's a birthday present for my daughter, and she likes lamb's wool a lot.

Christine: What size does your daughter wear?

Customer: Medium.

Christine: I can show you some pullovers. I hope we have a medium, though. They are the first ones to go.

Christine leaves the cash station and proceeds toward the racks with the customer following.

Christine: (pointing to a rack) Here are some of the vests. Maybe you can find a medium.

Customer: Do you have something in blue?

Christine: If it is not here, we don't have it. Here, this is sort of blue.

Customer: That's more violet than blue.

Christine: Why don't you look around some and see if there is anything you like.

Christine leaves the customer at the racks and goes back to the cash station. The customer leaves soon afterward.

Jack Sessions

A customer approaches Jack Sessions as he stands behind a counter.

Customer: Can you help me, please?

Jack: Surely, sir.

Customer: I would like to see the video camera you have on sale.

Jack: Which one? I don't know of any on sale.

Customer: The advertisement was in yesterday's *Winterthur Times*. It was the XXX brand.

Jack: Oh, that one. I will see if we have any in stock. I wouldn't recommend it, though.

Customer: What do you mean?

Jack: If I were you, I wouldn't buy that brand. I would recommend Brand YYY.

Customer: What's wrong with XXX?

Jack: It's not a great model. YYY has much better lenses.

Customer: I really don't need a fancy model. The basic model would do for me.

Jack: I will check if we have any in stock.

Customer: How can you not have any in stock? You just advertised it yesterday.

Jack: We sold a number of them yesterday.

Customer: And you still don't recommend it?

Jack: Well, I wouldn't recommend it.

Customer: Can you show it to me anyway?

Jack: Let me first show you YYY. It's right here.

Jack proceeds to the display area.

Customer: Could you show me the XXX brand?

Jack: Surely, I will, but let me show you this first.

Jack picks up Brand YYY from the display area.

Jack: This one has the best features. It has an f1.2 lens and a two-hour battery. You have to recharge the battery on the XXX after half an hour and it takes four hours. This one can be recharged in two hours. It's made in America, too.

Customer: Well, what's the price on this one?

Jack: Nine hundred ninety nine dollars.

Customer: That's two hundred dollars more than the other one.

Jack: It has more features. That's why it is higher priced. It can even take pictures in candlelight.

Customer: I am not a great photographer or anything like that. I just want a simple camera to take pictures of my daughter's birthday party and things like that.

Jack: I would still recommend this one.

Customer: Could you show me the other one?

Jack: Yes, but we have only one in stock now. We will have to give you a rain check. You can pick it up in a week or two.

Customer: But my daughter's birthday is next week.

Jack: Why don't you just buy this other one, then?

Customer: I am not sure I want to spend so much.

Jack: Actually, the prices will not be that different.

Customer: How come?

Jack: You have to buy a case for the other one for seventy dollars, and you definitely need a better battery. The two-hour battery is sixty dollars.

Customer: But your ad says "all inclusive price." Why do I need all these extra things?

Jack: You don't need them, but I would strongly recommend them. Moreover, you'll be buying American. We should all do that.

Customer: I will have to think about it more.

Jack: If you really insist on the other model, maybe I can find one in stock.

Jack goes to the back of store and returns with a box.

Jack: You are lucky. It looks like we do have one in stock.

Customer: Good, just wrap it up for me. You know if I hadn't promised my daughter I would record her birthday party on video, I don't think I would buy anything at this store again.

The customer pays and leaves.

Marilyn Peterson

Marilyn Peterson approaches a customer browsing in the dress department.

Marilyn: Aren't those dresses lovely? They just came in last week. They are made of the finest quality silk.

Customer: They are beautiful, but I am not sure they are for me.

Marilyn: Oh, they would look beautiful on you.

Customer: What I meant is that I am not sure I want to spend so much money.

Marilyn: They are the best quality, but if you are looking for something less expensive than that, you should look at these dresses here. They are good, too, but less expensive.

Marilyn moves to a different section of the department with the customer following.

Marilyn: Here we are. Look at the beautiful colors.

Customer: They are nice, but I prefer something less bright.

Marilyn: Let me find some for you.

Marilyn searches through racks.

Marilyn: These pastels look nice. Would a size 6 fit you?

Customer: Yes.

Marilyn: Would you like to try one on?

Customer: I would like to look at them first.

Marilyn: Let me put them side-by-side. It will be easier to compare that way.

Marilyn pulls out four dresses and puts them on top of the rack.

Customer: Oh, I don't know. It's so hard to choose.

Marilyn: The pink would look nice on you.

Customer: The only thing is, I bought a pink dress last month. Can I see that blue one instead?

Marilyn: Surely.

Marilyn pulls out the blue dress from the rack.

Customer: I like the blue better than the others.

Marilyn: Why don't we try this on and see how well it fits.

The customer and Marilyn proceed to the dressing room. After a few minutes the customer emerges from the dressing room.

Customer: It fits pretty well and I like it.

Marilyn: Should I wrap it up for you?

Customer: Well, I don't know. I still can't make up my mind.

Marilyn: The fabric and cut on this are excellent and at this price it is a great buy.

Customer: O.K. I will buy it.

Marilyn: I am sure you will enjoy it. Let me ring it up for you.

Marilyn proceeds to the teller station followed by the customer. On the way, she stops at the scarf rack.

Marilyn: This scarf would look beautiful with the dress.

Customer: I am not sure I need a scarf.

Marilyn: Why don't you just try it on and see how it looks. You don't have to buy it if you don't like it.

Customer: Oh, I like it all right. I just don't want to spend too much more.

Marilyn: It's on sale.

Customer: All right, I will take the scarf, too.

As she rings up the sale, Marilyn continues conversing with the customer.

Marilyn: Why don't I take down your name and address? I will drop you a note when the silk dresses go on sale.

Customer: I would really appreciate that. Thank you.

The customer departs with her dress and scarf.

Assignment

Write a report evaluating the performance of the three salespeople. The report should also recommend the kind of further training needed for each sales person.

Case 18
Dragon Fire

During his four years in college, Murray Austin had spent innumerable hours at the computer terminal. While his friends played Frisbee and basketball, he played computer games. Bored with most of the commercially available computer games, he started writing some of his own. His favorite was "Dragon Fire," which he wrote in his senior year. Fashioned after the dungeon games popular at many college campuses, its objective was to find treasures hidden inside a seemingly unending labyrinth of dungeons. On their way to the treasure, the players faced a number of obstacles including fire-breathing dragons and meteor showers.

On graduation from college, Murray accepted a sales position at a computer company, but his interest in computer games did not subside. In his spare time, he improved "Dragon Fire" by adding state-of-the-art graphics with multiple colors. He and his friends who had seen the game were sure that it was one of the best computer games around. One friend suggested that he sell the game through mail order.

After giving his friend's suggestion some thought, Murray Austin decided to sell two versions of "Dragon Fire," an intermediate and an advanced version, through direct mail. He would sell the separate versions on separate disks for use with a Macintosh computer. He set the price of each disk at $25.99, with a combined price for both disks of $45. This was considerably below the prices of other commercially available dungeon games.

A list broker suggested three possible mailing lists for mail offers: (a) a list of all recent college graduates, (b) a list of Macintosh computer owners, and (c) a list of persons who have previously bought software or computer peripherals through mail order. Since the number of names on each list was very large and the prices of lists varied, the list broker suggested that Murray use a limited number of names from each list for trial mailings.

Murray decided to buy 1,000 names from each list for his initial mailings. Each mailing included a short brochure explaining the game and a reply coupon for ordering. The average cost of the mailing was 32 cents and each brochure cost 25 cents.

As another option, he considered including a demonstration disk in each mailing. Although it cost 80 cents to produce a demonstration disk, Murray felt that including such a disk might increase the response rate. Besides the cost of the disk itself, including a demonstration disk raised mailing cost to 80 cents per unit. Unsure of whether the value of including the demonstration disk would compensate for the extra cost, Murray decided to include it in half of the mailings. He varied the designs of the return coupons so he could monitor the response from each mailing.

Three months after mailing out the 3,000 solicitation letters, Murray decided it was time to decide on the next step. In his typical methodical manner, he had organized all relevant information into two tables (see Exhibits 1 and 2). As he looked at the information he wondered whether he should continue with the venture and which list he should use if he did continue.

EXHIBIT 1   *Responses from Test Mailings*

| | Number of Orders for | | |
	Intermediate	Advanced	Both
List 1			
Demo disk	12	5	4
No demo	9	4	4
List 2			
Demo disk	24	19	12
No demo	16	10	8
List 3			
Demo disk	18	15	14
No demo	16	10	11

EXHIBIT 2   *Relevant Mailing Cost Information*

1. Producing and packaging each game disk cost $1.
2. Mailing a single disk cost $1.00 and mailing two disks cost $1.15.
3. For each list, 1,000 names and addresses cost: List 1: $60; List 2: $84; List 3: $100.

Assignments

1. Which of the three lists is best?
2. Is it cost effective to include the demonstration disk?
3. If Murray Austin mailed solicitation letters to 10,000 names from the best list, how much profit should he expect?

Case 19 (A)
Pamela's Flower Shop

As she looked at her calendar Pamela Rink counted once again the number of days before she graduated from school. It was exactly two more months to her last day of class. Her friends were all busy writing resumes and interviewing for jobs. But working for a big corporation was not Pamela's dream. She was committed to opening her own flower shop. "Retailing is in my blood," she explained. Her parents have owned and operated one of Evansville's three flower shops for over 20 years. Pamela has been working in her parent's store since she graduated from high school. During the last two years, she has been involved in almost every aspect of managing the store: from buying and selling to accounting and inventory management. By the time she was a junior at Evansville State College she had decided to go into retailing on her own after graduation.

Although her parents had offered her a formal management position in their store, Pamela wanted to embark on her own. Not wanting to compete directly with her parents, Pamela planned to open a flower shop in a neighboring town called Croton. A real estate broker had informed her of a vacancy in a relatively new small shopping center in Croton. The center had a supermarket and a drug store as anchor tenants. It also had a beauty salon, a dry cleaner, and a popular Chinese restaurant. The center is near a number of residential developments, and there is also a small office park within three miles. It is easily accessible from the a major highway linking Croton to downtown St. Charles.

The shopping center developer had recently conducted a customer spotting study in which 300 customers visiting the shopping center were intercepted and asked where they lived. The survey indicated that over 80 percent of the customers lived within a 5 mile radius of the shopping center. Clearly, the center does not draw much from the major city or the larger suburbs around Croton. Its clientele came mostly from the neighboring residential areas. It also attracted some lunch-time shoppers from the office park.

Pamela obtained a detailed map of Croton and plotted a 5-mile radius around the store location to identify the census tracts corresponding to the center's trade area. At the university library Pamela referenced the *Census of Population and Housing* to obtain a demographic and socioeconomic profile of the trade area residents. Exhibit 1 summarizes the information she obtained.

While working at her parent's store, Pamela had seen the results from a national survey of flower buyers undertaken by the flower sellers' trade association. According to that survey, all adults are potential flower buyers, but the propensity to buy depends on age. The primary age group for buying flowers, according to the survey, is between 25 and 54 years. Almost 60 percent of the people in this age group buy flowers at least once a year. Corresponding figures for the 20 to 24 age group and for people more than 54 years of age were 20 percent and 40 percent, respectively.

According to the survey, customers can be grouped into three segments: heavy, medium, and light buyers. Half the customers are light buyers who purchase flowers one to two times a year. The medium segment comprises 30 percent of the market. They buy flowers twice a

---

EXHIBIT 1   Croton Trade Area Study

Total Population	46,968
Population by age	
Less than 20 years	10.86%
20–24 years	12.23%
25–54 years	50.68%
Above 54 years	26.23%
Median Age	35.66
Estimated Household Income	
$50,000 or more	25.43%
$35,000–$49,999	15.43%
$25,000–$34,999	19.63%
$15,000–$24,999	20.54%
Less than $15,000	18.97%
Median HH income	$31,674

---

year, on an average. Heavy purchasers buy flowers about 4 times a year and represent 20 percent of all buyers.

From her experience Pamela knew that the average dollar value of purchases at her parent's store at Evansville was $10.00. She expected the number to be about the same for her store, too. She also hoped to get some business from companies located in the office park. Other potential customers included two gourmet restaurants in Croton that decorated tables with fresh flowers. Even with special price discounts, each represented about $2,500 of business annually, if she could get an exclusive service contract. Pamela was excited by the prospect of signing a service contract with at least one of the restaurants. Being realistic, however, she realized that this was highly unlikely until her store was well established.

There were no other full-service flower shops within five miles of her proposed location. But two supermarkets in Croton did sell flowers. Pamela did not consider the supermarkets to be serious competitors to her business. The quality of the flowers carried by the supermarkets was poor and the assortment was unpredictable. She did not expect the supermarkets to get more than 10 percent of the share of total flower sales in the trade area. She also estimated that 25 percent of the shoppers from her trade area will continue to buy from stores in St. Charles and Evansville.

The shopping center developer had quoted her a monthly rent of $1,700, but Pamela was in the process of negotiating a 10 percent reduction from that quote. While the landlord was agreeable to the reduced rent, he demanded on inserting a contingency payment clause in the lease in return. The clause would require Pamela to pay a "rent royalty" of half of one percent of annual sales above $600,000. According to a number of commercial real estate brokers such rent royalties are quite common for shopping center sites. The potential extra payment troubled Pamela. But she liked the shopping center's location. It was a well managed center with good visibility from the street. During her recent visits to the center, she noticed a constant stream of traffic both during weekdays and weekends. Moreover, because the center was relatively new, few leasehold improvements would be required.

Pamela planned to hire one full-time salesperson cum helper for $7 per hour. She also planned to hire some part-time workers to help during busy periods. She planned on 30 part-time hours a week at $5.00 an hour. In addition to salary she would have to pay benefits and payroll taxes equal to 20 percent of the total payroll. She estimated that she needed to draw $800 a month from the business for her personal expenses. Other estimated monthly expenses included: utilities and telephone $200 per month, insurance $150 per month, and supplies $225 a month.

Pamela planned a modest advertising and promotional program for the store. The objective of the advertising program was to inform Croton residents of the new store and let them know that they need not drive to St. Charles or Evansville anymore to buy flowers. Her proposed media plan included advertisements in local newspaper, Yellow Page listings, and flyers. The projected budget was around $300 per month (see Exhibit 2). In addition, she was also studying a proposal to participate in a cooperative direct mail campaign sponsored by a local media and marketing company. The direct mail piece, which would include a flyer from Pamela's along with flyers from a number of other local merchants, was to be distributed to 8,000 adults in Croton four times a year. The media company claimed that the direct mail campaign will generate a response rate of 3 percent over a 3-month period. The fee for participating in each mailing is $300. The company also suggested that Pamela could include a special introductory $2 rebate coupon with her flyer. The coupon could potentially increase the response rate by 50 percent.

Based on conversations with her father, Pamela estimated that she would need $15,000 to buy refrigerated cases, cash registers, and fixtures for her store. Although she intended to purchase mostly second-hand equipment, she did not think that she could get by with less. Equipment and fixtures could be depreciated completely over five years following the straight line method. Exhibit 3 lists the nonrecurring start-up expenses. These included such items as legal fees, initial inventory cost, and working capital requirements.

In the last four years Pamela had accumulated approximately $5,000 in savings. However, she did not want to put all of it into the store. Her parents had agreed with her on this and promised to give her $5,000 to invest in the store as a graduation present if she would invest half of her savings in the store, too. Her father also introduced her to the manager of the local bank who assured her that she could get a loan at 15 percent interest.

EXHIBIT 2   Planned Monthly Advertising Expense

Medium	Monthly Cost
1 column x 2″ Yellow Page listing	$55.00
2 insertions per month in local newspaper ($95 per insertion)	190.00
Flyers	50.00
Total	295.00

EXHIBIT 3   Start-Up Expenses

Item	Amount
Legal fees	$500
Office supplies	500
Initial inventory	8,000
Introductory announcements	200
Repainting, decorations, and signs	850
Labor for installation of fixtures	500
Rent deposit	3,200
Utility deposit	200
Working capital	8,500
Total	22,450

One of the most valuable experiences Pamela gained from working at her parent's store was her knowledge of flower wholesalers and wholesale prices. Wholesale prices accounted for 55 cents of every retail dollar. This did not include transportation costs, which typically came to 5 percent of retail sales. This left the store with a gross margin of 40 percent to cover all other expenses and to generate a profit. According to her experience, however, a 40 percent gross margin is somewhat optimistic. This margin is gained only if the entire inventory is sold at its regular price. Because flowers are extremely perishable, 10 percent of the inventory typically has no resale value.

Because of loss from spoilage, good inventory control was crucial in the floral business. The store manager must be able to predict the total amount and the types of flower that should be stocked with reasonable accuracy. This required a good inventory system that tracked sales patterns accurately and an intelligent forecasting system based on past sales and seasonal patterns. Pamela remembered seeing a brochure and price list from a retail software firm announcing a new P.O.S. system and software for flower shops. The brochure claimed that the system could reduce inventory spoilage at flower shops by 50 percent compared to the manual inventory tracking procedure. Although the price tag of $6,500 initially shocked her, she planned to look into the new system in more detail.

Assignments

1. What is the minimum level of sales the store must generate to cover all its expenses?
2. Estimate the potential sales of Pamela's Flower Shop. Will the store be able to break-even?
3. Prepare a projected first year income statement for the store.
4. Evaluate the pros and cons of the direct mail proposal. Should Pamela participate in the mailing? Is it worthwhile to include a $2 rebate coupon?
5. Is it worthwhile for Pamela to install the computerized inventory system?

Case 19 (B)
Pamela's Flower Shop

It was exactly one year ago that Pamela Rink opened her new flower shop in Croton. She sold $250,000 worth of flowers during the year. Although this was somewhat lower than what she had expected, she was relatively happy with the outcome. She realized, however, that greater challenges lay ahead of her. She had to find ways to increase her sales. One avenue she was contemplating was to add a delivery service. During the year there had been a number of requests for flower delivery. About half of the requests were from corporations that wanted flowers delivered to their business partners or employees. Most deliveries were to the local hospital. She had lost these sales because she had no delivery vehicle. Losing delivery sales was especially aggravating because the orders were typically for larger amounts. Delivery orders from individual customers were typically for $25, while corporate orders were $40, on the average.

Pamela was seriously considering adding delivery service. She could buy a used van for $10,000. Since most deliveries were intended for the local hospital, a part-time driver working 30 hours a week would suffice. She estimated a salary of $10 per hour for the driver. She estimated $1,200 a year for insurance, and $2,000 for maintenance and fuel. Her plan was to take a 60-month straight line depreciation for the van. The local bank had agreed to loan her the money for the van at 15 percent annual interest. She wondered how many delivery customers she required to justify the additional cost of delivery service.

Assignment

Should Pamela Rink add the Delivery service? Analyze the costs and potential benefits of adding the service and assess whether it will be profitable to add delivery service. Show your analysis and calculations in a table, clearly stating your assumptions. Use information from Pamela's Flower Shop (A) case, if necessary.

Case 20
Stafford Catalog Showrooms

The headline in the March 25, 1985 edition of *HFD*, the weekly home furnishings trade paper, read, "Feeling the Squeeze: Catalog Showrooms under Pressure." The story noted the unstable nature of the catalog showroom industry and reported dramatic industrywide personnel changes, slowing sales growth, and increasing competitive pressures among catalog showroom operators as well as from discounters and department stores.

The news came as no surprise to Ann Parkman, chief executive officer of Stafford Catalog Showrooms, a ten-store chain of retail outlets in the Midwest. Parkman had been in the industry since its inception in the mid-1960s and had seen the 20% annual sales growth of the 1970s come and go. She described the industry's and Stafford's current situation:

> The catalog showroom industry certainly has changed, but I'm convinced it's still a viable concept. It's just very hard to tell where the problem lies. We are caught between the discounters trading up and the department stores getting more promotional. What used to be a solid niche for the catalogers has been narrowed to a point where it's hard for anyone to make a profit. The last few years have been pretty tough for Stafford. It's bad enough to have two stores performing like the two we have in City A. They've never done as well as they should have in either sales or profits. But now, even our City B store sales are beginning to slow down. To make matters worse, BuySmart is opening five new discount stores in City B, one of them only a block from our showroom. The catalog showroom industry has always operated on volume, not margin, but if we don't get our sales growing again, we'll have to figure out how to be profitable at present volume levels.

CATALOG SHOWROOM OPERATIONS AND MERCHANDISING

First appearing in the 1960s, catalog showrooms were retail outlets comprising display areas, or showrooms, and adjoining warehouses. They sold brand-name appliances, electronics, luggage, giftware, sporting goods, toys, cameras, jewelry, and other assorted branded products for home and office that did not require delivery or installation. Originally, prices were well below those of traditional department stores.

Each September, showroom operators produced and distributed catalogs containing color photographs, descriptions, selling prices, and comparison prices (usually suggested retail prices) for most of the items available in their showrooms. Some operators also issued a spring catalog. It was common practice in the industry for groups of smaller noncompeting operators to share the production expenses of a joint catalog.

Although catalog showroom configurations and operations varied, two general formats were used. In the *mass merchandising* format, in all departments except jewelry backup stock was kept in the selling area and customers used shopping carts to bring their selections to checkout lines. *Sample-style* operators, on the other hand, stocked only sporting goods and toys on the selling floor. In the other departments, they displayed one sample of each item carried. Customers placed their orders for these items with order clerks and waited for their choices to be retrieved from the stock area. They then stood in a second line to pay for their purchases. Some sample-style operators provided clipboards and order forms at the showroom entrances so that customers could prepare their own orders as they examined the sample products.

Sample-style stores generally appeared more upscale, less cluttered, and less like discounters than the mass merchant-style outlets. In the mass merchant-style stores, however, product availability was readily apparent, and self-service made it unnecessary to stand in line twice. One major sample-style catalog chain, Service Merchandise, had installed easy-to-use computer terminals in many of its showrooms so that item availability could be determined and orders placed without assistance from order clerks.

The level of service in catalog showrooms depended primarily on product category. Jewelry was consistently a full-service area in both mass-merchandise and sample-style chains, while service levels in other departments differed. In mass merchant-style showrooms, where stock was kept on the selling floor, stockkeeping personnel frequently provided the limited sales assistance.

Traditionally, catalog showroom operations had been characterized by the unusual payment terms vendors made available to them. Forty percent of all showroom sales took place in November and December. Vendors desired even production runs throughout the year however, as well as reduced warehousing costs, and had allowed January payment for products delivered before June of the previous year. As industry sales had begun to slow in the 1980s, some catalogers had been forced to liquidate. Consequently, some vendors had become increasingly uneasy about the six-month terms and the prospect of having to chase their goods or money in bankruptcy court. Recently, some had required partial payments in November and December. Other vendors had stopped treating the catalog showrooms as a distinct line of trade and offered them the same credit terms available to discount merchants.

COMPETITION

Catalog showrooms competed with traditional department and specialty stores, discount stores (e.g., Target, K mart), general merchandisers (e.g., Sears, J.C. Penney's), and restricted-entry warehouse outlets (e.g., Price Club) (see Exhibit 1 and Appendix A). Catalog showrooms did not offer as wide an assortment of products as the discounters, but within the product lines they did carry, they offered a much larger selection of brands and models (see Exhibit 2). Many consumers, nevertheless, believed that because discounters carried a wider range of products, they also carried a wider selection of brands and models of each product. This misperception was considered a serious problem by catalog showroom operators.

EXHIBIT 1 *Stafford Catalog Showrooms: Leading Retail Channels for Selected Categories of Catalog Showroom Items*

	1984 Volume (millions)	% of Sales in Own Stores	% of Total Retail Volume
Consumer Electronics			
TV & Radio Stores	$7,852	66.5%[a]	45.9%[b]
Discount Stores	2,127	3.4	12.4
Department Stores	1,602	2.9	9.4
Household Appliance Stores	1,404	16.8	8.2
Catalog Showrooms	1,246	14.3	7.3
Camera/Photo Supplies			
Camera & Photo Supply Stores	$2,112	78.7%	30.2%
Discount Stores	1,418	2.3	20.3
Drugstores	1,307	3.1	18.7
Supermarket & Grocery Stores	759	0.3	10.9
Department Stores	718	1.3	10.3
Catalog Showrooms	497	5.7	7.1
Toys/Hobbies/Games			
Hobby, Toy, Game Stores	$3,806	78.0%	35.9%
Discount Stores	3,079	4.9	29.0
Department Stores	1,326	0.7	12.5
Drug & Proprietary Stores	590	1.4	5.6
Variety Stores	525	6.3	5.0
Supermarket & Grocery Stores	506	0.2	4.8
Catalog Showrooms	340	3.9	3.2
Jewelry & Watches			
Jewelry Stores	$8,295	87.1%	58.2%
Catalog Showrooms	2,588	29.7	18.2
Small Electric Appliances			
Discount Stores	$1,505	2.4%	31.7%
Department Stores	718	1.3	15.1
Drug & Proprietary Stores	675	1.6	14.2
Catalog Showrooms	593	6.8	12.5
Sporting Goods & Luggage			
Sporting Goods & Bicycle Shops	$6,158	75.1%	54.6%
Discount Stores	2,277	3.7	20.2
Catalog Showrooms	627	7.2	5.6
Housewares & Gifts			
Discount Stores	$4,136	6.7%	20.7%
Supermarkets & Grocery Stores	3,575	1.4	17.9
Department Stores	2,596	4.7	13.0
Gifts, Novelty & Souvenir Shops	2,570	51.0	12.9
Catalog Showrooms	1,795	20.6	9.0

[a]To be read: 66.5% of all 1984 TV and radio store sales were sales of consumer electronics.
[b]To be read: 45.9% of the total 1984 retail sales of consumer electronics were in TV and radio stores.

Source: Discount Merchandiser, May 1985.

EXHIBIT 2   *Stafford Catalog Showrooms: Assortment Comparison among Types of Outlets*

	Catalog Showrooms			Discount Stores			General Merchandisers		Dept. Stores
	Stafford	Service Merchandise	Wilson	Target	BuySmart	K mart	Ward's	Penney's	Dillard's
Golf Bags									
No. styles	8	14	4	9	9	12	11	10	0
High price	$64.97	$89.97	$79.99	$54.99	$39.99	$69.97	$139.99	$59.99	NA
Low price	$19.97	19.97	69.91	29.99	34.99	44.97	34.99	39.99	NA
Bicycles									
No. styles	14	22	20	10	6	12	12	0	0
High price	$119.97	149.95	139.88	129.99	149.99	149.97	279.99	NA	NA
Low price	$69.97	32.97	69.88	59.00	74.99	69.97	89.99	NA	NA
Irons									
No. styles	17	13	14	14	11	12	6	4	7
High price	$44.97	39.97	64.84	39.97	49.99	39.97	47.99	19.99	54.00
Low price	$14.94	16.86	15.94	14.94	17.44	13.97	16.88	14.99	19.00
Typewriters									
No. styles	14	13	10	7	4	4	4	9	0
High price	$479.90	319.97	499.90	299.97	279.00	439.97	319.00	299.99	NA
Low price	$69.90	149.00	59.90	159.99	219.00	229.00	259.00	79.95	NA
VCRs									
No. styles	7	5	8	10	0	11	8	4	8
High price	$499.90	496.00	599.99	599.99	NA	499.00	1,249.90	999.99	749.00
Low price	$319.77	259.00	249.90	279.99	NA	319.00	299.90	369.95	287.00

Originally, catalog showroom operators had been able to obtain some upscale brands unavailable to discount stores. Although vendors normally had restricted a few lines to traditional department and specialty stores, the catalog showroom operators had been able to offer most of the brand names carried in those outlets. While department stores had become more promotional, narrowing the catalog showrooms' price advantage, by 1975 repeal of the Fair Trade laws and changes in vendors' policies increasingly had allowed discounters to obtain the same brands as the catalog showrooms. Although the discounters generally carried lower-priced models with fewer features, access to the same brands had intensified the competition between the discount stores and the catalog showrooms.

One of the most successful discount chains was Target Stores, owned by Dayton Hudson. The following table gives some economic characteristics of a typical three-year-old Target Store and compares them with those of a leading warehouse-style retailer, Price Club.

	Target	Price Club
Square Feet	100,000	100,000
Annual Sales/sq. ft.	$160	$600
Gross Margin	31%	10%
Profit before Interest and Taxes		
$	$1.3m	$3.0m
% of Sales	8%	5%
Fixed Investment		
(Building, Fixtures, and Land)	$5.5m	$5.8m
Inventory, net at cost	$.6m	$(.1)m
Fixed Investment and Inventory	$6.1m	$5.7m
Pretax Return on		
Fixed Investment		
and Inventory	21%	53%
Inventory at Retail	$3.2m	$3.3m
Turnover	5X	18X

Source: Goldman Sachs

Traditionally, catalog showrooms had been bare-bones operations with attractive pricing on familiar brand-name merchandise. As many catalogers had made their showrooms more luxurious, restricted entry warehouse outlets had replaced them as the new bare-bones retailers of quality branded hard goods. Warehouse outlets bought only what was available from vendors at discounted prices. This merchandising policy resulted in a significant lack of depth in the assortment offered and little continuity of selection from week to week. However, it allowed the warehouse outlets to offer very low prices on familiar brand-name products. The industry leader, Price Club, operated strictly on a volume basis, with typical store sales of up to four times those of comparable Target outlets, as shown in the above table. Catalog showroom operators had begun to react to the competitive threats from discounters and warehouse stores by upgrading their assortments.

INDUSTRY DEVELOPMENT

During the 1970s the catalog showroom industry had experienced tremendous growth. New catalogers had begun operations, and existing chains had opened showrooms in many new markets. By 1980 the industry had established itself as a major retail channel, with 2,103 outlets and sales of $7.1 billion (Exhibit 1). Between 1980 and 1985, however, industry profitability and the number of stores had declined. In 1984 sales of $8.7 billion were made through 1,766 outlets. Individual company sales growth had increasingly come from acquisition. The increasing concentration in the industry brought into common ownership catalog showrooms with different retail operating systems. In addition, some chains had begun to invade geographic markets traditionally served by others.

In April 1985 Service Merchandise purchased H. J. Wilson to become the largest firm in the catalog showroom industry. Service

Merchandise and Best Products each had sales of over $2 billion and together controlled over 45% of all catalog showroom volume. Two other large catalog operators were the Canada-based Consumers Distributing Company, with 160 showrooms in the United States, and Carlson Catalog Showrooms, which operated 61 showrooms. Both had experienced declining earnings in 1984.

While many small unprofitable chains had been acquired by the larger operators, other small chains had remained profitable. Even L. Luria, however, a traditionally profitable Florida cataloger with high operating margins and a strong emphasis on jewelry, was experiencing less buoyant comparable store sales by mid-1985. W. Bell, an 18-store chain with outlets in Washington, D.C., Baltimore, Houston, and Chicago, had followed with uneven success a strategy of presenting a limited assortment of merchandise in upscale showrooms and providing strong sales help (see comparative performance statistics in Exhibit 3).

Industry studies had revealed that the catalog showroom industry was somewhat cyclical and was among the first lines of retail trade to be affected by economic changes. Its product mix emphasized discretionary items, whose purchase was most likely to be postponed during an economic downturn. In addition, catalog showrooms relied heavily on high-margin jewelry sales (see Exhibit 4). This reliance left operators at the mercy of gold price fluctuations. Short-term inventory buildup in preparation for the Christmas rush was often financed with bank credit (in addition to extended terms from vendors), and profits could be affected significantly by interest rates. Finally, the industry competed primarily on price, and its customers were thought to be especially sensitive to pricing and

---

EXHIBIT 3 *Stafford Catalog Showrooms: Selected Catalog Showroom Performance, 1981–1984 (millions)*

	FY 1981		FY 1982		FY 1983		FY 1984		No. Showrooms Dec. 1984
	Sales	NI	Sales	NI	Sales	NI	Sales	NI[b]	
Best Products[a]	$1,109	19.5	$1,582	26.1	$2,081	33.0	$2,253	13.6	204
Service Merch.	1,027	23.1	1,195	31.6	1,458	44.9	1,657	44.6	183
H. J. Wilson	403	12.7	458	5.6	514	8.8	521	(3.3)	79
L. Luria[c]	91	3.2	109	4.6	124	5.6	145	6.8	34
W. Bell [c]	107	2.4	135	1.4	125	2.7	138	2.7	17
Stafford	62	1.3	64	0.9	47	(0.8)	39	(0.7)	10
City A, 1	4	(0)	5	(0)	4	(0)	4	(0.1)	
City A, 2	3	(0.1)	3	(0.1)	3	(0)	3	(0.1)	
City B	11	0.5	11	0.3	10	0.3	9	0.1	

[a]Best acquired Basco in July 1982 and Modern Merchandising in October 1982. If 1982 sales of Best, Basco, and Modern had been combined for the entire year and not just from dates of acquisition, the sales increases for 1983 would be 5.9%. Sales include 40 jewelry and clothing nonshowroom retail outlets.
[b]Net income.
[c]Fiscal year ends last week in June.

EXHIBIT 4 *Stafford Catalog Showrooms: Net Sales and Selected Expenses by Product Category for Consolidated Company, 1984*

	Net Sale (000)	Gross Profit % Sales	Personnel Expense[a] % Sales	Building Expense[b] % Sales	Advertising Expense[c] % Sales	Interest Expense[d] % Sales
Jewelry	$8,958	45.5%	15.8%	4.7%	6.2%	5.6%
Pers/Appliances	5,059	15.6%	8.1%	3.8%	2.6%	2.8%
Luggage/Leather	881	32.0%	6.1%	7.1%	4.2%	3.6%
Dinner/Kitchen/Bath	1,860	29.5%	1.7%	7.8%	8.3%	3.9%
Silver/Crystal	774	37.3%	7.0%	11.3%	9.8%	3.0%
Clocks/Weather	557	28.5%	6.1%	2.8%	5.8%	4.5%
Games/Decor/Fire	1,196	33.9%	5.7%	18.6%	7.2%	3.3%
Lamps/Furniture	1,093	33.9%	7.0%	13.9%	6.3%	3.5%
Seasonal—Patio	1,445	15.7%	1.2%	9.2%	7.7%	−0.4%
Health & Beauty Aids (1/3 year)	837	34.9%	2.7%	22.9%	18.7%	3.5%
Seasonal—Christmas	300	28.0%	7.6%	44.3%	5.0%	0.0%
Home Ent./Computer	549	−7.3%	28.4%	7.5%	6.7%	5.2%
Toys	3,334	27.3%	7.5%	8.9%	5.3%	1.9%
Sports	2,421	25.4%	11.2%	9.2%	7.3%	2.2%
Juvenile	782	30.4%	11.3%	30.7%	7.3%	3.0%
Office	2,658	17.6%	3.3%	2.7%	3.5%	2.3%
Cameras	1,631	14.3%	5.4%	9.2%	2.2%	2.4%
Electronics	4,257	14.8%	5.3%	3.5%	2.3%	1.8%
Domestics	687	20.1%	9.5%	13.7%	3.3%	4.5%
Hardware	213	19.3%	5.3%	22.1%	1.5%	3.5%

[a]Allocation based on estimate of employee and management time expended on category.
[b]Allocation based on total square feet of floor space in building (showroom and warehouse) required by category.
[c]Allocation based on amount of space in both catalog and flyers devoted to category.
[d]Allocation based on amount and length of time inventory is carried for each category.

promotion. This price sensitivity became more acute during recessions.

STAFFORD CATALOG SHOWROOMS

The Catalog   Stafford was one of a group of four catalog showroom companies that jointly produced a common catalog. Stafford had assumed leadership in the merchandising deci-sions of the group, but each member contributed ideas and opinions. Except for some slight differences, for which participants paid extra, and different covers, the same catalog was used by each. Prices, however, were determined independently. Each member of the group served a different geographic market.

The catalog was issued in September, and its prices were guaranteed until January 31. A systematic review was conducted in early March for desired changes in product mix and prices. By

April, merchandising decisions for the next catalog had been made and production started. Some companies had experimented with multiple versions of their catalogs quoting different prices for different markets. Stafford, however, used one catalog, and its prices were the same in all markets served. The 1985 catalog was 448 pages long and contained over 7,000 items.

In recent years the number of pages in the Stafford catalog had been reduced, and the showrooms had begun to carry increasing numbers of items not included in the catalog. In 1984 approximately 10,000 current "not in catalog" (NIC) items were offered in the Stafford showrooms. Most of the NIC items were domestics, seasonal offerings, or health and beauty aids. However, 97% of the total current home entertainment and computer stockkeeping units (SKUs) did not appear in the catalog, and over half of the current camera and sports offerings were also NIC items. The luggage, clocks, lamps, and silver departments each had fewer than 10% NIC items. Best Products, Service Merchandise, and H. J. Wilson had slightly larger catalogs. Best and Service carried only half as many NIC items as Stafford, whereas H. J. Wilson carried significantly more.

Best Products and Service Merchandise mailed their catalogs; Stafford did not. It had, however, developed a customer list in each market, which was used in conjunction with purchased address lists for flyer mailings. Stafford's customer list was compiled from names on checks and jewelry sales documents. Customers who had bought nonjewelry items with cash were not represented, and only those who had made purchases within the previous three years were retained on the list. Customers could also ask to be put on the list by filling out a form available in the showroom. Stafford announced the availability of its catalog in the September promotional flyer and customers were invited to pick one up at a showroom. Ann Parkman was considering mailing the catalog so that Stafford could gain more control over when it actually reached consumers.

The catalog traditionally had been Stafford's primary method of advertising. In recent years the company had increased its use of flyers as promotional devices. In 1980 Stafford mailed seven flyers totalling 180 pages. In 1984 this had grown to nine flyers totaling 296 pages and 10 newspaper inserts totaling 160 pages. Except for the sale prices, flyers resembled minicatalogs and were normally 32 pages long. Customers apparently had become well aware of the company's promotional orientation and waited for sales. Some customers asked salespeople to call them when a particular item went on sale.

Flyers and newspaper inserts accounted for 70% of the advertising budget, the catalog itself for 25%, and television and radio for the remaining 5%. The industry advertising-to-sales ratio was 4.9%; the Stafford ratio was 5.4%.

Jewelry   Jewelry, always a mainstay of the catalog showroom industry, was consistently the highest-margin product category. In fact, many catalog showroom operators had evolved from jewelry retailers. Catalog showrooms in general, and Stafford in particular, had a reputation for good-quality jewelry at very reasonable prices. Stafford showrooms carried some individual pieces of diamond jewelry that retailed for up to $7,500. Moreover, the jewelry department was prominent in all Stafford showrooms: Customers had to pass it on their way to other departments. It was staffed by knowledgeable sales personnel who had successfully completed a company run training program. Some managers felt that many of Stafford's customers never shopped at Stafford for anything but jewelry.

Pricing   Stafford had always attempted to offer everyday low prices in its catalog. Consumers' ability to compare promotional prices with catalog prices put downward pressure on the promotional prices, and some Stafford merchandise managers had begun to raise catalog prices in anticipation of promotional markdowns. Jewelry experienced the greatest promotional activity, with markdowns of 21% (see Appendix B). Home entertainment and computers were marked down 19%, whereas personal appliances, luggage, clocks, toys, and cameras were all marked down less than 5%. To reduce price comparison and maintain margins, Stafford and many other catalogers had, over the years, carried and promoted an increasing number of unbranded items and items not included in the catalog. Furthermore, during the early 1980s inflation had led Stafford to lower the quality of its assortment in order to hold its price points.

Operations Unlike Best Products and Service Merchandise, Stafford mass-merchandised everything in its showroom. Shopping carts were provided, and customers took stock from the shelves and brought it to the checkout counter, as they would in a discount outlet. Stafford showrooms (including the attached warehouses) averaged approximately 45,000 square feet, compared with Best Products' full-size stores, which had traditionally been 65,000 square feet. (Although catalog showrooms were generally large stand-alone outlets, both Best Products and Service Merchandise had begun to tailor the sizes of their stores to particular markets and experiment with mall showrooms and outlets as small as 12,000 square feet.) Stafford showrooms were larger in relation to their adjoining warehouses than those of sample-style operators. Because stock could be stored more compactly in warehouses than on the selling floor, however, Stafford showrooms were not able to carry as much total on-hand inventory as comparably sized sample-style stores.

All product shipments passed through Stafford's central distribution center. There, large truckloads of individual products were broken down into smaller lot sizes, and trucks loaded with combinations of products proceeded to showroom warehouses. No inventory was kept in the distribution center. Because of the expense of double handling, Stafford rarely permitted interstore inventory transfers in response to local stockouts. Any such transfer required prior approval by the corporate merchandise manager of the department involved.

Inventory turned an average of 1.9 times in Stafford showrooms; the average for the industry's top-10 operators was 2.1 times. Stafford used a computerized inventory system, which recorded each transaction at the checkout register. Corporate merchandise managers received weekly reports on store-by-store inventory levels of each product in their department. It was their responsibility to ensure that enough inventory was maintained and that additional stock was available for items appearing in the promotional flyers. Store managers were told one month in advance what items would be promoted, but they were not aware of how much inventory, if any, was being shipped to their store for the promotion. Store managers had considered stockouts of promoted items a serious problem, but they felt the situation was improving. Consumers found stockouts in catalog showrooms especially annoying, because most had reviewed the catalog or flyers and come into the store for a particular item.

Noncurrent merchandise (merchandise from prior catalogs no longer in the current catalog, and NIC items not being reordered) had constituted over 22% of the total merchandise in Stafford showrooms in 1983, in contrast to only 10% on average for the industry's top-10 operators. In 1984 Stafford had reduced its noncurrent inventory to 14.5%.

PENBURY FARMS

Stafford had been purchased in 1977 by Penbury Farms, a large, privately held, diversified food processing and land development company. Penbury had become increasingly disappointed with its return from Stafford. Nevertheless, because most of the showrooms were at least eight years old and had begun to look quite run down, in 1983 Penbury undertook a selective renovation program. A full renovation, costing about $300,000, included new fixtures, wallpaper, carpet, and a few floor plan. A partial renovation, costing about $20,000, used the same fixtures but redesigned them making them lower and giving them a somewhat more modern appearance.

In an effort to improve Stafford's profitability, Penbury had imposed strict budgetary constraints. At the store level, these restrictions required managers to decrease payroll expenditures substantially. Also, between December 1982 and December 1984 Stafford had closed two of its least profitable showrooms. One more closing was planned for 1985. Neither of the stores in City A nor the one in City B was being considered for closing in 1985. Closing stores was extremely expensive (approximately $500,000) primarily because of the long-term lease obligations covering all the Stafford outlets. Exhibit 4 presents a summary of Stafford income and expenses by product category for 1984.

THE TWO MARKETS

The problems facing Stafford in City A and City B were typical of those of other stores in the chain. Although some showrooms had done well, others had never achieved expected sales or profitability. Management felt that some stores' lower gross margins resulted primarily from the mix of products sold and their customers' propensity to buy more on promotion.

When Stafford opened the stores in City A and City B, each was projected to sell in excess of $7 million per year. The City B store had exceeded that target, reaching a high of $11 million in 1981. The two stores in City A had never come close to the projection (see the following table for showroom sizes and sales and Exhibit 5 for statements of earnings).

In 1985 approximately 69,000 flyers were mailed in the City A market and over 88,000 in the City B market for each promotional period. Research had shown that the average Stafford showroom customer traveled fewer than six miles from home or work to the showroom. In both City A and City B, however, a substantial number of customers from more distant rural communities combined trips to the city for other reasons with visits to the Stafford showroom. Some customers who lived or worked near a showroom visited frequently during the year; many customers, however, shopped the showroom only during the Christmas season. This pattern appeared to hold equally in all three stores.

Showroom Sizes and 1984 Sales

	City A #1	City A #2	City B #1	1984 Catalog Showroom Average	1984 Discount Store Average
Size (Total sq. ft.)	50,000	54,500	54,250	34,936	64,874
Display Area	31,200	35,000	42,250	14,254	55,792
Warehouse Area	18,800	19,500	12,000	20,682	9,082
1984 Sales (millions)	$4.0	$2.8	$8.5	$5.0	$7.1

EXHIBIT 5 Stafford Catalog Showrooms: Earnings, Assets, and Liabilities, 1983, 1984 ($000s)

	City A, 1		City A, 2		City B		Consolidated Company Total		Consolidated Company % to Sales	
	1984	1983	1984	1983	1984	1983	(10 SRS)[a] 1984	(11 SRS) 1983	(10 SRS) 1984	(11 SRS) 1983
Net Sales	$4,024	$4,466	$2,857	$2,903	$8,545	$9,609	$39,492	$47,074	100.00	100.00
Cost of Sales (FIFO)	3,004	3,355	2,127	2,177	6,257	7,073	28,737	34,175	72.77	72.60
Gross Profit	1,020	1,111	730	726	2,288	2,536	10,755	12,899	27.23	27.40
Showroom Expenses										
Fixed	422	411	345	255	535	552	3,864	4,215	9.8	8.95
Variable	327	345	301	304	524	530	3,269	3,598	8.27	7.64
Advertising, Net	151	117	134	77	265	266	2,124	2,793	5.38	5.93
Total Operating Expenses	$900	$873	$780	$636	$1,324	$1,348	$9,257	$10,606	23.45	22.52
Showroom Income (Loss)	120	238	(50)	90	964	1,188	1,498	2,293	3.78	4.88
Interest Expenses, Net	(140)	(136)	(169)	(99)	(274)	(192)	(1,281)	(1,365)	(3.24)	(2.90)
Corporate Office Allocation	(210)	(180)	(150)	(117)	(447)	(386)	(2,091)	(2,428)	(5.29)	(5.16)
Operating Profit (Loss)	(230)	(78)	(369)	(126)	243	610	(1,874)	(1,500)	(4.75)	(3.19)
Discontinued Operation	0	0	0	0	0	0	(480)	(450)	(1.2)	(1.0)
Net Income, before Tax	(230)	(78)	(369)	(126)	243	610	(2,354)	(1,950)	(6.0)	(4.1)
Prov. for Income Taxes (Benefit)							(1,671)	(936)	(4.2)	(2.0)
Net Income (Loss)	(230)	(78)	(369)	(126)	243	610	$(683)	$(1,014)	(1.7)	(2.2)
ASSETS										
Total Inventories & Other Current Assets	$1,294	$1,867	$1,172	$1,404	$2,522	$2,692	$16,609	$19,859		
Total Property & Equip., Net of Depreciation	233	279	113	128	397	247	2,471	2,178		
TOTAL ASSETS	$1,527	$2,147	$1,284	$1,532	$2,919	$2,939	$19,081	$22,037		
LIABILITIES										
Total Current Liabilities	$462	$690	$429	$487	$833	$1,071	$5,743	$7,486		
Intercompany Stockholders' Investment	739	1,065	645	734	(3,781)	(3,929)	(4,982)	(4,098)		
Retained Earnings	325	392	210	311	5,867	5,797	18,320	18,650		
TOTAL LIABILITIES & STOCKHOLDERS' INVESTMENT	$1,527	$2,147	$1,284	$1,532	$2,919	$2,939	$19,081	$22,037		

Note: Year ended December 31.
[a] 10 showrooms in 1984, 11 showrooms in 1983.

CITY A

City A had a population of about 420,000 and was located in the Midwest. The residential areas ended abruptly at the city limits, and a substantial amount of farmland surrounded the city. City A's economy was dominated by four large machine tool manufacturers and a large army base. Annual sales of general merchandise in the City A market totaled about $360 million.

City A Showroom 1

Showroom 1 was located in Eastland Mall, a strip mall at the eastern edge of the city. The area immediately surrounding the mall consisted primarily of well-kept, middle-class residential neighborhoods, some upper-middle-class housing, and a large new luxury-apartment complex. There was a substantial amount of retailing on the nearby main roads. Less than a mile to the east, however, there were only farms and a machine tool factory. The mall was conveniently located on the main east-west highway, and during the 1970s it had been the most popular shopping center in the city. In 1980 Lincolnshire Mall, a large three-level enclosed mall, had opened directly opposite Eastland Mall, severely affecting Eastland. By 1985 Eastland had fallen into disrepair, and approximately one-third of its space was vacant.

Showroom 1 had opened in 1977 and had never been renovated. It had very high ceilings and still had the old-fashioned high fixtures. The departments were delineated by different wallpaper patterns on the outside walls (see Exhibit 6 for a breakdown of the percentage of catalog sales and floor space by product category for each of the City A and City B stores). In 1983 H. J. Wilson had opened a new sample-style showroom in the Lincolnshire Mall. It was only 30,000 square feet and had entrances off both the parking lot and the mall itself. It was supported by a small attached warehouse (included in the 30,000 square feet) and the substantially larger warehouse attached to a standard-size Wilson showroom on the west side of the city.

The Wilson showroom was considerably more upscale in appearance than Stafford Showroom 1 and featured attractive low fixtures arranged like those in a typical department store. Service on its selling floor was typical of the catalog showroom industry. Service personnel were more available than they were in the Stafford showrooms, and in the high-margin areas, such as jewelry and gifts, they were better trained. The employees wore distinctive sports jackets or uniforms. Exhibit 7 presents price comparisons between Stafford and various competitors on selected high visibility (high-volume) and low-visibility items.

A 70,000 square foot stand-alone Target outlet was adjacent to the Lincolnshire Mall. A clean and modern discount store, more upscale than K mart, Target offered lower-end models of quality brand name products at sharply discounted prices. Target was a self-service operation, but it provided some sales assistance in the form of stockkeeping personnel on the selling floor. Casual conversations between the casewriter and six customers in the Stafford showroom indicated that most felt Target was comparable to Showroom 1.

Other retailing outlets in the general vicinity included K mart, Penney's, Sears, and Dillard's. Although similar in service and appearance to Sears or Penney's, Dillard's was a department store that sold mainly brand name merchandise. During sales, Dillard's had very attractive prices.

City A Showroom 2

Showroom 2 was located in a small strip mall in the northwest part of City A, approximately

EXHIBIT 6 Stafford Catalog Showrooms: Percentage of Catalog, Sales, and Showroom Floor Space by Product Category (1984)

	% of Catalog[a]	City A, 1		City A, 2		City B	
		% Total Sales	% Showroom Selling Space[b]	% Total Sales	% Showroom Selling Space	% Total Sales	% Showroom Selling Space
Jewelry/Watches	23.5%	21.9%	10.6%	22.6%	7.2%	23.9%	11.2%
Personal Appliances	2.5	13.1	10.9	12.5	11.9	13.1	6.9
Luggage/Leather	4.2	2.3	5.8	2.0	3.8	2.6	5.1
Dinner/Kitchen/Bath	10.3	4.8	2.6	5.4	5.3	5.3	7.4
Silver/Crystal	3.9	2.1	2.0	2.3	4.6	3.0	2.0
Clocks/Weather	2.7	1.4	0.7	1.5	1.7	1.6	0.6
Games/Decor/Fireplace	4.6	3.1	7.7	3.2	9.7	3.3	4.9
Lamps/Furniture	5.4	3.4	7.8	2.8	6.3	3.0	8.9
Seasonal—Patio	0	4.0	6.9[c]	4.2	11.5	3.5	6.6
Health and Beauty Aids	0	2.1	3.8	2.6	3.6	2.1	4.2
Seasonal Christmas	0	0.8	6.9[c]	1.0	11.5	0.6	6.6
Home Entertainment/Computer	9.3	1.5	3.5	1.4	0.3	1.0	0.6
Toys	9.3	8.3	10.2	8.9	8.4	7.2	12.0
Sports	4.9	5.3	9.7	6.0	9.9	5.9	11.1
Juvenile	3.4	2.2	9.1	1.8	9.8	1.7	5.2
Office	4.7	7.0	0.7	6.4	1.8	7.0	2.2
Cameras	2.2	4.3	0.8	3.6	0.1	4.2	2.1
Electronics	7.4	10.4	1.5	10.0	0.3	9.3	3.9
Domestics	1.0	1.4	5.4	1.2	2.6	1.0	4.1
Hardware	0.7	0.6	0.3	0.6	1.2	0.7	1.0

[a] Percentage of catalog (not including flyers) devoted to each category.
[b] Percentage showroom selling space represents the proportion of selling floor footage devoted to each category, and does not include the warehouse storage space required by each category.
[c] Seasonal—Patio/Christmas occupy the same space and, therefore, should be counted only once.

EXHIBIT 7 Stafford Catalog Showrooms: Price Comparisons on Selected High- and Low-Visibility Items

	Catalog Showrooms			Discount Stores			General Merchandisers		Dept. Stores
	Stafford	Service Merch.	Wilson	Target	BuySmart	K mart	Ward's	Penney's	Dillard's
Jewelry									
(Hi) Casio Calendar Watch	$11.90	$12.97	NA	NA	23.99	NA	NA	NA	NA
Pers/Appliance									
(Hi) Oster Kitchen Center	149.90	139.87	148.97	NA	NA	139.87	NA	179.90	170.00
Luggage/Leather									
(Hi) Samsonite Attache	49.94	52.94	48.99	NA	NA	31.97	NA	NA	NA
Dinner/Kitchen Bath									
(Low) Pomerantz Tray	9.97	NA	16.97	NA	NA	NA	NA	19.99	NA
Silver/Crystal									
(Hi) Anchor Hocking 24-pc.	19.96	NA	NA	19.99	NA	NA	19.99	24.99	19.87
Clocks/Weather									
(Low) Spartus Digital Clock	19.97	19.82	NA	19.99	24.99	NA	21.99	24.99	NA
Lamps/Furniture									
(Hi) Pharmacy Lamp	34.90	NA	34.97	39.99	NA	34.96	50.00	89.99	NA
Seasonal—Patio									
(Low) Moss 52 Fan	59.90	59.97	89.97	59.00	99.99	80.00	99.99	NA	59.00
Health & Beauty Aids									
(Hi) Oil of Olay	3.99	NA	NA	3.89	4.19	3.89	NA	NA	5.09
Home Ent/Computer									
(Low) Commodore C-64	199.97	139.92	149.91	149.99	NA	139.92	169.99	NA	149.90
Toys									
(Low) See and Say	8.97	8.92	8.90	9.99	8.99	8.46	8.88	NA	10.99
Sports									
(Hi) BodyTone Rower	139.82	128.82	138.94	119.99	NA	169.97	159.99	159.99	NA
Juvenile									
(Hi) Century Car Seat	14.97	NA	NA	18.99	NA	19.97	24.00	NA	NA
Office									
(Low) T. I. Calculator	34.94	34.82	34.97	29.99	49.99	NA	39.99	NA	NA
Cameras									
(Low) Canon T50 SLR	158.94	169.97	188.48	154.99	NA	178.94	179.00	199.99	NA
Electronics									
(Hi) Emerson 5" TV	229.90	239.87	199.99	199.99	NA	NA	NA	NA	NA
Hardware									
(Low) Nut/Bolt Drawer	19.97	NA	NA	9.99	NA	19.97	12.99	NA	NA

eight miles from Showroom 1. It was surrounded by lower-middle-class houses built in the 1950s and some light industry. About a mile to the west, however, newer upper-middle-class housing had been built as the city expanded in that direction.

Showroom 2 had received a partial renovation in 1984, in which the existing fixtures had been rearranged and shortened. Workers in the immediate vicinity often browsed in the store on their lunch hours. The store manager had operated the store for four years and recognized many of the shoppers. Customers in Showroom 2 were less affluent than those in Showroom 1.

Four miles to the south and west of Showroom 2 was Riverview Mall, a mirror image of Lincolnshire Mall. In addition to a 60,000 square foot H. J. Wilson showroom (opened in 1980), it contained a Montgomery Ward and a Penney's. Freestanding K mart and Target outlets were adjacent to the mall. In early 1985 a warehouse club outlet very similar to Price Club had opened about half a mile south of the mall. Based on experience in other markets, its projected annual sales were approximately $40–50 million.

City B

Approximately 600,000 people lived in City B's metropolitan area. The midwestern city was about 60 miles from the state capital and was the site of several small colleges. Agriculture and health care were its major industries. In recent years new single-family homes and large luxury-apartment complexes had been extending the city west. Annual sales of general merchandise in the City B market totaled about $425 million.

City B Showroom

The City B showroom was located on a major east-west highway in the southwest section of the city, about one mile north of a heavily industrialized area. Northwest of the store were approximately four square miles of middle- to upper-middle-class homes. To the south and east of the showroom were modest homes in lower-middle-class neighborhoods. The vicinity immediately west of the showroom was entirely residential. However, a major new retailing area had grown up at an intersection about four miles west of the showroom, on the eastern edge of the new housing developments. In 1979, Target and in 1980, Service Merchandise had opened outlets in that area.

Even when compared with the fully renovated Stafford showroom, the Service Merchandise showroom looked relatively upscale. It included features such as a separate audio demonstration room and "Silent Sam," the computer ordering system. Sales help was moderate and comparable to that provided in the Stafford showroom. Directly across the highway from the Service Merchandise showroom was a 50,000 square foot Target outlet.

In 1984 BuySmart had opened a 90,000 square foot store one block south of the Stafford showroom. The BuySmart outlet was similar to a Target store in design, assortment, and operation. It offered low to moderate service and sharply discounted prices. About 40% of the product categories in BuySmart were carried in the Stafford showroom. BuySmart also stocked a wide assortment of soft goods, books, and records (see Exhibits 2 and 7).

Complete renovation of Stafford's City B showroom had been undertaken in August 1984 and had been finished just before the Christmas season. The renovation had greatly improved the appearance of the showroom, but lowering the fixtures had reduced the space available for stock on the selling floor significantly. This made it necessary to replenish stock more often at a time when payroll austerity was a high priority. The store manager attributed some of the decline in sales during the 1984 Christmas rush to the time it took to adjust to the new staffing requirements (see Exhibit 8).

CURRENT SITUATION

Ann Parkman felt strongly that, unless she was able to develop a viable long-range strategy for Stafford, the chain's situation would continue to deteriorate. She also felt that she didn't have much time. Parkman was scheduled to meet with John MacAloon, president of Penbury, in two weeks to discuss individual showroom performance and the future of Stafford in general. Parkman knew that MacAloon had doubts whether there was a place for catalog showrooms in the retailing environment of the 1980s. She was also convinced that a substantial long-term financial commitment from Penbury was necessary for Stafford's success and for her own future with the company.

MacAloon had been quite direct in his request for the meeting.

EXHIBIT 8   *Stafford Catalog Showrooms: Coverage and Allocation of Store Personnel*

12/15/84–12/21/84

	City A, 1		City A, 2		City B	
	No. of People	Total Hrs.	No. of People	Total Hrs.	No. of People	Total Hrs.
Housewares/Gifts	5	186	2	81	11	324
HBA/Lamps/Furn.[a]	1	39	1	41	3	116
Cameras/Radios	5	194	4	166	5	214
Jewelry	10	415	7	278	12	518
Sports/Toys	4	153	2	80	8	283
Customer Service	0	0	0	0	3	125
Cashiers	13	471	10	423	14	526
		1,458		1,069		2,106

4/13/85–4/19/85

	City A, 1		City A, 2		City B	
	No. of People	Total Hrs.	No. of People	Total Hrs.	No. of People	Total Hrs.
Housewares/Gifts	1	28	2	72	4	109
HBA/Lamps/Furn.	1	28	0	0	1	20
Camera/Radio	3	83	2	65	4	98
Jewelry	7	216	4	119	8	333
Sports/Toys	1	26	2	57	4	103
Customer Service	1	29	0	0	3	91
Cashiers	3	74	0	130	7	181
		484		443		935

Note: When primary departmental duties were not specifically assigned, personnel were allocated evenly over remaining areas.

[a]HBA = Health and Beauty Aids.

We are losing more money on Stafford all the time. You know the catalog showroom business inside and out. You tell me—is the catalog showroom still a viable concept? If this is a problem we can fix, let's fix it. If not, we have to figure out how to get out with minimal losses.

Parkman knew that MacAloon had already explored selling the business and had determined that a sale was very unlikely with Stafford's current financial condition. As Parkman prepared for the upcoming meeting, she reviewed a number of alternatives. She was unsure whether to focus on increasing sales, increasing margins, or reducing costs in her recommended strategy to improve Stafford's performance.

One alternative involved renovating all of the remaining stores. Seven stores required renovation. Full renovations for all seven would cost over $2 million. Parkman thought that the dingy appearance of many of the older stores could be contributing to the decline in sales. She doubted whether partial renovation was sufficient to alter the consumer's image of Stafford.

A second alternative involved a shift in product mix toward the higher-margin categories. Jewelry would take a central position in this strategy. The current product assortment would be reduced as the least profitable lines were dropped. Advertising would be focused to an even greater extent on jewelry and other high-margin items. Parkman believed that for this strategy to reach its full potential, a reduction in store size was required.

Another margin-increasing alternative called for a general upgrading of all existing product lines. However, Parkman felt this would necessitate a greater commitment to fashion, thereby risking an increase in the level of noncurrent inventory. Such an upgrading would probably require at least partial renovation of the stores, and production costs for the catalog and flyers were expected to increase by 50% under this strategy.

A very different approach involved, as Parkman called it, "a return to basics." This strategy assumed that Stafford's problem could be traced to the promotional trend of catalog showrooms. By returning to basics, Parkman meant pricing in the catalog as low as or lower than the discounters and drastically reducing the use of promotional flyers, thereby reestablishing a reputation for everyday low prices. She was aware, however, that many Stafford managers believed this would reduce sales in the short run by as much as 10%–15% and that it would take at least a year for the repositioning to alter consumer perceptions.

Finally, Parkman reviewed three cost-reducing strategies. The first was to discontinue the catalog. This had the added advantage of increasing pricing flexibility. The second involved an additional 10% reduction in store personnel, achieved by reducing hours of operation. The third involved the selective closing, in 1985, of the three least profitable stores (i.e., two more than currently planned). Each store had had an average net loss of over $100,000 in 1984. Under this alternative Store 2 in City A would be one of the three recommended for closing. To close all three stores would cost approximately $1.5 million.

Appendix A

Discount Stores, General Merchandisers, and Warehouse Outlets: Typical Format Characteristics

Discount stores (e.g., Target, K mart) were typically large retail chains which carried a wide assortment of products ranging from electronics to nonfashion-oriented clothing to houseware. They used a self-serve mass-merchandising format with little or no service support on the floor, and their product line rarely required delivery or set up.

General merchandisers (e.g., Sears, Penney's) were the successors to the nineteenth century general store. They had expanded originally through mail order, later to become huge chains with numerous retail outlets. Although originally focusing on hardware, their extremely wide assortment included everything from tools to clothing to jewelry. Although they carried some branded products, they sold mostly private label goods at moderate prices.

Restricted-entry warehouse outlets (e.g., Price Club) were deep discount combination retailer/wholesalers which originally operated out of large warehouses where they sold infrequently purchased hard goods to small retailers at wholesale prices. To be allowed entry, customers had to have membership cards which showed them to be retailers. Gradually, purchase privileges were extended to other groups (university employees, armed forces personnel, etc.). More recently, the warehouse operations had begun to sell directly to consumers, but they retained their restricted-entry image.

Appendix B

Retail Method of Inventory

Accounting convention requires that inventory be carried at cost or market, whichever is lower. In retailing, if markdowns are taken on a particular item, thereby reducing its retail selling price, the value at cost, as well as at retail, of all remaining (or ending) inventory of that product is adjusted downward.

Because the cost of goods sold is determined by subtracting ending inventory from the sum of opening inventory plus purchases, a decrease in the valuation of the ending inventory will result in a higher cost of goods sold in that period and a lower reported gross margin.

An example will illustrate the retail method of computing inventory. Assume that a retailer purchases 100 watches for $4,500 and the retailer's standard markup on watches is 55%.

The original intent, therefore, was to sell the watches for a total of $10,000. Assume that the retailer is unable to sell any of the watches for the intended retail price of $100 and marks the watches down to $89.50. The retailer, therefore, takes a markdown of $10.50 on each watch for a total markdown of $1,050. Assume that at the new price the retailer sells 56 watches for a total of $5,012 during the first year. One way to compute ending inventory would be to multiply the number of watches still in inventory (44) by their cost ($45) for a total of $1,980. This method, however, fails to recognize the decrease in the inventory's value exhibited by the required markdowns. The retail method of inventory solves that problem.

To compute ending inventory, cost of goods sold, and, therefore, gross margin, under the retail method:

1. Add the amount of markdowns to the retail sales revenue for the period to determine the total retail deductions ($5,012 + $1,050 = $6,062).
2. Subtract the total retail deductions from the sum of beginning inventory plus purchases at retail to determine the ending inventory at retail ($10,000 + $6,062 = $3,938).
3. Multiply the ending inventory at retail by the complement of the standard markup for the category to determine the ending inventory at cost ($3,938 × (1 − .55) = $1,772).
4. Subtract the ending inventory at cost from the sum of beginning inventory plus purchases at cost to determine the cost of goods sold ($4,500 − $1,772 = $2,728).
5. Subtract the cost of goods sold from the sales revenue to determine the gross margin ($5,012 − $2,728 = $2,284); gross margin percent is simply the gross margin divided by sales ($2,284/$5,012 = 45.6%).

Note that under the retail method ending inventory is $1,722 (not $1,980), cost of goods sold is $2,728 (not $2,520), and gross margin is $2,284 (not $2,492) or 45.6% of sales (not 49.7%).

Case 21
Shopfair Supermarkets (A)

In June 1980 Hal Huntley, vice-president of marketing for Shopfair Supermarkets, expressed concern about warehouse store competition in the Oxford area where his chain was headquartered. He described warehouse stores as "no-frills grocery stores which offer lower prices than conventional supermarkets. What enables warehouse stores to offer lower prices are substantially higher store volumes, reduced store services, fewer aesthetics, and more emphasis on high-turnover merchandise bought on deal at discount prices."

After experimenting with its own warehouse stores, Shopfair had, in June 1979, turned to a campaign that featured "warehouse specials" in its conventional supermarkets. Each week, about 250 staple grocery items were promoted at prices equivalent to, or lower than, those in warehouse stores. Now, one year later, Huntley had to decide whether to continue this campaign or to alter the marketing strategy.

THE ECONOMICS, FORMS, AND FORMATS OF WAREHOUSE STORES

Economics

Warehouse stores could set their retail prices as much as 20 percent below those of conventional

supermarkets, yet achieve similar operating profits for three main reasons. First, they bought a higher proportion of merchandise on deal. Second, they stocked a narrower assortment of merchandise by excluding slower-turnover and specialty items. Third, their no-frills format reduced store operating costs and investment requirements.

Deals   Deals were temporary discounts from regular prices, which manufacturers periodically offered to the trade to boost short-term sales volume. They hoped the trade would pass the discounts on to consumers by reducing retail prices an equivalent amount, by featuring the promoted brand in weekly newspaper advertisements, or by providing additional display support. Some allowances were payable only when the manufacturer received evidence, such as an affidavit, advertising tearsheet, or display photograph, that the required merchandising support had been performed. These were known as merchandising allowances. (In contrast, off-invoice allowances were straight deductions from list prices effective when orders were shipped and were not linked to performance requirements.)

The 1970s saw an increase in the frequency of these deals and their discount percentages due to several reasons: competitive pressures, the demands of the trade, and the artificial inflation of list prices. (For example, when the Nixon administration introduced wage and price controls, the federal government set the manufacturers' list prices in effect at the time as the allowable ceiling prices. As costs increased, manufacturers' margins were squeezed. After controls were lifted many manufacturers, determined to avoid a recurrence of this situation, set their list prices artificially high and offered more frequent and deeper discounts. By 1980 discounts of 10 percent to 20 percent on grocery products and health and beauty aids were common.) These occurrences continued even though manufacturers realized that this practice increased consumer price sensitivity and diverted funds which could otherwise have been spent on advertising to build brand loyalty.

By 1980 the availability of deals enabled warehouse store buyers to find at any time at least one national brand on deal in most product categories. The emphasis on deal buying, however, meant that the warehouse store could not offer the breadth or continuity of assortment found in a conventional supermarket. The merchandise mix could change from week to week depending on the brands and sizes offered on deal. When no national brands in a product category were available on deal, warehouse store buyers might take a private label or regional brand of comparable quality. Only in the case of a major national brand might a warehouse store stock an item on a continuing basis, even if this required some purchases at manufacturer's list prices.

Narrow Product Assortment   Because warehouse stores excluded low-turnover product categories and specialty items altogether and restricted the number of brands offered in the categories they did carry, some of them stocked as few as 500 items, compared with 10,000 items in a typical conventional supermarket. A 1980 survey of 72 warehouse stores reported that they could achieve between 29 and 42 inventory turns per year compared with a supermarket-industry average of 13.[1] The number of turns was lower in those warehouse stores that placed more emphasis on continuity of assortment because this policy required forward buying of deal merchandise in sufficient quantities to satisfy consumer demand until the next deal.

No-frills Operation   Cement floors, exposed beam ceilings, lack of windows, metal-framed display racks, and limited freezer space meant that the typical warehouse store's construction and equipment costs were lower than those of a conventional supermarket. (Exhibit 1 compares investment estimates for a new warehouse store with those for a new supermarket of similar size.) At the same time, weekly sales volume was typically much higher in the warehouse store. The 1980 survey of warehouse stores concluded that weekly sales per square foot averaged $9.10, compared with $6.49 for the supermarket industry as a whole. Warehouse stores achieving profit margins similar to those of conventional supermarkets consequently recorded higher returns on investment.

Operating costs for warehouse stores could be as low as 10 percent of sales, whereas those for conventional supermarkets might reach 20 percent. Labor productivity was especially high. In 1980 sales per labor hour in warehouse stores averaged $144—almost double the supermarket industry's average. Warehouse stores had six principal sources of labor savings:

1. Merchandise was simply dumped into baskets or sold directly from the cartons with the box lids removed. Inventory was typically stacked by forklift trucks on top of existing displays of merchandise. Efficient use of vertical space also increased sales per square foot and created a strong visual impact.
2. Where legally possible, merchandise was not individually price marked by store personnel.[2] Instead, prices were affixed to each display and sometimes summarized on weekly lists available at the store's entrance. The larger warehouse stores had electronic scanning systems which read the UPC codes on package labels.[3] Some claimed these systems had substantially increased their front-end productivity.
3. Warehouse stores often employed nonunion labor, in contrast to conventional supermarket chains, many of which were unionized.

EXHIBIT 1   *Investment Estimates for Warehouse Store Compared with Conventional Supermarket*

	New Warehouse Store	New Supermarket
Size of selling area (sq. ft.)	22,500	23,000
Annual sales	$10,000,000	$7,500,000
Investment		
Building	$450,000	$700,000
Land	225,000	230,000
Fixtures and equipment	350,000	570,000
Inventory[a]	350,000	575,000
Total	$1,375,000	$2,075,000

[a]Assuming 30 turns for warehouse store and 13 turns for conventional supermarket. Industry experts disagreed on the effects of warehouse store inventory turnover. Because warehouse store operators purchased large quantities of merchandise on deal, some alleged that the need to inventory the deal merchandise offset the favorable effect of volume on their inventory turnover. The result, these observers concluded, was a rate of inventory turnover for warehouse stores more or less comparable to that of the average supermarket.

Source: Industry estimates.

Per-hour labor costs were, therefore, often lower. In addition, store personnel could be more easily shifted from one task to another.

4. Warehouse stores used less labor in perishable departments, which traditionally required extensive customer service and merchandise preparation. (For example, few cut meat to a customer's order.)
5. Hours of operation in warehouse stores were sometimes shorter than those in conventional supermarkets, which often remained open until midnight or on a 24-hour basis.
6. Customers were required to bag their own merchandise, and some warehouse stores would not handle manufacturers' coupons. This reduced checkout time per customer, and fewer cashiers were needed to handle the same number of customers.

Additional savings on warehouse store costs were possible because of the following:

1. Advertising expenditures were a lower percent of sales. Some warehouse stores did no advertising beyond an opening promotion to generate awareness. Other chains continued advertising to educate consumers about the warehouse-store concept and to list their locations. Unlike conventional supermarkets, warehouse stores did not usually run weekly newspaper advertisements announcing prices on specific items.
2. Perishable departments were typically smaller than in conventional supermarkets, reducing the energy costs of freezer space.
3. Customers were charged for bags.
4. Check-cashing services were usually not offered, reducing bad-debt losses.

Limited Assortment Stores

By 1980 many forms of warehouse stores were evident, differing primarily in breadth of product assortments. Warehouse-type outlets with very narrow product selections were known as limited assortment stores or box stores. These usually had exceptionally small or sometimes no perishable departments and offered assortments of dry groceries skewed toward lower-quality controlled or private label items.

The first limited assortment store was opened by a German retail group in Iowa in 1976 under the Aldi (all discount) name. By 1980 there were almost 100 Aldi stores, often located adjacent to conventional supermarkets, and each stocking about 500 items, including some dairy and produce perishables. An expanded version of the limited assortment store was subsequently introduced by the A&P chain, which converted over 50 of its unprofitable conventional supermarkets to Plus (priced low, you save) Discount Foods stores. These outlets stocked 600–1,200 items, including some high-turnover health and beauty aids as well as key perishables.

Limited assortment store prices were up to 30 percent below those in conventional supermarkets; however, a significant fraction of the savings was attributable to the lower quality of the controlled and private label items emphasized in these outlets' dry grocery assortments.[4] Weekly sales volume ranged from $20,000 to $200,000, yielding gross margins of 9 percent to 12 percent. Limited assortment stores were believed to enjoy most success in inner-city areas and small towns, where conventional supermarkets had proven least likely to challenge their prices. In Chicago, however, the leading conventional supermarket chain, Jewel, was thought to have considerably slowed Aldi's market penetration by establishing a "store within a store" of deal merchandise in each of its outlets.[5]

Warehouse Store Formats

Like limited assortment stores, warehouse stores varied in size, stocking between 1,200 and 7,500 items. Weekly sales volume ranged from $70,000 to $700,000, providing gross margins of between 11 percent and 17 percent. There were two reasons for this diversity. First, many warehouse stores occupied buildings that had previously housed conventional supermarkets of varying sizes. Second, managers believed that the assortment mix in each store had to be closely adapted to the local competitive market. Industry analysts distinguished three warehouse store formats, based primarily on the number of items carried.

1. Heavy Deal Orientation   These stores carried between 1,200 and 2,500 items. National brands were only purchased on deal, so the proportion of private label merchandise was relatively high. Up to 85 percent of grocery sales were of merchandise purchased on deal. Most of these stores offered processed meat but not fresh meat and stocked only the 15 to 20 fastest-selling produce items.

2. Restricted Assortment   These stores carried between 3,000 and 3,500 items. The top national brands in major product categories were carried on a continuing basis regardless of whether they were available on deal. In most product categories, more than one brand was stocked. These stores typically offered a restricted selection of fresh meat cuts in family-size packages, thereby increasing the price per package and improving meat department productivity. The 75 highest-volume produce items were usually offered only in their raw, untrimmed state, to minimize produce department labor costs.

3. Representative Assortment   These stores, carrying 4,500 to 7,500 items, resembled no-frills conventional supermarkets minus some slow-moving specialty items. According to one industry analyst, these "hybrid stores" intended to give the customer "the best of both the warehouse-store and conventional-supermarket worlds." Perishable departments resembled those in conventional supermarkets, but offered less service and more aggressive pricing. Bakery and deli departments were included in the largest stores if they were self-supporting.

Table A compares the three formats.

EXHIBIT A   Warehouse Store Formats Compared

Approach	Number of Items	Sales Distribution (percent)[a]	Inventory per Square Foot ($)[b]
Heavy-deal orientation	1,200–2,500	70–80%	$11–13
Restricted assortment	3,000–3,500	67–75	11–16
Representative assortment	4,500–7,500	60–86	10–12

[a]Total grocery sales as a percentage of total store sales.
[b]Total inventory per square foot of store selling area.

Source: Willard Bishop Consulting Economists Ltd., Barrington, Ill.

Growth Prospects

Penetration of warehouse and limited assortment stores in the United States varied widely by geographic area (see Exhibit 2). The chains with the most outlets in 1980 were Prairie Markets, a division of Tradewell Stores (Kent, Washington), and Warehouse Market, a division of Nash Finch Co. (Minneapolis, Minnesota).

Industry analysts believed that warehouse stores had been especially successful in markets where the gross margins of conventional supermarkets were above the national average. The necessary price differential between a warehouse store and a conventional supermarket depended on the warehouse store assortment level. A warehouse store with a representative assortment could succeed with a differential of only 5 per-

EXHIBIT 2   Limited Assortment and Warehouse Store Penetration in the United States

	Limited Assortment Stores		Warehouse Stores	
	Number	$ of Total Supermarkets	Number	$ of Total Supermarkets
New England	0	0	96	5.5
Middle Atlantic	117	2.5	40	0.8
Southeast	172	2.0	110	1.3
East North Central	225	3.6	115	1.8
West North Central	135	4.3	170	5.4
West South Central	55	1.4	45	1.1
Mountain	15	0.8	90	4.8
Pacific	28	0.6	255	5.6
Total	747	2.1	921	2.6

Source: *Progressive Grocer*, 1980.

cent, but a store with a heavy deal orientation needed to show a differential of between 10 percent and 15 percent.

Some analysts thought the rate of new warehouse store openings might be slowed by the following factors:

1. An improvement in the economy reflected in increased real disposable income could reduce consumer price sensitivity and benefit conventional supermarkets.
2. Manufacturers might respond to declining inflation by cutting list prices and simultaneously reducing the frequency of deals and the level of percentage discounts offered.
3. Once warehouse stores captured 15 percent of a market's retail food volume, it was thought likely that new stores would cannibalize the sales of existing warehouse stores rather than steal incremental share from conventional supermarkets. In several major markets warehouse store shares already exceeded 10 percent.
4. Sites for new warehouse stores were becoming harder to find, and increases in land, construction, and labor costs required even higher sales volume projections to justify the investment.

Other industry experts believed that the current pace of warehouse store expansion would be sustained during the early 1980s, with the restricted and representative assortment formats showing the strongest growth rates.

THE OXFORD AREA MARKET

The Oxford market, in which two-thirds of Shopfair's stores were located, was one of the most densely populated metropolitan areas in the country. About two million people resided in the standard market statistical area (SMSA).[6] Approximately 4 million people lived within the greater metropolitan area. Population growth of 0.6 percent annually was below the national average. Food expenditures were thought to approximate $880 per capita in 1980. Weekly sales volume averaged almost $125,000 per store among the major conventional supermarket chains in the SMSA.

Conventional Supermarkets

Shopfair was the market-share leader in the Oxford area (see Exhibits 3 and 4). All seven conventional supermarket chains accepted manufacturers' coupons, cashed customers' checks, and bagged customers' purchases free of charge. Shopfair management believed, however, that its check-cashing and bagging services were superior. Union practices varied: Topval was unionized, Shopfair was not, Loring's had an in-house union.

In terms of sales mix, Shopfair and Topval led the other chains in grocery sales of private label and generic items by 11 percent and 4 percent respectively. Shopfair also led in percentage of sales in perishables; its management believed that the service and assortment in Shopfair's meat, deli, and produce departments reinforced the chain's positioning as the quality leader in the market.

Huntley described Shopfair's positioning strategy in the Oxford market: "We have always emphasized quality and service in our operations and advertising. Our problem is that, as a result, many consumers perceive our prices to be high."

A monthly tracking study (see Exhibit 5) which computed a price, quality, and perceived value index for the major chains in the market based on consumer interviews appeared to support this analysis. A second study showed that prices were, in fact, higher at Shopfair. A May 1980 price comparison of everyday prices of the same shopping basket at four stores showed the following:

EXHIBIT 3   *Comparative Data on Nine Chains in the Oxford SMSA, June 1980*

	Market Share[a] 1979	1980	No. of Stores in Oxford SMSA	Total No. of Stores	Av. Sq. Ft. of Selling Space	Avg. No. of Items per Oxford Store	Quality of Store Facilities[b]	Store Opening Hours[b]	Stores with Scanning System
Shopfair	15.1%	15.2%	30	55	22,500	12,000	Modern	Long	Some
Topval	14.5	12.7	26	140	23,500	12,000	Mixed	Long	Some
Galaxy	5.9	3.8	34	274	13,000	8,000	Old	Medium	None
Price-Lo	5.1	5.8	14	40	17,000	10,000	Mixed	Long	None
Loring's	na	2.4	4	37	26,000	10,000	Modern	Medium	All
Defina	na	2.9	4	24	28,000	12,500	Modern	Short	None
Roberts	na	2.9	4	6	20,000	11,000	Mixed	Short	None
Budget[c]	5.1	5.1	4	11	35,000	3,000	Warehouse	Long	Most
Foodmart[c]	2.2	3.0	5	21	19,000	3,000	Warehouse	Short	Some

[a]Data are for first half of 1980.
[b]Based on Huntley's qualitative assessment.
[c]Warehouse store chains.

Source: Company records.

Shopfair	100.0 (base)
Topval	99.5
Price-Lo	96.0
Loring's	96.0

Huntley believed, however, that the real difference in prices among these chains was narrower than the data suggested because of more weekly price specials at Shopfair and Topval.

Shopfair had made strenuous efforts to combat its high-priced image. It was the first chain in the Oxford market to introduce generic brands, and many of its outlets featured a generic "store within a store." It also led in offering low-priced substitutes for other fast-moving products. Shopfair regularly advertised its weekly price specials on broadcast media and in full-page advertisements of the Best Food Day editions of the two Oxford metropolitan dailies and local community newspapers.[7]

Huntley believed that the Shopfair customer mix, compared with that of the other chains, included a higher proportion of one- and two-member households, both young and old.

Shopfair has traditionally missed the large family with two or more kids. Although we have started to emphasize family packs in our meat department, for example, large families prefer to shop at chains such as Price-Lo and Loring's. Alternatively, they may shop at warehouse stores for their staples and buy their perishables and specialty items at Shopfair.

Huntley's Assessment of Shopfair's Competitors   Huntley reviewed each of Shopfair's major competitors in the Oxford market. In his opinion, Topval was suffering from an identity crisis. Although Topval, like Shopfair, advertised weekly price reductions on selected items, its advertising programs and positioning strategies were frequently changed, and the chain's credibility with the public was thought to be weakening as a result. Because Topval was

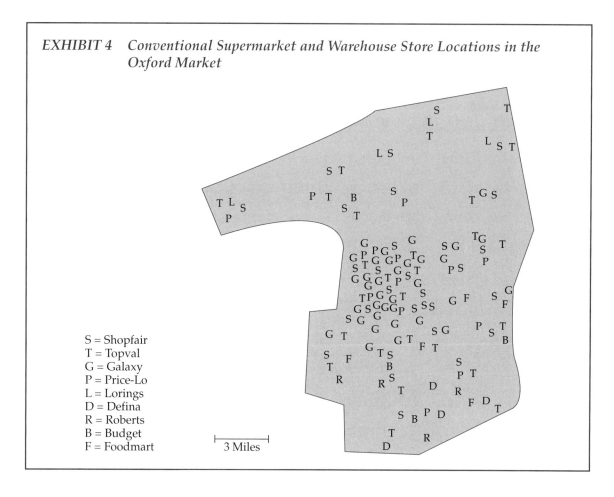

EXHIBIT 4   *Conventional Supermarket and Warehouse Store Locations in the Oxford Market*

S = Shopfair
T = Topval
G = Galaxy
P = Price-Lo
L = Lorings
D = Defina
R = Roberts
B = Budget
F = Foodmart

3 Miles

headquartered in Oxford, Huntley believed its management would be aggressively attempting to reverse its recent market share decline.

Like Shopfair, the Galaxy chain was owned by a large national food retailer, and it too advertised weekly price reductions on selected items. Many of its stores, however, were old, poorly located, and marginally profitable. It was rumored that the chain was considering selling some or all of its Oxford stores.

Price-Lo and Loring's followed a different pricing policy. Rather than offer deep discounts from regular list prices on a narrow range of items each week, they offered everyday low prices; up to 2,000 high-turnover items, often including several brands in the same product category, were continually offered below regular list price. To implement this policy, their buyers purchased between 65 percent and 70 percent of grocery merchandise on deal, compared with 50 percent and 55 percent by their counterparts at Shopfair and Topval. Conventional supermarket chains typically bought less than 50 percent of grocery merchandise on deal, except in highly competitive markets such as Oxford.

Huntley viewed Loring's as a well-managed chain with an excellent reputation for perishables, which could threaten Shopfair's market

EXHIBIT 5   *Consumer Perceptions of Supermarket Chains in the Oxford Market, 1978–1980*

	Price Index[a]			Quality Index[a]			Valued Index[a]		
	1978	1979	1980[b]	1978	1979	1980[b]	1978	1979	1980[b]
Shopfair	(3)	3	(8)	61	63	80	28	43	39
Topval	19	25	27	46	52	25	36	41	14
Galaxy	49	23	9	7	(3)	(5)	16	(3)	13
Price-Lo	50	59	36	44	62	45	60	73	43
Loring's	na	na	30	na	na	74	na	na	58
Defina	70	na	59	64	na	75	na	na	70
Roberts	79	85	60	82	90	68	72	89	62
Budget[c]	91	90	90	(8)	46	45	82	80	76
Foodmart[c]	na	84	73	na	37	36	na	74	6

[a]Indices were developed on the basis of an annual survey of 400 principal food purchasers in the Oxford market. Respondents were asked to name the best, second best, third best, worst, second worst, and third worst supermarkets on price, quality, and value. On the basis of each respondent's answers, points were assigned to each supermarket from +100 (best) to -100 (worst). Figures in the chart represent mean index scores across all respondents. Note that the value index is an independent measure; it is not based on a combination of the price index and quality index.
[b]As of June 1980.
[c]Warehouse store chains.

Source: Company records.

share in the northern end of the Oxford market. Loring's had recently announced it would open another store in the area.

The other two conventional supermarket chains of significance were Defina and Roberts. Defina had opened two new stores in 1979 and was known for its aggressive pricing of weekly specials on staple items. Store loyalty among Defina shoppers was strong, based partly on ethnic appeal. Huntley believed, however, that the Roberts chain was weakening and that regular Roberts' shoppers in increasing percentages were cross-shopping other stores.

In addition to the seven major conventional supermarket chains, which accounted for an unusually low 46 percent of sales in the Oxford market, many small independent supermarkets operated one to five outlets. They usually employed nonunion labor and, when linked to efficient food wholesalers, could obtain merchandise at close to the same prices as the major chains. Some independents competed on the basis of weekly price specials and convenience. Others emphasized high-quality perishables, product assortments closely tailored to the preferences of their local communities, and personalized customer service.

Warehouse Stores

The warehouse store formula had been introduced in the Oxford market in 1974 by an independent operator. It proved popular, partly because food prices were traditionally higher than in comparable cities, due to the Oxford area's higher labor and energy costs. By June 1980 there were about 25 warehouse stores in the market, accounting for almost 12 percent of retail food sales. (There were no limited assortment stores in the Oxford market.)

Two warehouse store chains, Budget and Foodmart, were responsible for over two-thirds of this volume. The Budget stores were operated by the owner of the Price-Lo supermarket chain; Foodmart stores were part of the Galaxy organization. Several Price-Lo and Galaxy supermarkets had been converted to warehouse stores since the first Budget outlet opened in 1976. Both companies were believed to view their warehouse operations as major sources of future sales and profit growth. Each was thought to be planning at least one new store opening by the end of 1980.

Shopfair and Topval were less committed to the warehouse-store concept. As of June 1980, Shopfair ran only two Foodrack outlets; Topval ran three Oxfarm stores. All were converted conventional supermarkets.

Budget's stores varied in size, carrying between 2,500 and 3,500 items. Prices on grocery products averaged 10 percent to 15 percent below Shopfair's. Budget's stores typically achieved over $400,000 in weekly sales volume from a 30,000-square-foot selling area. (Exhibit B presents estimated operating statements for Shopfair, Loring's, and Budget.) Shopfair's management estimated that 50 percent of Budget's expenses were fixed, and further noted that, although the Budget chain had the lowest gross margin, it recorded the highest operating profit. (Exhibit C compares departmental sales and gross margins for Budget's warehouse stores and Shopfair's supermarkets.)

WAREHOUSE STORE CONSUMER RESEARCH

In 1980 a national survey was taken of warehouse shoppers as they exited from warehouse stores. (A summary, shown in Exhibit 6, reveals consumer profiles and behavior by size of store.) Far from primarily low-income groups, a broad

---

EXHIBIT B   Estimated Comparative Operating Statements for Three Chains (% of gross sales)

	Shopfair[a]	Loring's	Budget
Gross margin	22.7	20.9	14.9
Expenses			
Payroll, taxes, benefits	12.1	11.0	5.5
Property rental	1.2	1.2	1.2
Utilities	1.1	1.1	0.9
Advertising	1.4	1.2	0.9
Supplies	1.2	1.1	0.5
Depreciation	0.8	0.8	0.7
Maintenance	0.7	0.6	0.5
All other[b]	2.1	2.0	2.3
Total expenses	20.6	19.0	12.5
Operating profit	2.1	1.9	2.4

[a]Excludes Foodrack stores.
[b]Includes insurance, taxes, licenses, equipment rentals, and other services.

Source: Company records and estimates.

EXHIBIT C   *Estimated Departmental Sales and Gross Margins for Shopfair and Budget (%)*

	Shopfair[a]		Budget	
	Sales	Gross Margin	Sales	Gross Margin
Grocery	56	18	68	13
Frozen food	6	20	5	15
Produce	8	30	7	20
General merchandise and health and beauty aids	6	30	4	15
Deli	7	35	3	25
Meat	17	25	13	20

[a]Excludes Foodrack stores.

Source: Company records and estimates.

cross-section of demographic and socio-economic groups was represented in the customer mix. Indeed, low-income consumers were underrepresented, because they were less likely to own automobiles and because they disliked stripped-down stores. In addition, the survey results supported the notion that warehouse stores appealed particularly to larger-sized families. Five percent of their volume was estimated to come from sales of complete cases of merchandise.

In 1980 Shopfair surveyed Oxford consumers (those who were the principal food purchasers in their households) about warehouse stores. Results are summarized in Exhibit 7. Huntley noted that 61 percent of respondents reported they were conveniently located near a warehouse store, compared with 36 percent in a 1979 survey. However, the likelihood of regularly shopping at a warehouse store had increased only marginally—the average on a 9-point scale moving from 5.26 in 1979 to 5.37 in 1980. Those who were less interested in shopping at warehouse stores cited inconvenient store locations, lack of

service, in-store congestion, and incomplete assortments as reasons that made one-stop shopping impossible.

Shopfair management believed that many warehouse store shoppers stocked up on staples at warehouse stores and shopped for perishables and specialty items at conventional supermarkets. Thus, the Shopfair survey asked respondents who had shopped at warehouse stores to characterize their last trip:

Regular shopping trip	20%
Fill-in shopping trip	55
Stock-up shopping trip	25

Huntley noted that, even though most visits to warehouse stores were viewed as fill-in trips, the average register total of $39 at Oxford warehouse stores greatly exceeded the $13 average figure for the entire food retailing industry.

The high average register total implied that Oxford's warehouse stores were achieving the same sales volumes as conventional supermarkets with smaller customer bases. Moreover, the warehouse store customer base was typically

EXHIBIT 6 National Survey of Warehouse Store Shoppers

| | Large | Medium | Small[a] | |
			Suburb	City
1. Source of awareness of this warehouse store				
Word-of-mouth	34%	32%	30%	26%
Newspaper	18	14	15	8
Radio	17	—	—	—
Saw store	23	48	44	60
2. Shopping frequency at this warehouse store				
Weekly	63%	51%	66%	67%
Every two weeks	23	19	17	13
Less often	11	19	11	3
First visit	3	10	6	15
3. Average transaction at this warehouse store	$37.84	$23.42	$11.93	$9.91
4. Perceived savings (shopping this warehouse store vs. conventional supermarket)	21%	30%	24%	24%
5. Do you buy your regular brand even when a comparable item is on special				9.
Always	21%	12%	10%	12%
Often	11	11	8	8
Seldom	17	29	18	22
Never	51	48	64	58

[a]Small warehouse stores here include limited-assortment stores.

Source: Willard Bishop Consulting Economists Ltd., 1980.

drawn from a wider geographic area. Huntley estimated that an average Budget warehouse store held a 15 percent market share within a circle of 10 minutes' driving time from the store, compared with 30 percent market share for an average Shopfair supermarket. Although very little of Shopfair supermarket's business came from customers beyond the 10-minute circle, over two-thirds of the warehouse store's business was derived from such customers.

	Large	Medium	Small[a]	
			Suburb	City
6. Do you shop another supermarket for products, brands, sizes (other than fresh meat) not available at the warehouse store?				
Always	1%	56%	42%	42%
Often	13	10	22	19
Seldom	73	20	19	21
Never	13	12	17	16
7. Number of persons in household				
1	6%	3%	5%	20%
2	20	22	19	23
3	24	22	14	23
4	26	23	29	18
5	15	17	21	14
6 or more	9	13	13	6
8. Occupation of household head				
White collar	48%	23%	37%	36%
Blue collar	40	55	53	30
Retired	11	11	7	23
Other	1	7	2	7
Employment status of nonhousehold heads				
Not employed	60%	55%	56%	52%
Employed part-time	22	30	24	27
Employed full-time	18	15	21	21
10. Annual household income				
Under $10,000	1%	19%	1%	13%
$10,000–$14,999	9	8	6	15
$15,000–$24,999	29	34	35	22
Over $25,000	46	31	38	32
Don't know/refused	15	8	19	18

SHOPFAIR'S RESPONSE TO WAREHOUSE STORES

In 1977 Shopfair had converted four of its conventional supermarkets in the Oxford suburbs to Foodrack warehouse stores. These supermarkets had become unprofitable through a combination of intense competition and either low population density in the immediate area or poor access from nearby higher density areas.

EXHIBIT 7   *Oxford Market Shoppers' Behavior and Attitudes toward Warehouse Stores (1980 Shopfair Survey)*

	Total Respondents	Respondents Who Shop Most at			
		Shopfair	Topval	Galaxy	Price-Lo
	(300)	(79)	(32)	(21)	(48)
1. Is there a warehouse store conveniently located for you to shop?					
Yes	61.0%	52.4%	50.4%	65.1%	71.2%
2. Have you been in a warehouse store in the past 12 months?					
Yes	62.4%	60.7%	45.2%	63.7%	69.1%
3. Average number of weeks since last visit to warehouse store	14.3	14.6	25.9	8.5	7.3
4. Average size of bill on last visit to warehouse store	$39.0	$29.0	$32.0	$53.0	$63.0
5. Average trip length from home to warehouse store					
Minutes	14.6	13.2	16.2	12.3	13.0
6. Chances of doing some of your shopping at a warehouse store regularly					
Mean score on a 9-point scale[b]	5.37	4.69	4.48	5.65	6.84

Consumers' Shopping Behavior, by Warehouse Chain

	Warehouse Store Last Shopped	Average Size of Bill on Last Shopping Trip to Warehouse Store
Budget	50.0%[c]	$59
Foodmart	30.5	34
Foodrack	5.0	26
Oxfarm	2.3	29
Other	12.2	31
Weighted average		40

[a]Includes warehouse stores.
[b]9 = definitely; 1 = definitely not
[c]Based on 187 respondents.

Source: Company records.

Other Chains	Other Stores[a]	Respondents Who Shopped at a Warehouse Store in the Past Month
(71)	(50)	(111)
68.3%	59.5%	93.5%
70.6%	57.3%	96.1%
14.6	16.4	1.8
$35.0	$31.0	$45.0
15.9	15.6	12.8
5.71	5.09	7.57

Average Time to Warehouse Store from Home (minutes)

16.4
12.8
11.9
16.5
11.6
14.2

The conversions were more a defensive move to reduce operating losses and preempt competing warehouse stores in these areas than an offensive move to diversify.

Each Foodrack warehouse store stocked about 3,000 items, selling on average at 10 percent below Shopfair prices. Advertising was minimal. By 1979 only two Foodrack warehouses were still in operation. Huntley explained that converted supermarkets could not always assume the appearance and full operating economies of warehouse stores. In addition, the warehouse store format could not compensate for inherently weak store locations. Huntley noted further that "Shopfair store managers were just not used to a no-frills format or to refusing customer requests to stock low-turnover items."

Shopfair's management rejected the ideas of either reviving the Foodrack operation or aggressively developing a new warehouse store chain. At the same time, they regarded the growing popularity of warehouse stores in the Oxford market as a serious threat to their continued market share leadership. Although some executives argued that warehouse store penetration in the market was probably approaching saturation, others believed that action was essential, because several Budget and Foodmart stores had been opened next to conventional Shopfair supermarkets.

The Warehouse Specials Campaign

As a result, Shopfair introduced its "warehouse specials" campaign in June 1979. About 250 items were offered each week in all Shopfair stores at dramatic discounts from regular list prices. These items were not all displayed in a single area but occupied their regular shelf positions, where they were flagged with shelf talkers and riser cards. (Shelf talkers were small signs attached to the front of the shelf on which the product was regularly stocked. Riser cards were attention-getting signs placed above the shelf.) The campaign became the focus of Shopfair's broadcast and print advertising.

Management hoped that the campaign would reinforce store loyalty among regular Shopfair customers and dissuade them from transferring all or part of their business to warehouse stores. In addition, they hoped that consumers would use warehouse special prices for price comparisons across chains and that Shopfair would thus be able to attract new customers. However, some executives believed the campaign detracted from Shopfair's quality image. They argued that business from periodic stock-up trips should be conceded to the warehouse stores. Management also found that stocking the shelves with the necessary inventories of items designated as warehouse specials added 0.2 percent to store payroll.

In June 1980 Shopfair's annual Oxford market consumer tracking study measured the impact of the warehouse specials campaign. Results are shown in Exhibit 8.

ALTERNATIVES FOR 1981

Shopfair's goal was to increase its share of the Oxford market to 17 percent in 1981. No new store openings were planned and, because all existing stores were operating profitably, there were no candidates for warehouse store conversion. Huntley had to decide on a strategy to achieve this goal. He also had to assess the vulnerability of each of Shopfair's competitors in the market to Shopfair's efforts to steal market share.

Shopfair's executives were split on what to do. One group believed Shopfair should focus exclusively on quality, discontinue the warehouse specials campaign, and emphasize a broader assortment, including more gourmet foods and general merchandise. A second group believed Shopfair should make no adjustments in its basic strategy and should continue the

EXHIBIT 8   Shopfair's Warehouse Specials Program: Summary Results of 1980 Consumer Research

	Total Respondents
	(300)
1. Which food stores have recently advertised "warehouse specials"?	
Shopfair	39.9%
Topval	16.7
Budget	6.1
Foodmart	15.0
2. What do "warehouse specials" mean?[a]	
Certain items are lower in price	13.1%
Consumers can buy in large quantities and save	8.8
Store buys in large quantities and consumers save	8.3
Brand items are less	20.0
Competition with food warehouse stores	3.5
Cheaper prices	23.9
Poor quality/overstock/ damaged goods	6.0
Items in cartons/no frills	5.1
3. Compared to shopping a regular warehouse food store, would shopping "warehouse specials" be . . . ?[a]	
Better	18.8%
Just as good	38.4
Not as good	29.4
4. Chances of taking advantage of Shopfair's "warehouse specials" next time you shop Mean score on a 9-point scale[c]	4.45

[a]Column figures for each question do not total 100 percent because of nonrespondents and the omission of low-frequency responses.
[b]Include warehouse stores.
[c]9 = definitely; 1 = definitely not.

Source: Company records.

	Respondents Who Shop Most at		Price-Lo	Other Chains	Other Stores[a]	Respondents Who Shopped at a Warehouse Store in the Past Month
Shopfair	Topval	Galaxy				
(79)	(32)	(21)	(48)	(71)	(50)	(111)
61.9%	51.1%	33.3%	29.3%	27.9%	28.1%	34.3%
11.4	26.1	10.4	29.8	10.9	17.4	15.0
1.7	1.8	3.8	10.8	9.9	6.6	12.6
13.0	28.8	35.5	13.0	13.6	1.9	24.3
18.6%	3.0%	22.1%	10.8%	11.5%	11.5%	11.9%
4.3	0.0	5.2	8.7	12.6	17.8	12.8
8.3	4.8	0.0	14.2	11.5	3.9	11.3
23.5	27.6	25.9	15.4	21.9	8.9	21.7
2.6	11.2	4.7	3.2	2.3	1.7	4.1
25.5	26.4	15.6	28.8	25.9	15.3	28.7
6.8	3.2	7.0	2.5	3.5	13.0	1.1
1.0	10.9	5.2	2.8	3.2	12.5	5.5
25.9%	19.7%	9.9%	14.4%	14.9%	20.3%	20.3%
37.4	45.4	25.3	28.8	40.8	46.9	36.9
26.9	27.6	45.5	44.4	29.0	14.3	36.2
6.00	4.30	3.58	3.57	4.09	3.91	4.71

warehouse specials for another year. They argued that, given time, the campaign would successfully combat the consumer perception of higher prices that seemed to be inevitably associated with Shopfair's quality image.

Other executives wanted to supplement the warehouse specials campaign with additional demonstrations of Shopfair's commitment to low prices. Suggestions included an increased emphasis on generic and private label brands; temporary introduction of double couponing (whereby Shopfair would double the face value of all manufacturers' coupons redeemed by customers at the checkouts); and a temporary double-the-difference program (in which Shopfair would guarantee to refund to any customer twice the difference in cost of filling an order at Shopfair versus a competitive supermarket chain).

Another group wanted to terminate the warehouse specials campaign, noting that Shopfair's market share had not increased over the previous year. Some of these executives argued for an everyday policy of low prices similar to those of Price-Lo and Loring's. Rather than offer a deep discount on only one item in 250 product categories each week, they argued that Shopfair should offer modest discounts on a continuing basis on 2,000 staple items, including more than one brand in many product categories. The prices of perishables were not to be affected. Advocates of this approach believed it would support a powerful and credible advertising campaign emphasizing Shopfair's low prices and value.

Finally, some executives believed that Shopfair had to confront the warehouse stores head on to halt their market share gains and discourage further openings. They wanted to match warehouse store prices on a much broader range of staples than were included in the warehouse specials campaign. As one executive put it, "We should declare open war on the warehouse operators. We have the resources to win."

PLANNING ISSUES

Three issues concerned Huntley as he assessed these different approaches. First, he knew Shopfair's traditional image was one of quality and service. To what extent should his strategy emphasize protecting this image versus improving consumer perceptions of Shopfair prices?

Second, he had to determine which, if any, of the alternatives would require changes in Shopfair's inventory and buying practices. In particular, would Shopfair buyers have to purchase a higher percentage of merchandise on deal rather than at regular prices, and would buying from one deal to the next require an increase in Shopfair's average inventories?

Third, Huntley had to decide how to gain the most flexibility. He could either adopt a single strategy for the entire Oxford market or tailor Shopfair's approach to the competitive situation in individual neighborhoods.

Notes

1. The supermarket-industry average was reported in the Cornell University study, Operating Results of Food Chains, 1979–1980. This figure included the warehouse store operations of those supermarket chains that participated in this survey conducted by Willard Bishop Consulting Economists Ltd., Barrington, Ill.
2. State law required that a price be marked on each item of merchandise in California, Connecticut, Massachusetts, Michigan, New York, and Rhode Island.
3. The universal product code (UPC) was a numerical bar code incorporated into the package design of most grocery products. Each product item had a unique code.
4. Price differences between limited assortment stores and conventional supermarkets on identical items averaged 15 percent.

5. The Jewel Companies, Inc., had opened over 100 limited assortment stores under the Jewel T and No-Frills names, principally in the southeast United States. None had been opened in the Chicago market, where the company was headquartered.

6. An SMSA denotes an economic unit formed by a city and surrounding area. The greater metropolitan area encompasses a larger territorial zone and more closely parallels the area covered by media emanating from the city.

7. Once a week (usually on Thursday), major daily newspapers carried a section devoted solely to food, which included recipes and editorial copy as well as advertising by food retailers and manufacturers.

Case 22
Ultra-Market, Inc.

In early July 1979, Gary Glass, President and Chairman of the Board of Ultra-Market, Inc. (U-M) in Fairfax, Virginia, was considering several alternatives for a marketing program and for future expansion of the company. U-M was a retail catalog grocery outlet selling prepackaged dry and frozen goods through a computerized order-taking system. The system involved the customer phoning in his order and either picking up his groceries already bagged or having them delivered to his home. Gary was not certain whether he should promote U-M as a discount grocery store, a service store specializing in and offering home delivery and ease of shopping, or a store offering price stability.

Gary had done no advertising to date. He wondered whether he should begin to advertise through media or direct mail, or continue not to advertise. Coupons had been used; another question was whether coupons should be continued as they were, changed, or dropped.

As soon as the year-old business broke even, Gary planned to enlarge either by setting up new distribution centers in other points on the east coast or by opening new pickup stations in the metropolitan Washington area. He was also considering some alterations at the Fairfax site: add-

ing milk and/or bread, increasing the product selection, and/or changing the warehouse operation to an automated picking system.

COMPANY HISTORY

Gary, 24, had the idea for U-M four years before it was put into operation. He and a friend, Kenneth Masters, 24, conceived of it while Gary was working in a Safeway supermarket and both were part-time students at Northern Virginia Community College.

One day in 1976 while Gary was working at the Safeway, Barbara Dodrill, 25, came through his line. Gary, a very friendly fellow, began to chat with her. The conversation ended by his setting up a time for him to show her some Amway products he was selling. Later, he did sell her some, but they spent most of the evening talking about his idea for a catalog grocery store. She typed up a report summarizing the ideas, and he showed it to friends and acquaintances who might be interested in supporting "G & M Markets" as it was first referred to.

Gary said he got the idea from his observations of customers at Safeway. He saw customers frustrated by two things: the long lines at the checkouts and having to look throughout the store for items that were moved about by an enterprising store manager or by manufacturers' reps or rack jobbers. He also noticed that shoppers picked up the same items week after week without comparison shopping. He believed that if he could eliminate some of these drawbacks, not only could he reduce overhead costs, which would allow him to charge lower prices, but also

This case was prepared by Isabella P. Long under the supervision of Professor Eleanor G. May of The Colgate Darden Graduate School of Business Administration, University of Virginia, Charlottesville, Virginia, as a basis for class discussion. Copyright 1979 by the Sponsors of the Darden Graduate School of Business. Reprinted with permission.

he could eliminate much of the inconvenience and tedium faced by food shoppers.

The initial idea for G & M Markets incorporated somewhat different concepts from those used for Ultra-Market. Gary and Kenneth envisioned a comfortable and decorative shopping area with "receptionists" to greet shoppers, where the customer could choose among produce, delicatessen meats and cheeses, party foods, and bakery products. The orders for nationally branded, prepackaged goods selected from the catalog would be placed either by telephone before the customer left home or in the store. The orders would be filled by a stock clerk in the warehouse. The idea was for a "faster, easier, and cheaper way to shop (in) a supermarket designed to incorporate the selection of fresh food and specialty items by the customer, with the selection of prepackaged items by store personnel."[1]

By January of 1977, the idea had evolved into a somewhat different form. The sales area was still to have produce and meat departments. In addition, there was to be "a computer system for ordering groceries, a catalog system for selecting groceries, and a conveyor system for processing groceries. Moreover, saving time, money and work (were) the Company's primary goals."[2]

Gary envisioned a number of benefits from catalog shopping both to the company and to the consumer. He believed that the customer would benefit by easily being able to compare brands, prices, and unit prices which would be plainly set out in the catalog. In times of rapid inflation, because the merchandise prices would be maintained for two to four months, Gary believed shoppers would welcome the promise of stable prices. Company benefits would result largely from cost control in a number of aspects of the operation. Fewer repetitious handling procedures would result in lower labor costs than in a regular supermarket. Shoplifting would be limited. As internal operations were increasingly au-

tomated, more attention could be paid to customer service.

Putting the idea into practice brought about further changes. "Ultra-Market," as it was called, opened in July 1978. Customers phoned in their orders, using a 94 page catalog. Orders were entered on the computer by the telephone answerer, and they were filled by U-M personnel in the warehouse. The customer shopped in the traditional sense only from two racks of items: one with potato chips and the like, and the other with marked down goods, items that were damaged or discontinued. No perishables except prepackaged frozen goods were sold. Before placing the first order, a customer had to come to the industrial park and pay a one-time charge of $6.00 to become a member and receive a catalog. Having the customer come to U-M was an effort to encourage pickup as the cheapest way to shop U-M, according to Gary. Also access to the location was quite complicated and it was felt best to have customers learn how to find U-M before starting to do business there.

The first computer used at U-M was a minicomputer with limited peripheral capacity and memory. It recorded orders and stored them for one week, and kept inventory records of a very simple nature (such as the number of items on hand).

The first catalog, printed by computer, was in a ring binder with section dividers. (See Exhibits 1 and 2 for a copy of the cover and a sample page.) It listed approximately 3,000 items. Each catalog cost between $2.50 and $3.00 to produce. The phrase used on the cover to characterize the operation was "Takes the work out of grocery shopping." In the front of the catalog several pages were used to explain the service, the hours of operation, methods of payment accepted, and other relevant aspects of the business.

The delivery charge was determined by the distance from the warehouse to the customer's home as follows:

EXHIBIT 1   Cover of First Catalog

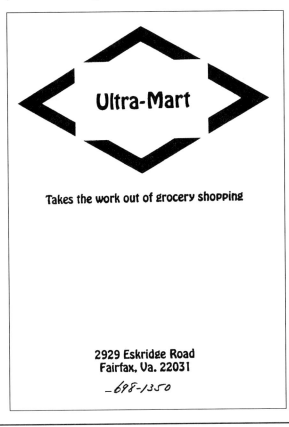

Ultra-Mart

Takes the work out of grocery shopping

2929 Eskridge Road
Fairfax, Va. 22031
_698-1350

Mileage to Home	Charge
0 to 3 miles	$2.25
3 to 5 miles	3.00
5 to 7 miles	3.75

Deliveries were not made if a person lived more than seven miles away. Orders had to be placed in advance of the desired delivery period as follows:

Delivery Period	Place Order Before
10 a.m. to 1 p.m.	8 p.m. of previous day
2 p.m. to 4 p.m.	12 noon of current day
6 p.m. to 9 p.m.	3 p.m. of current day

Cash coupons offered by U-M passed on to customers savings resulting from manufacturers' special price offers. Also discount coupons were offered by U-M on selected merchandise. In order to keep expenditures down, these coupons were designed by Gary and the copies were made in the office. These 4 inch × 3 inch pieces of paper were taped by U-M personnel to the items to which the offer applied. Manufacturer's coupons were accepted from customers also.

The prices in the first catalog remained effective for nine months, until the second was released in April 1979. From January through

---

EXHIBIT 2   Sample Page from First Catalog

		Size	Value	Price
TOMATO PASTE				
10552	Contadina Tomato Paste	6 oz	0.057	0.34
10563	Contadina Tomato Paste	12 oz	0.054	0.65
10574	Hunt's Tomato Paste	6 oz	0.057	0.34
10585	Hunt's Tomato Paste	12 oz	0.054	0.65
10596	Hunt's Tomato Paste	18 oz	0.051	0.91
VINEGAR				
19528	White House Cider Vinegar	32 oz	0.018	0.59
19530	White House Cider Vinegar	128 oz	0.015	1.89
19541	White House White Vinegar	16 oz	0.017	0.27
19552	White House White Vinegar	32 oz	0.015	0.49
ALUMINUM FOIL				
26111	Reynolds Aluminum Foil, 12"	25 ft	0.020	0.49
26122	Reynolds Economical Aluminum Foil	75 ft	0.016	1.19
26133	Reynolds Giant Aluminum Foil	200 ft	0.014	2.85
26144	Reynolds Heavy Duty Wrap	37.50 ft	0.025	0.95
26155	Reynolds Heavy Duty Wrap	100 ft	0.020	1.99
CANNING SUPPLIES				
24827	Ball Pint Jars	12's	0.249	2.99
24838	Ball Quart Jars	12's	0.291	3.49
24840	Ball Decorated Quart Jars	12's	0.333	3.99
24851	Certo	6 oz	0.165	0.99
24862	Fruit Fresh A-Acid	5 oz	0.330	1.65
24873	Gulf Wax	16 oz	0.037	0.59
24884	Sure Jell	1.75 oz	0.257	0.45
24895	Glad Freezer Wrap, 18 Inch	80 ft	0.012	0.99
24906	Reynolds Eskimo Freezer Paper, 18 Inch	75 ft	0.013	0.99
24917	Scot Freezer Tape, 3/4 Inch	90 ft	0.008	0.69
MISCELLANEOUS BAKING SUPPLIES				
28293	Reynolds Cooking Bags, 14x20	6's	0.125	0.75
28304	Reynolds Brown 'n Bag, 10x16	8's	0.111	0.89
32005	Colored Baking Cups	88's	0.003	0.23
32016	Foil Baking Cups	48's	0.007	0.35
32973	Broiler Blotters	6's	0.115	0.69

Page 3-14   June 1978 – Baking & Cooking Needs

March 1979, the catalogs were out of print; therefore, no one could join U-M in that period. By April, there were over 300 people on a waiting list for membership. Profit margins had slipped from 21 percent to 14 percent as cost of merchandise had risen, because retail prices had not been changed.[3]

FINANCING

Gary, Barbara, and Kenneth located a friend's father's friend, an attorney, who liked their idea for a catalog grocery store. The attorney agreed to cut his normal fees and to help draw up a memorandum for a stock offering and to arrange incorporation for $3,000. Each of the three friends put up $1,000. The memorandum took 18 months to prepare. The stock was offered between September and December 1977, but none of the $500,000 was raised. Gary stated that he believed that they were seeking too much money for such a speculative venture.

In January 1978, another stock offering was made, this time for only $30,000; in two weeks, all 30 shares were sold. But Gary found that this amount was not enough to operate the business, so $70,000 in additional shares was offered. By July, a total of $75,000 had been raised, and Ultra-Market opened for business. Later $25,000 worth of computer software made Data General, a computer company, the largest shareholder and entitled it to a representative on U-M's board. In February 1979, a further $100,000 of financing was obtained as a loan through the Small Business Administration.

MERCHANDISE

The selection of items was considerably smaller than in a traditional supermarket. The computer listed 2,787 items at the end of May 1979, but some additional items which were available had not yet been entered on the computer list. No perishable items were carried except for certain frozen foods: vegetables, meats, and ready-to-cook items. The choices were not limited to foods items; there were also toiletries, paper products, pet food, and bird seed, to name a few. Only two sizes of most items were carried.

PHYSICAL LAYOUT

U-M was located in an industrial park in Fairfax, Virginia. The offices for Gary, the secretaries, and the order-takers were in a building in the indus-

trial park, separate from the warehouse. The main frame of the computer and the cathode ray tubes were located in the office area. Across the hall from the office was a conference room that a neighboring business allowed Gary to use when he held meetings. His only obligation in return was to be sure the room was clean after use.

The warehouse (Exhibit 3) had a single garage door through which merchandise was both received from trucks and loaded into the delivery van. Gary tried to pre-arrange items for receiving merchandise so that he could have extra people on hand when the trucks arrived. Because suppliers did not always meet their obligations, inventory sometimes had to be left in the loading area until someone was free to unpack it and place it on the shelves. Total space in the warehouse was about 4,000 square feet and included a small work area for the Vice-President of Operations, a sales area, and the inventory storage area. The sales area was separated from the rest of the warehouse by a partition which did not reach the ceiling. If there was noise in the warehouse, customers in the sales area could hear it. Two cash registers for pickup sales, a bell to summon assistance, and a small food display of marked down items and snack foods comprised the sales area furnishings.

In the storage area, merchandise was placed on shelves totaling about 1,200 linear feet. Aisles between the shelves were wide enough for only one cart. Adjacent to the storage space was a 15 foot by 8 foot walk-in freezer with a map of its contents posted on the door. In front of the freezer were tables on which orders were assembled, checked, and bagged. Each bag was marked with the respective order number and the number of bags comprising the order; then the prepared orders were placed on two wooden shelves next to the freezer. If part of an order was for frozen food, that bag was marked with the

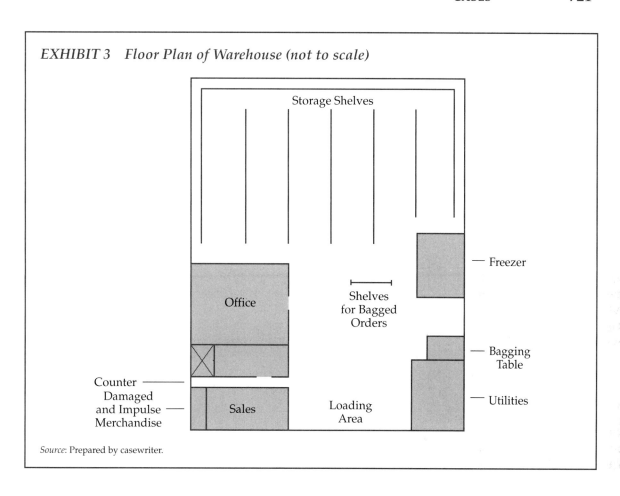

EXHIBIT 3   Floor Plan of Warehouse (not to scale)

Source: Prepared by casewriter.

same number and placed back in the freezer on the floor.

ORDER TAKING

Upon paying the $6.00, the customer received by mail a copy of the second catalog and an account number. Items could then be ordered by using the item numbers in the catalog. (See Exhibit 4.) The hours for taking orders were 9 a.m. to 8 p.m. Tuesday through Friday and 8 a.m. to 6 p.m. on Saturday. Orders could be left at any other time of the day or night and on Sunday on a recorder. The order taker punched the item numbers into one of two computer terminals. As the number was being entered, the item number, description, and price appeared on a C.R.T. screen. If an out-of-stock signal appeared by an item, the operator apprised the customer of this fact and inquired whether she wanted to substitute another item. Gary said that in the future when touch-tone would be in more widespread use than it was in 1979, the system would be expanded so

EXHIBIT 4   Sample Page from Second Catalog

	VEGETABLES - CANNED [Continued]	Size	Value	Price
14823	Green Giant Mexicorn	12 oz	0.038	0.45
14832	Manning's Hominy	20 oz	0.025	0.49
14841	Bush Chopped Kale	15 oz	0.019	0.29
14850	Bush Chopped Mustard Greens	15 oz	0.023	0.35
14869	Fine Fare Peas	17 oz	0.021	0.35
14878	Del Monte Early Sweet Garden Peas	17 oz	0.030	0.51
14887	Green Giant Peas	17 oz	0.030	0.51
14896	Kounty Kist Sweet Peas	17 oz	0.019	0.33
14906	Libby Sweet Peas	17 oz	0.029	0.49
14915	Del Monte Peas & Carrots	16 oz	0.031	0.49
14924	Libby Peas & Carrots	16 oz	0.031	0.49
14933	Luck Blackeye Peas	17 oz	0.029	0.49
14942	Green Giant Peas & Onions	17 oz	0.031	0.53
14951	Fine Fare Whole White Potatoes	16 oz	0.021	0.33
14960	Fine Fare Sliced White Potatoes	16 oz	0.021	0.33
14979	Betty Crocker Au Gratin Potatoes	5.80 oz	0.129	0.75
14988	Betty Crocker Hash Browns w/Onions	6 oz	0.125	0.75
14997	Betty Crocker Mashed Potatoes	28 oz	0.066	1.85
15006	Betty Crocker Potato Buds	16.50 oz	0.072	1.19
15015	Betty Crocker Scalloped Potatoes	5.50 oz	0.136	0.75
15024	Betty Crocker Sour Cream & Chives	4.75 oz	0.158	0.75
15033	Del Monte Whole White Potatoes	16 oz	0.029	0.47
15107	French's Big Tate Mashed Potatoes	16 oz	0.071	1.13
15336	Bush Turnip Greens	15 oz	0.199	2.99
15345	Hanover Whole White Potatoes	40 oz	0.017	0.69
18874	Idahoan Instant Potatoes	16 oz	0.056	0.89
18883	O & C Potato Sticks	7 oz	0.121	0.85
18902	Pillsbury Hungry Jack Potatoes	27 oz	0.065	1.75
20929	Libby's Sauerkraut	16 oz	0.027	0.43
23119	Libby Sauerkraut	27 oz	0.022	0.59
23128	Vlasic Sauerkraut	32 oz	0.025	0.79
23494	Fine Fare Spinach	15 oz	0.031	0.47
23852	Del Monte Leaf Spinach	15 oz	0.033	0.49
24237	Libby Cut Spinach, wtr pack	16 oz	0.031	0.49
24640	Fine Fare Tomatoes	16 oz	0.028	0.45
24668	Fine Fare Tomatoes	28 oz	0.023	0.65
24686	Fine Fare Stewed Tomatoes	16 oz	0.031	0.49
24695	Del Monte Stewed Tomatoes	16 oz	0.037	0.59
24732	Del Monte Stewed Tomato Wedges	14.50 oz	0.045	0.65
24741	Glen Park Tomatoes	28 oz	0.021	0.59
25171	Hunt's Whole Tomatoes	28 oz	0.032	0.89
25180	Hunt's Stewed Tomatoes	14.50 oz	0.039	0.57
25373	Hanover 3-Bean Salad	14.50 oz	0.048	0.69
25447	Fine Fare Mixed Vegetables	16 oz	0.022	0.35
25502	Veg-All Mixed Vegetables	16 oz	0.029	0.47
25511	Veg-All Mixed Vegetables	29 oz	0.025	0.73
	VEGTABLES - FROZEN			
44817	Bird's Eye Asparagus	10 oz	0.139	1.39
44826	Bird's Eye Bavarian Style Vegatables	10 oz	0.079	0.79
44835	Bird's Eye Broccoli Spears	10 oz	0.059	0.59
44844	Bird's Eye Broccoli Spears w/Cheese Sce	10 oz	0.079	0.79
44853	Bird's Eye Broccoli Spears w/Hollandaise	10 oz	0.089	0.29
44862	Bird's Eye Brussel Sprouts	10 oz	0.069	0.69
44871	Bird's Eye Cauliflower	10 oz	0.069	0.69
44880	Bird's Eye Chinese Style Vegetables	10 oz	0.083	0.83
44899	Bird's Eye Cut Corn	10 oz	0.049	0.49
44909	Bird's Eye Corn on the Cob	4 's	0.298	1.19
44918	Bird's Eye Danish Style Vegetables	10 oz	0.083	0.83

that orders could be taken directly by the computer. The customer would punch the item numbers into the home phone to place an order.

A study reported by Celanese in January 1979, which was conducted by Yankelovich in 1975, stated that of employed women, 20 percent were interested in the telephone ordering of food.

The U-M order taker asked whether the order was to be delivered or picked up. If it was to be delivered and the order was less than $50, there was a $1.50 delivery fee; if greater than $50, delivery was free. Delivery was offered within a certain area defined by zip code numbers; the distance ranged from 8 to 15 miles from U-M. If the order was to be picked up, the customer received a 2-percent discount on the order. The minimum order was $20.00.

ORDER PROCESSING

The actual filling of orders was not a complex process. After an order was taken, the computer printed an invoice (Exhibit 5) on one of the two printers in the warehouse and a picking slip (Exhibit 6) on the other printer. On the picking slip, items were classified into three categories: slow moving, fast moving, and "Gary missed these." Gary had judgmentally classified the items as slow moving or fast moving; any he had not yet

---

EXHIBIT 5   *Sample Invoice*

```
==========================================================================
: INFORMATION                                        ORDER PROCESSING :
:                        U L T R A  -  M A R K E T ,   I N C .          :
:  560-5040                                               698-1350     :
==========================================================================
:                                                                      :
: Ken\Ann Kalscheur            536 7821 (D)            Customer  3128  :
: 3267 Beue Heron Dr.             (N)                  Invoice   1024  :
: Falls, Church, Va  22042                             Map      15H8   :
==========================================================================
:                                                                      :
: Pickup Thu  5/31/79  5: 0 AM Routing add to previous order           :
:                                                                      :
==========================================================================
: ITEM : QTY :              DESCRIPTION         : SIZE  : PRICE : AMOUNT :
==========================================================================
: 41773 :  4 : MusMusselman's Apple Juice       : 46 oz : 1.05 :   4.20 :
: 15547 :  2 : Mr. Mushroom Stem & Pieces        :  4 oz : 0.69 :   1.38 :
: 18052 :  1 : Wesson Oil                        : 38 oz : 2.09 :   2.09 :
: 45577 :  1 : Welch's Grape Juice               : 12 oz : 0.85 :   0.85 :
: 35750 :  1 : Snyder's Rippled Potato Chips, Box: 13 oz : 1.35 :   1.35 :
: 11303 :  1 : Crystal Clear Dishwasher Detergent: 35 oz : 1.45 :   1.45 :
:                             Sub Total         :       :      : $11.32 :
:                             Tax               :       :      :  $0.45 :
:                             Pickup Discount    :       :      :  $0.24 :
:                                               :       :      : ------ :
:                             Total             :       :      : $11.54 :
:                                                                      :
==========================================================================
: Grocery  10       Grocery shopping designed for your time.  Frozen  0 :
```

EXHIBIT 6   Sample Picking Slip

Invoice: 1024	PICKUP: Thu 5/31/79 5: 0 AM	CUSTOMER: 3128

13—GARY MISSED THESE

11303	1 Crystal Clear Dishwasher Detergent	35 oz
15547	2 Mr. Mushroom Stem & Pieces	4 oz
18052	1 Wesson Oil	38 oz
35750	1 Snyder's Rippled Potato Chips, Box	13 oz
41773	4 Musselman's Apple Juice	46 oz
45577	1 Welch's Grape Juice	12 oz
	10 TOTAL ITEMS IN CATEGORY	

10 TOTAL ITEMS IN ORDER

---

classified were labeled "Gary missed these." The idea was ultimately to have a two-tier system, the lower tier for fast moving, the upper tier for slow moving. Entries in the third grouping would eventually be put in either of the first two categories.

After an order was printed, the picker, usually a high school student working part-time, punched a time card (Exhibit 7) on the time clock as he began to fill the order. He placed the picked items on a wheeled cart. Items were identified by a piece of tape on the shelf below them on which the catalog item numbers were marked. The order of item numbers did not correspond with the item category (slow or fast moving), but were arranged in numerical order. The picker had to scale the shelves like a monkey if the ordered item was located on a top shelf.

The loaded cart was then taken to the bagging table for the picked items to be checked. As the picker called out the name and size of each item, the checker, another picker, would match the item with those listed on the order. After the order was bagged, the order number identified, and the order placed on a shelf or in the freezer, the picker then punched the order out on the time card.

DELIVERIES

The driver for deliveries was required to punch in and out before and after a delivery run. He was another teenager who worked part-time. His job was to drive the one unrefrigerated, company-owned van during the three delivery periods each working day:

Tuesday through Friday	Saturday
10 a.m. to 12 p.m.	9 a.m. to 11 a.m.
1 p.m. to 3 p.m.	12 noon to 3 p.m.
6 p.m. to 9 p.m.	4 p.m. to 6 p.m.

Before going out on delivery, the driver collected the waiting invoices from a clipboard hung on the warehouse door. These invoices acted as his delivery list. Upon his return to the warehouse, the sales were rung up on a third cash register located in the Vice-President of Operation's office. If a delivery customer wished to pay by credit card, the driver was required to call in to the office and get approval before accepting the card.

Gary said that punching the clock actually had more use as a motivator than as a time-study device, and he was considering dropping the requirement.

EXHIBIT 7   Sample Time Card

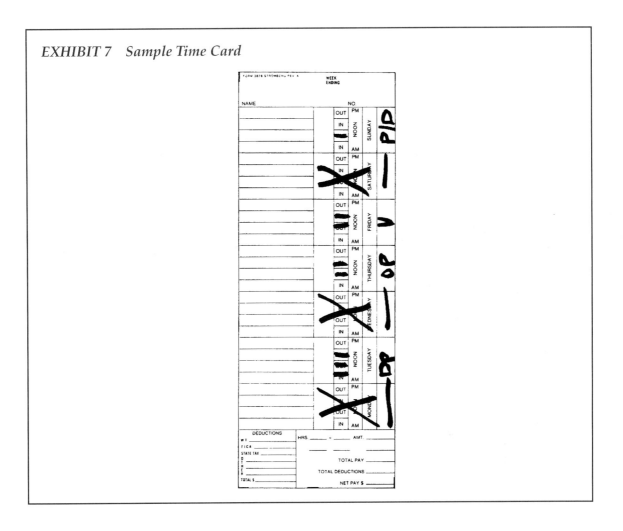

INVOICING

The salesperson was responsible for keeping invoices for delivery and pickup separate so that the pickup orders were rung up on separate registers from delivery orders.

Attached to each computer-printed invoice was a handwritten sales slip which listed any "amendments." One example of an amendment was the elimination of a delivery charge on an order. The computer added delivery charges automatically to each invoice for a delivery order. These charges had to be deducted if the second order was merely for items to be added to an order placed earlier. Invoices and sales slips for pickup orders were placed on clipboards in the warehouse until the orders had been filled, then the invoices and sales slips were moved to a basket in the office. Pickup orders were rung up as payment was received.

PERSONNEL

There were seven full-time people on the pay-roll (Exhibit 8): President and Chairman of the Board, Assistant to the President, Executive Vice-President, Vice-President of Marketing and Cus-tomer Service, Vice-President of Operations, As-sistant Director of Customer Services, and Ware-house Coordinator. Gary was an imposing young man, about six feet tall, full of enthusi-asm and drive. He and the rest of the staff worked long hours. He rarely left U-M before 9

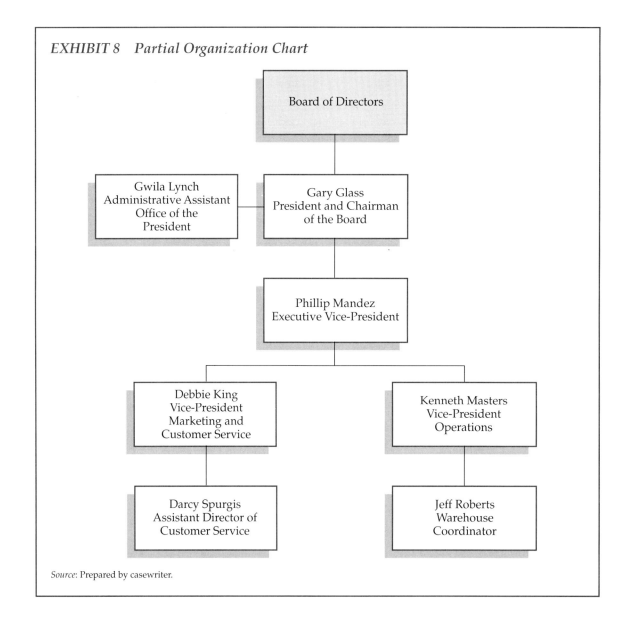

EXHIBIT 8   Partial Organization Chart

Board of Directors

Gwila Lynch
Administrative Assistant
Office of the
President

Gary Glass
President and Chairman
of the Board

Phillip Mandez
Executive Vice-President

Debbie King
Vice-President
Marketing and
Customer Service

Kenneth Masters
Vice-President
Operations

Darcy Spurgis
Assistant Director of
Customer Service

Jeff Roberts
Warehouse
Coordinator

Source: Prepared by casewriter.

or 10 p.m. Recently, his doctor had advised him to take things a little easier, so he had begun to take Sundays off. His responsibilities, and those of the other officers, were to carry out the decisions made by the Board of Directors.

Gary's right-hand man, Phillip Mandez, 22, the Executive Vice-President, was hired to fill in for Gary whenever Gary was busy elsewhere. In addition to the full-time employees, there were 10 to 12 part-time workers who included only two of the original employees. There was a high turnover, especially among the part-time workers. In the last three weeks in May, 17 people had left their jobs and had to be replaced. Phillip stated that he needed three people in the warehouse whenever it was in operation.

The Board of Directors, composed of the major investors and some of the officers (Exhibit 9), exercised control over the company and made operating decisions. The Board of Advisors (Exhibit 10) received no compensation and possessed no control over the operations of Ultra-Market. They met every two weeks to advise the officers and directors.

APRIL 1979 CATALOG

Ten thousand copies of a new catalog were produced in April 1979, at a cost of 50¢ each in the hopes of increasing the number of active customers to 10,000. It was expected that another catalog would be issued in August. On the first few pages, the April catalog stated the ground rules for shopping at U-M.

1. An order had to have been placed at least two hours prior to the beginning of the desired delivery period, or, if the desired period was 10 a.m. to 12 p.m., by 8 p.m. the night before.
2. Discounts of 2 percent were offered if the order was picked up.
3. Discounts of 3 percent were offered on case purchases, except for beverages.
4. Five to ten days' notice was required for case purchases so that the cases could be obtained from the supplier.
5. Manufacturers' coupons were honored, and U-M printed its own coupons when a manufacturer offered a cents-off label on a package. These coupons were redeemable for cash at any time prior to the expiration date.
6. Discount coupons in a Shopper's Guide attached to invoices were good for two weeks and were redeemable much like manufacturer's coupons.
7. Payment could be made by credit card (VISA or MasterCard), pre-approved check, or cash.

In a special offer, memberships were free from May 1 through June 30, 1979, and a 2-percent discount coupon was offered with the first order (Exhibit 11). As a part of the special offer, if a new

---

EXHIBIT 9 Board of Directors

Gary Glass, 24,
    President and Chairman
Phillip Mandez, 22,
    Executive Vice-President
Kenneth Masters, 24,
    Vice-President—Operations
Tom Haft, 28,
    Sales Manager, Kimberly Clark
    Businessman

Source: Prepared by casewriter.

EXHIBIT 10 Board of Advisors

Economist, 38
Accountant, 41
Lawyer, 32
Gary Glass, 24
Phillip Mandez, 22

Source: Prepared by casewriter.

EXHIBIT 11   *Special Promotion—April 1979 Catalog*

ULTRA-MARKET

REFER   A   FRIEND   OR   NEIGHBOR

Help your friends & neighbors receive

a FREE membership from ULTRA-MARKET &

Both of you can SAVE 2% on your grocery bill!

     Help us at ULTRA-MARKET to increase our membership
and to introduce our NEW Multi-Terminal Order Processing
System by telling a friend or neighbor about ULTRA-MARKET.
Increased memberships and sales mean increased savings and
services to you. Help us become a revolutionary success
in the grocery industry and you will introduce changes in
pricing and services found today.

* * *

     Call 560-5040 to become a member of ULTRA-MARKET
and we will send you a FREE catalog and a 2% discount
coupon to use on your first order. Please tell our
operator the referring member's name and account number
who told you about ULTRA-MARKET (shown at the bottom of
sheet) and this member will also receive a 2% discount
coupon to use on their order.

     By shopping at ULTRA-MARKET, both of you can receive
increased savings and services.

CALL   560-5040

Referring
Member's Name_____ Account #_____

     ACT NOW!!   Offer Expires June 30, 1979

member was referred by another member, the original member also received a 2-percent discount coupon for his next order. Gary stated that his target customers were families with working or nonworking mothers and four or more members. At the end of June, even though no advertising had been done, there were 1,500 members and an average of 50 orders per week.

Sales for the month of June were $12,000. Expenses usually were about $10,000 per month of which $7,000 was payroll and included health and life insurance for all full-time employees.

EXHIBIT 11 (Continued)

<u>MEMBERSHIP APPLICATION</u>

```
Name: _____ , _____        Acct. # _____
            Last          First
                                           Apt. # _____
Address: _____
                                           Zip: _____
City/State: _____
                                           Date: _____
Map: _ _ - _ _
                                           Amount Paid: _____
Day Phone: _____

Evening Phone: _____        ======================
                                                  DATA INPUT
Phone Type: _____
                                           D.P. Operator: _____
Family (# of Members) _____
                                           Date: _____
Referred By: _____


_____
Comments: _____

_____
```

The other $3,000 was for rent, telephone, utilities, delivery expenses, and computer rental. Total inventory was $45,000 at the end of May; 2,800 items were being carried in June.

When the April catalog came out, prices were raised to the equivalent of Safeway's and Giant's, according to Gary. U-M estimated that it lost 25 percent of its customers at that time.

Students at George Mason University did a study in May for Gary to see whether they could determine why he lost those customers (Exhibit 12). They interviewed by telephone a sample of 100 customers who had not shopped at U-M since January. Gary drew several conclusions from their findings. Some people interviewed said they no longer shopped at U-M because they forgot about it; therefore, Gary believed that advertising should be an important part of any promotional campaign. He also believed that the survey demonstrated that some respondents disliked having to shop two food stores because of U-M's lack of perishables. Out-of-stocks were another problem the survey identified, and Gary already had begun to require the employees in the warehouse to clean up their language and to dress more neatly.

With this catalog, the name of the organization was changed to Ultra-Market and a new logo was adopted (Exhibit 13). The slogan was changed to "Grocery shopping designed for your time." The name, the logo, and the slogan were the products of a newly appointed advertising agency. (All previous promotion, e.g., the early logo, flyers attached to door knobs, and solicitation of articles in local newspapers, had been handled by Gary.)

A similar operation, opened in April 1976 in Minneapolis, was called the Grocery Wagon. Customers were offered delivery only, no pickups were allowed. Management was highly experienced in the grocery industry. Although it had 20,000 customers and offered 6,000 items, the operation closed in April 1979. According to Gary, their capitalization was too high ($1.7 million in debt and stock), and they were not able to develop enough volume to support it.

EXHIBIT 12   Results of Telephone Survey

1. What aspects do you like about Ultra Mart?
   a. the prices are very reasonable ....87 percent
   b. the Ultra Mart idea is great ....40 percent
   c. the store is very convenient ....53 percent
2. What aspects don't you like about Ultra Mart?
   a. out of stock ....93 percent
   b. a wider selection of items needed ....21 percent
   c. the layout of the warehouse unbecoming of a professional operation (i.e., everyone
      in jeans, sometimes the language overheard was harsh, and the store was very plain) ..30 percent
   d. just forgot about shopping there ....40 percent
   e. too far of a distance to travel ....12 percent
   f. no perishables available ....37 percent
   g. like to see what they buy ....8 percent
   h. difficult ordering system ....3 percent
   i. poor arrangement of the catalog ....5 percent
3. What possible changes would you like to see at Ultra Mart?
   carry enough stock 1
   brighten up the check-out room 2
   carry produce 3
   advertise frequently 4

Source: Student survey.

PRESENT SITUATION

In June, Gary felt that the testing period for U-M was finally over. He believed that his idea had proved successful, so he wanted to move to the next stage of development. He had recently installed a new computer system, a $12,000 Data General mini-computer with nearly $50,000 worth of software. He believed that U-M had been prevented from reaching break-even sales volume because of the limited terminal capacity of the old system. With the new computer, that barrier was removed.

A number of computer programs, either on line or available for later installation, dealt with inventory control, order processing, order storage, customer data storage, manpower planning, and accounting. On an inventory control file, for example, the computer listed for each item the name, the quantity on hand, the reorder point, the size, and whether food stamps were acceptable. The reorder point was calculated judgmentally to be equivalent to three days of sales of an item. The computer was instructed on Wednesday nights to print out a list of those items whose quantities on hand were at or below the reorder quantity. On Thursdays, an order was placed with the supplier, and the merchandise was received and entered on the computer by Saturday. Information added to the computer later for each item was the pick sequence, the numbers for substitute items, the discount (whether a coupon was being offered for that item), units per case, number of requests

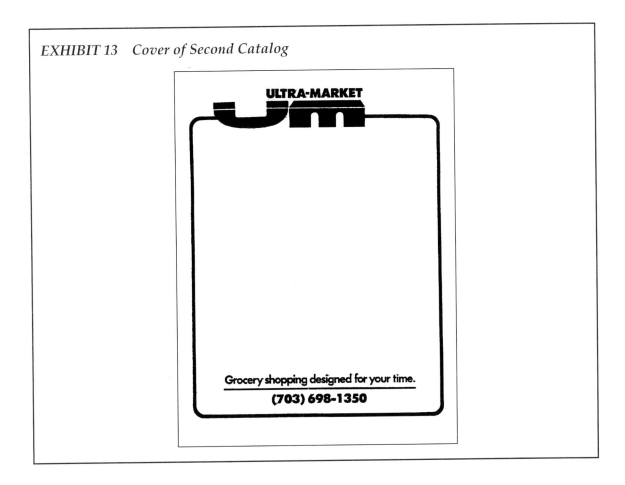

EXHIBIT 13   *Cover of Second Catalog*

ULTRA-MARKET

Grocery shopping designed for your time.
(703) 698-1350

when the item was out of stock, vendor, and vendor number. Gary expected the whole system to be in operation in two years.

Gary had a number of choices to make about how to promote U-M: whether to push discount prices, to advocate price stability, to promote service, or to use some combination of these. He believed that service was to become more important in the future because delivery would be even more popular as gas became more expensive and harder for consumers to obtain. In June, 65 percent of all U-M orders were delivered, and Gary hoped that the proportion would be about

the same in July. It seemed to him that most new customers wanted delivery.

Another question that kept coming up was about couponing. With the third catalog coming out in August, Gary wondered what he should do about the coupons he offered: discontinue them, emphasize them more, or continue as in the past.

Gary was considering using the ad agency to design a direct mail campaign to begin in late July. He said he had to decide whether this was the best way to reach his customers and to whom the mailing should go.

ALTERNATIVES FOR THE FUTURE

Gary wanted to be prepared for further development once the existing operation broke even and upon the successful completion of the second stock issue of $300,000. He expected these two events to occur by the end of the summer.

One alternative was to add bread and staple dairy products (butter and milk) to the product line. Such a move would call for buying a refrigerator for the warehouse (and finding space for it) at an estimated cost of $6,000.

Another possibility was to expand the product line so that a greater number of items were carried. It was reported in The Daily Progress (Charlottesville, Virginia) on January 30, 1978, that U-M carried about 4,000 items. At the end of June, that number had fallen to 2,800. Gary wondered whether he should increase the number again and, if so, what items should be added.

Gary was also considering investing in an automated picking system to speed up order filling and cut labor costs. It would involve installing a mezzanine level in the warehouse and using two conveyor belts to move the goods. Pickers would still be needed to remove the items from the shelves and put them on the belt. The cost for this system had been estimated in 1977 to be $8,000.

Another option that Gary was considering for some time after 1980 was expansion into other areas in metropolitan Washington. The idea involved pickup sites staffed by customer service personnel who could supply catalogs and answer customer questions, and people to process the orders after they arrived from the central warehouse. No inventory would be held at such a station. (See Exhibits 14A and 14B for data on the Washington market.)

Potential sites were to be selected on the basis of accessibility by the customer, size (2,000 to 3,000 square feet had been estimated as ad-

equate), and the demographics of the surrounding population. Some of the areas being considered were Roslyn (Arlington), Alexandria, and Reston-Herndon in Virginia, and Northwest Washington. (See the map in Exhibit 15.)

One idea was to use abandoned gas stations for pick ups. Customers would phone their orders to the main warehouse; based on their addresses, they would be directed to one of the pickup sites. Orders would be delivered from the warehouse to the pickup center where the customer would come to collect and pay for the items.

Because no personnel other than customer service and order processor staff would be needed, operating costs and the break-even sales volume for each center would be low, according to Gary. Each center would be responsible for developing its own sales and running its own advertising campaign. Contribution from sales would be used to cover the fixed costs of the center as well as any allocated overhead (including data processing and warehouse expenses) of the main operation.

A final option was to expand to other centers. Gary was considering opening at one site in the late summer. The site, located in Fort Lauderdale, Florida, had been suggested by an acquaintance, age 24, from Boston who was interested in operating it. A land developer in Fort Lauderdale had torn down a 25 year-old shopping center which had included the only grocery store within several miles. The new mall being built did not include a grocery store. In deference to demand, the developer was running buses to local supermarkets. The area residents, primarily retired but many having incomes in excess of $50,000 per annum, had boycotted the mall; thus they appeared to be natural customers for a catalog grocery store. Although they had time to shop, Gary stated he believed they would rather play cards and golf than shop for food.

EXHIBIT 14A *Distribution of Grocery Store Sales, Washington, DC–MD–VA, Standard Metropolitan Area*

	Number of Stores	Percentage of Market, Grocery Store Sales
Leading chains		89.0
Safeway	129	33.0
Giant Food	78	30.0
A&P	52	9.0
Grand Union	45	7.5
7-Eleven (c)	252	3.0
High's Dairy Stores (c)	175	1.5
MEMCO (div. Lucky Stores)	6	1.0
Food Fair (Pantry Pride)	7	1.0
Consumer Supermarkets	7	1.0
Acme (Super Saver)	7	1.0
Jumbo Food Stores	7	1.0
Leading independents		8.0%
Government commissaries	8	8.0
Sneider's	1	a
Larimer's	2	a
Magruder's	3	a
Other grocery stores	NA	3.0
Total	779+	100.0%

aIncluded in "Other Grocery Stores."
NA = Not available.
(c) = Convenience stores.

The second area was in the middle Atlantic, between Atlanta and Raleigh, North Carolina. A friend from South Carolina, aged 29, wanted to operate an Ultra-Market in this area. He was aware that the final choice of the location would be subject to the approval of Gary and the Board of Directors.

Gary had already obtained approval from the Board of Directors to raise capital to form a holding company. The plans for expansion into new markets were that the holding company would provide operation manuals (as yet not written), name, logo, national advertising, computer software, management organization and training, and market research and planning. The fee for these services would be 51 percent of the profits. In exchange, the subsidiary would supply $250,000 in capital, own 100 percent of the assets, and retain 49 percent of the profits.

With so many alternatives, Gary hardly knew where to turn next. He wondered how he could best use the $300,000 when it was raised.

Notes

1. From company records.
2. From company records.

EXHIBIT 14B *Distribution of Grocery Store Sales, DC-MD-VA, Standard Metropolitan Area*

	United States	SMA Total
Retail sales, 1976		
Total (millions)	$661,749	$10,374
Food store sales (millions)	$144,912	$1,978
Supermarket sales (millions)	$134,534	$1,852
Percentage of food store sales	92.8%	93.6%
Total number of food stores (1972)	173,084	1,972
Supermarket sales per capita	$623.19	$605.92
Population, 1976		
Total (thousands)	215,881.4	3,056.5
Total number of households (thousands)	74,002.4	1,057.3
Population by age of household head	8.3%	10.2%
Under 25 years	21.3%	28.2%
25–34 years	16.7%	19.5%
35–44 years	17.5%	18.0%
45–54 years	15.9%	13.3%
55–64 years	20.3%	10.8%
65 and over		
Number of persons per household	21.1%	22.7%
One	30.7%	28.2%
Two	17.1%	18.4%
Three	15.7%	15.9%
Four	8.3%	8.2%
Five	7.1%	6.6%
Six and over	2.92	2.89
Average household size		
Income, 1976		
Net effective buying income (millions)	$1,176,240	$22,361
Per capita EBI	$ 5,449	$ 7,316
Median household EBI	$ 13,781	$18,548
Housing units, 1970		
Total units (thousands)	67,699	938
Percent vacant	6.3%	4.2%
Percent occupied	93.7%	95.8%
Percent owner occupied	62.8%	46.0%
Percent renter occupied	40.2%	54.0%

Source: "Distribution Study of Grocery Store Sales in 289 Cities," *Supermarket News*, 1978.

EXHIBIT 15 *Map of Washington, DC–MD–VA Area*

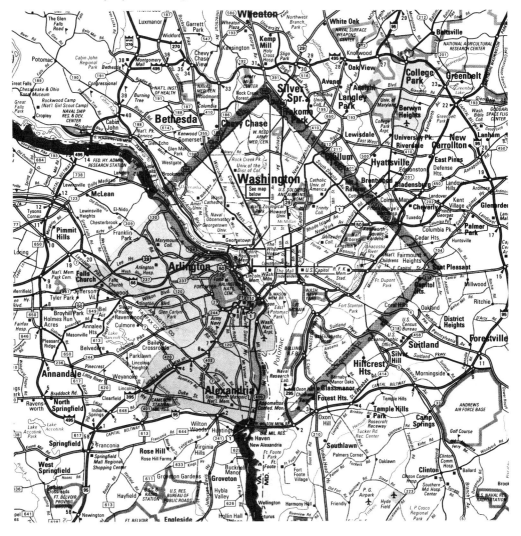

3. The July, 1979 *Chain Store Age* reported that the average gross margin for 1,500 supermarkets with minimum annual sales of $1 million were 22.7 percent of sales. Net profits as a percent of sales for selected stores were shown as 0.6 percent for Foodarama, 1.4 percent for Giant, 0.04 percent for A & P, 1.1 percent for Kroger, and 1.2 percent for Safeway.

4. The redemption rate was running at about 35%.

Case 23
Wendy's International, Inc.:
Wendy's Old Fashioned Hamburgers

"Does America need another hamburger chain?" was the question being asked as R. David Thomas opened the doors to his first Wendy's Old Fashioned Hamburgers restaurant at 257 East Broad Street in downtown Columbus, Ohio on November 15, 1969. At that time many food industry experts and some skeptical observers had commented that the fast-food growth curve had already peaked during the late 1960s and that the rapid expansion of the industry was over.

On March 21, 1978, after only eight years and four months, the thousandth restaurant in the Wendy's chain opened at 1000 Memorial Boulevard in Springfield, Tennessee. Never before had such an accomplishment been achieved in such a short period of time. During 1985, the company opened over 400 new units to bring the number of Wendy's Old Fashioned Hamburgers restaurants to approximately 3,400 at year end.

COMPANY BACKGROUND

Wendy's was founded by R. David Thomas, who was previously associated with Kentucky Fried Chicken and Arthur Treacher's Fish and Chips. Thomas presently serves as Senior Chairman of the Board. Robert L. Barney, currently Chairman and Chief Executive Officer, joined Wendy's in

Source: "Case 34, Wendy's International, Inc." from Cases and Exercises in Marketing, pp. 245–261, by W. Wayne Talarzyk, copyright © 1987 by The Dryden Press, a division of Harcourt Brace College Publishers, reprinted by permission of the publisher.

1970. He started in the fast-food business in 1962, when he became an owner of a Kentucky Fried Chicken franchise, later becoming a regional vice-president in charge of 135 restaurants. For a short period of time before joining Wendy's, he was vice-president of operations at Arthur Treacher's Fish and Chips. Ronald P. Fay is President and Chief Operating Officer. He was in charge of W. T. Grant's food service operations, one of the few profitable divisions for the company, until 1975 when he became a partner in a Wendy's franchise in Virginia Beach, Virginia. In December 1979, he sold his restaurants to Wendy's International and joined the corporation.

Much of Wendy's phenomenal success can be attributed to its large, well-run franchise organization and its low costs of operation along with quality and speed of service and upscale ambience. As a relative latecomer to the fast-food scene, Wendy's had a big advantage over the predecessor chains. But competition had a head start on restaurant development. McDonald's had started 14 years before Wendy's which gave it an advantage in market penetration. While McDonald's, Burger King, Burger Chef (now owned by Hardees), and many of the other fast-food pioneers had to build their franchise business from scratch, training managers with little or no restaurant experience, Wendy's drew from the ranks of former chain operators who were well acquainted with the business. Using a territorial franchise approach, the company emphasized those franchisees who could finance and manage their own "minichains" of five, ten, or more units. Franchisees pay a continuing 4 percent of sales franchise royalty, paid monthly to the parent company.

The second key to Wendy's success is its efficient operation. Initially the typical Wendy's building was about 30 × 76 feet, seating 90 to 100 people, with parking for 30 to 45 cars. Most units are built on half- to three-quarter-acre lots as opposed to a McDonald's or Burger King, which usually occupy an acre or more. Wendy's typically needs less land than the other two operations because a drive-in window accounts for 40 to 45 percent of a unit's total sales. Those customers who use the pick-up window obviously do not require parking spaces or inside eating areas. Exhibit 1 shows the new-image restaurant.

In 1984, 120 new Wendy's and 151 existing restaurants adopted the latest design change—the addition of a "greenhouse" at the front of the restaurant, or in some cases, along one or both sides. With more natural light, higher seating ca-pacity, and more attractive ambience, studies show that restaurants with greenhouses have higher sales than those without.

An average investment of $770,000 is required to construct a Wendy's unit. Of this total, about 50 percent goes for the building, another 30 percent for real estate, and the remaining 20 percent for equipment. The typical Wendy's outlet av-eraged $861,000 in annual sales in 1984. Selected financial data is presented in Exhibit 2.

In recent years, Wendy's has continued to focus attention toward opening company-owned outlets. This is being accomplished in two ways—either by buying back existing franchises or by constructing its own company-owned units. Of the 1,057 company-operated restau-rants at the close of 1984, 15 were acquired from franchise owners during the year. In 1984, 120 new company-operated restaurants were built. The company also operates a number of Sisters

EXHIBIT 1   *Picture of Wendy's New-Image Restaurant*

EXHIBIT 2 *Selected Financial Data—A Five-Year Financial Review (Dollars in thousands except per share data)*

	1984	1983	1982	1981	1980
Operations					
Retail sales	$ 877,269	$ 665,591	$ 560,516	$ 446,800	$ 310,067
Revenues	944,768	720,383	606,964	488,825	348,391
Company restaurant operating profit	166,383	126,367	101,717	74,832	54,385
Income before income taxes	126,882	99,476	80,031	64,897	54,804
Net income	68,707	55,220	44,102	36,852	30,096
Per share data:					
Net income	1.25	1.01	.84	.76	.67
Cash dividends	.25	.20	.15	.14	.13
Pro forma per share data:*					
Net income	.93	.76	.63	.57	.50
Cash dividends	.19	.15	.11	.11	.10
Cash flow from operations	135,850	97,885	75,985	66,857	58,345
Company restaurant operating profit margin	19.0%	19.0%	18.1%	16.7%	17.5%
Pre-tax profit margin	13.4%	13.8%	13.2%	13.3%	15.7%
Return on average assets	14.3%	14.0%	14.1%	15.2%	18.2%
Return on average equity	20.4%	19.3%	19.5%	22.0%	26.6%
Systemwide Wendy's sales	$2,423,000	$1,922,913	$1,632,440	$1,424,215	$1,209,314
Average sales per Wendy's restaurant:					
Company	869	754	706	702	665
Franchise	857	762	701	662	615
Systemwide	861	759	703	674	627
Financial position					
Total assets	$ 613,636	$ 506,713	$ 453,561	$ 375,469	$ 218,718
Property and equipment, net	498,593	377,911	327,442	281,008	174,235

*Reflects the effects of a 4-for-3 stock split declared in February 1985.

Chicken & Biscuits restaurants, through a wholly owned subsidiary, Sisters International. Most of the present 76 restaurants are company owned and operated with the rest being franchised.

INTERNATIONAL EXPANSION

In 1984, Wendy's continued to build on a base of international operations, with a focus on the long-term potentials of those markets. The top priority was one of improved penetration of existing franchised and company-operated markets. The firm opened eight company-operated restaurants in 1984, including four in Munich. The concentration of units in England, Spain, and West Germany enables Wendy's to advertise effectively in those company markets. Exhibit 3 provides a variety of data about Wendy's international operations.

	1984	1983	1982	1981	1980
Financial position (continued)					
Long-term obligations	105,005	86,671	103,070	97,956	42,418
Shareholders' equity	364,466	308,282	264,733	201,738	125,596
Shareholders' equity per share	6.63	5.67	4.87	3.95	2.80
Current ratio	.53	.65	.80	.58	.55
Ratio of debt to equity	29%	28%	39%	49%	34%
Ratio of debt to total capitalization	22%	22%	28%	33%	25%
Restaurant data (number open at year end)					
Domestic Wendy's:					
Company	1,014	887	802	734	502
Franchise	1,801	1,633	1,503	1,386	1,450
International Wendy's:					
Company	43	35	25	14	4
Franchise	134	118	100	95	78
Total Wendy's	2,992	2,673	2,430	2,229	2,034
Sisters:					
Company	26	21	17	10	4
Franchise	50	28	8	4	
Total Sisters	76	49	25	14	4
Other data					
Weighted average shares outstanding (000)	55,142	54,701	52,220	48,594	45,031
Number of shareholders at year end	31,000	25,000	20,000	19,000	18,000
Number of employees at year end	47,000	36,000	29,000	26,000	18,000

PRODUCT OFFERING

Wendy's places primary emphasis upon consistent quality in all areas of food preparation and presentation. The firm uses 100 percent pure beef, which is delivered in bulk and pattied fresh every morning in each of its restaurants. The patties are cooked slowly to retain their natural juices and flavors. Whether the customer orders the quarter-pound single, the half-pound double, or the three-quarter-pound triple, the hamburger is served directly from the grill. By mixing and matching the nine available condiments, a Wendy's customer can specify one of 1,024 different ways to have his or her hamburger served. Hamburgers account for about 40 percent of all sales and of these approximately 65 percent are singles, 33 percent doubles, and 2 percent triples.

Chili is also on the menu. In addition to being popular with customers, this product serves

---

EXHIBIT 3   Fact Sheet: International Development, 1984–1985

1984
Signed development agreements in Taiwan, Korea, New Zealand, and the Netherlands
Opened 24 new restaurants outside the United States: 8 company-operated restaurants and 16 franchise-operated restaurants.
At year-end, 177 restaurants served markets outside the United States.

International Restaurants

Australia	9	Philippines	2
Bahamas	1	Puerto Rico	13
Canada	71	Singapore	1
Hong Kong	1	Spain	11
Italy	3	Switzerland	4
Japan	24	United Kingdom	13
Korea	1	West Germany	2
Malaysia	4	Total	177

1985
April: Acquired Wendy's Restaurants of Canada, Inc., formerly a franchisee. Purchase included 71 existing restaurants.
Opened five more restaurants in Canada, for a total of 76 at year-end.

Restaurants Opened YTD 1985

Australia	2	Puerto Rico	2
Canada	5	Spain	2
Italy	1	Taiwan[a]	4[a]
Japan	1	Netherlands[a]	1[a]
Korea	3	United Kingdom[a]	1[a]
New Zealand[a]	1	West Germany	2
Philippines	1	Total	26

1986
Plan approximately 30 new restaurants in Canada as a result of an aggressive franchising program there.
Plan approximately 33 new restaurants elsewhere outside United States.
1986 total: over 60 international restaurants.

[a]First Wendy's in the country.

---

a unique secondary purpose. To keep the hamburgers fresh for customers, no cooked patties are kept on the grill for more than four minutes. In order to eliminate this potential meat waste factor, hamburgers not served within the four-minute time period are steamed in a kettle and used for the next day's chili. French fries, Frosties, coffee, tea, milk, and soft drinks round out the basic menu. The Frosty, a Wendy's exclusive, is a thick, creamy blend of chocolate and vanilla (much like a very thick milkshake) served with a spoon.

Addition of Salad Bars

In 1979, seeking ways to improve customer traffic, Wendy's turned to a strategy that had worked fairly well for other food service organizations—an expanded menu. The company's desire to diffuse its dependence on beef products and yet not interfere with its extremely efficient in-store operating setup led to salad bars as the first menu addition.

Salads represented a logical extension of the menu by being compatible with Wendy's operational system while enhancing the company's adult image. The salad bar also widened Wendy's appeal to families and increased its lunch and dinner business. Salads also helped attract the health- and weight-conscious and smaller-appetite consumers, both of which are growing market segments.

Other Menu Items

Wendy's also began testing a breakfast menu in May 1979 that included omelette and scrambled egg platters, bacon, sausage, biscuits, hashbrown potatoes, and french toast. Breakfast is prepared primarily on the grill, with relatively minor additions to kitchen equipment, and is compatible with Wendy's system. It is designed to utilize the restaurants from 7:00 to 10:30 a.m., before the lunch day begins. Breakfast represents an attractive opportunity to increase sales and utilization of the restaurants. Customers view Wendy's offering as a superior product. By late 1983 the breakfast menu, narrowed down to omelets, breakfast sandwiches, and french toast was offered in about 200 restaurants. Breakfast was implemented systemwide in June 1985.

Other significant developments evolving from changing strategies were three systemwide menu additions. First, a breaded filet of chicken breast sandwich, started in test in January 1980, was rolled out in most company and franchise stores. The second item was Wendy's Kids' Meal, a child-oriented meal. It consists of a smaller hamburger, smaller order of french fries, and a small Frosty or a small soft drink.

The third item was the Taco Salad, which incorporated several existing ingredients with no additional capital investment and minimal food preparation training: Wendy's uses lettuce, tomatoes, and cheese from the salad bar, plus the chili—the only new ingredients are taco chips and a special dressing. All of these product additions helped Wendy's sales volume by attracting new market segments and increasing the visit frequency of present customers. "Hot Stuffed" baked potatoes were introduced in late 1983 and became the most successful new product introduction to date. Exhibit 4 shows a television storyboard for Wendy's baked potatoes.

Testing of a full dinner menu began in 1982 in 29 Wendy's in Cincinnati. A successful dinner program has significant profit potential for the system. The test menu consists of five entrees, each competitively priced for family dinner business. Some of the dinner entrees are chopped beef and mushroom sauce, chicken parmesan, and country beef and gravy. The entrees include a side salad and dinner potatoes to provide a balanced meal. Entrees are based, for the most part, on products already in the restaurants. To date, customer feedback has been very favorable and testing is still in process.

ADVERTISING AND PROMOTION

To use the media to build overall awareness of Wendy's among potential as well as current customers (particularly adults from 18 through 34 years of age) Wendy's titled its 1982 advertising campaign "WKOP" ("Wendy's Kind of People"). The campaign goals were to create excitement, to generate increased store traffic, and to get consumers to try Wendy's products.

EXHIBIT 4   *Advertising—Hot Stuffed*

THE
WENDY'S
NATIONAL
ADVERTISING
PROGRAM,
INC.

TITLE: "HOT STUFFED II"

LENGTH: 30 SECONDS
COMM'L NO.: WOFH-3373

WHISPER: Ooh.

WHISPER: Hot

WHISPER: Hot, so hot.

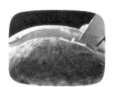

COOL ANNCR: Wendy's baked potatoes are

WHISPER: Hot stuff.

ANNCR: Wendy's stuffs 'em all kinds of ways.
WHISPER: Hot!
ANNCR: Like with cheese.

WHISPER: Oh, what a tease!

ANNCR: Or chili and cheese,

bacon and cheese

broccoli and cheese

WHISPER: Wendy's

ANNCR: Or sour cream and chives.

WHISPER: That makes five.

ANNCR: Wendy's stuffed baked potatoes.

They're hot!

For Wendy's kind of people.
WHISPER: Oooh.

Exhibit 5 presents some of the basic objectives and strategies for this campaign.

Wendy's uses coupons as a promotional device to increase sales and to heighten awareness on a short-term basis (a phenomenon which the firm hopes will retain some residual benefit in return customers). Coupons provide an opportunity for consumers to save money and also may encourage them to try new menu items. Coupons used by Wendy's generally offer a free item with the purchase of another one, or two menu items at the regular price of one, or a discount off the regular price of an item. From test situations, Wendy's has found that coupons distributed through newspaper inserts and direct mail are most frequently redeemed and are most effective for Wendy's because of the greater selectivity of saturation per dollar spent.

Wendy's also focuses on cultivating a good relationship with the public in each store's market. Local restaurants are encouraged to take part in public activities and community programs. Examples of such participation include fund raising for local charities, crime prevention programs, and sponsoring civil and cultural events.

"WHERE'S THE BEEF?"

Since 1982, the major hamburger fast-service chains have been fighting what the media dubbed the "Burger Wars." Wendy's, the world's third-largest hamburger chain, is outspent in advertising eight to one by its major competitors, McDonald's and Burger King. Accordingly, the company has been compelled to communicate using creative treatments and media extension techniques that break through the clutter and dramatize product benefits in a unique, often humorous and exaggerated manner.

At the start of 1984, when the Burger Wars began anew, the company again found itself in this position. McDonald's attacked with 39-cent hamburgers. Burger King came out swinging with its "flame-broiling versus frying" campaign. At the same time, research showed that consumers perceived McDonald's and Burger King's hamburgers to be larger, although in reality Wendy's Single contains more beef.

Seizing its size advantage, Wendy's created the "Where's the Beef?" campaign, spots for which first aired January 9, 1984. Its goal was to create consumer awareness of its larger-size hamburger and leverage a comparatively small ad budget to extend the reach and frequency of the ad message beyond purchased media impressions. In other words, use public relations to do more with less: Bring the advertising theme into the American vernacular, create awareness of Wendy's larger hamburger, and underscore the inherent value of all Wendy's menu items.

Objectives

Wendy's sought a unified marketing and public relations plan to create excitement and awareness for the campaign and the slogan. The public relations objectives for the campaign became to (1) build national and local media and consumer awareness and involvement in the campaign by making the slogan a news item and (2) persuade consumers that Wendy's offers them more beef in its hamburgers than other major competitors.

Once the initial objectives were achieved and "Where's the Beef?" took America by storm, Wendy's produced a sequel to satisfy the public's demand. Public relations objectives continued to focus efforts on extending the widespread awareness and impact of "Where's the Beef?"

Then, after a five-month leave of absence from the airwaves, "Where's the Beef?" was revived with a third campaign. Public relations activities paved the way for a triumphant return. The company added two elements—the

---

EXHIBIT 5   Media Objectives and Strategies for 1982

  I. *National/Local Media Objectives*
   During this crucial introductory period and the fall hamburger emphasis period, we recommend that local market media planning be guided by the following objectives:
   1. To make strategic and creative use of media at the local level (and in conjunction with Wendy's national advertising) to generate both broad and rapid as well as sustained awareness of Wendy's new "You're Wendy's Kind of People" campaign.
   2. To use media to build overall awareness of Wendy's among potential as well as current customers—particularly adults 18–34—to create excitement, generate increased store traffic trial of Wendy's products, and visit frequency during this important marketing period.
 II. *Media Strategy*
III. A. *Local Television*
   In order to execute these objectives, we are recommending that in all markets where affordable, spot television should serve as the primary local medium in support of this introduction. Spot television is recommended for several key reasons:
   1. Its proven ability to generate broad reach quickly is essential to the successful introduction of "You're Wendy's Kind of People" campaign.
   2. Television provides an excellent opportunity to present the strong people- and food-oriented visual messages which characterize the new campaign.
   3. When spot television is used selectivity and in combination with the network television schedule, the investment in both media is optimized to build awareness.
  B. Local Radio
   Radio is recommended as an effective local complement to the local spot television activity (in most markets) and as the primary medium only in those markets where spot television is not affordable for several reasons:
   1. Radio's strength as a frequency medium can be instrumental in reinforcing the new visual elements of Wendy's campaign as well as establishing in the consumer's mind the various musical executions of "Wendy's Kind of People."
   2. Radio provides an excellent opportunity to deliver long-copy messages to the consumer.
   3. Radio can be an effective reach-extender by reaching light TV viewers including the out-of-home audience, which can be an important target for our inside as well as Pick-Up Window business.

---

promotion of licensed "Where's the Beef?" products and an NFL "Where's the Beef?" Monday Night Football sweepstakes. Public relations plans supported these elements, as well. Exhibit 6 provides some additional information about this campaign and its results. A television storyboard for one of the later commercials is shown in Exhibit 7.

"FRESH" CAMPAIGN OVERVIEW

Based on Wendy's most extensive research ever, which determined that five out of the top ten fast-service attributes most valued by consumers had to do with freshness, Wendy's developed the campaign line, "Choose Fresh. Choose Wendy's." in 1985. After advertising freshness

    C. Local Newspapers

Where affordable, markets should also consider using newspapers, particularly where their use can be particularly effective in generating unusual interest or excitement in the new campaign. (See special "Teaser" campaign recommendations later.)

    D. Other Media

While a number of other media options may be available locally, we would recommend that their local use in the introductory plan be governed by the following:

1. The relative speed with which the medium's messages accumulate against the consumer, i.e., the more quickly a medium's audience builds over time, the more suitable it may be for introductory use.
2. The relative cost of using the medium and the degree to which its use would divert dollars from our primary media, i.e., spot television and radio.

III. National Advertising Plan

    A. New Campaign Introduction Flight

1. Prime-time Television

This network emphasis period will be supported on network television with 80 prime-time target (adults 18–34) GRPs per week for six consecutive weeks, highlighted by a Wendy's participation in the highest-rated program of the summer months—the Baseball All-Star game (and the pre-game program) on ABC, July 12, 1982. (A schedule of all Wendy's network appearances during the entire flight has been sent to all agencies.)

2. Network Radio

For six consecutive weekends, Wendy's will deliver 20 target GRPs/week through its 1/4 sponsorship of Mutual's Dick Clark National Music Survey.

    B. Hamburger Emphasis Period

1. Prime-time Television

This network emphasis period will be supported with 100 Prime-Time Target GRPs per week for each week of this six-week flight.

2. Network Radio

During this six-week flight, Wendy's will again deliver 20 Target points per week via Mutual's Dick Clark National Music Survey.

for over 16 years, Wendy's decided to put a more vigorous effort behind letting consumers know about its "unfair competitive advantage." More than 1,200 consumers (ages 18–49) were interviewed on their expectations of fast-service restaurants. Five of the top ten points included:

- Food served piping hot
- Food not precooked or reheated
- Food prepared the way I like it
- Food is fresh
- Food prepared with great care

Wendy's ranked significantly higher on these points. The top three hamburger chains rated similarly on the still-important categories of

---

EXHIBIT 6   Information on "Where's the Beef?" Campaign

Execution (Techniques and Materials)

Imagine receiving a plain box, marked "Perishable—Open Immediately!" that is filled with a large fluffy sesame seed bun. That is how the media first learned about "Where's the Beef?" The press materials, not the beef, were tucked between the 12-inch buns, along with a large magnifying glass.

While the teaser press kit was the key to gain media support, Wendy's created a fictional character and story to generate additional awareness. The character, Sheerluck Homes, helped media and customers solve "The Case of the Missing Beef" in key major markets.

Once the commercial ran, Wendy's focused efforts on maximizing exposure by using the slogan and the commercial's star, Clara Peller. Wendy's seized an opportunity for major news coverage with the filming of the second commercial at the Chicago studio of Director Joe Sedelmaier. Press were invited to view the last day of filming and to interview Clara and Wendy's spokespeople. One crew, trying for an exclusive, camped outside Sedelmaier's door for seven hours the previous day. Clara was ushered out a back entrance into a waiting car. On the evening news, the station covered the fact that its reporter had been duped by Wendy's "Where's the Beef?" people.

Public relations efforts focused heavily on national placements. Because of the popularity of Clara's photo, placed from the commercial's filming, AP had to run it three times to meet requests from its member newspapers. *Newsweek* ran an exclusive on its "Newsmakers" page. Subsequent photos of Clara with Muhammed Ali, with a "Where's the Beef?" cartoon caption, up to her waist in buns, and in front of the 1949 DeSoto used in the third commercial were placed with the wire services and national publications.

Video news releases and interviews with major national shows were arranged through careful planning. The result was coverage on news shows nationwide and interviews for Clara with scores of television hosts. Syndicated radio releases carried still more coverage.

Media events heralded more activity when "Where's the Beef?" returned, including the filming of the third campaign, Clara's Nashville recording debut as the "Where's the Beef?" record star, and the kickoff of the NFL Monday Night Football promotion.

Publicity manuals with how-to instructions and locally adaptable materials were distributed to the entire Wendy's system for each effort. These activities were designed to expand the national plan to the grassroots level. Licensees were kept informed through biweekly "Where's the Beef?" updates about the merchandising effort.

Results/Measurements

"Where's the Beef?" did more to raise Wendy's awareness and market share, and increase Wendy's sales and profit value, than any campaign in the company's history. Sales for 1984 increased 26 percent to $2.4 billion, compared with 1983 sales of $1.9 billion. Profits also rose 24 percent over 1983. Wendy's market share in the restaurant sandwich category increased 20 percent during the campaign's first four months, while restaurant name awareness rose 48 percent during the year. These results were achieved despite the company's being outspent by its major competitors.

Publicity efforts yielded more than 3.6 billion consumer impressions, which means each American was exposed to media coverage 16 times. The campaign accumulated more than 26,000 press clippings, more than 9,000 radio news stories and more than 1,200 television news stories. The campaign also made news throughout Europe and the Far East.

The commercial garnered three Clio Awards and was named the top commercial of 1984 by Video Storyboard Tests, Inc.

EXHIBIT 7   Advertising—Fluffy Bun

THE WENDY'S NATIONAL ADVERTISING PROGRAM, INC.

TITLE: "FLUFFY BUN"

LENGTH: 30 SECONDS
COMM'L NO.: WOFH-3386

CUST. #1: It certainly is a big bun.
CUST. #2: It's a very big bun.

CUST. #1: A big fluffy bun.

CUST. #2: It's a very...big...fluffy...bun.

CUST. #3: Where's the beef?
ANNCR: Some hamburger places give you a lot less beef on a lot of bun.

CUST. #3: Where's the beef?

ANNCR: At Wendy's, we serve a hamburger we modestly call a "Single"—and Wendy's Single has more beef than the Whopper or Big Mac. At Wendy's, you get more beef and less bun.

CUST. #3: Hey, where's the beef? I don't think there's anybody back there!

ANNCR: You want something better, you're Wendy's Kind of People.

"fast, friendly service," "reasonable prices," and "clean, comfortable environment."

Two television commercials created for this campaign include "Lamps," (Exhibit 8) a spot contrasting Wendy's freshly prepared salads, toppings, and sandwiches with prepackaged varieties at those "other"hamburger restaurants, and "Birthday," which questions the uncertain

EXHIBIT 8 Advertising—Fresh Lamp

THE
WENDY'S
NATIONAL
ADVERTISING
PROGRAM, INC

TITLE: "FRESH/LAMP"

LENGTH: 30 SECONDS
COMM'L NO.: YWDH-0460

ANNCR: You can choose pre-made, pre-packaged salads...

or you can choose to make one fresh.

Choose Fresh. Choose Wendy's.

ANNCR: You can choose frozen beef...

or you can choose fresh ground beef.

Choose Fresh. Choose Wendy's.

ANNCR: You can choose a hamburger warmed over under heat lamps...

or you can choose a hamburger served fresh, hot-off-the-grill.

Choose Fresh. Choose Wendy's.

age of hamburgers at "other" restaurants (Exhibit 9).

Two additional spots were developed. "Onions" tells the story of a man faced with a choice of "rehydrated" onions at the "other" hamburger restaurant, or fresh onions at Wendy's. "Express" laments the poor local hamburger, which stops before reaching its destination, the holding bin.

EXHIBIT 9 Advertising—Birthday

THE
WENDY'S
NATIONAL
ADVERTISING
PROGRAM,
INC

TITLE: "BIRTHDAY"

LENGTH: 30 SECONDS
COMM'L NO.: YWDH-0440

SINGERS: Happy Birthday to you, Happy Birthday to you —

Happy Birthday dear hamburger...

ANNCR: Order a hamburger at some places, chances are it's been sitting around getting old.

Wendy's believes no hamburger should grow old.

At Wendy's your hamburger

is always served immediately,

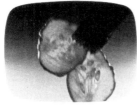

fresh hot-off-the-grill.

The other guys can't promise that.

SINGERS: How old are you now? How old...

(SFX: Candle blown out...)

ANNCR: Choose Fresh. Choose Wendy's.

The Wendy's Express, on the other hand, tells the story of speed.

A 30-second television advertisement aimed at blacks was called "The Will." It depicted a nephew who lost out on an inheritance because he took his uncle to restaurants that made hamburgers in advance and then put them in plastic boxes under heat lamps. Two Hispanic-oriented spots carried through with Wendy's theme of offering freshly prepared sandwiches that are not made from frozen beef or prepackaged and held under heat lamps. Both starred Don Cucufato, who tested well with Wendy's consumers and proved to be an effective spokesperson for Hispanic consumers.

NATIONAL TRACKING STUDY

The Wendy's National Tracking Study is an ongoing probability-sampling telephone survey of U.S. consumers. Exhibit 10 presents some selected results from the first quarter, 1985 study. Approximately 1,500 interviews are conducted each quarter among consumers aged 16–70 who have visited a restaurant serving mainly hamburgers at least once in the past month. The major objectives of the study are to:

- Define Wendy's market position relative to major competition.
- Monitor changes in the market position resulting from Wendy's advertising and sales promotion programs, competitive activity, economic conditions, etc.
- Detect and/or anticipate potential problem and opportunity areas.

EXHIBIT 10   Selected Results from Wendy's National Tracking Study (First Quarter, 1985)

Marketing Activity

Wendy's emphasized baked potatoes on network television during the first quarter of 1985 (1/7–2/3). This was followed by a video coupon in 85 percent of company markets (2/7–2/24) and a network television "Fresh Emphasis" (2/25–4/14). Wendy's emphasized the chicken sandwich during late fourth quarter of 1984 (11/19–12/23).

During the first quarter, the major competitive activities included:

    McDonald's: Double cheeseburger, "Hot Hand Warmin'," Filet-O-Fish emphasis, breakfast, 99¢ Big Mac

    Burger King: Croissanwich (2:1 preference over Egg McMuffin), 39¢ Hamburgers, 49¢ Cheeseburger, 99¢ Whoppers

    Hardee's: Fisherman's Filet, Roast Beef Combo Meal

Unaided Advertising Awareness

	1st Qtr. '84	4th Qtr. '84	1st Qtr. '85	**Point Change (percent)** 1st Qtr. '85 vs. 4th Qtr. '84	1st Qtr. '85 vs. 1st Qtr. '84
Wendy's	45.9%	50.2%	44.3%	− 5.9	− 1.6
Burger King	60.9	52.7	52.2	− 0.5	− 8.7
McDonald's	68.3	66.8	69.9	+ 3.1	+ 1.6
Hardee's	11.7	12.6	13.5	+ 0.9	+ 1.8
"Where's the Beef?"	71.2%	84.8%	83.0%	− 1.8	+11.8
"You Want Something Better, You're Wendy's Kind of People"	45.1	43.8	37.0	− 6.8	− 8.1
"Aren't You Hungry for Burger King Now?"	77.3	77.2	77.1	− 0.1	− 0.2
"It's a Good Time for the Great Taste at McDonald's"	N.A.	65.3	74.5	+ 9.2	N.A.
"It's all Here at Hardee's"	N.A.	23.0	27.3	+ 4.3	N.A.
Number of interviews	1,541	1,537	1,497		
Breakfast	18.4%	34.2%	46.7%	+12.5	+28.3
Chicken sandwich	43.5	48.0	56.5	+ 8.5	+13.0
Hot stuffed baked potatoes	70.5	75.5	82.0	+ 6.5	+11.5

Ever Tried Wendy's Products (among Total Customers)

	1st Qtr. '84	4th Qtr. '84	1st Qtr. '85	**Point Change (percent)** 1st Qtr. '85 vs. 4th Qtr. '84	1st Qtr. '85 vs. 1st Qtr. '84
Number of interviews	1,541	1,537	1,497		
Single hamburgers	N.A.	72.2%	75.7%	+3.5	N.A.
Chicken sandwich	18.0	21.5	23.4	+1.9	+ 5.4
Frosty	48.2	47.4	49.0	+1.6	+ 0.8
Breakfast	2.7	6.6	8.0	+1.4	+ 5.3
Apple dumplings	N.A.	7.8	9.0	+1.2	N.A.
Hot stuffed baked potatoes	25.2	34.7	35.8	+1.1	+10.6

Reasons for Going/Not Going to Wendy's

Food quality was cited most often (52.1 percent) during the first quarter of 1985 as the main reason for going to Wendy's. This was followed by convenience (30.4 percent).

Convenience was also cited most often (49.9 percent) as the main reason for not going to Wendy's more often. Cost was mentioned second most frequently (9.7 percent).

Ten Most Important Attributes
(10 = highest importance; 1 = lowest importance)

Rank	Attribute	Importance Rating
1	Hamburgers served fresh	9.18
2	Quality of food	9.08
3	Clean dining room	9.03
4	Fresh food	8.96
5	Taste of hamburgers	8.88
6	Food piping hot	8.86
7	Hamburgers served hot off the grill	8.86
8	Value for the money	8.57
9	Accuracy of order inside	8.53
10	Friendly service	8.53

Ratings on Ten Most Important Attributes
(10 = excellent; 1 = poor)

| Importance Rank | Attribute | Attribute Ratings | | |
		Wendy's	Burger King	McDonald's
1	Hamburgers served fresh	8.66[a]	8.09	7.40
2	Quality of food	8.17[a]	7.73	7.23
3	Clean dining room	8.51	8.19	8.29
4	Fresh food	8.34[a]	7.82	7.41
5	Taste of hamburgers	8.07[a]	7.76	6.82
6	Food piping hot	8.57[a]	8.00	7.70
7	Hamburgers served hot off the grill	8.51[a]	7.91	6.96
8	Value for the money	7.91	7.85	7.81
9	Accuracy of order inside	8.73[a]	8.49	8.33
10	Friendly service	8.25[a]	8.01	8.01
11	Clean restrooms	8.28[a]	8.05	8.05
12	Food not precooked or reheated	8.20[a]	7.62	7.03
13	Convenient location	7.07[b]	7.55	8.53
14	Accuracy of drive-through window	8.36	8.19	8.01
15	Order speed inside restaurant	8.27[a]	7.81	7.98
16	Taste of french fries	7.57[c]	7.46	8.19
17	Drive-through order speed	7.59	7.63	7.26
18	Appealing menu selection	8.19[a]	7.68	7.38
19	Overall menu prices	7.29[b]	7.68	8.11
20	Dining atmosphere	8.13[a]	7.61	7.66
21	Menu variety	8.14[a]	7.59	7.50
22	Nutritional food	7.94[a]	7.40	6.89
23	Roomy seating accommodations	7.93[b]	8.21	8.27

Ratings on Ten Most Important Attributes
(10 = excellent; 1 = poor)

Importance Rank	Attribute	Wendy's	Attribute Ratings Burger King	McDonald's
24	Suitable facilities for dining with children	7.75[b]	8.10	8.78
25	Hamburgers that are flame broiled	N.A.	N.A.	N.A.
26	Quality of salad bar	8.41[a]	7.50	N.A.
27	Price specials or discounts	6.45[b]	7.61	7.23
28	Restaurant appealing to children	6.77[b]	7.52	9.11
29	Community involvement	7.04[c]	7.12	8.33

[a]Wendy's significantly more acceptable than both competitors.
[b]Wendy's significantly less acceptable than both competitors.
[c]Wendy's significantly less acceptable than McDonald's, but comparable to Burger King.

Case 24
Zale Corporation

The assignment given Jack Olsen's marketing management class sounded easy enough when the instructor outlined the task. The assignment was to:

1. Choose a large, diversified corporation and prepare a description of its operations from published documents.
2. Describe the social, economic, technological, and competitive opportunity and threat environments in which it operates.

This case was prepared from published sources, including Zale Corporation annual reports and 10-K reports. The information presented in the case does not necessarily depict the explicit situation faced by Zale Corporation or past operating procedures but is introduced only for the purpose of class discussion. Financial data referenced from noncompany sources have not been validated as to accuracy. Data presented on the retailing environment are based on a variety of sources including *U.S. Census* data and the author's extrapolation of these data. The discussion of the retailing environment should not be interpreted as reflecting any research or views of the Zale Corporation. This case was prepared by Professor Roger A. Kerin, Edwin L. Cox School of Business, Southern Methodist University, solely as a basis for class discussion and is not designed to illustrate appropriate or inappropriate handling of administrative situations. This case appeared in *Strategic Marketing Problems*, 4/e, by Roger A. Kerin and Robert A. Peterson, pp. 652–665, © 1987, published by Allyn & Bacon, Inc. Reprinted with permission.

3. Outline a resource-allocation and market strategy statement for the corporation with particular emphasis on the firm's growth opportunities in the context of the overall portfolio of businesses.

Jack selected the Zale Corporation for two reasons. First, he was interested in a career in retailing, having worked part-time for a large, diversified retailing firm for two years. Second, he had just become engaged and had purchased the engagement ring at Zales Jewelers. The professionalism evident at Zales and the liberal credit terms provided him as a struggling student had impressed him.

Shortly after he began to piece together published information on the Zale Corporation, he realized that the assignment and firm were much larger than he had expected. Zale Corporation sales exceeded $1 billion and had operations spanning the globe. The corporation was indeed a diversified firm with a variety of businesses ranging from drugstores to jewelry stores. This is the kind of firm I would enjoy working for," he thought, "and now I'm going to chart its strategy for the 1980s."

ZALE CORPORATION

Zale Corporation is one of the largest diversified specialty retailing firms in the United States and the world's leading retailer of jewelry merchandise. Sales for combined operations exceeded $1 billion during the 1980 fiscal year ending March 31, 1980. A three-year financial summary is shown in Exhibit 1.

EXHIBIT 1   *Zale Corporation Consolidated Financial Statements ($000)*

Abbreviated Income Statements
(years ended March 31)

	1980	1979	1978
Sales $1,041,699	$904,464	$790,556	
Costs and expenses			
Cost of goods sold	662,359	600,856	527,939
Administrative, publicity, and selling	279,531	229,304	200,283
Interest	12,698	9,398	7,173
Amortization of gain on sale of			
corporate office building	1,950	10,549	—
Earnings from continuing operations before income taxes	89,061	75,455	55,161
Income taxes	35,036	32,450	26,808
Net earnings	$ 54,025	$ 43,005	$ 28,353

Abbreviated Balance Sheets

Assets	1980	1979	1978
Current assets			
Cash	$ 13,043	$ 15,166	$ 19,070
Trade receivables	175,106	131,331	115,143
Less allowance for doubtful accounts	(11,022)	(4,804)	(3,553)
Merchandise inventories	396,235	324,947	292,475
Other current assets	9,679	36,580	4,024
Total current assets	$583,041	$504,220	$427,159
Other assets	$ 33,536	23,198	19,088
Property and equipment (at cost), less accumulated			
amortization and depreciation	101,425	82,448	87,919
Total assets	$718,002	$609,866	$534,166
Liabilities and shareholders investment			
Current liabilities	$234,729	$173,012	$138,759
Long-term debt	103,433	55,046	54,745
Deferred gain from sale of corporate office building	10,287	12,237	—
Shareholders investment	369,553	369,571	340,662
Total liabilities and shareholders investment	$718,002	$609,866	$534,166

COMPANY BACKGROUND

The present-day Zale Corporation traces its beginnings to 1924, when Morris B. Zale and William Zale opened Zales Jewelers in Wichita Falls,

Texas. Both men remain as emeritus officers in the Zale Corporation.

From its beginnings, the company philosophy has rested on three pillars. Its merchandising philosophy held that Zales Jewelers would carry many types of goods other than jewelry.[1] Thus Zales Jewelers carried a brand line of merchandise—small appliances, cameras, cookware, and other complementary items—that set it apart from many competitors.

Its marketing philosophy emphasized two factors: heavy advertising and credit. On its opening day in Wichita Falls, Texas, Zales Jewelers recorded sales of $427.25, and of that amount $368.50 was on credit. Finally, the company has always placed great trust in its employees. This philosophy was and is unique in the jewelry business since jewelry, and particularly diamond goods, is exceptionally vulnerable to theft.

The company experienced a steady 36-year growth in sales volume following a strategy focused on jewelry and related items. However, in 1960 General Electric announced it had discovered a process for manufacturing synthetic diamonds. The possibility of a market glutted with synthetic diamonds prompted a diversification program in the 1960s aimed at acquiring firms engaged in specialized retailing in other fields.

The first acquisition was Skillern Drug Company, a regional specialty drugstore chain, in 1965. The diversification program continued during the 1960s to include Butler Shoe Company, a specialty shoe store chain, and a number of sporting goods firms, including Cullum and Boren, Cook, Zinik, and Housport. Levine's, a budget-fashion-merchandising store chain, was also acquired, as was Karotkin's, a furniture store chain. Zale Corporation subsequently sold Levine's in 1977 and Karotkin's in 1978.

In 1978 Zale Corporation formally articulated its mission, which emphasized a focus on specialty retailing and outlined its framework for long-range planning that promoted:

1. Strengthening and improving existing lines of business,
2. Pursuing additional lines of business,
3. Expansion in the international market,
4. Opportunism as a business attitude.

In 1979, the Zale Corporation prepared a detailed introspective study to assess its competitive position and in 1980 the company exceeded $1 billion in sales and achieved record earnings of $50 million. In addition to acquisitions of 34 additional jewelry units in 1980, the Zale Corporation recorded the largest increase in net new stores through internal expansion in a decade.

CURRENT OPERATING DIVISIONS

Zale Corporation has four primary lines of business as of March 31, 1980. They are: (1) jewelry, (2) foot wear, (3) drug, and (4) general merchandise. The corporation currently operates 1,845 retail stores in 49 states, the District of Columbia, Puerto Rico, Guam, and the United Kingdom. A brief description of each line of business is given below.

Jewelry

The jewelry business produced sales of $692.4 million, or 66.5 percent of total Zale Corporation sales, in fiscal 1980. About 11,000 persons are employed in the jewelry-related business. A four-year summary of the financial performance of the jewelry business is shown in Exhibit 2.

The business is divided into retail operations and other" operations. Retail operations consist of five divisions, each of which markets diamonds, gold jewelry, watches, silver, fine china, glassware, and complementary merchandise. The *Zale Jewelers Division* operates 760 outlets in 48 states and Puerto Rico, with the average store size being 2,000 square feet. The merchandise carried is principally in the medium price range. This division accounted for 51 percent of the

EXHIBIT 2 *Financial Summary of the Jewelry Business (thousands of dollars)*

	1980	**1979**	**1978**	**1977**
Sales	692,411	581,318	485,778	411,156
Operating profit	109,757	80,932	61,820	65,938
Assets	579,277	450,352	388,039	359,584
Net capital expenditures	24,373	14,774	7,002	10,461
Amortization and depreciation	10,035	7,655	6,626	5,840

Notes: 1. Operating profit and assets of the jewelry business on March 31, 1979 (end of fiscal year) reflect the change in pricing of certain nondiamond jewelry inventories from the FIFO (first in, first out) to the LIFO (last in, first out) method. This change had the effect of reducing operating profit and merchandise inventories by $2,004,000.

2. Operating profit and assets of the jewelry business at March 31, 1978 reflect the change in pricing of substantially all diamond merchandise inventories from the FIFO to the LIFO method. This change had the effect of reducing operating profit and diamond merchandise inventories by $27,379,000.

3. Operating profit was determined as follows. *Operating profits* are those contributed by the various merchandise groups without allocation of interest income, interest expense, profit-sharing contribution, corporate general and administrative expense, and income taxes. All significant intercompany sales and profits have been eliminated from the above calculations (Zale Corporation 1977 annual report). This definition of operating profit applies to all lines of business.

Source: Zale Corporation annual reports.

sales of the jewelry business. The *Fine Jewelers Guild Division* operates 305 stores and one leased department in 37 states and Guam under various trade names (Corrigans, Selco, Inc., Wiss & Lamberg, and Litwin Co.). The average store size is 3,200 square feet. The merchandise carried is in the higher price range. The *Leased Jewelry Division* operates 75 units in 14 states under the names of the stores in which they are located. This division also operates 18 stores under the name Mission Jewelers in five states. Merchandise in this division is principally in the popular price range, and the average store size is 2,000 square feet. The *Catalog Division* operates 13 showrooms (average showroom size is 30,000 square feet) in six states under the O. G. Wilson name. This division sells sporting goods, appliances, electronics, cameras, luggage, and other items in addition to items marketed through other jewelry divisions. The merchandise carried is in the medium to higher price range. *Zales Jewelers Limited* operates 60 stores in the United

Kingdom under the names Zales Jewelers, Maxwell Jewelers, and Leslie Davis Jewelers and sells merchandise principally in the medium price range. The average store size is 1,200 square feet.

Zale Corporation also engages in the purchasing, processing, and assembling of diamond and other jewelry-related merchandise. The corporation operates facilities in New York, Puerto Rico, and Tel Aviv for cutting and polishing diamonds and assembling jewelry items. The *Ross Watch Case Division* manufactures watch cases and other components for the company and sells to retailers and watch assemblers. In addition, the company, through its *International Diamond Division*, sells precious gems to retailers and suppliers throughout the world.

Drug

The drug business produced sales of $148.7 million in fiscal 1980, which represented 14.3 percent of total corporation sales. Approximately 3,000 persons were employed in this business. A four-year summary of the drug business is shown in Exhibit 3.

The drug business consists of two divisions. The *Skillern Drug Division* operates 146 drug stores in New Mexico and Texas. The average store contains 3,100 square feet. Skillern Drug Stores sell prescription and over-the-counter drugs, cosmetics, health and beauty aids, candy, tobacco, photographic supplies, and numerous complementary products. An article in *The Wall Street Journal* (October 15, 1980) stated that sales of this division were about $142.2 million in fiscal 1980. The *Aeroplex Division* operates 15 news, tobacco, and gift stands in the Dallas–Fort Worth Regional Airport. The average unit contains 800 square feet.

Footwear

The footwear business employed 4,000 persons and recorded sales of $136.8 million, or 13.1 percent of total corporation sales, in fiscal 1980. Exhibit 4 gives a four-year summary of the footwear business financial performance.

The footwear business is composed of two divisions. The *Butler Shoe Division* has 385 stores in 35 states, Washington, D.C., and Puerto Rico. The stores are variously named Butler's, Hot Feet, or Maling Brothers, and the average store size is 3,100 square feet. The merchandise in these units consists of ladies' and children's shoes, ladies' hosiery and handbags, and shoe cleaners. The *Self-Service Shoe Division* operates in 12 states with 30 leased departments under the name of the stores in which they are located. The typical size of a shoe department is 3,000 square feet. This division sells popular-price shoes for the entire family.

General Merchandise

The general merchandise business employed 1,000 persons and achieved sales of $63.8 million, or 6.1 percent of total corporation sales, in fiscal 1980. Exhibit 5 gives a four-year summary of the general merchandise business financial performance.

The general merchandise business consists of two divisions. The *Sporting Goods Division* operates 37 stores in nine states under a variety of store names (e.g., Cullum and Boren). The average store carries a complete assortment of sporting goods, including sportswear, and contains 14,000 square feet. According to a *Wall Street*

EXHIBIT 3   *Financial Summary of the Drug Business (thousands of dollars)*

	1980	1979	1978	1977
Sales	148,704	126,257	111,568	97,445
Operating profit	(291)	543	2,462	4,659
Assets	43,841	38,393	33,714	31,183
Net capital expenditures	933	1,864	630	2,619
Amortization and depreciation	1,160	1,051	1,010	820

Note: Operating profit and assets of the drug business on March 31, 1979, reflect the change in pricing of drug merchandise from the FIFO to the LIFO method. This change had the effect of reducing the operating profit and merchandise inventories by $1,379,000.

Source: Zale Corporation annual reports.

EXHIBIT 4   *Financial Summary of the Footwear Business (thousands of dollars)*

	1980	1979	1978	1977
Sales	136,827	123,089	116,927	98,001
Operating profit	17,567	15,486	15,696	11,499
Assets	56,083	47,850	41,382	36,669
Net capital expenditures	6,615	3,671	3,588	4,906
Amortization and depreciation	2,666	2,178	1,942	1,610

Source: Zale Corporation annual reports.

Journal article (September 22, 1982), the sporting goods division had about $35 million in sales in 1980. The *Sugarman Division* is a wholesaler of consumer electronics, jewelry, optical goods, and military insignia, and accessories. The *Home Furnishing Division*, consisting of 11 stores in Texas, was divested in 1978. This division produced sales of $29,556,000 in 1977.

The number of stores operated by the Zale Corporation in fiscal 1977 through fiscal 1980 is shown in Exhibit 6. Approximately 62 percent of the stores in the United States are located in the southern tier of states and California known as the Sunbelt.

Zale Corporation sales are seasonal, with peaks coinciding with major holidays such as Christmas, Easter, and Mother's Day and with the back-to-school selling season. The seasonality in sales requires large inventory levels to meet the demand at these sales peaks.

SELECTED PERFORMANCE MEASURES

Zale Corporation strives for balanced performance in three areas: (1) operating results, (2) asset management, and (3) investment performance. A summary of published performance measures is shown in Exhibit 7 for the 1978, 1979, and 1980 fiscal years.[2]

EXHIBIT 5   *Financial Summary of the General Merchandise Business (thousands of dollars)*

	1980	1979	1978	1977
Sales	63,757	73,800	76,283	71,225
Operating profit	939	(788)	1,163	2,949
Assets	28,385	25,589	35,387	38,263
Net capital expenditures	1,472	(989)	746	357
Amortization and depreciation	743	796	861	849

Note: During October 1978, Zale Corporation sold the inventory, receivables, and certain other assets of the Home Furnishing Division at a loss of approximately $700,000.

Source: Zale Corporation annual reports.

EXHIBIT 6   Number of Operating Stores

Division	1980	1979	1978	1977
Zale Jewelers Division	760	722	692	671
Fine Jewelers Guild Division	306	261	245	244
Leased Jewelry Division	93	65ᵃ	117	111
Catalog Division	13	12	11	13
Zales Jewelers, Ltd. (United Kingdom)	60	51	42	37
Home Furnishing Division	—	—	11	11
Sporting Goods Division	37	32	36	33
Aeroplex Division	15	14	13	13
Butler Shoe Division	385	359	349	351
Self-Service Shoe Division	30	45	47	48
Skillern Drug Division	146	143	117	112
Total	1,845	1,704	1,680	1,644

ᵃThe number of leased jewelry operations was reduced as the division completed its planned strategy of lessening its involvement in discount stores and placing more emphasis on department stores. Most of the discount store departments were in Woolco stores. Jewelry departments were subsequently opened in Dillard's Department Stores in the southwestern United States.

Source: Zale Corporation 10-K reports.

EXHIBIT 7   Selected Zale Corporation Performance Measures

	1978	1979	1980
Operating Results			
Sales growth	16.6%	14.4%	15.2%
Gross margin	33.2%	33.6%	36.4%
Operating expense ratio (percent of sales)	25.3%	25.4%	26.8%
Return on sales	3.6%	4.8%	5.2%
Asset Management			
Accounts receivable turnover	2.3	2.1	2.0
Inventory turnover	1.8	1.9	1.8
Long-term debt (millions)	$54.7	$55.0	$103.4
Investment Performance			
Dividends per share	$.91	$.98	$1.06
Earnings per share	$2.11	$3.21	$4.50
Return on shareholders investment	8.5%	12.1%	14.6%

Source: Zale Corporation annual report, fiscal 1980.

During the 1980 fiscal year, Zale Corporation, like all businesses, was faced with unprecedented interest costs. On March 31, 1980, the interest rate was 19.5 percent. These costs are reflected in the corporation's income statement. Furthermore, Zale Corporation, again like all businesses that provide extensive credit, experienced a sizable increase in bad debts. Furthermore, the collection time on accounts receivable increased.

THE RETAILING ENVIRONMENT

The retailing environment of the late 1970s and for the foreseeable future can be characterized as turbulent. The combination of recession, continuing inflation, and high interest rates during 1980 produced a bleak retail sales picture. Retail sales in the United States rose from an estimated $886 billion in 1979 to an estimated $948 billion in 1980—a 7 percent increase. By comparison, the Consumer Price Index increased 12 percent during the 1979–1980 period.

Inventory—typically a major current asset of retailers—has become a costly asset with rising interest rates. Accordingly, retailers have emphasized inventory turnover as a performance measure. The principal retailing strategy in recent years has been the move toward high-turnover and high-markup merchandise and away from slow-moving, low-markup products in an effort to increase sales per square foot and ultimately, turn on assets.

This retailing strategy is apparent in the growth of specialty retail stores and the popularity of leased departments in full-line department stores. The results of a recent study, examining the performance of local, regional, and national specialty stores for the period 1974–1978, are shown in Exhibit 8. The results reported include firms in a variety of retailing specialties. Leased departments currently account for about 6 percent of total department store sales. The most popular leased departments are sewing machines, wigs and hair goods, shoes, and watches and fine jewelry. About 65 percent of the 2,047 traditional department store companies in the United States lease out their shoe operations.[3]

Jewelry Retailing

Jewelry retailing faced a variety of shocks during the 1979–1980 period. The price of gold increased from $300 per ounce in June 1979 to $850 per ounce in January 1980. The escalating price of gold sparked widespread consumer interest in gold and gold jewelry, and jewelry retailers generally recorded extraordinary sales dollar gains even though unit volume remained stable or declined for many retailers. The price of gold continued to rise until the autumn of 1980, which made the financing of inventories at rising interest rates very costly. As the price of gold declined, jewelers were forced to offer substantial markdowns. A similar, though less dramatic, change occurred in silver prices. Silver was priced at $6 to $8 per ounce during most of 1979, but rose rapidly to $50 per ounce in January 1980, before falling to $10.80 per ounce in March 1980.

The uncertain economic picture resulted in greater popularity of "hard assets" among the buying public, however. The extent to which consumers will retain this hard asset" mentality is not known.

There are an estimated 35,000 jewelry stores in the United States. These stores accounted for $8 billion in retail sales. The Zale Corporation is purported to be the world's leading retailer of jewelry merchandise.

Drugstore Retailing

Three major drugstore chains in 1979 were Walgreens, Eckerd Drug, and Revco Discount Drug Centers. Walgreens operates approximately 690 drugstores, with a high percentage

EXHIBIT 8   *Selected Performance Measures of Specialty Retailers Arranged by Geographical Scope of Operations*

Operating Characteristic	Geographical Scope[a]		
	Local	Regional	National
Gross margin	36.6%	30.0%	42.2%
Inventory turnover (sales cost of goods sold ÷ average inventory)	3.1	4.2	2.8
Sales/store (thousands) (annual sales ÷ number of stores)	$2,608	$820	$883
Sales/total assets (annual sales ÷ total assets)	2.2	2.7	2.2
Return on sales (annual net profit after tax ÷ annual sales × 100)	0.23%	2.42%	4.45%
Return on assets (annual net profit ÷ total assets)	2.41%	5.81%	7.90%

[a]*Local specialty retailers* were those operating in up to five contiguous states whose markets and demographics were reasonably homogeneous. *Regional specialty retailers* were those who operated beyond five contiguous states or served demographically heterogeneous markets but did not serve all major regions and the top 20 SMSAs. *National specialty retailers* were defined as those firms that served all major regions and had representation in the top 20 SMSAs.

Source: Richard Miller, Strategic Pathways to Growth in Retailing," *Journal of Business Strategy*, (Winter 1981):16–29. Reproduced with permission of the author.

located in the Midwest. Eckerd Drug operates about 1,000 drugstores located primarily in Florida, North Carolina, and Texas. Revco Discount Drug Centers operates some 1,200 discount drugstores in a 24-state area, ranging from New York to Florida and from the eastern seaboard to Arizona.

Drugstores in the United States produced retail sales of approximately $30 billion. Drugstores affiliated with chains accounted for over half of this total (*Drug Store News*, May 1979). Texas and New Mexico alone accounted for about 2 percent of total drugstore sales. There were approximately 50,000 drugstores in the United States in 1977.

An evolution in drugstore retailing is under way.[4] The movement is away from the conventional drug store concept toward the super drugstore or combination food and drugstores. The conventional drug store chain unit operates with 7,500 square feet, generates annual sales of $1 million per unit, and has as its principal market focus health care and general merchandise. The super drugstore operates with 25,000 square feet, generates annual sales of $5 million per unit, and has as its principal market focus broad general merchandise at low prices. The combination food and drugstore located in or adjacent to a supermarket emphasizes one-stop shopping for a wide variety of food and general merchandise. The average size of a new drugstore exceeds 15,000 square feet (*Chain Store Age Executive*, August 1980).

Sporting Goods and Footwear Retailing

Sporting goods retailers are divided into two groups. General-line sporting goods stores carry a variety of merchandise including athletic equipment, sports wear, footwear, and related items. General-line sporting goods retailers number about 8,000 and produce sales of about $3 billion. Specialty sporting goods stores carry limited lines of merchandise and typically focus on a particular sport or complementary sports. These stores include golf shops, ski-related stores, and tennis, handball, and racquetball stores. Specialty sporting goods retailers number about 10,000 and produce sales of about $2.3 billion.

The estimated shoe store volume is $8 billion; approximately 30,000 shoe stores operate in the United States. Kinney Shoe Corporation, a division of F. W. Woolworth, is the largest shoe store chain under one name in the United States. The Melville Corporation is also a major competitor in footwear retailing with footwear departments in the K mart stores throughout the United States. The company also operates the popular-priced Thom McAn specialty shoe stores. The average size of new shoe stores is approximately 3,000 square feet.

Both sporting goods and footwear retailing practices are evolving, but in a direction directly opposite to drug retailing. Rather than broadened lines and larger units, as evident in drug retailing, sporting goods and footwear retailing is experiencing the "superspecialist." For example, *Tennis Lady* is a superspecialist store selling only ladies' expensive, high-fashion tennis apparel. *The Foot Locker* and *Athlete's Foot* are superspecialists in footwear retailing.

DRAFTING A RESOURCE ALLOCATION AND MARKET STRATEGY

Having completed the first two parts of his assignment, Jack began to consider how he might draft a resource-allocation and market strategy for Zale Corporation. His reading indicated that all Zale Corporation businesses were in specialty retailing of one form or another. Furthermore, all

businesses were in retailing sectors or geographical areas that were growing. He estimated that the annual growth of the U.S. retail jewelry business was about 13 percent; the retail drug business, 10 percent (12 percent in the Southwest); the retail footwear business, 10 percent; and the retail sporting goods business, 14 percent.[5] But the various businesses of Zale Corporation were quite different, he thought. For example, jewelry retailing was characterized by high retail margins and low inventory turnover when compared with drug retailing, which seemed to be a lower-margin, higher-turnover business. Jack had not decided how to include this factor in his analysis.

More important, Jack knew that whatever resource allocation and market strategy he recommended, it would have to include where and how Zale Corporation might grow in the 1980s. Was it in the jewelry business, the drug business, the footwear business, the general merchandise business, or in some combination of businesses? Where were the growth opportunities? Moreover, how could growth be accomplished? For example, should geographical expansion be considered since the majority of Zale Corporation store units were situated in the southern tier of states?

Underlying these considerations and others he had noted was the need for a clear understanding of Zale Corporation's distinctive competency before any recommendations could be made. Finally, he knew that any recommendation would necessitate all the financial documentation he could produce from the published data he had before him.

Notes

1. This strategy was modified in the late 1970s, when Zale Corporation removed nonjewelry merchandise from jewelry stores. Non-jewelry merchandise is now carried by other divisions.

2. The Zale Corporation adopted the LIFO (last-in, first-out) method of inventory valuation in 1978 fiscal year. Prior to 1978, the FIFO (first-in, last-out) method of inventory valuation was used. LIFO inventory valuation is based on the assumption that the last items acquired in inventory are the first items sold. FIFO is based on the assumption that the first items added to inventory are the first items sold. LIFO more closely matches current costs of inventory items with current revenues during periods of rising prices. LIFO is used for jewelry and drug merchandise inventories; FIFO is still used for footwear and general merchandise.

The effect of this change in inventory valuation during periods of rising prices (inflation) is to increase the cost of goods sold, thereby decreasing the gross margin percent. This in turn will decrease the return on sales percent. Inventory turnover is increased due to these changes. Fully 77 percent of all company inventories are valued using the LIFO method.

Therefore, performance measures such as gross margin percent, inventory turnover, return on sales, and return on shareholders investment for the 1979 and 1980 fiscal years are not comparable with those of previous fiscal years. Other performance measures discussed here are not materially affected by the method of inventory valuation.

3. L. Spalding, Footwear: To Lease or Own?" *Stores* (July 1979):16.

4. A. Bates, Three New Store Formats Will Soon Dominate Drug Retailing," *Marketing News* (March 7, 1980):9.

5. These growth rates were determined from the *1977 Census of Retail Trade*. Growth rates were extrapolated to 1980. The growth rates are not adjusted for inflation. All figures are based on total U.S. sales, except where indicated.

Case 25
La Quinta Motor Inns, Inc.:
National Advertising Campaign

In early 1979 Joyce Wilson, vice-president of marketing for La Quinta Motor Inns, Inc., was composing her thoughts prior to preparing an important memo. The memo was an assignment given to all upper-level executives who had attended a management conference conducted for the company by a team of professors from well-known business schools. The memo, directed to the president and chief executive officer, Sam Barshop, was to address the continued growth rate that top management recommended for the company over the next five years. Also, managers were to discuss the impact that growth would have on their departments and the role of their departments in achieving growth objectives.

Ms. Wilson knew the 22 percent compound annual growth rate in revenues and profits

This case was made possible through the cooperation of La Quinta Motor Inns, Inc. The case was prepared by Professors Roger Kerin and M. Edgar Barrett, Edwin L. Cox School of Business, Southern Methodist University, as a basis for class discussion and is not designed to illustrate effective or ineffective handling of administrative situations. The assistance of Ms. Phyllis B. Riggins, graduate student, in the preparation of this case is gratefully acknowledged. Issues raised at the end of the case are introduced solely for discussion purposes. They do not necessarily represent the opinions of La Quinta management. This case appeared in *Strategic Marketing Problems*, 4/e, by Roger A. Kerin and Robert A. Peterson, pp. 341–357, © 1987, published by Allyn & Bacon, Inc. Reprinted with permission.

achieved by La Quinta during its first 10 years would be a challenge to sustain. The next few years would see the chain's expansion into frontier" areas where it lacked the recognition achieved in the Southwest. She knew some top managers occasionally questioned the efficacy of the company's recent commitment to a national advertising campaign and the narrow market segment sought out by La Quinta. The national campaign was just entering its second year, and Ms. Wilson knew her comments on the campaign and target market would have implications for the role of both the campaign and market orientation in La Quinta's future.

NOTE ON THE LODGING INDUSTRY

According to the October 1978 *Wall Street Transcript* "Roundtable Discussion" on the lodging industry, the historic growth rate of the industry is something near 2 percent or a little less." Motels and motor hotels combined, however, have shown a larger growth rate than have hotels.

Occupancy rates were as high as 80 percent in the early 1960s. High occupancy rates made the industry attractive for investment, and supply began to seriously outstrip demand in the late 1960s and early 1970s. The recession of 1974 and the energy crisis that preceded it caused a slowdown in travel, and many financial institutions were forced to foreclose on lodging properties. By 1970 average industry occupancy rates approached 60 percent. The recovery proceeded slowly, and only in 1979 did industry occupancy rates approach 70 percent. Reluctance of financial institutions and investors to recreate the oversupply situation of the early 1970s served as a check during the recovery. Capacity actually declined in 1976. There were about 2.25 million lodging rooms in the United States in 1979. More than 60 percent of these rooms were over 10 years old. Holiday Inns accounted for approximately 12 to 15 percent of available rooms in 1974.

Four general motel classifications have emerged in the last 25 years: (1) small, individually owned tourist courts; (2) budget motels, such as Days Inn and Motel 6; (3) medium-priced chains, such as La Quinta and Rodeway; and (4) large, full-service chains such as Holiday Inn. The trend is away from small, independently owned units toward largely franchised, absentee-owned motels. With regard to the second classification, "One Howard Johnson executive predicted the budget motel would be to the motel industry what the Volkswagen was to autos. . . . How did the word 'budget,' perfectly respectable when applied to cars, airline flights, and department stores, fall into such disgrace in motels? Because many a budget motel was cheap as well as less expensive. . . . In a country where a clean, well-maintained room is the bare minimum the traveler requires, anything less is an insult."

LA QUINTA MOTOR INNS

The first La Quinta Motor Inn was built by the Barshop family in San Antonio, Texas, in 1968. Sam Barshop, referred to by *Forbes* in a June 1978 article as "the reluctant motelier," was heavily involved in the family real estate business and initially considered the lodging industry a sideline. The family built its first motel in 1961 after Ramada Inns had expressed interest in a piece of family property in San Antonio. When it was

announced that the 1968 World's Fair would be held in San Antonio, Sam and his brother, Phil Barshop, who had by then built other inns as franchises of Ramada and Rodeway, decided that "the occasion warranted a hotel with a different flavor." The first La Quinta Motor Inn was located across the street from Hemisfair '68. The name and architecture recalled San Antonio's Spanish Colonial heritage. Both characteristics have been retained in subsequent inns, as shown in Exhibit 1. La Quinta Motor Inns, Inc., was formed when Barshop Motel Enterprises offered stock for public sale in 1973.

Exhibit 2 summarizes the growth in the number of inns and rooms from fiscal years 1974 through 1979. Exhibit 3 shows La Quinta's income statements from 1975 through 1979.

La Quinta Service Concept

La Quinta's service concept is described in its 1978 annual report: "Because we define our primary market as the individual business traveler, we design and manage our inns to serve his or her needs: clean, quiet accommodations at a reasonable price." Every aspect of La Quinta's service is based on the company's perception of the business traveler's needs. Research conducted in early 1978 indicated that this service concept had worked effectively in attracting and satisfying these needs (see Appendix A).

The average La Quinta Motor Inn has about 120 rooms. There is a pool, color television, direct-dial telephone, a 24-hour switchboard, and one-day laundry service. La Quinta leases free-standing restaurant facilities, contiguous to the inns, to national restaurant chains, such as Denny's or Jojos, who operate them. These restaurants typically provide food service 24 hours a day. The inns are located on premium sites on major highways close to major industrial and office complexes, large retail shopping centers, and universities. Site selection is considered a key part of La Quinta's marketing strategy. Ac-

EXHIBIT 1   *La Quinta Motor Inn*

EXHIBIT 2   *La Quinta Motor Inns, Inc.—Number of Motor Inns and Rooms (fiscal 1974–1979)[a]*

	1979	1978	1977	1976	1975	1974
Motor Inns						
Company owned (50% or more)	64	55	49	49	45	36
Licensed	14	13	14	11	10	4
Total	78	68	63	60	55	40
Rooms						
Company owned (50% or more)	7,288	6,161	5,355	5,183	4,633	3,544
Licensed	1,770	1,638	1,776	1,388	1,267	596
Total	9,058	7,799	7,131	6,571	5,900	4,140

[a]Fiscal year ends May 31.

Source: Company records.

EXHIBIT 3   *La Quinta Motor Inns, Inc.—Income Statements (fiscal 1975–1979)*[a]

	1979	1978	1977	1976	1975
Revenues (000s)					
Motor inn	$44,682	$35,580	$27,256	$22,173	$16,272
Restaurant rental	1,881	1,545	1,127	990	790
Restaurant and club	1,094	1,029	960	1,084	1,097
Other	1,267	1,039	780	593	389
Total revenues	48,924	39,193	30,123	24,840	18,548
Operating Costs and Expenses (000s)					
Motor inn direct	22,958	18,410	15,139	12,762	9,602
Restaurant and club direct	1,038	988	1,013	1,113	1,166
Selling, general, and administrative	4,512	3,450	2,292	1,836	1,410
Depreciation and amortization	4,438	3,743	2,964	2,554	1,997
Total operating costs and expenses	32,946	26,591	21,408	18,265	14,175
Operating income	15,978	12,602	8,715	6,575	4,373
Other Income (deductions) (000s)					
Interest, net of capitalization	(6,172)	(4,946)	(3,922)	(3,499)	(2,803)
Gain on sale of assets, principally motor inns	1,477	553	501	215	289
Partners' equity in earnings and losses:					
Operations	(2,437)	(1,719)	(897)	(385)	(45)
Sales of motor inns	(589)	—	—	—	—
Total other income (deductions)	(7,721)	(6,112)	(4,318)	(3,669)	(2,559)
Earnings before income taxes	8,257	6,490	4,397	2,906	1,814
Income taxes	3,385	2,759	1,939	1,205	707
Net earnings (000s)	$ 4,872	$ 3,731	$ 2,458	$ 1,701	$ 1,107

[a]Fiscal year ends May 31.

Source: 1979 annual report.

cording to Sam Barshop: "Part of our company's marketing monies go toward purchasing a top notch site because all the advertising and publicity in the world can't change a bad site." As of 1979, Sam or Phil Barshop had personally selected every La Quinta Motor Inn site.

The majority of inns are managed by older married couples. Their duties include filing timely reports with the home office, keeping their inns clean and in good repair, and being friendly and courteous to customers. An article on "Husband/Wife Management Teams in Texas" in *Southwest Hotel-Motel Review* describes the advantage of these teams: "A husband and wife team gets to know their guest. . . . It's sort of a personal touch. . . . It builds a very great repeat business, which is important." La Quinta managers carry this personal touch to the point of calling each regular customer by name. *Input,* the company newspaper, is filled with letters that reflect the success of unit managers in creating this friendly feeling.

La Quinta has prospered using this service concept. Exhibit 4 shows the occupancy rate data

EXHIBIT 4   *La Quinta Motor Inns, Inc.—Percentage of Occupancy (fiscal 1974–1978)*

	1979	1978	1977	1976	1975	1974
Motor inns open one year or more	90.6%	89.1%	86.6%	82.1%	80.3%	81.4%
Overall	88.1	88.6	85.8	80.5	74.0	79.7

Source: Company records.

for new and existing La Quinta Motor Inns over the last six years. The company has consistently experienced some of the highest occupancy rates in the lodging industry.

Inn Location and Site Selection

Exhibit 5 shows the locations of La Quinta Motor Inns completed or under development as of late 1979. The company has expanded geographically by means of a three-part strategy. *Adjacency,* the first of these three, involves expansion to new cities of over 100,000 population within a 300-mile radius of an existing La Quinta Motor Inn property. This strategy can be observed in the existence of the various frontier" properties, such as Casper, Wyoming, and Salt Lake City, Utah. *Clustering*, the second part of the plan, consists of the construction of several inns in one city. Dallas and Houston are both examples of cluster cities. The third part, *filling in,* is the construction of inns in other, usually smaller, cities within an established market area. Seventy-eight company-owned or -licensed inns in the La Quinta Motor Inns chain would be operating in 20 states by the end of fiscal 1979. There were 25 inns under development in an additional four states at the time.

Price and Cost Structure

La Quinta's no-frills approach has enabled the company to minimize capital and operating costs and remain very reasonably priced. According to Sam Barshop, "La Quinta sells rooms, period . . . no atriums or meeting rooms to swell construction costs." La Quinta's price per room is typically 20 to 25 percent below comparable rooms at motor inns with more elaborate facilities. The average daily rate per occupied room in 1979 was $20.21.

In discussing the company's cost structure, Walter Bìegler, La Quinta's vice-president of finance and chief financial officer, mentioned the difficulty of performing a strict cost–profit analysis of their operations. He felt that some of the costs were actually semivariable with occupancy. Thus, he noted the variable cost component was not easy to isolate precisely. In general, however, he estimated the industry ratio of variable costs to revenue of 55 percent to be representative of La Quinta's situation.

Sales Force

La Quinta employs a small, but effective sales force under the direction of two divisional sales directors. The sales force is divided into eastern and western divisions.

The company employs eight sales representatives. These representatives made over 7,000 sales calls in 1979. Sales-call activity is heaviest during the period preceding and during new La Quinta Motor Inn openings. Sales representatives are responsible for calling on large corporations whose employees are potential customers of the entire network of La Quinta Motor

---

EXHIBIT 5   *La Quinta Motor Inn Locations as of Late 1979*

Alabama
Mobile
Arizona
+Flagstaff
+Kingman
Phoenix
Tucson
Arkansas
Little Rock (2)[a]
California
Costa Mesa[a]
Colorado
Denver (3)[a]
Florida
Jacksonville[a]
+Orlando
Tallahassee
+Tampa
Georgia
Atlanta
Columbus[a]
Illinois
Champaign[a]
+Moline
Indiana
Indianapolis (2)[a]
Merrillville
Kansas
Kansas City
Wichita

Kentucky
Louisville
Louisiana
New Orleans (2)
Mississippi
Jackson
Missouri
St. Louis
Nebraska
Omaha[a]
Nevada
Las Vegas
Reno[a]
New Mexico
Albuquerque
Ohio
+Cincinnati
Columbus[a]
+Dayton
Oklahoma
Oklahoma City
Tulsa
South Carolina
Charleston[a]
Columbia[a]
Greenville[a]
Tennessee
Memphis
Nashville

Texas
Abilene
Austin (3)
Beaumont
Brazosport
Bryan/College Station[a]
+Corpus Christi (2)
+Dallas/Fort Worth (14)[a]
Denton
El Paso (2)[a]
+Galveston
Houston (7)[a]
Killeen
Laredo
Lubbock
+McAllen
Odessa[a]
+San Angelo
San Antonio (7)
Texas City
Waco
Wichita Falls
Utah
Salt Lake City
Wyoming
Casper[a]
Cheyenne[a]

[a]Inns under development.
+Licensed property.
( )Number of inns located in each city.

Inns. Another function of the sales group is to assist unit managers in increasing occupancy rates of existing inns. Unit managers are also expected to make sales calls. The total numbers of prospective customers reached by all these efforts exceeded 25,000 in 1979.

Marketing and Advertising

Joyce Wilson joined La Quinta in 1975 to manage the newly formed marketing department. Her primary responsibilities at that time included assistance in formulating strategy, advertising, sale and promotion programs, and marketing research. In 1977 Ms. Sue Moore joined La Quinta as director of advertising to manage the company's in-house advertising agency. Creation of a marketing department and subsequent formation of an in-house advertising agency contributed to a more systematic approach to marketing and communications at La Quinta. Prior to that time, responsibility for advertising was dispersed among a variety of executives and often handled on an inn-by-inn basis.

The first formal advertising campaign was launched at the beginning of the 1977 fiscal year. The campaign's objectives were to enhance local or regional awareness (markets with existing inns), communicate the broader geographical scope of the chain, and further establish La Quinta's identity, or positioning, within the industry. Space in *Media Networks*, a mix of major weekly magazines with regional editions such as *Time, Newsweek, U.S. News and World Report,* and *Sports Illustrated,* was purchased for 15 La Quinta markets. (Markets relate to major cities and immediate environs.) Three to four full-page advertisements (depending on the market) were placed in the Southwest edition of both *The Wall Street Journal* (20 ads scheduled throughout the year) and *Business Week* (four ads scheduled throughout the year). The rationale for this selection and schedule was that these publications reached present and potential customers and would convey a "national image" for La Quinta even though their distribution was on a regional basis. Their readership also represented an "investor" audience. Two general-audience monthly magazines, *Southern Living* and *Texas Monthly,* carried three advertisements each that were scheduled for placement through out the year. Three advertisements were placed throughout the year in in-flight magazines published by Southwest, Ozark, and Texas International Airlines since these airlines service the majority of La Quinta markets. Finally, an advertisement was placed in each of several hotel and motel

reference books used by independent and corporate travel agencies, and two advertisements were placed in *Discovery,* a quarterly magazine with a circulation of one million for Allstate Insurance Company policyholders. The total media budget for this campaign was $135,000, with an estimated cost of 1 cent per reader per year. La Quinta executives believed that this effort achieved its objective.

The objective of the fiscal 1978 campaign was to retain the regional orientation, but take a step toward national recognition of La Quinta Motor Inns as inn locations expanded beyond states in the Southwest. This step was two-fold: (1) to reach feeder" markets for La Quinta cities, and (2) to create a higher level of awareness in new markets where La Quinta was building new inns. This national effort was reflected in the selection of *Time* magazine (B edition). This edition has a selective nationwide circulation focusing on subscribers classified as manager-professionals in addition to distribution to airlines and business offices. Four two-thirds-page advertisements were scheduled for placement throughout the year. The *Media Networks* purchase was timed to coincide with inn openings and included one advertisement each in five new markets. The number of insertions throughout the year in each of the remaining magazines is summarized below:

- *Business Week* (Southwest edition): 5 insertions
- *The Wall Street Journal* (Southwest edition): 6 insertions
- *Southern Living:* 2 insertions
- *Discovery:* 1 insertion
- Airline magazines: 3 insertions in Southwest, Ozark, and Texas International Airlines

Total funds invested in advertising in fiscal year 1978 declined from the previous year due to a reallocation of marketing expenditures within the company. Nevertheless, the $95,000 allocated to advertising space was viewed as getting more bang for the bucks" by Sue Moore. The reach of the 1978 plan was 17 percent higher than the previous year, and the estimated cost per subscriber per year had been reduced to slightly over six-tenths of a cent. The expanded coverage was showing increased inquiries about La Quinta Motor Inns from interested companies and individuals throughout the country.

The 1979 fiscal year advertising objectives were to accelerate the momentum begun in the 1978 campaign and further direct La Quinta's advertising toward a national audience. Two-thirds-page advertisements were placed throughout the year in *Business Week* (national edition) and *Time* (B edition). Each magazine carried five insertions. Sixteen insertions were scheduled throughout the year in *The Wall Street Journal* (Southwest edition), again with the investor community in mind. Examples of fiscal 1979 advertisements are shown in Appendix B. Total funds spent for advertising were $135,000. The cost per reader per year was approximately 1 cent. Although the company did not subscribe to a readership survey service, Sue Moore noted that the amount of qualified responses in terms of sales leads was very encouraging. Typical response letters reflected several key advertising goals: company letterhead, content of letters, titles of signees, city or state origin, and often, size of company sales force. A summary of the media allocation by year is shown in Exhibit 6.

MANAGEMENT MEMO

Thinking back over the growth La Quinta Motor Inns had achieved in the last decade and the crucial question of her department's role in sustaining that growth, Joyce Wilson began to list issues she would address in her memo to Mr. Sam Barshop.

One issue was the size of the advertising budget itself. Since 1975 La Quinta had sub-

---

EXHIBIT 6   La Quinta Motor Inns, Inc.—Allocation of Media Expenditures

	Fiscal 1977 June 1976– May 1977	Fiscal 1978 June 1977– May 1978	Fiscal 1979 June 1978– May 1979
The Wall Street Journal (Southwest edition)	$ 18,000	$ 3,000	$ 8,000
Time		56,000	77,000
Business Week (Southwest edition)	5,000	7,000	
Media Networks	85,000	12,000	
Business Week (national edition)			50,000
Hotel and motel reference books	6,100		
Southern Living	5,000	9,700	
Texas Monthly	5,000		
Discovery	4,600	3,000	
Airline magazines	6,400	4,300	—
Total	$135,000	$95,000	$135,000

Note: These figures do not include outdoor (billboard) advertising or miscellaneous promotional efforts of individual inns in La Quinta markets. Costs associated with these efforts are assumed by individual inns.

scribed to the policy of budgeting marketing and advertising expenditures on a per-room/per-day basis. This was a standard reporting procedure in the lodging industry. Each individual inn contributed a set amount for the marketing department, including the advertising budget. In 1975 the figure was 10 cents per room per day, which has since been raised to 12 cents per room per day for La Quinta. As a percentage of revenue, however, Ms. Wilson believed that other chains of similar or slightly larger size budgeted as much as $100,000 to $200,000 per year more for advertising than La Quinta. She knew that if she raised this issue, a sound economic justification would be necessary, since such additional funds would most likely be obtained from corporate funds rather than from individual inns.

A second issue was the national versus regional thrust of La Quinta advertising campaigns. Preliminary discussions with Ms. Moore indicated that national coverage would be proposed for the 1980 fiscal year campaign. However, company executives occasionally questioned this orientation on the grounds that La Quinta operated in 47 cities in 20 states. In reviewing a *Media Networks* local trade area audience plan, similar to the 1977 program, Ms. Moore determined that *Media Networks* offered their magazine combination in only 32 of the current La Quinta Inn cities and that one insertion for that geographical coverage would cost $87,000. Two insertions in each magazine would cost in the neighborhood of $150,000, with a volume discount, and so forth. These cities contained all but 15 La Quinta Motor Inns currently in operation. In the past, some company executives had expressed the opinion that the regional advertising approach would be more effective due to the regional aspects of the company's operations. Ms. Wilson felt that the memo provided a unique opportunity to address this issue, as well as the decision to insert advertisements throughout the year rather than focusing only on inn opening periods.

A third advertising-related issue was the number of vehicles La Quinta used to communicate its message. Since 1977 La Quinta had systematically reduced the number of vehicles so that in 1979, only *Business Week, Time,* and the Southwest edition of *The Wall Street Journal* were used. This focused effort was not only an advertising strategy related to the target audience, but also a result of the customer profile as portrayed by the company's 1978 market research. Other lodging chains around the country spread their advertising funds across many vehicles, including magazines, hotel and motel reference books, newspapers, direct mail, airline magazines, and occasionally spot and network radio and television, but their budgets were also larger. Expense was an important issue in this regard and supported the reduction of vehicles. However, Ms. Wilson felt that other arguments should be made as well. A broader issue was the topic of market targeting. Ms. Wilson was aware that some top-level managers had considered broadening the target market beyond the individual business traveler to include the entire family or pleasure traveler. Advocates of this strategy were concerned that La Quinta was losing these travelers by ignoring them in a direct advertising appeal. Arguments made in favor of expanding the target market were:

1. Room occupancy on weekends was lower than during the week. Friday, Saturday, and Sunday night occupancy rates were about 75 percent. If weekend occupancy were increased, overall occupancy rates would rise.
2. Broadening the target market might increase the trial of La Quinta Inns in frontier areas such as Casper, Wyoming.

Proponents of this strategy proposed that "weekend specials" of 25 percent off the average room rate be provided on Saturday and Sunday since other chains had done so. Furthermore, one-fourth of the media funds might be spent promoting the weekend business.

Such an approach was contrary to La Quinta's existing concept, but the idea was raised often enough that Ms. Wilson knew her memo must deal with it. Both she and Ms. Moore maintained that the "business travelers" appeal attracts pleasure travelers as well.

An issue related to the target market question was the creative strategy. La Quinta had rested its advertising message on four pillars: service, price, location, and no frills. If the target market were expanded, other messages would have to be communicated.

As Joyce Wilson sat back in her chair, she wondered aloud about what positions she should take on these and other issues. She was fully aware that Mr. Sam Barshop expected a thoughtful and thorough appraisal of the issues listed on her scratch pad.

APPENDIX A
Selected Results of March 1978 Customer Mail Survey[a]

1. Average number of different occasions a traveler stayed at La Quinta during the past twelve months: 10.2 times
2. Average number of nights stayed on most recent visit: 2.6 nights
3. Purpose of trip (percentages exceed 100% due to multiple answers)

Personal	9.5%
Business	79.8
Pleasure	12.2
Convention	3.5
Vacation	2.0

4. Frequency of staying at motels or hotels

Once a week or more	39.0%
Once every few weeks	21.7
About once a month	16.4
Less often than every few months	21.2

5. Type of trip and payment on most recent visit

Business trip paid for by the company	65.7%
Business trip paid for by self	16.4
Pleasure trip paid for by self	18.0

6. Rented a car on most recent trip

Yes	23.1%
No	75.9

7. Mode of travel on most recent trip

Airline	34.0%
Car	64.8

8. Reason for choice of a particular La Quinta Motor Inn on most recent visit (percentages exceed 100% due to multiple responses)

Close to next day's activities	47.5%
Saw it when ready to stop	5.7
Recommended by friend, relative, etc.	15.4
Specified by the company	7.3
Personal preference based on previous experience	48.1
Price	36.6
Stayed here before	40.9
Friendly and courteous personnel	27.9
Other motels full	3.1

9. Source of reservations

Self	55.4%
Secretary	13.3
Company	10.4
Travel agency	2.7
Association or convention	2.2
Relative, friend, etc.	4.7
No reservations	10.4

10. Person(s) sharing room on most recent visit (percentages exceed 100% due to multiple responses)

Spouse	21.6%
Children	5.2
Friends	3.4
Business associates	4.1
None, stayed alone	68.9

11. Likelihood of staying at a La Quinta Motor Inn on return visit to the city

Extremely likely	54.2%

Very likely	30.3
Somewhat likely	11.0
Not very likely	2.6
Not at all likely	1.0

12. Likelihood of staying at a La Quinta Motor Inn if one were available in another city visited

Extremely likely	45.5%

Very likely	35.4
Somewhat likely	15.3
Not very likely	2.3
Not at all likely	0.7

13. First stay in a La Quinta Motor Inn

Yes	27.0%
No	70.1

[a]Number of respondents = 5,600 of 10,000

APPENDIX B
Selected La Quinta Print Advertisements

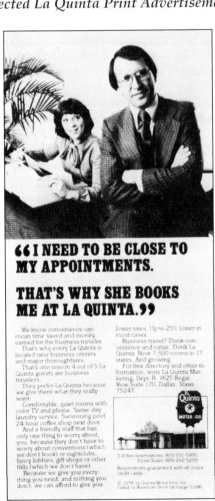

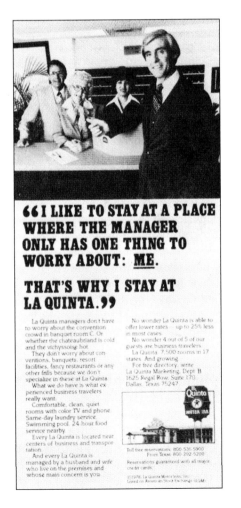

"I DON'T NEED CONVENTION MOBS, LONG CHECK IN AND CHECK OUT LINES, FANCY LOBBIES OR NIGHTCLUBS. I JUST WANT A CLEAN, QUIET ROOM AND PERSONAL SERVICE.

THAT'S WHY I STAY AT LA QUINTA."

At La Quinta, you'll never be jostled aside by conventioneers because we don't book conventions.

You won't be disturbed by a noisy nightclub, because we don't have nightclubs. Or any unnecessary frills for that matter.

We do have what the experienced business traveler really wants.

Comfortable, clean, quiet rooms with color TV and phone.

Same day laundry service. 24 hour coffee shop next door. Swimming pool.

And a staff trained to give you personal attention, supervised by husband and wife managers who live on the premises.

By cutting out the things you don't need, La Quinta can afford to give you lower rates. Up to 25% less in most cases.

No wonder 4 out of 5 of our guests are business travelers. La Quinta, 7,500 rooms in 17 states. And growing.

For free directory and other information, write La Quinta Marketing, Dept. T, 1625 Regal Row, Suite 120, Dallas, Texas 75247.

Toll free reservations: 800-531-5900. From Texas: 800-292-5200.

Reservations guaranteed with all major credit cards.

© 1978, La Quinta Motor Inns, Inc. Listed on American Stock Exchange (LQM).

"OUR SALESMEN ARE ON THE ROAD MORE THAN EVER. BUT OUR TRAVEL EXPENSES ARE DOWN.

WHERE ARE WE STAYING? LA QUINTA."

An independent survey of La Quinta guests proved 4 out of 5 are business travelers.

They know every motor inn on the road. And they prefer La Quinta over their second choice almost two to one.

Which shows us we're giving our preferred guests, business travelers, what they really want.

Metro locations close to business centers and transportation.

Big, comfortable, quiet rooms with color TV and phone. Same day laundry service. Swimming pool. 24 hour coffee shop next door.

And a helpful, courteous staff. (Headed by husband and wife managers who live on the premises.)

We don't book conventions. Nor court the vacation trade.

By cutting out the things you don't use, La Quinta can afford to give you lower rates. Up to 25% lower in most cases.

Business travel? Think La Quinta. Now 7,500 rooms in 17 states. And growing.

For free directory, write La Quinta Marketing, Dept. B, 1625 Regal Row, Suite 120, Dallas, Texas 75247.

Toll free reservations: 800-531-5900. From Texas: 800-292-5200.

Reservations guaranteed with all major credit cards.

© 1978, La Quinta Motor Inns, Inc. Listed on American Stock Exchange (LQM).

Appendix
Retail Management Careers

American retailing dates back to pioneer days when our earliest settlers bought feed and farm supplies from the general store. Today, a vast array of retail shops scattered across the horizon serve the material wants of millions of Americans. Sales by these merchants amounted to nearly 1.5 trillion dollars in 1991, almost 10 percent of the GDP. Increased employment opportunities for retail managers have paralleled this expansion of retail trade.

In general, college graduates of the 1990s will fare better than their counterparts in the 1970s and 1980s because of demographics. Whereas workers aged 16 to 24 comprised 20 percent of the labor force in 1986, by the year 2000 only 16 percent of the labor force will be in this age group. Because this age group will shrink as a percentage of the labor force, its members will be more in demand and can count on somewhat higher entry-level salaries.

Students preparing for careers in retailing should plan to work in an ever-changing environment. Trends and styles change, management philosophies change, store ownership changes, and new merchandising methods are constantly being tested.

Jobs in retailing are varied. Retail workers can be found in department stores or discount stores, owning franchises, or establishing small, independent businesses. This appendix seeks to profile management jobs and career paths in retailing, along with training programs provided by the major employers. Additionally, it presents ideas for conducting a job search, starting a retail franchise, and opening a small, independent retail business.

JOBS IN RETAILING

Behind the scenes, keeping the stores running smoothly, a cadre of talented workers exercise responsibility for buying and displaying merchandise, managing and hiring staff, and in general offering consumer service. These retail managers serve as department and store heads, buyers, and merchandising managers. A thumbnail sketch of each of these types of jobs appears below.

Department Manager   Most retailers start new college graduates as assistant buyers or department managers. Duties of department managers include:

- Scheduling sales staff work hours
- Motivating and leading sales staff
- Keeping records of sales and inventory
- Participating in merchandise selection
- Solving customer problems

To perform these duties, department managers need leadership skills, "people awareness," and some ability to work with numbers. These managers are chosen for promotion on the basis of how well they run their departments, and the profits they show.

Assistant Buyer   Assistant buyers train to select merchandise assortments for retail stores. They must learn how to spend money wisely, looking for the best quality for the least money. These trainees assist buyers with merchandising, marketing strategy, and financial management. Essentially, assistant buyers learn all the jobs of the buyer. Assistant buyers are promoted on the basis of how well they learn their jobs, and how well their divisions merchandise goods.

If they do well, department managers and assistant buyers rise to better jobs in the employment hierarchy. Typical career paths for retail employees are presented in Exhibit A.1 and A.2. Exhibit A.1 shows a career path within May Department Stores. Exhibit A.2 shows a career path within The Neiman-Marcus Group.

Most stores train beginning managers in both buying and department management. From that point on, the career path is two-pronged, with branches leading to careers in either store management or merchandising. Note, however, that The Neiman-Marcus Group maintains a crossover between merchandising and store management. Some of the jobs retail workers can perform as their careers advance are described below.

Department Group Manager   The department group manager directs several departments, performing many of the same duties as a department manager. While in training, these executives move from one part of the store to another and develop familiarity with different types of merchandise.

Store Manager   A store manager must be a "people person," ready to handle problems presented by customers and staff. These managers must make quick decisions and implement store policy. They oversee store layout and merchandise presentation, inventory control, and merchandise movement. These managers also motivate and coach staff and supervise store operations.

Director of Stores   A director of stores generally works at company headquarters, coordinating the efforts of all retail outlets in the chain. This person has responsibilities similar to those of the store manager, but for a number of stores.

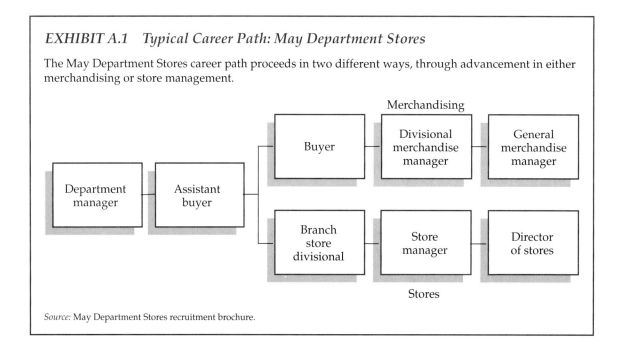

EXHIBIT A.1   Typical Career Path: May Department Stores

The May Department Stores career path proceeds in two different ways, through advancement in either merchandising or store management.

Source: May Department Stores recruitment brochure.

EXHIBIT A.2 *Typical Career path: The Neiman-Marcus Group*

From the position of Department Manager, Neiman-Marcus executives can advance to Buyer. The Buying position tests one's ability to engage in long-range planning and analysis as well as to establish priorities on a day-to-day basis. All Buyers are based in downtown Dallas.

From the position of Buyer, the preferred career path is to Assistant Store Manager and then to Divisional Merchandise Manager or Store Manager.

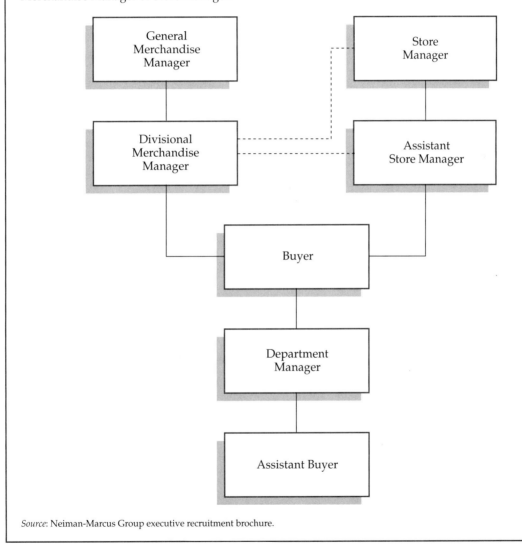

Source: Neiman-Marcus Group executive recruitment brochure.

Buyer Store buyers generally follow a merchandising career path. This might appear at first glance to be an exciting job, because some buyers shop in foreign cities like Paris and Hong Kong. Most buyers, however, work long hours shopping for wholesale merchandise within the

United States. Requirements for this job include a good eye for quality merchandise and a sixth sense for changes in consumer tastes and trends. Duties of the buyer include:

- Setting retail prices
- Buying merchandise on buying trips
- Responsibility for profit margins
- Leadership and training of department personnel
- Monitoring markups and markdowns

Division Merchandising Manager   The division merchandising manager is responsible for merchandise in a single division of all stores. For example a firm might employ managers for apparel, furniture, or housewares. The division merchandising manager coordinates the efforts of all buyers in his or her division to make certain inventories are sold, plan sales promotions, and lead the buying staff. Division merchandising managers report to the general merchandising manager.

General Merchandising Manager   These managers report directly to the company's chief executive officer. They are responsible for coordinating storewide or companywide merchandising efforts.

Nonselling Jobs   Retailing offers a variety of careers for personnel who are not suited to sales jobs in merchandising and store management. Retail firms employ financial analysts, accountants, credit controllers, systems analysts, computer programmers, customer service managers, and human resources personnel.

Retail Earnings   Beginning retail jobs pay between $20,000 and $25,000 per year. Salaries generally increase with promotions. A general merchandising manager, for instance, can earn up to $100,000 a year, depending upon the store and location. Divisional merchandising managers can earn up to $80,000 a year, again dependent upon the store and its location.

Jobs in Discount Stores   The job descriptions above pertain primarily to traditional department stores. Discount stores offer other retail jobs. Discount stores like Wal-Mart, K mart, Venture, and Zayre, are growing rapidly, and becoming an important part of retail merchandising. Jobs with discount companies resemble those in department stores, with variations by store.

Working Conditions   Retailing is a fast-paced world. Workers must be prepared to work extra hours to get ready for busy seasons. With stores open long hours, managers have extra work scheduling personnel. Managers sometimes work Saturdays and evenings to boost employee morale, or to give workers time off. Buying trips can be fun, but imagine shopping all day long for several days! This fast-paced job requires great stamina. The variety of jobs that each manager must do, plus rapidly changing consumer markets and responsibility for profit margins, means that retail managers must be high-energy people with the ability to work under pressure.

THE JOB SEARCH

When you begin your job search, you will be looking for employment for at least the next few years. It will help you and your employer if you know the kind of retailing job you want, and what you can contribute to that job. Therefore, as you begin looking for work, it is a good idea to review the types of jobs available in retailing, your own background, and any special skills you have that will benefit your employer.

Retailers are looking for special types of individuals. Specifically, they want flexible people who can predict the future, leaders and planners with acute social awareness.

The retail environment is constantly changing. Yesterday's successful leading market item may be today's disaster. For this reason, retailers need employees who are ready for change and adapt smoothly to new situations.

Additionally, retailers must predict what people will buy next season with some accuracy. Thus, retailers want to hire forward-looking individuals who eagerly anticipate new trends and developments in marketing and retail sales.

Retail managers also need leadership and planning skills. Buyers must know how much and what kinds of merchandise to buy. Department managers need to accurately assess how much inventory to order. As buyers or department managers, employees need social skills that help them to manage people, and they need to play a leadership role, helping others to see and work toward overall company goals.

If you have developed any of the skills retailers look for in employees through employment, schooling, and extracurricular activities, be sure to stress this in all phases of your job search.

Steps in a job search include: writing a resume, finding job leads, developing a powerful cover letter, and managing the interview.

The Resume   Most job seekers do best with single-page resumes outlining a desired job description, education, work experience, and extracurricular activities that show interests and skills employers seek. The job description can help you target your career choices and reach the people most likely to employ you.

Most employers request a chronological resume listing all of your activities and experiences consecutively in time, beginning with your most recent job or school endeavor. Employers believe that chronological lists show whether you have held increasingly responsible jobs, and are geared for the challenge of upward mobility.

If you are a recent college graduate, your education will be one of your strongest selling points, so a description of your education belongs at the top of the resume. If you have been out of college for some time, work experience is more important than college and belongs at the top of your resume.

A short, accurate resume gives future employers a full picture of your abilities and requires

very little time to read. As you write it, don't forget that it is a selling tool. Employers are most likely to develop a favorable impression if the resume is targeted to the job description, showing that you have the skills to be successful doing that job.

Finding Job Leads   You can uncover job leads in several different ways. One of the most successful, networking, involves talking to everyone you know who is associated with retailing to make them aware of your search for a job. A college recruitment office can become part of your network. These leads are especially important because many employers recruit on campus, which shows a definite interest in new employees.

A second way to uncover job leads is to conduct an unsolicited mailing campaign. Such a campaign requires finding people in retail establishments who are likely to hire people in the near future and writing to them about your qualifications. This type of campaign works best if you target people with responsibility for hiring. You can find their names from library indexes or journals, or a telephone call to the company.

The want ads in newspapers can also help you uncover leads, as can advertisements in trade journals.

Cover Letters   A third step in the job search process is preparing a cover letter. A good cover letter starts by reminding the employer of the company's needs. You can discover the employer's needs from the want ads, ads in trade journals, your college placement office, company recruiting brochures, and your general knowledge of retailing jobs.

Once you have reminded the employer of his or her staffing needs, the next step is to tell that person how you are especially suited to filling those needs. Suggest how your background, education, and work experience suit you to the employer's job.

The cover letter should close with a paragraph stating your interest in the position and your availability.

The Interview   The interview is the most important step in your job campaign. When you are face-to-face, you and the employer can form accurate impressions of one another. Your job in this situation is to sell yourself.

To help yourself to remain calm and confident in the interview, prepare for it beforehand. A list of the 15 most commonly asked interview questions appears in Exhibit A.3. Be prepared to give a brief answer to each of these questions. Another way to prepare for the interview is to reassess the employer's needs and job description, and review your attributes as they pertain to the job.

After the employer asks the first few questions, it's your turn. Employers expect that you will want to know more about the job for which you are interviewing. You may want to prepare a list of questions to ask beforehand. Inquire first about job duties and training. Reserve questions

about compensation until the last interview. Try to develop an accurate picture of the job. Take notes, including questions that occur to you during the interview.

When you finish asking questions, it's time to let the employer know how specific skills, experience, and education fit his or her employment needs. This is the part of the interview that counts. Listen carefully for the interviewer's reaction, and make certain you have answered all of his or her questions.

From this point, the employer will tell you what happens next. Some jobs require several interviews. If you have made a good impression, you will be hired, or asked to return for a second interview.

In the final interview, the employer should raise the subject of salary. To answer questions about how much you expect to earn, try to find out how much the job pays. Employers generally have a figure in mind about what they will pay. If the salary is given as a range, try to show how your experience qualifies you for the top of the range. If the salary the employer offers

---

EXHIBIT A.3   The 15 Most Frequently Asked Interview Questions

1. Why did you choose your academic major?
2. What courses did you like best? Least? Why?
3. In what kinds of extracurricular activities did you participate?
4. What kind of job do you want?
5. How did your college career prepare you for this type of work?
6. Have you had summer work or other previous employment in this or a related field?
7. What have you learned from your work experience?
8. Why are you interviewing with our company?
9. What are the most important considerations for you in choosing a job?
10. What do you see yourself doing five years from now? Ten years from now?
11. What do you do in your leisure time?
12. What are your strengths and weaknesses?
13. What are your ideas on salary?
14. Why should we hire you?
15. Do you have any questions?

Source: Susan Barnard and Gretchen Thompson, *Job Search Strategy for College Grads* (Boston: Bob Adams Inc., 1984), p. 147.

proves unacceptable, you can make this clear. If you are comfortable with the salary, you can let that be known as well.

TRAINING PROGRAMS

Many employers operate in-service employee development and training programs. Management studies have demonstrated that employees perform better when they sense that their companies have such a commitment to them. Therefore, as you choose your future employer, seek to understand the components of the training programs you will be offered.

The following quotes support the idea of retailers making commitments to training programs.

Neiman-Marcus

A key factor in our ability to maintain the Neiman-Marcus standards of excellence has been a commitment to the development of highly competent professionals. Neiman-Marcus offers a carefully designed program that assures career growth to those who are able to meet the demands of our business.

Length and components of training programs vary, but a good training program gives each trainee a combination of on-the-job training and classroom or seminar experience. Good training programs are practical and teach individuals how to handle all aspects of the job. Sketches of some company training programs follow.

Bloomingdale's

An executive trainee position in our Merchandising Division involves a diverse experience with a career path leading to the position of Buyer. Bloomingdale's Executive Training Program is designed to be self-paced combining a comprehensive training manual, classroom instruction and challenging on-the-job training assignments. Bloomingdale's Executive Trainees are exposed to all facets of retailing. The Executive Trainee Manual provides technical information about merchandising and store operations. As you progress through the training program you will have many opportunities to apply your knowledge. You then will be placed in the position of Assistant Department Manager in the New York store. The career path for the merchandising executive is geared for individuals with a strong desire to succeed, proven leadership ability, business acumen, effective communication skills as well as senior management potential.

All promotions are based on individual performance and merit.

Dayton Hudson

Store management opportunities at Dayton Hudson begin with our Store Management Trainee Program. One of the best in retailing, the program provides our new executives with well-developed, structured orientation and training. We update the program regularly so that it meets your needs as well as the needs of the organization. Our 20 week program provides both classroom and on-the-job experience to prepare you for future assignments in the company. Your first eight weeks will be spent in the heart and center of our business: the selling floor. There you experience first-hand our emphasis on personal selling skills, customer service and the value we place on our front-line sales force. Your next four weeks will teach you merchandising basics, including price changes, floor layout/presentation, inventory control and merchandise processing.

The Merchandising Training Program at Dayton Hudson is a 24-week program, providing both classroom and on-the-job training.

As you start the training program, you will receive an orientation to the Dayton Hudson Department Store company philosophies and policies. You'll spend time in one of our stores, learning how the stores and merchandising organization work hand in hand.

During the bulk of your time as a merchandising trainee, you will be assigned to a buying office where you will work under the guidance of a Senior Buyer. At that time, you will learn how the buying office interacts with other areas of the organization.

You will also learn the details of the buying function. This includes planning seasonal goals, inventory control, product development, advertising, trend merchandising and assisting in buying and reordering of merchandise. In addition you will learn to use our advanced computer systems in order to plan, analyze and react to the business.

The May Company Department Stores

May is committed to helping associates succeed; training and development are key tools. The May Executive Training Program is the beginning of a career development process designed to facilitate long-term success. Starting with your first day as an executive trainee and at each step along the way, May is teaching and training you to be a business executive.

Your first step in the program is as an executive trainee—spending an intensive, 12-week period learning in the classroom, the buying office and the stores. This corporate-wide program has been implemented in all of our department store, discount store, and specialty shoe store divisions.

Classroom work combined with hands-on experience in the buying office and the stores eases the transition from a college to a business environment. The classroom training orients executive trainees to May, its strategic mission, culture and priorities, as well as its sophisticated systems and philosophy of retailing.

In the buying office and the stores, these new skills are put into operation as executive trainees work with experienced executives on specific assignments as part of the merchandising organization.

Our executive training program provides maximum exposure to the retailing industry to prepare new executives not just for that first position, but for a career with May.

BUSINESS OWNERSHIP

As an alternative to working for others, many people choose to own their own retail businesses. Most advisors recommend that business owners work for someone else before starting their own companies to gain experience. Two popular forms of business ownership are the franchise and starting a small, independent company.

The Franchise   Franchising has become a common business practice in the United States over the past three decades. Owners of franchises like McDonald's, 7-Eleven, Computerland, and Pier One Imports buy the opportunity to do business under a recognized name from a franchisor. The International Franchise Association defines a franchise as follows:

> A franchise is a continuing relationship between franchisor and franchisee in which the sum total of the franchisor's knowledge, image, success, manufacturing and marketing techniques are supplied to the franchisee for a consideration.[1]

Reasons to Buy a Franchise   Individuals buy franchises for a variety of reasons. One significant advantage of owning a franchise is doing business as a recognizable, reputable firm. An owner of a Kentucky Fried Chicken or 7-Eleven franchise starts out with the advantage of being known. Franchisors spend money on advertising to bring franchised goods and services to the attention of the public. A well-run franchise's reputation for a good product and service helps the franchisee gain customers and become established.

For one reason or another, most small, independent businesses do not survive beyond the first few years of operation. A business franchise minimizes this risk. Franchisors have developed proven methods of doing business. New business owners need not flounder while developing systems and procedures because these are provided by the franchisor to help reduce the odds of business failure. In addition to providing systems for doing business, franchisors often provide training programs for their franchisees to promote good business practices and protect their vested interests in the success of their franchisees.

A final reason individuals purchase franchises is to be their own bosses with operating independence. Many individuals do not want to work for others, but prefer instead the self-esteem of owning their own businesses. Franchisors cater to these people.

Franchisors are typically paid for the advantages they afford new business startups. These fees vary among franchises and generally include an initial fee, an ongoing percentage of royalties, and an ongoing contribution to advertising expenses.

Evaluating a Franchise Deciding whether or not a given franchise opportunity is for you requires estimating projected financial rewards from doing business as a franchisee, deciding whether or not you are suited to the type of business, and evaluating the franchisor's package.

Estimating future financial rewards is a tricky business. It involves forecasting sales, then subtracting projected business costs as well as franchise costs. You can forecast sales on the basis of subjective guesses, performance of other franchisees in this business, and marketing information for retail sales of your product or service in your marketing area.

Franchisors should provide a fairly accurate picture of how much it will cost to do business. Any business venture begins with relatively low sales and relatively high costs. Therefore most businesses do not begin to show a profit until they have been established for several months, or a year. After subtracting franchise royalties from your revenue projections, you should be in a good position to judge what your profits will be and whether or not you are willing to work for this rate of return.

A person suited to owning a franchise is generally someone with managerial experience and excellent motivational skills. To succeed in a business requires having both an interest in the business and a willingness to make it work. Franchisees therefore need organizational skills, the ability to plan, and social awareness—many of the same attributes companies want from executive trainees.

Making the decision to buy a franchise requires taking a close look at the franchisor and its offer. Dennis L. Foster, a franchise consultant with The Development Group, has prepared the checklist in Exhibit A.4 to evaluate a franchise opportunity.

The Independent Business Starting a small, independent business is definitely the riskiest way to find a job in retailing, but it can also be the most rewarding. In addition to the benefits of the franchise, especially being your own boss, an independent business affords the owner the advantages of retaining all of the profits since no royalties are paid to a franchisor, and the pride in having developed a totally unique line of merchandise and service.

A Checklist for Going into Business Are you likely to succeed at starting your own business? The U.S. Small Business Administration, Office of Business Development, has prepared the checklist in Exhibit A.5 to help you answer this question.

The Business Plan In much the same way that franchising requires developing projections of

EXHIBIT A.4   Evaluating the Ingredients of a Franchise

Franchise Identity

Is the franchise trade name well-known? If not, it is catchy or unique?

Is the name so similar to another business name or trademark that it might cause confusion?

Is anyone else already using the name or a similar name or trademark in your trading area? If so, can you obtain the right to use the name or trademark from the party already using it? How much will it cost?

Is the image of the business conducive to your own personality and self-esteem?

How do you feel about being known as the owner or president of a business?

Operating System

Does the franchisor offer a training program? If so, how long is it? What topics does it cover?

Will the franchisor help you select a site for the business?

Does the franchisor provide a franchise operating manual? If so, what subjects are included?

    Grand opening?
    Setting up books and records?
    Accounting and reports?
    Advertising and publicity?
    Purchasing inventory?
    Marketing and sales?
    Daily operating procedures?
    Cleanliness and grooming?
    Employee policies and procedures?
    Technical information?

Does the franchisor provide predesigned signs, menus, fixtures, decorations, etc.? If not, will he or she help you procure them?

Can the franchisor help you purchase equipment, supplies, or inventory at a discount? Is it really a discount?

Financial Relationship

Is there an initial franchise fee?

Does the fee vary from one location to another? If so, what is the amount of the fee for the location or territory you have in mind?

Does the franchisor charge an ongoing franchise royalty? If so, what is the percentage?

Is the royalty set for the entire term of the franchise, or can it be raised or lowered in the future?

If the royalty is not set, what factors will the franchisor use to determine it?

Does the franchisor charge a co-op advertising royalty set for the entire term of the franchise, or can it be raised or lowered in the future?

Source: Dennis L. Foster, *The Complete Franchise Book* (Rocklin, Calif.: *Prima Publishing and Communications*, 1988), pp. 38-40.

EXHIBIT A.5   Independent Business Checklist

1. Are you a self-starter?
   _____ I do things on my own. Nobody has to tell me to get going.
   _____ If someone gets me started, I keep going all right.
   _____ Easy does it. I don't put myself out until I have to.
2. How do you feel about other people?
   _____ I like people. I can get along with just about anybody.
   _____ I have plenty of friends—I don't need anyone else.
   _____ Most people irritate me.
3. Can you lead others?
   _____ I can get most people to go along when I start something.
   _____ I can give the orders if someone tells me what we should do.
   _____ I let someone else get things moving. Then I go along if I feel like it.
4. Can you take responsibility?
   _____ I like to take charge of things and see them through.
   _____ I'll take over if I have to, but I'd rather let someone else be responsible.
   _____ There is always some eager beaver around wanting to show how smart he is. I let him.
5. How good an organizer are you?
   _____ I like to have a plan before I start. I'm usually the one to get things lined up when the group wants to do something.
   _____ I do all right unless things get too confused. Then I quit.
   _____ You get all set and then something comes along and presents too many problems. So I just take things as they come.
6. How good a worker are you?
   _____ I can keep going as long as I need to. I don't mind working hard for something I want.
   _____ I'll work hard for a while, but when I've had enough, that's it.
   _____ I can't see that hard work gets you anywhere.
7. Can you make decisions?
   _____ I can make up my mind in a hurry if I have to. It usually turns out O.K., too.
   _____ I can if I have plenty of time. If I have to make up my mind fast, I think later I should have decided the other way.
   _____ I don't like to be the one to decide things.
8. Can people trust what you say?
   _____ You bet they can. I don't say things I don't mean.
   _____ I try to be on the level most of the time, but sometimes I just say what's easiest.
   _____ Why bother if the other fellow doesn't know the difference?
9. Can you stick with it?
   _____ If I make up my mind to do something, I don't let anything stop me.
   _____ I usually finish what I start—if it goes well.
   _____ If it doesn't go right away, I quit. Why beat your brains out?
10. How good is your health?
    _____ I never run down!
    _____ I have enough energy for most things I want to do.
    _____ I run out of energy sooner than most of my friends seem to.

Now count the checks you made.
How many checks are there beside the first answer to each question?
How many checks are there beside the second answer to each question?
How many checks are there beside the third answer to each question?

If most of your checks are beside the first answers, you probably have what it takes to run a business. If not, you're likely to have more trouble than you can handle by yourself. Better find a partner who is strong on the points you're weak on. If many checks are beside the third answer, not even a good partner will be able to shore you up.

Now you can answer this question: "Are you likely to succeed at owning your own business?"

Source: Checklist for Going into Business, U.S. Small Business Administration, Office of Business Development, (Management Aid 2.016), pp. 2-3.

sales and costs, starting a small business involves creating a detailed business plan. The business plan includes sales projections and an estimate of costs of doing business. Sales projections are a function of where you choose to locate, the market niche you decide to fill, your advertising campaign, and how well your competitors are doing.

Sources of marketing information include:

Your local Chamber of Commerce

The National Retail Merchants Association
100 West 31st Street
New York, New York 10001

Survey of Buying Power
published annually in June by
Sales Management, Inc.
630 Third Avenue
New York, New York 10007

The Editor and Publisher Market Guide
published annually in September by
Editor and Publisher Co.
850 Third Avenue
New York, New York 10002

Costs of doing business vary according to the type of small business you choose to start. As an initial investment, a retail business requires a store front rental, a starting inventory, furniture, and fixtures, a deposit for utilities, operating capital, and advertising for a grand opening. A trade association for your particular type of business can help you estimate costs of doing business.

When you have estimated sales revenues and costs, you will notice that costs and disbursements will exceed revenues during the startup period and during slow sales seasons. During this time you may need to borrow money from a bank to cover the costs of doing business. These loans can be repaid with revenues earned as the business matures during busy seasons. To apply for a loan, you will need a business plan. For more detailed information on how to prepare a business plan, contact your local Small Business Administration Office.[2]

Involvement with Government   As soon as you open the doors of your business, you are legally responsible to meet the requirements of all government agencies that regulate your type of business. In choosing a location for your business, for instance, you will need to find a building that is zoned by your local government for commercial use.

Some states require that businesses be licensed or registered. To find out if this applies to your business, you can call your state's Department of Commerce or Department of Economic Development.

As a retailer, you must also pay numerous taxes, including any state sales tax and withholding taxes for state income tax that may apply. Contact your state's Department of Revenue to find out if you are responsible for any of these taxes, and if so, how to collect and record them.

If you have one or more employees, you will need to obtain a Federal Employer Identification number from the U.S. Treasury, Department of Internal Revenue. This is the number you will use to pay the employer's share of unemployment compensation and social security taxes. These payments are due quarterly, and employers are fined for late payments. Failure to comply with the U.S. Department of Internal Revenue regulations can result in repossession of your business, large fines, or imprisonment. It is a good idea to get into the habit of paying withholding taxes for all employees regularly.

Some counties require that you register your business name. Be sure to contact your local county clerk to see if this is a requirement in your state.

Notes

1. Dennis L. Foster, *The Complete Franchise Book* (Rocklin, Calif.: Prima Publishing and Communications 1988).
2. Rewritten from *Business Plan for Retailers*, Small Business Administration, Management Assistance (Management Aid 2.020).

Index